Lecture Notes in Computer Science 11337

Commenced Publication in 1973
Founding and Former Series Editors:
Gerhard Goos, Juris Hartmanis, and Jan van Leeuwen

More information about this series at http://www.springer.com/series/7407

Jaideep Vaidya · Jin Li (Eds.)

Algorithms and Architectures for Parallel Processing

18th International Conference, ICA3PP 2018
Guangzhou, China, November 15–17, 2018
Proceedings, Part IV

 Springer

Editors
Jaideep Vaidya
Rutgers University
Newark, NJ, USA

Jin Li
Guangzhou University
Guangzhou, China

ISSN 0302-9743 ISSN 1611-3349 (electronic)
Lecture Notes in Computer Science
ISBN 978-3-030-05062-7 ISBN 978-3-030-05063-4 (eBook)
https://doi.org/10.1007/978-3-030-05063-4

Library of Congress Control Number: 2018962485

LNCS Sublibrary: SL1 – Theoretical Computer Science and General Issues

This Springer imprint is published by the registered company Springer Nature Switzerland AG
The registered company address is: Gewerbestrasse 11, 6330 Cham, Switzerland

Preface

Welcome to the proceedings of the 18th International Conference on Algorithms and Architectures for Parallel Processing (ICA3PP 2018), which was organized by Guangzhou University and held in Guangzhou, China, during November 15–17, 2018.

ICA3PP 2018 was the 18th event in a series of conferences devoted to research on algorithms and architectures for parallel processing. Previous iterations of the conference include ICA3PP 2017 (Helsinki, Finland, November 2017), ICA3PP 2016 (Granada, Spain, December 2016), ICA3PP 2015 (Zhangjiajie, China, November 2015), ICA3PP 2014 (Dalian, China, August 2014), ICA3PP 2013 (Vietri sul Mare, Italy, December 2013), ICA3PP 2012 (Fukuoka, Japan, September 2012), ICA3PP 2011 (Melbourne, Australia, October 2011), ICA3PP 2010 (Busan, Korea, May 2010), ICA3PP 2009 (Taipei, Taiwan, June 2009), ICA3PP 2008 (Cyprus, June 2008), ICA3PP 2007 (Hangzhou, China, June 2007), ICA3PP 2005 (Melbourne, Australia, October 2005), ICA3PP 2002 (Beijing, China, October 2002), ICA3PP 2000 (Hong Kong, China, December 2000), ICA3PP 1997 (Melbourne, Australia, December 1997), ICA3PP 1996 (Singapore, June 1996), and ICA3PP 1995 (Brisbane, Australia, April 1995).

ICA3PP is now recognized as the main regular event in the area of parallel algorithms and architectures, which covers many dimensions including fundamental theoretical approaches, practical experimental projects, and commercial and industry applications. This conference provides a forum for academics and practitioners from countries and regions around the world to exchange ideas for improving the efficiency, performance, reliability, security, and interoperability of computing systems and applications.

ICA3PP 2018 attracted over 400 high-quality research papers highlighting the foundational work that strives to push beyond the limits of existing technologies, including experimental efforts, innovative systems, and investigations that identify weaknesses in existing parallel processing technology. Each submission was reviewed by at least two experts in the relevant areas, on the basis of their significance, novelty, technical quality, presentation, and practical impact. According to the review results, 141 full papers were selected to be presented at the conference, giving an acceptance rate of 35%. Besides, we also accepted 50 short papers and 24 workshop papers. In addition to the paper presentations, the program of the conference included four keynote speeches and two invited talks from esteemed scholars in the area, namely: Prof. Xuemin (Sherman) Shen, University of Waterloo, Canada; Prof. Wenjing Lou, Virginia Tech, USA; Prof. Witold Pedrycz, University of Alberta, Canada; Prof. Xiaohua Jia, City University of Hong Kong, Hong Kong; Prof. Xiaofeng Chen, Xidian University, China; Prof. Xinyi Huang, Fujian Normal University, China. We were extremely honored to have them as the conference keynote speakers and invited speakers.

ICA3PP 2018 was made possible by the behind-the-scene effort of selfless individuals and organizations who volunteered their time and energy to ensure the success of this conference. We would like to express our special appreciation to Prof. Yang Xiang, Prof. Weijia Jia, Prof. Yi Pan, Prof. Laurence T. Yang, and Prof. Wanlei Zhou, the Steering Committee members, for giving us the opportunity to host this prestigious conference and for their guidance with the conference organization. We would like to emphasize our gratitude to the general chairs, Prof. Albert Zomaya and Prof. Minyi Guo, for their outstanding support in organizing the event. Thanks also to the publicity chairs, Prof. Zheli Liu and Dr Weizhi Meng, for the great job in publicizing this event. We would like to give our thanks to all the members of the Organizing Committee and Program Committee for their efforts and support.

The ICA3PP 2018 program included two workshops, namely, the ICA3PP 2018 Workshop on Intelligent Algorithms for Large-Scale Complex Optimization Problems and the ICA3PP 2018 Workshop on Security and Privacy in Data Processing. We would like to express our sincere appreciation to the workshop chairs: Prof. Ting Hu, Prof. Feng Wang, Prof. Hongwei Li and Prof. Qian Wang.

Last but not least, we would like to thank all the contributing authors and all conference attendees, as well as the great team at Springer that assisted in producing the conference proceedings, and the developers and maintainers of EasyChair.

November 2018   Jaideep Vaidya
                                                                                             Jin Li

Organization

General Chairs

Albert Zomaya   University of Sydney, Australia
Minyi Guo   Shanghai Jiao Tong University, China

Program Chairs

Jaideep Vaidya   Rutgers University, USA
Jin Li   Guangzhou University, China

Publication Chair

Yu Wang   Guangzhou University, China

Publicity Chairs

Zheli Liu   Nankai University, China
Weizhi Meng   Technical University of Denmark, Denmark

Steering Committee

Yang Xiang (Chair) Swinburne University of Technology, Australia
Weijia Jia   Shanghai Jiaotong University, China
Yi Pan   Georgia State University, USA
Laurence T. Yang St. Francis Xavier University, Canada
Wanlei Zhou   Deakin University, Australia

Program Committee

Pedro Alonso   Universitat Politècnica de València, Spain
Daniel Andresen   Kansas State University, USA
Cosimo Anglano   Universitá del Piemonte Orientale, Italy
Danilo Ardagna   Politecnico di Milano, Italy
Kapil Arya   Northeastern University, USA
Marcos Assuncao Inria, France
Joonsang Baek   University of Wollongong, Australia
Anirban Basu   KDDI Research Inc., Japan
Ladjel Bellatreche LIAS/ENSMA, France
Jorge Bernal Bernabe University of Murcia, Spain
Thomas Boenisch High-Performance Computing Center Stuttgart,
         Germany

Contents – Part IV

Internet of Things and Cloud Computing

Dynamic Task Scheduler for Real Time Requirement in Cloud Computing System

Yujie Huang, Quan Zhang, Yujie Cai, Minge Jing[✉], Yibo Fan,
and Xiaoyang Zeng

State Key Laboratory of ASIC and System, Fudan University,
Shanghai 201203, China
mejing@fudan.edu.cn

Abstract. In such an era of big data, the number of tasks submitted to cloud computing system becomes huge and users' demand for real time has increased. But the existing algorithms rarely take real time into consideration and most of them are static scheduling algorithms. As a result, we ensure real time of cloud computing system under the premise of not influencing the performance on makespan and load balance by proposing a dynamic scheduler called Real Time Dynamic Max-min-min (RTDM) which takes real time, makespan, and load balance into consideration. RTDM is made up of dynamic sequencer and static scheduler. In dynamic sequencer, the tasks are sorted dynamically based on their waiting and execution times to decrease makespan and improve real time. The tasks fetched from the dynamic sequencer to the static scheduler can be seen as static tasks, so we propose an algorithm named Max-min-min in static scheduler which achieves good performance on waiting time, makespan and load balance simultaneously. Experiment results demonstrate that the proposed scheduler greatly improves the performance on real time and makespan compared with the static scheduling algorithms like Max-min, Min-min and PSO, and improves performance on makespan and real time by 1.66% and 17.19% respectively compared to First Come First Serve (FCFS).

Keywords: Cloud computing · Dynamic scheduler · Real time

1 Introduction and Analysis of Related Work

With the widespread use of cloud computing [1], the number of tasks submitted to cloud computing system grows rapidly which leads to the congestion of cloud computing system, but users' real-time requirement for cloud computing system becomes much higher [10]. However the existing algorithms pay more attention to makespan and load balance while rarely taking real time into consideration. And most of them are static scheduling algorithm which do not schedule tasks until all tasks are submitted [10]. Some representative algorithms are described below.

First come first server (FCFS) is a dynamic task scheduling algorithm which first assigns the first arrived task to a free host. It ignores the characteristics of hosts and tasks, such as task size and host processing capacity [2, 3].

© Springer Nature Switzerland AG 2018
J. Vaidya and J. Li (Eds.): ICA3PP 2018, LNCS 11337, pp. 3–11, 2018.
https://doi.org/10.1007/978-3-030-05063-4_1

Min-min algorithm first assigns the smallest task in the task list to the host where the completion time of the smallest task is minimum while Max-min algorithm first assigns the biggest one [2, 3]. Max-min achieves better performance on makespan than Min-min.

Intelligent algorithm, like Genetic Algorithm (GA) [4, 5] and Particle Swarm Optimization (PSO) [6, 7, 9], is applied in task scheduling because task scheduling is a Non-deterministic Polynomial Complete problem (NP-C problem) where intelligent algorithm is suitable [5, 6]. Intelligent algorithm can have good performance on many aspects, like makespan and load balance, but its scheduling time is long [6].

When users make new demands, such as security of immediate data, task scheduling algorithm should also take them into consideration without affecting makespan and load balance as much as possible [8].

Except FCFS, all above algorithms are static scheduling algorithm which need the information of all tasks before scheduling in order to achieve better performance [9]. But in fact, waiting for all tasks to be submitted before scheduling has a severe impact on the real time performance because tasks are submitted one by one at an indefinite intervals [10]. Real time of cloud computing system requires the waiting time it takes for a task to be submitted to execution should be as short as possible. As a result, the real time performance of the system can be measured by the total waiting time of all the tasks. Hence, we propose a dynamic task scheduler called Real Time Dynamic Max-min-min (RTDM) which takes makespan, load balance, and the total waiting time into consideration.

The remainder of this paper proceeds as follows: Sect. 2 states the workflow and architecture of RTDM, experiment results are shown in Sect. 3 and Sect. 4 concludes this paper.

2   Real Time Dynamic Max-Min-Min

Figure 1 shows the architecture of RTDM which includes two parts: dynamic sequencer and static scheduler. Dynamic sequencer is used to store and sort the tasks submitted by users; Static scheduler fetches first n tasks from dynamic sequencer and assigns them to the local task lists of suitable hosts when there is a vacant host. We take global consideration of tasks' characteristics by adjusting the value of n according to the tasks' estimated submission intervals. Each host owns a local task list, and it executes the tasks in the list in turn. The detailed description of dynamic sequencer and static scheduler is as follows.

2.1   Dynamic Sequencer

Once one task is submitted, it will be pushed into the dynamic sequencer and the tasks in the sequencer will be rearranged according to their priority values. The task with highest priority will be fetched first by the static scheduler. Regarding to the priority value of a task, the execution time of the task should be considered together with the submission time. In principal, the tasks submitted earlier should be scheduled first which will improve the real time performance. And prioritizing large tasks can help

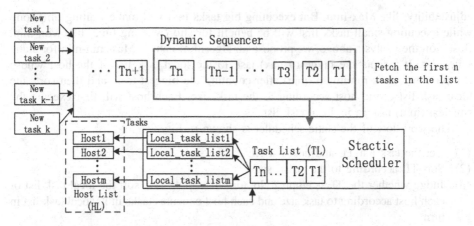

Fig. 1. The architecture of real time dynamic max-min-min

reduce makespan, like Max-min. Therefore the priority value should be calculated as Eq. (1).

$$PriorValue_i(t) = a \cdot ExeTime_i + b \cdot WaitTime_i(t) \qquad (1)$$

Where t means the current time, $PriorValue_i(t)$ means the priority value of $task_i$ at time t, a indicates the weight of execution time of a task, b is the weight of waiting time of a task, $ExeTime_i$ means the execution time of $task_i$ performed on the standard host and $WaitTime_i(t)$ means the time $task_i$ has waited at time t which is calculated as Eq. (2) where $SubmitTime_i$ means the submission time of $task_i$. The values of a and b are determined by the estimated ranges of all tasks' submission intervals and execution times.

$$WaitTime_i(t) = t - SubmitTime_i \qquad (2)$$

2.2 Static Scheduler

If the number of tasks in the dynamic sequencer is greater than n, static scheduler fetches the first n tasks from dynamic sequencer. Otherwise static scheduler fetches all the tasks in dynamic sequencer. As shown in Fig. 1, all the fetched tasks are sent to the task list (TL) in the static scheduler. We can take the tasks in TL as static tasks where we can apply static scheduling algorithm. Considering the data independence of tasks, a static scheduling algorithm with the best load balance property will achieve minimum makespan, because only when all the hosts are fully utilized, the minimum makespan will be achieved.

As a result, the static scheduler needs to make the difference between the completion times of all hosts as small as possible. In this sense, it is an average allocation problem. It is known that giving more priority to the bigger task in task scheduling will enhance the task uniformity of different hosts because small tasks have stronger adjustability, like Max-min. But executing big tasks first will make waiting time long while executing small tasks first will be benefit for short waiting time, like Min-min. Based on the analysis above, we propose an algorithm named Max-min-min for static scheduler. It assigns the biggest (max) task to the local task list of the host whose completion time is minimum (min) after counting the biggest task, and then sorts the local task list of the host according to the task size. Each host will first execute the smallest (min) task in its local task list.

The workflow of the static scheduler is shown in Fig. 2:

(1) Get the task list TL and host list HL.
(2) Sort TL according to the tasks' size.
(3) Judge whether the TL is empty? No, turn to step 4; Yes, sort the local task list of each host according to task size and each host executes tasks in its local task list in turn.
(4) Take out the biggest task from TL and assign it to the local task list of the host whose completion time will be minimum after counting the biggest task. Turn to step 3.

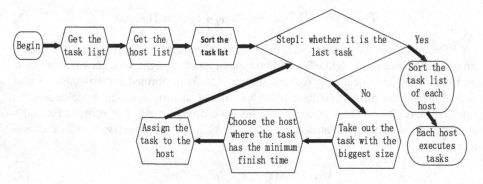

Fig. 2. The workflow of the static scheduler

2.3   A Tiny Example for Real Time Dynamic Max-Min-Min

Here is a tiny example for RTDM. Assume that we have five tasks and one host and the host is vacant at the beginning. So we let n be equal to 1. The execution time, and submission time of each task is shown in Table 1. If the factor of waiting time is not considered in dynamic sequencer, i.e. $a = 0.1$ and $b = 0$, the execution order is (task id: 1, 3, 4, 5, 2). It can be seen that the task 2 cannot be executed since its priority always is lowest, so its waiting time reaches maximum 100 s and the total waiting time of all tasks is 150 s. In the case of $a = 0.1$ and $b = 1$, the execution order of tasks is (task id: 1, 2, 3, 4, 5) and the max waiting time and total waiting time of all tasks are 50 s and 90 s respectively.

We can find that taking waiting time into consideration ($a = 0.1$ and $b = 1$) in dynamic sequencer can reduce max waiting time and total waiting time by 50% and 40% respectively compared to ignoring waiting time ($a = 0.1$ and $b = 0$).

Table 1. Waiting time, execution time and submission time of tasks

Task ID	1	2	3	4	5
Execution time (s)	20	10	20	40	30
Submission time (s)	0	10	20	30	40
Waiting time (s) (a = 0.1, b = 1)	0	10	10	20	50
Waiting time (s) (a = 0.1, b = 0)	0	100	0	10	40

3 Experiment and Results

In order to evaluate the proposed scheduler, we establish a cloud computing system simulation model and implement RTDM, FCFS, Max-min, Min-min, Max-min-min and PSO with python. The specific information of the tasks and hosts in the experiment is as follows: (1) Each task includes two parameters: its execution time performed on the standard host and its submission time. (2) Each host includes one parameter: the ratio of its processing capacity to the standard host's (PCR). The number of hosts in the experiment is 10 and their parameters are listed as {2, 0.8, 0.4, 0.8, 1.1, 0.9, 1.2, 0.8, 0.4, 1.6}. The execution time of one task performed on one host is calculated as Eq. (3) where ET_{ij} means the execution time of $task_i$ performed on $host_j$, ET_{is} means the execution time of $task_i$ performed on the standard host and PCR_{js} means the ratio of $host'_{j}s$ processing capacity to the standard host's.

$$ET_{ij} = \frac{ET_{is}}{PCR_{js}} \qquad (3)$$

3.1 Experiment in the Case of Static Tasks

In this section, we verify the superiority of Max-min-min in the case of static tasks by comparing its makespan, load balance, and waiting time with other algorithms when the submission interval of each task is 0. All experimental data are the average of 1000 experiments. In each experiment we generate 100 tasks whose execution time performed on the standard host is a random number from 0.1 s to 100 s, then schedule the tasks with Min-min (executing smallest tasks first), Max-min (executing biggest tasks first), FCFS, Max-min-min and PSO, and get their makespans, coefficients of load balance (CLB), scheduling times and total waiting times. CLB is represented by the ratio of the variance of all hosts' completion times to the average completion time of all hosts. CLB can be calculated as Eq. (4) where NH means the number of hosts and ct_i means the completion time of $host_i$.

$$CLB = \frac{\frac{1}{NH} \cdot \sum_{i=1}^{NH} \left(ct_i - \frac{1}{NH} \cdot \sum_{j=1}^{NH} ct_j\right)^2}{\frac{1}{NH} \cdot \sum_{i=1}^{NH} ct_i} \qquad (4)$$

The results are shown in Figs. 3, 4 and 5, and the results of PSO is obtained after 100 iterations.

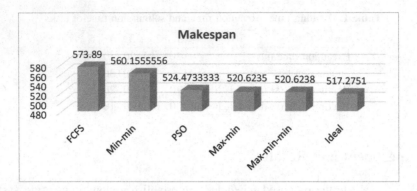

Fig. 3. Makespans of different algorithms

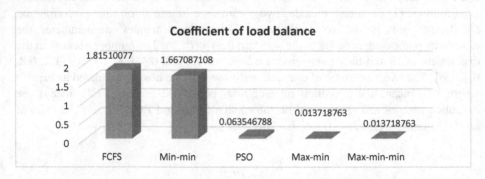

Fig. 4. Coefficients of load balance of different algorithms

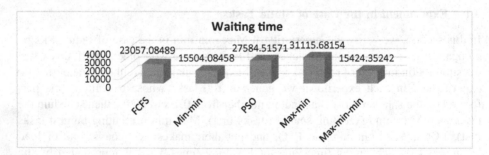

Fig. 5. Waiting times of different algorithms

As shown in Fig. 3 where *Ideal* means the minimum makespan in the ideal case of totally average allocation which can be calculated as Eq. (5), Makespan of FCFS, Min-min, PSO, Max-min, Max-min-min is 10.95%, 8.29%, 1.39%, 0.65%, 0.65% more than the minimum makespan separately. The difference between Max-min and Max-min-min is 0.0003 s, because Max-min-min spends extra time sorting the local task list of each host to change the execution order of the assigned tasks.

$$Ideal = \frac{\sum_i^{NT} ET_{is}}{\sum_j^{NH} PCR_{js}} \qquad (5)$$

As shown in Fig. 4, CLB of FCFS, Min-min and PSO is 132.23, 121.52 and 4.63 times of Max-min-min separately. Max-min and Max-min-min have the same CLB because the tasks assigned to the same host with both algorithms are the same.

As shown in Fig. 5, we can find that the total waiting time of Max-min is 1.35, 1.13, 2.01 and 2.02 times of FCFS, PSO, Min-min and Max-min-min separately.

As shown in Fig. 6, The scheduling time of PSO is 121.83, 108.11 and 138.78 times of Max-min, Max-min-min and Min-min separately while FCFS takes only 2.566×10^{-6} s.

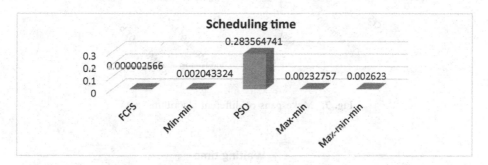

Fig. 6. Scheduling times of different algorithms

We can find that Max-min-min can achieve good performance not only on makespan and load balance, but also on waiting time. It also can be seen that an algorithm with good load balance achieves shorter makespan in the case of static tasks.

3.2 Experiment in the Case of Dynamic Tasks

In this section we verify the superiority of RTDM in the case of dynamic tasks. We create one thousand tasks whose execution time on the standard host is a random number from 0.01 s to 100 s. Each task is submitted to the cloud computing system at a random interval from 1 s to 10 s. We let a = 0.01, b = 1, n = 5 after considering the task sizes and submission intervals.

The comparison of RTDM, Max-min, Min-min, PSO (100 iterations) and FCFS is shown in Figs. 7 and 8.

As shown in Fig. 7, RTDM (a = 0.01, b = 1) improves performance on makespan by 98.06%, 97.12%, 97.14% and 1.66% separately compared to Min-min, Max-min, PSO and FCFS. RTDM (a = 0.01, b = 1) loses 0.12% performance on makespan compared to that RTDM (a = 0.01, b = 0).

As shown in Fig. 8, the waiting time of Min-min, Max-min, PSO and RTDM (a = 0.01, b = 1) is 22.25, 31.6, 28.07 and 2.85 times of RTDM (a = 0.01, b = 1) respectively and RTDM (a = 0.01, b = 1) reduces waiting time by 17.19% compared to FCFS.

In general, RTDM can improve the performance on makespan and waiting time simultaneously.

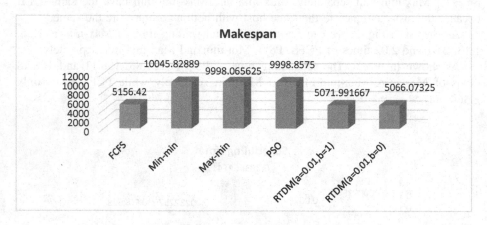

Fig. 7. Makespans of different algorithms

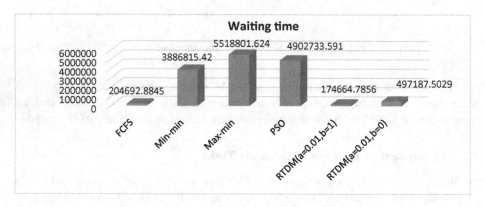

Fig. 8. Waiting times of different algorithms

4 Conclusion

In this paper, we proposes a dynamic scheduler named Real Time Dynamic Max-min-min (RTDM) which takes real time, makespan and load balance into consideration. RTDM consists of dynamic sequencer and static scheduler. In dynamic sequencer, we prioritize each task in it based on the task's waiting time and execution time to ensure the performance on makespan and real time. After the tasks are fetched from the dynamic sequencer to the static scheduler, they can be seen as static tasks. So in static scheduler, we propose an algorithm named Max-min-min which has good performance on makespan, load balance and real time in the case of static tasks. Experiment results demonstrate that RTDM can improve the performance on makespan, load balance and waiting time simultaneously.

References

1. Mell, P., Grance, T.: The NIST definition of cloud computing. National Institute of Standards and Technology (2014)
2. Teena, M., Sekaran, K.C., Jose, J.: Study and analysis of various task scheduling algorithms in the cloud computing environment. In: International Conference on Advances in Computing, Communications and Informatics, pp. 658–664 (2014)
3. Bhoi, U., Ramanuj, P.N.: Enhanced max-min task scheduling algorithm in cloud computing. Int. J. Appl. Innov. Eng. Manag. 2(4), 259–264 (2013)
4. Wei, X.J., Bei, W., Jun, L.: SAMPGA task scheduling algorithm in cloud computing. In: Chinese Control Conference, pp. 5633–5637 (2017)
5. Makasarwala, H.A., Hazari, P.: Using genetic algorithm for load balancing in cloud computing. In: Electronics, Computers and Artificial Intelligence, pp. 49–54 (2016)
6. Alla, H.B., Alla, S.B.: A novel architecture for task scheduling based on dynamic queues and particle swarm optimization in cloud computing. In: Cloud Computing Technologies and Applications, pp. 108–114 (2016)
7. Liu, X.F., Zhan, Z.H., Deng, J.D.: An energy efficient ant colony system for virtual machine placement in cloud computing. IEEE Trans. Evol. Comput. PP(99), 1 (2016)
8. Chen, H., Zhu, X.: Scheduling for workflows with security-sensitive intermediate data by selective tasks duplication in clouds. IEEE Trans. Parallel Distrib. Syst. 28(9), 2674–2688 (2017)
9. Gupta, S.R., Gajera, V.: An effective multi-objective workflow scheduling in cloud computing: a PSO based approach. In: International Conference on Contemporary Computing (2016)
10. Zhu, X., Yang, L.T., Chen, H., Wang, J., Yin, S., Liu, X.: Real-time tasks oriented energy-aware scheduling in virtualized clouds. IEEE Trans. Cloud Comput. 2(2), 168–180 (2014)

CGAN Based Cloud Computing Server Power Curve Generating

Longchuan Yan[1,2,3](✉), Wantao Liu[1,3], Yin Liu[4], and Songlin Hu[1,3]

[1] Institute of Information Engineering, Chinese Academy of Sciences,
Beijing 100093, China
yanlongchuan@iie.ac.cn
[2] State Grid Information and Telecommunication Branch,
Beijing 100761, China
[3] School of Cyber Security, University of Chinese Academy of Sciences,
Beijing 100049, China
[4] Beijing Guoxin Hengda Smart City Technology Development Co., Ltd.,
Beijing 100176, China

Abstract. For a better power management of data center, it is necessary to understand the power pattern and curve of various application servers before server placement and setup in data center. In this paper, a CGAN based method is proposed to generate power curve of servers for various applications in data center. Pearson Correlation is used to calculate the similarity between the generated data and the real data. From our experiment of data from real data center, the method can generate the power curve of servers with good similarity with real power data and can be used in server placement optimization and energy management.

Keywords: Generative Adversarial Nets
Conditional Generative Adversarial Nets · Cloud computing
Power curve generating

1 Introduction

With the increasingly wide application of Internet and Internet of things, the global demand for computing resources and storage resources is gradually increasing. A large number of new IT devices are put into the data center, and data centers consume a large amount of power, of which IT equipment and refrigeration are the two main types of energy source [1, 2]. Server is the most deployed IT device in data center. It is also the foundation of data center's service and an important part of energy management. In recent years, because of the development of demand driven and energy management technology for different types of services in the cloud computing, the cloud computing server presents new usage rules and energy consumption characteristics. The new and old equipment are working together, the energy consumption of new equipment is increasing gradually. With new model of server energy consumption coming with new applications, it is necessary to research and mater of the characteristics of energy

© Springer Nature Switzerland AG 2018
J. Vaidya and J. Li (Eds.): ICA3PP 2018, LNCS 11337, pp. 12–20, 2018.
https://doi.org/10.1007/978-3-030-05063-4_2

consumption of the cloud computing servers. According to the configuration and usage of the server, we can predict and generate the typical energy consumption curve of the cloud computing server automatically in advance, which is very important for the energy efficiency management and optimization of the data center.

There are two ways to model server energy consumption, one is component based modeling, and the other is performance counting based modeling. The server energy consumption model based on component usage is mainly based on the calculation of the total energy consumption of the server based on the usage of each component [3]. The server energy consumption model based on component usage is one of the classic modeling methods. The modeling method based on CPU usage rate is the earliest job. Some researchers have expanded the model and introduced the parameters of environment temperature, bus activity and processor frequency to the model, in order to improve the accuracy and applicability of the model. Recently, with the extensive application of deep learning and GPU, researchers have introduced high energy consuming components such as GPU into the model to improve the applicability of the model. Paper [4] discusses the modeling of static and dynamic energy consumption in multi-core processors. The energy consumption of the processor is divided into four parts: dynamic kernel energy consumption, non-kernel dynamic energy consumption, kernel static energy consumption and non-kernel static energy consumption. The four parts are modeled respectively. Finally, the total energy consumption is calculated. The paper further studies the effect of DVFS on processor energy consumption, and finds that not low frequency will bring low energy consumption.

These modeling methods are based on the running state of the device, and do not take into account the energy consumption characteristics of different services and applications at the data center level, and cannot predict the power needed for an application to run on a new server. This is needed for data center planning, server deployment and energy management. From the actual needs of data center, this paper studies how to generate the power curve of the server for various applications in advance, which can provide reference and guidance for energy consumption planning and management.

GAN (Generative Adversarial Nets) is a recently developed training method for generative models [5], which has been widely applied in the field of image and vision. The researchers have made a variety of improvements to the model. It has been able to generate objects such as digital number, face and some objects, and form a variety of realistic indoor and outdoor scenes, recover the original image from the segmentation image, color the black and white images, restore the object image from the object contour, and generate the high resolution image from the low resolution image, etc. [6–10].

In this paper, the generation method of energy consumption curve of server based on GAN is studied, and the advantages of GAN in estimating the probability distribution of sample data are used for the generation of server energy consumption. The energy consumption curves generated by the model can be used in the energy management of data centers such as server placement planning, Power Capping energy consumption management and room temperature optimization. It is of great significance for the resource scheduling and energy consumption optimization of the cloud computing data center.

Specifically, this paper makes the following contributions:

1. A CGAN based power generating model is proposed to enhance the quality of server power curve generation.
2. An evaluation method for the similarity of server energy consumption curve is proposed.

2 Analysis and Management of Server Power

2.1 Server Power Analysis

The server is one of the major energy consuming devices in the cloud computing data center, which accounts for about 40% of the energy consumption of the data center. The energy consumption of the server is closely related to many factors such as manufacturer, hardware configuration, application system type, resource usage and etc. A large number of servers in the data center show different energy consumption characteristics. The working day and non-working day have various energy consumption patterns. In the non-working day of the enterprise data center, the power consumption of the server is low than that of the working day.

It is shown that the energy consumption curves of the working day Web and DB servers of application system and computing and storage servers of big data processing system in Fig. 1. The Web server has a rapid increase in power in the morning and afternoon in the working day. There is a strong correlation between the power curve of the DB server and the Web server. The energy consumption of the database server is

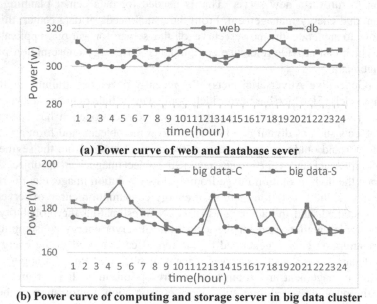

(a) Power curve of web and database sever

(b) Power curve of computing and storage server in big data cluster

Fig. 1. Server power curve of various applications

mainly due to the power rise caused by the user access of the working day and the backup of the non-working day. The energy consumption of big data cluster is mainly related to computing task.

The energy consumption of equipment can be divided into two parts: basic energy consumption (idle energy consumption) and dynamic energy consumption. The basic energy consumption is mainly related to the model and configuration of equipment. The dynamic energy consumption is related to the dynamic use of components such as CPU, memory, I/O and disk.

When the server is installed and deployed, we need to estimate the energy consumption characteristic and power curve of the server according to the server's manufacturer, model, configuration, and the type of application service, which can provide and guide the server's most deployment in the machine room and the management of the energy consumption of the cabinet.

From 2000 to now, the power characteristics of server are changing.

1. For the different needs of cloud computing, big data processing and artificial intelligence, GPU, FPGA, MIC and more acceleration cards are widely used in the server. New servers, such as computing servers, storage servers, deep learning computing servers and other servers with different configurations and functions, have emerged.
2. The storage and computing density of servers is getting higher and higher, which requires that the power supply capability of new data centers can be improved continuously.
3. Some vendors have integrated storage node, computing node and management node in a single machine cabinet, and designed an integrated machine for big data processing, cloud computing and deep learning.

The new development trends and features of these servers, as well as the mixed use of new and old equipment, increase the complexity of power supply, refrigeration, energy consumption management and adjustment of the server room, which brings new challenges to the energy consumption optimization of the cloud computing data center. So we need to research the power characteristics and pattern of the servers used in various application fields for a better energy management.

2.2 Application Scenarios of Server Power Curve

The data center is a scarce resource. It is a very economical mean for data center operation to deploy more servers and ensure its safe operation under the constraints of the limited physical space, power and temperature. Some researchers proposed many technologies to improve the efficiency of data center power, such as cluster scheduling [11], server power capping [12], reducing power fragmentation [13], dynamic voltage frequency scaling (DVFS) and power management in data center [12].

Server power curve and characteristics is needed in the above technologies to find the optimal server placement in racks, set the value of power capping in advance, or schedule the servers according the power utilization pattern.

The energy consumption data of servers in data center is monitored, which contain energy consumption characteristics and probability distribution in these data with the server. Understand and grasp the hidden information consumption pattern can describe the server's predictive generation server energy consumption curve.

In this paper, the power data of different types of servers in an enterprise data center is used to train an improved CGAN model to obtain statistical characteristics of servers for generating server power cure in advance. The research results will be used for power capping setting in advance and server placement planning and etc.

3   Server Power Generative Model

3.1   GAN

There are at least two modules in the GAN framework: the generation model (GM) and the discriminative model (DM). The purpose of the generation model is to learn the real data distribution as much as possible, and the purpose of the discriminative model is to determine the input data from the real data as far as possible. The two models compete with each other, generating models and finally producing fairly good output. The computation procedure and structure of GAN is shown in Fig. 2. G and D represent the generation model and the discriminative model respectively in this paper.

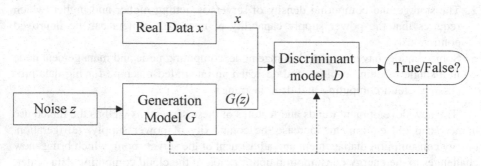

Fig. 2. Computation procedure and structure of GAN

The model training process is actually a zero sum game about G and D. Then the loss function of the generating model G is ObjG (θ G) = −ObjD (θD, θG). So the optimization problem of GAN is a two-player min-max problem. The objective function of GAN can be described as follows:

$$\min_G \max_D V(D, G) = E_{x \sim P_{data}(x)}[\log D(x)] + E_{z \sim P_z(z)}[\log(1 - D(G(z)))] \quad (1)$$

In GAN theory, it is not necessary to require that G and D are all neural networks. They only need to be able to match the corresponding generating and discriminating functions. But in practice, deep neural networks are commonly used as G and D. A GAN application of excellent needs a good training method. Otherwise, the output of the neural network model will not be ideal due to the freedom of the neural network model.

3.2 Conditional GAN

Conditional GAN (CGAN) [6] proposed to add additional information y to G model, D models, and real data to train the model, where y can be tagging or other auxiliary information. In generator the prior noise p(z), and y are combined together as input. In discriminator x and y are presented as input and to a discriminative function. The objective function of a CGAN would be as follows.

$$\min_G \max_D V(D, G) = E_{x \sim P_{data}(x)}[logD(x|y)] + E_{z \sim P_z(z)}[\log(1 - D(G(z|y)))] \quad (2)$$

3.3 Server Power Generative Model

In this paper, CGAN is used to generate server power curve for data center IT equipment management. Some related parameters of server are used as extra information, such as server brand, server model, application type, working-day and non-working day info and etc. The power generative model can learn the pattern of various servers by the control of the extra information. We can use the model generate new server power curve that can be used in server placement optimization, power capping, energy management and etc.

In this model, auxiliary information y and x are combined together as input of generative model G, and auxiliary information y is also sent to the discriminative model D.

4   Experimental Results

The power data of servers collected from the monitoring system in our data center by Intelligent Platform Management Interface (IPMI). There are over 120 servers in our power data generating experiment. We collect the server power data every 3 min, with a total of 480 data points per day. The time of data collect is about 2 weeks.

4.1 Result of GAN Experiment

In this paper, GAN network is used to generate the power curve of the server firstly. The generator uses a three layer fully connected neural network. The number of neurons in each layer is 100, 128 and 480 respectively. The discriminator uses three layers of neural networks. The number of neurons in each layer is 480, 128 and 1, respectively. The activation function of the first layer of the generator and discriminator is Relu, and the third layer activation function is Sigmod. The loss function is cross entropy and the training algorithm is Adam algorithm.

In this case, two types of servers are trained, one is the server with high power fluctuation and the other is the server with low power fluctuation. As shown in Fig. 3, the server power curve generated by the GAN network shows that the generated server power curve amplitude is very similar to the original power.

The disadvantage of GAN is unable to control the power curve corresponding to the server model or the application type, which limit the practical application of GAN.

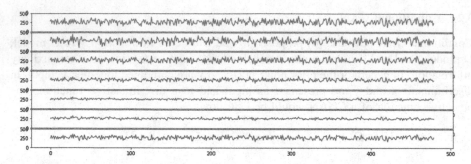

Fig. 3. Server power curve generated by GAN (Watt)

4.2   Result of CGAN Experiment

For a better practical application, CGAN is used to generate the power curve of server in data center. In our experiments, the data of application type, server model and wording day are used as auxiliary information in CGAN. There are four kinds of server applications in our experiments, such as application server, VM host, database server and big data processing system server. Due to working day has different power pattern with the non-working day, working day information is also used. There are 6 kinds of server in this test. Some configuration and primary power information of the server is listed in Table 1.

Table 1. Configuration and power information of various servers.

Server model	Number of CPU	Number of Disk	Capacity of RAM (GB)	Min and Max power in data set (Watt)
IBM 3650	2	2	32	110, 146
Hanbai C640	2	2	128	166, 249
Inspur NF8560	4	4	32	458, 555
Inspur NF8470	4	4	128	215, 477
Sugon I840	4	4	128	247, 353
Sugon I980	4	4	128	933, 1187

In this CGAN experiment, the structure of the natural network is similar to the above experiment. The generator uses a three layer fully connected neural network. The number of neurons in each layer is 112, 128 and 480 respectively. The discriminator uses three layers of neural networks. The number of neurons in each layer is 492, 128 and 1, respectively. Activation function and training method is the same to the above GAN experiment.

There are five power curves is shown in Fig. 4, which was generated by CGAN. From top to down, the corresponding servers of these pictures are NF8470 as VM host, NF8470 as application server, IBM 3650 as database server, NF8470 as database server and I840 as database server respectively in working day.

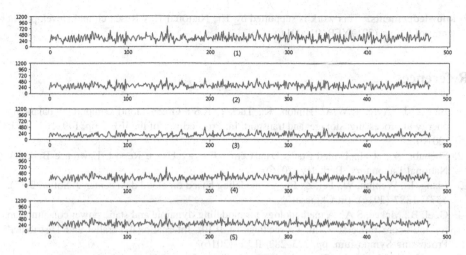

Fig. 4. Server power curve generated by CGAN (Watt)

Pearson Correlation is a kind of measure of similarity widely used in statistical analysis of data. In this paper, Person Correlation is used to calculate the similarity between the generated power curve and the real data. The definition of Pearson Correlation is listed in Eq. (3).

$$\rho(X, Y) = \frac{E[(X - \mu_X)(Y - \mu_Y)]}{\sqrt{\sum_{i=1}^{n}(X_i - \mu_X)^2}\sqrt{\sum_{i=1}^{n}(Y - \mu_Y)^2}} \tag{3}$$

We calculated the Pearson Correlation between the generated power curve and the real power data in the same server model and application type. The value of Pearson Correlation is between 0.65–0.72, which indicates that the generated power curves have good similarity with the real power data from data center.

5 Conclusions

For the server power curve prediction issue in cloud computing, a CGAN based power curve generating model is proposed in this paper. The model integrated some auxiliary information to control the curve pattern. The extra information is used to improve the accuracy of server power curve prediction under various servers. From our experiments, the proposed method can generated the power curves with good similarity with the real power data.

In future, we will explore the finer auxiliary information to boost the model. The proposed method will be used in power capping setting, server scheduling and power management in cloud data center to save energy consumption and support more servers.

Acknowledgements. This work is supported by The National Key Research and Development Program of China (2017YFB1010001).

References

1. Baliga, J., Ayre, R.W.A., Hinton, K., Tucker, R.S.: Green cloud computing: balancing energy in processing, storage, and transport. In: Proceedings of the IEEE, pp. 149–167. IEEE (2010)
2. Shehabi, A., et al.: United States Data Center Energy Usage Report. Lawrence Berkeley National Laboratory, Berkeley (2016)
3. Liang, L., Wenjun, W., Fei, Z.: Energy modeling based on cloud data center. J. Softw. **25**(7), 1371–1387 (2014). (in Chinese)
4. Goel, B., Mckee, S.A.: A methodology for modeling dynamic and static power consumption for multicore processors. In: Proceedings of IEEE International Parallel and Distributed Processing Symposium, pp. 273–282. IEEE (2016)
5. Goodfellow, I., et al.: Generative adversarial nets. In: Advances in Neural Information Processing Systems, vol. 27, pp. 2672–2680. NIPS (2014)
6. Mirza, M., Osindero, S.: Conditional Generative Adversarial Nets, arxiv:1411.1784 (2014)
7. Radford, A., Metz, L., Chintala, S.: Unsupervised representation learning with deep convolutional generative adversarial networks. In: Proceedings of International Conference on Learning Representations, arxiv:1511.06434 (2016)
8. Chen, X., Duan, Y., Houthooft, R., Schulman, J., Sutskever, I., Abbeel, P.: Infogan: interpretable representation learning by information maximizing generative adversarial nets. In: Advances in Neural Information Processing Systems, vol. 29, pp. 2172–2180. NIPS (2016)
9. Zhao, J., Mathieu M., Lecun, Y.: Energy-based generative adversarial network. In: Proceedings of International Conference on Learning Representations, arxiv:1609.03126 (2017)
10. Berthelot, D., Schumm, T., Metz, L.: BEGAN: boundary equilibrium generative adversarial networks, arxiv:1703.10717 (2017)
11. Wong, D.: Peak efficiency aware scheduling for highly energy proportional servers. In: Proceedings of International Symposium on Computer Architecture, pp. 481–492. IEEE (2016)
12. Wu, Q., et al.: Dynamo: facebook's data center-wide power management system. In: Proceedings of ACM/IEEE International Symposium on Computer Architecture, pp. 469–480. IEEE (2016)
13. Hsu, C.-H., Deng, Q., Mars, J., Tang, L.: SmoothOperator: reducing power fragmentation and improving power utilization in large-scale datacenters. In: Proceedings of the Twenty-Third International Conference on Architectural Support for Programming Languages and Operating Systems, pp. 535–548. ACM (2018)

One-Sided Communication in Coarray Fortran: Performance Tests on TH-1A

Peiming Guo[✉] and Jianping Wu

School of Meteorology and Oceanology,
National University of Defense Technology, Changsha 410073, China
gpmnudt@163.com

Abstract. One-sided communication mechanism of Messaging Passing Interface (MPI) has been extended by remote memory access (RMA) from several aspects, including interface, language and compiler, etc. Coarray Fortran (CAF), as an emerging syntactic extension of Fortran to satisfy one-sided communication, has been freely supported by the open-source and widely used GNU Fortran compiler, which relies on MPI-3 as the transport layer. In this paper, we present the potential of RMA to benefit the communication patterns in Cannon algorithm. EVENTS, a safer implementation of atomics to synchronize different processes in CAF, are also introduced via classic Fast Fourier Transform (FFT). In addition, we also studied the performance of one-sided communication based on different compilers. In our tests, one-sided communication outperforms two-sided communication only when the data size is large enough (in particular, inter-node transfer). CAF is slightly faster than the simple one-sided routines without optimization by compiler in MPI-3. EVENTS are capable of improving the performance of parallel applications by avoiding the idle time.

Keywords: One-sided communication · Coarray Fortran · MPI

1 Introduction

In the presence of ever-increasing requirements for accessing and processing large-scale data sets, Message Passing Interface (MPI) that has long been a language-free communication protocol with supports for point-to-point communication and broadcast is suffering from the following issues: (1) the burden of explicitly calling communication functions and directives increases the difficulty of programming; (2) A time-consuming global computation is needed for data transmission to issue the matching operations; (3) Limited execution control statements for managing the completion of asynchronous operations. To solve the above problems, a new communication mechanism named as one-sided communication has evolved in the last few years.

Point-to-point (two-sided) communication mechanism is mainly composed of sending and receiving operations, and the messages transferred by these operations include not only data, but also an envelope containing source, destination, tag and communicator [1]. The envelope indicates the information which is used by processes to distinguish and selectively receive data they need. There are two basic communication modes for point-to-point data transfer: blocking and non-blocking. A blocking

© Springer Nature Switzerland AG 2018
J. Vaidya and J. Li (Eds.): ICA3PP 2018, LNCS 11337, pp. 21–33, 2018.
https://doi.org/10.1007/978-3-030-05063-4_3

way means the synchronous execution of processes and the other means asynchronous execution of processes. In blocking mode, the sender cannot modify the local send buffer until the messages have been safely stored in receive buffer. However, non-blocking mode allows communication functions return as soon as the data transfer has been invoked, which is beneficial for overlapping communication and computation.

One-sided communication mechanism was first extended by remote memory access (RMA) in MPI-3 and serves as a mechanism that allows a single communication caller, whether sending side or receiving side, to specify all communication parameters. MPI-3 becomes more usable comparing with MPI-2 as the consequence of a substantial improvement in RMA [2]. In the traditional message-passing model, the communication and synchronization operations are often tied together (e.g., blocking/non-blocking communication), while RMA separates these two functions through remote writing, remote reading, and synchronization operations, etc. As a result, the explicit identification of the completion of an asynchronous operation becomes highly feasible in one-sided communication.

RMA allows users to directly access and update remote data without sending the data back to local cache or memory. In other words, RMA provides a convenient and faster mechanism for data transfer between different images without the hand-shake operation in two-sided communication modes [3]. From this point of view, one-sided communication using RMA mechanisms can avoid the time-consuming global computation or explicit polling for communication requests in point-to-point communication. In the field of one-sided communication, there have been many researches based on different compilers and transport layers [4, 5].

1.1 MPI-3 Interface for One-Sided Communication

Coincident with the development of one-sided communication, several significant extensions in MPI version 3.0 including RMA communication calls and Fortran 2008 bindings were defined and implemented by the MPI Forum in September 21, 2012. For example, MPI_PUT performs the dater transfer from the origin memory to the target memory and MPI_GET transfer data from the target memory to the origin memory in contrast. Being similar with MPI-2, one-sided communication in MPI-3 has also defined the gather and scatter operations between source and destination. However, conflicting operations to the same memory location are not allowed. Namely, when a RMA operation is performed, the local communication buffer should not be updated. In particular, a get call will lock the local memory buffer and it should not be accessed by any remote process.

To meet the requirements for remote memory access, MPI-3 currently provides active and passive routines to support one-sided communication [6]. Active target communication ensures the synchronization between origin and target process, but it will also bring ineffective implementations caused by WAIT operations. Passive target communication shows more efficient than the active routine without regard to the ordering of continuous communication calls (e.g., MPI_PUT, MPI_GET), therefore it is usually an unsafe way to transfer data when a single process is involved in different RMA operations.

1.2   Syntactic Extensions in Fortran 2008: CAF

In recent years, Coarray Fortran is increasingly applied in large-scale scientific computing and expected to optimize communication mechanism as well as to simplify the structure of code [7, 8]. Generally, we call it as CAF which emerged as a highly usable tool for one-sided communication. CAF was first added into Fortran 2008 as a data entity to support Partitioned Global Address Space (PGAS) programming model which takes advantage of one-sided communication for data transfer [9]. When a Fortran program containing coarray starts to run, it will be replicated itself into many duplicates, which are executed asynchronously [10]. The number of duplicates can be set at run-time, from the environment variables or compiler options. Each duplicate can be viewed as an image residing on a processor or node with its own data entity. Fortran syntax introduces image index in square brackets to reference coarray distributed across individual images, and coarray without square brackets means local data.

CAF coincides with MPI-3 on the demand of one-sided communication with a clear difference between them. The message-passing interface is a portable communication interface standard, not a specific programming language [11]. Therefore, people who use MPI-3 to transfer data should be proficient in the static structure of the library with the form of invoking functions. Unlike MPI-3, CAF relics on the architecture of a particular compiler to implement the Partitioned Global address Space model (PGAS) [12], which means that the users can make use of the optimization from compiler itself which is unavailable to MPI-3.

1.3   Freely Supported by Specific Compiler: GNU

Commercial compilers such as Intel Fortran compilers have restricted the development of CAF for a long time. There was almost no free, open-source compiler to fully support CAF until the OpenCoarrays (an open-source software project collecting transport layers to support CAF in GNU Compiler) was released, which provides a one-sided communication library to GNU Fortran (Gfortran) version 5.1. OpenCoarrays contains two runtime library: one based on MPI-3, widely covers the extended coarray features in Fortran 2008, and the other based on GASNet, for more professional users. Our experiments therefore chose MPI-3 as the underlying library of CAF programming for one-sided communication.

OpenCoarrays serves the purpose that providing an application binary interface (ABI) to convert high-level communication and synchronization into elegance calls to the underlying library [13]. After the installation of OpenCoarrays, an external library (libcaf_mpi) related to multi-image execution is generated. Gfortran improves the multi-image support for coarrays through the underlying libraries (e.g., GasNet and MPI-3) [14]. In addition, CAF was used in the open-source OpenUH compiler to develop data-intensive applications for the porting of reverse time migration in seismic exploration [15], and Notified Access in CAF provided by a run-time library (LIB-CAF_MPI) was proposed to associate coarray variables with event variables [16]. Intel Fortran has implemented coarrays as well as corresponding synchronization constructs and outperforms Gfortran only on intra-node scalars transfers [17]. Furthermore, MPI-3 extended the communication between sender and receiver with synchronization operations [18]. Generally speaking, the performance of CAF in large-scale parallel computation relies not only on the architectures of supercomputers, but also on the combinations of compiler and library. However, the comparative study of CAF and MPI-3 is rare, which prompts our research.

Our research aims to study the performance of one-sided communication based on GNU compiler and several comparative experiments are presented in this paper. Besides, we also present the performance of CAF based on OpenUH compiler and the new proposed explicit synchronization mechanism (EVENTS) in CAF is introduced in the following sections. This paper will contribute to the development of large-scale integral operations in Numerical Weather Prediction (NWP) and our research can also remove the inefficiency incurred by implicit synchronization mechanism.

This paper is organized as follows. In Sect. 2 we provide an overview of Cannon algorithm and Fast Fourier Transform is introduced in Sect. 3. Then in Sect. 4, we present the performance comparisons from three aspects: communication models (CAF vs. MPI-3), compilers (Gfortran vs. OpenUH) and synchronization mechanisms (SYNC ALL vs. EVENTS). The implementation of CAF involves Cannon algorithm, Fast Fourier Transform and the EPCC CAF Micro-benchmark suite running on multiple cores on the leadership HPC platform: TH-1A. Finally in Sect. 5, we report our conclusions.

2 Cannon Algorithm to Solve Matrix Multiplication

Cannon algorithm is designed to perform matrix multiplication in parallel, which represents one of the most common communication patterns in scientific computing: the halo exchange [19]. The main idea is to divide the whole matrix into small ones, and each one resides on a single patch. Then the data on separate patches is driven to perform cyclic shift along the rows and columns, avoiding the many-to-many communication in block-by-block multiplication. If there are 16 processors and the two-dimensional matrices are of size 100 * 100, the corresponding cannon algorithm employing CAF consists of these three parts:

2.1 Data Arrangement

In order to take advantage of RMA mechanism, data on all processors should be defined as coarrays so that they could be easily accessed by other images. Both matrix A and matrix B are split into 16 small matrices of size 25 * 25 and are evenly distributed to 16 processors.

2.2 Cyclic Shift and Calculation

Considering the characteristics of Cartesian topological structure, cycle operations is depicted as follow: First, we move the block matrix A_{ij} in this column left with displacement of i and the block matrix B_{ij} in this row up with displacement j, respectively. Then the multiplication of the present A and B blocks is performed. The shifts are repeated 4 times. In the remaining 3 cycles, every cycle is divided into two parts: shift and computation. The result of every cycle is stored in the local processor. After 4 cycles, we can get the last result C_{ij} on processor P_{ij}.

According to the aforementioned Cannon algorithm, every image needs to obtain data from the right and bottom boundaries. Adjacent images can use halos for data exchange.

As shown in Fig. 1, the part surrounded by blue box represents the halo space of the image 10. All the data in this halo space will be obtained by image 10 before its computation in every step. Since the array in the halo region is not contiguous, the two-sided communication strategy employing MPI could not consistently send the data from separate memory to image 10. This prompts users have to call the sending and receiving functions twice in order to complete the transfer of data. In addition, unless the halo width is the same as the block matrix's order, it always bring out inefficiency that a time-consuming global data transfer is performed because of the lack of support for "stride transfer" in two-sided communication. CAF has syntax to support efficient non-contiguous array transfer by using buffers on both sender and receiver.

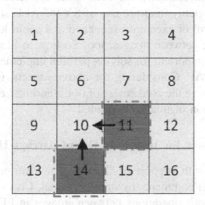

Fig. 1. Halos in Cannon algorithm

3 Explicit Management for Asynchronous Operations in FFT

For the sake of completeness, we also studied the new fine grain synchronization mechanism known as EVENTS in CAF through an application on FFT, and analyze the identification of the completion which is essential for asynchronous processes.

The underlying library (libcaf_mpi) produced by Opencoarrays employs the passive target categories, where the target images have no explicit participation in communication. The robustness and effectiveness of this strategy turn out to be a puzzle when two RMA operations from different images have the same target. This puzzle is particularly evident in the butterfly operations of Cooley-Tukey FFT.

3.1 Implicit Management Brings Incorrectness and Inefficiency

In the previous studies based on MPI-2 to solve Cooler-Tukey FFT, a butterfly operation involving two processes will be carried out in the same node. The communication between different nodes must be considered before the computations in every step which means that synchronization statements (e.g. MPI_BARRIER, MPI_WAIT) followed by communication and computations are needed. As a result of that, redundant idle time caused by the implicit management for the completion of asynchronous operations will be inevitably produced.

For example, the FFT at 8 points requires three levels of butterfly operations and each point resides on one image. Each level includes 4 butterfly operations and needs to specify the combinations of images to transfer data before computations. Therefore, the results of each step are highly data dependent, and the source and target images of communication changes dynamically in different levels. In this case, the use of general synchronization statements in MPI-2 shows a poor performance on the control of execution sequence and could lead to deadlock between images.

SYNC ALL is a robust synchronization mechanism for execution control in CAF. The execution of the segment before SYNC ALL statement precedes the execution of the segment following the SYNC ALL statement. However, images executed asynchronously in FFT remain unknown for each other and different tasks on odd-even images complete unpredictably, and the use of SYNC ALL statements shows a poor performance on the control of execution sequence and could lead to a lot of idle time and unexpected deadlock between images, too. So how to identify the completion of the tasks on all images is important for solving parallel implementation of FFT problem in a parallel way with CAF. Considering the above aspects, in order to improve the parallel efficiency and ensure the correctness of our algorithm, explicit management for the asynchronous execution of images is needed.

3.2   Explicit Management for Images in OpenCoarrays Using EVENTS

Gfortran (version 5.1+) with support of OpenCoarrays currently supports EVENTS which is competitive with commercial compilers (Intel, Cray). Before identifying the completion of asynchronous operations between images in FFT techniques, we must declare event variables as coarrays which could be accessed remotely. An event variable is equivalent to a counter that can be atomically accumulated by any image through EVENT POST statement, and the image invocating EVENT WAIT will wait for the local event variable reaching a certain threshold. This is a robust way to manage asynchronous operations in FFT.

Different from the traditional messaging-passing way, we split the butterfly operation into two parts: task1 and task2, each of which is performed by a single node. The data transfer between different nodes follows RMA routines. Figure 2 illustrates the first level butterfly operation between image1 and image2 using EVENTS variables to synchronize different tasks in them. First, image1 calls EVENT_WAIT to wait for image2 to get data from image1. Once image2 complete task2, it will call EVENT_POST to notify image1 to receive data from image2 and to finish the left computations. Then, both image1 and image2 keep on waiting for the next level butterfly operation.

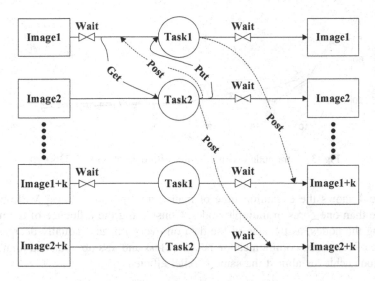

Fig. 2. Cooler-Tukey FFT using EVENTS

4 Result

CAF is now available on GNU compiler. In this section, we present several comparative experiments on the performance of one-sided communication and synchronization operations in CAF. All the tests are based on Cannon algorithm and Cooler-Tukey FFT. For the purpose of our investigation, we run our codes on 4 compute nodes equipped with Intel Xeon at 2.6 GHz in TH-1A. We conducted ten iterations for every test and select peak values as the experiment result.

4.1 Comparisons Between CAF and MPI-3

It is worth mentioning that MPI-3 support both one-sided communication and two-sided communication, thus, the comparative study between CAF and MPI-3 could be divided into two parts: (1) Comparison of communication mechanisms: one-sided communication vs. two-sided communication; (2) Whether one-sided communication is optimized by GNU compiler or not: CAF vs. MPI-3. The codes were generally the same except for the communication patterns, which is beneficial to the corresponding comparative experimental study.

As shown in Fig. 3, MPI represents the traditional interface for two-sided communication. This figure shows the execution time of matrix multiplication using MPI and CAF with more than one cores in a single node, which means that the influence of the network connecting the nodes is not involved. As we can see from the Fig. 2, when the data size on each image is not very large, the execution time of the algorithm using CAF is always shorter than that using MPI within a single node.

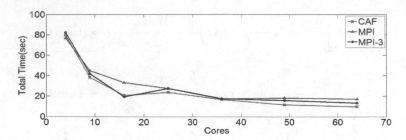

Fig. 3. Intra-node execution time with data of 3360 * 3360

Figure 4 shows the execution time of matrix multiplication using MPI and CAF with more than one cores in multiple nodes. Considering the influence of the network connecting the nodes, as the size of the data on every image gradually decreases, the advantage of one-sided communication becomes less and less obvious and finally these two methods achieves almost the same parallel efficiency.

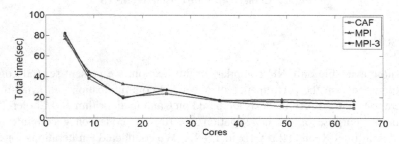

Fig. 4. Inter-node execution time with data of 3360 * 3360

In our experiments, the codes of CAF used one-sided communication defined by coarray whereas the codes of MPI-3 called MPI_Get functions to access remote memory. The results from averaging ten iterations on TH-1A are shown in Figs. 3 and 4. Both CAF and MPI-3 improve the execution speed relative to two-sided communication and the performance differences between CAF and MPI-3 are weakly measurable because CAF is usually but not always faster than MPI-3. As described in Sect. 1, CAF relies on Gfortran to implement one-sided communication which is a compiler-based approach but MPI-3 is a library-based approach that does not rely on any compiler. Therefore, it is easier to port MPI-3 to other compilers to enhance the scalability of one-sided communication. CAF can make use of the optimizations based on Gfortran to show a slight performance improvement.

To study further the impacts of data size and the network connecting the nodes on one-sided communication, we carried out the experiments of cannon algorithm for two-dimensional arrays of different orders on single node and multiple nodes. The experimental results are presented in Fig. 5. It shows a similar phenomenon with Figs. 1 and 2. We can see that on whether a single node or multiple nodes, it requires enough computation and communication to demonstrate the performance differences between

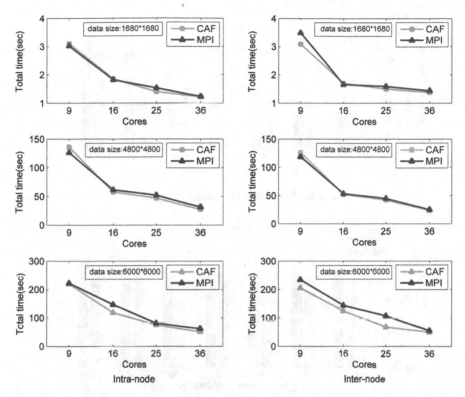

Fig. 5. Intra/inter-node execution time with data of different sizes

one-sided communication and two-sided communication. In particular, the network between nodes in TH-1A is more prone to the saturation of data than that in a single node. Therefore, we can conclude that one-sided communication outperforms two-sided communication only on large transfers, and inter-node transfers demands a larger scale of data to maintain these advantages on execution time.

4.2   Comparisons Between Gfortran and OpenUH

OpenUH is an open source compiler including numerous optimization components based on the infrastructure of Open64. In our research, the EPCC CAF Micro-benchmark suite [20] was applied to testing the optimization effect of Gfortran and OpenUH. We measured the latency and bandwidth of the single point-to-point put operation on one node, which means a best case to study the performance of compilers because the network connecting multiple nodes is ignored. Here we present the tests performed on a single node of TH-1A.

This test employed 16 images to complete the put operation. Image 1 communicates only with image 2 and all the other images keeps waiting until the end of the code execution. Figures 6 and 7 show that OpenUH outperforms Gfortran when the data size is small, namely that OpenUH has advantages in small transfers such as scalars in the absence of resource competition.

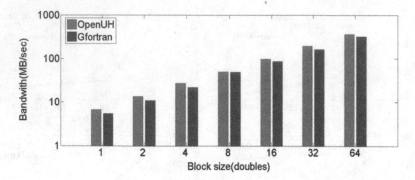

Fig. 6. Bandwidth put small block size

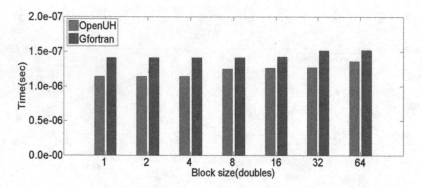

Fig. 7. Latency put small block size

As the data size increases, the relationship between the two is reversed and the trend of liner growth becomes unstable. Figure 8 shows that Gfortran outperforms OpenUH when the data size is large. Through experimental comparison, we find that the performance of these two compilers for one-sided communication is different depending on the data size. In the applications of HPC, Gfortran is therefore an option worth considering to use one-sided communication technology to perform super large scale array operations.

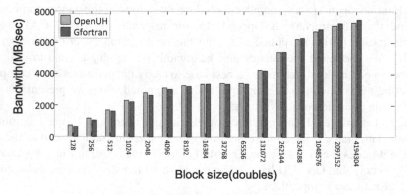

Fig. 8. Bandwidth put large block size

4.3   Comparisons Between SYNC ALL and EVENTS

In our experiments, the code using EVENTS only differs from that using SYNC ALL in synchronization mechanisms, therefore these two methods produce the same computation time. We can see that the latency of SYNC ALL shows an exponential growth as the number of images increases in Fig. 9 EVENTS can save a lot of idle time because both the EVENT POST and EVENT WAIT statements are non-blocking and the efficiency of global synchronization is avoided by explicitly identifying the completions of different tasks in a counting way.

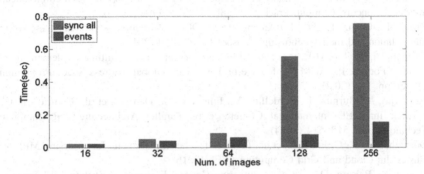

Fig. 9. Execution time of FFT

5   Conclusion

One-sided communication is a new communication mechanism to enhance the performance of parallel algorithms. CAF and MPI-3 promote the development of this style of communication respectively from the language layer and interface layer In our research, a series of comparative experiments was conducted to study the potential of RMA mechanism to reduce communication time and improve parallel efficiency. In addition, we compare OpenUH with Gfortran for the basic operation of CAF from the EPCC CAF Micro-benchmark.

Both CAF and MPI-3 which employ one-sided communication outperform the traditional interface that employs two-sided communication, and CAF slightly outperform MPI-3 in intra-node transferring as a result of compiler optimization. Affected by the network connecting different nodes, the difference in inter-node transfers between CAF and MPI becomes less obvious except when the data size is large enough. OpenUH has an advantage over Gfortran in small transfers but presents inferiority in large transfers. Implementing EVENTS to synchronize images in CAF applications provides a performance improvement on TH-1A and FFT. This research confirms the robustness of CAF in parallel computing and it should be developed for the future super large scale parallel computing platforms.

Acknowledgments. This work is funded by NSFC (41875121, 61379022). The authors would like to thank Gcc team for providing compiler resources to carry out this research and the editors for their helpful suggestions.

References

1. Ghosh, S., Hammond, R., et al.: One-sided interface for matrix operations using MPI-3 RMA: a case study with elemental. In: International Conference on Parallel Processing, pp. 185–194. IEEE (2016)
2. Dinan, J., et al.: An implementation and evaluation of the MPI 30 one-sided communication interface. Concurr. Comput. Pract. Exp. **28**(17), 4385–4404 (2016)
3. Guo, M., Chen, T., et al.: An improved DOA estimation approach using coarray interpolation and matrix denoising. Sensors **17**(5), 1140 (2017)
4. Eachempati, D., Jun, H.J., et al.: An open-source compiler and runtime implementation for Coarray Fortran. In: ACM Conference on Partitioned Global Address Space Programming Model, pp. 1–8 (2010)
5. Fanfarillo, A., Burnus, T., Cardellini, V., Filippone, S., Dan, N., et al.: Coarrays in GNU Fortran. In: IEEE International Conference on Parallel Architecture and Compilation Techniques, pp. 513–514 (2014)
6. Dosanjh, M.G.F., Grant, R.E., et al.: RMA-MT: a benchmark suite for assessing MPI multi-cluster. In: Cloud and Grid Computing. IEEE (2016)
7. Garain, S., Balsara, D.S., et al.: Comparing Coarray Fortran (CAF) with MPI for several structured mesh PDE applications. Academic Press Professional, Inc. (2015)
8. Rouson, D., Gutmann, E.D., Fanfarillo, A., et al.: Performance portability of an intermediate-complexity atmospheric research model in Coarray Fortran. In: PGAS Applications Workshop, pp. 1–4 (2017)
9. Jin, G., Mellorcrummey, J., Adhianto, L., Iii, W.N.S., et al.: Implementation and performance evaluation of the HPC challenge benchmarks in Coarray Fortran 2.0. In: IEEE International Parallel & Distributed Processing Symposium, pp. 1089–1100 (2011)
10. Zhou, H., Idrees, K., Gracia, J.: Leveraging MPI-3 shared-memory extensions for efficient PGAS runtime systems. In: Träff, J.L., Hunold, S., Versaci, F. (eds.) Euro-Par 2015. LNCS, vol. 9233, pp. 373–384. Springer, Heidelberg (2015). https://doi.org/10.1007/978-3-662-48096-0_29
11. Fanfarillo, A., Hammond, J.: CAF events implementation using MPI-3 capabilities. In: ACM European MPI Users' Group Meeting, pp. 198–207 (2016)
12. Iwashita, H., Nakao, M., Murai, H., et al.: A source-to-source translation of Coarray Fortran with MPI for high performance. In: The International Conference, pp. 86–97 (2018)
13. OpenCoarrays. http://www.opencoarrays.org
14. GNU Compiler Collection. https://gcc.gnu.org
15. Eachempati, D., Richardson, A., Liao, T., Calandra, H., et al.: A Coarray Fortran implementation to support data-intensive application development. Cluster Comput. **17**(2), 569–583 (2014)
16. Fanfarillo, A., Vento, D.: Notified access in Coarray Fortran. In: European MPI Users' Group Meeting, pp. 1–7 (2017)
17. Fanfarillo, A., Rouson, D., et al.: OpenCoarrays: open-source transport layers supporting Coarray Fortran compilers. In: ACM International Conference on Partitioned Global Address Space Programming MODELS, pp. 1–11 (2014)

18. MPI Forum: A Message-Passing Interface Standard. University of Tennessee, pp. 403–418 (2012)
19. Yang, C., Murthy, K., Mellor-Crummey, J.: Managing asynchronous operations in Coarray Fortran 2.0. In: 27th International Parallel and Distributed Processing Symposium, vol. 36, no. 2, pp. 1321–1332. IEEE (2013)
20. Henty, D.: Performance of Fortran coarrays on the Cray XE6. In: Proceedings of Cray Users Groups. Applications, Tools and Techniques on the Road to Exascale Computing, pp. 281–288. IOS Press (2013)

Reliable Content Delivery in Lossy Named Data Networks Based on Network Coding

Rui Xu[✉], Hui Li[✉], and Huayu Zhang

Shenzhen Key Laboratory of Information Theory and Future Network
Architecture, Future Network PKU Laboratory of National Major Research
Infrastructure, PKU Institute of Big Data Technology,
Shenzhen Engineering Lab of Converged Networking Technology,
Shenzhen Graduate School, Peking University,
Beijing, People's Republic of China
xurui.stone@foxmail.com, lih64@pkusz.edu.cn,
geb.mmp@gmail.com

Abstract. Named Data Networking (NDN) is a new content transmission and retrieval network architecture, its network cache and request mechanism can improve network transmission performance and reduce transmission delay. Network coding has been considered as especially suitable for latency and lossy network, providing reliable multicast transport without requiring feedback from receivers. However, for network coding, the best practical advantage is robustness and adaptability, without caring the change of networks. The purpose of this paper is to improve the reliability of content delivery in lossy NDN networks by network coding. In this paper, we use network coding as an error control technique in NDN. We analyze the performance of network coding compared with automatic repeat request (ARQ) and forward error correction (FEC) technique in lossy NDN networks. We confirm that network coding can reduce the number of packets retransmitted in lossy NDN networks. Extensive real physical emulation shows that network coding reduces the number of packet retransmission and improves the reliability of content delivery in lossy NDN networks.

Keywords: Named Data Networking · Network coding
Reliable content delivery · Lossy networks

1 Introduction

In the current Internet network architecture, communication sides transmit IP packets through a single transmission link to complete communication. However, taking into consideration that future Internet application mainly focuses on distribution and sharing of content, traditional client-server mode exposes more and more disadvantages. Information-centric networking (ICN) [1, 2] is a new communication paradigm that aims at increasing the security and efficiency of content delivery. The NDN [1] architecture proposed by Zhang et al. is one of the most popular ICN architectures. Different from current transmission way that uses IP to identify location of content, NDN names content directly, which makes content become the first entity in network.

© Springer Nature Switzerland AG 2018
J. Vaidya and J. Li (Eds.): ICA3PP 2018, LNCS 11337, pp. 34–46, 2018.
https://doi.org/10.1007/978-3-030-05063-4_4

NDN routes by content name, caches content in router and gets content nearby [1], so it can achieve fast content transmission and retrieval.

The most important point in NDN is communication mode, which is mainly driven by content consumers. To receive content, consumer shall send out interest packets that carry the name of desired content [2]. The same interest packets sent by different multiple consumers may meet in a node and be merged before being forwarded [16]. Data packet takes the same path as interest packet forwarded, but in the reverse direction. It is in this process, consumer only cares what the content is rather than where the content comes from and locates.

Network coding was first proposed by Ahlswede et al. [3, 4] in 2000, In traditional network, intermediate nodes only transmit received packet to next node, that is to say, storage and forwarding. Network coding is a kind of channel coding technology that combines routing with coding. The role of intermediate node is not only storage or forwarding, but also processing data received from input channel linearly or nonlinearly, and then transmitting the processed data to associated nodes through output channel, it concludes that intermediate nodes play the role of encoder/decoder. Network coding is also widely used in various fields such as file sharing, reliable storage, wireless network, network security and so on. The purpose of this paper is to improve the reliability of content delivery in lossy NDN networks by network coding. We can also see from Fig. 1 to understand our work.

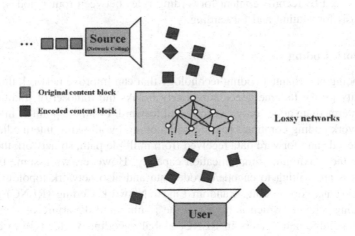

Fig. 1. A schematic diagram of our work in linear multicast, general lossy networks [6].

In lossy networks, network coding can improve the reliability of transmission by reducing packet retransmission frequency. After that, many studies have analyzed the reliable gain of network coding. While Ghaderi [5] and other researchers analyzed the reliable gain of network coding compared with ARQ and FEC under tree topology, also proved that network coding can reduce packet retransmission frequency in lossy networks compared with ARQ. In this paper, we try to extend this result to a more practical NDN network. We analyze the reliable gain of network coding compared with other error control technique in nontree topology. It will verify the advantage of network coding so as to extend the application of network coding in NDN to a wider field.

In this paper, we adopt network coding as an error control technique in lossy NDN networks to reduce packet retransmissions and improve the reliability of content delivery. We also develop an encoder/decoder that suits NDN to process real file by network coding. Then we build a real physical emulation environment to verify the reliable gain in lossy NDN networks by network coding. We also make main codes of our encoder/decoder open source in [26].

2 Background and Related Work

2.1 NDN Network Model

NDN is a kind of ICN architecture, which focuses on content itself, not location of content. Content name is the only unique identity used for routing and transmission, also network cache is one of the most important features in NDN architecture. The router in NDN has three important data structures [1, 2]: Content Store (CS), Pending Interest Table (PIT) and Forwarding Information Base (FIB). CS is the content storage part in NDN router, its main function is providing content cache. PIT records the name of interest packets that have been forwarded and the faces of these interest packets enter the router node. FIB records content forwarding rules between router nodes, which is the main basis for routing and forwarding.

2.2 Network Coding

Network coding is a channel coding technology that can improve network through-put and reliability [3, 4]. Its emergence completely breaks the mindset of traditional network that intermediate nodes only can store and forward. From the point of information theory, network coding combines routing with coding by allowing intermediate nodes to encode/decode and forward data received from multiple path, so network throughput can achieve the maximum communication capacity. However, we assume that intermediate nodes are willing to encode/decode data and also network topology is static when adopting network coding. Random Linear Network Coding (RLNC) is a very popular coding scheme, which is robust to the joining and departure of source node. There are two important vectors in RLNC, global encoding vector (GEV) and local encoding vector (LEC). This paper we want to verify that network coding can improve the reliability of content delivery in lossy NDN networks, then we use RLNC to process real files, which is very practical and useful.

2.3 Network Coding for Information Centric Networking

Network coding is suitable for ICN has been pointed out in [9] for the first time, network coding allows faces to request multiple encoded replicas content from multiple faces asynchronously [11, 13, 18], thus improving the efficiency of content delivery. RLNC is used for linear combination of original data packets rather than sending original data packets directly. RLNC also increases diversity of data packets, so received data packets have a higher diversity. Network coding is also suitable for improving cache hit rate [17, 20], this is due to recoding process performed by intermediate nodes. In addition, interest packets are forwarded randomly to maximize overall cache hit rate.

2.4 Analysis of Existing Work

In spite of the existing work [10–22], they do not consider the impact of modifications and limitations in ICN. Most works use additional headers for network coding and handle similar messages compared with regular network traffic, these works also ignore content name is the most important part in ICN, therefore, the process of matching data packets should be based on content name rather than the logo in data packet.

Most of the existing works also assume a very ideal experiment environment, modification of ICN may make these works not such useful in a practical environment. The existing works [10–13] and [15–19] do not take into consideration that the safety aspect of ICN. Because content publishers sign each segment, recoding through network coding is equivalent to generate new data packet with new signature. Therefore, recoding cannot be carried out transparently in intermediate node without requester node notices it. If the generated data packets are not signed, malicious nodes can interfere with communication by introducing a single pseudo message. If an encoding node will sign the message, a transitive trust model is needed.

3 Named Data Networking with Network Coding in Lossy Networks

3.1 Network Model and Analysis

Error control technique mentioned in this paper includes the following four kinds: end-to-end ARQ, end-to-end FEC, link-to-link ARQ and network coding (link-to-link FEC) [5].

In this part, we define the successful transmission of a packet to the user as the packet transmission. Suppose there are two mutually independent *userA* and *userB* in the NDN network. The probability of packet loss in one independent user is p_n, $n \in \{A, B\}$ and packet loss event follows the Bernoulli principle. We define the number of packet transmissions in ARQ and network coding mode is η_{ARQ} and η_{NC}, according to [7], we have the following result.

$$\eta_{ARQ} = \frac{1}{1 - p_A} + \frac{1}{1 - p_B} - \frac{1}{1 - p_A p_B} \tag{1}$$

Proposition 1: The packet transmissions in lossy NDN networks with network coding are

$$\eta_{NC} = 1 + \frac{p_A}{1 - p_A} + \frac{p_B}{1 - p_B} - \frac{p_A}{1 - p_A p_B} \tag{2}$$

Proof: The source node sends N packets to user node, the probability that the number of lost packets at receiver *userA* is smaller than that of receiver *userB*, so we have $Np_A \leq Np_B$. Let X_A and X_B be the random variables denoting the numbers of transmission attempts before a successful transmission for the combined and uncombined packets. This implies that, on average, one can combine Np_A pairs of lost packets since $Np_A \leq Np_B$. As a result, there are $Np_B - Np_A$ lost packets from *userB* that needed to be retransmitted alone. Therefore, the total number of transmissions that are required to deliver all N packets successfully to two receivers are

$$m = N + Np_A E[X_A] + N(p_B - p_A)E[X_B] \tag{3}$$

Now, $E[X_B] = \frac{1}{(1-p_B)}$, since p_B follows a geometric distribution, from (1), we have

$$E[X_A] = \frac{1}{1 - p_A} + \frac{1}{1 - p_B} - \frac{1}{1 - p_A p_B} \tag{4}$$

Replacing $E[X_A]$ and $E[X_B]$ in (1) and dividing m by N, we have

$$\eta_{NC} = 1 + \frac{p_A}{1 - p_A} + \frac{p_B}{1 - p_B} - \frac{p_A}{1 - p_A p_B} \tag{5}$$

3.2 Core Architecture Design

Name. Since RLNC is adopted in NDN, content name and CS table need to be modified correspondingly. In NDN architecture, content name is hierarchical, and each individual name is composed of multiple components related to the character. Because of RLNC, we need to modify content name. There are two new components in content name shown in Fig. 2, also we design encoded content block shown in Fig. 3. Each encoded block has three components, includes generation, GEV and payload.

Fig. 2. Naming mechanism when NDN meets RLNC.

In our architecture, each content block has a new name, we introduce two components **gen_g** and **en_n** in name part to recompose content name, **gen_g** represents the id of generation when adopting RLNC to process real file, **en_n** is the id of encoded content block, but **en_n** may be changed, because of the intermediate node can recode. We also

Fig. 3. Encoded content block component. Generation occupies one byte in each encoded content block and generation technology is used to reduce encoding/decoding computation in our work.

describe the process of naming an encoded content block. Source node cut the original file shown in Fig. 4 **/www/pkusz/edu/cn/videos/movie.rmvb** into **/www/pkusz/edu/cn/videos/movie/rmvb/g/k**, **g** is the id of generation and **k** is the id of original content block, then before transmission it encodes original content block into **/www/pkusz/edu/cn/videos/movie.rmvb/g/n** $(n \geq k)$. The id **g** will not change under transmission, but id **n** will change because intermediate node recodes, so we can use a random number to take the place of id **n**.

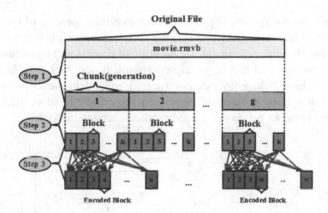

Fig. 4. The process of cutting real file and encoding. Step 1: cut real file *movie.rmvb* into $Chunk_1,\ldots,Chunk_g$. Step 2: cut every content chunk into $Block_1,\ldots,Block_k$. Step 3: encode $Block_1,\ldots,Block_k$ into $EncodedBlock_1,\ldots,EncodedBlock_n (n \geq k)$.

CS. Before we process real file, we redesign the architecture of CS table shown in Fig. 5, in traditional NDN architecture, CS table stores original content block, and each content block has a unique name. But the adopting of RLNC and generation technology, some encoded content blocks may share a common name, each encoded content block has all the information of original content block in the same generation, so each encoded content block may look like the same in the same generation. However, we can also see from Fig. 4 to find the real file cutting and encoding process, the exact matching (EM) lookup algorithm in CS table can be changed into longest prefix matching (LPM) lookup algorithm, we only need to choose the encoded content block from generation range. As a result, CS table should be changed into one content name with a generation encoded content block.

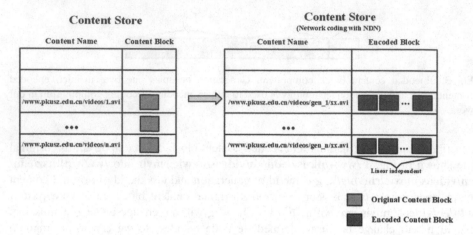

Fig. 5. Redesigned structure of CS table when adopting RLNC.

System Process. In our system, Fig. 6 shows the execution process of our testbed and Fig. 7 shows the main interactive process, we follow the main interactive process of NDN. In our real physical experiment, we do not use simulators to generate simulation data any more, we use real files to generate network flows. As CS table and content name mechanism have changed, we do not use traditional data packet process in NDN. Our real physical testbed is aimed at improving the reliability of content delivery in lossy NDN networks, so we do not consider other changes in NDN.

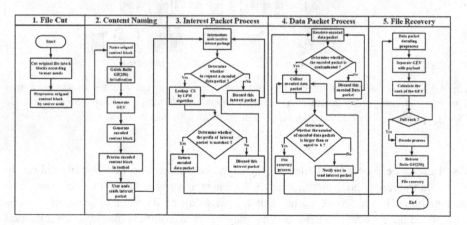

Fig. 6. The main execution process of our testbed. The process of interest packet and data packet not in the execution follows the original NDN architecture.

4 Experiments

4.1 Testbed Implement

In order to confirm the reliable gain, we build a real physical testbed. We build our system following NDN Forwarding Daemon (NFD) [23, 24] code database, a core component of the NDN platform for deploying a system on a computer rather than a simulator. In order to suit real physical machines, use more API to better build our system and process real files, we change the main codes in NFD into JAVA codes, we build the testbed on Linux OS, Windows OS and use seven real physical machines to confirm the reliable gain. We have modified and followed the main module of NFD to implement our system. In the following part, we will introduce our real file process module.

4.2 Real File Process Module

In this part, we introduce the process of real file, we follow and modify Kodo C++ library [25] to enable RLNC to process real file, we also use JAVA to implement this module. First, we implement a real file encoder/decoder and use its main part to implement our system. In our encoder/decoder, there are seven important modules and the execution process of our encoder/decoder is shown in Fig. 8, the main module of our encoder/decoder includes *FileCut.java, MutiplyPro.java, Galois.java, InverseM atrix.java, DecodingInit.java, Recode.java and DecodingAnswer.java.*

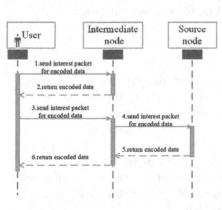

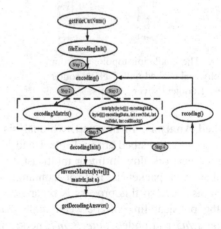

Fig. 7. Main interactive process relates to our testbed.

Fig. 8. The execution process of encoder/decoder. Step 1: initialize file process. Step 2: generate GEV. Step 3: adopt GF(256) to encode. Step 4: generate LEV. Step 5: decoding process.

4.3   Emulation and Analysis

File Process Analysis. In this part, we analysis the performance of encoder/decoder. we use real file *movie.rmvb* to test the performance of encoder/decoder. Our physical experiment is built on a win10 pro PC, the CPU parameter: AMD FX(tm)-6300 Six-core Processor, the RAM parameter: 8 GB, the storage size parameter: 1 TB, the file size parameter: 37.1 MB. We cut original file into 20 original content blocks and encode them into 30 encoded content blocks in every generation to do this experiment, then we change the generation parameter into 10, 20, 30, 40, 50, 60, 70, 80, 90. The generation occupies only one byte length in each encoded content block, so its range is [0, 255]. From Fig. 11 we can see that, we only encode/decode in the same generation and when generation becomes lager, each encoded content block becomes smaller, so each encoded content block costs less time to encode/decode.

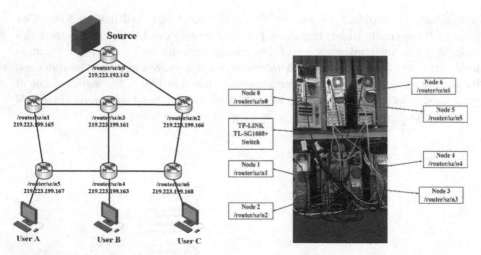

Fig. 9. The emulation topology of our real physical testbed with 7 NDN router nodes, 1 content sever, 3 users.

Fig. 10. Our physical testbed.

Testbed Analysis. In this part, we analysis our testbed, the physical parameter and topology of our testbed are in Table 1 and Fig. 9. We also use real file *movie.rmvb* to generate network flow in linear multicast, the experiment parameter is in Table 2. We set that if a packet is lost or contaminated in network transmission, we need to retransmit it, so this process is regarded as a packet retransmission. We randomly cut the physical link off between node */router/sz/n1* and node */router/sz/n5*, node */router/sz/n3* and node */router/sz/n4*, node */router/sz/n2* and node */router/sz/n6* to test our physical environment under transmission. We can also see from Fig. 12 to see the result of $\eta_{ARQ} - \eta_{NC}$, η_{NC} is lower than η_{ARQ} (Fig. 10).

Table 1. Physical machine configuration.

Node name	IP address	CPU(core)	OS	RAM	STORAGE
/router/sz/n0	219.223.193.143	AMD A8-5600K APU with Radeon(tm) HD Graphics @ 3.6 GHz	Win10 pro (x64)	4 GB	500 GB
/router/sz/n1	219.223.199.165	Intel(R) Core(TM) i3-4150 CPU @ 3.50 GHz	Ubunt16.04 (x64)	4 GB	500 GB
/router/sz/n2	219.223.199.166	Intel(R) Core(TM) i3-4150 CPU @ 3.50 GHz	Ubunt16.04 (x64)	4 GB	500 GB
/router/sz/n3	219.223.199.161	Intel(R) Core(TM) i3-4150 CPU @ 3.50 GHz	Ubunt16.04 (x64)	4 GB	500 GB
/router/sz/n4	219.223.199.163	Intel(R) Core(TM) i3-4130 CPU @ 3.40 GHz	Ubunt16.04 (x64)	4 GB	500 GB
/router/sz/n5	219.223.199.167	Intel(R) Core(TM) i3-4150 CPU @ 3.50 GHz	Ubunt16.04 (x64)	4 GB	500 GB
/router/sz/n6	219.223.199.168	Intel(R) Core(TM) i3-4150 CPU @ 3.50 GHz	Ubunt16.04 (x64)	4 GB	500 GB

Table 2. Experiment parameters.

Parameter	Values
Link rate	100–10000 kbps
Network topology	Seven nodes
Content size	37.1 MB
Number of content blocks	20
Number of encoded content blocks	30
Zipf	0.8
CS size	1000
Generation size	60
Galois field size	256
Primitive polynomial	0×01
Generating element	0×03
Cache strategy	Leave Copy Everywhere (LCE)
CS replacement policy	Least Recently Used (LRU) [8]

We test the end-to-end ARQ compared with end-to-end FEC until we successfully get recovery file. In end-to-end case, we set node */router/sz/n0* as source node and node */router/sz/n5*, */router/sz/n4*, */router/sz/n6* as user node. Next in end-to-end FEC case, intermediate nodes don't participate in encoding/decoding. then we change the number of users from one to three and get the result of retransmissions. From Fig. 13, we can see network coding reduces the packet retransmissions in end-to-end case.

Then we test link-to-link case, its test process mostly like end-to-end case. We follow end-to-end case, set node */router/sz/n0* as source node and node */router/sz/n5*, */router/sz/n4*, */router/sz/n6* as user node and then node */router/sz/n1*, */router/sz/n3*, */router/sz/n2* as intermediate node. In link-to-link case, intermediate node participates in encoding/decoding, they just act as encoder/decoder.

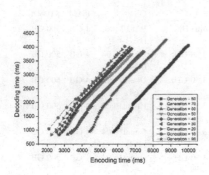

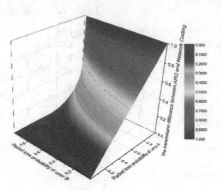

Fig. 11. The encoding/decoding performance of our encoder/decoder.

Fig. 12. Difference result of ARQ and network coding mode in two users case, $p_A, p_B \in (0, 1)$.

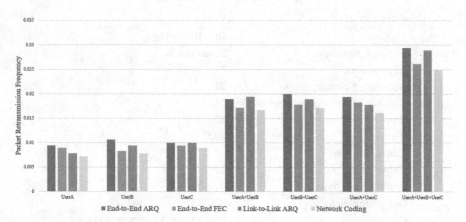

Fig. 13. Result of our experiment. Packet retransmission frequency is defined in per thousand packets that needs to be retransmitted.

We also change the number of users from one to three and get the result of retransmissions. From Fig. 13, we can also see that in link-to-link case, network coding performs better than ARQ.

5 Conclusions

In this paper, we use network coding as an error control technique in lossy NDN networks and build a real physical experiment environment to confirm the reliable gain. To suppose this real physical environment, we also develop a real file encoder/decoder, then we test our testbed compared with other error control techniques, our extensive evaluations show that network coding benefits NDN, while at the same time network coding reduces packet retransmissions. In our future work, we can build NDN router with network coding on MAC layer to test the system and gains.

Acknowledgment. The authors would like to thank sponsors of National Keystone R and D Program of China (No. 2017YFB0803204, 2016YFB0800101), Natural Science Foundation of China (NSFC) (No. 61671001), Guangdong Key Program GD2016B030305005, Shenzhen Research Programs (JSGG20150331101736052, ZDSYS201603311739428, JCYJ201703060 92030521), this work is also supported by the Shenzhen Municipal Development and Reform Commission (Disciplinary Development Program for Data Science and Intelligent Computing).

References

1. Zhang, L., et al.: Named data networking (NDN) project. Relatrio Tcnico NDN-0001, Xerox Palo Alto Research Center PARC (2010)
2. Jacobson, V., Smetters, D.K., Thornton, J.D., Plass, M.F., Briggs, N.H., Braynard, R.L.: Networking named content. In: Proceedings of the 5th International Conference on Emerging Networking Experiments and Technologies, pp. 1–12. ACM (2009)
3. Li, S.Y., Yeung, R.W., Cai, N.: Linear network coding. IEEE Trans. Inf. Theory **49**(2), 371–381 (2003)
4. Ahlswede, R., Cai, N., Li, R., Yeung, R.W.: Network information flow. IEEE Trans. Inf. Theory **46**(4), 1204–1216 (2000)
5. Ghaderi, M., Towsley, D., Kurose, J.: Reliability gain of network coding in lossy wireless networks. In: IEEE INFOCOM, pp. 196–200 (2008)
6. Huang, J., Liang, S.T.: Reliability gain of network coding in complicated network topology. In: The 7th Conference on Wireless Communications Network and Mobile Computing, Wuhan, China (2011)
7. Nguyen, D., Tran, T., Nguyen, T., et al.: Wireless broadcast using network coding. IEEE Trans. Veh. Technol. **58**(2), 914–925 (2009)
8. Laoutaris, N., Che, H., Stavrakakis, I.: The LCD interconnection of LRU caches and its analysis. Perform. Eval. **63**(7), 609–634 (2006)
9. Montpetit, M.J., Trossen, D.: Network coding meets information centric networking: an architectural case for information dispersion through native network coding. In: Proceedings of the ACM NoM, South Carolina, USA (2012)
10. Anastasiades, C., Thomos, N., Strieler, A., Braun, T.: RC-NDN: raptor codes enabled named data networking. In: Proceedings of the IEEE ICC, London, UK (2016)
11. Saltarin, J., Bourtsoulatze, E., Thomos, N., Braun, T.: NetCodCCN: a network coding approach for content centric networks. In: Proceedings of the IEEE INFOCOM, San Francisco, CA, USA, April 2016
12. Wu, D., Xu, Z.W., Chen, B., Zhang, Y.J.: Towards access control for network coding based named data networking. In: Proceedings of the IEEE GLOBECOM, Singapore (2017)
13. Saltarin, J., Bourtsoulatze, E., Thomos, N., Braun, T.: Adaptive video streaming with network coding enabled named data networking. IEEE Trans. Multimed. **19**(10), 2182–2196 (2017)
14. Wu, Q.H., Li, Z.Y., Tyson, G., et al.: Privacy aware multipath video caching for content centric networks. IEEE J. Sel. Areas Commun. **34**(8), 2219–2230 (2016)
15. Bourtsoulatze, E., Thomos, N., Saltarin, J.: Content aware delivery of scalable video in network coding enabled named data networks. IEEE Trans. Multimed. **20**(6), 1561–1575 (2018)

16. Zhang, G., Xu, Z.: Combing CCN with network coding: an architectural perspective. Comput. Netw. **94**, 219–230 (2016)
17. Liu, W.X., Yu, S.Z., Tan, G., Cai, J.: Information centric networking with built-in network coding to achieve multisource transmission at network layer. Comput. Netw. (2015)
18. Wang, J., Ren, J., Lu, K., Wang, J., Liu, S., Westphal, C.: An optimal cache management framework for information centric networks with network coding. In: IEEE IFIP Networking Conference, pp. 1–9 (2014)
19. Ramakrishnan, A., Westphal, C., Saltarin, J.: Adaptive video streaming over CCN with network coding for seamless mobility. In: IEEE International Symposium on Multimedia, pp. 238–242. IEEE (2016)
20. Wu, Q., Li, Z., Xie, G.: CodingCache: multipath aware CCN cache with network coding. In: Proceedings of the ACM ICN, Hong Kong, China, pp. 41–42, August 2013
21. Matsuzono, K., Asaeda, H., Turletti, T.: Low latency low loss streaming using in network coding and caching. In: Proceedings of the IEEE INFOCOM, Atlanta, GA, USA, May 2017
22. Chou, P.A., Wu, Y., Jain, K.: Practical network coding. In: Proceedings of the Allerton Conference on Communication (2003)
23. Afanasyev, A., et al.: NFD developers guide, named data networking. Technical report, NDN-0021 Revision 7, October 2016. https://named-data.net/publications/techreports/ndn-0021-7-nfd-developer-guide/
24. Named Data Networking Project: Named data networking forwarding daemon (2017). https://github.com/named-data/NFD
25. Pedersen, M., Heide, J., Fitzek, F.H.P.: Kodo: an open and research oriented network coding library. In: Proceedings of the IFIP NETWORKING, Valencia, Spain, pp. 145–152, May 2011
26. https://pan.baidu.com/s/1e-yzTAETbLrUBc1jFDpP1w

Verifying CTL with Unfoldings
of Petri Nets

Lanlan Dong[ID], Guanjun Liu[✉][ID], and Dongming Xiang[ID]

Department of Computer Science, Tongji University, Shanghai 201804, China
liuguanjun@tongji.edu.cn

Abstract. There are many studies on verifying Computation Tree Logic (CTL) based on reachable graphs of Petri nets. However, they often suffer from the state explosion problem. In order to avoid/alleviate this problem, we use the unfolding technique of Petri nets to verify CTL. For highly concurrent systems, this technique implicitly represents all reachable states and greatly saves storage space. We construct verification algorithms and develop a related tool. Experiments show the advantages of our method.

Keywords: Computation Tree Logic · Model checking · Petri nets
Unfolding

1 Introduction

Model checking is an automatic verification technique based on finite state machines. It has a great advantage compared with other techniques such as simulation, testing, and deductive reasoning. With the improvement of the automatic verification ability, model checking has been used in many large-scale systems such as sequential circuits [1], computer hardware system [2], communication protocols [3], integrated systems [4] and authentication protocol [5].

The first step of model checking is to use some formal models, e.g. labeled transition system or Petri net, to represent the behaviors of a system. Petri net is a modeling tool proposed by Petri in his doctoral thesis [6] and has been widely used to model concurrent systems.

The second step is to describe the system design requirements or to-be-checked properties. With the development of computer technologies and the expansion of computing scales, it is necessary to verify temporal behaviors of a system. Therefore, the temporal logic is introduced into computer science. The branching-time temporal logic CTL is one of the most popular temporal logic languages. It was firstly applied to model checking by Clarke et al. [7]. It has two path operators, A and E, which are used to describe the branching structure of a computation tree.

The third step is to verify system properties based on the models. But there is a problem, i.e., the state space explosion. At present, there are some solutions to the problem, e.g., symbolic model checking and partial order reduction.

© Springer Nature Switzerland AG 2018
J. Vaidya and J. Li (Eds.): ICA3PP 2018, LNCS 11337, pp. 47–61, 2018.
https://doi.org/10.1007/978-3-030-05063-4_5

The method of symbolic model checking is based on Bryant's Ordered Binary Decision Diagram (OBDD) [8]. When combining CTL with OBDD in [9], system states can be more than 10^{20}. Later, some improved techniques can verify a system with 10^{120} states [10]. The partial order reduction technique focuses on the independence of concurrent events. Two events are relatively independent to each other when they can occur in any order that leads to a number of identical states [11–13]. In addition, symmetric technique [14] and abstraction technique [15] [16] can also alleviate the problem of state explosion.

Petri-nets-based model checking generally uses a Petri net to model a concurrent system, and then generate its reachable graph, because the reachable graph can be viewed as a special labeled transition system. However, the number of states of a reachable graph usually grow exponentially with the increase of the Petri net size. The unfolding technique is another way to represent the states of a Petri net and their transition relations. It can save space especially for a Petri net in which there are many concurrent events. We use the unfolding technique of Petri nets to check soundness, deadlock, and data inconsistency [17–19]. Esparza et al. use unfolding to check LTL [20]. To the best of our knowledge, no one proposes an unfolding-based method to check CTL. In this paper, we use the unfolding technique to verify CTL except for the operator ¬. We design the related algorithms and develop a tool. Our experiments show that our tool is effective for millions of states.

2 Basic Notations

2.1 Petri Net

In this section, we recall the definitions of Petri nets, unfoldings, and CTL. For more details, one can refer to [21].

$(P, T; F, M_0)$ is a *Petri net* where *places* set P and *transitions* set T are finite and disjoint, $F \subseteq (P \times T) \cup (T \times P)$ is the *arcs* set, and M_0 is the *initial marking*, for $p \in P$, $M_0(p) = k$ means that there are k *tokens* in *place* p. For $x \in P \cup T$, ${}^\bullet x = \{y \mid y \in P \cup T \land (y, x) \in F\}$ and $x^\bullet = \{y \mid y \in P \cup T \land (x, y) \in F\}$ are called *preset* and *postset* of x, respectively.

Definition 1. Let $N = (P, T; F, M)$ be a Petri net, *transition firing rules* are defined as follows:

(1) if $t \in T$ satisfies:

$$\forall p \in P : p \in {}^\bullet x \to M(p) \geq 1$$

then t is *enabled* at the marking M, which is denoted as $M[t\rangle$.
(2) firing an enabled t at marking M leads to a new marking M' (denoted as $M[t\rangle M'$) such that $\forall \, p \in P$:

$$M' = \begin{cases} M(p) - 1 & p \in {}^\bullet t - t^\bullet \\ M(p) + 1 & p \in t^\bullet - {}^\bullet t \\ M(p) & \text{others} \end{cases} \tag{1}$$

In this paper, we have two assumptions: (1) all Petri nets are safe, which means that each place has at most one token in any reachable marking; (2) every transition has a non-empty preset and a non-empty postset.

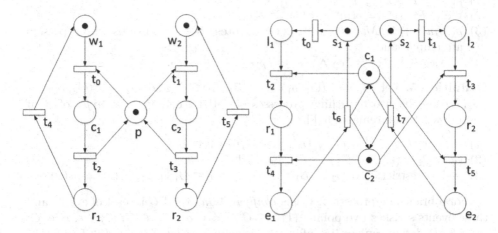

Fig. 1. Two exclusive processes   **Fig. 2.** Two philosophers dining

Figure 1 is a Petri net of two exclusive processes where place p represents a shared resource. Figure 2 is a Petri net of two philosophers dining problem in which place c_i means the chopstick on the left of ith philosopher.

Definition 2. Let $N = (P, T; F)$ be a Petri net, and $x, y \in P \cup T$ satisfy, $x \neq y$.

(1) if there is a path from x to y in the net, then they are in *causal relation* that is denoted as $x < y$;
(2) if there are two paths $p \rightarrow t_1 \rightarrow \cdots \rightarrow x$ and $p \rightarrow t_2 \rightarrow \cdots \rightarrow y$ such that they start at the same place p, and $t_1 \neq t_2$, then they are in *conflict relation* that is denoted as $x \# y$;
(3) if neither $x < y$ nor $y < x$ nor $x \# y$, then they are in *concurrent relation* that is denoted as x co y.

Definition 3. Let $N = (P, T; F)$ be a net. N is an *occurrence net* if the following conditions hold:

(1) $\forall p \in P : |{}^{\bullet} b | \leq 1$;
(2) there is no cycle in the net;
(3) $\forall x \in P \cup T$: the set $\{y \mid y \in P \cup T \wedge y < x\}$ is finite and
(4) $\forall x \in P \cup T : \neg(x \# x)$.

The relation between any two nodes in $P \cup T$ is either causal or conflict or concurrent. The elements of P and T are often called *conditions* and *events* in the occurrence net, respectively. For readability, an occurrent net is denoted as $O = (B, E; G)$.

Definition 4. Let $N = (P, T; F, M_0)$ be a Petri net, $O = (B, E; G)$ be an occurrence net, ρ be a *labeling function*: $B \cup E \to P \cup T$. $\beta = (O, \rho) = (B, E; G, \rho)$ is a *branching process* of N if

(1) $\rho(B) \subseteq P, \rho(E) \subseteq T$;
(2) $\forall e \in E$: $\rho(e^\bullet) = \rho(e)^\bullet \wedge \rho(^\bullet e) = ^\bullet \rho(e)$;
(3) $\rho(Min(O)) = M_0$, where $Min(O)$ denotes those conditions whose presets are empty; and
(4) $\forall e_1, e_2 \in E$: $^\bullet e_1 = ^\bullet e_2 \wedge \rho(e_1) = \rho(e_2) \to e_1 = e_2$.

Definition 5. Let $\beta_1 = (O_1, \rho_1) = (B_1, E_1; G_1)$ and $\beta_2 = (O_2, \rho_2) = (B_2, E_2; G_2)$ be two branching processes of a Petri net. β_1 is a *prefix* of β_2 if the following requirements hold:

(1) $(e \in E_1 \wedge ((c, e) \in G_2 \vee (e, c) \in G_2)) \to c \in B_1$;
(2) $(c \in B_1 \wedge (e, c) \in G_1) \to e \in E_2$; and
(3) ρ_1 is a restriction of ρ_2 to $B_1 \cup E_1$. i.e., $\forall x \in B_1 \cup E_1$: $\rho_1(x) = \rho_2(x)$.

For a branching process β, C is a *configuration* of β if C is a set of events and these events satisfies two points: (1) $e \in C \wedge e' < e \to e' \in C$; (2) $\forall e, e' \in C$: $\neg (e \# e')$. *local configuration* of event e is defined as $[e] = \{ e' \mid e' \in E \wedge (e' \le e) \}$. A set of conditions $S \subseteq B$ is called a *co-set* of a branching process β, if $\forall b, b' \in S$: b co b'. A maximal co-set is a *cut* of β, i.e., S is a cut if there is no co-set S' such that $S \subset S'$. A configuration and a cut are closely related. Let C be a configuration of β, then the co-set $cut(C)$ is a cut, where $cut(C) = (Min(O) \cup C^\bullet) \setminus (^\bullet C)$. It is obvious that $cut(C)$ is a reachable marking, which denoted as $Mark(C)$. $Mark(C)$ is a marking by firing all events in the configuration C in a specific order.

Definition 6. Let $\beta = (O, \rho)$ be a branching process of $N = (P, T; F, M_0)$. branching process β is *complete* if for every reachable marking M in net N, there is a configuration C of β such that

(1) $Mark(C) = M$;
(2) $\forall t \in T$: if $M[t\rangle$, then there exists a new configuration $C' = C \cup \{e\}$ such that $e \notin C \wedge \rho(e) = t$.

Definition 7. Let $\beta = (O, \rho)$ be a branching process of $N = (P, T; F, M_0)$, $t \in T$, and X be a *co-set* of β. (t, X) is a *possible extension* of β if it satisfies:

(1) $\rho(X) = ^\bullet t$; and
(2) (t, X) does not already belong to β.

Adding a possible extension of β and its output conditions can form a new branching process, and the original branching process is a prefix of the new one. All branching processes of a Petri net form a partially ordered set under the prefix relation, and the maximum element is called its *unfolding*. It is easy to understand that the unfolding of a Petri net is infinite if the Petri net is unbounded or has an infinite firing transition sequence. For examples, Figs. 3 and 4, are unfoldings of Figs. 1 and 2, respectively.

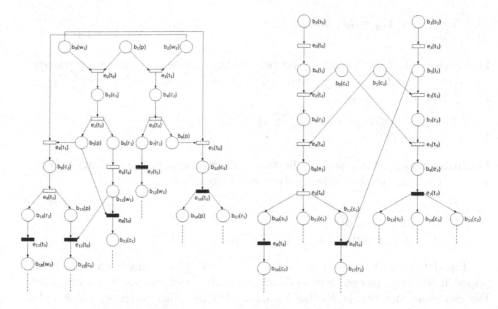

Fig. 3. Unfolding of Fig. 1   **Fig. 4.** Unfolding of Fig. 2

Definition 8. A partial order $\prec$ on the finite configuration of the unfolding of a Petri net is an *adequate order* if

(1) $\prec$ is well-founded;
(2) $C_1 \subset C_2$ implies $C_1 \prec C_2$;
(3) $\prec$ is preserved by finite extensions: if $C_1 \prec C_2$ and $Mark(C_1) = Mark(C_2)$, then the isomorphism I_1^2 satisfies $C_1 \oplus E \prec C_2 \oplus I_1^2(E)$ for all finite extensions $C_1 \oplus E$ C_1.

Definition 9. Let $\prec$ be an adequate order on the configuration of the unfolding of a net, and β be a prefix of the unfolding containing an event e. The event e is a *cut-off event* of β if β contains a local configuration $[e']$ such that

(1) $Mark([e]) = Mark([e'])$; and
(2) $[c'] \prec [e]$.

In the Figs. 3 and 4, the black events are all cut-off events.

If a finite prefix of an unfolding is complete, we called the prefix as *finite complete prefix* (FCP). Hence, the key problem is to identify all cut-off events in the unfolding such that the remainder after cutting off them is an FCP. In this paper, we adopt the complete finite prefix algorithm proposed by Esparza [22].

Definition 10. Let E_1 and E_2 be two events sets where $\phi(E_1) = t_{1,1}t_{1,2}\cdots t_{1,n_1}$ and $\phi(E_2) = t_{2,1}t_{2,2}\cdots t_{2,n_2}$. $\phi(E_1) \ll \phi(E_2)$ if $\exists\, 1 \le i \le n_1$:

1) $\forall\, 1 \le j < i$: $t_{1,j} = t_{2,j}$; and
2) $t_{1,i} \ll t_{2,i}$.

Definition 11. Let C_1 and C_2 be two configurations of a branching process, $FC(C_1) = C_{1,1}C_{1,2}\cdots C_{1,n_1}$, and $FC(C_2) = C_{2,1}C_{2,2}\cdots C_{2,n_2}$. $FC(C_1) \ll FC(C_2)$, if $\exists\, 1 \le i \le n_1$:

1) $\forall\, 1 \le j < i$: $\phi(C_{1,j}) = \phi(C_{2,j})$; and
2) $\phi(C_{1,i}) \ll \phi(C_{2,i})$.

Definition 12. Let C_1 and C_2 be two configurations of a branching process. $C_1 \prec_F C_2$ if one of the following three conditions holds:

1) $|\, C_1 \,| < |\, C_2 \,|$;
2) $|\, C_1 \,| = |\, C_2 \,|$ and $\phi(C_1) \ll \phi(C_2)$;
3) $\phi(C_1) = \phi(C_2)$ and $FC(C_1) \ll FC(C_2)$.

The definitions of *Foata normal form FC* and $\phi(C_1)$ come from [22]. In this paper, it has been proved that $\prec_F$ is an adequate order and also is a total order. We can construct two FCPs like Figs. 3 and 4 by using order $\prec_F$. The index of conditions and events denotes the sequence of being appended to the prefix (Note that the order is not unique). In Fig. 1, we define $t_0 \ll t_1 \ll t_2 \ll t_3 \ll t_4 \ll t_5$, and in Fig. 2, $t_0 \ll t_1 \ll t_2 \ll t_3 \ll t_4 \ll t_5 \ll t_6 \ll t_7$.

2.2   CTL Definitions

For a finite state model $\mathcal{M}=(S,T,L,AP)$(Kripke structure), S is a finite set of states, $T \subseteq S \times S$ is a state transition relation, $L\colon S \to 2^{AP}$ is a state marking function, $L(S)$ denotes the set of true atomic proposition in S, and AP represents the set of all atomic propositions. A CTL formula ψ characterizes one property of $\mathcal{M}$. The symbol $\mathcal{M},s \vDash \psi$ denotes that the property in state s is true. Denote $\pi = s_1, s_2, s_3, \cdots$ as a path in $\mathcal{M}$, and path($\mathcal{M}$) as the set of paths.

The syntax of CTL is defined: $\varphi\colon\colon = p \mid \neg\alpha \mid \alpha\wedge\beta \mid \alpha\vee\beta \mid EX\alpha \mid AX\alpha \mid EF\alpha \mid AF\alpha \mid EG\alpha \mid AG\alpha \mid E(\alpha U\beta) \mid A(\alpha U\beta)$ where $p \in AP$. A (**A**ll) means all paths; E (**E**xists) means some paths. $X\ \alpha$ holds if α holds at the (ne**X**t) state; $F\alpha$ holds if α holds at one state in the (**F**uture); $G\alpha$ holds if α holds for (**G**lobal) states in the future; $\alpha U\beta$ holds if eventually β holds and α holds (**U**ntil) then. Given a CTL formula φ, a *syntax parser tree*, as shown in Fig. 5, the leaves represent the atomic propositions, the non-leaf nodes represent the CTL operators, the root node is the formula φ itself, each child node of a non-leaf node is its operand (it may be an atomic proposition or an operator).

3   Model Checking of CTL via FCP

FCP of a Petri net can perfectly represent all the reachable states and firing transition sequences of the Petri net. Our basic idea of CTL over FCP: when we need some specific reachable states, we can get these states via the unfolding. Therefore, the first question is how to utilize FCP to obtain all the reachable

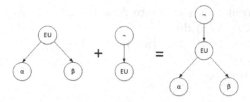

Fig. 5. Syntax parser tree

states that contain a particular atomic proposition p. As we all know, for concurrent systems, the number of conditions usually is smaller than the number of reachable markings in the reachable graph. Therefore, we store the concurrent relation between any two conditions by using a two-dimensional boolean matrix. If we regard the matrix as an adjacency matrix of one graph, then the problem mentioned above can be converted into a problem of finding all maximal cliques of the graph (namely maximum complete subgraph). In this paper, we adopt the famous Bron-Kerbosch algorithm [23] to find these cliques. Given FCP $(B,E;G)$ and a condition $p \in B$, we denote $con(p) = \{c \mid c \in B \wedge c\ co\ p\}$ as the set of concurrent vertexes according to concurrent relation. For two vertex x, $y \in con(p)$: if $x\ co\ y$, then there is an undirected edge from x to y. Therefore, to compute all the cuts containing condition p is equivalent to find all the maximal cliques of a subgraph containing the vertexes in $con(p)$.

Algorithm 1. Find all cuts containing a given condition in FCP

Input: FCP $O = (B, E; F, \rho)$, a condition p and a concurrence relation matrix *matrix*
Output: $sat(p)$
```
 1: function FINDALLAUTS(O, b, matrix)
 2:     sat(p) ← ∅, con(p) ← ∅, P ← ∅, X ← ∅, R ← ∅;
 3:     for all p′ ∈ B do
 4:         if matrix[p][p′] is true then
 5:             con(p) ← con(p) ∪ p′;
 6:         end if
 7:     end for
 8:     P ← con(p) ∪ p;
 9:     sat(p) ← BRONKERBOSCH(P, R, X);
10:     return sat(p);
11: end function
12:
13: function BRONKERBOSCH(P, R, X)
14:     result ← ∅;
15:     if P = ∅ ∧ X = ∅ then
16:         result ← result ∪ R where R is a maximal clique;
17:     end if
18:     choose a pivot vertex u in P ∪ X;
```

19:        add all adjacent points of u into $N(u)$;
20:    **for all** $v \in P \setminus N(u)$ **do**
21:        BRONKERBOSCH(P $\cap$ $N(u)$, R $\cup$ v, X $\cap$ $N(u)$);
22:        P $\leftarrow$ P $\setminus$ v;
23:        X $\leftarrow$ X $\cup$ v;
24:    **end for**
25:    **return** result
26: **end function**

Algorithm 1 is about finding all cuts containing a given condition in FCP. For a subformula φ, like $\neg (E(\alpha \ U \ \beta))$, how to solve $sat(\varphi)$? Given a Petri net and a CTL formula φ, we use a syntax parser tree to represent a CTL formula. Therefore, we take the bottom-up traversal approach to decide each subformula until the whole formula. For a subformula φ, we save the "important" states satisfying the formula and these states denoted as $sat(\varphi)$. If node φ' is the parent of the node φ, then we can use $sat(\varphi)$ to compute φ', and execute the corresponding algorithm to get $sat(\varphi')$. The CTL model checking based on FCP is shown in Algorithm 2 and the computations of sat(φ) for different operators are shown in Algorithms 3–8.

Algorithm 2. CTL model checking based on FCP

Input: A complete finite prefix $O = (B, E; F, \rho)$, and a CTL formula φ
Output: true or false
 1: generate syntax parser tree of φ, *tree* $= \{\varphi, \varphi_1, \varphi_2, \cdots, \varphi_n\}$;
 2: $sat(\varphi) \leftarrow \varnothing$, $sat(\varphi_1) \leftarrow \varnothing$, $sat(\varphi_2) \leftarrow \varnothing$, $\cdots$, $sat(\varphi_n) \leftarrow \varnothing$;
 3: *visited* $\leftarrow$ leaf nodes of *tree*, *unvisited* $\leftarrow$ non-leaf nodes of *tree*;
 4: **while** *unvisited* $\neq \varnothing$ **do**
 5:     choose a node φ' in *unvisited* such that all of its children are in *visited*;
 6:     execute the corresponding algorithm according to the operator that node φ' represented, denoted the result as *result*;
 7:     $sat(\varphi') \leftarrow$ *result*;
 8:     *unvisited* $\leftarrow$ *unvisited* $\setminus \varphi'$;
 9:     *visited* $\leftarrow$ *visited* $\cup \varphi'$;
10: **end while**
11: **if** $Min(O) \in sat(\varphi_1)$ **then**
12:     return true;
13: **else**
14:     return false;
15: **end if**

Because of the difference of operators' semantics, we put forward a specific algorithm for every CTL operator. The similar point of these algorithms is backtracking, i.e., by searching possible states(or *cuts*) on the FCP within the bottom-up approach, mark state s if $\mathcal{M}, s \vDash \varphi$. Furthermore, one of the different points of these algorithms is that for AX, AF, AG, and AU, a related formula must be true for all paths starting at the initial marking. Therefore we must add extra steps to judge whether every marking s' that can reach the current marking s satisfies $\mathscr{M},s' \vDash \varphi$(i.e., if all are satisfied, then $\mathscr{M},s \vDash \varphi$. Note that we use ${}^\bullet s$ to represent all markings that can reach s. In the same way, we use $s^\bullet$ to represent all markings reachable from s. We divide CTL into two part, one is that there only is path operator A such as AX, AF, AG, and AU, (which is called $ACTL$), the other is that there only is path operator E such as EX, EF, EG, and EU, (which is called $ECTL$).

3.1   Model Checking of ECTL

Model checking of $\varphi = EX\ \varphi_1$

Algorithm 3. Model checking of $\varphi = EX\ \varphi_1$

Input: $sat(\varphi_1)$
Output: $sat(\varphi)$
1: $sat(\varphi) \leftarrow \varnothing$;
2: **for all** cut $s \in sat(\varphi_1)$ **do**
3:      **for all** cut $s' \in {}^\bullet s$ **do**
4:         $sat(\varphi) \leftarrow sat(\varphi) \cup s'$;
5:      **end for**
6: **end for**

Model checking of $\varphi = EF\ \varphi_1$

Algorithm 4. Model checking of $\varphi = EF\ \varphi_1$

Input: $sat(\varphi_1)$
Output: $sat(\varphi)$
1: $pre \leftarrow \varnothing, sat(\varphi) \leftarrow sat(\varphi_1), newAdded \leftarrow sat(\varphi_1)$;
2: **while** $newAdded \neq \varnothing$ **do**
3:      **for all** cut $s \in newAdded$ **do**
4:         $pre \leftarrow pre \cup {}^\bullet s$;
5:      **end for**
6:      $newAdded \leftarrow \varnothing$;
7:      **for all** cut $s' \in pre \setminus sat(\varphi)$ **do**
8:         $sat(\varphi) \leftarrow sat(\varphi) \cup s'$;
9:         $newAdded \leftarrow newAdded \cup s'$;
10:      **end for**
11: **end while**

Model checking of $\varphi = E\ (\varphi_2\ U\ \varphi_1)$

Algorithm 5. Model checking of $\varphi = E(\varphi_2\ U\ \varphi_1)$

Input: $sat(\varphi_1)$, $sat(\varphi_2)$
Output: $sat(\varphi)$
1: $pre \leftarrow \varnothing, sat(\varphi) \leftarrow sat(\varphi_1), newAdded \leftarrow sat(\varphi_1)$;
2: **while** $newAdded \neq \varnothing$ **do**

3:     **for all** cut s ∈ *newAdded* **do**
4:         *pre* ← *pre* ∪ •s;
5:     **end for**
6:     *newAdded* ← ∅;
7:     **for all** cut s′ ∈ *pre* \ *sat*(φ) **do**
8:         **if** s′ ∈ *sat*(φ_2) **then**
9:             *sat*(φ) ← *sat*(φ) ∪ s′;
10:            *newAdded* ← *newAdded* ∪ s′;
11:        **end if**
12:    **end for**
13: **end while**

3.2   Model Checking of ACTL

Model checking of $\varphi = AX\ \varphi_1$

Algorithm 6. Model checking of $\varphi = AX\ \varphi_1$

Input: *sat*(φ_1)
Output: *sat*(φ)
1: *sat*(φ) ← ∅;
2: **for all** cut s ∈ *sat*(φ_1) **do**
3:     **for all** cut s′ ∈ •s ∧ (s′)• ⊆ *sat*(φ) **do**
4:         *sat*(φ) ← *sat*(φ) ∪ s′;
5:     **end for**
6: **end for**

Model checking of $\varphi = AF\ \varphi_1$

Algorithm 7. Model checking of $\varphi = AF\ \varphi_1$

Input: *sat*(φ_1)
Output: *sat*(φ)
1: *pre* ← ∅, *sat*(φ) ← *sat*(φ_1), *newAdded* ← *sat*(φ_1);
2: **while** *newAdded* ≠ ∅ **do**
3:     **for all** cut s ∈ *newAdded* **do**
4:         *pre* ← *pre* ∪ •s;
5:     **end for**
6:     *newAdded* ← ∅;
7:     **for all** cut s′ ∈ *pre* \ *sat*(φ) ∧ (s′)• ⊆ *sat*(φ) **do**
8:         *sat*(φ) ← *sat*(φ) ∪ s′;
9:         *newAdded* ← *newAdded* ∪ s′;
10:    **end for**
11: **end while**

Model checking of $\varphi = A\ (\varphi_2\ U\ \varphi_1)$

Algorithm 8. Model checking of $\varphi = A(\varphi_2\ U\ \varphi_1)$

Input: $sat(\varphi_1)$, $sat(\varphi_2)$
Output: $sat(\varphi)$
 1: $pre \leftarrow \varnothing$, $sat(\varphi) \leftarrow sat(\varphi_1)$, $newAdded \leftarrow sat(\varphi_1)$;
 2: **while** $newAdded \neq \varnothing$ **do**
 3:     **for all** cut s $\in newAdded$ **do**
 4:        $pre \leftarrow pre \cup {}^{\bullet}s$;
 5:     **end for**
 6:     $newAdded \leftarrow \varnothing$;
 7:     **for all** cut s$'$ $\in pre \setminus sat(\varphi)$ **do**
 8:        **if** s$' \in sat(\varphi_2) \wedge (s')^{\bullet} \subseteq sat(\varphi)$ **then**
 9:           $sat(\varphi) \leftarrow sat(\varphi) \cup s'$;
10:           $newAdded \leftarrow newAdded \cup s'$;
11:        **end if**
12:     **end for**
13: **end while**

Because of $EGf = \neg AF\neg f$ and $AGf = \neg EF\neg f$, the model checking of the operator EG and AG can be converted into the model checking of EF and AF. However, model checking of the operator $\neg$ is based on global state space, which cannot utilize the advantages of FCP. Therefore the three operators are not considered in this paper.

4   Experiments

4.1   Model Checker

According to the algorithms above, we develop a model checker, as shown in Fig. 6. Based on the open software PIPE (Platform Independent Petri Net Editor) [24], we add two new modules to it: one is a generator of the FCP of a Petri net, and another is a model checker for CTL over FCP. Our checker only needs to input a Petri net and a CTL formula, and then it can output the result and the checking time. Figure 6 shows the Petri net model of 2-philosophers' dining problem, the CTL formula: EXR_1, the FCP, and the checking result.

4.2   Experimental Results

Table 1 shows the sizes of FCPs and reachable graphs of Petri nets of N dining philosophers where N is from 2 to 11. Note that Fig. 2 shows the Petri net model of 2 dining philosophers. Obviously, there is a space explosion problem for reachable graphs with the increasing of N. It is obvious that FCP greatly reduces storage space.

We do experiments on a server, with Intel(R) Xeon(R) CPU and 64 GB RAM. Our experiments consist of three parts. In the first part, we just consider

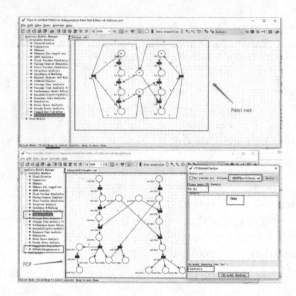

Fig. 6. The illustration of our checker

Table 1. Data comparison between reaching graph and FCP

N	FCP			Reachable graph	Petri net	
	Conditions	Events	*Cut-off events*	Nodes (markings)	Places	Transitions
2	18	10	3	13	10	8
3	27	15	5	45	15	12
4	35	19	6	161	20	16
5	43	23	7	573	25	20
6	51	27	8	2041	30	24
7	59	31	9	7269	35	28
8	67	35	10	25889	40	32
9	75	39	11	92205	45	36
10	83	43	12	328393	50	40
11	91	47	13	1169589	55	44

the simple formula such as $EX\ \alpha$, $E(\alpha\ U\ \beta)$ and so on, which only contains atomic propositions. Table 2 shows the spent time (ms). It is obvious that for 11 philosophers process, it spent approximately 30 min on $E(l_1\ U\ r_1)$ and $A(l_1\ U\ r_1)$. Most of the time is spent on computing $sat(l_1)$ and $sat(r_1)$.

In the second part, we try to detect deadlock in philosopher's dining problem based on our methods. As we all know, there exists a deadlock in the philosophers dining problem when every philosopher holds the left chopstick and then waits for the right chopstick. We can describe this situation with CTL. For the model

Table 2. The first group of experiments

N	EXr_1	EFr_1	$E(l_1\ U\ r_1)$	AXr_1	AFr_1	$A(l_1\ U\ r_1)$
2	1.806	0.499	2.448	2.098	0.212	2.432
3	2.132	2.320	5.855	2.342	0.742	5.608
4	6.331	10.813	21.320	7.260	3.844	20.134
5	32.705	62.543	82.074	40.281	17.562	79.261
6	97.656	214.120	392.132	90.531	95.736	393.956
7	614.742	1250.983	2251.039	582.560	751.261	2272.928
8	3354.148	7804.289	11765.532	6094.413	3477.288	13845.131
9	22062.357	50996.521	61203.888	19359.999	18190.530	62478.147
10	92715.560	272337.395	315414.734	108087.381	99573.543	324438.840
11	451405.112	1347042.300	1632404.379	462159.711	460256.197	1584963.188

of n philosophers dining $\mathscr{M}_n$, let $\varphi = EF(r_1 \wedge r_2 \wedge \cdots \wedge r_n)$. If φ is true, this means that there is a deadlock, otherwise no deadlock. Note that the initial marking is $m_0 = (s_1, s_2, \cdots, s_n)$. What we need to do is to verify whether $\mathscr{M}_n, m_0 \models \varphi$ holds. Our tool outputs true for this formula and Table 3 shows the spent time (ms).

Table 3. The second group of experiments

N	2	3	4	5	6	7
-	1.171	1.041	3.627	10.398	36.638	106.627
N	8	9	10	11	12	13
-	660.840	3375.862	17784.927	86442.395	443150.014	2360197.824

At the last part, we compare our tool with INA (Integrated Net Analyzer) [25], an excellent model checker based on the reachable graphs of Petri nets. We do the same experiment on this tool. Because INA doesn't have a timer which can output the exact time of CTL model checking, we get the approximate time by stopwatch on the mobile phone manually. Table 4 shows the results (ms). When N is small, for example, N < 5, the time is so short that we can not record manually. When N is 12, there are 4165553 reachable states, it spends more

Table 4. The third group of experiments

N	2	3	4	5	6	7
-	< 330	< 330	< 330	330	730	2940
N	8	9	10	11	12	13
-	5310	40910	305190	3600000	> 9 h	–

than nine hours. When N is 13, the experiment terminates because of memory exhausted. Noting that, with the increment of N, it is obvious that our tool performs better.

5   Conclusions

In this paper, we present a series of algorithms of CTL model checking based on the unfolding technique of Petri nets. On the one hand, the method allows us to check large systems with millions of states; on the other hand, the method saves space greatly. The insufficiency of algorithms is that for operator ¬, we cannot get an overall method to check it. In the future, we plan to improve our method. and take the complemented place to represent operator ¬.

Acknowledgments. Authors would like to thank reviewers for their helpful comments. This paper is partially supported by the National Natural Science Foundation of China under grant no. 61572360.

References

1. Dai, Y.Y., Brayton, R.K.: Verification and synthesis of clock-gated circuits. IEEE Trans. Comput.-Aided Des. Integr. Circuits Syst. **PP**(99), 1 (2017)
2. Griggio, A., Roveri, M.: Comparing different variants of the IC3 algorithm for hardware model checking. IEEE Trans. Comput.-Aided Des. Integr. Circuits Syst. **35**(6), 1026–1039 (2016)
3. Gnesi S, Margaria T.: Practical applications of probabilistic model checking to communication protocols, pp. 133–150. Wiley-IEEE Press (2013)
4. Wang, H., Zhao, T., Ren, F., et al.: Integrated modular avionics system safety analysis based on model checking. In: Reliability and Maintainability Symposium, pp. 1–6. IEEE (2017)
5. Hegde, M.S., Jnanamurthy, H.K., Singh, S.: Modelling and verification of extensible authentication protocol using spin model checker. Int. J. Netw. Secur. Its Appl. **4**(6), 81–98 (2012)
6. Petri, C.A.: Kommunikation mit Automaten. Ph.D. Thesis, Institut Fuer Instrumentelle Mathematik (1962)
7. Clarke, E.M., Grumberg, O., Hiraishi, H., et al.: Verification of the Futurebus+ cache coherence protocol. Form. Methods Syst. Des. **6**, 217–232 (1995)
8. Bryant, R.E., Bryant, R.E.: Graph-based algorithms for boolean function manipulation. IEEE Trans. Comput. **35**(8), 677–691 (1986)
9. Burch, J.R., et al.: Symbolic model checking: 10 20, states and beyond. Inf. Comput. **98**(2), 142–170 (1992)
10. Burch, J.R., Clarke, E.M., Long, D.E.: Symbolic model checking with partitioned transition relations. Computer Science Department, pp. 49–58 (1991)
11. Valmari, A., Hansen, H.: Stubborn set intuition explained. In: Koutny, M., Kleijn, J., Penczek, W. (eds.) Transactions on Petri Nets and Other Models of Concurrency XII. LNCS, vol. 10470, pp. 140–165. Springer, Heidelberg (2017). https://doi.org/10.1007/978-3-662-55862-1_7
12. Flanagan, C., Godefroid, P.: Dynamic partial-order reduction for model checking software. ACM SIGPLAN Not. **40**(1), 110–121 (2005)

13. Boucheneb, H., Barkaoui, K.: Delay-dependent partial order reduction technique for real time systems. Real-Time Syst. **54**(2), 278–306 (2018)
14. Si, Y., Sun, J., Liu, Y., Wang, T.: Improving model checking stateful timed CSP with non-zenoness through clock-symmetry reduction. In: Groves, L., Sun, J. (eds.) ICFEM 2013. LNCS, vol. 8144, pp. 182–198. Springer, Heidelberg (2013). https://doi.org/10.1007/978-3-642-41202-8_13
15. Podelski, A., Rybalchenko, A.: ARMC: the logical choice for software model checking with abstraction refinement. In: Hanus, M. (ed.) PADL 2007. LNCS, vol. 4354, pp. 245–259. Springer, Heidelberg (2006). https://doi.org/10.1007/978-3-540-69611-7_16
16. Nouri, A., Raman, B., Bozga, M., Legay, A., Bensalem, S.: Faster statistical model checking by means of abstraction and learning. In: Bonakdarpour, B., Smolka, S.A. (eds.) RV 2014. LNCS, vol. 8734, pp. 340–355. Springer, Cham (2014). https://doi.org/10.1007/978-3-319-11164-3_28
17. Liu, G., Reisig, W., Jiang, C., et al.: A branching-process-based method to check soundness of workflow systems. IEEE Access **4**, 4104–4118 (2016)
18. Liu, G., Zhang, K., Jiang, C.: Deciding the deadlock and livelock in a petri net with a target marking based on its basic unfolding. In: Carretero, J., Garcia-Blas, J., Ko, R.K.L., Mueller, P., Nakano, K. (eds.) ICA3PP 2016. LNCS, vol. 10048, pp. 98–105. Springer, Cham (2016). https://doi.org/10.1007/978-3-319-49583-5_7
19. Xiang, D., Liu, G., Yan, C., et al.: Detecting data inconsistency based on the unfolding technique of petri nets. IEEE Trans. Ind. Inform. **13**, 2995–3005 (2017)
20. Esparza, J., Heljanko, K.: Implementing LTL model checking with net unfoldings. In: Dwyer, M. (ed.) SPIN 2001. LNCS, vol. 2057, pp. 37–56. Springer, Heidelberg (2001). https://doi.org/10.1007/3-540-45139-0_4
21. Katoen, J.-P.: Principles of Model Checking. The MIT Press, Cambridge (2008)
22. Esparza, J., Vogler, W.: An improvement of McMillan's unfolding algorithm. LNCS **1099**(3), 285–310 (2002)
23. Himmel, A.S., Molter, H., Niedermeier, R., et al.: Adapting the BronCKerbosch algorithm for enumerating maximal cliques in temporal graphs. Soc. Netw. Anal. Min. **7**(1), 35 (2017)
24. Bonnet-Torrés, O., Domenech, P., Lesire, C., Tessier, C.: EXHOST-PIPE: PIPE extended for two classes of monitoring petri nets. In: Donatelli, S., Thiagarajan, P.S. (eds.) ICATPN 2006. LNCS, vol. 4024, pp. 391–400. Springer, Heidelberg (2006). https://doi.org/10.1007/11767589_22
25. Roch, S., Starke, P.H.: INA: Integrated Net Analyzer (2002). https://www2.informatik.hu-berlin.de/~starke/ina.html

Deep Q-Learning for Navigation of Robotic Arm for Tokamak Inspection

Swati Jain[1(✉)], Priyanka Sharma[1(✉)], Jaina Bhoiwala[1(✉)],
Sarthak Gupta[1], Pramit Dutta[2], Krishan Kumar Gotewal[2],
Naveen Rastogi[2], and Daniel Raju[2,3]

[1] Department of Computer Engineering, Institute of Technology,
Nirma University, Ahmedabad, Gujarat, India
{swati.jain,priyanka.sharma,jaina.bhoiwala,
14bce105}@nirmauni.ac.in
[2] Institute of Plasma Research, Bhat, Gandhinagar, Gujarat, India
{pramitd,kgotewal,Naveen,raju}@ipr.res.in
[3] Homi Bhabha National Institute, Mumbai, Maharashtra, India

Abstract. Computerized human-machine interfaces are used to control the manipulators and robots for inspection and maintenance activities in Tokamak. The activities embrace routine and critical activities such as tile inspection, dust cleaning, equipment handling and replacement tasks. Camera(s) is deployed on the robotic arm which moves inside the chamber to accomplish the inspection task. For navigating the robotic arm to the desired position, an inverse kinematic solution is required. Such closed-form inverse kinematic solutions become complex in the case of dexterous hyper-redundant robotic arms that have high degrees of freedom and can be used for inspections in narrow gaps. To develop real-time inverse kinematic solver for robots, a technique called Reinforcement Learning is used. There are various strategies to solve Reinforcement problem in polynomial time, one of them is Q-Learning. It can handle problems with stochastic transitions and rewards, without requiring adaption or probabilities of actions to be taken at a certain point. It is observed that Deep Q-Network successfully learned optimal policies from high dimension sensory inputs using Reinforcement Learning.

1 Introduction

Different types of interior observations are done by robotic systems due to the hostile situations inside the nuclear reactor. Maintenance of the same is one of the main challenges, which is somehow responsible for guaranteeing the validity and safety of fusion reaction [1]. International Atomic Energy Agency stated the nuclear and radiation accident as "an event that has led to significant consequences to people, the environment or the facility". The problems caused due to this nuclear and radiation accidents are fatal effect to individual and huge radiation release to the atmosphere or melting of the reactor core. If proper maintenance is not provided than running a nuclear power plant is very risky [2]. To carry out this maintenance activity we need an inspection robot or robotic arm.

© Springer Nature Switzerland AG 2018
J. Vaidya and J. Li (Eds.): ICA3PP 2018, LNCS 11337, pp. 62–71, 2018.
https://doi.org/10.1007/978-3-030-05063-4_6

The main task of that robotic arm is to carry inspection tool like a camera for the inspection of the wall inside the reactor vessel. Because the plasma facing components consist of graphite tiles, plasma diverters, limiters, diagnostics and plasma control coils; constrained location can be monitored by hyper-redundant manipulators which are an alternative to serial manipulators [1]. A Great number of Degree of Freedoms (DOFs) are there in hyper-redundant manipulators that enable it in entering/reaching difficult areas and avoids obstacles with improved agility. Entering the constrained location makes a system more complex to be managed. To make it easily manageable, an auto navigation system can be used for the robotic arm that ensures auto widespread scanning of the inner walls, however, the existence of great number of DOFs has the hostile effect of puzzling the kinematics and dynamics for these manipulators.

"Kinematically redundant" robots are those having more than minimum number of DOF. It is also known as simply "redundant" robots. Whereas Hyper redundant robots are those with a very large degree of kinematic redundancy. Snakes, elephant trunks, and tentacles are the examples with which they are equivalent in morphology and operation [3]. Figure 1 shows the hyper-redundant manipulator as discussed in [4]. All the joints in the hyper-redundant manipulator are similar to universal joints and they are defined in the spherical workspace. As you can see each link has a connection to the other link and with the motor.

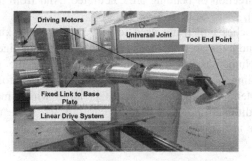

Fig. 1. Hyper redundant manipulator [4]

The hollow links are connected using tendons and are pulled by motors which are placed outside the structure of the robotic arm to lighten the weight. Due to this structure of hyper-redundant manipulator, we can stimulate links in a 3D workspace. There is a tool end point where our camera is mounted for monitoring purpose [4].

The concept of kinematic modeling is there for the movement of the robotic arm. If by the specified values of the joint parameter, the position of the end effector is calculated than it is called forward kinematics. To reach a particular point, the configuration parameters for all the joints are to be calculated and to achieve a particular configuration, actuation parameters are to be calculated termed as inverse kinematics.

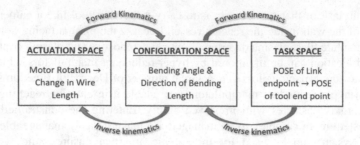

Fig. 2. Kinematic model [4]

Figure 2 [4] shows the kinematic model in which when we consider the forward kinematics, the actuation space is converted to the configuration space i.e. the motor rotates and the length of tendon changes which leads to the bending angle and the direction of bending of the arm. After that configuration space tends to task space which leads to the position of each link's end point as well as the position of tool endpoint. Whereas if we consider inverse kinematics, then the task space is converted to configuration space and which eventually leads to actuation space. So, in the inverse kinematics, the destination or the position of endpoint are known and accordingly the bending angle and direction of bending are calculated. And from that, the rotation of motor takes place [4].

Numerical approaches which are used to solve the inverse kinematics are computationally heavy, and it may be time-consuming. Artificial Intelligence is faster for all these calculations. Numerous solutions are not known for the same. So, we use Reinforcement Learning, it is considered as a better approach for planning the trajectory. In our problem, the number of states is large which makes this situation difficult to use a traditional approach like Q-Learning. To solve this Reinforcement learning problem, we use an algorithm namely Deep-Q-Network.

2   Literature Survey

Wang [1] designed a tokamak flexible in-vessel inspection Robot. The objective was to increase the efficiency of remote maintenance using a corresponding trajectory planning algorithm to complete the automatic full coverage scanning of the Complex tokamak cavity. To get the clear images of the first wall which could be obtained with using as less time as possible. They proposed two different trajectory planning methods namely RS which is rough scanning and another is FS which is fine scanning. Wand et al. [5] proposed the software and hardware solution which is designed and implemented for tokamak in-vessel viewing system that installed on the end-effector of flexible in-vessel robot working under vacuum and high temperature. The new feature consists of two parts namely binocular heterogeneous vision inspection tool and first wall scene emersion based augment virtuality method for visual inspection.

An underwater mobile robot is proposed in [2] that consist of, a laser positioning unit and a main control station. The laser positioning unit guides the underwater mobile robot with the precision of $0.05°$. Here the concept used is little different in which the mobile robot moves on reactor vessel wall with four magnetic wheels. To perform remote control operation in radiation, [6] Radiation hardened material and components are used to build the AARM tool. Basically this system extends the life of reactor by replacing the pressure and fuel tube. After removing the tube all the maintenance activities can be carried out with AARM tool.

Flexibility is the desired characteristic in the constrained environment inside the reactor. To design Flexible in-vessel inspection robot that moves smoothly without any shrill effects to the actuators during the review procedure FIVIR (Flexible in-vessel inspection robot) was proposed [7]. FIVIR has easy control and good mechanics property.

Robotic arms with motors in every joint makes it heavy resulting into the bending effect at the end effector. Hence design concept and control mechanism of a 3 link tendon driven hyper-redundant inspection system [4]. The paper details the structural design, kinematic modelling, control algorithm development and practical implementation of the hyper-redundant robot with experiments. Hyper-redundant robots give higher degree of flexibility with an increased complexity in solving the inverse kinematics for the same. Attempts has been made to use ANN for modelling the inverse kinematics in hyper redundant arms in two dimensions [8, 9].

One more design is proposed in which they used a robotic arm with 7 DOF [10] and trained it for 3D simulations. Real world experiments were done to gather sufficient training data. For this concept of Q-Learning and deep Q-Networks are used. Getting it done efficiently they used a reward function, which was designed with some intermediate rewards by calculating the Q-values.

A deep Q- network that is implemented on gaming environment [11], that takes pixels and game score as input and outperforms of all previous algorithms. Assorted array of challenging tasks can be learned by the artificial agent. They incorporated replay algorithm which successfully integrates reinforcement learning with deep network architecture.

3 Proposed Approach

To implement the inverse kinematics Machine Learning Algorithms can be employed. To solve the problem of inverse kinematics in hyper-redundant robots, Reinforcement Learning technique can be used. In Reinforcement Learning paradigm, the algorithm goes through exploration and exploitation phases. In exploration, the agent learns about the environment and in exploitation it takes decision based on learning in the earlier phase.

3.1   Reinforcement Learning

The theory of reinforcement learning is inspired by the psychological and neuroscientific perspectives of human behavior [11], concerned with the problem of selecting an appropriate action from a set of actions in an environment, to maximize some cumulative reward. Reinforcement Learning is not given the explicit path, instead, it uses trial and error to reach the goal initially, but later uses its past experience to take the optimal path, in the problem an agent decides the best action only on the basis of its current state, this is best described by Markov Decision Process. Figure 3 shows the pictorial representation of Reinforcement Learning, where the reinforcement Learning model consists of the following things:

- A set of environment and agent states S.
- A set of actions A of the agent.
- Policies of transitioning from states to actions.
- Rules that determine the scalar immediate reward of a transition
- Rules that describe what the agent observes.

Fig. 3. Reinforcement learning

Figure 4 shows the image of the proposed approach. In which a machine learning technique namely Reinforcement learning is for the trajectory purpose. And after reaching a particular destination the raw data is gathered of damaged tiles and then image processing is applied to get the resultant data.

3.2   Deep Q Network Architecture

Training consists of few parameters like [s, a, r, s_, done] and is stored as agent's experience, where, *s* is current state, *a* is action, *r* is the reward, *s_* is next state and *done* is a Boolean value to check whether the goal is reached or not. The initial idea was to take (state, action) as an input to the neural network, and the output should be the value representing how that action would be at the given state. The same concept is shown in Fig. 5.

The issue with this approach is, for each (state, action) pair we need to train it separately which is time-consuming. Suppose, three actions possible from state 's' are −1, 0, +1. If we have 3 actions possible we need to train it 3 times to choose the best action at state 's'. We will get three values from the three (state, action) pair.

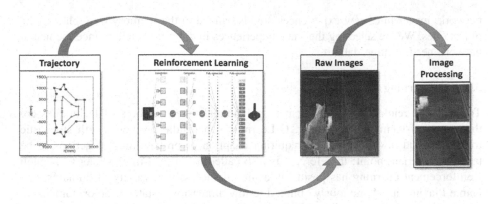

Fig. 4. Proposed approach

We will get value1, value2 and value 3 for the (state, action) pairs (s, +1), (s, 0) and (s, −1) respectively. Now, action with the maximum value is selected i.e. max (value1, value2, value3).

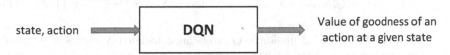

Fig. 5. Deep Q network model

Another better approach is to take a state as an input and output would be (action, value) pair which also gives the action with the value representing the goodness of an action. Figure 6 explains the same concept. The same is explained in [11].

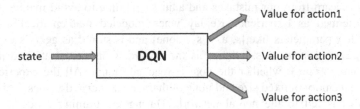

Fig. 6. This figure shows architecture of the deep Q network.

We have (s, a) using which we can find the next state 's_', immediate reward is calculated using a function _r_func () and a Boolean value named 'done' is used to check whether the goal is reached or not. [s, a, r, s_, done] tuple is the experience which is stored in memory until the memory is full. Once the memory is full, we take a batch of random experiences (In our case batch of 16 experiences is taken into consideration) to avoid the overfitting problem. These experiences are used to train and evaluate the network, meanwhile, new experiences are also added to the memory by replacing the oldest ones. We are selecting the same experiences in different batches since the neural network needs a huge dataset.

3.3 Q-Learning

To solve the reinforcement problem in polynomial time, numbers of techniques are there; one of them is Q-Learning. Q-Learning can handle problems with stochastic transitions and rewards, without requiring adaption or probabilities of actions to be taken at a certain point; therefore, it is also called as "model-free" strategy. Though Reinforcement Learning has positively achieved success in a variety of domains, like Game Playing, it is "previously" limited to low dimensional state space or domains in which features can be assigned manually. In our approach we use a Deep Neural network with Q-Learning – so-called Deep Q Network (DQN).

Q-Learning is one of the techniques of reinforcement learning. So, Q-Learning also has agent, environment and, rewards like reinforcement learning. They are: Arm is *Agent*; Tokamak (Nuclear reactor) is *Environment* and *Rewards* are inversely proportional to the distance of current position from the desired position.

$$Q(S_t, a_t) \leftarrow Q(S_t, a_t) + \alpha \cdot \left(r_{t+1} + \gamma \cdot \max_a Q(S_{t+1}, a) - Q(S_t, a_t) \right) \qquad (1)$$

Equation (1) shows the calculation of Q values are calculated. Where S is an actual and instant situation of an agent, α is learning rate, γ is a discount factor and $Q(S_t, a_t)$ is Q value to reach the state S by taking an action a.

Reinforcement starts with hit and trial, as it gets trained, it gets the experience and it takes the decisions on the basis of its policy values. That leads to increase the reward value.

3.4 Experience Replay (Replay Memory)

The ability to learn from our mistakes and adjust next time to avoid making the same mistake is termed as Experience Replay when modeled mathematically. Training consists of few parameters like [s, a, r, s_, done] and is stored as agent's experience, where, *s* is current state, *a* is action, *r* is the reward, *s_* is next state and *done* is a Boolean value to check whether the goal is reached or not. All the experiences are stored in the memory of fixed size and none of them are associated values. This is just a raw data that is fed to the neural network. During the training process, once the memory is full random batches of a particular size are selected from this fixed memory. Whenever the new experiences are added, and if the memory is full than the old ones are discarded. Experience relay helps to avoid the overfitting problem and to deal with the problem of lack of training data, the same data can be used numerous times for training the network.

3.5   Frozen Target Network

We are using the Q network's output as our regression target. We run the post-state $s\_t + 1$ through our Q function, a maximum value is selected and added to the immediate reward. This sum is called the regression target. This is an issue in optimization because the parameters are updated at every step that leads to the change in the regression target at every step. To solve this problem delayed/frozen network is used because it updates its parameters after a few steps, to provide the stable regression target.

4   Experimental Setup and Results

This section includes the experimental setup for this work. The robotic arm used in the work is of 3 hollow links and a camera. All the links are of 63 mm link diameter, 80 mm link flange diameter with the length of 90 mm and all the links are connected with a universal joint. At the end of the third link, a camera is deployed. Because the motor which operates the robotic arm is outside the body of the robotic arm it lightens the weight of the robotic arm, and so are operated with tendons. The tendons are connected to the motor which is outside the structure of the robotic arm [4].

To see how the three links robotic arm works, we created the visualization of the same by defining the environment with the blue square/point moving in it, and the agent is three arms. The goal is to make the end connector reach the blue point, following such a path maximizes the cumulative reward.

We define the reward function as:

(a) The reward is initialized to the value of $-(d/200)$ for each episode, where d is the distance between the end connector and blue point.
(b) With every step in an episode, if arm reaches to the blue point and is still stable there, reward = reward + 10, implies goal is reached.
(c) If arm touches the blue point, but not stable, reward = reward + 1, implies it can do better
(d) With every step arm takes, we reduce the reward by -1/30, so that it takes less number of steps to reach the goal.

We define action as:

- During training, the arm can take any value between $(-2/pi, 2pi)$ from its current position.

We define our state as:

- There are many ways to define the state, depends on the number of observations, as long as the state or observation is representative and helpful in finding the goal.

We define the goal as:

- blue point (i.e. goal), the distance between end-point of all the arms and blue, the distance of end-connector and blue point.

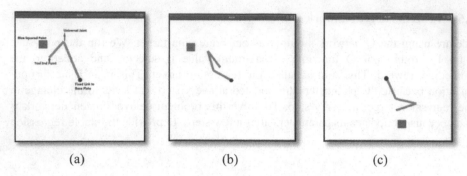

Fig. 7. This figure shows the training examples. (Color figure online)

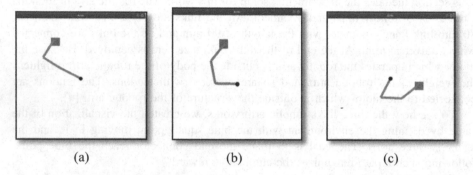

Fig. 8. This figure shows the testing examples. (Color figure online)

As shown in Fig. 7, we created a visualization of a three link robotic arm with 6 Degree of Freedoms (DOFs) with the Deep Q-Learning concept that initially explores each and every possible way to reach the destination which is called training. The number of experiences are gathered in a fixed memory and trained in the random batches of fixed size. During testing, the robotic arm reaches the destination without any flickering in the defined space. It is observed that DQN successfully learned optimal policies from high dimension sensory inputs using Reinforcement Learning [5]. Figure 7(a, b, c) shows the training scenario where the robotic arm is getting trained and it flickers a lot to reach to the destination. Figure 8(a, b, c) shows the testing scenario where the robotic arm reaches the destination without flickering.

5   Conclusions

The inverse kinematics of hyper-redundant robot is a complex process. The inverse of the forward kinematics model may lead to multiple solutions, and hence the best solution needs to be estimated. Machine Learning algorithms can be deployed for such problems. In the paper, we used reinforcement Deep Q learning approach for training to estimate the configuration parameters to reach the desired position in the task space.

We created a visualization of three links robotic arm with 6 DOF for visualizing the manipulator's response during training and testing. This initially explores each and every possible way to reach the destination and accumulates the positive and negative rewards, which is called training. The number of experiences are gathered in a fixed memory and trained in the random batches of fixed size. During testing, the robotic arm exploits the gathered experience during the exploration phase. The configuration parameters estimated by the system leads to the manipulator in the desired position in the task space. It is observed that DQN successfully learned optimal policies for high dimension sensory inputs using reinforcement learning.

In this work, so far we have only included the movement of the robotic arm, in two dimensional. This work can be extended with more number of links and in three dimensions.

Acknowledgment. This work is conducted at Nirma University, Ahmedabad underfunded research project by the Board of Research in Nuclear Sciences under Department of Atomic Energy.

References

1. Wang, H., Chen, W., Lai, Y., He, T.: Trajectory planning of tokamak flexible in-vessel inspection robot. Fusion Eng. Des. **98–99**, 1678–1682 (2015)
2. Vijayakumari, D., Dhivya, K.: Conceptual framework of robot with nanowire sensor in nuclear reactor. Int. J. Inf. Futur. Res. **1**(11), 146–151 (2014)
3. Hyper-Redundant Robotics Research. http://robby.caltech.edu/ ~ jwb/hyper.html. Accessed 15 Feb 2018
4. Dutta, P., Gotewal, K.K., Rastogi, N., Tiwari, R.: A hyper-redundant robot development for tokamak inspection. In: AIR 2017, p. 6 (2017)
5. Wang, H., Xu, L., Chen, W.: Design and implementation of visual inspection system handed in tokamak flexible in-vessel robot. Fusion Eng. Des. **106**, 21–28 (2016)
6. Andrew, G., Gryniewski, M., Campbell, T.: AARM: a robot arm for internal operations in nuclear reactors. In: 2010 1st International Conference on Applied Robotics for the Power Industry, CARPI, pp. 1–5 (2010)
7. Peng, X., Yuan, J., Zhang, W., Yang, Y., Song, Y.: Kinematic and dynamic analysis of a serial-link robot for inspection process in EAST vacuum vessel. Fusion Eng. Des. **87**(5), 905–909 (2012)
8. Liu, J., Wang, Y., Li, B., Ma, S.: Neural network based kinematic control of the hyper-redundant snake-like manipulator. In: Advances in Neural Networks – ISNN 2007, vol. 4491, pp. 339–348, April 2015
9. Liu, J., Wang, Y., Ma, S., Li, B.: RBF neural network based shape control of hyper-redundant manipulator with constrained end-effector. In: Wang, J., Yi, Z., Zurada, Jacek M., Lu, B.-L., Yin, H. (eds.) ISNN 2006. LNCS, vol. 3972, pp. 1146–1152. Springer, Heidelberg (2006). https://doi.org/10.1007/11760023_168
10. James, S., Johns, E.: 3D Simulation for Robot Arm Control with Deep Q-Learning, p. 6 (2016)
11. Mnih, V., et al.: Human-level control through deep reinforcement learning. Nature **518**, 529–533 (2015)

The Design and Implementation of Random Linear Network Coding Based Distributed Storage System in Dynamic Networks

Bin He[1], Jin Wang[1,2]([✉]), Jingya Zhou[1,2], Kejie Lu[3], Lingzhi Li[1,2], and Shukui Zhang[1,2]

[1] Department of Computer Science and Technology, Soochow University, Suzhou, People's Republic of China
wjin1985@suda.edu.cn
[2] Provincial Key Laboratory for Computer Information Processing Technology, Soochow University, Suzhou, People's Republic of China
[3] Department of Computer Science and Engineering, University of Puerto Rico at Mayagüez, Mayagüez, USA

Abstract. Nowadays, different end devices with different computation and bandwidth capabilities acquire data from Internet. To improve efficiency of data storage and retrieve, in this paper, we study how to use random linear network coding to construct an efficient distributed storage system to reduce the traffic cost in a dynamic network. In order to balance the success ratio of recovery traffic cost and traffic speed, we firstly introduce a random network coding scheme and implement a practically available distributed storage system in the actual environment. We then adjust different parameters, e.g., finite fields, link bandwidth, node computing capabilities, etc., to evaluate the proposed system. Finally, experiment results show the efficiency of the proposed designs.

Keywords: Random linear network coding
Distributed storage system · Dynamic networks

1 Introduction

Starting with the use of *Redundant Array of Independent Disks* (RAID) systems, people have been using coding to help enhance the reliability of the storage

S. Zhang—This work was supported in part by the National Natural Science Foundation of China (No.61672370, 61572310), Natural Science Foundation of the Higher Education Institutions of Jiangsu Province (No. 16KJB520040), Suzhou Key Laboratory of Converged Communication (No. SZS0805), Prospective Application Foundation Research of Suzhou of China (No. SYG201730), Six Talent Peak high-level personnel selection and training foundation of Jiangsu of China (No. 2014-WLW-010), Shanghai Key Laboratory of Intelligent Information Processing, Fudan University (No. IIPL-2016-008) and Postgraduate Research & Practice Innovation Program of Jiangsu Province (No. SJCX17_0661).

© Springer Nature Switzerland AG 2018
J. Vaidya and J. Li (Eds.): ICA3PP 2018, LNCS 11337, pp. 72–82, 2018.
https://doi.org/10.1007/978-3-030-05063-4_7

system [1]. In the past, RAID systems were widely used in backup solutions. However, RAID systems have many limitations. For example, RAID systems require that the hard disks have the same storage space and data transfer speed. Moreover, once a storage node is unavailable, to regenerate a new node, it is necessary to collect enough data to decode the whole original data first, which increases the cost of network transmission.

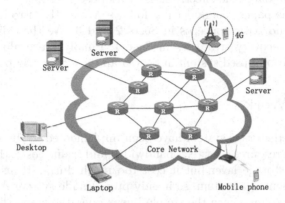

Fig. 1. Distributed storage system in dynamic networks

Since the traditional view is that "processing data on intermediate nodes will not bring benefits", routers do not process the received packets. Therefore in the scheme, routers are generally routers that use the "store-forward" mechanism. On the other hand, network coding was first proposed by Ahlswede et al. [2], which allows routers encode the required data packets to increase the network throughput. Network coding can directly recode the coded data to generate new coded data without breaking code integrity, which is better than traditional coding solutions. From the research on network coding based distributed storage system have mainly focused on the problem of code regeneration [3, 4], which have been proven that network coding can not only reduce the download time but also require less storage space. Many researcher studied how to implement a distributed storage system [5–9]. However, most current distributed storage solutions are designed for static network structures, in which the storage nodes have the same storage sizes and the same interfaces. They overlooked the highly dynamic factors in the network, in which different nodes, e.g., mobile phones, tablets, etc., have different bandwidths and computational capabilities. Moreover, in such dynamic networks, most terminal devices are mobile devices, there may be failures such as node leaving, dropping, and damage at any time. As shown in Fig. 1, a network contains a phone, PDA, laptop, etc., as end users, which may disconnect with this network at any time.

In this paper, we will address the challenging problem of implement an actual distributed system based on network coding in dynamic networks. The main contributions of the paper are summarized as follows:

Problem Modeling: We design an novel distributed storage system model based on network coding and analyze the model's quality.

Storage Strategy: We propose a distributed storage strategy based on *Random Linear Network Coding* (RLNC) and apply this strategy to our model.

System Implementation: We implement an actual system, evaluate the performances and validates the effectiveness of proposed designs.

The rest of the paper is organized as follows. We firstly introduce the related work of others and basic concepts in Sects. 2 and 3. We then discuss the system model and recovery strategies in Sect. 4. Finally, we evaluate the actual performance with proposed system in Sect. 5 and conclude the paper in Sect. 6.

2　Related Work

Actual distributed storage system have been implemented in [10,11]. These systems cost system resource a lot (e.g. bandwidth and traffic cost). [10] have implemented a cloud storage layer but it cost too much during transmission, while [11] have implemented a system, so it only provides file system APIs.

For network coding, since the simple linear operations and distributed execution, most actual distributed system designs have considered *Random Linear Network Coding* (RLNC), which leads to lower bandwidth and recover cost in distributed storage system. [12] uses RLNC to design regenerating code for distributed storage system. [13] have utilized RLNC to implement a cloud storage service. No matter in [12] or in [13], performance evaluation is either through a simulation or a client running on traditional servers. In this era of the *Internet of Things* (IOT), all nodes in the network have different computing powers and storage capacities. it is necessary to design a more general distributed storage system, in which not only traditional servers but also different devices can be a storage nodes or end users. Shwe *et al.* have proposed a scalable distributed cloud data storage service [16], but their system is not easy to deploy and not adapt to dynamic networks, because their system is non-portable.

For distributed storage system, Alexandros G. Dimakis *et al.* have showed that RLNC based regenerating codes can significantly reduce the repair bandwidth and shows that there is a fundamental trade-off between storage cost and repair bandwidth [14]. Although their designs consider the highly dynamic requirement, they haven't implemented a proof-of-concept prototype to measure its actual performance. On the other hand, Henry C. H. Chen *et al.* have implemented a proof-of-concept prototype of NCCloud and deployed it atop both local and commercial clouds [15]. Although the solution is suitable for large-scale systems, it is too complicated for ubiquitous computing, e.g. edge computing.

Therefore, in this paper, we try to design and implement a distributed storage system based on RLNC, it is suitable for either complex computing or ubiquitous computing. Moreover, it meets highly dynamic requirements in real environment.

3   Random Linear Network Coding Basics

The core idea of linear network coding is that the routers can encode the received data packets to generate newly coded data packets and send out to next hop routers [2–4]. Based on this idea, network throughput can be significantly improved. Moreover, it can improve network reliability and security [17–19]. *Random Linear Network Coding* (RLNC) uses random coding coefficients from a finite field to linearly combines original data into coded data [20]. In distributed storage system, the total number of coded data blocks are larger than the total number of original data blocks to keep redundancy. As long as an end user obtain a sufficient number of coded blocks, it can decode and obtain all the original data block [20]. This feature simplify the content download process, especially in dynamic network environment. Moreover, once a storage node is unavailable, it can regenerate the coded data blocks to keep redundancy as long as it receives a number of coded data blocks from other available storage nodes. The original data blocks are not necessary to be recovered before regenerate the coded data blocks in the new storage node [20]. In other word, RLNC can recode the coded data to generate new coded data, which reduce the cost of repair cost.

In particular, given an $n \times m$-dimension coefficient matrix A ($n >= m$) and a vector X contains m unknown numbers($x_1, x_2, \ldots, x_m$), assuming $AX = T$, we can solve X, only need any m linearly independent equations in the system.

The finite field is a filed which only contains a limited number of elements. It has been widely used in *cryptography*. Our coding work is performed on finite field. All elements in our code matrix are randomly selected from a finite field.

In this paper, we use RLNC based on finite field to encode and decode data. The specific coding process is as follows:

Split into Generation and Blocks: We split the file streams into generations which present the smallest unit of encoding. The generations' size is fixed, it may be 8 MB, 16 MB, *etc.* Then we split each generation into blocks, these blocks are called original blocks. After that, arrange these blocks into a matrix whose dimension is $m \times l$ (each block expands in bytes as a row).

Generate Coefficient Matrix: We generate an $n \times m$-dimension coefficient matrix randomly in a selected finite field ($n >= m$). When the finite field is lager enough, we can ensure any m rows in this matrix are linearly independent.

Encode: Now there are two matrices: a coefficient matrix C and the original data matrix O. We multiply these matrices and then get a $n \times l$-dimension matrix M, in mathematics, it is expressed as: $C \times O = M$. Any m rows in M are linearly independent because of C's feature. We regard each row as a coded block.

Storage: Store these coded blocks to storage entities, since they are linearly independent, we can store them randomly.

Decode: According to the feature of the matrix, we can take out any m rows from matrix C, and then take the corresponding m rows from matrix M, assemble these rows in succession, we call these two new matrix C' and M', then there

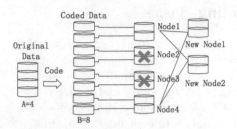

Fig. 2. Model of the dynamic distributed storage system

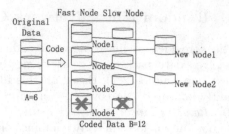

Fig. 3. Model of the dynamic distributed storage system with uneven speed and storage

are $O = C'^{-1} \times M'$. Based on this principle, if there are original data to recover, we can combine any m rows (m blocks) and then multiply the inverse of related coefficient matrix, after that, we can get the original data.

4 Model and Strategies

4.1 System Model

Nowadays, there are two different distributed storage system models:

Client-Proxy-Server Model: The system is composed of several servers with storage, the client connects to these servers through a proxy server, and each server node can be calculated independently, any node can adjust the file blocks by itself, but the disadvantage is: if these servers use two kinds of *Operation System* (OS) or more, we should deploy two or more solutions on them.

Client-Proxy/Server-Storage Unit Model: The system is composed of simple storage units. The server and proxy server would be in charge of the controlling of storage units, the client only communicates with the server, all leaf nodes are storage units, thus they would only be charge of storaging file. The server performs the task of file block adjustments.

It is clear that the second model is less complex and more universal, thus we this model to finish our experiment.

In Figs. 2 and 3, we describe two different strategies using network coding for distributed storage system. Our main focus is whether to consider the speed of the node in the strategy while using *Random Linear Network Coding* (RLNC). As given in Fig. 2, we assume all nodes have the same speed, we consider that the original data is splitted into A blocks and code them into B coded blocks, in this scenario, we can see that 2 nodes are broken, the number of remaining blocks is greater than or equal to the number of original blocks, thus we can use *Node 1* and *Node 4* to generate two new nodes named *New Node 1* and *New Node 2*. We further assume that the storage node may be a cell phone, a pad, or other mobile device, they have different speeds. We refer to these nodes as *slow nodes* and normal server nodes as *fast nodes*, as shown in Fig. 3. Suppose there are the same number of fast node and slow node, the fast node has two units of space but the slow node has only one. Considering the stability of the fast node, whether it is a fast node crash or a slow node crash, we generate new nodes from the remaining fast nodes as much as possible.

We have three indicators for evaluate performance:

Recovery Possibility: Recovery possibility means the probability of recovering complete data after multiple processes "broken then node-repair".

Traffic Cost: Suppose there are A original blocks and then they are coded into B linearly independent coding blocks. traffic cost means the amount of transmitted data when we generate a new node. It is worth noting that the number of transmitted coded blocks is greater than or equal to A, otherwise the original data cannot be recovered.

Recovery Time: Because of the existence of slow nodes, we must also consider the time taken for recovery.

4.2 Recovery Strategies

We generate new nodes from remaining fast nodes as much as possible unless there were not enough fast nodes. Suppose there are n fast nodes and t slow nodes, original data is splitted into m blocks, and we need k redundant blocks. In order to increase the recovery probability and reduce the amount of redundancy, we use Algorithm 1 to calculate the relationship among n, m and k. After that, we find that the bigger n/m is, the small k is. Since the coding coefficient table is stored in proxy node, we can first detect the linear correlation of the newly generated coding matrix and increase the recovery possibility when regenerate the code. This is reflected in Algorithm 2. We ensure the consistency of files in different file systems through the consistency of metadata. In addition, we can also use metadata to reproduce and restore files. This is shown in Algorithm 3.

Algorithm 1. Required redundancy algorithm

Input:
  Fast nodes: n, Slow nodes: t, Original blocks: m
Output:
  Redundant blocks: k
1: Dim $last := -10000$, k
2: **while** $last <= m$ **do**
3:    $t := (m + k)/n$
4:    $last := m + k - t$
5:    **if** $(m + k)$ MOD $n <> 0$ **then**
6:       $last := last - 1$
7:    **end if**
8: **end while**
9: **return** k

Algorithm 2. Regeneration algorithm

Input:
  Coding coefficient Matrix T ($m \times (m + k)$-dimension)
1: Dim set<Matrix> q: Full arrangement matrix($m \times m$) in matrix(T)
2: **for** each i in q **do**
3:    **if** $rank(i) = m$ **then**
4:        REGENERATION and BREAK
5:    **end if**
6: **end for**
7: Take an *element* from set q randomly and regeneration

Algorithm 3. Metadata verification algorithm

Input:
  Nodes: $n = \{n_1, n_2, ..., n_p\}$
  Original metadata: md_o
1: regenerate full file and get new metadata md_n
2: **while** $md_o <> md_n$ **do**
3:    It shows defeat, regenerate full file again.
4:    **if** out of time **then**
5:        BREAK
6:    **end if**
7: **end while**
8: Rebuild coded blocks on new node

For example, if there is a node broken, in order to regenerate a new node, we have to do: **first**, detect if there are enough fast nodes, if fast nodes are not enough, use slow nodes instead; **then**, in server, flag exist coefficient vector, use Algorithm 2 to get a random coefficient matrix, regenerate it, at the same time, check the consistency of files using metadata, and verify the metadata by Algorithm 3; **finally**, mapped the relationship of the coefficient matrix and regenerate the coded data. After that, we can regenerate a new node and reserve the possibility of recovery.

5   Implementation and Performance

5.1   Implementation

We implement this system using $C\#$ on traditional server and *java* on mobile device, we set the size of the finite field to the smallest unit of $C\#/java$, which is 2^8. The system's architecture is shown in Fig. 4. This system is composed of server and client. Server program (Control plane) is running on proxy and client program (Data plane) is running on nodes. It has four modules, index database module records the file structure and speed detect module is used to distinguish between fast and slow nodes. The metadata detect module ensures the file consistency. Moreover, encode/decode module is the core of entire system, it controls all encode and decode operations. In client program, there are only two types of data, data blocks present the content of coded blocks while metadata is used to ensure the file consistency. We experiment on traditional server ($i5 - 6400$) and mobile device ($Snapdragon - 835$), then we get different results by adjusting experimental parameters.

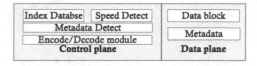

Fig. 4. Overall architecture of system

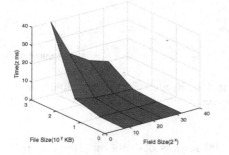

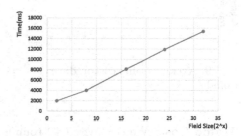

Fig. 5. The relationship of file size, field size and coded time

Fig. 6. The relationship of matrix size and coded time

5.2   Performance and Results

We implement RLNC encoding on different finite fields (the size of finite field is 2^q, $q = 8, 16, 32, etc.$), then we change the parameters q, original file size and encoding matrix size, and we gain two figures, Figs. 5 and 6. In these two figures, we see the encoding time is affected by file size, field size and encoding matrix size. The reason of this is that the larger finite field size and encoding matrix size is, the more complex calculation is. In this section we provide actual performance measured in experiment. If not specified otherwise, the field size F is chosen to be 2^8. Finally, our experimental results are as follows:

Recovery Possibility: In the same environment with Subsect. 5.1, we test the possibility of recovery by changing number of blocks per node and number of original blocks. After that, we draw two figures, Figs. 7 and 8. It is seen from these figures that when bigger number of blocks per node/original blocks is, the bigger recovery possibility is. Bigger number of blocks per node/original blocks means files are divided into smaller blocks, which would increase the probability of linear independence. So we can recovery entire file easier. When the recovery possibility is high enough, it can meet the needs of the dynamic networks.

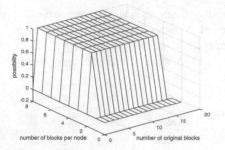

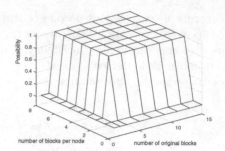

Fig. 7. After 10 rounds   **Fig. 8.** After 100 rounds

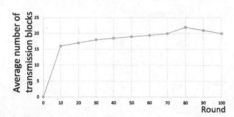

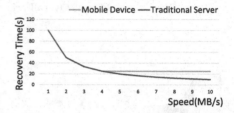

Fig. 9. Average traffic cost in different rounds

Fig. 10. Recovery time in different speeds

Traffic Cost: We conducted 10 rounds to 100 rounds of tests on the system. Figure 9 shows the experimental result. (Assume the original data is splitted into 16 blocks and in every round, only one node is broken). We can see in the regeneration process, the average traffic cost is stable.

Recovery Time: We try to recovery 100 MB original data under different speeds, and measure time to evaluate performance. Assume there are enough fast nodes. The result is shown in Fig. 10. Limited by the performance of mobile devices, the recovery speed of mobile devices is limited by the decoding speed when the network speed reaches a certain level. Therefore, increasing the encoding and decoding speed is still a key factor for our exploration.

6   Conclusion

In this paper, we have introduced the network coding and used a strategy of RLNC to implement an actual distributed storage system, then we have researched parameters related to network coding in order to improve the performance of system and evaluated the actual performance. In addition, we have promoted this system to different devices, making it suitable for mobile devices.

References

1. Buyya, R., Cortes, T., Jin, H.: A Case for Redundant Arrays of Inexpensive Disks (RAID), vol. 17, no. 3, pp. 109–116. ACM (1988)
2. Ahlswede, R., Cai, N., Li, S.Y.R., Yeung, R.W.: Network information flow. Proc. IEEE Trans. Inf. Theory **46**(4), 1204–1216 (2000)
3. Dimakis, A.G., Godfrey, P.B., Wainwright, M.J., Ramchandran, K.: Network coding for distributed storage systems. In: Proceedings of IEEE International Conference on Computer Communications (INFOCOM), vol. 56, pp. 2000–2008 (2007)
4. Dimakis, A.G., Ramchandran, K., Wu, Y., Suh, C.: A survey on network codes for distributed storage. Proc. IEEE **99**(3), 476–489 (2011)
5. Liu, F., Shen, S., Li, B., Li, B., Jin, H.: Cinematic-quality vod in a p2p storage cloud: design, implementation and measurements. IEEE J. Sel. Areas Commun. (JSAC) **31**(9), 214–226 (2013)
6. Zhang, Y., Dragga, C., Arpaci-Dusseau, A.C., Arpaci-Dusseau, R.H.: Viewbox: integrating local file systems with cloud storage services. In: Proceedings of File and Storage Technologies, vol. 49, pp. 119–132 (2014)
7. Weil, S.A., Brandt, S.A., Miller, E.L., Long, D.D., Maltzahn, C.: Ceph: a scalable, high-performance distributed file system. In: Proceedings of Operating Systems Design and Implementation, pp. 307–320 (2006)
8. Hu, W., Yang, T., Matthews, J.N.: The good, the bad and the ugly of consumer cloud storage. ACM SIGOPS Oper. Syst. Rev. **44**(3), 110–115 (2010)
9. Muthitacharoen, A., Chen, B.: A low-bandwidth network file system. In: Proceedings of Symposium on Operating Systems Principles, vol. 35, no. 5, pp. 174–187 (2001)
10. Bowers, K.D., Juels, A., Oprea, A.: A high-availability and integrity layer for cloud storage. In: Proceedings of Computer and Communications Security (CCS), pp. 187–198 (2009)
11. Shvachko, K., Kuang, H., Radia, S., Chansler, R., Shvachko, K.: The hadoop distributed file system mass storage systems and technologies. In: Proceedings of Mass Storage Systems and Technology (MSST) (2010)
12. Fitzek, F.H.P., Toth, T., Szabados, A., Pedersen, M.V.: Implementation and performance evaluation of distributed cloud storage solutions using random linear network coding. In: IEEE International Conference on Proceedings of Communications Workshops (ICC), pp. 249–254. IEEE (2014)
13. Sipos, M., Fitzek, F.H.P., Lucani, D.E., Pedersen, M.V.: Distributed cloud storage using network coding. In: Proceedings of Consumer Communications and Networking Conference (CCNC), pp. 127–132 (2014)
14. Dimakis, A.G., Godfrey, P.B., Wainwright, M.J., Ramchandran, K.: Network coding for distributed storage systems. IEEE Trans. Inf. Theory **56**(9), 4539–4551 (2010)
15. Chen, H.C.H., Hu, Y., Lee, P.P.C., Tang, Y.: NCCloud: a network-coding-based storage system in a cloud-of-clouds. IEEE Trans. Comput. **63**(1), 31–44 (2014)
16. Shwe, H.Y., Chong, P.H.J.: Scalable distributed cloud data storage service for internet of things. In: Ubiquitous Intelligence and Computing, Advanced and Trusted Computing, Scalable Computing and Communications, Cloud and Big Data Computing, Internet of People, and Smart World Congress, pp. 869–873 (2016)
17. Wang, J., Wang, J., Lu, K., Xiao, B., Gu, N.: Optimal linear network coding design for secure unicast with multiple streams. In: Proceedings of Information Communications (INFOCOM), pp. 2240–2248 (2010)

18. Wang, J., Wang, J., Lu, K., Xiao, B., Gu, N.: Modeling and optimal design of linear network coding for secure unicast with multiple streams. IEEE Trans. Parallel Distrib. Syst. **24**(10), 2025–2035 (2013)
19. Wang, J., Wang, X., Zhang, S., Zhu, Y., Jia, J.: An efficient reliable communication scheme in wireless sensor networks using linear network coding. Int. J. Distrib. Sensor Netw. pp. 487–513 (2012)
20. Chuang, C., Yung, K.: Network dynamics, network resources and innovation. In: Proceedings of Academy of Management Annual Meeting (2008)

Security and Privacy in Computing

Forward Secure Searchable Encryption Using Key-Based Blocks Chain Technique

Siyi Lv[1], Yanyu Huang[1], Bo Li[1], Yu Wei[1], Zheli Liu[1(✉)], Joseph K. Liu[2], and Dong Hoon Lee[3]

[1] College of Computer and Control Engineering, Nankai University,
Tianjin 300071, China
lv_si_yi@163.com, onlyerir@163.com, nankailibo@163.com,
suifengrudao@outlook.com, liuzheli@nankai.edu.cn
[2] Computer Science, The Monesh University, Melbourne, Australia
joseph.liu@monash.edu
[3] Information Security, Korea University, Seoul, Korea
donghlee@korea.ac.kr

Abstract. Searchable Symmetric Encryption (SSE) has been widely applied in the encrypted database for exact queries or even range queries in practice. In spite of it has excellent efficiency and complete functionality, it always suffers from information leakages. Some recent attacks point out that forward privacy is the vital security goal. However, there are only several schemes achieving this security. In this paper, we propose a new flexible forward secure SSE scheme referred to as "FFSSE", which has the best performance in literature, such as fast search operation, fast token generation and $O(1)$ update complexity. It also supports both *add* and *delete* operations in the unique instance. Technically, we exploit a novel "key-based blocks chain" technique based on symmetric cryptographic primitive, which can be deployed in arbitrary index tree structures or key-value structures directly to guarantee forward privacy.

Keywords: Searchable encryption · Keyword search
Forward privacy · Searchable Symmetric Encryption

1 Introduction

Data encryption currently is used to ensure data privacy in outsourcing data to the cloud. However, encryption breaks the data availabilities, such that keyword search, range query or other functions cannot be directly applied over the ciphertext. Searchable encryption (SE) is the mechanism to allow querying the encrypted data without leaking data privacy to the cloud server. Searchable Symmetric Encryption (SSE) is designed on symmetric cryptographic primitives and thus has very good performance (when compared to public key searchable encryption [1–3]). It allows a client to store encrypted documents on the server and then retrieve all documents containing a certain keyword (or collection of keywords) at a later point.

© Springer Nature Switzerland AG 2018
J. Vaidya and J. Li (Eds.): ICA3PP 2018, LNCS 11337, pp. 85–97, 2018.
https://doi.org/10.1007/978-3-030-05063-4_8

1.1   Leakages and Attacks of SSE

Although SSE can protect the data content to a certain level, the deterministic encryption used in SSE makes the cloud server observe the repeated queries and other information easily. These leakage can be modeled as *size pattern*, *search pattern* and *access pattern*. *Size pattern* [7] means that a server can know the number of keyword-document pairs. *Search pattern* [8] means that a server can know the repeated deterministic tokens. *Access pattern* [8] means that a server can know the search results, including matching document identifiers of a keyword search and the document identifiers of the added/deleted documents.

1.2   Requirement of Forward Privacy

As we all known, even small leakage can be leveraged by an attacker to reveal the client's queries. Especially in the dynamic database, the server could inject new documents to obtain more advantages. Zhang et al. [9] showed that the file-injection attack can be devastating. They consider both adaptive and non-adaptive attacks. In this paper, we do not consider the non-adaptive attack. The adaptive attack refers to whether the server injects documents before or after the client's query is made. It is more effective, however, it cannot be applied to the forward secure schemes [7]. This fact highlights the importance of forward privacy in any real-world deployment.

Forward privacy means a malicious server cannot learn whether a newly added document matches previous search queries. Most of existing schemes [6,7, 10–13] suffer from inefficiencies, while among them, $\Sigma o\phi o\varsigma$ [11] is very efficient in practice for both searches and updates.

Table 1. Comparison with typical forward private SSE schemes. N is the number of entries (i.e. the number of keyword-document pairs) in the database, while $\mathcal{W}$ is the number of distinct keywords, $\mathcal{D}$ is the number of documents and $\mathcal{M}$ is the length of search token. The n_w is the size of the search result set for keyword w and a_w is the number of times the queried keyword w was historically added and deleted to the database. Denote $\mathcal{AE}$ as asymmetric encryption, $\mathcal{SE}$ as symmetric encryption, μ as the length of data identifier, λ as the security parameters and $\mathcal{TT}$ as tree traverse operation.

Scheme	Computation				Communication		Client storage
	Search	Update	Token generation		Search	Update	
			Search	Update			
SPS14 [7]	$O(\min\{\frac{a_w + \log N}{n_w \log^3 N}\})$	$O(\log^2 N)$	$O(1) \cdot \mathcal{SE}$	$O(2^\ell) \cdot \mathcal{SE}$	$O(\log N +n_w)$	$O(\log N)$	$O(N^\alpha)$
TWORAM [12]	$\tilde{O}(a_w \log N + \log^3 N)$	$\tilde{O}(\log^2 N)$	$O(n_w) \cdot \mathcal{SE}$	$O(n_w) \cdot \mathcal{SE}$	$\tilde{O}(\log^3 N +a_w \log N)$	$\tilde{O}(\log^3 N)$	$O(\log N)$
$\Sigma o\phi o\varsigma$-B [11]	$O(a_w) \cdot (\mathcal{AE} + \mathcal{TT})$	$O(1)$	$O(a_w) \cdot \mathcal{AE}$	$O(a_w) \cdot \mathcal{AE}$	$O(n_w)$	$O(1)$	$O(\mathcal{W}(\log \mathcal{D} + \log \mathcal{M}))$
$\Sigma o\phi o\varsigma$ [11]	$O(a_w) \cdot (\mathcal{AE} + \mathcal{TT})$	$O(1)$	$O(a_w) \cdot \mathcal{AE}$	$O(a_w) \cdot \mathcal{AE}$	$O(n_w)$	$O(1)$	$O(\mathcal{W} \log \mathcal{D})$
FFSSE	$O(a_w) \cdot (\mathcal{SE} + \mathcal{TT})$	$O(1)$	$O(1) \cdot \mathcal{SE}$	$O(1) \cdot \mathcal{SE}$	$O(n_w)$	$O(1)$	$O(\mathcal{W}(\mu + \lambda))$

1.3   Motivation

$\Sigma o\phi o\varsigma$ has some limitations of performance and application scopes. The TDP technique in $\Sigma o\phi o\varsigma$ relies on the asymmetric cryptographic primitive. However, asymmetric primitive is more expensive than symmetric primitive. Therefore we focus on *how to exploit the new technique based on symmetric cryptographic primitive which has the same effect as TDP, as to further improve its performance.*

The storage position in $\Sigma o\phi o\varsigma$ must be generated based on the repeated operation by the private key of the asymmetric primitive. It means TDP in $\Sigma o\phi o\varsigma$ conflicts with the storage structure with its own index generation rule. This limitation would limit its application scopes. Therefore we also focus on *how to exploit the new technique independent of token generation rule, to provide forward private security for the existing structures with its own index generation rule.*

1.4   Our Contributions

We construct a flexible forward secure searchable encryption scheme based on the symmetric primitives, denoted as "FFSSE", which supports both add and delete operations in the unique instance. As shown in Table 1, the contribution includes: (1) FFSSE and $\Sigma o\phi o\varsigma$s ($\Sigma o\phi o\varsigma$-B and $\Sigma o\phi o\varsigma$) have the same asymptotic complexity in search and update. But experiments show that FFSSE improves $4\times$ search and $300\times$ update than $\Sigma o\phi o\varsigma$-B ($100\times$ search and at least $300\times$ update than $\Sigma o\phi o\varsigma$), owing to the adopted symmetric cryptographic primitive; (2) FFSSE has the most efficient token generation among all the forward private SSE schemes.

Technically, we exploit a novel "key-based blocks chain" (KBBC) method based on symmetric cryptographic primitive. Without relying on the index generation rule, it can be deployed in arbitrary index tree structures or key-value structures to provide forward private security.

2   Related Work

2.1   Searchable Symmetric Encryption

The first practical searchable encryption scheme was introduced by Song et al. [5] in 2000. Subsequently, many schemes were proposed. Among them, the approach based on inverted index is the most widely used. In this approach, an index is in the form of (*key*, *value*), where the *key* is a keyword and the *value* consists of a list of document identifiers associated with the keyword. Compared to other approaches, it achieves the sublinear search time. When searching for a keyword, it will return the list of document identifiers matching the keyword immediately. In 2006, Curtmola et al. [8] firstly introduced this approach and subsequent schemes such as [4,7,11,14–16] are proposed.

2.2   Trapdoor Permutation Technique

We review the trapdoor one-way permutations described in [17]. In $\Sigma o\phi o\varsigma$, TDP is built by the asymmetric primitive. The client maintains a counter c and its search token $ST_c(w)$ for each keyword w. When adding a keyword-document pair for keyword w, client will first produce a search token by $ST_{c+1}(w) \leftarrow \pi_{sk}^{-1}(ST_c(w))$ and then produce a storage position (called as update token) $UT_{c+1}(w)$ using a keyed hash. Finally update its client state and store the document identifier into $UT_{c+1}(w)$ in the server. Since the latest search token is stored in client, the malicious server cannot know where the $UT_{c+1}(w)$ is produced from.

3   Preliminaries

3.1   Notations

Denote $\mathrm{negl}(\lambda)$ as a negligible function, where λ is the security parameter. Denote $E_k(m)$ as the symmetric encryption of the message m by key k, $D_k(c)$ as the symmetric decryption of the ciphertext c by key k. Moreover, denote $\mathbf{H}(k, m)$ as a keyed hash function with key k and message m as input.

Denote $\mathbb{W}$ as the keyword set and $\mathcal{W}$ as the number of distinct keywords ($\mathcal{W} = |\mathbb{W}|$). Denote $\mathbb{W}_x \subseteq \{0,1\}^*$ as the x-th keyword and thus $\mathbb{W} = \bigcup_{i=1}^{\mathcal{W}} \mathbb{W}_i$. Denote $ind_x \in \{0,1\}^\mu$ as the x-th document identifier with the bit length of μ.

In general, denote w as the keyword, $\mathrm{DB}(w)$ as the set of documents containing keyword w in *database* DB and N as the total number of keyword-document pairs which database supports. Denote $\mathbf{Hist}(w)$ as the history of keyword w. It lists all the modifications made to $\mathrm{DB}(w)$ over the time.

3.2   Dynamic Searchable Symmetric Encryption

We review the general definition of *dynamic searchable encryption scheme* in [11], $\mathcal{DSSE} = (\mathbf{Setup}, \mathbf{Search}, \mathbf{Update})$, containing an algorithm and two client-server protocols. $\mathbf{Setup}(\mathrm{DB})$ is an algorithm for setting up the whole encrypted database supporting keyword search. It takes as input DB and outputs a pair (EDB, K, σ), where EDB is the encrypted database, K is the secret key contained by client and σ is the client's state. $\mathbf{Search}(K, q, \sigma; \mathrm{EDB}) = (\mathrm{Search}_C(K, \sigma, q), \mathrm{Search}_S(\mathrm{EDB}))$ is a client-server protocol for performing a search query. The client takes the key K and its state σ as inputs, outputs a query q. The server takes the EDB as input, outputs the results as document identifiers matching the query q. $\mathbf{Update}(K, \sigma, op, in; \mathrm{EDB}) = (\mathrm{Update}_C(K, \sigma, op, in), \mathrm{Update}_S(\mathrm{EDB}))$ is a client-server protocol supporting update operations. The client takes as inputs the key K, an operator $op(add, del,$ the addition and the deletion of a document/keyword pair respectively), client's state σ and an input in parsed as the index ind and a set W of keywords. The server takes as input the EDB.

3.3   Forward Privacy Security

Leakage Definition. Define $\mathcal{L} = (\mathcal{L}^{Setup}, \mathcal{L}^{Search}, \mathcal{L}^{Update})$ as the leakage function, describing what protocols in $\mathcal{FFSSE}$ leak to the adversary. More formally, the leakage function $\mathcal{L}$ will keep as state the *query list* Q: the list of all queries issued so far and for a search query on keyword w, entries are (i, w), or for an **op** update query with input **in**, entries are $(i, \mathbf{op}, \mathbf{in})$. The integer i is a timestamp, initially set to 0 and it increments with the query times. Define $\mathbf{sp}(x)$ as the search patterns, formally, $\mathbf{sp}(x) = \{j : (j, x) \in Q\}$ (only matches search queries).

Definition 1. *(Forward privacy). A $\mathcal{L}$-adaptively-secure SSE scheme Σ is forward private if the update leakage function $\mathcal{L}^{Update}$ can be written as $\mathcal{L}^{Update}(\boldsymbol{op}, \boldsymbol{in}) = \mathcal{L}'(\boldsymbol{op}, \{(ind_i, u_i)\})$, where $\{(ind_i, u_i)\}$ is the set of modified documents paired with the number u_i of modified keywords for the updated document ind_i.*

4   Key-Based Blocks Chain

We propose "key-based blocks chain" (KBBC) technique, which can link arbitrary number of data blocks in a set $\mathcal{B}$ as a chain $\mathcal{C}$ while hiding their relations.

4.1   Notations and Definitions

Define $\mathbb{B}$ as the data block set, $\mathbb{B} = \{b_0, \cdots, b_n\}$ where $|\mathbb{B}| = n$. Define data block as $b = (id, value, key, ptr)$, where id and $value$ are data identifier and data value, the ptr and key are data identifier and encryption key of its next block. Denote $\mathcal{C}$ as a chain built over the subset $\mathcal{B}$ in $\mathbb{B}$. Denote n_c as the number of chains over the set $\mathbb{B}$. Assuming a block can only belong to one chain, then $1 \leq n_c \leq n$.

Block Definitions. We define three types of blocks: *head block*, *tail block* and *internal block*, which are the first block, last block and other blocks in a chain $\mathcal{C}$, denoted by $\mathcal{C}.head$, $\mathcal{C}.tail$ and $\mathcal{C}.internal$, respectively.

4.2   KBBC Algorithms

There are three algorithms (*Init, AddHead, Retrieve*) in KBBC. *Init*() initializes a blocks chain. It takes none input but outputs a description $\mathcal{C}$ for this chain. $AddHead(\mathcal{C}, id, value, 1^\lambda)$ adds a *head block* to the chain. It takes $\mathcal{C}$, id, $value$ and security parameter 1^λ as inputs and outputs a new head block b. It has four steps: (1) generate a block as $b = (id, value, \mathcal{C}.head.key, \mathcal{C}.head.id)$; (2) sample a random key k from $\{0,1\}^\lambda$; (3) utilizes k to encrypt contents of b except id; (4) store b in the server. $Retrieve(\mathcal{C}, id, k)$ retrieves a next block in the chain. It takes $\mathcal{C}$, id and k as inputs and outputs id and k of the next block. It has tree steps: (1) find the block b by its id; (2) decrypt b by its k; (3) output the obtained identifier $b.ptr$ and key $b.key$.

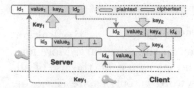
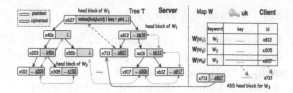

Fig. 1. An example of key-based blocks chain. There are four blocks with data identifiers of id_1, id_2, id_3 and id_4, whose encryption keys are key_1, key_2, key_3 and key_4 respectively. The *head block* in the chain is the id_1 whose encryption key is maintained in the client; the id_2 is an *internal block* and its key is stored in the previous block id_1; the *tail block* is the id_4, whose key is stored in the previous block id_2, however, its *ptr* value is $\perp$ because it is the end of this chain.

Fig. 2. Storage structure and operations of FFSSE. Here, we eliminate the XOR part. There are three keywords (W_1, W_2 and W_3) and their inverted index lists ($\mathcal{L}_{W_1}$, $\mathcal{L}_{W_2}$ and $\mathcal{L}_{W_3}$) in a *database* DB. The client stores the encryption key, identifier of *head block* of each list and a counter in the map **W**. The server stores each document identifier in these lists into the *value* part of a data block in a node of the tree $\mathcal{T}$. The root node shows the whole parts of a data block.

Build a Blocks Chain. To build a blocks chain, we first execute $Init()$ to initialize the chain $\mathcal{C}$. Then, for each block $b_i \in \mathcal{B}$ ($\mathcal{B} \subseteq \mathbb{B}, 0 \le i \le |\mathcal{B}| - 1$), we execute $AddHead(\mathcal{C}, b_i.id, b_i.value, 1^\lambda)$ repeatedly, until all blocks are added to chain $\mathcal{C}$. Figure 1 shows an example of a chain built from blocks with identifiers of id_1, id_2 and id_4.

4.3   Forward Privacy

Obviously, KBBC algorithms can ensure forward privacy for the newly added block, because its next block identifier is encrypted by a random key stored in the client.

Theorem 1 *(AddHead leaks no information). Define* $\mathcal{L}_S = (\mathcal{L}_S^{Retrieve}, \mathcal{L}_S^{AddHead})$, *where* $\mathcal{L}_S^{Retrieve} = (n_c, num_c, \textbf{Hist}(\mathcal{C}))$, $\mathcal{L}_S^{AddHead} = \perp$, *KBBC is* $\mathcal{L}_S - forward - privacy$.

Proof. If $\mathcal{C}$ has already been retrieved, the adversary knows the number of blocks which have already been in $\mathcal{C}$ (denote as num_c) and $\textbf{Hist}(\mathcal{C})$. If all the chains of $\mathbb{B}$ have been retrieved, it leaks the number of chains over the set $\mathbb{B}$ (denote as n_c). Therefore, $\mathcal{L}_S^{Retrieve} = (n_c, num_c, \textbf{Hist}(\mathcal{C}))$.

In the *AddHead* algorithm, when we add a new *head block* to $\mathcal{C}$ which has already been retrieved, we will generate a new block as $b=(id^*, value^*, \mathcal{C}.head.key, \mathcal{C}.head.id)$, which is encrypted by a new key k stored in the client side. Without k, adversary cannot decrypt b, so that the added *head block* and blocks of $\mathcal{C}$ are indistinguishable. Moreover, the adversary can only know that we add a block into $\mathbb{B}$, but cannot know which chain it belongs to and whether generate a new chain. Therefore, $\mathcal{L}_S^{AddHead} = \bot$. The adversary cannot get any advantage to learn more additional information through $AddHead$ operation.

4.4 Independent of Index Generation Rule

In KBBC, the index (data identifier) can be generated by random selection or some algorithms according to application requirements. It is flexible and valuable for some other designs with the consideration of forward security.

In fact, we can regard each block as a **"key-value"** structure, where the id with clear text is **key**, which may be the index or position in the concrete storage structure, other encrypted parts are **value**. So that, KBBC can be applied in many popular index tree (like AVL, B-tree) or key-value storage structures to provide the forward private security. In other words, it is suitable for both relational databases and NoSQL databases.

5 The FFSSE Construction

In this section, we describe our forward secure searchable encryption scheme (denoted as "FFSSE"), which is very flexible for the usage of "key-based blocks chain".

5.1 Storage Structure

Like the $\Sigma o\phi o\varsigma$, we consider the SSE construction with inverted index scheme. For each keyword $w \in \mathbb{W}$, denote $\mathbb{L}_w$ as an indexed list to store the document identifiers $(ind_0, \cdots, ind_{n_w})$ containing the keyword w, where $n_w = |\mathbb{L}_w|$.

Based on KBBC technique, the block in FFSSE is like $b = (id, (ind \| op \| key_{next} \| id_{next}) \oplus mask)$, where id is the identifier in $\mathcal{T}$, ind is the document identifier, key_{next} is the encryption of the next block, id_{next} is the identifier of the next block in $\mathcal{T}$ and $mask$ is the sign.

In server, we adopt the binary search tree $\mathcal{T}$ as an example to store the data blocks defined in Sect. 4. Each node stores a data block. We denote $\mathcal{T}[id]$ as the node indexed by id, and $\mathcal{T}[id].data$ as the stored data. Each element (document identifier) in the list $\mathbb{L}_w$ is stored in the $value$ part of a data block. As a result, there are total $\mathcal{W}$ inverted lists containing $\mathcal{N}$ nodes stored in $\mathcal{T}$, whose depth is $\log \mathcal{N}$.

In client, we adopt a map $\mathbf{W}$ to store the state which can be defined as the tuples of $st_w = (id, key)$ of each keyword w, where id and key are data identifier and encryption key of the *head block* in the inverted list $\mathbb{L}_w$. The default value of id is $\bot$.

Figure 2 shows this storage structure which we eliminate the XOR part. FFSSE supports both add and delete operations. More specifically, "$ind \| add$" denotes add operation but "$ind \| del$" denotes delete operation for document ind, where "$\|$" denotes the concatenation of two strings. See the root node in tree $\mathcal{T}$ of Fig. 2 as an example. Moreover, besides the map $\mathbf{W}$, the client should securely store the secrete key uk.

5.2 Our Construction

Figure 3 gives the formal description of FFSSE scheme. It allows only insertion of data block into tree $\mathcal{T}$, and supports both *add* and *delete* operations.

Setup()
1: $uk \xleftarrow{\$} \{0,1\}^{\lambda}$
2: $\mathbf{W} \leftarrow empty\ map,\ \mathcal{T} \leftarrow empty\ tree$
Search(w, σ; EDB)
Client:
  1: $(id, key) \leftarrow (\mathbf{W}[w].id,, \mathbf{W}[w].key)$
  2: Send token (id, key) to the server.
Server:
  3: $\mathbf{S} \leftarrow empty\ set,\ i \leftarrow 0$
  4: repeat
  5: $mask \leftarrow H(key, id)$
  6: $b \leftarrow \mathcal{T}[id].data \oplus mask$
  7: $id \leftarrow b.ptr,\ key \leftarrow b.key$
  8: $ind\|op \leftarrow b.value$
  9: $\mathbf{S}[i++] \leftarrow ind\|op$
  10: until ($b.ptr ==\perp$)
  11: $\mathbf{S} \leftarrow Merge(\mathbf{S})$ // merge the same
       ind with *add* and *del* operations
  12: Send each ind in $\mathbf{S}$ to the client.

Update(op, w, ind, σ; EDB)
Client:
  1: $(id, key) \leftarrow (\mathbf{W}[w].id, \mathbf{W}[w].key)$
  2: $r \xleftarrow{\$} \{0,1\}^{\lambda}$
  3: $id^* \xleftarrow{\$} \{0,1\}^{\lambda}$
  4: $key^* \leftarrow F_{uk}(r)$
  5: $mask \leftarrow H(key^*, id^*)$
  6: $b \leftarrow (id^*, (\text{"}ind\|op\text{"}\|key\|id)$
                                $\oplus mask)$
  7: $\mathbf{W}[w].id \leftarrow id^*$
  8: $\mathbf{W}[w].key \leftarrow key^*$
  9: Send block b to the server.
Server:
  10: Insert block b into the tree $\mathcal{T}$.

Fig. 3. FFSSE: Forward private SSE scheme supporting both add and delete operation

Update Operation. When client wants to update a document (with identifier ind) matching w, it runs KBBC.$AddHead(\mathbb{L}_w, \cdot)$. More specifically, it firstly produces a new data block b, whose identifier $b.id^*$ is generated based on a random value sampled from $\{0,1\}^{\lambda}$. The $b.value$ is set to the document identifier and its operation, i.e., $ind\|op$; the $b.key$ and $b.ptr$ are set to $\mathbf{W}[w].key$ and $\mathbf{W}[w].id$ respectively, that is, encryption key and data identifier. Then, the client samples a symmetric key key^* and utilizes it to generate the sign $mask$. Next, it sends the block $b = (b.id^*, (b.value, b.key, b.ptr) \oplus mask)$ to server, and updates the state of keyword w as $\mathbf{W}[w].id = b.id^*$ and $\mathbf{W}[w].key = key^*$. Finally, the server will insert this block into the tree $\mathcal{T}$ to finish this process. Figure 2 shows the details of inserting a new keyword-document pair into the inverted list of $\mathbb{W}_3$.

Search Operation. When the client performs search query on w, it will issue a search token t that will allow the server to retrieve the document identifiers matching w. To do so, the client can only generate the search token as the keyword state stored in the map $\mathbf{W}[w]$, i.e., $t \leftarrow (\mathbf{W}[w].id, \mathbf{W}[w].key)$. After receiving t, server can retrieve the blocks chain one by one by running KBBC. $Retrieve(\mathbb{L}_w, \cdot)$ repeatedly, until the *tail block* is visited. For each node in the chain, the server decrypts its *value* and obtains the stored document identifier. If a document identifier has both the *add* and *del* operators, it should be ignored. In Fig. 3, a function $Merge$ is defined to merge the same document identifier with different operations. In the end, the server returns all the document identifiers matching w to client to finish this process.

5.3 Security Analysis

The adaptive security of FFSSE can be proven in the Random Oracle Model.

Theorem 2 *(Adaptive security of FFSSE). Define* $\mathcal{L}_S = (\mathcal{L}_S^{Search}, \mathcal{L}_S^{Update})$, *where* $\mathcal{L}_S^{Search} = (sp(w), \mathbf{Hist}(w))$, $\mathcal{L}_S^{Update}(op, w, ind) = \perp$, *FFSSE is* $\mathcal{L}_S - adaptive - secure$.

Proof. Let λ be the security parameter. Deriving some games from real world game will help to prove the theorem.

Game G_0. G_0 is the real world FFSSE security game $SSEReal_A^{FFSSE}(\lambda)$. That is to say, $P[SSEReal_A^{FFSSE}(\lambda) = 1] = P[G_0 = 1]$.

Game G_1. When generating key^*, G_1 picks a new random key instead of calling F. We store it in a table Key, when queried w for the next time, we can use the content in Key. Therefore, we can build a reduction able to distinguish between F and the truly random function. That is to say, there exists an efficient adversary A, $P[G_0 = 1] - P[G_1 = 1] \leq Adv_{F,A}^{prf}(\lambda)$.

Game G_2. In Fig. 4, we remove the code which has nothing to do with the hash function $\mathbf{H}$. Therefore, Fig. 4 are single roundtrip protocols.

For each **update** operation, we output fresh random strings. For **search** operation, we get next id, key from the current block. Specifically, with $id_c, key_c, mask_c$, we decrypt the head block and retrieve all the blocks in a blocks chain which matches keyword w. For $mask$, we can use the function $\mathbf{H}$ to get all the $mask$ we need. Therefore, we can conclude that $P[G_1 = 1] - P[G_2 = 1] = 0$.

The Simulator. We can divide the code of G_2 into two parts, one is the leakage function and the other is the simulator. Figure 5 describes the simulator. In simulator, we store the block state σ which can be parsed as key, id, $value$ at time u in table $Bkey^*$, Bid^*, $Bdata$ respectively. In simulator, it uses the counter $\overline{w} = min\ sp(w)$ uniquely mapped from w using the leakage. $SSEIdeal_{A,S,\mathcal{L}_S}^{FFSSE}$ and G_2 are identical. Therefore, $P[G_2 = 1] - P[SSEIdeal_{A,S,\mathcal{L}_S}^{FFSSE}(\lambda) = 1] = 0$.

Conclusion. Combine the contributions which come from G_0, G_1, G_2 and S, we can conclude that $P[SSEReal_A^{FFSSE}(\lambda) = 1] - P[SSEIdeal_{A,S,\mathcal{L}_S}^{FFSSE}(\lambda) = 1] \leq Adv_{F,A}^{prf}(\lambda)$, by stating that $\mathbf{H}$ is a hash function.

Setup()
1: $uk \xleftarrow{\$} \{0,1\}^\lambda$, $\mathbf{W} \leftarrow empty\ map$
2: $\mathcal{T} \leftarrow empty\ tree$, $\mathbb{S} \leftarrow empty\ map$
Search(w, σ; EDB)
Client:
1: $key_w \leftarrow \text{Key}[w]$
2: $((id_0, key_0, mask_0), \ldots,$
    $(id_c, key_c, mask_c), c) \leftarrow \mathbf{W}[w]$
3: $if((id_0, key_0, mask_0), \ldots,$
    $(id_c, key_c, mask_c), c) = \bot$
4:    $return\emptyset$
5: $end\ if$
6: $(ind_0\|op_0, \ldots, ind_c\|op_c) \leftarrow \mathbf{Hist}(w)$
7: $for\ i = head\ to\ 0$
8:    $mask_{k-1} \leftarrow H(key_i, mask_i)$
9: $end\ for$
10: Send $(id_c, key_c, mask_c)$ to server.

Update(op, w, ind, σ; EDB)
Client:
1: $key_w \leftarrow \text{Key}[w]$
2: $((id_0, mask_0, key_0), \ldots,$
    $(id_c, mask_c, key_c), c) \leftarrow \mathbf{W}[w]$
3: $if(((id_0, mask_0, key_0), \ldots,$
    $(id_c, mask_c, key_c), c) = \bot)then$
4:    $mask_0 \xleftarrow{\$} \{0,1\}^\lambda \mathcal{M}, c \leftarrow -1$
5: $else$
6:    $mask_{c+1} \leftarrow H(key_c, mask_c)$
7:    $key_{c+1} \xleftarrow{\$} \{0,1\}^\lambda$
8: $end\ if$
9: $\mathbf{W}[w] \leftarrow ((id_0, mask_0, key_0), \ldots,$
    $(id_c, mask_{c+1}, key_{c+1}), c+1)$
10: $b \leftarrow (id, (ind\|op) \oplus mask)$
11: Send b to the server.
Client:
12: $Insert\ b\ into\ tree\ \mathcal{T}$

Fig. 4. *Game G_2*

Setup()
1: $Bkey^* \leftarrow emptymap$
2: $Bid^* \leftarrow empty\ map$
3: $Bdata \leftarrow empty\ map$
4: $\mathcal{T} \leftarrow empty\ tree$
Search($\mathbf{sp}(w)$, $\mathbf{Hist}(w)$)
Client:
1: $\overline{w} \leftarrow min\mathbf{sp}(w)$
2: $(u_0, u_1, \ldots, u_{head})\ \mathbf{Hist}(\overline{w})$
3: $for\ i \leftarrow head\ to\ 1$
    $Program\ H\ s.t.$
    $H(Bid^*[u_i]\|Bkey^*[u_i]) \leftarrow$
    $Bdata[u_{i-1}] \oplus (ind\|op\|$
        $Bkey^*[u_{i-1}]\|Bid^*[u_{i-1}])$
4: $end\ for$
5: Send token $(Bid^*[u_{head}],$
        $bkey^*[u_{head}])$ to server.

Update()
Client:
1: $Bkey^*[u] \xleftarrow{\$} \{0,1\}^\lambda$
2: $Bid^*[u] \xleftarrow{\$} \{0,1\}^\lambda$
3: $Bdata[u] \xleftarrow{\$} \{0,1\}^{2\lambda+\mu+1}$
4: $Send\ block\ (Bid^*[u], Bdata[u])\ to\ server.$
5: $u \leftarrow u + 1$
Server:
6: $Insert\ block\ b\ into\ tree\ \mathcal{T}$

Fig. 5. *Simulator S*

6   Experiments and Evaluations

We implement the FFSSE scheme and evaluate its functionality and efficiency. The experiments shows that FFSSE has excellent performance exceeds $\Sigma o\phi o\varsigma$.

6.1 Implementation Details

We implemented FFSSE' core functions and benchmarks in C/C++. All the cryptographic primitives implementation in FFSSE uses the third party's code provided by $\Sigma o\phi o\varsigma$ [11]'s open source code. For keyed hash function, we use HMAC. The keyed permutation $\mathcal{P}$ and symmetric encryption are instantiated using AES in counter mode.

Experiment Environments. We use the same keyword-document pairs generation rules that $\Sigma o\phi o\varsigma$ does. Also, we use RocksDB as underlying server side's storage to store tree $\mathcal{T}$ as $\Sigma o\phi o\varsigma$ does. To note that, aside from the chosen for pairs generation rules and cryptographic components, we drop RPC machinery in implementation and don't take timings of underlying database operations into account. These considerations attempt to guarantee the accurate measurements and comparison of operations for our schemes and $\Sigma o\phi o\varsigma$'s.

We run our experiments on a desktop computer with a single Inter Core i7-7700 3.60 HZ CPU, 8 GB of RAM running on ubuntu 14.0.4. Our codes have been opened in GitHub: https://github.com/liuzheli/FFSE.

Parameter. For our schemes, we set λ, the length of symmetric keys, to 256 bits. The N_{max}, the maximum number of keyword-document pairs, is determined by concrete benchmarks ranging from 140 to 14000000. The length of identifiers, μ, can be set from λ and N_{max} according to the above-mentioned descriptions.

Data sets. We adopt the part of Wikipedia data dumps as the source of data sets.

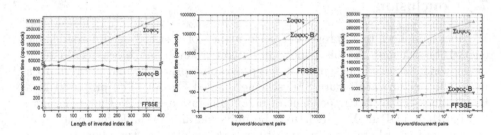

Fig. 6. Comparison of token generation in update operation. X-axis is the number of times that keyword w has been queried, i.e., a_w.

Fig. 7. Comparison of search operation. Average execution time of one search operation over database with keyword-document pairs range from 100 to 100000.

Fig. 8. Comparison of update operation. Average execution time of one update operation over database with keyword-document pairs range from 100 to 1000000.

6.2   Evaluation

Token Generation. We evaluated the performances of token generation algorithms in update operation. Figure 6 shows the experiment results. We can conclude that our token generation algorithms have significantly better performance than $\Sigma o\phi o\varsigma$'. FFSSE is at least $300\times$ faster than $\Sigma o\phi o\varsigma$-B. Specially, we can see that the token generation in the client is very expensive for $\Sigma o\phi o\varsigma$ when the length of indexed list is long.

SSE Operations. We evaluated execution times of completed search and update operations to compare performances of different schemes. We tested each scheme on the basis of the same keyword-document pairs, keyword sets and benchmarks. Concretely, we first run the update operation benchmarks and construct the databases at the same time. Then, we run the search operation benchmarks on them. The experiment results can be shown in Figs. 7 and 8. We can conclude that no matter search or update operation, FFSSE has significantly better performance than $\Sigma o\phi o\varsigma$s.

About search operation, FFSSE is average $4\times$ better than $\Sigma o\phi o\varsigma$-B. Despite our search algorithm only contains symmetric key encryption, the reason why our advantage is not obvious is due to the facts: there is no token generation operation and RSA public key-based evaluation in $\Sigma o\phi o\varsigma$-B is only $5\times$ slower than symmetric encryption in FFSSE.

About update operation, the differences in their performances stem mainly from the token generation and block encryption. We can see that FFSSE is average $300\times$ better than $\Sigma o\phi o\varsigma$-B.

7   Conclusion

We focus on how to improve the performance of forward secure searchable encryption schemes. In this paper, we exploit a key-based blocks chain technique which is based on symmetric cryptographic primitive and apply it to a more efficient forward secure SSE scheme, named FFSSE. The proposed key-based blocks chain is independent of index generation rule, so that it is more flexible than TDP in $\Sigma o\phi o\varsigma$. It may be universal and valuable for some other schemes of forward security. In our future work, we plan to study how to design the forward secure order-preserving encryption scheme based on key-based blocks chain technique.

Acknowledgment. This work was supported by the National Natural Science Foundation of China (No. 61672300), and National Natural Science Foundation of Tianjin (No. 16JCYBJC15500).

References

1. Fu, Z., Wu, X., Wang, Q., Ren, K.: Enabling central keyword-based semantic extension search over encrypted outsourced data. IEEE Trans. Inf. Forensics Secur. **12**(12), 2986–2997 (2017)
2. Fu, Z., Wu, X., Guan, C., Sun, X., Ren, K.: Toward efficient multi-keyword fuzzy search over encrypted outsourced data with accuracy improvement. IEEE Trans. Inf. Forensics Secur. **11**(12), 2706–2716 (2016)
3. Xu, P., Wu, Q., Wang, W., Susilo, W., Domingo-Ferrer, J., Jin, H.: Generating searchable public-key ciphertexts with hidden structures for fast keyword search. IEEE Trans. Inf. Forensics Secur **10**(9), 1993–2006 (2015)
4. Cash, D., et al.: Dynamic searchable encryption in very-large databases: data structures and implementation. In: NDSS vol. 14, pp. 23–26 (2014)
5. Song, X.D., Wagner, D., Perrig, A.: Practical techniques for searches on encrypted data. In: S&P (2000)
6. Demertzis, I., Papadopoulos, S., Papapetrou, O., Deligiannakis, A., Garofalakis, M.: Practical private range search revisited. In: SIGMOD, pp. 185–198 (2016)
7. Stefanov, E., Papamanthou, C., Shi, E.: Practical dynamic searchable encryption with small leakage. In: NDSS, pp. 23–26 (2014)
8. Curtmola, R., Garay, J., Kamara, S., Ostrovsky, R.: Searchable symmetric encryption: improved definitions and efficient constructions. CCS **19**(5), 895–934 (2011)
9. Zhang, Y., Katz, J., Papamanthou, C.: All your queries are belong to us: the power of file-injection attacks on searchable encryption. In: USENIX Security (2016)
10. Chang, Y.-C., Mitzenmacher, M.: Privacy preserving keyword searches on remote encrypted data. In: Ioannidis, J., Keromytis, A., Yung, M. (eds.) ACNS 2005. LNCS, vol. 3531, pp. 442–455. Springer, Heidelberg (2005). https://doi.org/10.1007/11496137_30
11. Bost, R.: Σοφος—forward secure searchable encryption. In: CCS, pp. 1143–1154 (2016)
12. Garg, S., Mohassel, P., Papamanthou, C.: TWORAM: round-optimal oblivious RAM with applications to searchable encryption. Cryptology (2015)
13. Lai, R.W.F., Chow, S.S.M.: Forward-secure searchable encryption on labeled bipartite graphs. In: Gollmann, D., Miyaji, A., Kikuchi, H. (eds.) ACNS 2017. LNCS, vol. 10355, pp. 478–497. Springer, Cham (2017). https://doi.org/10.1007/978-3-319-61204-1_24
14. Kamara, S., Papamanthou, C., Roeder, T.: Dynamic searchable symmetric encryption. In: CCS, pp. 965–976 (2016)
15. Kurosawa, K., Ohtaki, Y.: UC-secure searchable symmetric encryption. In: Keromytis, A.D. (ed.) FC 2012. LNCS, vol. 7397, pp. 285–298. Springer, Heidelberg (2012). https://doi.org/10.1007/978-3-642-32946-3_21
16. Naveed, M., Prabhakaran, M., Gunter, C.A.: Dynamic searchable encryption via blind storage. In: S&P, pp. 639–654 (2014)
17. Lysyanskaya, A., Micali, S., Reyzin, L., Shacham, H.: Sequential aggregate signatures from trapdoor permutations. In: Cachin, C., Camenisch, J.L. (eds.) EUROCRYPT 2004. LNCS, vol. 3027, pp. 74–90. Springer, Heidelberg (2004). https://doi.org/10.1007/978-3-540-24676-3_5

Harden Tamper-Proofing to Combat MATE Attack

Zhe Chen[1], Chunfu Jia[1,2,3]($\boxtimes$), Tongtong Lv[1], and Tong Li[4]

[1] College of Computer, Nankai University, Tianjin 300350, China
cfjia@nankai.edu.cn
[2] Information Security Evaluation Center of Civil Aviation,
Civil Aviation University of China, Tianjin 300300, China
[3] Key Laboratory on High Trusted Information System in Hebei Province,
Baoding 071002, China
[4] School of Computer Science, Guangzhou University, Guangzhou 500016, China

Abstract. The malicious modification on software is a major threat on software copyright. As a common protection method, tamper-proofing can detect and respond the malicious modification. However, existing works consider less about the security of tamper-proofing itself. When launching MATE (Man-At-The-End) attacks based on reverse engineering to the software equipped with embedded tamper-proofing, adversary is enabled to obtain all privileges to the execution code and device configure, which lead tamper proofing being attacked. In this paper, we design a novel tamper-proofing scheme to ensure the code integrity. Different from previous works, our tamper-proofing technique has executed in an isolated zone, Intel SGX (Software Guard Extension) enclave instances, such that the MATE attacks cannot compromise the tamper-proofing functions. Moreover, our scheme performs considerably high execution efficiency since it only introduces the constant extra cost of time and space. We deploy our work on SPECint-2006 benchmark suit. The experimental results demonstrate our scheme is light-weight for computation and storage.

Keywords: Tamper proofing · Trusted execution
Software Guard Extension

1 Introduction

According to the BSA (Business Software Aliance), illegitimate or unlicensed software still bring huge economic losses [1]. Code cracking and pirating are serious threat to software industry. The MATE attacks is the most serious threat

This project is partly supported the National Natural Science Foundation of China (No. 61772291), the Science Foundation of Tianjin (No. 17JCZDJC30500), the Open Project Foundation of Information Security Evaluation Center of Civil Aviation, Civil Aviation University of China (No. CAAC-ISECCA-201702).

© Springer Nature Switzerland AG 2018
J. Vaidya and J. Li (Eds.): ICA3PP 2018, LNCS 11337, pp. 98–108, 2018.
https://doi.org/10.1007/978-3-030-05063-4_9

to the code integrity. The implementers of MATE attacks are end-users, which leads to that identifying whether an end-user has malicious property is beyond code publisher's ability [2]. In MATE attacks scenario, an adversary could highly control whole binary code and the adversary has unrestricted resource to do reverse engineering. To prove the integrity of software running on untrusted hosts, tamper-proofing is one of the representative techniques for software protection.

Tamper-proofing is a protection method to ensure the integrity of executable code, even in the presence of attackers attempt to modify the execution sequence. According to the definition which is presented by Collberg [3,4], a whole tamper-proofing system has two components: checking module and responding module. Checking module has monitored the whole execution states and qualified these information as a check-sum. Responding module gives a response to tampering. However, to our best knowledge, it seems that the existing works rarely considers the security of tamper-proofing itself. The nice-looking design philosophy still has potential safety hazards. As a part of software, tamper-proofing code is unavoidable to being exposed to MATE attacker. Attacker may analyze the explicit tamper-proofing code and disable its function. Hence the tamper-proofing is vulnerable under MATE attacks.

To mitigate this problem, it would be ideal if the tamper-proofing is hardened by powerful methods, such as trusted execution environment. SGX technique can provide secure virtual/physical memory (called enclave) in which the code executes securely. SGX mechanism guarantees the isolation of secure virtual/physical memory, and encrypts the memory pages to write on disk. In previous works of protecting software by SGX, researchers write all executable code into SGX enclaves [5-7]. These heavy-weight methods increase the size of trusted environment base. From a practical point of view, the challenge of constructing light-weight tamper-proofing is how to minimize the size of trusted code. Using these trusted code, a tamper-proofing technique can be constructed.

The primary contribution of this work is that proposed a novel tamper-proofing technique to protect executable code. Different from design philosophy of previous works, our tamper-proofing code have been revealed by reverse engineering. The security of presented work is proved by powerful secure hardware, Intel SGX. The major advantages of presented work are as follows.

- The work process of tamper-proofing is isolated from operating system, which can deal with most threats.
- Randomly reading memory can prevent leaking memory reading pattern.
- Light-weight tamper-proofing provides a relative good execution performance.

Under the detailed security analysis, our work can resist possible attack forms: check-sum forgery attack, pre-computation attack and impersonation attack. We have deployed this novel tamper-proofing on SPECint-2006 benchmarks. The evaluation shows that our work is a light-weight scheme for time and space overhead.

Organization. The remainder of our paper is organized as follows. We minutely summarize the existing works of software tamper-proofing and significant property of Intel SGX in Sect. 2. In Sect. 3, the design overview is introduced. We analyze the security of this technique in Sect. 4 and show the evaluation results in Sect. 5. Finally the discussion is in Sect. 6.

2   Related Works

2.1   Software Tamper-Proofing

Tamper-proofing is a technique which prevents software being malicious modified [4,8]. The mainstreams of tamper-proofing are static tamper-proofing(based on code transform) and dynamic tamper-proofing (based on check-respond). In narrow sense, we only consider the tamper-proofing based on check-respond.

Researchers always use integrity checking to show whether the software is being compromised. The oblivious hash [9–11] is a mature way about integrity checking. It has certain on account of its code has similar structure with normal code. However, it need huge space to store the hash value when software has multiple execution states. The NULL-pointer response [12] has caused abnormal code pattern, and it only works on C/C++ programming. Chen [13] et al. have hardened the oblivious hash based on control flow obfuscation. By regarding the comparison of hash value as classification in machine learning, researchers have integrated this comparison and program's branches into neural networks. Another hardening technique is self-en/decrpyt code [14–16] in program runtime. The encrypted code is decrypted only when it passes the integrity verification. To crack this protection, attackers can dump the decrypted code by dumping the virtual memory. As a conclusion, hardening the tamper-proofing cannot just rely on traditional code protection methods.

2.2   Intel SGX and Its Application

Intel Software Guard Extension. The Intel Software Guard Extension (SGX) is a special x86-64 instructions extension that provides trusted processor and isolated physical memory region [5,17,18]. The processor and the code in isolated memory are enough to construct a trusted computing base. As the latest iteration of trust computing, SGX enables software to protect themselves from malicious hosts, operating systems or hypervisors. The isolated memory region is called *enclave*. The enclave runs in ring 3 (user mode) of operating system, but its has been invoked by non-enclave code only the SGX hardware guarantees the integrity of entire software stack. Using Intel SGX, developers can complete remote/locate attestation and date sealing by SGX SDK.

Application of SGX. Benefiting from being isolated from potential-malicious operating system, researchers have more convenience on building security protocols and applications. The security model may extend the property of cloud server from "honest and curious" to "potential-malicious". Haven [6] is a SGX-based system that enables user securely executing applications in cloud servers. Other similar works include Graphene-SGX [7] and SGXKernel [19], which enable users execute unmodified applications in SGX enclaves. Wang et al. [20] have hardened AES encryption algorithm in enclaves and build a special system call to invoke the SGX instructions. Schuster et al. [21] have proposed a system that allows users run security and complete MapReduce computation in cloud servers. Ohrimenko et al. [22] have proposed high performance data-oblivious machine learning algorithms for several classification and cluster algorithms. For another purpose, SGX has enabled to improve the security of Tor [23] and protect the distributed sandbox [24].

3   Design Overview

Our technique is motivated by the reversing view of secure remote computation. In secure remote computation, a cryptograph algorithm is a "private plots" in untrusted cloud service providers. In the contrast, software providers also desire the "private plots" to run their products in untrusted hosts. As the Fig. 1 shows that, although the end-hosts are potential malicious, we still have the security base, SGX enclaves.

In our work, protection is provided by monitoring the virtual memory. The tamper proofing code is programmed into SGX enclave. We divide the protected software into three parts: non-enclave part, enclave part and sealed addresses table. The detailed design is as follows.

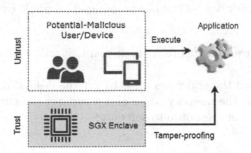

Fig. 1. The working flow of tamper-proofing

3.1   Non-enclave Part

To perform a relatively good execution efficiency, our work does not rewrite any origin code into SGX enclave. We insert some check points at the location where we want to execute tamper-proofing. These check points trigger the tamper-proofing code in enclaves. They bridge the non-enclave part and enclave part through SGX ECALL and OCALL. The whole non-enclave part includes origin code, check points and the essential SGX routine functions.

3.2 Enclave Part

The enclave part is the core of our tamper-proofing framework. It has realized most of tamper-proofing work. The enclave completes three functions: memory pages reading, check-sum computation, and tampering response. When software executes to a check point, the enclave will be created.

The memory pages reading function will read the words from the specific range of virtual addresses ⌊addr-start, addr-end⌋. To avoid attacker guessing the memory read pattern, we introduce Coupon Collector's Problem [25], which help to obfuscate read pattern. If we want check m bytes in once check, we have randomly sampled the memory pages for $m \ln m$ times. Check-sum computation function is realized by a general message-digest algorithm such as SHA-1. This function uses the words of memory pages as inputs and computes a current check-sum. The responding code gives the response if tampering is detected. The possible response may include halting its execution or causing the software crash.

3.3 Sealed Addresses Table

As local variables are stored as plaintext in SGX .dll file, the checked addresses and the corresponding check-sums cannot be directly written into enclave. We use SGX SDK to seal these information to a sealed addresses table. The content of addresses table include the addresses of checked memory pages ⌊addr-start, addr-end⌋ and the corresponding check-sums. When tamper-proofing works, it unseals the data to get the checked addresses and the correct check-sum.

Figure 2 is the work flow of tamper-proofing. The whole execution process is as follows.

1 When the software executes to a check point, it will create enclave to start tamper-proofing.
2 The enclave unseal the addresses table to get the desired data.
3 The enclave reads the memory pages and computes the current check-sum.
4 The enclave gives the response to software.

4 Security Analysis

In this section, we first present the attacking scenario on our technique and the goals of attackers, then we state how our works combat the attacks.

4.1 Attack Model and Some Assumption

We consider the reverse engineering methods that attacker possibly use. The host is off-line so that software provider cannot execute any remote checking mechanism in anytime. All the security of software only relies on built-in protection. We assume that attacker has controlled whole binary code and the design of

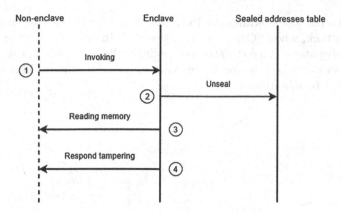

Fig. 2. The framework of protected software

tamper-proofing technique is unconcealed. Attacker has all privilege to reverse, modify and transform the target software. We only consider the adversary in OS level. If attacker has bypassed the tamper-proofing or disabled tamper-proofing, the cracking is success.

Meanwhile, we have unconditional trust to SGX enclave. The SGX enclave is "black box" to attacker from OS-level and we has assumed that SGX hardware is unconditioned secure. In our work, the side-channel attack and micro architectural attack [26] are out of our consideration. The tamper-proofing will correctly realize the functions and cannot be modified by attacker. The only way to attack software is trying to fake the tamper-proofing by modifying the memory.

4.2 Attacks Against Tamper-Proofing

In order to fake the check about untampered execution, the attacker must fake the correct check-sums, modify the tamper-proofing code or change the memory pages. These attacks forms can be classified to three types: check-sum forgery attack, impersonation attack and pre-computation and relay attacks.

Check-Sum Forgery Attacks. The attacker needs to forgery the check-sum by modifying the memory contents being checked or to fake the tamper-proofing by using a false check-sum. The categories of this attack are as follows

Memory Copy Attack. When we only want to check several bytes of the memory, the memory copy attack must be faced. As Figs. 3 and 4 shows two forms of memory copy attack. In Fig. 3, attacker injects their malicious code at other location in memory. Attacker changes the program counter (PC) register pointing to malicious code. After completing executing the malicious code, the PC points to the correct code. In Fig. 4, the malicious code usurps the location of the correct code. The correct code has been moved to another location. When checking the

memory, attacker also modifies the PC register to fake the tamper-proofing. To
detect this attack, when SGX is invoked, the SGX instructions will preserve the
values of all registers. Once the attacker modifies the PC register, this operation
may lead the error when the hardware exits from enclave mode. This attack will
cause software termination.

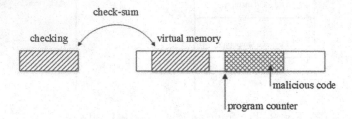

Fig. 3. One form of memory copy attack

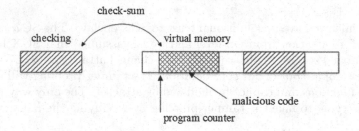

Fig. 4. Another form of memory copy attack

Code Blocks Transform Attack. An attacker may deploy the code block rear-
rangement and replace some of blocks by their own code. When tamper-proofing
sequentially read these code blocks, attacker will re-replace the code blocks by
using the origin ones. To mitigate such attack, we design our tamper-proofing
by reading these code blocks by pseudorandom pattern. Hence, the only way to
get the pattern is cracking the pseudorandom algorithm, which has been proved
the enough resistance against attack.

As a matter of luck, attacker only replace several memory pages to pray
these bytes may escape being checked. To ensure tamper-proofing can read all
location in memory, we introduce the Coupon Collector's Problem. The result
of Coupon Collector's Problem is that: if we want to check n bytes and we only
pseudorandomly read several bytes every time, the expectation of each memory
byte being read at least once is $n\ln n$. After executing $n\ln n$ times memory read,
all the memory bytes has been read with high probability (almost 100%).

Impersonation Attack. In this attack, we assume that attacker also have his own malicious enclave. He use his own enclave to fake the correct enclave. If the correct enclave is force to trust the malicious enclave, the attacker can optionally bypass the tamper-proofing. To complete this attack, attacker must crack the attestation mechanism of SGX. The difficulty of impersonation attack is equal to cracking the cryptographic algorithms which are used by SGX. To our best knowledge, the cryptographic algorithms used by SGX are general algorithms, which have the enough strength against general attack types.

Pre-computation and Relay Attacks. Attacker may attempt to compute the check-sums over all possible memory region before executing the tamper-proofing. Later, when tamper-proofing checks the memory, attacker fakes the tamper-proofing by pre-computation value. The premise of launching pre-computation and relay attack is that attacker can fake the enclave and reveal the addresses table. In fact, the process of reading memory pages is completed under enclave mode, such that attacker cannot pre-compute the check-sum. Moreover, the computation is also completed in enclave mode, injecting the pre-computation check-sum is beyond attacker's ability.

5 Implementation and Evaluation

5.1 Implementation

We implement our work in C++ for Windows10 64-bit system. The tamper-proofing code is whole programmed by Intel SGX SDK. The hash algorithm is realized by SHA-1 in SGXSSL library. The memory reading process is completed by pointer and the random reading pattern is provided by SGX function.

We present evaluation on our tamper-proofing technique. We have measured the overhead in terms of program's performance and program's size. We deploy our work in five benchmarks from SPECint-2006: 999.specrand, 401.bzip2, 429.mcf, 456.hmmer, 458.sjeng and 470.lbm. The environment of experiment is Intel Core i7-7700 CPU with 8 GB RAM. The enclave size is default setting, 32 MB.

5.2 Impact on Program's Performance

We evaluate the time cost by inserting 8 check points. Table 1 shows the time cost of 5 benchmarks by inserting 8 check points. The increased overhead is caused by execution of enclave code, especially reading memory page from virtual memory to enclave. Because the memory requirement of these benchmarks are far less than the EPC (enclave page cache), the major effect of SGX programming, pages swap between EPC and DRAM, does not occur. This claims that our work is better than programming all software code into SGX enclaves. The experiments on these benchmarks show that the time overhead of our work is acceptable.

Table 1. The evaluation on time cost

Benchmark	Origin	Tamper-proofing	Increment
specrand	1.001280 s	3.936236 s	2.934956 s
sjeng	11.410403 s	15.41242 s	4.002017 s
mcf	3.978625 s	5.067415 s	1.08879 s
lbm	6.178057 s	8.150352 s	1.972295 s
bzip2	0.090153 s	2.109811 s	2.019658 s

5.3   Impact on Program's Size

The Table 2 gives the space cost of inserting 8 check points. After being protected, origin programs are treated as non-enclave parts. Besides the SGX invoking instructions, no extra code or data have been inserted in non-enclave parts. The size increment of non-enclave part is caused by inserting SGX invoking code. The non-enclave parts of benchmarks have few size increment. The size of enclave is 211 KB. The increasing size of whole protected software is about 212 KB, which can be negligible for modern hard disk. We believe the issue of program's size does not present a problem to protecting software. The evaluation present a good performance about time and space cost.

Table 2. The evaluation on space cost

Benchmark	Origin	Non-enclave	Enclave
specrand	37 KB	37 KB	211 KB
sjeng	266 KB	267 KB	211 KB
mcf	59 KB	60 KB	211 KB
lbm	63 KB	64 KB	211 KB
bzip2	179 KB	180 KB	211 KB

6   Discussion

Because the premise of MATE attacks is that software provider allows attacker get whole binary code, so only code obfuscation or other semantic-preserving transform to protect tamper-proofing is not solid enough. The trusted execution environment isolated the potential threat in operating system level. The MATE attacks based on reverse engineering can hardly reverses the hardened tamper-proofing code. Cracking our hardened tamper-proofing technique needs a great price. In existing technology, the size of enclave is less than most software. If we hard all functions of software, frequent missing page interruption may greatly influence the execution efficiency. Our work only edits the tamper-proofing into enclaves, which presents a relatively good performance in execution efficiency.

Obviously, our technique is incompatible with address space lay-out randomization (ASLR) and self-en/decrypt code. The checked memory pages are represented by fixed virtual address. This means when the ASLR works, our technique may possibly produce false positives. The self-en/decrypt code modifies the virtual memory pages on occasion, which may also lead to false positives. This limitation still exists in binary code level tamper-proofing schemes. Another limitation is that user's hosts must support the SGX. It needs 6th generation Intel Core processor or later based platform and SGX-enabled BIOS. Old configuration hosts cannot execute the protected software.

7 Conclusion

In this work, we design a novel software tamper-proofing technique. Different with existing works, we construct tamper-proofing based on Intel SGX enclaves. Benefiting from SGX, our work can directly read/write virtual memory without any system invocation and be isolated from MATE attacks. The experimental results present the security and practicability of our work.

References

1. Business Software Alliance: BSA global software survey (2016). http://globalstudy. bsa.org/2016/index.html
2. Akhunzada, A., et al.: Man-at-the-end attacks: analysis, taxonomy, human aspects, motivation and future directions. J. Netw. Comput. Appl. **48**, 44–57 (2015)
3. Collberg, C., Thomborson, C.: Software watermarking: models and dynamic embeddings. In: Proceedings of the 26th ACM SIGPLAN-SIGACT Symposium on Principles of Programming Languages, pp. 311–324. ACM (1999)
4. Nagra, J., Collberg, C.: Surreptitious Software: Obfuscation, Watermarking, and Tamperproofing for Software Protection. Pearson Education (2009)
5. Arnautov, S., et al.: Scone: secure Linux containers with Intel SGX. In: USENIX Symposium on Operating Systems Design and Implementation, vol. 16, pp. 689–703. USENIX Association (2016)
6. Baumann, A., Peinado, M., Hunt, G.: Shielding applications from an untrusted cloud with haven. ACM Trans. Comput. Syst. **33**(3), 1–26 (2014)
7. Tsai, C., Porter, D.E., Vij, M.: Graphene-SGX: a practical library OS for unmodified applications on SGX. In: 2017 USENIX Annual Technical Conference (USENIX ATC 2017), pp. 645–658. USENIX Association (2017)
8. Jain, R., Trivedi, M.C., Tiwari, S.: Digital audio watermarking: a survey. In: Bhatia, S.K., Mishra, K.K., Tiwari, S., Singh, V.K. (eds.) Advances in Computer and Computational Sciences. AISC, vol. 554, pp. 433–443. Springer, Singapore (2018). https://doi.org/10.1007/978-981-10-3773-3_42
9. Chen, Y., Venkatesan, R., Cary, M., Pang, R., Sinha, S., Jakubowski, M.H.: Oblivious hashing: a stealthy software integrity verification primitive. In: Petitcolas, F.A.P. (ed.) IH 2002. LNCS, vol. 2578, pp. 400–414. Springer, Heidelberg (2003). https://doi.org/10.1007/3-540-36415-3_26

10. Chen, H.Y., Hou, T.W., Lin, C.L.: Tamper-proofing basis path by using oblivious hashing on Java. ACM Sigplan Not. **42**(2), 9–16 (2007)
11. Jacob, M., Jakubowski, M.H., Venkatesan, R.: Towards integral binary execution: implementing oblivious hashing using overlapped instruction encodings. In: Proceedings of the 9th workshop on Multimedia & security, pp. 129–140. ACM (2007)
12. Tan, G., Chen, Y., Jakubowski, M.H.: Delayed and controlled failures in tamper-resistant software. In: Camenisch, J.L., Collberg, C.S., Johnson, N.F., Sallee, P. (eds.) IH 2006. LNCS, vol. 4437, pp. 216–231. Springer, Heidelberg (2007). https://doi.org/10.1007/978-3-540-74124-4_15
13. Chen, Z., Wang, Z., Jia, C.: Semantic-integrated software watermarking with tamper-proofing. Multimed. Tools Appl. **77**(9), 11159–11178 (2018)
14. Cappaert, J., Preneel, B., Anckaert, B., Madou, M., De Bosschere, K.: Towards tamper resistant code encryption: practice and experience. In: Chen, L., Mu, Y., Susilo, W. (eds.) ISPEC 2008. LNCS, vol. 4991, pp. 86–100. Springer, Heidelberg (2008). https://doi.org/10.1007/978-3-540-79104-1_7
15. Sharif, M.I., Lanzi, A., Giffin, J.T., Lee, W.: Impeding malware analysis using conditional code obfuscation. In: The Network and Distributed System Security Symposium. ISOC (2008)
16. Ren, C., Chen, K., Liu, P.: Droidmarking: resilient software watermarking for impeding android application repackaging. In: Proceedings of the 29th ACM/IEEE International Conference on Automated Software Engineering, pp. 635–646. ACM (2014)
17. Intel software guard extensions. https://software.intel.com/en-us/sgx/
18. Costan, V., Devadas, S.: Intel SGX explained. IACR Cryptology ePrint Archive **2016**, 86 (2016)
19. Tian, H., Zhang, Y., Xing, C., Yan, S.: SGXKernel: a library operating system optimized for Intel SGX. In: Computing Frontiers Conference, pp. 35–44. ACM (2017)
20. Wang, S.,Wang, W., Bao, Q.,Wang, P.,Wang, X.,Wu, D.: Binary code retrofitting and hardening using SGX. In: Proceedings of the 2017 Workshop on Forming an Ecosystem Around Software Transformation, pp. 43–49. ACM (2017)
21. Schuster, F., et al.: VC3: trustworthy data analytics in the cloud using SGX. In: IEEE Symposium on Security and Privacy, pp. 38–54. IEEE (2015)
22. Ohrimenko, O., et al.: Oblivious multi-party machine learning on trusted processors. In: USENIX Security Symposium, pp. 619–636. USENIX Association (2016)
23. Kim, S.M., Han, J., Ha, J., Kim, T., Han, D.: Enhancing security and privacy of Tor's ecosystem by using trusted execution environments. In: 14th USENIX Symposium on Networked Systems Design and Implementation, pp. 145–161. USENIX Association (2017)
24. Hunt, T., Zhu, Z., Xu, Y., Peter, S., Witchel, E.: Ryoan: a distributed sandbox for untrusted computation on secret data. In: USENIX Conference on Operating Systems Design and Implementation, pp. 533–549. USENIX Association (2016)
25. Kobza, J.E., Jacobson, S.H., Vaughan, D.E.: A survey of the coupon collectors problem with random sample sizes. Methodol. Comput. Appl. Probab. **9**(4), 573–584 (2007)
26. Schwarz, M., Weiser, S., Gruss, D., Maurice, C., Mangard, S.: Malware guard extension: using SGX to conceal cache attacks. In: Polychronakis, M., Meier, M. (eds.) DIMVA 2017. LNCS, vol. 10327, pp. 3–24. Springer, Cham (2017). https://doi.org/10.1007/978-3-319-60876-1_1

A Fast and Effective Detection of Mobile Malware Behavior Using Network Traffic

Anran Liu[1,2], Zhenxiang Chen[1,2]([✉]), Shanshan Wang[1,2], Lizhi Peng[1,2],
Chuan Zhao[1,2], and Yuliang Shi[3]

[1] School of Information Science and Engineering, University of Jinan, Jinan 250022,
Shandong, China
czx@ujn.edu.cn
[2] Shandong Provincial Key Laboratory of Network Based Intelligent Computing,
Jinan 250022, Shandong, China
[3] School of Software, Shandong University, Jinan 250100, Shandong, China

Abstract. Android platform has become the most popular smartphone
system due to its openness and flexibility. Similarly, it has also become
the target of numerous attackers because of these. Various types of
malware are thus designed to attack Android devices. All these cases
prompted amounts of researchers to start studying malware detection
technologies and some of the groups applied network traffic analysis to
their detection models. The majority of these models have considered the
detection primarily on network traffic statistical features which can distinguish malicious network traffic from normal one. However, when faces
a large amount of network traffic on the detection stage, especially some
of the network flows are quite huge as a result of containing too many
packets, feature extraction can be extremely time consuming. Therefore,
we propose a malware detection approach based on TCP traffic, which
can quickly and effectively detect malware behavior. We first employ the
traffic collection platform to collect network traffic generated by various
apps. After preprocessing (filtering and aggregating) the collected network traffic data, we get a large number of TCP flows. Next we extract
early packets' sizes as features from each TCP flow and then send it
to detection model to get the detection result. In our method, the time
it takes to extract features from 53108 network flows is reduced from
39321 s to 18041 s, which is a reduction of 54%. Meanwhile, our method
achieves a detection rate of 97%.

Keywords: Malware detection · Network traffic · Machine learning

Supported by the National Natural Science Foundation of China under Grants No.
61672262, No. 61573166 and No. 61572230, the Shandong Provincial Key R&D Program under Grant No. 2016GGX101001, No. 2016GGX101008, No. 2018CXGC0706
and No. 2016ZDJS01A09, the TaiShan Industrial Experts Programme of Shandong
Province under Grants No. tscy20150305, CERNET Next Generation Internet Technology Innovation Project under Grant No. NGII20160404.

J. Vaidya and J. Li (Eds.): ICA3PP 2018, LNCS 11337, pp. 109–120, 2018.
https://doi.org/10.1007/978-3-030-05063-4_10

1   Introduction

Due to the portability of smartphones, more and more people prefer to using smartphones to handle everything that can be handled, and smartphones therefore carry a large amount of users' privacy information. Attackers thus began to attack smartphones to steal users' private information, and use it to make profits. The most common way they use to attack smartphones is to design various types of malware, and the way malware is developed differs depending on the operating system.

Smartphones can be classified into several different categories according to their operating systems. Among them, smartphones equipped with Android operating systems have become the most widely accepted and used devices because of their openness and the diversity of apps they provided. According to the report released by Gartner in May 2017 [2], the market share of Android platform has reached 86.1%. In order to attack more devices and obtain more users' privacy information, most attackers thus consider Android platform as their target. Recent report has pointed that more than 99% of malware designed for mobile devices targets Android devices [1].

In March 2018, the number of the apps in Google Play has reached 3.6 million [3], which will only be much larger in third-party market. It is very difficult for users to identify whether an app is malicious or not when faced with such a large number of apps. Therefore, the need to detect Android malware has risen sharply. Amounts of researchers have thus studied malware detection techniques which can be roughly categorized into static and dynamic groups. In addition, with more and more malware relying on network interfaces to interact with attackers, network traffic based detection starts to be used to identify Android malware. Compared to static analysis detection, like [6,11,13], which is difficult to identify malicious variants due to code obfuscation [15], and dynamic analysis detection, like [10] and [21], which needs to deploy a detection environment on the mobile phone, detection based on network traffic doesn't need to deploy on the Android devices and is adaptable to the variants. Network traffic based detection extracts features from network traffic and employs machine learning method to identify mobile malicious behavior. But when faces a large amount of network traffic on the detection stage, especially some of the network flows are huge as a result of containing too many packets, feature extraction can be extremely time consuming. And this will directly increase the time overhead of detection stage. Therefore, we propose our method, a fast and effective detection approach of mobile malware behavior using network traffic.

In our method, we first collect a large amount of network traffic using a traffic collection platform and then filter all the non-TCP traffic out. After that, we aggregate the remaining traffic into flows and perform feature extraction on each flow. Finally, we send the extracted feature tuple to detection model to get the detection result.

The detection model used in our method is a model based on TCP packet size feature. In consideration of the fact that encrypting network traffic between application layer and transport layer is gradually becoming a popular trend, we choose TCP, one of the most popular transport layer protocols, to analyze. And in order to deal with the time consumption problem we pointed out above, we chose the sizes of the first few packets of a network flow and some statistics of those sizes as features since we won't have to deal with the entire network flow when we extract a feature tuple from it. Furthermore, for encrypted network traffic, we won't have to separate them out and decrypted them for analysis, but to treat them equal to unencrypted network traffic and then extract the same features from them. This is to some extent also reduces the overall detection time as well.

In this paper, we mainly make the following contributions:

- **Network traffic based malware detection in a time saving way.** Our experimental results show that our method can effectively identify mobile malicious behavior with a low time consumption.
- **A lightweight detection system.** We proposed a prototype system which allows us to identify mobile malicious behavior on the server side without consuming the resources of users' mobile devices.
- **An effective encrypted traffic classification method without infringing users' privacy.** Our method can identify encrypted network traffic quite precisely without decrypted those encrypted network flows, which can save a lot of time and also protects users' privacy.

The rest of the paper is organized as follows: related work is introduced in Sect. 2. Section 3 presents the methodology of our method in detail and the evaluation of our method is introduced in Sect. 4. Section 5 concludes the paper.

2   Related Work

The network traffic analyzed by the researchers in traffic-based malware detection method is roughly divided into two parts, namely application layer traffic and transport layer traffic.

Application Layer Traffic Based Analysis. In mobile devices, most apps use DNS protocol for domain name resolution and HTTP protocol for data transfer. Therefore, almost all application-level traffic based malware detection methods are implemented by analyzing DNS traffic or HTTP traffic. Wei et al. [20] proposed a malware detection method based on domain name resolution behavior. Their method can analyze DNS flows generated by apps automatically and determine whether the app is malicious based on the geospatial information of the resolved IP address. Zaman et al. [22] record the domain names accessed by the app through the URL in HTTP request message and then compare them with the known domain name blacklist. The app that communicates with the domain name in the blacklist is considered as a malicious app. Wang et al. [19] treat each HTTP flow generated by an app as a text file, and then leverage natural language processing to extract text-level features that can distinguish between normal apps and malware. Although these methods achieve high detection rates, they are severely limited by SSL/TLS encryption. Attackers can use SSL/TLS encryption to hide the information carried by application layer traffic easily.

Transport Layer Traffic Based Analysis. The two most important protocols at transport layer are TCP and UDP, and the majority of the transport layer traffic is transmitted over TCP. Thus, researchers usually leverage TCP traffic to explore malware detection method, and most of them analyze the statistical features of TCP flows [4]. Shabtai et al. [17] proposed anomaly-based malware detection method with automatic update capability. This method uses statistical features extracted from TCP flows to generate normal app traffic patterns and then identify all the apps whose traffic patterns are deviated from the normal pattern as malware. Wang et al. [18] use six TCP statistical features and combined with machine learning algorithm to detect Android malware. However, none of these methods takes into account the time consumption problem in feature extraction phase in malware detection process.

Arora et al. [5] proposed an algorithm to prioritize network traffic features, which gave a high detection accuracy and reduced both training and testing time. However, some of the final 9 features chosen in that paper, such as Average Packet Size, Packets Sent per Flow and Maximum Packet Size, still are flow statistic features which need to traverse the whole network flow to be extracted, and this will increase the time cost of feature extraction phase in detection process. Lizhi et al. [14] pointed out that the sizes of early stage packets are effective enough to achieve ideal traffic identification performances. Bernaille et al. [7] used the first four to five packets to classify TCP-based apps and achieved high accuracy. Since malware detection is a subcategory in traffic classification, we decided to use early packet sizes as features to detect Android malware behavior.

3 Methodology

In our method, network traffic generated by the apps are collected from the traffic collection platform. After preprocessing the collected network traffic data, we get a large number of TCP flows. Next, we extract the sizes of the early packets of a network flow and some statistics of those sizes as features and then send the feature tuple to detection model to get the detection result. The whole detection approach is detailed in the following sections.

3.1 Traffic Collection

Network Trace Capture. In our method, we use the active traffic generation and collection platform proposed in [9] to collect traffic data. The platform consists of four parts, namely foundation platform, traffic generator, traffic collector and network proxy/firewall respectively. Foundation platform is built based on Android Virtual Device (AVD), and traffic generator is designed to install and activate malware samples to generate network traffic automatically. The function of traffic collector is to collect inbound and outbound network traffic with tcpdump tool, and then the traffic mirroring technology is employed to mirror traffic to the server side. During the whole process, the attack behavior is carefully monitored and controlled by proxy/firewall. On the server side, we collect traffic traces and store them in pcap format for the next preprocessing step.

Traffic Data Preprocessing. Since our work only focuses on TCP traffic, we need to filter the traffic data collected in the previous step and remove all packets whose transport layer protocol is not TCP. After that, we aggregate the packets in each traffic trace according to the definition of TCP flow, and store all flows in pcap format separately. The whole process is implemented using a combination of Python script and T-shark command.

3.2   Feature Extraction

The features used in our method are the sizes of the first n packets of a TCP flow and 4 statistics (i.e. average, standard deviation, minimum and maximum values) of the sizes. The number of selected packets is a parameter that is to be determined and we will describe the determination of this parameter in detail in Sect. 4.2. It should be noted that the order of the features extracted from a TCP flow must be consistent with the order of the packets. That is, the first feature in the feature tuple is the size of the first packet in this TCP flow, the second feature is that of the second packet, and so on. Beyond this, these four statistical features are also arranged in order in the feature tuple. Namely, the (n+1)st feature in the feature tuple is the average of the first n features, the (n+2)nd feature is the standard deviation of the first n features, and so on. In addition, if a TCP flow contains fewer than n packets, we will use an integer 0 to fill in the feature tuples extracted from this flow (the last 4 features of the feature tuple are still the values of these 4 statistics). Thus, the length of the feature tuples extracted from each network flow is n+4. The entire feature extraction process is illustrated in Fig. 1.

We chose the first few packets sizes of a TCP flow as features for the following reasons. On the one hand, Este et al. [12] had proved that packet size is the most effective feature for early stage network traffic identification; on the other hand, we only have to traverse the first few packets of a TCP flow and ignore the rest part of the TCP flow to get features, which will significantly reduce the time cost of feature extraction process.

3.3   Learning-Based Detection

Machine learning can be used to automatically discover the rules by analyzing data, and the rules are helpful for us to predict unknown data. In our research, we leverage machine learning method to analyze features extracted from TCP flows and generate the rules which can determine whether a flow is malicious or

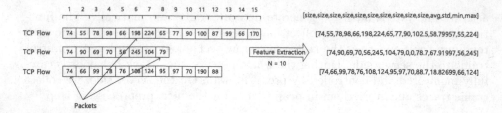

Fig. 1. Feature extraction process.

not. If we determine that the flow is malicious based on the generated rules, the app corresponding to this flow is then considered to be malware. Through this process, we can achieve the purpose of malware detection.

The learning method we chose is Random Forest [8], which uses several decision trees to train the data set and then gets the prediction rule. The construction process of Random Forest is roughly as follows. First, bootstrapping method [16] is used to randomly select samples from the original training set, which is a resampling with replacement. This procedure will be repeated several times to generate multiple training sets. The number of the training sets is a parameter. And then for each training set, a decision tree will be generated. It should be noted that, for each node of the decision tree in a Random Forest, the feature set used for the selection of the optimal feature is only a subset of the feature set of this node. Finally, each decision tree will vote for the prediction result and the result is a majority vote of all single predictions given individually by each decision tree. In our method, we built the classifiers in Python using the scikit-learn machine learning libraries, using $criteria = gini$, $max\_features = auto$, and $n\_estimators = 10$ as parameters.

3.4   Lightweight Detection Architecture

The prototype system shown in Fig. 2 is a lightweight detection system, which only requires users to install an app on their mobile devices and won't need to get root permissions for we just identify the malicious behavior by the network traffic mirrored from the user side. After the detection, the final result will be returned to the app.

Additionally, in order to improve model's adaptability to new types of malware, we designed a model updating framework. We store the traffic and the labels we predicted on the storage server. After collecting a certain amount of labeled flows, we cluster these flows and check the labels of each cluster. If all the flows in a cluster belong to the same category, we will randomly select several flows from this cluster and then detect them manually. If all manually detected flows also belong to this category, then we add all the flows in the cluster to training set and update the model. It should be noted that the model updating process is off-line and therefore does not occupy any user's mobile device resources.

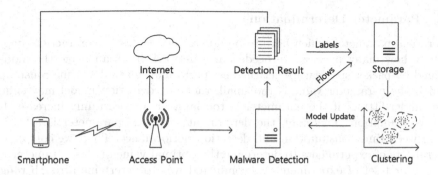

Fig. 2. Lightweight detection architecture.

By using this detection architecture, we can detect multiple apps on a single device, as well as multiple apps on multiple devices at the same time. Within the LAN (local area network), diverse apps might execute network behavior simultaneously, therefore we can collect the network traffic generated from them and then identify these apps in a short time. In addition, the features we used in our method can also guarantee the real-time performance of the detection, for we only need the sizes of early packets in a TCP flow.

4   Evaluation

4.1   Data Sets

Our malicious apps are downloaded from public malware database, VirusShare. Our normal apps are downloaded from multiple popular app markets by app crawler. Consider there might be some potential malicious apps in app markets which can cause the impurity of our normal app set, thus all the normal apps we downloaded from the markets are sent to VirusTotal to test whether these apps are malicious or not and then the apps whose test results are normal will be added to our normal app set. We get a normal app set of 8321 samples and a malware set of 2839 samples.

In order to train and evaluate the detection performance of our model, we use the automatic mobile traffic collection system which is introduced in Sect. 3.1 to collect traffic data. For traffic generated by normal apps, we label it as benign. Since most malware are taking the form of repackaging malicious behavior into normal apps, the traffic generated by malware contains both malicious traffic and normal traffic (most of which is normal traffic and only a small amount of traffic is malicious). In order to improve the accuracy of our labels, we extract the target IP filed of each flow generated by malware and upload it to VirusTotal. If the filed is detected as malicious, we will label the corresponding flow as malicious.

Finally, we get 1.03 GB network traffic data generated by normal apps as well as 219 MB malicious network traffic data, and then we extract features from those traffic data. Finally, 53108 feature tuples are extracted from the traffic we collected to train and test the model.

4.2   Parameter Determination

There is a parameter which have to be determined in feature extraction stage, namely how many packets are needed in a network flow can make the model trained by packet size feature get the best performance at a low time consumption. If the parameter value is too small, then the detection model may suffer from under-fitting; if the parameter is too large, it will certainly increase the time consumption. Therefore, the determination of the parameter is a trade-off between time consumption and detection performance. Thus, we conducted several sets of experiments to determine the optimal value of this parameter.

The first set of experiments we conducted was to determine a rough range of the parameter. Firstly, for each instance in the data set, we extract the size of the first 10, 30, 50, 100, and 200 packets separately and record the time cost of each extraction process. Considering that for most TCP flows, the number of packets contained in it is usually less than 200, so as the value of the parameter (number of packets) further increased, early packet feature extraction will be the same with the extraction of the entire flow. And thus, we only took a maximum of 200.

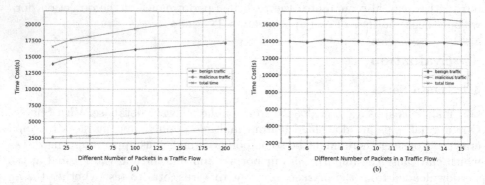

Fig. 3. Time costs of feature extraction process. (a) Time costs of the extraction of the packet sizes of first 10, 30, 50, 100 and 200 packets. (b) Time cost of the extraction of the packet sizes of first 5–15 packets.

The time we recorded is shown in Fig. 3(a). From this figure we can clearly see that there is a growing trend with the increment of the parameter and when the number of packets is 10, the time cost is the minimum. Thus in the next set of experiments, we extracted the size of the first 5–15 packets from each instance in the data set separately, and generated 11 feature sets. Choosing to extract the size of the first 5–9 packets is due to time considerations while the extraction of the size of the 11–15 packets is in consideration of the model performance. Similarly, we also recorded the time required to generate each feature set and the results are shown in Fig. 3(b).

From Fig. 3(b) we can find out that there is no obvious trend in this figure, and the data is fluctuating up and down without an optimal value. Additionally,

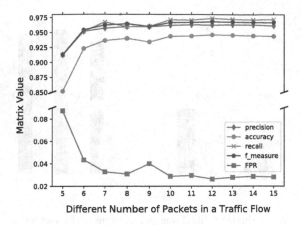

Fig. 4. Matric values of each parameter.

the time cost of generating the sizes of first 5 packets feature set even is a little larger than the time cost of generating the sizes of first 15 packets feature set. Thus, in this session, the time cost indicator is not taken into account.

Next, we trained and tested 11 detection models using ten-fold crossover method on the extracted 11 feature sets. We measured the results in terms of five indicators, including accuracy, precision, recall, F-measure score and FPR, and the detection performance is illustrated in Fig. 4. We can see from the Fig. 4 that when the value of the parameter is 12, five indicators have all reached the optimal value (the first four indicators are the highest under all parameters, the last indicator is the lowest under all parameters). Therefore, we chose 12 as the value of the parameter.

4.3   Comparative Evaluation

In order to evaluate the performance of our detection model, we reconstructed the flow statistics model proposed by TrafficAV [18] to compare with the proposed model, for the statistical features it used are typical and required to traverse the entire flow to be extracted. Our evaluation is conducted from two aspects of time performance and detection performance.

Time Performance. We extract packet size feature set from the whole data set and recorded the time consumption in the meanwhile. Additionally, we extract the flow statistic features used in TrafficAV from our data set and also record time consumption as a control. We didn't add the time it took to train and test the detection model because when compared with the time cost in feature extraction phase, the time cost in training phase and testing phase only account for a small proportion.

These two time records are shown in Fig. 5(a). We can see that our method greatly reduces the time required for feature extraction. It takes us 27324 s to

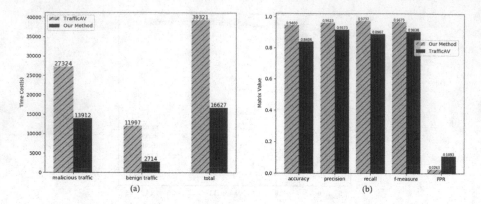

Fig. 5. Comparative evaluation. (a) Time performance. (b) Detection performance.

extract flow statistic features used in TrafficAV from the whole data set, and the number is only 15009 in our method, which is a reduction of 54%.

We believe that when there are more huge flows which contains great amounts of packets, the advantage of our method will be more prominent since if we want to extract the flow statistic features used in TrafficAV from a network flow, we have to traverse the entire flow, while extracting the features used in our method only requires traversing the first few packets of this network flow.

Detection Performance. We employed ten-fold crossover method to evaluate the detection performance of our detection model. Next, we implemented the flow model proposed in TrafficAV based on our data set, and employed ten-fold crossover method to evaluate this detection model as well. The detection performance of these two models is shown in Fig. 5(b). It shows that our method also get a better detection performance than TrafficAV does.

4.4   Encrypted Network Traffic Classification

We collected 735 benign TLS flows and 4 malicious TLS flows as test data set in order to estimate our method's ability to identify encrypted network flows. We extracted feature tuples from these encrypted network flows and then use the model we have trained by the data set we introduced in Sect. 4.1 to classify these network flows. These two data sets are non-overlapping.

At last, our model identified 733 encrypted network flows correctly, including 730 benign TLS flows and 3 malicious TLS flows. This illustrates our method has a certain ability to classify encrypted network flows. In addition, through our method, we won't have to separate the encrypted traffic from a pile of traffic and then analyze them separately in detection stage. Instead, we treat these network traffic equal to unencrypted traffic, extract the same features from them and then send feature tuples to the model for detection. In this respect, our method saves the time as well.

5   Conclusion

The increasing number of Android malware brings mobile users a elevating security risk, and makes the detection of mobile malware a greater challenge. Multiple methods are thus proposed to identify malicious behavior of Android apps and network traffic based method is one of the most popular methods. However, when faces a large amount of network traffic, feature extraction phase in detection process can be extremely time consuming. In this paper, we propose a method which is able to identify malware without violating user's privacy, and can achieve relatively rapid detection on the premise of ensuring a high detection rate. We proved that: by using packet size based analysis, we can quickly detect Android malware behavior with a high accuracy. Furthermore, we designed a device-level lightweight prototype system which can identify a collection of malware on multiple mobile devices in a short time and have the self-update ability. In the future, we will make our efforts to implement the prototype system and try to extend our work to recent Android malware samples.

References

1. Another reason 99% of mobile malware targets androids (2017). https://safeandsavvy.f-secure.com/2017/02/15/another-reason-99-percent-of-mobile-malware-targets-androids/
2. Gartner: Q1 worldwide smartphone sales growth 9% (2017). http://smartcity.asmag.com.cn/xfdz/4345.html
3. Number of available applications in the google play store from December 2009 to March 2018 (2018). https://www.statista.com/statistics/266210/number-of-available-applications-in-the-google-play-store/
4. Arora, A., Garg, S., Peddoju, S.K.: Malware detection using network traffic analysis in android based mobile devices. In: 2014 Eighth International Conference on Next Generation Mobile Apps, Services and Technologies (NGMAST), pp. 66–71. IEEE (2014)
5. Arora, A., Peddoju, S.K.: Minimizing network traffic features for android mobile malware detection. In: Proceedings of the 18th International Conference on Distributed Computing and Networking, p. 32. ACM (2017)
6. Arp, D., Spreitzenbarth, M., Hubner, M., Gascon, H., Rieck, K., Siemens, C.: DREBIN: effective and explainable detection of android malware in your pocket. In: Ndss, vol. 14, pp. 23–26 (2014)
7. Bernaille, L., Teixeira, R., Akodkenou, I., Soule, A., Salamatian, K.: Traffic classification on the fly. ACM SIGCOMM Comput. Commun. Rev. **36**(2), 23–26 (2006)
8. Breiman, L.: Random forests. Mach. Learn. **45**(1), 5–32 (2001)
9. Chen, Z., et al.: A first look at android malware traffic in first few minutes. In: 2015 IEEE Trustcom/BigDataSE/ISPA, vol. 1, pp. 206–213. IEEE (2015)
10. Enck, W., et al.: TaintDroid: an information-flow tracking system for realtime privacy monitoring on smartphones. ACM Trans. Comput. Syst. (TOCS) **32**(2), 5 (2014)
11. Enck, W., Ongtang, M., McDaniel, P.: On lightweight mobile phone application certification. In: Proceedings of the 16th ACM Conference on Computer and Communications Security, pp. 235–245. ACM (2009)

12. Este, A., Gringoli, F., Salgarelli, L.: On the stability of the information carried by traffic flow features at the packet level. ACM SIGCOMM Comput. Commun. Rev. **39**(3), 13–18 (2009)

13. Felt, A.P., Chin, E., Hanna, S., Song, D., Wagner, D.: Android permissions demystified. In: Proceedings of the 18th ACM Conference on Computer and Communications Security, pp. 627–638. ACM (2011)

14. Lizhi, P., Bo, Y., Yuehui, C., Tong, W.: How many packets are most effective for early stage traffic identification: an experimental study. China Commun. **11**(9), 183–193 (2014)

15. Moser, A., Kruegel, C., Kirda, E.: Limits of static analysis for malware detection. In: 2007 Twenty-Third Annual Computer Security Applications Conference, ACSAC 2007, pp. 421–430. IEEE (2007)

16. Opitz, D.W., Maclin, R.: Popular ensemble methods: an empirical study. J. Artif. Intell. Res. (JAIR) **11**, 169–198 (1999)

17. Shabtai, A., Tenenboim-Chekina, L., Mimran, D., Rokach, L., Shapira, B., Elovici, Y.: Mobile malware detection through analysis of deviations in application network behavior. Comput. Secur. **43**, 1–18 (2014)

18. Wang, S., et al.: TrafficAV: an effective and explainable detection of mobile malware behavior using network traffic. In: 2016 IEEE/ACM 24th International Symposium on Quality of Service (IWQoS), pp. 1–6. IEEE (2016)

19. Wang, S., Yan, Q., Chen, Z., Yang, B., Zhao, C., Conti, M.: Detecting android malware leveraging text semantics of network flows. IEEE Trans. Inf. Forensics Secur. **13**(5), 1096–1109 (2018)

20. Wei, T.E., Mao, C.H., Jeng, A.B., Lee, H.M., Wang, H.T., Wu, D.J.: Android malware detection via a latent network behavior analysis. In: 2012 IEEE 11th International Conference on Trust, Security and Privacy in Computing and Communications (TrustCom), pp. 1251–1258. IEEE (2012)

21. Yan, L.K., Yin, H.: DroidScope: seamlessly reconstructing the OS and dalvik semantic views for dynamic android malware analysis. In: USENIX Security Symposium, pp. 569–584 (2012)

22. Zaman, M., Siddiqui, T., Amin, M.R., Hossain, M.S.: Malware detection in android by network traffic analysis. In: 2015 International Conference on Networking Systems and Security (NSysS), pp. 1–5. IEEE (2015)

A Scalable Pthreads-Compatible Thread Model for VM-Intensive Programs

Yu Zhang$^{(\boxtimes)}$ and Jiankang Chen

University of Science and Technology of China, Hefei, China
yuzhang@ustc.edu.cn

Abstract. With the widespread adoption of multicore chips, many multithreaded applications based on the shared address space have been developed. Widely-used operating systems, such as Linux, use a per-process lock to synchronize page faults and memory mapping operations (e.g., mmap and munmap) on the shared address space between threads, restricting the scalability and performance of the applications. We propose a novel Pthreads-compatible multithreaded model, PATHREADS, which provides isolated address spaces between threads to avoid contention on address space, and meanwhile preserves the shared variable semantics. We prototype PATHREADS on Linux by using a proposed character device driver and a proposed shared heap allocator *IAmalloc*. Pthreads applications can run with PATHREADS without any modifications. Experimental results show that PATHREADS runs 2.17×, 3.19× faster for workloads hist, dedup on 32 CPU cores, and 8.15× faster for workload lr on 16 cores than Pthreads. Moreover, by using Linux Perf, we further analyze critical bottlenecks that limit the scalability of workloads programmed by Pthreads. This paper also reviews the performance impact of the latest Linux 4.10 kernel optimization on PATHREADS and Pthreads, and results show that PATHREADS still has advantage for dedup and lr.

1 Introduction

With the widespread adoption of multicore chips, many multithreaded applications based on the shared address space have been developed. Such shared address space, however, requires the kernel virtual memory (VM) subsystem to synchronize concurrent address space operations (i.e., page faults or mmap, munmap and mprotect system calls) launched by either application code or the called libraries, e.g., libc. Widely-used operating systems such as Linux often use a single read-write lock per process to serialize address space operations, limiting the scalability of multithreaded VM-intensive applications [9]. For example, on a 32-core Linux system mentioned in Sect. 5, histogram (hist) from Phoenix [20] consumes up to 40% and 50% of the execution time in the kernel per-process lock on 16 and 32 cores[1], respectively.

---

[1] The number of threads (workers) equals to the number of CPU cores enabled.

© Springer Nature Switzerland AG 2018
J. Vaidya and J. Li (Eds.): ICA3PP 2018, LNCS 11337, pp. 121–137, 2018.
https://doi.org/10.1007/978-3-030-05063-4_11

Some research efforts try to improve scalability of multithreaded software. Clements *et al.* propose a scalable address space by using RCU balanced trees [9]. Kleen *et al.* think that processes scale better than threads since a process does not share the address space with others [15]. Psearchy from MOSBENCH [7] was modified to use processes instead of threads. However, due to shared variables between threads, it is quite difficult to migrate a multithreaded workload from the shared address space to thread-private address space. In addition, super page is also used to reduce the number of page faults so as to ease contentions [9], but cannot benefit from many small address regions.

Unlike the above work, we propose a new scalable thread model, PATHREADS (<u>P</u>rivate <u>A</u>ddress space based <u>threads</u>), which adopts isolated address space for each thread to avoid contentions on address space operations, but keeps shared variable semantics on the heap and globals. Like Pthreads, each thread in PATHREADS has its own stack, and can synchronize with other threads via locks, condition variables or barriers using the same Pthreads API. Thus, Pthreads applications can be built and run with PATHREADS without any code modifications.

To reduce contentions on the shared heap, we design a novel shared heap allocator, called *IAmalloc* (<u>I</u>solated <u>A</u>ddress space based <u>malloc</u>). *IAmalloc* provides each thread an isolated address range for allocation, but allows all threads to read or write the whole heap. The isolation of the allocation area can avoid synchronous operations at the time of allocation, and can further provide good spatial locality when allocated heap objects are only visited by the thread that created them.

We prototype PATHREADS on Linux by emulating each thread using a single-threaded Linux process, where private copy-on-write (COW) memory mappings of a process can further be changed to meet the mapping requirement of PATHREADS via a proposed character device driver CDEV. Thus, users only need to install the device module in their own kernel without any kernel modifications. We further prototype *IAmalloc* by adopting Doug Lea's *dlmalloc* [16] with minor modification, and implement Pthreads synchronization API for PATHREADS using algorithms similar to Pthreads.

The main contributions of this paper are as follows:

- We analyze the reason why the VM-intensive multithreaded program has the performance bottleneck in the shared address space (see Sect. 2).
- We propose a scalable PATHREADS model and a shared *IAmalloc* allocator, providing thread-private address space but keeping shared variable semantics (see Sect. 3).
- We propose a solution to implement PATHREADS on Linux using well-designed "thread emulated by process" policy and character device driver (see Sect. 4).
- We prototype PATHREADS and demonstrate its effectiveness on a 32-core machine with Linux 3.2.0 and 4.10 kernels (see Sect. 5).

On Linux 3.2.0 kernel, it achieves up to 3.19×, 2.17× faster than Pthreads for dedup, hist on 32 CPU cores, respectively. PATHREADS with *IAmalloc* can also reduce false sharing and improve the performance of non-VM-intensive programs, e.g., achieving 8.15× faster than Pthreads for linear_regression (lr) on 16 cores. Although the latest Linux kernel has significant improvement on the kernel locking mechanism, PATHREADS still has advantage for some Pthreads programs, e.g., achieving up to 2.99× faster than Pthreads for dedup on 32 cores, and 7.45× faster for lr on 16 cores.

2   Background and Motivation

In this section, we first introduce the VM management in Linux Kernel, then describe VM-intensive programs and their performance bottlenecks.

VM Management and Contention in Linux Kernel. In most widely used operating systems such as Linux, an address space shared among threads principally consists of a set of memory mapping regions and a page table tree. Linux uses struct *mm_struct* to manage the whole address space among threads, and struct *vm_area_struct* (VMA) to describe a memory mapping region including its start address, end address and flags to determine access rights and behaviors.

The *mm_struct* includes a red-black tree to store VMAs in order to enable the OS kernel to quickly find a region containing a particular virtual address. Linux provides system calls for memory mapping operations: mmap, munmap and mprotect. The mmap creates a memory mapping region and adds it to the tree, the munmap removes a region from the tree, and the mprotect updates the permission of a region by modifying the relative VMA. In addition, when a soft page fault is triggered, the handler looks up the tree and checks whether the faulting virtual address is mapped.

To ensure correct behavior when threads perform memory mapping operations and page faults concurrently, Linux uses a per-process read-write semaphore *mmap_sem* to serialize those operations launched by different threads. Therefore, a thread need acquire the semaphore in *write* mode before executing a memory operation in order to prohibit other threads performing address space operations. And the page fault handler need acquire the semaphore in *read* mode and can proceed with other page faults in parallel. Consequently, contentions on *mmap_sem* become intense when running an application with a large number of threads, leading to speedup degradation.

Performance Bottleneck of VM-Intensive Programs. The VM-intensive program is a very important class of multithreaded programs, and its main feature is to contain a large number of address space operations. For example, programs frequently trigger page faults, or programs containing frequent or bulk heap operations would frequently call memory mapping operations. A page fault causes to acquire *mmap_sem* in read mode, while a memory mapping operation need acquire *mmap_sem* in write mode. Performance bottlenecks of the VM-intensive program in read or write modes are different. We next analyze them using the evaluation methodology in Sect. 5.

Contention in Read Mode. In order to find out the main reason of the performance loss, we test the overhead of hotspot functions for the workload. We find that the first two hotspot functions of `hist` are `down_read_trylock()` (trylock for reading) and `up_read()` (release a read lock) from Linux kernel. As shown in Fig. 1(a), overheads brought by the two functions increase heavily as CPU core count grows, and even reach up to 30% and 20% of total runtime on 32 cores, respectively. We then use Linux Perf [19] to find that these function calls are all derived from page faults. From the process of `do_page_fault()` shown in Fig. 1(b)), we know that with high CPU core count, the lock contention would be further aggravated by page faults.

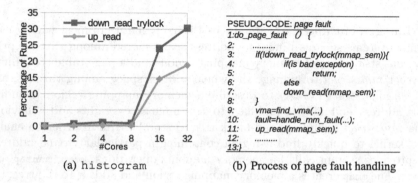

(a) histogram   (b) Process of page fault handling

Fig. 1. Overhead of contention in read mode and the process of page fault handling.

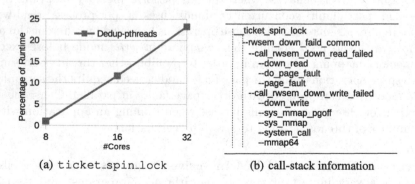

(a) ticket_spin_lock   (b) call-stack information

Fig. 2. Overhead of contention in write mode and the call stack information.

Contention in Write Mode. `dedup` from PARSEC [3] is a typical VM-intensive program. It suffers from serious lock contention, where the kernel `ticket_spin_lock()` occupies 24.7% of total execution time on 32 CPU cores, as shown in Fig. 2(a). Call-stack information in Fig. 2(b) generated by Linux Perf shows that `ticket_spin_lock()` is mainly invoked by the Linux kernel function `rwsem_down_failed_common()` (wait for a lock to be granted). There are two main sources of `rwsem_down_failed_common()`: one is caused by page fault handler if it fails to contend *mmap_sem* in read mode, and the other is caused by memory mapping system calls such as `mmap`, `mproctect` if they fail to contend *mmap_sem* in write mode. Thus we can draw a conclusion that the *mmap_sem* becomes a serious bottleneck for `dedup` using Pthreads.

3   The PATHREADS Model

3.1   Design of the Thread Model

To tackle the above performance issues caused by the contention on per-process read-write semaphore, we propose a novel thread model, PATHREADS in Fig. 3, which follows Pthreads programming interface but strives to achieve the following goals.

G1. Avoid contentions on the address space. We address the issue by confining threads in separate address spaces. Each thread has readonly (RO) text (code) segment and its own stack but occupies the same address segment (① in Fig. 3).

G2. Preserve the sharing semantics on heap objects and globals like Pthreads in order to support Pthreads programs without modification. We address the issue by designing mechanisms to change the VM mapping properties of the same address ranges in different address spaces, and to implement Pthreads synchronization API.

G3. Reduce contentions on the shared heap. We address the issue by letting each thread allocate heap objects in a disjoint subheap, but allow other threads accessing all subheaps (② in Fig. 3, where the bold line means allowing allocation).

Isolated Address Space. Each PATHREADS thread has its own memory mapping structure (*mm_struct*) to manage its isolated address space without interference from other threads. Thus, there is no contention on the semaphore *mmap_sem* when performing address space operations even with high CPU core count.

However, the isolated address spaces among threads bring challenge in preserving the shared variable semantics among threads under good performance. In the next subsections, we introduce features of PATHREADS to obtain the above G2 and G3.

3.2   Preserving Shared Variable Semantics

Threads running with Pthreads library share all memory except for the stack. Even if each thread has its own stack to maintain the control flow, a thread

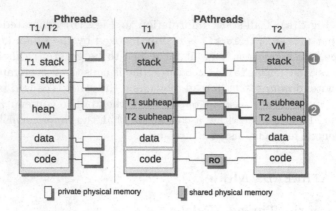

Fig. 3. Different thread models: Pthreads vs. PATHREADS

can read and write the stack content of other threads due to the shared address space. Changes to memory immediately become visible to all other threads. In general, threads often share two types of data with each other, i.e., globals in data segment and objects in heap segment, while the situation of stack sharing (especially write sharing) is relatively uncommon [17]. Improper use of stack write-sharing can cause significant security risks.

By contrast, since PATHREADS runs threads in separate address spaces, we have to consider how PATHREADS explicitly manage various shared data resources.

Stack. In view of the rareness and error-proneness of stack write-sharing, PATHREADS does not support stack write-sharing across threads, so any updates to stack variables are only locally visible. As shown in Fig. 3, Pthreads has to allocate a disjoint address range from the shared address space as each thread's stack. This causes that Pthreads cannot scale as the number of threads increases. But in the PATHREADS model, stacks of all threads occupy the same address range in their own address spaces, so as to effectively use the limited address space to support a large number of threads. When a child thread is created by its parent thread, it can directly inherit the stack status from the parent thread, accordingly supporting some meaningful and common stack read-sharing.

Globals and the Heap. In OSes such as Linux, a process invokes `fork()` to create a *child* process, which is an almost exact duplicate of the calling process, the *parent*. The two processes execute the same program text, but have separate copies of the stack, data and heap segments. The kernel employs COW mapping technique to avoid wasteful page copying but to allow each process modifying its private copies without affecting the other process. Multiple threads within a process share the process's address space and page tables, directly sharing globals and heap objects.

Nevertheless, in PATHREADS, in order to share globals and heap objects among threads, data and heap segments in each thread's separate address space should not be private COW mappings like Pthreads, but shared writable mappings. That is, the page-table entries for these segments in one thread refer to the same physical memory pages as the corresponding page-table entries in the other threads. As shown in the right side of Fig. 3, although threads T1 and T2 have their own address spaces, the data and heap segments belonging to T1 and T2 will map to the same shared physical pages. Thus, the shared variable semantics could be ensured in PATHREADS.

Code. Similar like Pthreads, the text segment of each thread in PATHREADS is marked as read-only, and is mapped to a common set of physical pages.

Synchronization Algorithms and Primitives. PATHREADS should support programs that invoke Pthreads synchronization API, such as locks, condition variables and barriers. All these synchronization algorithms should be similar to Pthreads, but are built atop the separate address spaces of PATHREADS, rather than the shared address space.

3.3   The Heap Allocator

In PATHREADS, due to the thread-private address space, it is impossible to ensure heap sharing semantics by using legacy allocators. To address the problem, a new heap allocator, *IAmalloc*, is proposed to apply to the PATHREADS. *IAmalloc* need ensure that a heap object allocated by one thread can be read or written correctly by the other threads, and it also need effectively support dynamic memory allocation, access and recycling.

To achieve the above requirements, *IAmalloc* first makes each thread occupy the same address range as its heap segment; then it divides the whole heap segment into several subheaps, and each subheap can only be used to respond allocation requests from a single thread; finally, *IAmalloc* ensures that all allocated heap objects in different subheaps can be read and written by each thread. Thus, *IAmalloc* avoids synchronization when allocating heap objects. Moreover, since heap objects allocated by a thread are in the same subheap, the spatial locality can be improved especially when the heap objects allocated by a thread would not be accessed by the other threads.

4   Implementing PATHREADS on Linux

Prototyping PATHREADS in a proof-of-concept OS or existing OS kernel is direct, but faces compatibility and practical issues. To prototype rapidly and make it practical, we implement PATHREADS using a proposed character device driver on Linux.

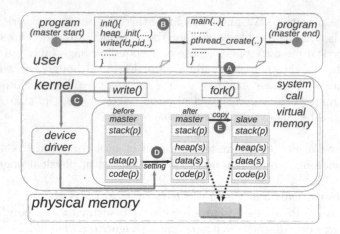

Fig. 4. Program execution flow, where *(p)* or *(s)* represent that the region is private or shared memory mapping, respectively.

4.1 Spawning a PATHREADS Thread

We emulate a PATHREADS thread using a single-threaded Linux process by invoking `fork()` in the implementation of `pthread_create()`. As mentioned in Sect. 3.2, a forked process has a private address space, which is an almost exact duplicate of its parent process via COW mappings. The forked process satisfies G1 (Sect. 3.1), but cannot support the shared variable semantics (G2) required by PATHREADS. Therefore, the **key** to implement PATHREADS is how to change the VM mapping attributes before any `pthread_create()` call in a Pthreads program.

To obtain shared globals in data segment and the shared heap, we first prohibit the main thread to execute COW on its data and heap segments, and set them shared. Subsequently, with the child threads created (Ⓐ in Fig. 4), they will have shared data and heap segments inherited from the main thread (Ⓔ in Fig. 4).

In order to prohibit COW, we need modify the properties recorded in VMAs of the master thread from private to shared. It is not practical to directly modify the source code of Linux kernel, because it will lead to rebuild the Linux kernel. To modify the kernel lightly, we develop a character device driver, CDEV, which follows the Linux device driver interface. Thus, users only need install the CDEV module into their own Linux kernel without any kernel modifications.

As depicted in Fig. 4, a special `init()` function (Ⓑ in Fig. 4) is added to perform the attribute modification of memory mappings. Such a function is decorated with GCC constructor attribute `__attribute__((constructor))`, so that it can be called automatically before entering `main()`. In the `init()`, we initialize the heap and then hijack the `write()` system call to access to the CDEV driver. Through `write()` (Ⓒ in Fig. 4), CDEV can get the process ID (PID) of the master thread, and find its *mm_struct*. CDEV then finds the VMA of the data and heap segments in the *mm_struct* and changes the mapping properties of the VMA from private to shared (Ⓓ in Fig. 4).

4.2 Heap Allocator *IAmalloc*

Due to the isolation among threads, traditional shared heap allocators such as *ptmalloc* [14] in `glibc` cannot apply to PATHREADS. We then develop *IAmalloc* to preserve shared heap semantics among separate address spaces basing on Doug Lea's *dlmalloc* [16]. The **key point** is how to share heap between threads with good efficiency.

Heap Allocation Policy. Performing concurrent dynamic memory allocation and de-allocation in a single shared heap requires synchronization control each time, and would inevitably serialize all allocation and de-allocation operations, badly hurting the scalability [2]. The layout of the heap can have a significant impact on how fast the program is running [13]. To obtain efficiency, *IAmalloc* separates the entire heap into several subheaps, and each thread can get a subheap for thread-local allocation but can read or write any objects in the whole heap. Thus, it is unnecessary to synchronize dynamic allocations, and objects allocated by the same thread also have good spatial locality, accordingly improving the performance and scalability of programs.

In the implementation of *IAmalloc*, each subheap has corresponding metadata in the global structure shared among threads, and has a relative *mspace* structure managed by *dlmalloc*. *IAmalloc* directly reuses *mspace* memory management in *dlmalloc*. When a thread invokes `malloc()`, it first finds the *mspace* from its relative subheap without contention, then gets the desired memory block from the *mspace*. As shown in Fig. 5, threads T1 and T2 allocate space from their subheaps to store variables `x1` and `x2`, respectively. After that, both T1 and T2 can access `x1` or `x2`; and each thread can free a heap object allocated by another, e.g., T1 can free `x2`. In this situation, *IAmalloc* would search the global metadata of subheaps to find the target subheap including the to-be-freed memory address and then reclaim the memory block into the target.

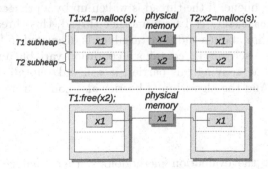

Fig. 5. T1 and T2 malloc x1 and x2, respectively; then T1 frees x2.

The Source of Chunks and Pad Allocation. In *dlmalloc*, if there is not enough memory in an mspace, the allocator would invoke sbrk() or mmap() to allocate a chunk from the address space. However, frequent accesses to the kernel must be a performance defect. To avoid this problem, we modify the algorithm of *dlmalloc*, that is, if a thread finds there is not enough virtual memory in the mspace, the thread would split a chunk with fixed size from an available pre-assigned subheap and then save it into the mspace.

False sharing occurs when processors access different data objects within the same cache line in parallel [5]. This false sharing can cause serious performance degradation. To reduce or even avoid false sharing, except for allocating in thread-local subheap, *IAmalloc* also pads the allocation, that is, makes the heap allocated addresses aligned.

4.3   Thread Management and Synchronization

Thread Management. When pthread_create() is called in application code, the PATHREADS runtime would invoke fork() to create a child process (Ⓐ and Ⓔ in Fig. 4), assign a subheap to the child, and give the child a deterministic thread ID. Calling pthread_self() will return the assigned thread ID instead of the PID given by Linux. In order to implement pthread_join(), PATHREADS maps the deterministic thread ID to PID returned by fork(), and invokes waitpid() to wait for the specified thread. The PATHREADS runtime maintains both global and private meta-data for each thread, including PID, thread ID, the relative subheap, etc.

Synchronization. The implementation of *mutex* in PATHREADS is similar to that in Pthreads, but works between multiple Linux processes rather than multiple threads within a Linux process. The PATHREADS runtime lets a thread sleep instead of keeping busy while waiting for a mutex, and the algorithm of mutex is mentioned in [12].

A *condition variable* has a waiting queue and a mutex pointer in PATHREADS. When a thread invokes pthread_cond_wait(), it need release the mutex and then sleep in the waiting queue. If the thread is waken up by a pthread_cond_signal() or pthread_cond_broadcast() call from another thread, this thread will contend the mutex. Algorithm about condition variables is discussed in [4].

In PATHREADS, each *barrier* contains a condition variable and a mutex. If a thread is the last one arriving this barrier, it will wake up all threads sleeping in waiting queue. And the algorithm of barrier also comes from [12].

5   Evaluation

We first introduce the evaluation methodology, then analyze the evaluation results.

5.1   Evaluation Methodology

We chose some workloads from Phoenix [20] and PARSEC [3] benchmark suites, which can be built and run with Pthreads or PATHREADS. Table 1 lists some detailed information about these workloads, where the first six workloads come from Phoenix, and the last four come from PARSEC. Columns 2–5 are profiling data collected by running each workload with 32 threads using the input dataset size given in Column 6, where *lock, wait, signal, barrier* in the title of Columns 2–4 represent numbers of pthread_mutex_lock, pthread_cond_wait, pthread_cond_broadcast/signal, and pthread_barrier function calls; *heap* refers to total bytes allocated in the heap segment. From the table, we find that only pca, flui and dedup take advantage of Pthreads synchronization function calls in application code. dedup is a typical VM-intensive application that consumes a lot of heap space and invokes many synchronization operations. PATHREADS does not support Ad Hoc synchronizations [22] and stack write-sharing like Pthreads-compatible multithreading systems such as Dthreads [17], so it cannot support workloads such as x264 from PARSEC.

Table 1. Benchmarks and their profiling data when running with 32 threads.

Benchmark	Lock	Wait/signal	Barrier	Heap (B)	Dataset
string_match (sm)	0	0	0	8243	500 MB
histogram (hist)	0	0	0	3014	1.4 GB
linear_regression (lr)	0	0	0	208	500 MB
matrix_multiply (mm)	0	0	0	4000256	2000
kmeans	0	0	0	2420832	100000
pca	2016	0	0	32040384	4000
swaptions (swap)	0	0	0	5431	Large
fluidanimate (flui)	22949710	1756/80	3411	36001	Large
blackscholes (black)	0	0	0	678	Large
dedup	258340	1044/69485	0	886135061	Large

Evaluation Methodology. We conducted all workloads on a 32-core Intel 4× Xeon E7-4820 system equipped with 128 GB of RAM. The OS is 64-bit executable Ubuntu 12.04 with kernel 3.2.0 and 4.10. All benchmarks and shared dynamic libraries are compiled by GCC v4.6.3 with optimization flag -O3. We logically disable CPU cores by Linux's CPU hotplug mechanism, which allows to disable or enable individual CPU cores by writing 0 or 1 to a special file (/sys/devices/system/cpu/cpuN/online), and the number of workers equals to the number of CPU cores enabled [23]. Each workload is executed 10 times. To reduce the effect of outlier, the lowest and the highest runtimes for each workload are discarded, thus each result is the average of the remaining 8 runs.

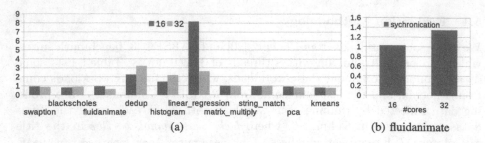

(a)   (b) fluidanimate

Fig. 6. (a) Runtime ratio: Pthreads relative to PATHREADS; (b) synchronization overhead ratio: PATHREADS relative to Pthreads for `flui`

5.2   Performance

We first compare the performance of PATHREADS with Pthreads. Figure 6(a) shows the runtime ratio of Pthreads relative to PATHREADS for each workload running with 16 and 32 cores, respectively. PATHREADS outperforms Pthreads in 3 workloads, including `hist`, `lr` and `dedup`. Two VM-intensive workloads built with PATHREADS run faster than with Pthreads, e.g., reaching up to 2.17× and 3.19× faster than Pthreads for `hist` and `dedup` on 32 cores, respectively. Although `lr` is not VM-intensive, PATHREADS greatly improves its performance, e.g., running 8.5× faster than Pthreads on 16 cores, due to eliminating false sharing. Reasons for this improvement are analyzed in Sect. 5.3.

Workloads `mm` and `sm` with PATHREADS show similar performance as those with Pthreads. Compared to Pthreads, however, PATHREADS has no advantage for the rest five workloads, where `flui` contains many Pthreads synchronization calls unlike the others, i.e., `swap`, `black`, `pca` and `kmeans`. For `flui`, PATHREADS cannot obtain the performance improvement on 32 cores, because the synchronization algorithm of mutex, barrier and so on, brings some performance overhead. As shown in Fig. 6(b), the synchronization overhead from PATHREADS is much higher than that from Pthreads. For the other four workloads, all of them have smaller calculation, so the overhead of thread creation has great impact on the program performance. Pthreads calls `clone()` to create child thread, while PATHREADS calls `fork()`. However, the overhead from `fork()` is higher than `clone()` in many different cores.

5.3   Performance Analysis in Detail

We further use Linux Perf to deeply analyze the reason why PATHREADS runs faster than Pthreads for `hist`, `dedup` and `lr`.

Locking Overhead in Linux Kernel. As analyzed in Sect. 2, hotspot kernel functions related to contention in read mode or write mode are different. The performance bottleneck of `hist` is contention on *mmap_sem* in read mode. When running `hist` with PATHREADS, overheads of two relative hotspot functions `down_read_trylock()` and `up_read()` are significantly reduced, both less than 0.5%

of the total execution time. But for `dedup`, the performance bottleneck is contention in write mode, and the relative hotspot function is `ticket_spin_lock()`. PATHREADS can also significantly reduce the overhead of spinlock for `dedup` to less than 2.37% on 32 cores. Significant reduction in kernel lock overhead indicates that per-thread isolated address space enabled by PATHREADS can effectively reduce contentions in Linux kernel.

More Linux Perf Data Analysis. Linux perf provides some underlying indicators, such as task-clock (TC), context-switch (CS), instructions per cycle (IPC) and stalled cycles per instruction (SCPI), to describe the internal execution of the application. TC represents the time spent on calculation. SCPI indicates the number of empty clock cycles, which can be caused by many reasons, such as cache, physical memory [1,8].

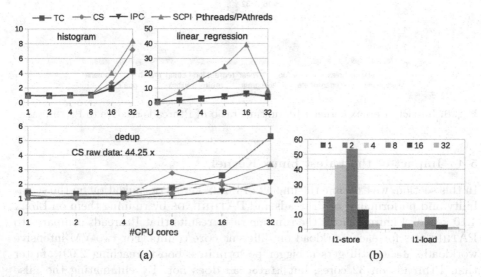

Fig. 7. (a) The ratio of L1 cache miss rate for `lr`: Pthreads/PATHREADS; (b) perf data about underlying execution: ratio - Pthreads/PATHREADS

By analyzing results collected by Perf, we find `hist` and `dedup` built with Pthreads generate large number of SCPI, due to the serious contentions on shared *mmap_sem*; while `lr` built with Pthreads has poor cache performance, due to false sharing.

We further compare the value ratio of Pthreads relative to PATHREADS. As shown in Fig. 7(a), for `hist`, the number of SCPI in Pthreads is 8× more than PATHREADS on 32 cores. `hist` with Pthreads suffers from serious lock contention, which generates many cycles stalled, leading to lower CPU utilization. The CPU utilization is greatly improved on PATHREADS since IPC on PATHREADS is 4× more than Pthreads.

For **dedup**, as core count increases, the ratios of IPC and SCPI (Pthreads/PATHREADS) also increase. Serious contentions on *mmap_sem* result in lower execution efficiency and higher memory latency for Pthreads. Especially, the ratio of context-switch is very high, where Pthreads is 132× higher than PATHREADS (CS ratios in Fig. 7(a) should be magnified by 44.25 times). Due to reducing contention in **dedup**, PATHREADS greatly enhances the efficiency of the task, where TC on Pthreads is 5× slower than PATHREADS.

For **lr**, the ratio of SCPI is extremely high, reaching 40× on 16 cores. Figure 7(b) further shows the ratio of cache miss rate (Pthreads/PATHREADS). We see that the load miss rate and store miss rate on Pthreads achieve 8× and 52× higher than PATHREADS, respectively. So the bad SCPI for **lr** is due to waiting for cache resources.

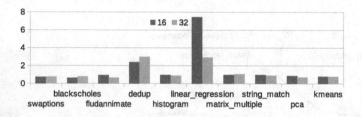

Fig. 8. Impact of Linux kernel 4.10: runtime ratio of Pthreads relative to PATHREADS

5.4   Impact of the Latest Linux Kernel

In this section, we examine the impact of Linux kernel optimization on the scalability and performance of Pthreads and PATHREADS by running them on Linux 4.10 kernel. Figure 8 shows the runtime ratio results that Pthreads compares to PATHREADS for each workload on different core counts. For two VM-intensive workloads, **dedup** still gets a bigger performance boost, reaching 2.99× faster than Pthreads on 32 cores, but **histogram** does not. By eliminating the false sharing, PATHREADS still greatly improve the performance of **lr**, reaching up to 7.45× faster than Pthreads on 16 cores.

To analyze the performance behavior in depth, we further use Linux Perf to collect information of hotspot functions for workloads. For **histogram** built with Pthreads, results show that **down_read_trylock** and **up_read** just occupy 0.17% and 0.13% of the total runtime on 32 cores. This indicates that the latest Linux kernel 4.10 has been able to effectively reduce the contentions in read mode, because since Linux kernel 3.15, address space competition has been reduced by optimizing VMA cache [11].

For **dedup**, the overhead of **_raw_spin_lock** in the 4.10 kernel is only 0.5% of the total time for Pthreads. This is because the 4.10 kernel uses a better queue spinlock [10] rather than the ticket spinlock. The hotspot functions for **dedup** with Pthreads on the 4.10 kernel are **flush_tlb_func()**, **_default_send_IPI_dest_field()**, occupying 3.46%, 2.26% of the total time, respectively. So frequent TLB refresh and communication between threads on *mmap_sem* still seriously affect the application performance on the latest Linux kernel.

6   Related Work

To avoid contentions caused by shared data structures, it is not uncommon for programmers to modify their applications, e.g., Psearchy from MOSBENCH [7] emulating threads by processes. However, it is difficult to modify the application from shared memory based to only private memory based. Furthermore, it cannot support legacy code directly.

Clements *et al.* [9] use super pages to improve scalability. On the X86-64, this can greatly reduce the number of page faults, dropping the contention on the read/write semaphore that manages address space. However, many multi-threaded applications often map small virtual memory regions, which cannot benefit from this solution. Furthermore, as memory consumes and CPU core count grows, using super pages would result in the same scalability problem. [7] analyzes seven system applications running on Linux on a many core computer, and points out that all applications trigger scalability bottlenecks inside Linux kernel. Boyd-Wickizer *et al.* [6] point out shared data structures used in kernel limit the application performance. And they argue that application should control sharing: the kernel should arrange each data structure so that only a single processor need update it. Wentzlaff *et al.* [21] find that page fault handling in Linux does not scale beyond 8 CPU cores.

The shared address space has a cost, for example, kernel VM operations such as handing soft page faults, allocating VM regions via mmap/sbrk, can degrade the performance and scalability of applications. Clements *et al.* [9] propose a new design to increase the concurrency of kernel operations on a shared addressed space by exploiting RCU [18], so that soft page faults can both run in parallel with operations that mutate the same address space and avoid contending with other page faults on shared cache lines. But this way still cause contentions on the coarse-grained lock.

7   Conclusions

This paper presents a Pthreads-compatible thread library PATHREADS and a shared heap allocator *IAmalloc*. Experimental results show that PATHREADS can improve the performance of VM-intensive application compared with the Pthreads. Strategies such as allocating in thread-local subheap and pad allocation employed in *IAmalloc* can improve the locality and eliminate false sharing. By our evaluation, we also give some analysis about underlying execution and access features. In the future work, we will try to enhance PATHREADS by reducing thread creation and synchronization overhead among separate address spaces.

Acknowledgment. This work was partly supported by the grants of National Natural Science Foundation of China (No. 61772487) and Anhui Provincial Natural Science Foundation (No. 1808085MF198).

References

1. Anderson, J.M., Berc, L.M., Dean, J., et al.: Continuous profiling: where have all the cycles gone? ACM Trans. Comput. Syst. **15**(4), 357–390 (1997). https://doi.org/10.1145/265924.265925
2. Baldassin, A., Borin, E., Araujo, G.: Performance implications of dynamic memory allocators on transactional memory systems. In: 20th PPoPPACM SIGPLAN Symposium on Principles and Practice of Parallel Programming, pp. 87–96. ACM (2015). https://doi.org/10.1145/2688500.2688504
3. Bienia, C., Kumar, S., Singh, J.P., Li, K.: The PARSEC benchmark suite: characterization and architectural implications. In: 17th PACT International Conference on Parallel Architectures and Compilation Techniques, pp. 72–81, October 2008
4. Birrell, A.: Implementing condition variables with semaphores. In: Herbert, A., Jones, K.S. (eds.) Computer Systems: Theory, Technology, and Applications. Monographs in Computer Science, pp. 29–37. Springer, New York (2004). https://doi.org/10.1007/0-387-21821-1_5
5. Bolosky, W.J., Scott, M.L.: False sharing and its effect on shared memory performance. In: USENIX Systems on USENIX Experiences with Distributed and Multiprocessor Systems, vol. 4, p. 3. USENIX Association, Berkeley (1993)
6. Boyd-Wickizer, S., Chen, H., Chen, R., et al.: Corey: an operating system for many cores. In: 8th OSDIUSENIX Conference on Operating Systems Design and Implementation, pp. 43–57. USENIX Association, Berkeley (2008)
7. Boyd-Wickizer, S., Clements, A.T., Mao, Y., et al.: An analysis of Linux scalability to many cores. In: 9th OSDIUSENIX Conference on Operating Systems Design and Implementation, pp. 1–8. USENIX Association, Berkeley (2010)
8. Browne, S., Dongarra, J., Garner, N., Ho, G., Mucci, P.: A portable programming interface for performance evaluation on modern processors. Int. J. High Perform. Comput. Appl. **14**(3), 189–204 (2000)
9. Clements, A.T., Kaashoek, M.F., Zeldovich, N.: Scalable address spaces using RCU balanced trees. In: 17th ASPLOS International Conference on Architectural Support for Programming Languages and Operating Systems, pp. 199–210, ACM, New York (2012). https://doi.org/10.1145/2150976.2150998
10. Corbet, J.: MCS locks and qspinlocks, March 2014. https://lwn.net/Articles/590243/
11. Corbet, J.: Optimizing VMA caching, March 2014. https://lwn.net/Articles/589475/
12. Drepper, U.: Futexes are tricky, November 2011. https://www.akkadia.org/drepper/futex.pdf
13. Evans, J.: A scalable concurrent malloc(3) implementation for FreeBSD. In: BSD-Can Conference, Ottawa, Canada, May 2006
14. Gloger, W.: Dynamic memory allocator implementations in Linux system libraries, May 2006. http://www.malloc.de/en/index.html
15. Kleen, A.: Linux multi-core scalability. In: Linux Kongress, October 2009
16. Lea, D.: Dlmalloc: a memory allocator (2012). http://g.oswego.edu/dl/html/malloc.html. Accessed 24 Sept 2012

17. Liu, T., Curtsinger, C., Berger, E.: DTHREADS: efficient deterministic multi-threading. In: 23rd SOSPACM Symposium on Operating Systems Principles, pp. 327–336, October 2011
18. McKenney, P.E.: Exploiting deferred destruction: an analysis of read-copy-update techniques in operating system kernels. Ph.D. thesis, Oregon Health & Science University (2004)
19. de Melo, A.C.: Performance counters on Linux. In: Linux Plumbers Conference, September 2009
20. Ranger, C., Raghuraman, R., Penmetsa, A., et al.: Evaluating MapReduce for multi-core and multiprocessor systems. In: 13th HPCA IEEE International Symposium on High Performance Computer Architecture, pp. 13–24. IEEE Computer Society, Washington, DC, February 2007. https://doi.org/10.1109/HPCA.2007.346181
21. Wentzlaff, D., Agarwal, A.: Factored operating systems (fos): the case for a scalable operating system for multicores. SIGOPS Oper. Syst. Rev. **43**(2), 76–85 (2009). https://doi.org/10.1145/1531793.1531805
22. Xiong, W., Park, S., Zhang, J., Zhou, Y., Ma, Z.: Ad Hoc synchronization considered harmful. In: 9th OSDIUSENIX Conference on Operating Systems Design and Implementation, pp. 1–8. USENIX Association, Berkeley (2010)
23. Zhang, Y., Cao, H.: DMR: A deterministic MapReduce for multicore systems. Int. J. Parallel Prog. 1–14 (2015). https://doi.org/10.1007/s10766-015-0390-5

Efficient and Privacy-Preserving Query on Outsourced Spherical Data

Yueyue Zhou, Tao Xiang[(⊠)], and Xiaoguo Li

College of Computer Science, Chongqing University, Chongqing 400044, China
txiang@cqu.edu.cn

Abstract. Outsourcing spatial database to the cloud becomes a paradigm for many applications such as location-bases service (LBS). At the same time, the security of outsourced data and its query becomes a serious issue. In this paper, we consider 3D spherical data that has wide applications in geometric information systems (GIS), and investigate its privacy-preserving query problem. By using an approximately distance-preserving 3D-2D projection method, we first project 3D spatial points to six possible 2D planes. Then we utilize secure Hilbert space-filling curve to encode the 2D points into 1D Hilbert values. After that, we build an encrypted spatial index tree using B^+-tree and order-preserving encryption (OPE). Our scheme supports efficient point query, arbitrary polygon query, as well as dynamic updating in the encrypted domain. Theoretical analysis and experimental results on real-word datasets demonstrate its satisfactory tradeoff between security and efficiency.

Keywords: Outsourcing · Privacy-preserving query · Spherical data
B^+-tree · Hilbert curve

1 Introduction

Spherical data is a kind of 3D spatial data and has wide applications in the real world. As we know, the earth we live can be regarded as a sphere, and a large number of spatial data objects of the earth are on the spherical surface. Therefore, spherical dataset has wide applications in geometric information systems (GIS) and location-bases service (LBS). The Google's S2 library [3] represents all data on a 3D sphere and provides a solution of spherical data processing. It is used in many databases and applications such as Google Maps and MongoDB.

The security of outsourced spatial data is of great importance, but little attention has been paid to spherical data in the existing literature. Because the cloud may be untrustworthy, spatial data cannot be outsourced to the cloud in its plain form. Traditional encryption schemes do not support querying on the cloud directly or induce too much overhead in decryption, therefore it is imperative to find a way of querying on outsourced spatial data in private manner. However, most of the work in the existing literature focuses on 2D spatial data [9,12,13], little attention has been paid to 3D spatial data such as spherical data.

© Springer Nature Switzerland AG 2018
J. Vaidya and J. Li (Eds.): ICA3PP 2018, LNCS 11337, pp. 138–152, 2018.
https://doi.org/10.1007/978-3-030-05063-4_12

It is more difficult to enable privacy-preserving query on spherical data. Compared with 2D spatial data, it is more complicated to query on 3D spherical data because we usually need to calculate the relation of data points (e.g. find the k-nearest neighbors of a data point) on the spherical surface rather than a plane. Therefore, it is not easy to directly extend the solutions of privacy-preserving query on traditional 2D plane to 3D spherical surface.

In this paper, we target on 3D spherical data and investigate the problem of how to query on its encrypted form in the cloud. We propose an efficient spatial index as follows. By utilizing an approximately distance-preserving 3D-2D projection, we first transform 3D data on a unit sphere to six planes. Then we encode the 2D data into 1D representation by secure Hilbert space-filling curve. After that, we create a B^+-tree for the 1D data. The index is encrypted by order-preserving encryption (OPE) and then outsourced to the cloud together with the encrypted spatial data. We also propose a method of querying and updating directly on the encrypted index. Our method supports point query and arbitrary polygon (as long as the Hilbert cell is tiny enough) query.

Our contributions are summarized as follows:

- To the best of our knowledge, we study the problem of privacy-preserving query on 3D spherical data for the first time.
- We build spatial index efficiently and query the encrypted data efficiently. Our scheme supports point query and arbitrary polygon (as long as the Hilbert cell is tiny enough) query, as well as dynamic updating.
- We analyze the security of the proposed scheme and conduct extensive experiments on real-word data to evaluate the performance of the proposed scheme. Theoretical analysis and experimental results show its satisfactory balance between security and efficiency for practical deployment.

2   Related Work

The work about privacy-preserving query on spatial data can be generally classified into several categories according to the employed cryptographic tools: homomorphic encryption, searchable encryption, order-preserving encryption, and secure transformation.

Homomorphic encryption (HE) can be used in privacy-preserving query since it supports calculations on ciphertext. In [20], an improved HE technique over a composite order group is used for outsourced LBS data in the cloud. In [19], similar technique is adopted for supporting polygon spatial query. In [18], based on the Paillier public-key cryptosystem, a solution is proposed for the mobile user to preserve his location and query privacy in approximate kNN queries.

Searchable encryption (SE) can perform queries on encrypted data without revealing privacy. In [17], two symmetric-key SE schemes are proposed for supporting circular range search on spatial dataset. In [15], by leveraging an R-tree based SE scheme and adding a trusted third party, the authors proposed a solution for privacy-preserving circular range search on spatial data. In [14], the authors proposed a symmetric-key SE scheme for geometric range search on encrypted spatial data by converting point in geometric range test into vector-matrix computations.

Order-preserving encryption (OPE) [4] is proposed in database community and has been widely used for privacy-preserving querying. In [16], OPE is utilized to encrypt the transformed spatial data, and trusted user can issue spatial range queries to SP directly on the encrypted Hilbert index. In [7], a dynamic index for spatial data on the cloud is proposed, where spatial transformation is applied to the data and the spatial index is encrypted using OPE. It supports secure query processing and dynamic data updating on cloud service provider.

Secure transformations are also used for protecting the query privacy in outsourced spatial data. In [12,13], two spatial transformations, i.e. hierarchical space-division transformation and error-based transformation, are proposed to redistribute the location data. Only trusted user with correct key can reconstruct the exact original data points from the transformed points. In [9], Hilbert-curve based cryptographic transformation is proposed to protect data privacy and to improve the efficiency of the query processing in outsourced databases.

3   Preliminaries

3.1   Approximately Distance-Preserving 3D-2D Projection

We introduce an approximately distance-preserving projection technique which maps the points on a 3D sphere to the six planes of a cube in distance-preserving manner, and the same method is also used in the Google's S2 library [3]. For simplicity, we assume the sphere is a unit sphere, i.e. its radius $r = 1$, and its circumscribed cube encloses the sphere in the space of $[-1, 1] \times [-1, 1] \times [-1, 1]$ as shown in Fig. 1(a). The point on the sphere surface is denoted by $p(u, v)$, where u is the latitude afasdnd v is the longitude.

First, we transform the coordinate of point $p(u, v)$ into Cartesian coordinate $p(x, y, z)$. Second, for a given point on sphere surface, we decide which plane (or face) of the cube it should be projected to. As Fig. 1(a) shows, we divide sphere surface by six planes that is decided by the equations $|x| = |y|$ and $|y| = |z|$. Figure 1(b) shows one of the projected faces. Third, we project the points on sphere surface into the six faces of the cube in approximately distance-preserving manner. As shown in Fig. 1(c), if we directly project a point p to the cube face as p', the distance relationship on the sphere will change after its projection because the map is nonuniform. Therefor, we adjust the projected coordinate of p' by a quadratic nonlinear transformation [3], so that the points on the sphere can be approximately uniformly projected to the six planes of the cube.

3.2   Hilbert Curve

A Hilbert curve is a continuous fractal space-filling curve first introduced by [6]. It can map the data in multi-dimensional space to one-dimensional space and has higher clustering properties than other space-filling curves. The steps of Hilbert

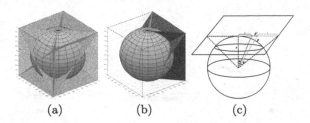

(a)   (b)   (c)

Fig. 1. Sphere surface projection.

curve filling in 2D space are as follows: First, we divide a region into $2^n \times 2^n$ grids, where n is the order and each grid is a Hilbert cell. Next, beginning with a starting point (e.g. the bottom left Hilbert cell), we use a continuous curve to traverse each Hilbert cell by the following rules: (1) each Hilbert cell is traversed by only once; (2) only vertically and horizontally neighbored Hilbert cells are allowed to be traversed; (3) the Hilbert curve has the same orientation when it is viewed at any lower order.

We can label the Hilbert cells by its traversed sequence starting from zero. When a point $p(x, y)$ is located in a Hilbert cell, we call the label of that Hilbert cell as its *Hilbert value* $H(p)$. The Hilbert curve can be determined by a tuple of parameters (x_0, y_0, θ, n) where x_0, y_0 is the starting point, θ represents the orientation, and n is the order [10].

3.3 Order-Preserving Encryption

Order-preserving encryption (OPE) is a deterministic encryption scheme that preserves the numerical order of the plaintext [4]. Specifically, let OPE = (Key-Gen, Enc, Dec) be the syntax of an OPE scheme, where KeyGen is the key generation algorithm, Enc the encryption algorithm, and Dec the decryption algorithm. For any key k and two plaintexts x and y, if $x < y$, then $\mathsf{Enc}(x, k) < \mathsf{Enc}(y, k)$. Thereby OPE allows us do comparison operations (e.g. ==, MAX, MIN) directly on the encrypted database.

4 Models

4.1 System Model

Our system model is shown in Fig. 2. It includes three entities: data owner (DO), service provider (SP) and trusted user (TU). SP (also known as the cloud) possesses powerful computing and storage capabilities. DO firstly outsources encrypted spatial data and its index to SP. After that, DO can send an update request with updated encrypted data to SP, and SP handles the request on ciphertext directly and updates the encrypted data structure. DO also needs to authorize the user who wants to query on the outsourced data by sending secret key to TU. Once TU has a query request, he can send it to SP and SP is responsible for returning the query result.

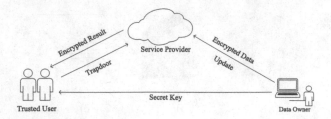

Fig. 2. System model.

4.2 Security Model

We assume the cloud (SP) is honest but curious. We adopt the two threat models considered in [11] as follows where the adversary is able to acquire some information on the communication channel. In both models, the adversary's goal is to learn the location information that TU queried.

Offline Model: The adversary can obtain a dump of SP's encrypted spatial database, but he cannot observe any query made by TU.

Online Model: The adversary can see both the encrypted spatial database, TUs queries, and SP's responses.

5   Our Scheme

5.1   Framework

At a high level, our scheme mainly contains the following algorithms:

- Setup(1^λ): On input the security parameter λ, DO runs this algorithm to output a secret key $K = (K_1, K_2)$. $K1$ is an AES encryption key that is used to encrypt data object. $K2 = (K_{OPE}, K_{AES}, HSK)$ where K_{OPE} is the OPE key, K_{AES} is another AES encryption key used to generate the encrypted face index FI. $HSK = (x_0, y_0, \theta, n)$ is the Hilbert secret key that determines the parameters of a Hilbert curve.
- BuildIndex(OP, K): On input a set of origin points OP and the secret key K, DO runs this algorithm to output the encrypted spatial index ESI.
- Outsource(ESI, OP): After building the encrypted index ESI, DO encrypts data objects OP by AES with the key $K1$, and then outsources ESI and the encrypted data to SP.
- Trapdoor($QW, K2$): On input $K2$ and a query window QW, TU runs this algorithm to output a query token set T.
- Query(T, ESI): On receiving the trapdoor information T and the encrypted spatial index ESI, SP runs this algorithm to query the encrypted spatial data. It invokes different sub-procedure for point query and range query. The output is the encrypted data ED.
- ReceiveData($ED, K1$): On receiving the encrypted result ED from SP, TU invokes this algorithm to decrypt the plaintext by AES decryption key $K1$.
- Update(ND): In the input an update request ND, SP runs this Algorithm to securely insert a new data to ESI.

5.2 Spatial Index Construction

Suppose DO has a spherical dataset OP and he wants to build its index under secret key K generated by the Setup algorithm, our index construction consists of the following steps. The procedure is also described in Algorithm 1.

1. **3D to 2D Projection:** DO first projects the data points in OP from 3D spherical surface to six 2D planes as described in Sect. 3.1. We use $P = \{P_i | i = 1, \ldots, 6\}$ to represent the set of projected 2D data points on six planes, i.e. P_i contains all the points projected on face i.
2. **2D to 1D Transformation:** For each plane that contains 2D data points P_i, DO builds a Hilbert curve by the secret parameter HSK and gets the corresponding set of Hilbert values for all the data points in P_i.
3. **Index Construct:** For each set of Hilbert values of P_i, DO constructs a B$^+$-tree BT_i. After that, DO gets the set of B$^+$-trees $BT = \{BT_i | i = 1, \ldots, 6\}$, then DO uses a list to connect six face index i and its corresponding B$^+$-tree BT_i, and gets the constructed index in plaintext.
4. **Index Encryption:** DO encrypts the constructed index. First, he encrypts each face index i by AES under the key K_{AES}. Then, he encrypts all the nodes in BT by the OPE scheme in [4] under the key K_{OPE} and gets the encrypted B$^+$-trees EBT. Finally, DO gets the encrypted spatial index ESI.

Algorithm 1. BuildIndex

Input: OP, K
Output: ESI
    $ESI \leftarrow \phi$;
 1: **for** i=0 to 6 **do**
 2:     $P_i, BT_i \leftarrow \phi$;
 3: **end for**
 4: **for all** $p \in OP$ **do**
 5:     $i \leftarrow$ FACE_PRO(op);
 6:     $p' \leftarrow$ Project p to face i;
 7:     Append p' to P_i;
 8: **end for**
 9: **for** i=0 to 6 **do**
10:     **for all** $p \in P_i$ **do**
11:         Add Hilbert value $H(p, HSK)$ to B$^+$ tree BT_i;
12:     **end for**
13: **end for**
14: **for** i=0 to 6 **do**
15:     $(e_i, EBT_i) \leftarrow (\text{Enc}_{AES}(i, K_{AES}), \text{Enc}_{OPE}(i, K_{OPE}))$;
16:     Add (e_i, EBT_i) to ESI;
17: **end for**
18: **return** ESI;

5.3 Trapdoor Generation

Once TU wants to launch a query (point query or range query), he needs to generate a query token first. TU should also have the knowledge of $K2 = (K_{OPE}, K_{AES}, HSK)$. Suppose the set of query points is $QW = \{p_i | i = 1, \ldots, n\}$, where $n = 1$ for point query and $n \geq 2$ for range query. That is to say, in the case of point query, QW only contains one point; while in the case of range query, it contains two or more points that describe the boundary of the queried polygon. The generated threshold $T = \{t_i | i = 1, \ldots, n\}$ is a set of query token for each Hilbert cell that is contained in the query point or polygon. Each t_i consists of two parts, i.e. $t_i = (t_{i1}, t_{i2})$. t_{i1} is the AES encryption of p'_i under the secret key K_{AES}, where p'_i is the approximately distance-preserving 3D-2D projection of p_i as described in Sect. 3.1. t_{i2} is the OPE encryption of p'_i's Hilbert value under the secret key K_{OPE}. This procedure is shown in Algorithm 2.

Algorithm 2. Trapdoor

Input: $QW, K2$
Output: T

   $T \leftarrow \phi$;
1: **for all** $p_i \in QW$ **do**
2:    $j \leftarrow$ FACE_PRO(p_i);
3:    $p'_i \leftarrow$ Project p to face j;
4:    $(t_{i1}, t_{i2}) \leftarrow (j, H(p'_i, HSK))$;
5:    Append (t_{i1}, t_{i2}) to T;
6: **end for**
7: Find all Hilbert cells contained in the polygon determined by T and add their tuples of face index and Hilbert value to T;
8: **for all** $t_i \in T$ **do**
9:    $(t_{i1}, t_{i2}) \leftarrow (\mathsf{Enc}_{AES}(t_{i1}, K_{AES}), \mathsf{Enc}_{OPE}(t_{i2}, K_{OPE}))$;
10: **end for**
11: **return** T

5.4 Query Processing

Upon receiving the query request from TU with the trapdoor T, SP searches the encrypted spatial data and returns the encrypted query result back to TU. In our paper, we consider two types of query: point query and range query.

Point Query. For point query, given a point, SP should return all the points that fall in the same Hilbert cell, or have the same Hilbert value in other words. T contains only one query token $t_1 = (t_{11}, t_{12})$ that is generated by the Trapdoor algorithm. SP can first determine which of six B$^+$-trees the queried point is in by t_{11} since it is the value of encrypted face index. Then, SP can traverse that B$^+$-tree by depth-first search to find the encrypted Hilbert value of queried point by t_{12}. Finally, SP returns the encrypted data ED corresponding to this encrypted Hilbert value. This process is described in Algorithm 3.

Algorithm 3. Point_Query

Input: T, ESI
Output: ED
1: $(t_{11}, t_{12}) \leftarrow T$;
2: Find the B$^+$-tree $EBT_{t_{11}}$ in ESI;
3: $node \leftarrow$ root of $EBT_{t_{11}}$;
4: $key \leftarrow$ Find the maximal key that is not greater than t_{12} in $node$;
5: **if** $key == null$ **then**
6:     **return** ϕ;
7: **end if**
8: **if** $node$ is a leaf node **then**
9:     **if** $t_{12} == key$ **then**
10:         $ED \leftarrow$ The data associated with key's pointer;
11:     **else**
12:         $ED \leftarrow \phi$;
13:     **end if**
14:     **return** ED;
15: **else**
16:     Recursively search the subtree of $node$;
17: **end if**

Range Query. The range query in our scheme supports arbitrary polygon (as long as the Hilbert cell is tiny enough). It means TU can request for querying on an arbitrary polygon by giving its boundary points, e.g. three vertices for a triangle and four vertices for a rectangle, and SP should return all the points that fall in the Hilbert cells covered by the boundary points. The Trapdoor algorithm can find out all the Hilbert cells contained in the polygon and creates query tokens for all of them. After receiving the query tokens, SP can retrieve ESI to find out all the data filled in those Hilbert cells.

A trivial way to do this is converting range query to point query, i.e. querying each Hilbert cell by point query independently and aggregating all the results of point query, but the performance is unsatisfactory. Here, we introduce a optimized traversing method to accelerate the search. The basic idea is as follows. If we have a set of values S in ascending order to be searched in a B$^+$-tree, starting from the first key of a currently visited node, we find out all the values in the set that are not greater than the key. We view these found values as a new set S', and remove them from S. Then we search S' in the subtree corresponding to the key and add the searched result as a part of output. We repeat this process with the updated S starting from the next key until all the keys are visited.

In order to make the above-mentioned optimized traversing, we need to do some preparations. First, we need to divide the threshold set $T = \{t_i | i = 1, \ldots, n\}$ into six possible subsets based on the value of encrypted face index t_{i1} of each query token t_i. After that, we sort the elements in each subset by t_{i2} in ascending order. Finally, we can perform the optimized traversing in ESI to search each subset. The entire range query process is described in Algorithm 4.

Algorithm 4. Range_Query
___
Input: T, ESI
Output: ED
 1: $L \leftarrow \phi$; $//L$ is a key-value list where each value is a point to a set;
 2: $ED \leftarrow \phi$;
 3: **for all** $t_i \in T$ **do**
 4:    $(t_{11}, t_{12}) \leftarrow t$;
 5:    Add t_{12} to $L[t_{11}]$ in ascending order;
 6: **end for**
 7: **for all** $(k, S) \in L$ **do**
 8:    Find the B$^+$-tree EBT_k in ESI;
 9:    $node \leftarrow$ root of EBT_k;
10:    **for all** $key \in node$ **do**
11:      $S' \leftarrow$ Find all elements in S that is not greater than k;
12:     **if** $node$ is a leaf node **then**
13:       **if** $S'! = \phi$ **then**
14:         **if** $k \in S'$ **then**
15:           Add the data associated with key's pointer to ED;
16:         **end if**
17:       **end if**
18:     **else**
19:       Recursively search S' in the subtree of $node$;
20:     **end if**
21:     $S \leftarrow S - S'$;
22:    **end for**
23: **end for**
24: **return** ED

5.5 Dynamic Update

Our scheme supports dynamically updating data and its index at SP in the encrypted domain. Dynamic updating includes deleting, inserting, adding, and replacing. We only take inserting operation as an example in the following statements because other operations are similar.

If DO wants to insert a new point np into the outsourced dataset on SP, he first encrypts it by AES with the key $K1$ and gets enp. By the same way in Sect. 5.3, he then generates the trapdoor information of np, i.e. get the encrypted values of its projected face and Hilbert value. After this preparation, DO issues an inserting request along with enp and the generated trapdoor information. Upon receiving the request, SP traverses ESI by using the same method described in Sect. 5.4 to find out the leaf node that has the same encrypted Hilbert value with enp. Finally, SP inserts a pointer pointing to the address of enp in the node. If the capacity of the leaf node exceeds its maximum, overflow should be handled by splitting the leaf node into two subtrees. The inserting operations performed by SP can be described in Algorithm 5.

Algorithm 5. Insert

Input: t, eop, ESI
1: $(t_1, t_2) \leftarrow t$;
2: Find the B$^+$-tree EBT_{t_1} in ESI;
3: $leaf \leftarrow$ Find t_2 in EBT_{t_1};
4: Add the pointer to eop in $leaf$;
5: **if** The capacity of $leaf$ exceeds its maximum **then**
6:    Split $leaf$ into two subtrees;
7: **end if**

6 Security Analysis

In this section, we analyze the security of our proposed scheme. The security of our scheme includes two aspects: the security of encrypted spatial index and the security of spatial data objects. First, because the spatial data objects are encrypted by AES, its security can be well guaranteed under proper secret key length. Second, the security of encrypted spatial index is related to Hilbert curve and OPE. For Hilbert curve, in [8], the authors have proved that the complexity of a brute-force attack to find the Hilbert secret key is $O(2^{4p})$ where p is the number of bits used to discretize each parameter. As for OPE, in [5], the authors gave the first formal security definitions for OPE, and proved that OPE is indistinguishable under the ordered chosen plaintext attack (IND-OCPA).

Based on the above analysis, our scheme achieves a good balance between security and efficiency, and can protect the location of spatial data in the online and the offline models defined in Sect. 4.2. In the offline model, the adversary can only acquire the dump of encrypted spatial database. Because all the data points are encrypted by AES, it is infeasible for the adversary to get any useful information about the plaintext. In the online model, the adversary can further obtain the communication packages between TU and SP so he knows TU's queries and SP's responses, i.e. the encrypted query tokens and the encrypted query results. Given the encrypted query tokens, the adversary can get some knowledge about the size of query window as well as the result, but he is unable to acquire any other more information about the query or the returned result because the spatial index is encrypted by Hilbert curve and OPE.

7 Experiments

In this section, we conduct experiments to evaluate the performance of our proposed scheme and compare our work with DISC, which is a dynamic index for spatial data proposed in closely related work in [7]. We adopt two publicly-available real-word spatial databases California Road Network (CRN) [2] and Gowalla [1] in our experiments. Our experiments are conducted on a computer with 2.6 GHz Intel i5 CPU and 8 GB 1600 MHz DDR3 memory.

7.1 3D to 2D Projection

Since we project 3D spherical data to 2D planes, we need to evaluate the performance of our projection. We randomly select 2,000 points from CRN and Gowalla datasets and record their time costs respectively. The results are shown in Table 1. Although the numbers of selected points are the same, the result on Gowalla dataset is worse. Because the records in Gowalla cover wider sphere surface and the points are projected to more different planes, it takes more time to handle the projection transformation in different planes.

Table 1. Time cost of 3D to 2D projection

Dataset	Number of points	Projection time (us)
CRN	2,000	87
Gowalla	2,000	497

7.2 Spatial Index Construction

Both our scheme and DISC use tree structures (we use B^+-tree and DISC uses R-tree) to construct spatial index. Because the node capacity affects the height of constructed tree and thus has the impact on index construction, we evaluate the time cost of index construction under different node capacities. We set the node capacities of B^+-tree in our scheme and R-tree in DISC as 20, 40 and 60 respectively. We use the entire CRN dataset and randomly select 100,000 points from Gowalla dataset, and record their time costs of spatial index construction. The results are shown in Fig. 3. The performance of our scheme is similar to that of DISC on CRN dataset in Fig. 3(a) and (b) our scheme performs much better than DISC on Gowalla dataset containing larger number of points and covering wider sphere surface.

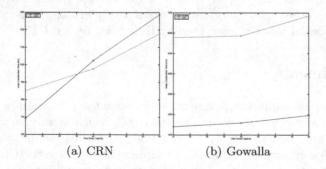

(a) CRN   (b) Gowalla

Fig. 3. The time cost of index construction under different node capacities.

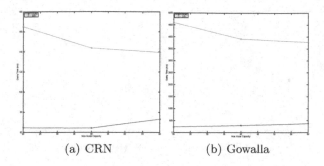

(a) CRN   (b) Gowalla

Fig. 4. The time cost of point query under different node capacities.

7.3 Queries

The time cost of query in our scheme consists of two parts: the trapdoor generation by TU and the search operation by SP, so we take the sum of these two parts as the query overhead. We test the time costs of point query and range query under different node capacities. Still, we set the node capacities of B^{+}-tree in our scheme and R-tree in DISC as 20, 40 and 60 respectively.

- **Point Query.** We randomly generate 2,000 query points on CRN and Gowalla datasets, and test the time costs of point query under different node capacity of trees by using our scheme and DISC. The results are shown in Fig. 4, where we can see that our scheme performs much better than DISC. The time cost of point query on Gowalla dataset is higher than that on CRN dataset. Because Gowalla contains more records and the height of its index tree is higher, it takes more time to query on Gowalla dataset.
- **Range Query.** The time cost of range query is not only related to the spatial index structure (e.g. the node capacity), but only related to the size of query window. Without lose of generality, we only consider the situation where the queried polygon is a rectangle. We randomly generate 1,800 query windows in each group of experiments. The results are shown in Figs. 5 and 6. Figure 5 demonstrates the time cost of range query under different node capacities on two datasets, and it shows that our proposed scheme is much more efficient than DISC. Figure 6 illustrates the impact of query window size, where the node capacity of tree is set to 40. It indicates that our scheme has much better performance on Gowalla dataset.

7.4 Dynamic Update

The time cost of update in our scheme consists of two parts: the trapdoor generation by TU and the update operation by SP, so we take the sum of these two parts as the update overhead. Taking insert as an example, we randomly select 2,000 points on the spatial index tree as updating points, and test the time costs

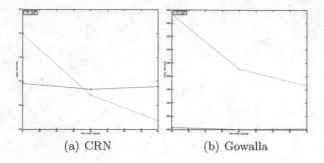

(a) CRN   (b) Gowalla

Fig. 5. The time cost of range query under different node capacities.

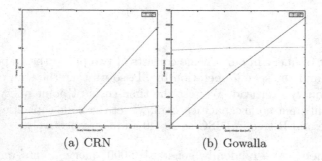

(a) CRN   (b) Gowalla

Fig. 6. The time cost of range query under different query window sizes.

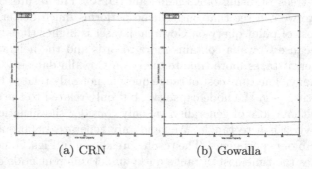

(a) CRN   (b) Gowalla

Fig. 7. The time cost of insert on different datasets.

of insert under different node capacity of trees by using our scheme and DISC. The results are given in Fig. 7. It is observed that our scheme is much more efficient on both two datasets.

8   Conclusion

In this paper, we explore the problem of privacy-preserving query on outsourced 3D spherical data. In our solution, data owner (DO) encrypts the original data by

AES and builds its encrypted spatial index by approximately distance-preserving 3D-2D projection and secure Hilbert space-filling curve. Service provider (SP) only stores the encrypted data and its encrypted index. Once the truster user (TU) launches a query request, SP can perform the query, including point query, arbitrary polygon query and dynamic updating, on the encrypted index. Our scheme is suitable for large-scale geometric spatial dataset and can achieve good balance between security and efficiency.

Acknowledgments. This work was supported by the National Natural Science Foundation of China (No. 61672118) and Graduate Scientific Research and Innovation Foundation of Chongqing, China (No. CYB16046).

References

1. Gowalla. https://snap.stanford.edu/data/loc-gowalla.html
2. Real spatial datasets. http://www.cs.utah.edu/~lifeifei/SpatialDataset.htm
3. S2Geometry. http://s2geometry.io/
4. Agrawal, R., Kiernan, J., Srikant, R., Xu, Y.: Order preserving encryption for numeric data. In: Proceedings of ACM SIGMOD International Conference on Management of Data (SIGMOD), pp. 563–574 (2004)
5. Boldyreva, A., Chenette, N., Lee, Y., O'Neill, A.: Order-preserving symmetric encryption. In: Joux, A. (ed.) EUROCRYPT 2009. LNCS, vol. 5479, pp. 224–241. Springer, Heidelberg (2009). https://doi.org/10.1007/978-3-642-01001-9_13
6. Hilbert, D.: Über die stetige abbildung einer linie auf ein flächenstück. Math. Ann. **38**, 459–460 (1891)
7. Kamel, I., Talha, A.M., Aghbari, Z.A.: Dynamic spatial index for efficient query processing on the cloud. J. Cloud Comput. **6**(1), 5 (2017)
8. Khoshgozaran, A., Shahabi, C.: Blind evaluation of nearest neighbor queries using space transformation to preserve location privacy. In: Papadias, D., Zhang, D., Kollios, G. (eds.) SSTD 2007. LNCS, vol. 4605, pp. 239–257. Springer, Heidelberg (2007). https://doi.org/10.1007/978-3-540-73540-3_14
9. Kim, H.I., Hong, S.T., Chang, J.W.: Hilbert-curve based cryptographic transformation scheme for protecting data privacy on outsourced private spatial data, pp. 77–82 (2014)
10. Ku, W.-S., Hu, L., Shahabi, C., Wang, H.: Query integrity assurance of location-based services accessing outsourced spatial databases. In: Mamoulis, N., Seidl, T., Pedersen, T.B., Torp, K., Assent, I. (eds.) SSTD 2009. LNCS, vol. 5644, pp. 80–97. Springer, Heidelberg (2009). https://doi.org/10.1007/978-3-642-02982-0_8
11. Lewi, K., Wu, D.J.: Order-revealing encryption: new constructions, applications, and lower bounds. In: Proceedings of the 2016 ACM SIGSAC Conference on Computer and Communications Security, pp. 1167–1178 (2016)
12. Lung, M.Y., Ghinita, G., Jensen, C.S., Kalnis, P.: Outsourcing search services on private spatial data, pp. 1140–1143 (2009)
13. Lung, M.Y., Ghinita, G., Jensen, C.S., Kalnis, P.: Enabling search services on outsourced private spatial data. VLDB J. **19**(3), 363–384 (2010)
14. Luo, Y., Fu, S., Wang, D., Xu, M., Jia, X.: Efficient and generalized geometric range search on encrypted spatial data in the cloud. In: IEEE/ACM Conference on Quality of Service (IWQoS), pp. 1–10 (2017)

15. Ren, H., Li, H., Chen, H., Kpiebaareh, M., Zhao, L.: Efficient privacy-preserving circular range search on outsourced spatial data. In: IEEE Conference on Communications (ICC), pp. 1–7 (2016)
16. Talha, A.M., Kamel, I., Aghbari, Z.A.: Enhancing confidentiality and privacy of outsourced spatial data, pp. 13–18 (2015)
17. Wang, B., Li, M., Wang, H., Li, H.: Circular range search on encrypted spatial data. In: IEEE Conference on Distributed Computing Systems (ICDCS), pp. 794–795 (2015)
18. Yi, X., Paulet, R., Bertino, E., Varadharajan, V.: Practical approximate k nearest neighbor queries with location and query privacy. IEEE Trans. Knowl. Data Eng. 28(6), 1546–1559 (2016)
19. Zhu, H., Liu, F., Li, H.: Efficient and privacy-preserving polygons spatial query framework for location-based services. IEEE Internet Things J. 4(2), 536–545 (2017)
20. Zhu, H., Lu, R., Huang, C., Chen, L., Li, H.: An efficient privacy-preserving location-based services query scheme in outsourced cloud. IEEE Trans. Veh. Technol. 65(9), 7729–7739 (2016)

Detecting Advanced Persistent Threats Based on Entropy and Support Vector Machine

Jiayu Tan and Jian Wang[✉]

College of Computer Science and Technology,
Nanjing University of Aeronautics and Astronautics, Nanjing, China
{styletjy,wangjian}@nuaa.edu.cn

Abstract. Advanced Persistent Threats (APTs) have become the critical issue in high security network. The high pertinence, disguise and phasing make it even more ineffective to be discovered by traditional detection technologies. APTs continuously gather information and data from targeted objects, using various of exploits to penetrate the organization. The current threat detection methods take advantage of machine learning algorithm using statistical and behavioral characteristics of the network traffic. The key problem using machine learning algorithm is to find a appropriate feature vector to be fed into the learner. This paper presents an entropy-based detection using support vector machine, aiming to find the traffic containing APT attack, so that attacking stream will be restricted in a smaller range of network traffic which makes it much easier to be found in further analysis. The experimental results show that the proposed method can more effectively and efficiently distinguish the traffic containing ATP streams from the normal.

Keywords: Advanced persistent threats · Machine learning
Entropy · Detection · Traffic

1 Introduction

In the past decades, global Internet network has been developed rapidly. In the meantime, cyber-attack also evolved a lot in quantities and attacking means. In 2010, the notorious cyber-attack, Stuxnet, lurked and did preparation for a long term, and finally broke into the industrial control system which was physically isolated, resulting the delaying of the nuclear plan of Iran [4]. Advanced Persistent Threats (APTs) are more and more frequently appeared in people's vision ever since. APTs are human-driven infiltrations, long-term penetration, customized for the targeted organization after some intelligence analyses, maybe on open sources, and even can leverage unknown exploits to penetrate vulnerable systems. APT attackers are usually highly equipped with penetration skills and tools and have considerable financial resources. What's more, the attackers work often in group and are well-organized. This is a threat under the instruction

© Springer Nature Switzerland AG 2018
J. Vaidya and J. Li (Eds.): ICA3PP 2018, LNCS 11337, pp. 153–165, 2018.
https://doi.org/10.1007/978-3-030-05063-4_13

of a specific target, rather than simply hacking the network through malicious programs on the random targets.

In recent years, many works related to APTs detection have been carried out, however, most of them concentrate on distinguishing the exact malicious network stream, which we think will result in low precision and raise higher false alert. Due to the surreptitious feature of APTs, the patterns keep changing and therefore it is hard to find a specific nature of it to identify this kind of cyber-attack [3]. So we hold the view that finding a precise attacking stream will be much more difficult. Consequently, in this paper, we focus on recognizing whether there exists attacking stream in a volume of network traffic. In this way, attacking stream can be restricted in a certain network traffic within a particular time interval, so that precision of further detection can be improved a lot.

We found that the traffics sent from APTs payloads are different from normal traffics in the way establishing connections. In APTs traffics, they may keep a long period TCP session in order to communicate with attackers and transfer data in low volumes of traffic which will lead to a little difference in the distribution of some particular features of network traffic. While this kind of deviation cannot be easily noticed in common detection method, so unlike what many other APT detection approaches did, we first introduce the entropy concept, invoked in information theory, to make it more uncovered.

The main **contribution** of this paper is that the problem of APT detection is considered to be solved by two steps: (1) find which volume of network traffic contains attacking stream, (2) analyze the suspect traffics and find out the specific malicious stream. What we mainly discuss here is the first step, so we proposed entropy based detection and our experimental results showed remarkable performance of it.

The rest of this paper is organized as follows. Section 2 presents related works. Section 3 introduces the details of our approach. An experiment is presented and the results are analyzed in Sect. 4. Finally, Sect. 5 concludes the paper and sketches out the recommendation for the future work.

2   Related Work

2.1   Anomaly Traffic Detection

Anomaly network traffic detection is very helpful to our research. It provides a basic way to deal with the network traffic classification which has a certain significance for detection of APTs as well. They usually use Sniffer, NetFlow, fprobe or flow-tools to collect traffic data and extract useful features from these high volumes of network traffic [5]. Commonly used ways to extract features are as follow,

1. Using headers of network traffic flow directly as the properties of data, e.g. source or destination IP, source or destination port, type of protocols.
2. Using statistics features of network traffic as the properties of data, e.g. traffic bytes transferred between two hosts, number of packets or flows. These

methods offered basic idea to detect anomaly traffic, but detection concerning to APT attack is quite different.

Moreover, we have also taken guidance on how to choose proper features for the classification algorithm. An environment for network traffic research was introduced by Ferreira et al. [6], and they used it to propose a set of recommended features for traffic classification and anomaly detection based on meta-analysis of main papers published in the past years. In paper [7], the authors proposed a feature selection method and their experiments revealed the existence of irrelevant features, as well as a high redundancy among some features and interdependencies that account for a considerable group of anomalies.

However, APT detection is quite different from anomaly traffic detection in some aspects. APTs will try to behave like normal applications and lurk for a long period in order to avoid being discovered. Even more, some APT attacks are shrewd enough to remain undetected using zero-day exploits. As a result, the common anomaly detections are incompetent to discover APT attacks.

2.2 APT Detection

Since APT attacks have drawn lots of people's attentions, hundreds of security experts devoted themselves to analyzing this kind of malicious attack strategy. Big data analysis and machine learning algorithms are popular and diffusely applied to the detection of APTs. The authors in the report [2] discovered the presence of and revealed a report about a malware found on the Internet that exposes noticeable similarities to Stuxnet. They deeply analyzed the structure, and design philosophy of the malware sample. Technical report [16] took a survey on an unclassified data sets to figure out the middle infrastructure i.e. the system of hops, distribution points, the command and control servers, exploited during a APT attack.

Most of recent works try to discern malicious network traffic like C&C communications or payload downloading. These works [8,18] both focused on communication traffic of command and control. Article [8] found that when the APT payloads communicate with the C&C servers, the commands for control are sent with a fixed time interval which has a strong correlation with the type of malicious payloads. Then they employed machine learning GBDT methods for classification in the flow. And article [13] also hold the belief that anomaly traffic would be definitely generated between the attacker's machine and victim's host via Remote Access Tool, a communication approach in APT attack. Instead of recognizing communication traffic, article [18] found a new feature that the access of C&C domains tends to be independent, while legal web domains are accessed correlatively, which is able to efficiently tell the difference between C&C domains and legal domains. Based on this feature, the authors used a 1×3 vector to represent the relationship between an internal host and an external domain, and apply classification algorithm to detect C&C. However, these approaches are limited due to the long period of time of the detection execution, which turns out to delay the opportunity to discover APT attacks.

Other papers place emphasis on detecting common network traffic. Work [1] paid attentions to the behaviors of HTTP requests and used Genetic Programming (GP), two Decision Tree Classifier (DTC), namely CART and Random Forests, and Support Vector Machines (SVM) to train the classifier, and then was tested with a new set of data in purpose of evaluating its performance. Article [17] implemented a fractal based machine learning algorithm to detect the presence of APTs using TCP based network connections attributes and compared it with a standard machine learning algorithm. And the results have shown that fractal method provides better performance in the comparison, but it's still low in precision, which means it will raise much higher false alarm rate.

Some other detection approaches need expert analysis, which are comparatively effective methods so far. The authors in [10] designed and estimated a novel framework that is tailored to support security analysts in detecting APTs, which used multi-factor approaches where big data analytics methods are applied to internal and external information to support human specialists. And the proposed approach represented a step forward with respect to the state-of-the-art and paves the way to novel methods for early detection and mitigation of APTs. Article [9] focused on detecting the few hosts that show suspicious activities, like data exfiltration, out of thousands hosts in a large organization. In this way, security analysts are allowed to be more efficient since they could focus their capability and attention on a limited amount of hosts. And its experiments demonstrate that the proposed approach is an improvement with respect to common-ranking. And the framework is able to identify and rank suspicious hosts very likely involved in data exfiltration related to APTs. But this method need a high performance machine to analyze the big data, otherwise, it will bring down the efficiency of the detection method.

3   Our Approach

Our proposal integrated entropy theory with support vector machine, using Contagio malware database [14] aiming to find a volume of network traffic that contains attacking stream. Support vector machine, known as widely used binary classification algorithm, is suitable to be applied in this work, due to its high performance in two-class classification and the application of kernel function mapping the data samples into a higher dimensional feature space. For the purpose of building SVM classification model, we synthesized the traffic data, calculated their entropy values as the training and testing data, and then the key problem becomes a non-linear classification problem in which the network traffic can be labeled as two categories: (1) containing attack and (2) not containing attack. By this means, we can highly accurately classify the APT traffic from the normal ones. The results showed that our method can achieve a better precision and accuracy. The detailed steps will be demonstrated in the following subsections.

3.1 Feature Extraction

The feature vector used in the classification involving three metrics that can describe the volumes of traffic and the state of the network: the first one is the number of data packets transferred during a single session, the second one is the total bytes delivered in the same single session, and the last one is the duration of a complete TCP session. It is reported in [11] that APT activity generated a small number of data packets in short-term TCP window/session or small count in a large TCP window/session, whereas, normal Internet traffic presents patterns of large numbers of packets in a short period of time.

3.2 Entropy Computation

Background. Information entropy is defined as the mean amount of information generated by a random data source. It is a measurement of its average information content, or equivalently, of unpredictability of the state. In fact, the entropy could be viewed as how much useful information content the message actually contains.In general, entropy refers to disorder or uncertainty, and the definition of entropy used in information theory is directly similar to the definition mentioned in statistical thermodynamics. The concept of information entropy was brought in by Claude Shannon in his 1948 paper [15].

It is an information-theoretical measure of the degree indeterminacy of a random variable. If X is a discrete random variable defined with possible values $\{x_1, ..., x_n\}$ and probability mass function $P(X)$ as:

$$H(X) = E[I(X)] = E[-\log(P(X))], \tag{1}$$

where E is the expected value operator, and I is the information content of X, $I(X)$ is itself a random variable. The entropy can demonstratively be written as:

$$H(X) = \sum_{i=1}^{n} P(x_i)I(x_i) = -\sum_{i=1}^{n} P(x_i) \log_b P(x_i), \tag{2}$$

here b is the base of the logarithm used above 2, Euler' number e, and 10 are the most commonly used values of b, and the corresponding units of entropy are the bits for $b = 2$, *nats* for $b = e$, and *bans* for $b = 10$. In our paper, we choose $b = 2$ as the base of the logarithm to simplify the calculation.

We can tell from the formula that, the entropy of discrete random variable $H(X)$ is non-negative, because the possibility $P(x_i)$ of each possible value x_i is not negative. Particularly, we define the result of the expression $P(x_i) \log P(x_i)$ is 0 while the possibility $P(x_i) = 0$ or 1. With the basic knowledge concerning to information theory, let's consider the value of possibility P_{x_i} corresponding to the symbol x_i, we can deduce that the derivative of entropy formula (2) is,

$$H'(P_{x_i}) = -\log_2 P_{x_i} - \frac{1}{\ln 2}, \tag{3}$$

and,

$$H''(P_{x_i}) = -\frac{1}{P_{x_i} \ln 2} \left(1 \geq P_{x_i} \geq 0\right). \tag{4}$$

As we know, $H'(P_{x_i})$ is a decreasing function when P_{x_i} is between 0 and 1 for the reason that $H''(P_{x_i})$ is always less than 0. Therefore it is easy to draw a conclusion that when the possibility getting closer to 1, the derivative would be smaller. And there's a noticeable fact that the possibility of each symbol x_i will not higher than $2^{-\frac{1}{\ln 2}}$ if the width of each bin can be chosen appropriately in the possibility distribution. That means the slope will down to 0 from positive infinity when P_{x_i} ranges from 0 to $2^{-\frac{1}{\ln 2}}$. We all know that the slop describes the steepness of the line tangent to the curve at the point. So we can conclude that within a certain possibility distribution, if there is a tiny change happened in a lower possibility interval, it will significantly affect the final entropy of the system, in comparison to the situation where the same change happened in a higher span. As we can tell from Fig. 1 that if an unusual connection established which will bring a change in the lower possibility interval, it may lead to an inconspicuous difference to the whole distribution, but when it refers to the entropy there would be much more obvious deviation.

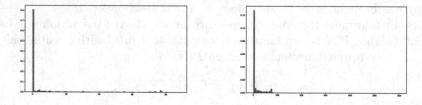

Fig. 1. Possibility distribution of duration

Entropy Computation. The key issue for computing each sample of traffic is to obtain the possibility of every flow. Thus we draw a possibility distribution histogram of each feature like Fig. 1, actually we won't display the picture in the computation procedure. Thence, we get a series of possibilities corresponding to the features we mentioned before. Later then, by using the formula (2) we obtain the entropy value of each sample file. And we labeled the record as 1 if the malicious traffic is contained in the traffic file, otherwise, we labeled it as 0.

3.3   Building SVM Model

There are lots of machine learning libraries, in this paper, the authors used Tensorflow as the machine learning engine. It is widely used in variety of fields, such as computer vision, speech recognition and language translation. Through the above steps, we prepared the data for training and testing. Using the Gaussian kernel function, we can map these training data into a higher dimensional feature space. And taking the advantage of support vector machine, we find the most optimized hyperplane between two categories. While using Tensorflow, Gaussian kernel function should be declared firstly, and then, we need to create a prediction function. After that, training data can be fed to the prediction function. We divide the data set into two parts, 1000 randomly chosen records for training and another 1000 samples from the rest of data set for testing. With generations of training, we finally obtained a well-trained SVM model that can be used to classify the two categories of network traffic data.

4   Experiment and Results

Before carrying out the experiment, we need to prepare the data set for training and testing the classification model. As mentioned before, the experiment was implemented in a few steps. Last but not least, we analyzed the results and explained the excellent performance.

4.1   Data Set

The data set applied in our experiment is synthetic packet capture files obtained from two main sources. The anomaly traffic data files were collected from Contagio malware database contributed by Parkour [14]. The non-malicious data is gathered from the central switch in our school. We are aware of that it is unrealistic to totally identical with real APT attack, so we try to mimic the mechanism of APT attack in the way establishing connections i.e. low and slow in a long period relatively. We also take reference on how to generate a combined data set from a report by researchers at Carnegie Mellon University [16], Contagio blog [14] and McAfee white paper [11], which provided information on how APT guarantee low and slow activity to prevent being discovered from firewall and intrusion detection technologies. More importantly, the anomaly traffics are designed so that they are not prominent in the normal business and are not discovered by maintaining a very stable hiding on a larger time scale. In addition, they also maintain a very slow speed.

A brief overview of Contagio malware database is shown in Table 1 We can see various kinds of sets of APTs have been included in the capture file. Moreover, since the duration of APTs is often spread over days and months, sophisticated techniques are used to detect their obfuscation. One of these techniques is the use of variation of the same APT like Gh0st RAT which has a number of variants and therefore the dataset comprises of its two variants to ascertain the viability of the proposed algorithm.

4.2   Experiment

In this section the synthetic data was used to test the performance of our method. The experiment was carried in a computer with four 3.30 GHz cores, 8 GB of

Table 1. Overview of Contagio malware database

Taidoor	Xtreme RAT
Darkcomet	Gh0st gif
IXESHE	Vidgrab
LURK	Poison Ivy
DNS watch	9002
Pingbed	Variant Letsgo
Mediana	Gh0st v2000 var
Hupigon	Scieron
Sanny	Netraveler

RAM, 3.5TB hard drive. The programming language was Python 3.6 and the machine learning engine is Tensorflow 1.4.0. Our experiment would be operated as following steps:

1. Pre-process. Before we apply the data set to machine learning algorithm, we ought to remove the meaningless noise in our experiment. Two categories of packets are going to be eliminated:
   - Elimination of the TCP packets with zero length, because they actually do nothing when server and client exchange data to each other.
   - Elimination of the re-transmitted data packets, since they may be discarded if they have already been received or be kept in case the original packets were not received at the receiver end. Essentially the total count of the data packets won't change.

   Afterwards, the data is preliminarily ready before being fed to the classification algorithm. We finally generated 1132 normal traffic files and 29 malicious traffic files containing more than 30 million sessions by using Tshark [19], a command line tool extensively utilized for the analysis of PACAP files.
2. Combining packet capture files. In this synthesis, the malicious traffic accounts for only less than 0.01% in every sample, which is much lower than paper [8]. There are about 20,000 to 30,000 sessions of each non-malicious capture file, we randomly chose one file from the APT network traffic capture files, and mixed it with the non-malicious file. In this way, we finally generated more than 1000 capture files containing APT network traffics.
3. Feature extraction. We extracted the features mentioned before from the original capture files. One of the samples after feature extraction looks like Table 2:
4. Entropy computation. As mentioned before, we calculated the entropy of each sample file, and created a csv file to store the entropy results of all traffic files which contains more than 2,000 records. Here is an overview in Table 3 of the final input file that is ready to be applied into the machine learning algorithm,
5. Building classification model. Input the csv file generated previously into the support vector machine algorithm. As referenced in [12], we build a non-linear classifier, and the classification results demonstrate outstanding performance of out method.

Table 2. Table feature extraction sample

SessionID	Packets	Bytes	Duration
1	19961	13397272	91.3377
2	18970	18469524	21.6573
3	16593	12419778	91.3352
4	16589	15878012	49.5196
5	15086	19845618	0.8771
6	14641	12934430	91.3227
7	14280	13054640	91.3370
8	12813	12173855	90.2782
9	12431	9637389	91.3103
10	10886	9380560	48.2295
...	...	...	...

Table 3. Overview of entropy computation result

SampleID	Ep_Packets	Ep_Bytes	Ep_Duration	flag
1	1.62997396765	1.13345078829	7.70188552486	0
2	1.78184835782	1.28551262413	7.58384103902	0
3	1.57602566801	1.26045873852	7.59871075104	0
4	1.5038066539	1.11866129103	7.61297338541	0
5	0.857692417697	1.08692115226	7.49951444943	0
6	1.35267371528	1.06295780204	4.06730153977	1
7	1.14233680811	0.910838676236	4.64659436002	1
8	1.13322375711	0.859611891072	1.74121380584	1
9	1.16824141086	0.924556446934	4.19911894912	1
10	1.46715712526	0.950601469679	2.39754954179	1
...	...	...	...	...

6. For the purpose of assessing performance measure, we introduce the following metrics,

$$Accuracy = \frac{TP + TN}{N}, \tag{5}$$

$$Precision = \frac{TP}{TP + FP}, \tag{6}$$

$$Recall = \frac{TP}{TP + FN}, \tag{7}$$

$$F1 = \frac{2 \times Precision \times Recall}{Precision + Recall}, \tag{8}$$

where, TP, FP, TN, FN represent the count of true positive, false positive, true negative, false negative respectively, and obviously to see that $N = TP + FP + TN + FN$.

4.3   Results and Analysis

As indicated in Table 4, our method shows illustrious performance by combining entropy theory and machine learning. F-measure, also known as balanced F score, is an indicator of how accurate the algorithm is in the binary classification model.

As Fig. 2 shown, precision, accuracy, recall and balanced F score are increasing as the iteration goes. And the trend of confusion matrix as shown in Fig. 3 also confirms the remarkable effect of support vector machine based on entropy theory.

Table 4. Classification performance

	Our method
True positive rate	94.48%
True negative rate	92.17%
False positive rate	7.83%
False negative rate	5.52%

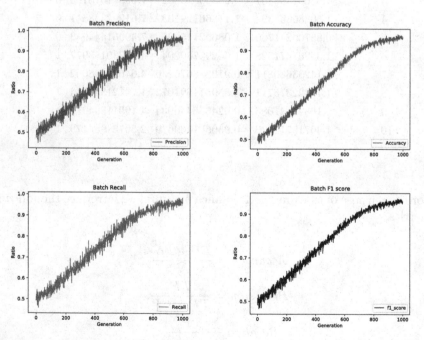

Fig. 2. Performance metrics for SVM algorithm

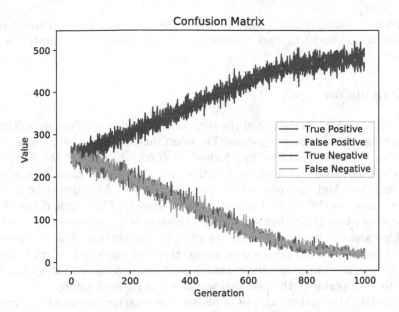

Fig. 3. Confusion matrix per generation

Table 5. Classification performance metrics

Metric	Correlation fractal dimension [17]	Our work
Precision	15.02%	92.03%
Accuracy	94.42%	93.30%
Recall	93.25%	94.47%
F1 score	29.99%	93.24%

We give a comparison to [17] with the final classification result in Table 5. Work [17] focuses on recognizing the exact anomalous network stream which leads to a low precision result, while our approach concentrates on detecting if a certain volume of network traffic contains malicious stream. We are aware of that it may be not appropriate to compare these two works in the circumstance that we have different detection strategies. But the emphasis is clear that we considered APT detection as two comparatively easier steps, and the first step could largely constrain the analysis scope, making the precision and accuracy promoted a lot.

Our approach generated new features by utilizing entropy theory and the new features can describe the distribution of a volume of network traffic in a time period. Thus we could do the classification in a better performance due to the deduction of quantity of data which will bring higher efficiency. We can see from the figures and tables that the application of entropy transformed the inconspicuous anomaly into relatively noticeable changes, which made it much easier for SVM model to find the optimized hyperplane to separate the two categories.

5   Conclusion

In our work, we have investigated the detection of Advanced Persistent Threats by taking numerous reference papers. The main innovation in this paper is introducing the concept of entropy in information theory to convert the features of traffic data into brand new characteristics and then apply them into support vector machine. And the approach we proposed divides APT detection into two steps reducing the difficulty of detecting APT attacks. Our method transforms Gigabytes or even Trillionbytes data into thousands of records of entropy values, which greatly decreases the complexity of computation. The experimental results demonstrate that our method is effective and efficient to alert if there is APT traffic exists in the specific network. And the detection strategy has been proved to be superior to the previous works we mentioned before.

Meanwhile, the further analysis of finding the attacking stream is going to be our next central issue in the future work. And we must notice that our assessment was carried with data that is simulated as APT attack traffic though most of the samples were adopted in the past APT cases, however, in practical situation, most APT attacks contains zero-day exploits, which means the consequent remains to be verified.

References

1. Barceló-Rico, F., Esparcia-Alcázar, A.I., Villalón-Huerta, A.: Semi-supervised classification system for the detection of advanced persistent threats. In: Abielmona, R., Falcon, R., Zincir-Heywood, N., Abbass, H.A. (eds.) Recent Advances in Computational Intelligence in Defense and Security. SCI, vol. 621, pp. 225–248. Springer, Cham (2016). https://doi.org/10.1007/978-3-319-26450-9_9
2. Bencsáth, B., Pék, G., Buttyán, L., Félegyházi, M.: Duqu: a stuxnet-like malware found in the wild. CrySyS Lab Tech. Rep. **14**, 1–60 (2011)
3. Brewer, R.: Advanced persistent threats: minimising the damage. Netw. Secur. **2014**(4), 5–9 (2014)
4. Chien, E., O'Murchu, L., Falliere, N.: W32.Duqu: the precursor to the next stuxnet. In: LEET (2012)
5. Devi, S.R., Yogesh, P.: A hybrid approach to counter application layer DDoS attacks. Int. J. Crypt. Inf. Secur. (IJCIS) **2**(2), 45 (2012)
6. Ferreira, D.C., Vázquez, F.I., Vormayr, G., Bachl, M., Zseby, T.: A meta-analysis approach for feature selection in network traffic research. In: Proceedings of the Reproducibility Workshop, pp. 17–20. ACM (2017)
7. Iglesias, F., Zseby, T.: Analysis of network traffic features for anomaly detection. Mach. Learn. **101**(1–3), 59–84 (2015)
8. Lu, J., Zhang, X., Junfeng, W., Lingyun, Y.: APT traffic detection based on time transform. In: 2016 International Conference on Intelligent Transportation, Big Data & Smart City (ICITBS), pp. 9–13. IEEE (2016)

9. Marchetti, M., Pierazzi, F., Colajanni, M., Guido, A.: Analysis of high volumes of network traffic for advanced persistent threat detection. Comput. Netw. **109**, 127–141 (2016)

10. Marchetti, M., Pierazzi, F., Guido, A., Colajanni, M.: Countering advanced persistent threats through security intelligence and big data analytics. In: 2016 8th International Conference on Cyber Conflict (CyCon), pp. 243–261. IEEE (2016)

11. McAfee: Combating advanced persistent threats-how to prevent, detect, and remediate APTs (2011). www.write-angle.com/wp-content/uploads/2011/04/Combating-Advanced-Persistent-Threats.pdf

12. McClure, N.: Tensorflow machine learning cookbook (2017)

13. Ng, S., Bakhtiarib, M.: Advanced persistent threat detection based on network traffic noise pattern and analysis. J. Adv. Res. Comput. Appl. **21**, 1–18 (2016)

14. Parkour, M.: Contagio malware database (2013). www.mediafire.com/folder/c2az029ch6cke/TRAFFIC_PATTERNS_COLLECTION

15. Shannon, C.E.: A mathematical theory of communication. Bell Syst. Tech. J. **27**(3), 379–423 (1948)

16. Shick, D., Horneman, A.: Investigating advanced persistent threat 1 (APT1) (2014)

17. Siddiqui, S., Khan, M.S., Ferens, K., Kinsner, W.: Detecting advanced persistent threats using fractal dimension based machine learning classification. In: Proceedings of the 2016 ACM on International Workshop on Security and Privacy Analytics, pp. 64–69. ACM (2016)

18. Wang, X., Zheng, K., Niu, X., Wu, B., Wu, C.: Detection of command and control in advanced persistent threat based on independent access. In: 2016 IEEE International Conference on Communications (ICC), pp. 1–6. IEEE (2016)

19. Wireshark: (2015). www.wireshark.org/docs/man-pages/tshark.html

MulAV: Multilevel and Explainable Detection of Android Malware with Data Fusion

Qun Li[1,2], Zhenxiang Chen[1,2(✉)], Qiben Yan[3], Shanshan Wang[1,2], Kun Ma[1,2], Yuliang Shi[4], and Lizhen Cui[4]

[1] School of Information Science and Engineering, University of Jinan, Jinan 250022, Shandong, China
[2] Shandong Provincial Key Laboratory of Network Based Intelligent Computing, Jinan 250022, Shandong, China
czx@ujn.edu.cn
[3] University of Nebraska Lincoln, Lincoln, NE 68588, USA
[4] Shandong University, Jinan 250101, Shandong, China

Abstract. With the popularization of smartphones, the number of mobile applications has grown substantially. However, many malware are emerging and thus pose a serious threat to the user's mobile phones. Malware detection has become a public concern that requires urgent resolution. In this paper, we propose MulAV, a multilevel and explainable detection method with data fusion. Our method obtain information from multiple levels (the APP source code, network traffic, and geospatial information) and combine it with machine learning method to train a model which can identify mobile malware with high accuracy and few false alarms. Experimental result shows that MulAV outperforms other anti-virus scanners and methods and achieves a detection rate of 97.8% with 0.4% false alarms. Furthermore, for the benefit of users, MulAV displays the explanation for each detection, thus revealing relevant properties of the detected malware.

Keywords: Android malware detection · Data fusion · Multilevel Result explanation

1 Introduction

Android is a popular platform for smartphones today. From December 2009 to December 2017, the number of Android applications grew from 16,000 to

Supported by the National Natural Science Foundation of China under Grants No. 61672262, No. 61573166 and No. 61572230, the Shandong Provincial Key R&D Program under Grant No. 2016GGX101001, No. 2016GGX101008, No. 2018CXGC0706 and No. 2016ZDJS01A09, the TaiShan Industrial Experts Programme of Shandong Province under Grants No. tscy20150305, CERNET Next Generation Internet Technology Innovation Project under Grant No. NGII20160404.

© Springer Nature Switzerland AG 2018
J. Vaidya and J. Li (Eds.): ICA3PP 2018, LNCS 11337, pp. 166–177, 2018.
https://doi.org/10.1007/978-3-030-05063-4_14

3,500,000 in the Google Play Store [5]. Since the first mobile malware appeared in 2004 [10], smartphones have gradually become the targets of hackers. The well-known mobile malware DroidDream had infected more than 260,000 terminals before it was purged by Google [19]. Researchers have studied amounts of methods to analyze and detect Android malware and can be roughly categorized into three approaches, namely static analysis, and dynamic analysis and network traffic based analysis.

In this study, we present MulAV, a multilevel and explainable Android malware detection method with data fusion. MulAV exploits source code information, network traffic and geospatial information to detect Android malware. Moreover, MulAV is equipped with an additional functionality which can explain each result for users.

We evaluated our approach using 18,365 benign samples and 10,560 malware samples. Result shows that MulAV outperformed related methods and popular anti-virus scanners. Furthermore, MulAV achieves an accuracy of 97.8%, precision of 98% and the false positive rate (FPR) of 0.4%. To the best of our knowledge, MulAV is the first method to detect malware using data fusion and the relationship between any two features.

The contributions of this paper are as follows:

- We discovered the relationship between codes and network traffic through URLs, and also discovered the relationship between network traffic and the geospatial information through the IP.
- We provide the relationship among the code, network traffic, and geospatial levels, then we use these relationship to fuse data and train a detection model with high accuracy and few false alarms.
- MulAV provides users and researchers with detection results and explanations, which reveals the potential reasons for the malicious behaviors. Users and researchers can get a deep understanding of malicious behaviors with the help of result explanation.

The rest of this paper is organized as follows: Related work is introduced in Sect. 2. Section 3 introduces the MulAV in detail and the evaluation is discussed in Sect. 4. Section 5 concludes the paper.

2   Related Work

Researchers have contributed significantly to the area of Android malware detection. The detection methods are introduced in the subsequent sections.

Detection Using Static Features. Static analysis is a fast and relatively inexpensive technique for detecting malware. Arp et al. [6] presented Drebin, which combines machine learning with static features extracted from the *Manifest.xml* file and source codes to obtain a detection model. However, it cannot prevent infections with mobile malware in most cases. Static analysis has been successfully used in Android malware detection, but often produces false positives. To resolve this problem, Octeau et la. [12] trigged the static analysis results with a probabilistic model. Suarez-Tangil et al. [15] proposed DroidSieve, an Android malware classifier which is based on static analysis, and is resilient to obfuscation; however, their analysis only scales to a large number of apps without addressing the performance bottlenecks.

Detection Using Dynamic Features. Dynamic analysis refers to the analytic method of observing run-time behavior by executing the application on a simulator or actual smartphone. Wong and Lie [18] presented IntelliDroid, a targeted input generator, that can be configured to produce inputs specific to a dynamic analysis tool, for the analysis of any Android application. Saracino et al. [13] detected and stopped malicious behaviors with a host-based malware detection system, that can be paired with full-system dynamic analysis tools such as TaintDroid [9], an system-wide dynamic taint tracking and analysis system.

Detection Using Network Traffic Features. In recent years, the combined use of network traffic and machine learning method has also been applied in Android malware detection. Narudin et al. [11] selected various network traffic features, and combined them with machine learning methods to detect malware. Coincidentally, Wang et al. [17] extracted features from HTTP and TCP packets and combined them with C4.5 decision tree algorithm to train models which can detect Android malware. Researchers believe that each malware can be classified into a malware family in terms of their properties. For instance, Chakraborty et al. [8] integrated supervised learning and unsupervised learning to identify Android malware families with high accuracy.

Detection Using Hybrid Features. The above methods use only one level of features to detect Android malware. Thus, they all have limitations. For instance, static analysis cannot deal with malware variants, and dynamic analysis can detect malware variants but consumes additional resources. Hence, some researchers proposed malware detection methods which use hybrid features. Tong et al. [16] proposed a method which adopts both dynamic and static analysis. Similarly, Spreitzenbarth et al. [14] combined static and dynamic analysis with machine learning method to detect malware. However, these approaches only

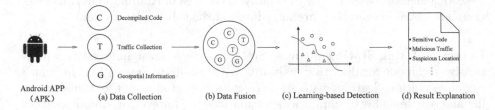

Fig. 1. Schematic depiction of the analysis steps performed by MulAV

combine the analysis methods and ignore the relationship between them. Our method focus on the relation between static and network traffic features which can be used to detect Android malware.

3 Methodology

To detect Android malware, MulAV requires a comprehensive representation of applications, which helps the identification of typical indications of malicious activities. Thus, our approach uses data fusion which extracts feature sets from multiple levels to detect malware. This process is illustrated in Fig. 1 and outlined as follows.

1. **Data Collection.** MulAV gathers the APP source codes, network traffic, and geospatial information of an Android application (Sect. 3.1).
2. **Data Fusion.** MulAV uses data fusion to fuse information extracted from codes, network traffic and geography levels (Sect. 3.2).
3. **Feature Extraction.** MulAV extracts features from disassembled code, collected network traffic, and geospatial information (Sect. 3.3).
4. **Result Explanation.** MulAV calculates the explanations and presents them to users (Sect. 3.4).

3.1 Data Collection

Data is collected from code level, network traffic level, and geospatial level.

Disassembled Code. The function of an application depends on its codes, and code analysis is a vital step in application analysis. To extract features from the codes of the inspected application, the application should be decompiled. We utilized a framework [2] to decompile the application, which can effectively obtain the source codes of the application in a short time. We integrate the decompiling function of the framework into MulAV so that we can decompile amounts of applications automatically.

Traffic Collection. We utilize an active traffic generation and collection framework [7] to collect the network traffic generated by the application in the real network environment. The framework consists of four parts, namely, foundation platform, traffic generator, traffic collector and network proxy/firewall. The foundation platform is built on the basis of the *Android Virtual Device*, and the rest of the parts are built on the foundation platform. Then, the traffic generator installs and activates applications to generate network traffic automatically. Meanwhile, the traffic collector gathers inbound and outbound network traffic with the *tcpdump* tool and then mirrors all the network traffic to a server. Finally, the proxy/firewall monitors the attack behavior and prevents attacks. With this network traffic collection framework, we can collect the traffic of Android applications (benign or malicious) in the real network environment.

Geospatial Information Collection. To help detect malicious applications accurately, we also need geospatial information. However, we cannot simply determine the geographic location information of APP on the basis of its introduction. We should identify the information according to APP's behavior. In order to obtain geospatial information, we combine the collected network traffic and geographic information database GeoIP [1] to access to relevant information of the APP. We confirm the malicious domain name in the traffic and determine the IP address of this domain name. The DNS server may return multiple IP addresses for this domain name but we should record only the IP addresses that are interacting, and this can be confirmed from the HTTP package. After obtaining the IP address of the malicious domain name, we can find and record relevant geospatial information from GeoIP.

3.2 Data Fusion

In the detection with data fusion, we need to first discover the relationship among the multiple levels of Android applications, namely, the code, network traffic, and geography levels. The use of URL and IP in mining is the most intuitive and easiest to understand; thus is the method we use.

First, we need to extract the URL in the disassembled code, using the framework [2]. In addition, we use code scanning and regular expression to discover the missing URL as a supplement.

Second, all URLs should be extracted from the network traffic and used for succeeding relationship. We can collect the domain name or URL from DNS protocol packet. However, only the primary domain name can be obtained in this manner. The primary domain name is insufficiently detailed for relationship. The complete URL extraction algorithm is shown in Algorithm 1.

Third, we obtain two URL sets, one from the disassembled code and another from the network traffic. Then we should match the complete URL in both sets. Once a match is successfully made, we record the function declaration (including function type, return value type, parameter type and number of parameter) from the disassembled code. The URL and corresponding IP (the one used to establish a communication) are also recorded, and then used to extract the feature.

Fourth, we should fuse geospatial information to detect malware. In this process, we deploy a database of geographic information, that is, GeoIP, which can return the latitude, longitude and country name through the IP. Then we combine the IP we recorded before and GeoIp, to obtain the geospatial information.

Finally, our data set leverages three levels, namely, the code, network traffic and geospatial levels. The code and network traffic levels have a corresponding relationship through the URLs, and the network traffic and geospatial levels acquire their relationship through the IP. Each piece of data is formed with three levels of features.

Algorithm 1. URLs extraction in Network traffic

Input: Network traffic in $PCAP$ format
Output: All urls in Network Traffic

1: **for** each packet in $PCAP$ file **do**
2:    **if** is DNS request packet **then**
3:        $D[c, d] \leftarrow$ Request code c of domain d;
4:    **end if**
5:    **if** is DNS response packet **then**
6:        **if** response code $\in D[c, d]$ **then**
7:            $IP[ip, d] \leftarrow$ resolved ip of domain d;
8:        **end if**
9:    **end if**
10:   **if** is $HTTP$ packet **then**
11:       **if** destination IP $\in IP[ip, d]$ **then**
12:           sub $\leftarrow$ URL path in HTTP packet;
13:           $L[url] \leftarrow d + sub$;
14:       **end if**
15:   **end if**
16: **end for**
17: **return** L;

3.3 Feature Extraction

During feature extraction, we extract features from the fused data. A script written in Java language is used to extract the features of each level from the fused data. The features are shown in Table 1.

Table 1. Feature sets and description

Id	Feature	Description
1	Invocation path	The path of a function invoke or invoked with other functions
2	Primary domain	The name of a computer or group of computers on the Internet
3	URL path	The rest level of primary domain
4	IP	Internet protocol, a protocol designed for communication between computer networks
5	Location	Latitude and longitude
6	Country	The country where the server is located

3.4 Result Explanation

Most malware detection models provide a detection result, during the detection of unknown applications but do not provide reasons. However, we apply the feature selection algorithm to calculate the contribution of each feature to the detection result; consequently, each feature is given a different weight, and then an explanation is provided.

To achieve this goal, we define six sets for each feature extracted from the code and the network traffic. Set $S1$ saves all the sensitive invocation paths extracted from the malware. All malicious primary domains are stored in set $S2$. Set $S3$ represents the URL path that belong to the malicious server. Set $S4$ refers to the IP strings that correspond to the domain names. All sensitive location and country name are falls in sets $S5$ and $S6$, respectively.

Each feature has a different contribution to the detection result. Thus every feature has a weight. We apply the *information gain algorithm* to calculate the weight of each feature, and then we obtain the vector of weight (W), which can be defined in our method as $W = <W_1, W_2, W_3, W_4, W_5, W_6>$, and the malicious score $F(X)$ can be calculated through the formula: $F(x) = <U, W>$.

Finally, we can obtain the malicious score of an unknown application with $F(x)$. Every application may have many samples, and each sample has its own malicious score. The sum of the scores of the samples belonging to the same application is the score of this application. The higher the score, the more confident we are that this application is a malware.

4   Evaluation

After presenting MulAV in detail, we evaluate its performance from the following aspects. We mainly conduct the following experiments.

1. **Detection Performance.** We conduct related experiments on the detection performance of our data set and compare its performance against those of other models, which train with other machine learning algorithms, as well as calculate the detection performance using only a single level of information. We also compare its performance with that of anti-virus scanners (Sect. 4.2).
2. **Result Explanation.** In another experiment, we analyze the explanations provided by MulAV to verify whether they relate to the actual characteristics of the malware (Sect. 4.3).

4.1   Data Set

For our experiments, we collect a data set that contains benign and malicious applications. We use a crawler script written in Python to crawl China's application market. We obtain over 20,000 applications. To ensure that the software are benign, we upload all the samples to VirusTotal [4], to remove applications deemed malicious by any of these detection engines to determine the data set as benign. We remove adware, because classifying it as benign or malicious is ambiguous. Finally, we have 18,365 benign applications to evaluate. The malicious application comprises two parts: one part has 5,560 malicious applications from Drebin and the other has 5,000 malicious applications downloaded from VirusShare [3]. Although they have been identified as malicious applications, we still send them for VirusTotal testing to ensure that all applications are indeed malicious.

4.2   Detection Performance on Malicious APP

In our first experiment, we evaluate the performance of the detection model on the Drebin and Virusshare datasets. For this experiment, we apply 10 folder-validation. The detection model and respective parameters are determined on the basis of the training set, which can distinguish the benign and malicious applications. The model is then used to detect the data in the test set. We repeat the process 10 times and average the results.

Detection Result of MulAV. The detection rate of malicious samples is not equal to the detection rate of malicious applications, because one application may have more than one correspondence with the code and the network traffic. Furthermore, the network traffic generated by the malware is a mixture of benign and malicious traffic, and the code of the malware is a mixture of benign and malicious code. Thus we determine the application as malware if it contains malicious traffic or code. In this manner, we calculate the accuracy, precision, recall rate, and FPR of our detection model, namely, 97.8%, 98.0%, 99.6%, 97.5% and 0.4%.

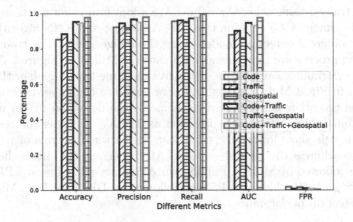

Fig. 2. Performance of different models with SVM algorithm

Comparison with Different Models. In our next experiment, we compare the detection performance of the model trained using different features. MulAV is trained with data fusion and the SVM algorithm. In our evaluation experiment, we use different combinations of features to train the detection model.

As shown in Fig. 2, MulAV, which combines data fusion with the SVM algorithm has the best performance, whereas the model trained using geospatial features has the worst performance in different metrics. This finding may indicate that geospatial features have a low contribution to malware detection. MulAV exhibits the best performance in seven different feature combinations with the same machine learning algorithm.

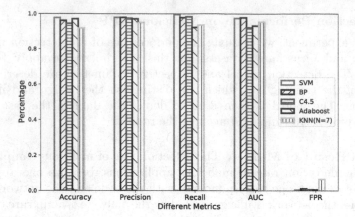

Fig. 3. Comparison with different algorithms

Comparison with Different Algorithms. In our third experiment, we compare the detection performances of the model trained using the SVM algorithm with those trained using other algorithms. We adopt four other machine learning algorithms, namely, C4.5 decision tree, BP, Adaboost and KNN algorithms. We obtain four different detection models using these algorithms. The training data and training process are the same as with those of MulAV's. Figure 3 shows the detection performance comparison of the five machine learning algorithms.

As seen in Fig. 3 MulAV is slightly more accurate than the detection models that use the other algorithms. Furthermore, the detection model using the BP algorithm achieves the same precision as MulAV, whereas the rest of the detection models show lower precisions than the latter. In terms of recall rate, MulAV also achieves the highest score. In AUC metrics, BP shows the highest score and is followed by MulAV. Finally, MulAV achieves the lowest FPR; meanwhile, KNN shows the highest FPR and followed by BP. Therefore, MulAV has the best detection performance.

Comparison with AV Scanners. Although MulAV performs better than related algorithms, it should still compete with common scanners used in practice. Hence, we also compare it against eight popular anti-virus scanners on the Drebin project and VirusShare data set. The detection results of the eight anti-virus scanners are shown in [6]. The eight popular anti-virus scanners are AntiVir, AVG, Bit-Defender, ClamAV, ESET, F-Secure, Kaspersky, and McAfee, we added an anti-virus scanner named 360, which is a common scanner in China. The comparison results of MulAV and Drebin and the nine other anti-virus scanners are shown in Table 2. The detection rates of the anti-virus scanners vary considerably. For the Drebin data set, the best scanners detect over 95% of the malware whereas three scanners (including Kaspersky and McAfee) detect less than 50% of the malicious applications. For the VirusShare dataset, the best scanners detect over 95% of the malicious samples; only a few scanners demonstrate a low detection rate, such as the 360 anti-virus scanner, which detect only 29.5% of the malware. MulAV provides the best performance with a detection rate of 97.9%.

Table 2. Detection rates of MulAV and other anti-virus scanners

	MulAV	AV1	AV2	AV3	AV4	AV5	AV6	AV7	AV8	AV9
Drebin	97.9%	96.4%	93.7%	84.7%	84.5%	78.4%	64.2%	48.5%	48.3%	95.4%
VirusShare	95.6%	95.1%	92.2%	89.3%	87.7%	72.7%	75.4%	50.4%	41.6%	29.5%

Detection in the Wild. To further prove the validity of MulAV, we use MulAV to detect apps in the wild. These apps does not exist in the data set for the training MulAV. In the wild app sets of 463 apps, 218 apps are malicious which filtered by Virustotal [4], we defined the app is malware if one of 60 anti-virus detect that app is malicious, however, only few part of them can detect malware, for example, the anti-virus *F-secure* only detect 17.4% of 218 malware, other malware detection was contributed by other anti-virus scanners. By contrast, MulAV can identify 139 out of 218 apps, the detection rate is much higher than most of the anti-virus scanners', thereby verifying the capability of MulAV to detect wild apps.

Fig. 4. The result of explanation

4.3   Result Explanation

Another advantage of MulAV is the interpretative result provided for the detection, which can help users obtain a thorough understanding of malware. We use the feature selection algorithm named information gain algorithm to calculate the contribution of each feature to the detection result, and assign a weight to each feature, namely, 0.977, 1.546, 1.351, 1.546, 0.471, 0.274 for each feature. Finally, we assign each malicious software a malicious score. The higher the score, the more confident we are that it is a malware. As seen in Fig. 4, there is an example to illustrates MulAV's result explanation.

5   Conclusion

The emergence of Android malware poses a tremendous threat to the public at an alarming rate. Thus researchers have made significant contributions to the detection of malware. As a remedy, we present MulAV, a multilevel and explainable Android malware detection method with data fusion. MulAV exploits code, network traffic, geospatial information and machine learning, thereby successfully keeping pace with malware development. Furthermore, our evaluation demonstrates the potential of MulAV. Our results show that the proposed technique outperforms related detection methods and identifies malware with only a few false alarms. Furthermore, MulAV provides two advantages for malware detection. On the one hand, this method detects malware using data fusion with a detection rate of 97.8% and a few false alarms, thus showing its precision as a detection model. On the other hand, MulAV not only identifies malicious applications, but also provides detailed explanation of the detection results.

In the future, we aim to overcome MulAV's limitations. For data fusion, we will attempy to combine the dynamic analysis method and MulAV to detect malicious applications. When running an application, all application functions come from code. Then, the dynamic behaviors are generated. Finally, communication is established with a destination server through network traffic. Thus, adding dynamic detection methods should enhance our method's detection capabilities.

References

1. Geoip. https://dev.maxmind.com/zh-hans/geoip/legacy/geolite/
2. Mobile-security-framework. https://github.com/MobSF/Mobile-Security-Framewo rk-MobSF
3. Virusshare. https://virusshare.com/
4. Virustotal. https://www.virustotal.com/
5. Number of available applications in the google play store. Technical report. https://www.statista.com/statistics/266210/number-of-available-applications-in-the-google-play-store (2017)
6. Arp, D., Spreitzenbarth, M., Hubner, M., Gascon, H., Rieck, K., Siemens, C.: DREBIN: effective and explainable detection of android malware in your pocket. In: Ndss, vol. 14, pp. 23–26 (2014)

7. Cao, D., et al.: Droidcollector: a high performance framework for high quality android traffic collection. In: 2016 IEEE Trustcom/BigDataSE/ISPA, pp. 1753–1758. IEEE (2016)

8. Chakraborty, T., Pierazzi, F., Subrahmanian, V.: EC2: ensemble clustering and classification for predicting android malware families. IEEE Trans. Dependable Secur. Comput., 1 (2017)

9. Enck, W., et al.: TaintDroid: an information-flow tracking system for realtime privacy monitoring on smartphones. ACM Trans. Comput. Syst. (TOCS) 32(2), 5 (2014)

10. Hypponen, M.: Malware goes mobile. Sci. Am. 295(5), 70–77 (2006)

11. Narudin, F.A., Feizollah, A., Anuar, N.B., Gani, A.: Evaluation of machine learning classifiers for mobile malware detection. Soft Comput. 20(1), 343–357 (2016)

12. Octeau, D., et al.: Combining static analysis with probabilistic models to enable market-scale android inter-component analysis. In: ACM SIGPLAN Notices, vol. 51, pp. 469–484. ACM (2016)

13. Saracino, A., Sgandurra, D., Dini, G., Martinelli, F.: MADAM: effective and efficient behavior-based android malware detection and prevention. IEEE Trans. Dependable Secur. Comput. 15, 83–97 (2016)

14. Spreitzenbarth, M., Schreck, T., Echtler, F., Arp, D., Hoffmann, J.: Mobile-Sandbox: combining static and dynamic analysis with machine-learning techniques. Int. J. Inf. Secur. 14(2), 141–153 (2015)

15. Suarez-Tangil, G., Dash, S.K., Ahmadi, M., Kinder, J., Giacinto, G., Cavallaro, L.: DroidSieve: fast and accurate classification of obfuscated android malware. In: Proceedings of the Seventh ACM on Conference on Data and Application Security and Privacy, pp. 309–320. ACM (2017)

16. Tong, F., Yan, Z.: A hybrid approach of mobile malware detection in android. J. Parallel Distrib. Comput. 103, 22–31 (2017)

17. Wang, S., et al.: TrafficAV: an effective and explainable detection of mobile malware behavior using network traffic. In: 2016 IEEE/ACM 24th International Symposium on Quality of Service (IWQoS), pp. 1–6. IEEE (2016)

18. Wong, M.Y., Lie, D.: IntelliDroid: a targeted input generator for the dynamic analysis of android malware. In: NDSS, vol. 16, pp. 21–24 (2016)

19. Zhang, J.: Research of Android application security. Ph.D. thesis, Beijing University of Posts and Telecommunications (2013)

Identifying Bitcoin Users Using Deep Neural Network

Wei Shao[1], Hang Li[1], Mengqi Chen[1], Chunfu Jia[1(✉)], Chunbo Liu[2], and Zhi Wang[1]

[1] College of Cyberspace Security, Nankai University, Tianjin 300350, China
cfjia@nankai.edu.cn
[2] Information Security Evaluation Center of Civil Aviation,
Civil Aviation University of China, Tianjin 300300, China

Abstract. In Bitcoin user identification, an important challenge is to accurately link Bitcoin addresses to their owners. Previously, some heuristics based on transaction structural rules or observations were found and used for Bitcoin address clustering. In this paper, we propose a deep learning method to achieve address-user mapping. We define addresses by their transactional behaviors and seek concealed patterns and characteristics of users that can help us distinguish the owner of a certain address from millions of others.

We propose a system that learns a mapping from address representations to a compact Euclidean space where distances directly correspond to a measure of address similarity. We train a deep neural network for address behavior embedding and optimization to finally obtain an address feature vector for each address. We identify owners of addresses through address verification, recognition and clustering, where the implementation relies directly on the distance between address feature vectors.

We set up an address-user pairing dataset with extensive collections and careful sanitation. We tested our method using the dataset and proved its efficiency. In contrast to heuristic-based methods, our model shows great performance in Bitcoin user identification.

Keywords: Bitcoin · Blockchain · Deep learning · Bitcoin privacy

1 Introduction

Bitcoin, introduced in 2008 by Nakamoto [23], is a cryptocurrency that entirely changes the role people play in trading scenarios, from clients outside of a transaction black box to participators of ledger decisions. Bitcoin owns most of its

C. Jia—Address all correspondence related to this paper to this author. This project is partly supported the National Natural Science Foundation of China (No. 61772291), the Science Foundation of Tianjin (No. 17JCZDJC30500), the Open Project Foundation of Information Security Evaluation Center of Civil Aviation, Civil Aviation University of China(No. CAAC-ISECCA-201702).

J. Vaidya and J. Li (Eds.): ICA3PP 2018, LNCS 11337, pp. 178–192, 2018.
https://doi.org/10.1007/978-3-030-05063-4_15

reputation to user privacy protection. There is no central authority or supervisor having overall manipulations over others, which makes Bitcoin favored by many. Unlike filling piles of identity information sheets before opening bank accounts, users of Bitcoin need only a pseudonym, a.k.a an address or a hashed public key, to participate the system. (We refer to pseudonyms, addresses and hashed public keys interchangeably for expressive convenience.) Unless willingly revealed, it is hard to uncover the true identity or any personal information of a certain pseudonym owner just from the Blockchain.

However, the pseudonym mechanism is not a guarantee for anonymity. Transaction graph analysis is a common method for Bitcoin de-anonymization. Since the transaction data are fully recorded on the Bitcoin blockchain, it is feasible to construct a bitcoin flow graph through transactions. Followed by address clustering and address-user mapping, quantitative analysis and address tracing become realistic. Yet the result of Bitcoin address clustering remains unsatisfactory over the years due to the inaccuracy of heuristics used in the process. To identify owners of millions of Bitcoin addresses with more accuracy, we intend to seek alternative methods.

Deep learning allows computational models to learn the representation of data with high-level abstraction and to discover information hidden in large datasets [16]. In our scenario, we define an address by the transactions it made and we intend to unearth the relation between addresses and their owner. Different from conventional supervised learnings but similar to face recognition, our target is to learn a discriminative feature for each address, which can be regarded as an embedding of address behaviors in the Bitcoin system. Once we obtain the embeddings, the three-progressive targets of address verification, recognition and clustering become simple distance calculation. In face recognition, a well-designed loss function, such as Center Loss [32], Range Loss [34], AM-Softmax [31], helps the network to embed each face image into a continuous, linear-separable feature space and enhances its discriminative power. The similarity between our task and face recognition inspires us to follow the same pattern for our system. In this paper, we propose a pipeline for Bitcoin address behavior featuring. It converts raw data from the blockchain to primary address vectors that our network could process. Then we find the optimal loss function and use it to guide our training process. Moreover, to obtain optimal results from a deep learning model, we need abundant data samples [9] and well-designed training strategies, both of which can be challenging to acquire in Bitcoin user identification. The amount of ground truth is limited due to the reluctance of users to reveal their addresses. Unlike using abundant and well-examined datasets for training and testing for other typical deep learning problems, we set up a novel address-user dataset from all possible sources.

In summary, we propose a unified system for Bitcoin address identification using a deep learning method. Our contributions are:

- A user-address dataset that is collected and sanitized that conforms with the address distribution against users in reality.

- A pipeline for Bitcoin address featuring that converts raw address features into a primary address vector to be learned by deep learning models.
- A delicately-designed deep learning system that realizes Bitcoin user identification progressively by address verification, recognition and clustering.
- We test the model with extensive experiments and compare our results with address clustering using heuristics.

The paper is organized as follows. In Sect. 2, we introduce Bitcoin terminologies as background. In Sect. 3, heuristics used for transaction graph analysis are introduced as related work. We describe our designs for the address featuring pipeline and the model in Sect. 4. Section 5 presents the experiments we conduct to verify the performance of our deep learning model and the results. Finally, in Sect. 6, we conclude the paper.

2   Bitcoin Terminologies

The data recorded on the Bitcoin blockchain provide sources for our featuring. Therefore we give an overall review of the Bitcoin system and define Bitcoin terminologies.

- Bitcoin Users. Bitcoin users indicate real-world individuals or organizations that possess identities in reality as well as numerous addresses in the Bitcoin system. The Bitcoin system runs on a peer-to-peer network that has no mechanism for node registration or management. Any user with a pair of ECDSA keys can join the network and involve in transactions.
- Bitcoin Addresses. The identity of a transaction participator is represented by his hashed ECDSA public keys, knowing as 'addresses'. In this paper, when we refer to an 'address', we regard it as an account name of a user or a label of a sample but never its assigned hash value.
  It is certain for all addresses that knowing a corresponding secret key to a hashed public key indicates the ownership of the address and the unredeemed coins in it. The addresses are meant to assure user anonymity since they contain no links to their owner. However, specified in [23], users' pseudonyms provide full-anonymity for users on two conditions. First, users must always use a new pseudonym for every transaction they send; second, users must never voluntarily reveal links of their real-world identity and pseudonyms. But in reality, few people have followed the rules, giving chances for Bitcoin transaction analysts to conduct transaction graph analysis and eventually de-anonymize some Bitcoin users.
- Bitcoin Transactions. A verified transaction on the longest chain is the record that proves the existence and legitimacy of a coin transfer between addresses. When users make a transaction, they redeem unspent coins from previous transactions and spend them by distributing coins to output addresses. The transaction then will be broadcast to the whole network and be recorded on the blockchain by a specific miner if it's valid. A standard transaction contains the information shown in Fig. 1. The transactions that an address

Attribute		Interpretation
Version No.		The version of the Bitcoin system in use.
Lock Time		The transaction verification time or the block height.
Input count m		The number of inputs, $m \geq 1$.
Input (m)	Hash (PrevTx)	A hash points to unspent transaction outputs.
	ScriptSig	The script indicating the rightfulness of the redemption.
Output count n		The number of outputs, $n \geq 1$.
Out-puts (n)	value	The value to spend.
	ScriptPubkey	The script indicating the condition for coin redemption.

Fig. 1. The content of bitcoin transactions. We list the attributes and their interpretation.

participates and their attributes partially define the address in our address abstraction.

- The Blockchain. Once transactions are validated, a certain miner packs them in a block and appends it to the end of the longest hash-linked blockchain. In this paper, we discuss little about the complicated process of transaction verification and block mining but concern more about the actual information recorded on the Blockchain. Thanks to online and offline Bitcoin parsing tools such as [1] and [2], we can obtain interpreted blocks and transactions from raw hashes with ease.

3   Related Work

Graph analysis is a common way for Bitcoin address identification. Transaction graphs are often constructed from raw transaction data to indicate the flow of bitcoins through all transactions. Then, several empirical heuristics are used to cluster addresses that belong to the same user and a user graph can be obtained, where a vertex represents a user and a directed edge represents a transaction between them. Finally, with vertex-user labelings, we are able to de-anonymize some addresses and uncover their whole Bitcoin history.

In the process, address clustering is the most significant part, as the more effective the algorithms are, the more addresses will be clustered and the less false linking there will be between them. There are some address clustering heuristics that have been researched and evaluated in previous work.

- The Multi-input Heuristic. The most acknowledged and used heuristic is the multi-input heuristic, which was first mentioned in [23] by Nakamoto as a nature of multi-input transactions. The heuristic has then been studied and widely used in user graph construction and Bitcoin transaction pattern analysis [5,10,11,14,18,20,25–27,30]. The heuristic assumes that a transaction can only be initiated by one user no matter how many inputs are included. Therefore, the input addresses of a transaction should all belong to the sender who starts the transaction. With this transitive heuristic, we can merge inputs of all transactions and form clusters for input addresses that have ever appeared in the same transaction. We can identify the owner of an address cluster by mapping the owner to any address in it.

- The Shadow/Change Address Heuristic. Shadow address heuristic was first mentioned in [5] and was refined as Change address in [20]. In Bitcoin transactions, users usually have an output for changes and the change address should belong to the one sending the transaction. The heuristic is less robust than the multi-input heuristic since the recognition of shadow addresses is based on conservative observation instead of concrete fact. The two are often used together as address clustering rules [5,20,24,30].
- Other Heuristics. In [6,15], instead of analyzing the Blockchain and transactions, the authors try to breach Bitcoin user privacy via the network. They use network-layered methodologies to trace addresses to the IP address of their transaction originator. Other heuristics derived from wallet behaviors and typical transaction patterns have also been discussed but are less acknowledged or proved.

We should notice that the mentioned heuristics provide barely satisfactory clustering in experiments. In [24], the mean wallet recall of the first two heuristics for wallet-address mapping is approximately 0.693, while the result raises no more than 1% if combined with other heuristics. In [6], experiments show that heuristics for IP-address mapping links 59.9% addresses to their owner's IP in the best case, let along the linking failure if VPNs or Mixing services [28] are used.

4   Methods

In this section, we propose the detailed design of our deep learning model, including the extraction of features for addresses.

4.1   Address Featuring

We categorize address features into **address statistical features**, including the average time interval of an address be used, the most frequent transaction type an address involved in etc., and **address transaction history features** which are transaction behaviors of an address extracted both automatically and manually. We require not only exact statistics for address statistical features but also carefully-designed feature engineering for address transaction history features.

The transaction history of an address allows us to describe it by its transactional behaviors, as input or output or even both. It is an important feature of an address since it directly shows the patterns of an owner when interacting with the Bitcoin system. For a simple instance, if an address has never paid any fees other than Bitcoin enforcement in its whole transaction history, it is highly unlikely that it belongs to a user that constantly pay extra transaction fees out of self-willingness to speed up the transaction confirmation.

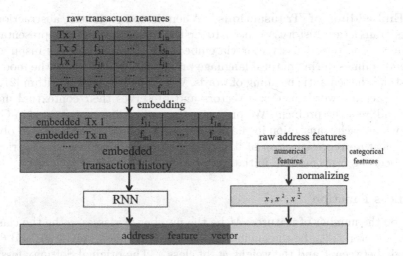

Fig. 2. The pipeline for address featuring. We first embed address transaction features and concatenate it with the corresponding manually extracted features. Then we use a Gated Recurrent Unit RNN to obtain a fixed-length vector. The concatenation of the transaction history vector and the address feature vector is our primary representation of an address.

Figure 2 shows our featuring pipeline for address transaction history features. Raw transaction features cover the entire transaction history of an address. Inspired by the Youtube recommendation learning model [8], in our model, we first use a one-hot embedding to embed transaction history and get a dense vector representation (a pink unit). Then we append the corresponding manually-extracted features of the transaction to its embedding, such as the time of the transaction, the input/output amount, the fee etc. (a navy unit). Therefore we obtain the transaction history feature represented as a variable-length sequence where each element is a concatenation of an embedded transaction and its manually-extracted features. The length of the sequence is the size of the transaction history. We observe that the transaction history is a time-sequenced feature. Recurrent Neural Networks (RNNs), first introduced in the 80s and further researched in [7,12], are specialized in exhibiting dynamic behaviors for a time sequence. We therefore use an RNN to extract a fixed-length transaction history representation.

As for address statistical features that have continuous values, we normalize the values and also provides their square and square root to accelerate our model's convergence since deep learning networks are sensible to the scaling and distribution of their inputs.

Finally, the embedded and trained transaction history feature vector, along with normalized address statistical features concatenate into a primary feature vector of an address. It is a 173-dimension vector that is ready to be fed into our feed-forward neural network.

The Embedding of Transactions. When it comes to the abstraction of address transaction history, we need to first convert the sparse representation of a transaction to a dense vector via embedding. The process was inspired by word embeddings during natural language processing, which allows the model to understand the semantic meaning of words. We use Word2Vec algorithm [21,22], which represents words as dense vectors and preserves their contextual meanings, to address the problem. We pre-train the embedding matrix in skip-Gram mode, where each transaction in the training set is treated as a word, and obtain a dense feature representation of it. With the pre-training, we have extricated our embedding from random initiation.

4.2   Loss Function

Let N be the number of features, M be the number of classes, y_i be the class of a feature vector f, θ_{y_i} be the angle between f and its class weight w_i, and θ_j be the angle between f and the weight w_j of class j. The original Softmax loss can be formulated as (1) after normalization:

$$L_s = -\frac{1}{N} \sum_{i=1}^{N} \log \frac{e^{\cos(\theta_{y_i})}}{\sum_{j=1}^{M} e^{\cos(\theta_j)}} \tag{1}$$

Softmax loss is widely used in classification tasks because of its efficiency and succinctness. However, since our task is not confined to mere classification but to distinguish the potential and unknown address owners that have never appeared in our training set, simply using Softmax to train our network is barely a good solution. In the case of binary-class ($M = 2$), Softmax defines the decision boundary as $\theta_1 = \theta_2$ as Fig. 3(a) because it only requires $\cos(\theta_{y_i}) > \cos(\theta_j)$ for every other class j. However, it causes a problem as samples near the decision boundary may have smaller angels between samples in another class. The problem hinders our results as samples from different classes may be identified as similar by our model.

Additive Margin Softmax. Since the problem is caused by different classes sharing the same decision boundary, it is reasonable to adjust the decision boundary of different classes accordingly. In [31], Wang et al. replace $\cos(\theta_{y_i})$ with $\cos(\theta_{y_i}) - m$ in (2), where m is the cosine margin, and scale the cosine values using a hyper-parameter s to facilitate the network optimization. The additive margin Softmax loss (AM-Softmax) can be formulated as

$$L_{AMS} = -\frac{1}{N} \sum_{i=1}^{N} \log \frac{e^{s \cdot (\cos(\theta_{y_i}) - m)}}{e^{s \cdot (\cos(\theta_{y_i}) - m)} + \sum_{j=1, j \neq y_i}^{M} e^{s \cdot \cos(\theta_j)}} \tag{2}$$

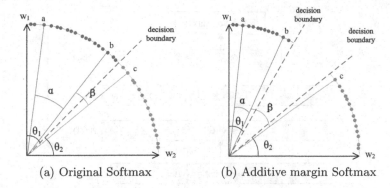

(a) Original Softmax   (b) Additive margin Softmax

Fig. 3. Comparison between original Softmax and additive margin Softmax. α is the angle of sample a and b belonging to same class, and β is the angle of b and c belonging to two different classes. In (a), since β is smaller than α, our model will mistakenly predict b and c to be similar. While in (b), the problem is addressed as α is smaller than β.

The additive margin Softmax loss modifies the decision boundary of different class. L_{AMS} requires $\cos(\theta_{y_i}) - m > \cos(\theta_j)$ for a sample to be classified in class y_i. m forces the network to learn more compact features within a class therefore enhance its discriminative power. In Fig. 3(b), samples near the decision boundary now are distant from samples in different classes. Notice that even the above analysis is built on a binary-class case, it is trivial to generalize this analysis to multi-class cases. Therefore, in our model where similarity decisions are crucial, we use additive margin Softmax.

4.3 The Model Architecture

The purpose of our model is to learn a discriminative representation of an address to a compact Euclidean space where distances directly correspond to a measure of address similarity. It takes the input of our pre-processed primary address feature vectors as input and outputs 120-D feature vectors that can be used for address owner identification.

We use a 3-layered fully-connected architecture called the *MainNet*. Shown in Fig. 4, in the *MainNet* we apply a leakyReLU activation function to the first two layers and a linear one to the third. Then an AM-Softmax is applied on the output feature vectors for loss calculation and parameter adjustment.

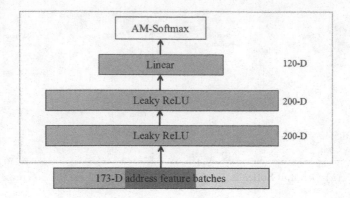

Fig. 4. The architecture of our model. It is a 3-layered model that is trained to learn address feature vectors for optimized abstraction.

5   Experiments and Results

We propose our experiment scheme in this section and evaluate our model with multiple evaluations.

5.1   The Dataset

Unlike image classification or face recognition where datasets are abundant [13, 33], the proper dataset of Bitcoin addresses labeled with user identify information is a lot harder to find. We must build a dataset from scratch.

Data Collection. We only target users who own at least three addresses. Crawling information down from popular Bitcoin forums or social networks is the way we collect data. Blockchain.info [3] has been collecting addresses with exposed owner information for years and is considered as one of our reliable sources. Moreover, we have referred to a helpful self-organized website Bitcoin-WhosWho.com [4], whose owners are dedicated to track Bitcoin addresses and prevent Bitcoin scams.

Manual sanitation is conducted for collected samples. Firstly, we remove samples with a non-owner label. For example, we remove address 1RedzZR6wRwczYjhv2s6PCn6Qq2gEroJt from Bitcoin-WhosWho.com, which is labeled 'Bitcoin_Roulette.com' just because it has appeared on the website but not because 'Bitcoin_Roulette' owns it. We also merge samples with labels that are different in literal but same in semantics. For example, address 1EuMa4dhfCK8ikgQ4emB7geSBgWK2cEdBG and address 13UcxXvmrW8WAsEQMmUw1R8eQAwUjuYETv are labeled 'Mt Gox' and 'MtGox from Reddit' respectively by Blockchain.info while they actually both belong to MtGox. We carefully performed semantic checkings to prevent high false negative rate in later experiments. After careful sanitation, finally we fix our dataset to the size of 8986 sample addresses and 66 user labels in total, which are corresponded to 350196 transactions that took place from Jan. 2009 to Sept. 2016.

Data Distribution. The distribution of our dataset is shown in Fig. 5. Over 60% of addresses are owned by a few users and over 90% of users own less than 10 addresses. It is consistent with the real Bitcoin address distribution according to both common knowledge and research results [27].

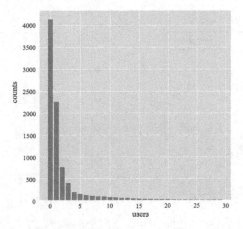

Fig. 5. Full distribution of addresses against users

The Open-Set Mode. It is worth stressing that we train our model in open-set protocol [17] because it has more resemblance to real practice. It enforces our model to blind predictions since the training set does not intersect with the test set at all. We separate the dataset to ensure that both testing samples and their labels never appear in the training set. The model learns only the rules to discriminatively represent addresses but knows no label of any address to be tested.

As a result, we have 6235 addresses **(70% of total)** with 49 users in the training set, while the test set contains the rest.

5.2   Result and Evaluation

We implement the system and experiment it with our dataset for Bitcoin user identification. The results for address verification, recognition and clustering are evaluated in this section.

Verification. Given two addresses of unknown users, the system determines whether they belong to the same owner by address verification.

To test our system, we generate 3582625 address pairs with 25666383 negative pairs and 1216242 positive pairs from the test set. The model outputs the abstracted 120-D address feature vectors of these address pairs and calculates their cosine similarity. Figure 6(a) shows the distribution of address pairs where the horizontal axis denotes the cosine similarity of feature vectors for every address pair. The pink columns represent pairs belonging to different users and the blue columns represent pairs belonging to the same. There is a clear division line around $p = 0.55$. It means that when we set the similarity threshold as p, our model can perform verification of two addresses in great effectiveness.

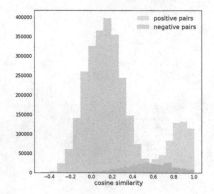

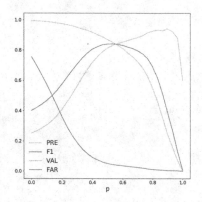

(a) The distribution of address pairs

(b) The evaluation curves under different similarity threshold

Fig. 6. (a) The distribution of address pairs where the pink columns represent pairs belonging to different users and the blue columns represent pairs belonging to the same. (b) The graph of VAL, PRE, F_1 and FAR for p in [0, 1]. (Color figure online)

To be specific about the threshold and obtain the optimum result, we use *validation rate* VAL(p), *false accept rate* FAR(p), *precision* PRE(p) and $F_1(p)$ as our result evaluations [29]. They are defined as

$$\text{VAL}(p) = \frac{|\text{TA}(p)|}{|P_{same}|}, \quad \text{FAR}(p) = \frac{|\text{FA}(p)|}{|P_{diff}|}, \quad \text{PRE}(p) = \frac{|\text{TA}(p)|}{|T_{same}|},$$

$$F_1(p) = \frac{2 * \text{VAL}(p) * \text{PRE}(p)}{\text{VAL}(p) + \text{PRE}(p)}$$

where $|P_{same}|$ denotes all pairs (i, j) of the same user and $|P_{diff}|$ denotes all pairs of different users. $|T_{same}|$ denotes all pairs (i, j) the model predicted to be owned by the same user.

We define *true accepts* TA(p) and *false accepts* FA(p) as

$$\text{TA}(p) = \{(i, j) \in P_{same}, with\ cosine(x_i, x_j) \leq p\},$$

$$\text{FA}(p) = \{(i,j) \in P_{diff}, with\ cosine(x_i, x_j) \le p\},$$

where $cosine(x_i, x_j)$ is the cosine similarity between x_i and x_j while p is the similarity threshold.

We expect higher VAL(p), PRE(p), $F_1(p)$ with lower FAR(p) for better verification performance. In Fig. 6(b), we fit the curve of the four with p in $[0, 1]$. We prioritize $F_1(p)$ and FAR(p) and find the best performance with similarity threshold at 0.50 in Table 1.

Table 1. The optimal result of address verification when $p = 0.50$

Criteria	Value
VAL(0.50)	0.869
PRE(0.50)	0.813
F_1(0.50)	0.840
FAR(0.50)	0.051

Table 2. The result of K-NN address recognition when k = 1, 2, 3, ...

k	ACC	REC	PRE	F1
1	0.911	0.772	0.855	0.787
2	0.905	0.721	0.842	0.753
3	0.877	0.603	0.656	0.611
...	...	...	...	...

Recognition. In recognition task, we need to recognize an unknown address from a given test gallery which contains its true label. With address feature vectors, we regard address recognition as a simple k Nearest Neighbors (k-NN) classification.

The evaluations of recognition are *accuracy* ACC, *recall* REC, *precision* PRE and F_1 in the usual way of multi-class classification. As shown in Table 2, taking the top-k similar addresses into account, we found the obvious best result when k = 1. Our training model behaves amazingly in recognizing address owners from the test gallery as it can effectively cage the correct address owner with ACC of 0.911.

Clustering. For address clustering, the system clusters addresses of the same labels. For better demonstration, we first applied PCA to the 120-D feature vectors and preserve 95% of the vector component. Then we applied t-SNE to reduce the vector dimension to 3 and obtained Fig. 7. We selected five representative user labels that vary in sample amounts. In Fig. 7, the addresses of the same user (denoted by dots in the same color) form clusters with short distances and clear boundaries, despite the number of samples a label owns. We use *recall* REC = 0.836, *precision* PRE = 0.766 for clustering as the evaluations [19].

Discussion. Bitcoin addresses are clustered according to heuristics in previous research, while our system predicts clusters by its learned rules. We discuss the difference between our method and the heuristics in this section.

In our model, an address is represented by its full attributes. The address feature vector reflects not only its relation with transactions but also its behavior

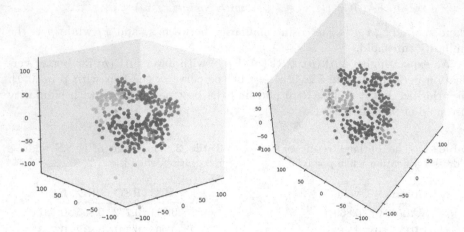

Fig. 7. Cluster result shown in different angles. The dots of the same color denote addresses of the same owner. The color purple, blue and light green represent users who own 184, 100, and 60 addresses respectively, while the orange and the dark green represent ones owning 8 and 4 addresses. (Color figure online)

patterns such as timing, balance and network information, which are predictable to our model to some extend. The Heuristics, on the other hand, discard too much information and some even are from mere observations. We often need to combine many heuristics and implement them very conservatively to avoid false linkings.

In addition, our model learns address features with transaction information that is fewer but more comprehensive. The training requires only thousands of samples and the analysis requires only the transactions an address involved. But the heuristics must traverse all transactions in a time period, which usually contains millions of transactions, and only applies under their conditions. For example, the multi-input heuristic only applies to input addresses, which may accounts for a small percentage of all the addresses the algorithm traverses.

However, both our system and the multi-input heuristic are affected by the size and distribution of the dataset. Neither has good performance when the transaction history is insufficient.

6   Conclusion

We propose a unified system using deep learning that is capable of identifying Bitcoin address owners with eligible results. We have gone through large amounts of test experiments so that the architecture, the feature engineering, the loss function and the parameters lead to optimum results.

The featuring of addresses is the foundation for the good performance. With the proposed Bitcoin address feature engineering pipeline, the deep learning model is able to learn massive information from the primary address features and finally outputs discriminative feature vectors for all addresses. After the test experiments of address verification, recognition and clustering on our test dataset, we conclude that the embedded address behaviors indeed conceal information of its owner.

For future work, we will keep on expanding our address-user dataset and unearth more information from the Bitcoin network by deep learning. We will also dig deep in mechanisms that can withstand the deep learning model for Bitcoin address analysis.

References

1. Bitcoin-abe. https://github.com/bitcoin-abe/bitcoin-abe
2. Bitcoin blockchain info. https://blockchain.info
3. Bitcoin blockchain info tags. https://blockchain.info/tags
4. Bitcoin whos who. https://bitcoinwhoswho.com/
5. Androulaki, E., Karame, G.O., Roeschlin, M., Scherer, T., Capkun, S.: Evaluating user privacy in bitcoin. In: Sadeghi, A.-R. (ed.) FC 2013. LNCS, vol. 7859, pp. 34–51. Springer, Heidelberg (2013). https://doi.org/10.1007/978-3-642-39884-1_4
6. Biryukov, A., Khovratovich, D., Pustogarov, I.: Deanonymisation of clients in bitcoin P2P network. In: Proceedings of the 2014 ACM SIGSAC Conference on Computer and Communications Security, pp. 15–29. ACM (2014)
7. Cho, K., et al.: Learning phrase representations using RNN encoder-decoder for statistical machine translation. ArXiv Preprint ArXiv:1406.1078 (2014)
8. Covington, P., Adams, J., Sargin, E.: Deep neural networks for YouTube recommendations. In: Proceedings of the 10th ACM Conference on Recommender Systems, pp. 191–198. ACM (2016)
9. Deng, J., Dong, W., Socher, R., Li, L.J., Li, K., Fei-Fei, L.: ImageNet: a large-scale hierarchical image database. In: Proceedings of the IEEE Conference on Computer Vision and Pattern Recognition, pp. 248–255. IEEE (2009)
10. Fleder, M., Kester, M.S., Pillai, S.: Bitcoin transaction graph analysis. ArXiv Preprint ArXiv:1502.01657 (2015)
11. Harrigan, M., Fretter, C.: The unreasonable effectiveness of address clustering. In: International Conference on Ubiquitous Intelligence & Computing, Advanced and Trusted Computing, Scalable Computing and Communications, Cloud and Big Data Computing, Internet of People, and Smart World Congress (UIC/ATC/ScalCom/CBDCom/IoP/SmartWorld), pp. 368–373. IEEE (2016)
12. Hochreiter, S., Schmidhuber, J.: Long short-term memory. Neural Comput. 9(8), 1735–1780 (1997)
13. Huang, G.B., Ramesh, M., Berg, T., Learned-Miller, E.: Labeled faces in the wild: a database for studying face recognition in unconstrained environments. Technical Report 07-49, University of Massachusetts, Amherst (2007)
14. Kondor, D., Pósfai, M., Csabai, I., Vattay, G.: Do the rich get richer? an empirical analysis of the bitcoin transaction network. PloS One 9(2), e86197 (2014)
15. Koshy, P., Koshy, D., McDaniel, P.: An analysis of anonymity in bitcoin using P2P network traffic. In: Christin, N., Safavi-Naini, R. (eds.) FC 2014. LNCS, vol. 8437, pp. 469–485. Springer, Heidelberg (2014). https://doi.org/10.1007/978-3-662-45472-5_30
16. LeCun, Y., Bengio, Y., Hinton, G.: Deep learning. Nature 521(7553), 436 (2015)

17. Liu, W., Wen, Y., Yu, Z., Li, M., Raj, B., Song, L.: SphereFace: deep hypersphere embedding for face recognition. In: Proceedings of the IEEE Conference on Computer Vision and Pattern Recognition, vol. 1. IEEE (2017)
18. Maesa, D.D.F., Marino, A., Ricci, L.: Data-driven analysis of bitcoin properties: exploiting the users graph. Int. J. Data Sci. Anal., pp. 1–18 (2017)
19. Manning, C.D., Raghavan, P., Schtze, H.: An Introduction to Information Retrieval. Cambridge University Press, Cambridge (2008)
20. Meiklejohn, S., et al.: A fistful of bitcoins: characterizing payments among men with no names. In: Proceedings of the 2013 Conference on Internet Measurement Conference, pp. 127–140. ACM (2013)
21. Mikolov, T., Grave, E., Bojanowski, P., Puhrsch, C., Joulin, A.: Advances in pre-training distributed word representations. ArXiv Preprint ArXiv:1712.09405 (2017)
22. Mikolov, T., Karafiát, M., Burget, L., Černockỳ, J., Khudanpur, S.: Recurrent neural network based language model. In: Eleventh Annual Conference of the International Speech Communication Association (2010)
23. Nakamoto, S.: Bitcoin: a peer-to-peer electronic cash system. Consulted (2008)
24. Nick, J.D.: Data-driven de-anonymization in bitcoin. Master's thesis, ETH-Zürich (2015)
25. Ober, M., Katzenbeisser, S., Hamacher, K.: Structure and anonymity of the bitcoin transaction graph. Future Internet 5(2), 237–250 (2013)
26. Reid, F., Harrigan, M.: An analysis of anonymity in the bitcoin system. In: Altshuler, Y., Elovici, Y., Cremers, A., Aharony, N., Pentland, A. (eds.) Security and privacy in social networks, pp. 197–223. Springer, New York (2013). https://doi.org/10.1007/978-1-4614-4139-7_10
27. Ron, D., Shamir, A.: Quantitative analysis of the full bitcoin transaction graph. In: Sadeghi, A.-R. (ed.) FC 2013. LNCS, vol. 7859, pp. 6–24. Springer, Heidelberg (2013). https://doi.org/10.1007/978-3-642-39884-1_2
28. Ruffing, T., Moreno-Sanchez, P., Kate, A.: CoinShuffle: practical decentralized coin mixing for bitcoin. In: Kutyłowski, M., Vaidya, J. (eds.) ESORICS 2014. LNCS, vol. 8713, pp. 345–364. Springer, Cham (2014). https://doi.org/10.1007/978-3-319-11212-1_20
29. Schroff, F., Kalenichenko, D., Philbin, J.: FaceNet: a unified embedding for face recognition and clustering. In: Proceedings of the IEEE Conference on Computer Vision and Pattern Recognition, pp. 815–823. IEEE (2015)
30. Spagnuolo, M., Maggi, F., Zanero, S.: BitIodine: extracting intelligence from the bitcoin network. In: Christin, N., Safavi-Naini, R. (eds.) FC 2014. LNCS, vol. 8437, pp. 457–468. Springer, Heidelberg (2014). https://doi.org/10.1007/978-3-662-45472-5_29
31. Wang, F., Liu, W., Liu, H., Cheng, J.: Additive margin softmax for face verification. ArXiv Preprint ArXiv:1801.05599 (2018)
32. Wen, Y., Zhang, K., Li, Z., Qiao, Y.: A discriminative feature learning approach for deep face recognition. In: Leibe, B., Matas, J., Sebe, N., Welling, M. (eds.) ECCV 2016. LNCS, vol. 9911, pp. 499–515. Springer, Cham (2016). https://doi.org/10.1007/978-3-319-46478-7_31
33. Wolf, L., Hassner, T., Maoz, I.: Face recognition in unconstrained videos with matched background similarity. In: Proceedings of the IEEE Conference on Computer Vision and Pattern Recognition, pp. 529–534. IEEE (2011)
34. Zhang, X., Fang, Z., Wen, Y., Li, Z., Qiao, Y.: Range loss for deep face recognition with long-tailed training data. In: Proceedings of the IEEE Conference on Computer Vision and Pattern Recognition, pp. 5409–5418. IEEE (2017)

A Practical Privacy-Preserving Face Authentication Scheme with Revocability and Reusability

Jing Lei[1], Qingqi Pei[1], Xuefeng Liu[2(✉)], and Wenhai Sun[3]

[1] State Key Lab of Integrated Service Networks,
School of Telecommunications Engineering, Xidian University,
Xi'an, Shaanxi, China
[2] School of Cyber Engineering, Xidian University, Xi'an, Shaanxi, China
liuxf@mail.xidian.edu.cn
[3] Department of Computer and Information Technology, Purdue University,
West Lafayette, IN 47906, USA

Abstract. Revocability and reusability are important properties in an authentication scheme in reality. The former requires that the user credential stored in the authentication server be easily replaced if it is compromised while the latter allows the credentials of the same user to appear independent in cross-domain applications. However, the invariable biometrics features in the face authentication poses a great challenge to accomplishing these two properties. Existing solutions either sacrifice the accuracy of the authentication result or rely on a trusted third party. In this paper, we propose a novel privacy preserving face authentication scheme without the assistance of an additional server, which achieves both revocability and reusability as well as the same accuracy level of the plaintext face recognition that uses Euclidean distance measure. Moreover, we rigorously analyze the security of our scheme using the simulation technique and conduct the experiment on a real-world dataset to demonstrate its efficiency. We report that a successful user authentication costs less than a second on a smartphone with common specs.

Keywords: Face authentication · Revocability · Reusability

1 Introduction

Face authentication is gaining momentum in many commercial mobile applications as a convenient and user-friendly access control method. For example, users are able to login into the apps and authenticate the purchases with Face ID [3]. Recently, digital payment platform Alipay of Ant financial launches the *smile to pay* service [2], which only requires a customer to smile at the camera to make the payment for both offline and online purchases. In contrast to the traditional password-based authentication, users are released from the tedious memorization [26], and instead, able to access their accounts by simply taking

© Springer Nature Switzerland AG 2018
J. Vaidya and J. Li (Eds.): ICA3PP 2018, LNCS 11337, pp. 193–203, 2018.
https://doi.org/10.1007/978-3-030-05063-4_16

a *selfie*. However, user passwords, crypto-keys or PINs are relatively easy to be revoked and replaced when the system is compromised. The user is also encouraged and able to adopt distinct passwords or tokens for different applications to break the identity linkability and avoid extra revocation cost when a breach occurs in one application. On the other hand, a biometric-based authentication, such as the studied face authentication in this work, inherently does not have the above merits, which in turn becomes a significant barrier for their further widespread deployment in reality [14,20,25]. Specifically,

- *for one particular application, facial features cannot be directly revoked or canceled due to its uniqueness.* Unlike key/password-based approaches, a user's face feature is permanently associated with him/her and usually difficult to be modified [12,19];
- *for different applications, the bio-features of a user's face cannot achieve cross-application variance.* The invariability of user biometrics inevitably leads to the cross-matching or collision attack. In order to mitigate this threat, face authentication is expected to be reusable [6], i.e., it remains secure even when a user utilizes the same or correlated face feature multiple times in different applications.

The core technique used in the face authentication is the template matching [5], where the correlation between the user query and enrolled features (or template) can be efficiently verified by an authentication server. Previous work that focuses on biometric-based authentication and supports reusability and revocability can be generally divided into two categories based on the adopted specific techniques: (1) data transformation [15,28] and (2) fuzzy extractor [4,6-8,16,24].

Unfortunately, the randomness introduced by data transformation for the privacy preservation inevitably cause the result accuracy degradation, which adversely impacts the effectiveness and usability of the face authentication in the sense that an illegal user may have a good chance to be misidentified as an authorized user. Fuzzy extractor is also not suitable for face authentication because its distance metric used to measure the similarity of feature vectors only supports hamming distance, edit distance, and their variants, while facial features are usually high-dimensional, and the commonly used distance metrics include Euclidean distance, cosine distance and so on.

Other schemes of privacy-preserving face recognition based on two-party computation [9,21,28] target at a different problem from ours. They consider a two-party computation model, where the server owns a database of face images and a user wants to know whether the queried face image is in the database. The security objective here is to hide two parties' input from each other. In addition, we adopt an entirely different design strategy and do not rely on a trusted third party [10], because we believe that such assumption is quite strong and may not be fulfilled easily in reality.

Our Contributions: Motivated by the aforementioned reasons, we in this work propose a novel privacy-preserving face authentication protocol with recoverability and reusability. The main contributions can be summarized as follows.

- We innovatively combine the secret sharing and additive homomorphic encryption to protect the user enrolled face features and the queried features, against the authentication server. As such, the sensitive user bio-information are hidden from the server throughout the entire authentication phase, which further makes the face credential of the user revokable. In addition, we generate the noise vectors that are used to mask the original face features to be fully independent in different applications and thus realize the reusability property. Moreover, our scheme enjoys the same accuracy level with the plaintext face recognition that uses Euclidean distance measure in practice.
- We rigorously prove the security of our scheme using the simulation technique. In the presence of a semi-honest adversary, both the bio-template and the queried features are well protected. The advantage of unauthorized users to pass the authentication is negligible. We also do the experiment on the real-world dataset to demonstrate its effectiveness and efficiency. Specifically, a successful user authentication costs less than a second on a smartphone with common specs.

2 Problem Formulation

In this section, we formulate the studied problem by giving the background, system model and design goals.

2.1 Background

We firstly briefly describe a plaintext face authentication system without considering privacy issues. A typical face authentication scheme in general contains two basic steps, feature extraction and similarity measure.

Face Feature Extraction. In machine learning and pattern recognition, feature extraction algorithm derives feature vectors from initial data to reduce the dimensionality [10]. A host of approaches have been proposed in the literature so as to extract the human facial features, such as principal component analysis [9] and DeepID [17,22,23]. Our proposed scheme is compatible with all the face feature extraction algorithms as long as the extracted features forms a vector. Note that we will not further consider this standard step in our following protocol elaboration since it is orthogonal to the proposed security and privacy design.

Similarity Measure. As the enrolled template and the query are represented by two feature vectors respectively, we can compute the distance between them to measure the image similarity [13,27]. A match is found if the distance is within a predefined threshold value. In practice, Euclidean distance is the most widely used similarity measure in the face authentication system [11]. Given the template vector X and the query vector $\overline{X}$, their similarity τ can be calculated by

$$\tau^2 = \|\overline{X} - X\|^2 = (\overline{x}_1 - x_1)^2 + (\overline{x}_2 - x_2)^2 + \ldots + (\overline{x}_n - x_n)^2$$

2.2 System Model

Our system consists of two entities, a mobile user and an authentication server (AS) as shown in Fig. 1. In order to access the intended resources, the user has to interact with the AS to pass the face authentication. We assume that the user owns an intelligent device with a camera, such as a smartphone to capture the user face image, from which the corresponding facial features of the user can be obtained by running a feature extraction algorithm on the device.

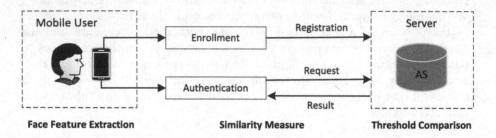

Fig. 1. System model

In the enrollment phase, the mobile user first needs to randomly divide the extracted feature into two parts and submits the masked one part to the AS as the user template for the subsequent authentication in the future. To authenticate the user, a smart device is used to extract a new set of the user facial features as the query and generate an authentication request. Finally, through a round of interaction, the AS checks if the obfuscated Euclidean distance between the template vector and query vector is within a predefined threshold to verify the user identity without knowing the underlying bio-information. In addition, the server is honest-but-curious to the user. More concretely, AS will execute strictly according to a protocol providing reliable authentication service, but it is curious about the face features of a user for other purposes.

2.3 Design Goals

With respect to the functionality and performance, our presented scheme is expected to achieve the following goals.

- *Revocability.* A user's enrolled features can be revoked if it is compromised.
- *Reusability.* The user enrolled features are independent in cross-domain applications, and the server cannot obtain a user's query features during the authentication phase.
- *Result accuracy.* The proposed scheme should achieve the same level of accuracy with the plaintext face recognition scheme that uses Euclidean distance as similarity measure.
- *Efficiency.* The proposed authentication should be efficient in terms of computation and communication costs at both user and server sides.

Regarding security, our proposal should satisfy three properties as below.

- *Completeness.* A registered legitimate user can always convince the honest authentication server to grant him/her the access to the system.
- *Soundness.* An unauthorized user can successfully cheat the honest authentication server into accepting his/her identify with negligible probability.
- *Privacy* Besides the final result, the server should learn nothing about the private user facial features.

3   The Proposed Scheme

3.1   Main Idea

Reusability and revocability are necessary for a face authentication system in practice, which means that neither enrolled feature nor query feature can be disclosed. In our proposed scheme, the enrolled feature of a mobile user is randomly divided into two parts and shared with the AS to ensure the security of original feature. To preserve use's query feature privacy during the authentication process, additive homomorphic encryption (e.g. Paillier [18]) is incorporated into the design of the proposed protocol.

3.2   Scheme Details

Our scheme includes three parts: System Initialization, User Enrollment and Face Authentication. A detailed description is presented in Fig. 2.

System Initialization: In this phase, the server runs algorithm *Setup* to generate a pair of public and private keys, which enables to correctly compute the Euclidean distance between user enrolled feature and query feature in a secure way.

User Enrollment: In order to prevent the server from learning registered features, the user calls algorithm *FeatureMask* to split the original feature vector into two vectors, and the original complete feature vector will be discarded. In addition, the user computes the norm of the original feature vector as an auxiliary value, which will be used in the authentication phase. A random number is introduced to mask the auxiliary value.

Face Authentication: To verify the authenticity of a user, the idea behind protocol *SimilarityMeasure* is as follows: (1) Combining the data owned by the AS, the user is capable of computing correct the Euclidean distance between enrolled feature and queried feature; (2) A dishonest user can pass the verification by fabricating a small value $[dis']$ for $dis' \leq T$. To defend against this attack, the server chooses a random number r as a challenge in each authentication.

After the protocol *Similarity Measure*, the server runs *Threshold Comparison* to recover masked similarity using $\tau = dis \cdot r^{-1}$ (Note that r^{-1} represents the inverse of r) and compare τ with a global threshold T.

Assuming $pk = N$ is the server's public key, we use Z_N to denote the message space. Let $\boldsymbol{X}$ denote the original n-dimensional feature and each entry $x_i, a_i \in Z_{2^l}$ is an l-bit value, where Z_{2^l} is a ring that integers modulo $2^l < N$. $\boldsymbol{X}$ and $\overline{\boldsymbol{X}}$ be the extracted user facial features at two different time. And we use $[\cdot]$ to describe the from of ciphertexts encryted by pk. For instance, given a plaintext x, its ciphertext is presented as $[x]$.

- **Setup**(1^λ): Given a security parameter λ, the server computes and outputs

$$(pk, sk) \leftarrow Paillier.GenKey(1^\lambda)$$

- **FeatureMask**($\boldsymbol{X}$, $\boldsymbol{a}$, R): Given a n-dimensional face enrolled feature vector $\boldsymbol{X} = (x_1, x_2, \ldots, x_n)$, a n-dimensional random vector $\boldsymbol{a} = (a_1, a_2, \ldots, a_n)$ and a random number $R \in Z_N$, the mobile user first computes

$$\boldsymbol{X} - \boldsymbol{a} = (x_1 - a_1, x_2 - a_2, \ldots, x_n - a_n)$$

$$\|\boldsymbol{X}\|^2 + R = x_1^2 + x_2^2 + \cdots + x_n^2 + R.$$

Then let

$$s_1 = \boldsymbol{X} - \boldsymbol{a}; s_2 = \boldsymbol{a}; s_3 = \|\boldsymbol{X}\|^2 + R; s_4 = R,$$

and outputs $((s_1, s_3), (s_2, s_4))$, where (s_1, s_3) is secret held by the user and (s_2, s_4) is held by the server.

- **SimilarityMeasure**: A protocol with two rounds of interactions run by the mobile user and the server, and outputs dis that denotes masked distance of two face feature vectors $\overline{\boldsymbol{X}}$ and $\boldsymbol{X}$. For details,

Input: User has pk, s_1, s_3, $\overline{\boldsymbol{X}}$; Sever has pk, sk, s_2, s_4;

Output: User outputs $\perp$ ($\perp$ means empty); Server outputs d;

1. The server chooses a random number r, computes ciphertext $[r]$, $[rs_2] = [r\boldsymbol{a}] = ([ra_1], [ra_2], \ldots, [ra_n])$, $[rs_4] = [rR]$, and then sends $([r], [rs_2], [rs_4])$ to the user;
2. The user utilizes $\|\overline{\boldsymbol{X}}\|^2 = \overline{x}_1^2 + \overline{x}_2^2 + \cdots + \overline{x}_n^2$ and $\overline{\boldsymbol{X}} \cdot s_1 = \overline{\boldsymbol{X}} \cdot (\boldsymbol{X} - \boldsymbol{a})$ to compute $[dis] = [r(\|\overline{\boldsymbol{X}}\|^2 + s_3 - 2\overline{\boldsymbol{X}} \cdot s_1) - 2\overline{\boldsymbol{X}} \cdot rs_2 - rs_4]$ by the additive homomorphic properties, as follows

$$[dis] = [r]^{(\|\overline{\boldsymbol{X}}\|^2 + s_3 - 2\overline{\boldsymbol{X}} \cdot s_1)} [rs_2]^{(N - 2\overline{\boldsymbol{X}})} [rs_4]^{(N-1)}$$

where N represents the module of plaintext in Paillier, and then sends $[dis]$ to the server;
3. The sever decrypts $[dis]$;
4. **RETURN**: dis.

- **ThresholdComparison**(dis, r, T): Given the dis, the random r determined by the above protocol and a threshold T, the server computes similarity

$$\tau = dis \cdot r^{-1}.$$

And then the server compares the similarity τ with the threshold T. If $\tau \leq T$, then the server returns res=1 to the user; otherwise, the server returns res=0.

Fig. 2. Details of our scheme

4 Security Definitions and Analysis

We now analyse and prove the security of our proposed scheme.

Completeness: The following equation holds in plaintext, thus if the user is registered and legal, the honest sever will return the result of successful authentication.

$$
\begin{aligned}
d &= r(\|\overline{X}\|^2 + s_3 - 2\overline{X} \cdot s_1) - 2\overline{X} \cdot rs_2 - rs_4 \\
&= r(\|\overline{X}\|^2 + \|X\|^2 + R - 2\overline{X} \cdot (X - a)) - 2\overline{X} \cdot ra - rR \\
&= r\|\overline{X} - X\|^2
\end{aligned}
$$

Soundness: A malicious mobile user attempts to pass the authentication by sending a fake value $[dis']$. In the proposed scheme, the challenge r^{-1} makes the probability of $dis' \cdot r^{-1} < T$ is $\frac{T}{N}$, where N is the server's public key. In practice, N is usually a 1024-bit or 2048-bit number while T is a small value. Thus, the probability that an attacker successfully passes the authentication is negligible.

Privacy: The proposed protocol includes algorithms *Setup*, *FeatureMask*, *SimilarityMeasure*, and *ThresholdComparison*. According to Sect. 4, only the protocol *SimilarityMeasure* that require user-server interactions needs to be proven.

Definition 1. *Protocol* SimilarityMeasure *securely computes the functionality*

$$
f((pk, s_1, s_3, \overline{X}), (pk, sk, s_2, s_4)) = (\bot, dis)
$$

in the presence of static semi-honest adversaries.

Proof. Firstly, we consider the case that the user is corrupted. In the protocol, the user receives a message $([r], [rs_2], [rs_4])$. Formally, S_1 is given $(pk, s_1, s_3, \overline{X})$ and works as follows:

1. S_1 chooses three random numbers r_1, r_2 and r_3.
2. S_1 encrypts r_1, r_2, r_3 with pk to obtain $[r_1]$, $[r_2]$, $[r_3]$.
4. S_1 outputs $((pk, s_1, s_3, \overline{X}), [r_1], [r_2], [r_3])$.

Because paillier is semantically secure, we have $[r_1] \overset{c}{\equiv} [r]$, $[r_2] \overset{c}{\equiv} [rs_2]$, $[r_3] \overset{c}{\equiv} [rs_4]$. That is, any two ciphertexts encrypted by Paillier cannot be computationally distinguished. Thus, we have $S_1(x, [r_1], [r_2], [r_3]) \overset{c}{\equiv} view_1^\pi(x, [r], [rs_2], [rs_4])$, where x represents the input of S_1 that is $(pk, s_1, s_3, \overline{X})$.

Next, we proceed to the case that the server is corrupted, and construct a simulator S_2. In the protocol, the server receives a message $[dis]$ denoted by c. Simulator S_2 receives for input (pk, sk, s_2, s_4) and output dis. Then:

1. S_2 chooses a random number r'.
2. S_2 encrypts d with pk to obtain $c' = [dis]$.
3. S_2 outputs $((pk, sk, s_2, s_4), r', c')$.

As mentioned above, paillier is semantically secure, which any two ciphertexts are indistinguishable. At the same time, we say that two random numbers are also indistinguishable. Thus, there are following equation holding: $r' \overset{c}{\equiv} r$, $c' \overset{c}{\equiv} c$. Thus, we have $S_2(y, r', c') \overset{c}{\equiv} view_2^\pi(y, r, c)$, where y represents the input of S_2 that is (pk, sk, s_2, s_4).

5   Performance Evaluation

5.1   Experiment Setup

To evaluate the performance, our scheme is implemented in JAVA. User-side computation is performed on a smartphones running Android OS 5.0, and a computer with a 3.2 GHz Intel i5 6500 CPU and 8 GB RAM running Windows.7 is used as the AS. We adopt the popular CASIA-WebFace database from Center for Biometrics and Security Research [1]. The DeepID is exploited as the feature extraction algorithm. 3000 pairs data of highly compact 160-dimensional vectors that contain rich identity information are used as a test set, which has marked indicating whether a pair of data belongs to the same person. And some pre-processing operations are performed for feature vectors.

5.2   Evaluation

We evaluate the performance of the proposed scheme in terms of communication overhead and computation efficiency. Since no prior work can achieve the same functionality and security guarantee with ours, we only compare the proposed scheme with the plaintext face authentication schemes.

Firstly, the round complexity of our protocol is two. Sending a authentication request, ID of the user, or receiving the result of face authentication from $\{0/1\}$ only takes negligible bandwidth. The challenge message sent by the server includes $n + 2$ BigIntegers in Z_N, where n denotes the dimension of feature vectors. The response message contains only one ciphertext. Then, in terms of computation efficiency, the time costs of highly efficient operations are omitted, thus we mainly measure the computational complexity about all steps of the protocol *SimilarityMeasure* in Sect. 4. We can note that a major part of the computation efforts comes from computing encryptions, decryption, and homo-morphic operations, which requires a complex modular exponentiation (ME) and modular multiplication (MM), shown in Table 1.

Table 1. Communication and computation overhead

	Comm.overhead	Comp.overhead
The mobile user	$(n + 2)BigInteger$	$(n + 1)T_{ME} + (n + 1)T_{MM}$
The server	$(1)BigInteger$	$(n + 2)T_{enc} + T_{dec}$

The time cost of the cryptography primitive operations is investigated on different smartphones. The smartphone 1 has a 1.7 GHz processor and 2 GB RAM and another one with a 2.0 GHz processor and 4 GB RAM is better. We take into account the effect of the dimension of feature vectors on latency, combined with different key-lengths and smartphones. Both Figs. 3 and 4 show that the time cost for authentication is proportional to the dimension of feature vectors. From Fig. 3, we deduce that the higher the security level, the longer the authentication time delay on the same smartphone, such as smartphone 1. As shown in Fig. 4, given different smart phone performance parameters, the authentication cost depends on the frequency and memory of the smart phone, and the dimension has dominant impact to computation efficiency. In fact, one protocol execution needs less than 1 s on a smartphone with common specs. Therefore, the proposed authentication protocol offers efficient user authentication in reality.

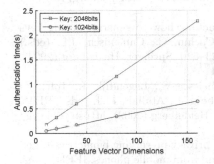

Fig. 3. Different key lengths   **Fig. 4.** Different smart phones

6 Conclusion

We design a practical privacy-preserving face authentication with revocability and reusability by using secret sharing and lightweight addition homomorphic encryption. We address all the drawbacks in the previous solutions, and make the privacy-preserving face authentication practical on applications. In addition, we rigorously analyse the security of our scheme in the presence of semi-honest adversaries. Our scheme can support secure distance metric such as Euclid distance in general, and the methodology is also compatible with other similarity measure (e.g., cosine similarity).

Acknowledgments. This work is supported by the National Key Research and Development Program of China under Grant 2016YFB0800601, the Key Program of NSFC-Tongyong Union Foundation under Grant U1636209 and the Key Basic Research Plan in Shaanxi Province under Grant 2017ZDXM-GY-014.

References

1. Casia-webface-database. http://www.cbsr.ia.ac.cn/english/Databases.asp
2. Smile to pay. https://www.antfin.com/report.htm. Accessed 16 Mar 2015
3. Your face is your secure password. https://www.apple.com/iphone-x/#face-id
4. Boyen, X.: Reusable cryptographic fuzzy extractors. In: Proceedings of the 11th ACM Conference on Computer and Communications Security. ACM (2004)
5. Brunelli, R.: Template Matching Techniques in Computer Vision: Theory and Practice. Wiley, Hoboken (2009)
6. Canetti, R., Fuller, B., Paneth, O., Reyzin, L., Smith, A.: Reusable fuzzy extractors for low-entropy distributions. In: Fischlin, M., Coron, J.S. (eds.) EUROCRYPT 2016. LNCS, vol. 9665, pp. 117–146. Springer, Heidelberg (2016). https://doi.org/10.1007/978-3-662-49890-3_5
7. Cui, H., Au, M.H., Qin, B., Deng, R.H., Yi, X.: Fuzzy public-key encryption based on biometric data. In: Okamoto, T., Yu, Y., Au, M.H., Li, Y. (eds.) ProvSec 2017. LNCS, vol. 10592, pp. 400–409. Springer, Cham (2017). https://doi.org/10.1007/978-3-319-68637-0_24
8. Dodis, Y., Reyzin, L., Smith, A.: Fuzzy extractors: how to generate strong keys from biometrics and other noisy data. In: Cachin, C., Camenisch, J.L. (eds.) EUROCRYPT 2004. LNCS, vol. 3027, pp. 523–540. Springer, Heidelberg (2004). https://doi.org/10.1007/978-3-540-24676-3_31
9. Erkin, Z., Franz, M., Guajardo, J., Katzenbeisser, S., Lagendijk, I., Toft, T.: Privacy-preserving face recognition. In: Goldberg, I., Atallah, M.J. (eds.) PETS 2009. LNCS, vol. 5672, pp. 235–253. Springer, Heidelberg (2009). https://doi.org/10.1007/978-3-642-03168-7_14
10. Gunasinghe, H., Bertino, E.: PrivBioMTAuth: privacy preserving biometrics-based and user centric protocol for user authentication from mobile phones. IEEE Trans. Inf. Forensics Secur. 13(4), 1042–1057 (2018)
11. Guo, F., Susilo, W., Mu, Y.: Distance-based encryption: how to embed fuzziness in biometric-based encryption. IEEE Trans. Inf. Forensics Secur. 11(2), 247–257 (2016)
12. Li, J., Li, J., Chen, X., Jia, C., Lou, W.: Identity-based encryption with outsourced revocation in cloud computing. IEEE Trans. Comput. 64(2), 425–437 (2015)
13. Li, J., Sun, L., Yan, Q., Li, Z., Srisa-an, W., Ye, H.: Significant permission identification for machine learning based android malware detection. IEEE Trans. Industr. Inf. 14, 3216–3225 (2018)
14. Li, P., Li, T., Ye, H., Li, J., Chen, X., Xiang, Y.: Privacy-preserving machine learning with multiple data providers. Future Gener. Comput. Syst. 87, 341–350 (2018)
15. Liu, K., Kargupta, H., Ryan, J.: Random projection-based multiplicative data perturbation for privacy preserving distributed data mining. IEEE Trans. Knowl. Data Eng. 18(1), 92–106 (2006)
16. Matsuda, T., Takahashi, K., Murakami, T., Hanaoka, G.: Fuzzy signatures: relaxing requirements and a new construction. In: Manulis, M., Sadeghi, A.R., Schneider, S. (eds.) ACNS 2016. LNCS, vol. 9696, pp. 97–116. Springer, Cham (2016). https://doi.org/10.1007/978-3-319-39555-5_6
17. Ouyang, W., et al.: DeepID-Net: deformable deep convolutional neural networks for object detection. In: Proceedings of the IEEE Conference on Computer Vision and Pattern Recognition (2015)

18. Paillier, P.: Public-key cryptosystems based on composite degree residuosity classes. In: Stern, J. (ed.) EUROCRYPT 1999. LNCS, vol. 1592, pp. 223–238. Springer, Heidelberg (1999). https://doi.org/10.1007/3-540-48910-X_16

19. Patel, V.M., Ratha, N.K., Chellappa, R.: Cancelable biometrics: a review. IEEE Signal Process. Mag. **32**(5), 54–65 (2015)

20. Ratha, N.K.: Privacy protection in high security biometrics applications. In: Kumar, A., Zhang, D. (eds.) ICEB 2010. LNCS, vol. 6005, pp. 62–69. Springer, Heidelberg (2010). https://doi.org/10.1007/978-3-642-12595-9_9

21. Sadeghi, A.R., Schneider, T., Wehrenberg, I.: Efficient privacy-preserving face recognition. In: Lee, D., Hong, S. (eds.) ICISC 2009. LNCS, vol. 5984, pp. 229–244. Springer, Heidelberg (2010). https://doi.org/10.1007/978-3-642-14423-3_16

22. Sun, Y., Liang, D., Wang, X., Tang, X.: Deepid3: face recognition with very deep neural networks. arXiv preprint arXiv:1502.00873 (2015)

23. Sun, Y., Wang, X., Tang, X.: Deep learning face representation from predicting 10,000 classes. In: Proceedings of the IEEE Conference on Computer Vision and Pattern Recognition (2014)

24. Takahashi, K., Matsuda, T., Murakami, T., Hanaoka, G., Nishigaki, M.: A signature scheme with a fuzzy private key. In: Malkin, T., Kolesnikov, V., Lewko, A.B., Polychronakis, M. (eds.) ACNS 2015. LNCS, vol. 9092, pp. 105–126. Springer, Cham (2015). https://doi.org/10.1007/978-3-319-28166-7_6

25. Wu, Z., Liang, B., You, L., Jian, Z., Li, J.: High-dimension space projection-based biometric encryption for fingerprint with fuzzy minutia. Soft Comput. **20**(12), 4907–4918 (2016)

26. Wu, Z., Tian, L., Li, P., Wu, T., Jiang, M., Wu, C.: Generating stable biometric keys for flexible cloud computing authentication using finger vein. Inf. Sci. **433–434**, 431–447 (2018)

27. Xia, Z., Xiong, N.N., Vasilakos, A.V., Sun, X.: EPCBIR: an efficient and privacy-preserving content-based image retrieval scheme in cloud computing. Inf. Sci. **387**, 195–204 (2017)

28. Zhuang, D., Wang, S., Chang, J.M.: FRiPAL: face recognition in privacy abstraction layer. In: 2017 IEEE Conference on Dependable and Secure Computing. IEEE (2017)

Differentially Private Location Protection
with Continuous Time Stamps
for VANETs

Zhili Chen[1], Xianyue Bao[1], Zuobin Ying[1(✉)], Ximeng Liu[2,3], and Hong Zhong[1]

[1] School of Computer Science and Technology, Anhui University, Hefei, China
{zlchen,yingzb}@ahu.edu.cn
[2] School of Information Systems, Singapore Management University,
Singapore, Singapore
[3] University Key Laboratory of Information Security of Network Systems
(Fuzhou University), Fuzhou, Fujian, China

Abstract. Vehicular Ad hoc Networks (VANETs) have higher requirements of continuous Location-Based Services (LBSs). However, the
untrusted server could reveal the users' location privacy in the meantime. Syntactic-based privacy models have been widely used in most of
the existing location privacy protection schemes. Whereas, they are suffering from background knowledge attacks, neither do they take the continuous time stamps into account. Therefore we propose a new differential
privacy definition in the context of location protection for the VANETs,
and we designed an obfuscation mechanism so that fine-grained locations and trajectories will not exposed when vehicles request location-
based services on continuous time stamps. Then, we apply the exponential mechanism in the pseudonym permutations to provide disparate
pseudonyms for different vehicles when making requests on different time
stamps, these pseudonyms can hide the position correlation of vehicles on
consecutive time stamps besides releasing them in a coarse-grained form
simultaneously. The experimental results on real-world datasets indicate
that our scheme significantly outperforms the baseline approaches in data
utility.

Keywords: LBS · VANETs · Location privacy
Continuous time stamps · Differential privacy

1 Introduction

In recent years, as the popularity of LBSs in VANETs, a large quantity of location
data of vehicles are inevitably upload to LBS providers every day. However,
locations of personal vehicles are normally sensitive, since they are likely to
expose their owners' physical health, lifestyle, personal beliefs, etc. This may
in turn exposes them to adversary attacks, including unwanted location-based
spams/frauds, extortions, or even physical dangers [18]. For example, if a driver

© Springer Nature Switzerland AG 2018
J. Vaidya and J. Li (Eds.): ICA3PP 2018, LNCS 11337, pp. 204–219, 2018.
https://doi.org/10.1007/978-3-030-05063-4_17

frequently visits a specialist hospital on Monday morning, an attacker can easily infer that the driver has probably suffered a certain disease recently [9]. As a result, location privacy issues in VANETs have already drawn great attention worldwide.

A large amount of research works have been made on location privacy protection of VANETs, the main technologies which have been applied in VANETs could be divided into:cryptography [7,13], and Mix-zone [14,22], information-distortion [15–17].

For example, Yi et al. used a fully homomorphic encryption technology to protect the database when searching for private information and proposed an K-anonymous mixed-zone scheme that tolerates delays [20]. Lim et al. used similar routes between two vehicles to achieve path confusion [10]. Ying et al. presented a location privacy protection scheme (DMLP) using dynamic mix-zone [21]. Shin et al. proposed an anonymous method of trajectory [17], which divides the trajectory into segments so that they can be anonymous from other segments. Cui et al. [3] proposed that the information of randomly selecting an auxiliary vehicle at each request is advanced together with the requesting vehicle as a request parameter so that the server cannot distinguish the real requester.

Unfortunately, most of them are based on syntactic privacy models, lacking of rigorous privacy guarantee [18]. Moreover, they mainly focus on location protection in static scenarios, or at single time stamp, leaving alone the case with continuous time stamps. Thus various inference attacks can be launched on location generalization or location perturbation with side information like road constraints or users' moving patterns [2,12].

Differential privacy [5] has became a standard for privacy preservation to guarantee its rigorous privacy and can balance the security of user location protection and the effectiveness of user location as a request parameter, also, it has been proven to be effective against attackers with arbitrary side information [1,4], and has been applied to location protection in several ways. The first is to protect locations at a single time stamp to ensure geo-indistinguishability [1]. The second is to protect historical locations or trajectories in a data publishing or data aggregation setting, to guarantee user-level differential privacy [8], where a user opting in or out of a dataset affects little on the output. The third is to protect locations with continuous time stamps, requiring location protection on the fly for a single user. This is the case which we are focusing on. Xiao and Xiong put forward an elegant scheme to address this location protection problem, guaranteeing differential privacy under temporal correlations [18]. Nevertheless, retaining these temporal correlations may still enable attackers to infer location information. In the context of VANETs, there are few location privacy protection technologies based on differential privacy. As far as we known, only a few researches used differential privacy in vehicle's information aggregation [19], but the protection of location privacy in the continuous position request have not been studied.

In this paper, we resolve the problem of location protection under continuous time stamps for VANETs in a completely different way by hiding temporal correlations across time stamps, looking for a effective balance between the privacy and the utility of LBSs. Specifically, we first design a location perturbation mechanism to ensure location differential privacy for vehicles requesting services at the same time from the same Roadside Units (RSU). Then, we apply a pseudonym permutation mechanism to randomly permute the IDs of all vehicles within the range of each RSU for each time stamp, so that one vehicle uses the ID of another in the range of the same RSU at the same stamp, and location correlations across the continuous time stamps are completely hidden. As a result, our scheme can well protect locations within the range of a RSU (in a fine granularity) to ensure the privacy of users, while it can correctly release locations in term of the ranges of RSU (in a coarse granularity) for other potential purposes (e.g. research).

The contributions of this paper can be summarized as follows:

1. We introduce a new definition of differential privacy in the context of VANETs to reasonably use local sensitivities, and propose an effective location perturbation mechanism called convergence mechanism to protect location privacy for requesting vehicle which could realize a better utility toward LBSs than the baseline methods under the same privacy level.
2. We design a pseudonym permutation scheme with the exponential mechanism, so as to hide location correlations of vehicles across continuous time stamps. Compared to the general scheme of randomly choosing a pseudonym, the exponential mechanism selection not only satisfies randomness but also has an utility function, which makes the vehicle farther from the requesting vehicle more likely to be selected as a substitute to maximize the protection of the positional safety of the substitute vehicle.
3. Taking into account the demand for location privacy of the requesting vehicle under continuous time stamps and the LBS server's demand for data, we combine the convergence with the pseudonym permutation mechanism, which well protects locations in fine granularity while releases them in coarse granularity. The experiment demonstrates that our scheme achieves a better location utility than the baseline schemes.

The remainder of this paper is organized as follows. Section 2 introduces the models and preliminaries of this paper. Section 3 introduces the basic concepts and definitions of differential privacy used in this work. We provide the detailed description of our scheme in Sect. 4. Section 5 gives our experimental results and the related analysis. Finally, we conclude the paper and provide future work in Sect. 6.

2   Models and Preliminaries

In this section, we introduce some special symbols and their definitions, then introduce the privacy problem model and the techniques needed to solve the privacy problem (Table 1).

Table 1. Notations

X	A collection of all vehicle locations in an RSU
id_i	The number that uniquely identifies a vehicle V_i
$(x_i, y_i) \in X$	The true location of the vehicle V_i in RSU
r	The privacy requirements of the mobile user in the vehicle
ϵ	Privacy budget
req	The requested positional parameters of the request
z	The result of the request

2.1 System Model

As depicted in Fig. 1, a typical LBS system usually consists of three major components:active vehicle requesting service, trusted RSU with the capabilities data processing and data storage, and untrusted third-party LBS servers. The RSU collects requests for active vehicles within its range at regular intervals. After collecting the request parameters containing the identity information and location information of the active vehicles, the RSU forwards the information to the LBS server. The LBS server sends the request results to the RSU, and the RSU then returns the result of the request to the requesting active vehicle.

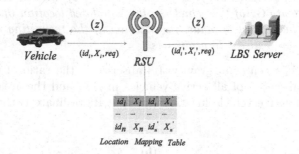

Fig. 1. System model: active vehicle, RSU, and LBS server

2.2 Threat Model

In the system model of this paper, the LBS server is incompletely trusted which would be compromised by attackers to eavesdrop the vehicle's location information. But the attackers that will not tamper with the communication message before requesting information to reach the server are belong to passive attackers. If the vehicle directly appends its real-time location to the LBS request and sends the request to RSU or LBS server, the attacker can continuously obtain and analyze the information in the LBS request from the LBS server to track the trajectory information of the requesting vehicle. However, even the vehicle can use a pseudonym-based signature and change pseudonym every message, attackers can still infer the travel route of the vehicle based on the frequently updated location, speed, direction and road condition. Therefore, how to ensure the vehicle's location privacy under the premise of providing accurate LBS service to vehicles is an important issue, which needs to be addressed in this paper.

2.3   Preliminaries Statement

Definition 1 (Location set). *As shown in Fig. 2(a), we define the privacy circle as the circle with the request vehicle as the center and the privacy requirement r as the radius. We have two location sets at here, when the i-th user issues a location-based service request, $\triangle V_i$ denotes a set of locations of all active vehicles other than the requesting vehicle within privacy circle at the current time, and $\triangle V_i'$ indicates the union of $\triangle V_i$ and the currently requested vehicle's location $Q_i(x_i, y_i)$.*

$$\triangle V_i = \{S_j^i | PointsLength(S_j^i, (x_i, y_i)) \leq r, S_j^i \in X\}.$$
$$\triangle V_i' = \triangle V_i \cup (x_i, y_i). \tag{1}$$

S_j^i represents the location of user j in $\triangle V_i$. Let $PointsLength()$ indicate the distance from S_j^i to the location (x_i, y_i) of the requesting vehicle.

Definition 2 (r-location set). *Before the request of the i-th vehicle, we use the center of gravity G_i of the vehicle as the simulated location of the requested vehicle. When the request is made, the location of the requesting vehicle is Q_i, then Q_i and G_i are called r-location sets.*

G_i is the $\triangle V_i$'s center of gravity. Its abscissa is the ratio of the weighted average of the abscissas of all active vehicles in $\triangle V_i$ and the area of polygons composed of all active vehicle locations in $\triangle V_i$; Its ordinate is the ratio of the

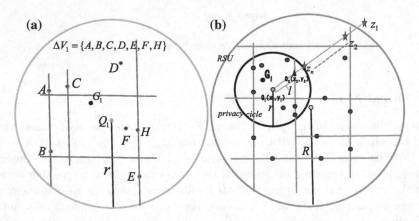

Fig. 2. (a) Privacy circle (b) convergence model

weighted average of the ordinates of all active vehicles in $\triangle V_i$ and the area of the polygons composed of all active vehicle position points in $\triangle V_i$. We use GetPolygonCenter($\triangle V_i$) to represent the function to find the center of gravity.

3   Differential Privacy in VANETs

As shown in Fig. 2(a), we use Q_1 to indicate the location of the requesting vehicle. $\triangle V_1$ is the location set when Q_1 sends the request, when $\triangle V_1$ is not empty, G_1 represents the center of gravity of $\triangle V_1$, and Q_1 and G_1 are a pair r-location sets. When $\triangle V_1$ is empty, Q_1 and the arbitrary virtual location point on the edge of privacy circle are a pair r-location sets. And, we use z_t to represents the position after added noise at the current time.

Definition 3 (Differential privacy on r-location set). *A randomized mechanism $\mathcal{A}$ satisfies ϵ-differential privacy in the privacy circle if, for any output z_t as well as the position of the Q_1 and the G_1, the following holds:*

$$\frac{Pr(\mathcal{A}(Q_1) = z_t)}{Pr(\mathcal{A}(G_1) = z_t)} \le e^\epsilon.$$

Definition 4 (Global Sensitivity). *In the privacy circle centered on request vehicle Q_i at any moment, the maximum distance between the center of gravity G_i and the request vehicle Q_i is the global sensitivity of the confusion mechanism.*

Definition 5 (Local Sensitivity). *In the privacy circle centered on the request vehicle Q_i at the current moment, the current distance between the center of gravity G_i of $\triangle V_i$ and the requesting vehicle Q_i is the local sensitivity of the confusion mechanism.*

Definition 6 (Laplace Mechanism [6]). *Given a data set D, assuming a function $f: D \rightarrow R^d$ with a sensitivity of $\triangle f$, then the stochastic algorithm $M(D) = f(D) + \eta$ satisfies ε-difference privacy, where $\eta \propto e^{\frac{-\epsilon \|\eta\|}{\triangle f}}$ indicates that η is a random noise that follows the laplacian distribution with scale parameter $\triangle f / \varepsilon$.*

Definition 7 (Exponential Mechanism [11]). *Suppose the input of algorithm M is a dataset D, the output is an entity object $r \in Range$, $q(D, r)$ is the utility function, $\triangle q$ is the sensitivity of function $q(D, r)$, and if algorithm M chooses r from Range by the probability proportional to $exp(\frac{\epsilon q(D,r)}{2\triangle q})$, then Algorithm M satisfies ε-differential privacy.*

3.1   Utility Metrics

To measure the utility of our scheme, we use the Euclidean distance between the pre-confused location Q_1 of requester and the confounded location z to represent the utility of our obfuscation mechanism, this distance we use drift to indicate.

$$drift = \sqrt{((Q_1.x - z.x)^2 + (Q_1.y - z.y)^2)}.$$

Definition 8 (Trajectory distortion). *If the trajectory* $T = C_1, C_2, ..., C_n$ *is a trajectory issued in place of the base trajectory* $T_0 = c_1, c_2..., c_n$, *then its trajectory distortion metrics is defined as:*

$$D(T) = \frac{\sum_{i=1}^n r(C_i)}{n}.$$

Where $r(C_i)$ represents the radius of the area covering one location point on T_0 and T, and at least one location point is simultaneously covered by C_i for every moment on T and T_0. If $D <= R$ (the radius of a RSU), the trajectories T and T_0 are said to be approximate trajectories and the two trajectories have the same coarse-grained trajectories. Then, we can use this trajectory T instead of T_0's coarse-grained trajectory to publish. Obviously, the smaller D is, the closer T is to the true trajectory of T_0 (Algorithm 1).

4   Design Details and Proofs

4.1   Design Details

Framework. The overall framework of the system is shown in Fig. 1. The vehicles mentioned in the following are all active vehicles at the current time and sending their own information to the RSU. We assume that a temporary database is configured on the RSU, the temporary database stores the information of the vehicle that requests the service within the scope of the RSU at the current moment. The RSU selects a vehicle's id from the database as the requesting vehicle's pseudonym id by Algorithm 2. The RSU builds a table in the database for the correspondence between the true id and the pseudonym id'_i. Then, adding noise to the location of the requesting vehicle at the current moment to get a new location point X'_i, the RSU sends the processed information to the LBS

Algorithm 1. Framework

Input: $\mathbb{ID}$: the *id* of the N requesting vehicles $\mathbb{V}$ within the RSU at the current time.
   $(\mathbb{X}, \mathbb{Y})$: the location of the N requesting vehicles $\mathbb{V}$ within the RSU at the current time.
   r: user-defined privacy requirements.
   id_j: the *id* of the $j-$th vehicle v_j in $\mathbb{V}$.
   $LOC_{id_j} = (x_j, y_j)$: the location of the $j-$th vehicle v_j in $\mathbb{V}$.
   ϵ_1, ϵ_2: privacy budget.
Output: (x'_i, y'_i): the sanitized version of the location $(x_i, y_i) \in (\mathbb{X}, \mathbb{Y})$ of the requested vehicle.
   id_j: the pseudonym $id_j \in \mathbb{ID}$ of the requested vehicle v_i.
1: $id_j \leftarrow$ ALGORITHM1(ϵ_2, $(\mathbb{X}, \mathbb{Y})$, r);
2: $(x'_i, y'_i) \leftarrow$ ALGORITHM3(ϵ_2, $(\mathbb{X}, \mathbb{Y})$);
3: **return** $(id_j, (x'_i, y'_i))$;

---

server. The information includes: the id of the RSU, the pseudonym id'_i of the request vehicle, the location X'_i after the noise is added and request body. After receiving the request, the server returns the request result to the RSU according to the RSU's id id_{RSU}. Finally, the RSU looks up the ID mapping table, finds the id in the same row as id'_i, and returns z to the vehicle id_i. At this point, a location-based service is completed, the data collected by the server during this process includes: id'_i, X'_i, and id_{RSU}, and the specific location of the RSU can be obtained by id_{RSU}. Providers can recover accurate coarse-grained trajectories of substitute vehicles from these service data, and these service data can be used to study value-added services.

Algorithm 2. ID Replacement (IDR)

Input: $\mathbb{ID}$: the id of the N requesting vehicles $\mathbb{V}$ within the RSU at the current time.
   $(\mathbb{X}, \mathbb{Y})$: the location of the N active vehicles $\mathbb{V}$ within the RSU at the current time.
   r: user-defined privacy requirements.
   id_i: the id of the $i-$th vehicle v_i in $\mathbb{V}$.
   $LOC_{id_i} = (x_i, y_i)$: the location of the i-th vehicle v_i in $\mathbb{V}$.
   ϵ_1: privacy budget.
Output: id_j: the pseudonym of the requested vehicle v_i.
   for $(j = 1$ to $N)$ **do**
2:    RSU received $(id_j, (x_j, y_j))$ from the vehicle v_j;
      $Dis_\mathbb{V}[j] \leftarrow Dis(v_i, v_j)$; $\lhd$ Distance from request vehicle v_i to other active vehicles
4:    $\triangle f_1 \leftarrow MAX(Dis_\mathbb{V}[j])$; $\lhd$ The sensitivity
   end for
6: $Pr(M_{EX}(id_i, Dis_\mathbb{V}[j], \mathbb{ID}) = id_j) \leftarrow \dfrac{exp(\frac{\epsilon_1 Dis(id_i, id_j)}{2\triangle f_1})}{\sum_{id'_j \in \mathbb{ID}} exp(\frac{\epsilon_1 Dis(id_i, id'_j)}{2\triangle f_1})}$;
   $id_j \leftarrow M_{EX}(id_i, Dis_\mathbb{V}[j], \mathbb{ID})$; $\lhd$ Exponential mechanism to randomly choose a substitute
8: **return** id_j;

ID Replacement. We use the randomness of the exponential mechanism to select the substitute id, but compared with the traditional method of random selection, the exponential mechanism can also design utility functions to filter out the best results to meet the needs of location privacy of users. Because the added noise location is more likely to be around the currently requested vehicle, the closer the substitute vehicle is, the closer the noised location is to the real location of the substitute vehicle, which is not conducive to protecting the original intention of all requests for vehicle fine grained trajectories. Here we let M_{EX} denote the mechanism selecting id_j, and we use the distance $Dis(v_i, v_j)$ between the substitute and the request vehicle as a utility function of the exponential mechanism. This can make the active vehicle farther away from the requesting vehicle be selected as an substitute, because the farther this distance is, the safer the substitute vehicle is to replace the requesting vehicle. The sensitivity of utility function is the maximum value of any distance from the requested vehicle to the substitute. According to the exponential mechanism, the probability distribution of the pseudonym id_j can be computed as follows.

$$Pr(M_{EX}(id_i, Dis_V[j], \mathbb{ID}) = id_j) = \frac{exp(\frac{\epsilon_1 Dis(id_i, id_j)}{2\Delta f_1})}{\sum_{id'_j \in \mathbb{ID}} exp(\frac{\epsilon_1 Dis(id_i, id'_j)}{2\Delta f_1})}. \tag{2}$$

Algorithm 3. Convergence mechanism

Input: (x_i, y_i): the location of the requested vehicle V_i.
  $\mathbb{V}'$: m vehicles other than the requested vehicle V_i in the privacy circle.
  $(\mathbb{X}', \mathbb{Y}')$: coordinates of $\mathbb{V}'$.
  ϵ_2: privacy budget.
Output: Sanitized version (x'_i, y'_i) of the location $(x_i, y_i) \in (\mathbb{X}', \mathbb{Y}')$ of the requested vehicle V_i;
 1: $G_1 \leftarrow$ GetPolygonCenter$((\mathbb{X}', \mathbb{Y}'))$;◁ Calculate the position of the center of gravity of $(\mathbb{X}', \mathbb{Y}')$
 2: **if** $m=0$ **then**
 3:     $\Delta f_2 \leftarrow r$; ◁ the *sensitivity_2*
 4: **else**
 5:     $\Delta f_2 \leftarrow$ Dis$((x_i, y_i), G_1)$;◁ distance from vehicles to G_1 in $\mathbb{V}'$
 6: **end if**
 7: sample noise vector η_j with pdf $P(\eta_j) \propto e^{\frac{-\epsilon_2 \|\eta_j\|}{\Delta f_2}}$ $(j = 1, 2)$;
 8: $z_1.x \leftarrow x_i + \eta_1$;◁ Add laplace noise to the abscissa
    $z_1.y \leftarrow y_i + \eta_2$;◁ Add laplace noise to the ordinate
 9: **if** Dis$((z_1.x, z_1.y), (x_i, y_i)) \leq r$ **then**
10:     return $(z_1.x, z_1.y)$;
11: **else**
12:     $x'_i = x_i + \frac{fmod(Dis(z_1, Q_1), r)}{\sqrt{(\frac{z_1.y - Q_1.y_i}{z_1.x - Q_1.x_i})^2 + 1}}$;
        $y'_i = y_i + \frac{z_1.y - Q_1.y_i}{z_1.x, Q_1.x_i} \frac{fmod(Dis(z_1, Q_1), r)}{\sqrt{(\frac{z_1.y - Q_1.y_i}{z_1.x - Q_1.x_i})^2 + 1}}$;
13:     return $Q_2(x'_i, y'_i)$;
14: **end if**

Convergence Mechanism. Because we protect the privacy of users within the scope of privacy requirements, and the scope of privacy requirements is limited, and the random noise generated is uncertain. Therefore, we need to introduce locations beyond privacy requirements into the privacy requirements. We propose a convergence mechanism (CM) that satisfies differential privacy. The detailed process is as follows.

We first explain how to build the location set ΔV_i, RSU constructs a location set for each active vehicle based on the location information. If a vehicle is in the privacy circle and a location-based request is issued, the vehicle is active vehicle and included in the location set ΔV_i. In Fig. 3, the circle with radius R is the range of RSU, and the center of the privacy circle r is the location of the requesting vehicle Q_1. All red "•" make up the location set V_1 and the G_1 is the center of gravity of V_1. $z_1, z_2, ..., z_n$ are the locations beyond the privacy circle after the noises is added and Q_2 is the location to release after the convergence.

Then we calculate the center of gravity of the polygon that consists of the location of each vehicle in the location set. Laplace noise is then added to the location of the requesting vehicle, and then according to the following Eq. (3) converged into the privacy circle.

$$x_i' = x_i + \frac{fmod(Dis(z_1, Q_1), r)}{\sqrt{(\frac{z_1.y - Q_1.y_i}{z_1.x - Q_1.x_i})^2 + 1}}.$$

$$y_i' = y_i + \frac{z_1.y - Q_1.y_i}{z_1.x, Q_1.x_i} \frac{fmod(Dis(z_1, Q_1), r)}{\sqrt{(\frac{z_1.y - Q_1.y_i}{z_1.x - Q_1.x_i})^2 + 1}}.$$

$$(3)$$

In the Eq. (3), fmod represents the modulo operation, $Dis()$ represents the distance between of z_1 and Q_1, Q_1 represents the requested vehicle position (x_i, y_i), z_1 represents the noise-added position, and (x', y') is the location of publishing.

4.2 Theorems and Proofs

Theorem 1. *For every request, Algorithm 2 is ϵ_1-differentially private.*

Proof. Our goal is to make the ratio of the probability that two different requesting vehicles pick the same active vehicle as a substitute at any time is less than e^{ϵ_1}, even if the adversary knows that the requesting vehicle uses a pseudonym, it cannot distinguish between which active vehicle sent the request, it means that this mechanism satisfies differential privacy:

$$\frac{Pr(M_{EX}(id_i, Dis_V[j], \mathbb{ID}) = id_j)}{Pr(M_{EX}(id_i', Dis_V[j], \mathbb{ID}) = id_j)} = \frac{\frac{exp(\frac{\epsilon_1 Dis(id_i, id_j)}{2\Delta f_1})}{\sum_{id_j' \in \mathbb{ID}} exp(\frac{\epsilon_1 Dis(id_i, id_j')}{2\Delta f_1})}}{\frac{exp(\frac{\epsilon_1 Dis(id_i', id_j)}{2\Delta f_1})}{\sum_{id_j' \in \mathbb{ID}} exp(\frac{\epsilon_1 Dis(id_i', id_j')}{2\Delta f_1})}}$$

$$= (\frac{exp(\frac{\epsilon_1 Dis(id_i, id_j)}{2\Delta f_1})}{exp(\frac{\epsilon_1 Dis(id_i', id_j)}{2\Delta f_1})})(\frac{\sum_{id_j' \in \mathbb{ID}} exp(\frac{\epsilon_1 Dis(id_i', id_j')}{2\Delta f_1})}{\sum_{id_j' \in \mathbb{ID}} exp(\frac{\epsilon_1 Dis(id_i, id_j')}{2\Delta f_1})})$$

$$(4)$$

$$\leq exp(\frac{\epsilon_1}{2})(\frac{\sum_{id_j' \in \mathbb{ID}} exp(\frac{\epsilon_1}{2}) exp(\frac{\epsilon_1 Dis(id_i, id_j')}{2\Delta f_1})}{\sum_{id_j' \in \mathbb{ID}} exp(\frac{\epsilon_1 Dis(id_i, id_j')}{2\Delta f_1})})$$

$$\leq exp(\frac{\epsilon_1}{2}) exp(\frac{\epsilon_1}{2})(\frac{\sum_{id_j' \in \mathbb{ID}} exp(\frac{\epsilon_1 Dis(id_i, id_j')}{2\Delta f_1})}{\sum_{id_j' \in \mathbb{ID}} exp(\frac{\epsilon_1 Dis(id_i, id_j')}{2\Delta f_1})}) = exp(\epsilon_1).$$

Therefore, Algorithm 2 is ϵ_1-differentially private.

Theorem 2. *Algorithm 3 is ϵ_2-differentially private on r-location set.*
Proof. In this algorithm, G1 and Q1 are a pair of r-position sets, and the probability of each location point Q_2 being released within the scope of privacy requirements consists of two probabilities: (1) The probability that Q_2 is a new point after Q_1 and G_1 is confused by laplace noise, we call it the base probability $P'_{G_1}(Q_2)$ (2) z is a new point after Q_1 and G_1 is confused by laplace noise, but z be converged to Q_2 by the convergence mechanism. In addition, we need to know that the Laplace Mechanism satisfies ϵ-differentially private. That is to say:

$$\frac{P_{G_1}(z)}{P_{Q_1}(z)} \leq exp(\epsilon_2). \tag{5}$$

$$\frac{P'_{G_1}(Q_2)}{P'_{Q_1}(Q_2)} \leq exp(\epsilon_2);. \tag{6}$$

As shown in Fig. 2(b): $Q_2(x'_i, y'_i)$ in the privacy circle, $z_1, z_2, ..., z_n$ is the point outside the little circle that can converge to Q_2.
We can get the following inequalities from (5):

$$\frac{P_{G_1}(z_1)}{P_{Q_1}(z_1)} \leq exp(\epsilon_2); \quad \frac{P_{G_1}(z_2)}{P_{Q_1}(z_2)} \leq exp(\epsilon_2); ...; \frac{P_{G_1}(z_n)}{P_{Q_1}(z_n)} \leq exp(\epsilon_2).$$

We convert the above inequality to $\frac{xx_0}{yy_0} \leq exp(\epsilon_2)$; Corresponding: $\frac{xx_1}{yy_1} \leq exp(\epsilon_2)$; $\frac{xx_2}{yy_2} \leq exp(\epsilon_2)$; ... $\frac{xx_n}{yy_n} \leq exp(\epsilon_2)$; And, there are two ways of forming Q_2 points: the point directly selected by the publishing mechanism; Other locations are selected by the publishing mechanism but converge to the Q_2 point. So,

$$\frac{P_{G_1}(Q_2)}{P_{Q_1}(Q_2)} = \frac{P'_{G_1}(Q_2) + P_{G_1}(z_1) + ... + P_{G_1}(z_n)}{P'_{Q_1}(Q_2) + P_{Q_1}(z_1) + ... + P_{Q_1}(z_n)}$$

$$= \frac{xx_0 + xx_1 + ... + xx_n}{yy_0 + yy_1 + ... + yy_n}$$

$$\leq \frac{yy_0 \cdot exp(\epsilon_2) + yy_1 \cdot exp(\epsilon_2) + ... + yy_n \cdot exp(\epsilon_2)}{yy_0 + yy_1 + ... + yy_n} \leq exp(\epsilon_2).$$

Therefore, Algorithm 3 is ϵ_2 differentially private on r-location set.

5   Experimental Evaluation

5.1   Datasets

Considering our research mainly focuses on VANETs environment, we used a real-world datasets.

This dataset contains the GPS trajectories of 10,357 taxis during the period of Feb. 2 to Feb. 8, 2008 within Beijing [23]. The total number of points in this dataset is approximately 15 million and the total distance of the trajectories reaches to 9 million kilometers. The average sampling interval is approximately 177 s with a distance of about 623 m. Each file of this dataset, which is named by the taxi ID, contains the trajectories of one taxi.

5.2   Experiment Setting

We call our proposed mechanism CM, and we did a simulation experiment for CM, it is performed on a 64-bit Windows 7 desktop with Intel(R) i5 CPU @ 3.30 GHz and 8GB of memory. In order to show the continuity of the trajectory, we filter the data in the dataset, we extract user location data from 8am to 11am on the February 3. We perform k-means clustering on the vehicle's location according to distance, iterate ten times. In our solution, the location of the RSU where the user's vehicle is located should be used as the coarse-grained location of the user's vehicle, but the deployment method of the RSU is not detailed here, and we will deploy the location of the RSU in the center of the cluster, and we set an RSU range to 3 km in our experiment. And, in order to outline the location of the vehicle in a two-dimensional map, we use the COORD coordinate transformation software to transfer the latitude and longitude coordinates to the Beijing 54 Coordinate System. We calculate the position of the center of gravity of all the vehicles in the privacy requirement range and add noise to the position of requester. After confusion, we perform the convergence. And, the two steps loop have been executed 100 times, then we calculated the average distance between the noise-added position and the position of the inquired vehicle. This average distance is called the average drift. The drift reflects the quality of data availability guaranteed by our mechanisms while protecting the privacy of service requesters. The smaller the drift is, the closer the location of the request parameter is to the real location of the requesting vehicle, and the request result is closer to the real request result.

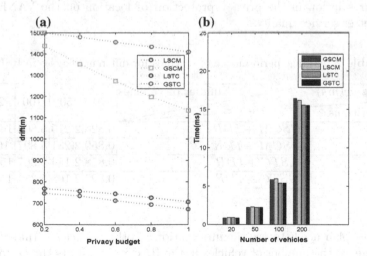

Fig. 3. (a) Average drift vs. privacy budget (b) effectiveness vs. number of vehicles

5.3   Experiment Results

(1) Andrs et al. proposed a laplace mechanism coordinates that satisfies geo-indistinguishability in polar [1], it truncates the reported location outside the scope of privacy requirements and replaces the reported location with the vertices of the square area nearest to the reporting position within the privacy requirement range. But, under the same size of privacy requirements, experiments have shown that our mechanism can also reduce the amount of noise while satisfying differential privacy. As shown in Fig. 3(a), the privacy budget is used to balance the security and utility of our solution. the drift denotes the amount of noise under different privacy budgets, that is, the error caused by the newly generated position of these methods instead of the real position of the requesting vehicle. Drift decreases as the privacy budget increases, which indicates that the utility of the new location generated by the CM is increasing. However, the security of the location privacy of the real requesting vehicle is also reduced and vice versa. LSCM indicates that the sensitivity we use during the noise generation phase is local sensitivity, and we use our convergence mechanism to converge the reported position outside the privacy requirements into the privacy requirement range; LSTC denotes using local sensitivity to add noise and uses the truncation mechanism to introduce reported location into the privacy requirements. GSCM and GSTC indicated that they used global sensitivity when adding noise, and used our convergence mechanism and the truncation mechanism of Andrs et al. to introduce privacy points beyond the privacy requirements. We can see that the local noise-sensitivity method produces less noise than the global sensitivity method, and our LSCM produces less error than the LSTC, this shows that the use of our solution in the privacy protection of location on the VANETs can obtain better service quality.

Table 2. Average performance of schemes for different vehicles in RSU

$runtime(ms)$ Algorithms	20	50	100	200
$GSCM + IDR$	0.826	2.215	5.804	16.381
$LSCM + IDR$	0.859	2.231	5.897	16.13
$LSTC + IDR$	0.858	2.184	5.367	15.522
$GSTC + IDR$	0.827	2.168	5.382	15.476

(2) Our plan needs to use the information of other vehicles within the same RSU range, so the number of vehicles in the RSU range affects the performance of our solution. As shown in Fig. 3(b) and Table 2, the runtime refers to the sum of the time of adding the noise in different ways and the time of selecting the substitute id in our testbed (with the unit in millisecond (ms)), it increases as the number of vehicles in the RSU increases. But this time is very small, almost negligible when the number of vehicles is in milliseconds. While our LSCM

satisfies security requirements, the error is the smallest of the four noise adding methods, and, when the number of vehicles reaches 200, the LSCM differs from other methods in efficiency within a millisecond. It shows that our scheme is feasible in terms of efficiency.

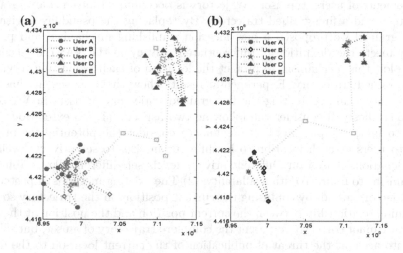

Fig. 4. (a) Real trajectories (b) coarse-grained trajectories

(3) We randomly select five users and show their true trajectories recorded every 20 min between 8am and 11am as shown in Fig. 4(a). In order to provide the service provider with the required coarse-grained trajectory, we allow the service provider to obtain the id of the mobile user as a substitute and the id of the RSU where the user is located when each request arrives, this can get the coarse-grained trajectory of the mobile user. And, as shown in Fig. 4(b), this coarse-grained trajectory is represented by the position of successive RSUs. Although the substitute vehicle is also a mobile user, our coarse-grained trajectory is displayed across the RSU. Such a trajectory does not expose the fine-grained trajectory and real location of the substitute vehicle, and the range of this granularity can be adjusted according to actual conditions. And, according to the definition of trajectory distortion in Definition 8, we can obtain that the trajectory distortion between the coarse-grained trajectories of the substitutes vehicle and the real trajectories of the substitutes vehicle is obviously less than R, because each time the pseudonym is selected within an RSU range. These two results reflect the security and effectiveness of our solution, while protecting the fine-grained trajectory of the currently requested user and the real location of the currently requested user, the service provider is provided with coarse-grained trajectories of other requesting users that are also in the same privacy circle.

6   Conclusion and Future Work

In this paper, we propose a privacy protection method based on differential privacy and pseudonym permutation for the problem of trajectory privacy protection in location-based services for VANETs. Under the personalized privacy requirements of users, the user's trajectory is decomposed into a coarse-grained trajectory and a fine-grained trajectory. By replacing the pseudonym with the coarse-grained we proposed a new location publishing mechanism and proved that it meets the definition of differentiated privacy in the ,VANETs scenario. We exploit this mechanism to protect the location of each requesting service in a fine-grained trajectory. Experimental results show that our scheme has better usability while protecting the fine-grained trajectory of users in VANETs. Future studies will consider the following two aspects: (1) To extend our approach to more complex applications and to consider the potential for privacy leaks to users at each location to be different in size, to set privacy levels for those locations, based on Different privacy levels set different data publishing mechanisms to improve data availability. (2) The existing methods of protecting the trajectory are all by confusing the current position on the trajectory so that the timing relationship between the current position and the position at the next moment cannot correctly represent the complete trajectory of a user, but seldom take into account the threat of publication of the current location to the user's true location at the next moment. Our goal is tantamount to design a solution to solve or optimize this problem.

Acknowledgment. The work is supported by the Natural Science Foundation of China under Grant No. 61572031 & U1405255. We thank the anonymous reviewers for their valuable comments that helped improve the final version of this paper.

References

1. Andrés, M.E., Bordenabe, N.E., Chatzikokolakis, K., Palamidessi, C.: Geo-indistinguishability: differential privacy for location-based systems. In: Proceedings of the 2013 ACM SIGSAC Conference on Computer & Communications Security, pp. 901–914. ACM (2013)
2. Chow, C.-Y., Mokbel, M.F.: Enabling private continuous queries for revealed user locations. In: Papadias, D., Zhang, D., Kollios, G. (eds.) SSTD 2007. LNCS, vol. 4605, pp. 258–275. Springer, Heidelberg (2007). https://doi.org/10.1007/978-3-540-73540-3_15
3. Cui, J., Wen, J., Han, S., Zhong, H.: Efficient privacy-preserving scheme for real-time location data in vehicular ad-hoc network. IEEE Internet Things J. (2018)
4. Dewri, R.: Local differential perturbations: location privacy under approximate knowledge attackers. IEEE Trans. Mob. Comput. **12**(12), 2360–2372 (2013)
5. Dwork, C.: Differential privacy: a survey of results. In: Agrawal, M., Du, D., Duan, Z., Li, A. (eds.) TAMC 2008. LNCS, vol. 4978, pp. 1–19. Springer, Heidelberg (2008). https://doi.org/10.1007/978-3-540-79228-4_1
6. Dwork, C., McSherry, F., Nissim, K., Smith, A.: Calibrating noise to sensitivity in private data analysis. In: Halevi, S., Rabin, T. (eds.) TCC 2006. LNCS, vol. 3876, pp. 265–284. Springer, Heidelberg (2006). https://doi.org/10.1007/11681878_14

7. Ghinita, G., Kalnis, P., Khoshgozaran, A., Shahabi, C., Tan, K.L.: Private queries in location based services: anonymizers are not necessary. In: Proceedings of the 2008 ACM SIGMOD International Conference on Management of Data, pp. 121–132. ACM (2008)
8. Jorgensen, Z., Yu, T., Cormode, G.: Conservative or liberal? Personalized differential privacy. In: 2015 IEEE 31st International Conference on Data Engineering (ICDE), pp. 1023–1034. IEEE (2015)
9. Krumm, J.: Inference attacks on location tracks. In: LaMarca, A., Langheinrich, M., Truong, K.N. (eds.) Pervasive 2007. LNCS, vol. 4480, pp. 127–143. Springer, Heidelberg (2007). https://doi.org/10.1007/978-3-540-72037-9_8
10. Lim, J., Yu, H., Kim, K., Kim, M., Lee, S.B.: Preserving location privacy of connected vehicles with highly accurate location updates. IEEE Commun. Lett. 21(3), 540–543 (2017)
11. McSherry, F., Talwar, K.: Mechanism design via differential privacy. In: 48th Annual IEEE Symposium on Foundations of Computer Science, FOCS 2007, pp. 94–103. IEEE (2007)
12. Mouratidis, K., Yiu, M.L.: Anonymous query processing in road networks. IEEE Trans. Knowl. Data Eng. 22(1), 2–15 (2010)
13. Mouratidis, K., Yiu, M.L.: Shortest path computation with no information leakage. Proc. VLDB Endow. 5(8), 692–703 (2012)
14. Palanisamy, B., Liu, L.: Attack-resilient mix-zones over road networks: architecture and algorithms. IEEE Trans. Mob. Comput. 14(3), 495–508 (2015)
15. Pan, X., Meng, X., Xu, J.: Distortion-based anonymity for continuous queries in location-based mobile services. In: Proceedings of the 17th ACM SIGSPATIAL International Conference on Advances in Geographic Information Systems, pp. 256–265. ACM (2009)
16. Pan, X., Xu, J., Meng, X.: Protecting location privacy against location-dependent attacks in mobile services. IEEE Trans. Knowl. Data Eng. 24(8), 1506–1519 (2012)
17. Shin, H., Vaidya, J., Atluri, V., Choi, S.: Ensuring privacy and security for LBS through trajectory partitioning. In: 2010 Eleventh International Conference on Mobile Data Management (MDM), pp. 224–226. IEEE (2010)
18. Xiao, Y., Xiong, L.: Protecting locations with differential privacy under temporal correlations. In: Proceedings of the 22nd ACM SIGSAC Conference on Computer and Communications Security, pp. 1298–1309. ACM (2015)
19. Yang, W.D., Gao, Z.M., Wang, K., Liu, H.Y.: A privacy-preserving data aggregation mechanism for vanets. J. High Speed Netw. 22(3), 223–230 (2016)
20. Yi, X., Kaosar, M.G., Paulet, R., Bertino, E.: Single-database private information retrieval from fully homomorphic encryption. IEEE Trans. Knowl. Data Eng. 25(5), 1125–1134 (2013)
21. Ying, B., Makrakis, D., Mouftah, H.T.: Dynamic mix-zone for location privacy in vehicular networks. IEEE Commun. Lett. 17(8), 1524–1527 (2013)
22. Yu, R., Kang, J., Huang, X., Xie, S., Zhang, Y., Gjessing, S.: MixGroup: accumulative pseudonym exchanging for location privacy enhancement in vehicular social networks. IEEE Trans. Dependable Secur. Comput. 13(1), 93–105 (2016)
23. Zheng, Y.: T-drive trajectory data sample, August 2011. https://www.microsoft.com/en-us/research/publication/t-drive-trajectory-data-sample/

Fine-Grained Attribute-Based Encryption Scheme Supporting Equality Test

Nabeil Eltayieb[1], Rashad Elhabob[2], Alzubair Hassan[1], and Fagen Li[1(✉)]

[1] Center for Cyber Security, School of Computer Science and Engineering,
University of Electronic Science and Technology of China, Chengdu 611731, China
fagenli@uestc.edu.cn
[2] School of Information and Software Engineering,
University of Electronic Science and Technology of China, Chengdu 611731, China

Abstract. The data of user should be protected against untrusted cloud server. A simple way is to use cryptographic methods. Attribute-based encryption (ABE) plays a vital role in securing many applications, particularly in cloud computing. In this paper, we propose a scheme called fine-grained attribute-based encryption supporting equality test (FG-ABEET). The proposed scheme grants the cloud server to perform if two ciphertexts are encryptions of the same message encrypted with the same access policy or different access policy. Moreover, the cloud server can perform the equality test operation without knowing anything about the message encrypted under either access policy. The FG-ABEET scheme is proved to be secure under Decisional Bilinear Diffe-Hellman (DBDH) assumption. In addition, the performance comparisons reveal that the proposed FG-ABEET scheme is efficient and practical.

Keywords: Cloud server · Attribute-based encryption
Equality test · Decisional Bilinear Diffe-Hellman

1 Introduction

Cloud computing becomes prevalent, and all the institutions turn to use it for storing their data. By outsourcing data, the cloud users enjoy a very low price, scalability, and vast computation capabilities. Although the benefits, users usually abstain from storing their sensitive data in the cloud for security concerns. To alleviate concerns, the users should encrypt the data before outsourcing. Therefore, encryption techniques provide flexible access control mechanisms over these encrypted data in cloud computing. Recently, attribute-based cryptography has attracted the data owners to use it as a secure algorithm for protecting the data. The concept of attributed-based encryption (ABE) was first suggested by Sahai and Waters [15], which provides data privacy and fine-grained access control. The users' secret keys and ciphertexts are associated with user's attributes. The users can only access the encrypted data if their attributes match the access policy, that created the ciphertext. There exist two kinds of ABE: key-policy

© Springer Nature Switzerland AG 2018
J. Vaidya and J. Li (Eds.): ICA3PP 2018, LNCS 11337, pp. 220–233, 2018.
https://doi.org/10.1007/978-3-030-05063-4_18

attribute-based encryption (KP-ABE) [6] and ciphertext-policy attribute-based encryption (CP-ABE) [3,5]. Then, many authors have presented several research papers using the applications of ABE. For example, ABE is used to achieve fine-grained access control [8,9,24]. ABE used for data auditing when the user is losing the control of data, and at the same time, he wants to check whether the cloud has stored the data securely [16,17]. Searchable encryption [18] guaranteed to the user secure search over remote cloud data if he lost the physical control. The data owner encrypts his data with keywords and sends it to the cloud. The users create trapdoor associated with the keywords. When the cloud receives the trapdoor, it performs the search processes, and it returns the search results to the users. To allow a user to search over encrypted data, there are many schemes using ABE [7,25]. Despites, there are some deficiencies in these searchable schemes. Because they used the trapdoor for searching ciphertexts only in case the attributes match the access policies of the ciphertexts. Recently, a new type of searchable encryption has been introduced by Yang et al. [23]. This kind of search helps the user checking if the ciphertexts encrypted by different access policies include the same message, which can be used to support keywords search on encrypted data trivially. In this paper, we present a fine-grained attribute-based encryption scheme supporting equality test (FG-ABEET). Our scheme is based on the scenario shown in Fig. 1. The data owner encrypts his private data with corresponding trapdoors and stores it in the cloud. Suppose there is a user intends to search in the data owner's ciphertexts, he sends a request using specific trapdoor to the cloud. When the cloud receives the request of searching, it can decide whether two different ciphertexts are encryptions of the same plaintext. The aim of this work is to allow the users an easy search of ciphertexts, to reach secure fine-grained, and access control in the cloud.

1.1 Related Work

Searchable encryption technique has many traits such as protecting data privacy of data owners and allowing the users to search over the encrypted information. The first one who suggested the concept of a public key encryption with a keyword search (PKE-KS) is Boneh et al. [4]. Subsequent, identity based encryption keyword search (IBE-KS) has attracted a lot of researchers in this field [1]. ABE has also competed in searchable encryption; it can perform searching over encrypted data. Besides, it can achieve fine-grained access control [12,14,27]. In spite of this, the above three schemes PKE-KS, IBE-KS and ABE-KS have some limitations, because they only perform an equivalence test on ciphertexts based on a fixed public key. The concept of public key encryption with equality test (PKE-ET) was introduced by Yang et al. [23]. The purpose of his scheme is to investigate if two user's ciphertexts include the same message. To improve Yang's scheme by adding some new features such as authorization, Tang [19] suggests an enhanced FG-PKEET to achieve a fine-grained authorization. The test operation can be done by authorized two users with the help of a trusted authority. After that Tang [20] suggested another scheme called an all-or-nothing PKEET.

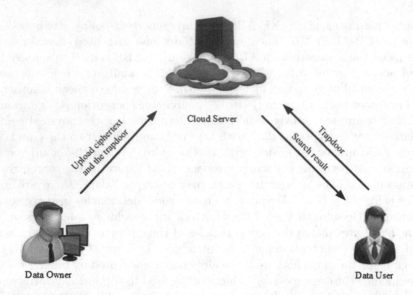

Fig. 1. Application scenario for ABE-ET in cloud computing

This scheme provides a new authorization method to specify who can do a plaintext equality test based on ciphertexts. Then, a new concept of PKEwET and identity-based encryption was proposed by Ma [13], under the name identity-based encryption with equality test (IBEET). To decrease the computational time cost in the previous scheme, Wu et al. [22] designed a scheme for this purpose. Recently, ABE supports the concept of equality test, because it supports the functionality of search and tests on the ciphertext based on different access policies [21]. A KP-ABE with equality test (ET) scheme was proposed by Zhu et al. [26], which provides testing if the ciphertexts include the same information based on the sets of different attributes. But, it only realizes one-way against chosen-ciphertext attack. Liao et al. [11] claimed that Zhu et al.'s scheme isn't secure for a test under chosen ciphertext attack. They proposed a new scheme to solve one-way against chosen-ciphertext attack. As we know, there is no explicit CP-ABE fine-grained access control scheme with equality test.

1.2 Organization

In Sect. 2, we introduce both the bilinear map and hardness problem for security analysis. Then, the definitions of FG-ABEET such as system models, properties, and security models are given in Sect. 3. We present our construction in Sect. 4. The security analysis is demonstrated in Sect. 5. In Sect. 6, we compare our scheme with other schemes. Finally, a conclusion of our works is given in Sect. 7.

2   Preliminaries

In this section, we briefly describe the basic definition and properties of the bilinear pairings, the Decisional Bilinear Diffie Hellman (DBDH) assumption, access tree, and the lagrange coefficient.

2.1   Bilinear Map

Let $\mathbb{G}_1$ and $\mathbb{G}_2$ be two multiplicative cyclic groups of prime order p. Suppose that g is a generator of $\mathbb{G}_1$. A bilinear map $e : \mathbb{G}_1 \times \mathbb{G}_1 \rightarrow \mathbb{G}_2$ with mentioned below properties:

1. Bilinearity: $e(g^a, g^b) = e(g, g)^{ab}$ for all $g, g \in \mathbb{G}_1$, $a, b \in \mathbb{Z}_p^*$.
2. Non-degeneracy: We have $g, g \in \mathbb{G}_1$ such that $e(g, g) \neq 1$.
3. Computability: An efficient algorithm to evaluate $e(g, g)$ for all $g, g \in \mathbb{G}_1$ is provided.

2.2   The Decisional Bilinear Diffie Hellman (DBDH) Assumption

The security of our scheme is established under the Decisional Bilinear Diffie Hellman (DBDH) assumption. Let $a, b, c, z \in \mathbb{Z}_p^*$. The decisional BDH assumption is that no probabilistic polynomial time adversary $\mathcal{B}$ can distinguish the tuple $(A = g^a, B = g^b, C = g^c, e(y, y)^{abc})$ from the tuple $(A = g^a, D = g^b, C = g^c, e(g, g)^z)$ with non-negligible advantage.

2.3   Monotone Access Structure

Suppose there is a set of attributes $\{P_1, P_2, \ldots, P_n\}$, we say a selection of attributes $S \in 2^{\{P_1, P_2, \ldots, P_n\}}$ is monotone if $\forall B, C : B \in A$ and $B \subseteq C$ then $C \in S$, the monotone access structure is known as a group collection of non-empty subsets $S \in 2^{\{P_1, P_2, \ldots, P_n\}} \setminus \{\emptyset\}$. We denote the authorized sets by S (qualified set), and the sets which are not in S are called the unauthorized sets. We emphasize that the monotone access structures [2] must be used in our scheme.

2.4   Access Tree

Let τ be a tree representing the security policy to access the data; we denote $node_x$ for the node x, τ_x is a subtree of τ at node x, $(node_R)$ the root node R, γ is the set of attributes, and we say γ satisfies the tree τ if $\tau(\gamma) = \tau_R(\gamma) = 1$, the tree τ consists of many nodes where each $node_x$ has one parent $(parent_x)$ and one or many children $child_x$, n_x is the number of children for the $node_x$ so $n_x = |child_x|$, k_x is the threshold of $node_x$ which is a minimum number of children are required to satisfy (pass) $node_x$ and to go to the parent node $parent_x$, each node x in the tree has assigned unique number arbitrarily which is known as an $index(x)$.

2.5   The Lagrange Coefficient

Lagrange was defined for attribute-based encryption with Fine-Grained Access Control by Goyal and Sahai in [6], for each $i \in \mathcal{Z}_p$ we denote $\triangle_{i,S}$ and a set S will be computed as in Eq. 1:

$$\triangle_{i,S}(x) = \prod_{(j \in S, i \neq j)} \frac{x-j}{i-j} \tag{1}$$

3   The Framework of FG-ABEET Scheme

In this section we formalize the model of Fine-Grained Attribute-Base Encryption Equality Test (FG-ABEET).

3.1   System Model

Based on the scenario in Fig. 1. our scheme involves several entities: key authority (KA), data owner (DO), data user (DU), cloud server (CS).

1. Key Authority (KA). The KA is in charge of generating system public parameters that will be used by the CS and data owners.
2. Data Owner (DO). The DO encrypts his secrets data before outsourcing to the cloud, and creates the trapdoor for test purpose.
3. Data User (DU). The DU decrypts the ciphertexts or tests the ciphertexts if he is a legitimate user.
4. Cloud Server (CS). The CS stores the resulting ciphertexts, and performs the equality test algorithm without decrypting ciphertexts.

3.2   Definition of FG-ABEET

The proposed scheme consists of the following algorithms (Setup, KeyGen, Encrypt, Decrypt, Trapdoor, Test). Where M is plaintext space and CT ciphertext space.

1. **Setup** (λ): KA takes security parameter λ, then returns public parameter PK and keeps master secret key MSK secret.
2. **KeyGen:** An access structure τ, the master key MSK, and the public parameter PK are taken by KA. The decryption key dk is outputted by KA.
3. **Trapdoor:** KA takes as inputs an access structure τ, the master key MSK and the public parameter PK. It outputs a trapdoor td.
4. **Encrypt** (PK, M, γ): DO takes as inputs the public parameters PK, a message M, and a set of attributes γ. Then, the algorithm will encrypt M and will produce a ciphertext CT.
5. **Decrypt** (PK, CT, dk): DU takes as inputs the public parameters PK, a ciphertext CT, which contains an access structure τ, and a decryption key dk. If the set γ of attributes fulfills the access structure τ, then the algorithm will decrypt the ciphertext CT and will return a message M. Otherwise, it returns symbol $\perp$.

6. **Test** (CT_i, td_i, CT_j, td_j): Assume that we have U_i and U_j where i, j are user index $(1 \leqslant i, j \leqslant N)$ and N denotes the number of users, we define $Test$ algorithm to determine whether two users ciphertexts contain the same message or not. CSP takes as inputs U_i's ciphertexts C_i , trapdoor td_i and U_j's ciphertexts CT_j , trapdoor td_j. If the set γ of attributes fulfills the access structure τ. The algorithm outputs 1 if CT_i and CT_j include same message. Otherwise, it returns symbol $\perp$.

3.3   Security Model

Definition 1. *Our FG-ABEET scheme is secure against selective chosen-plaintext attack if no adversary can win the following game.*

Setup. The set of attributes γ are declared by the adversary $\mathcal{A}$ in order to be challenged. The setup algorithm of FG-ABEET is run by the challenger $\mathcal{C}$. In addition, the public parameters are sent to $\mathcal{A}$.

Phase 1. The $\mathcal{A}$ makes many queries for decryption key for many access structures τ_{se}, where $\gamma \neq \tau_{se} \forall se$. the $\mathcal{C}$ generates decryption key dk and corresponding trapdoor td for the $\mathcal{A}$.

Challenge. The $\mathcal{A}$ selects two messages m_0, m_1 with equal lengths, and sends it to $\mathcal{C}$. $\mathcal{C}$ replies to $\mathcal{A}$ with challenge ciphertext CT by calling Encrypt (PK, M_b, γ), where $b \in \{0, 1\}$.

Phase 2. It is the same as **Phase 1**.

Guess. The $\mathcal{A}$ outputs a guess bit b' of b. $\mathcal{A}$ wins the game if $b' = b$. The advantage of $\mathcal{A}$ is indicated as $Adv(\mathcal{A}) - \Pr[b' - b] - 1/2$.

3.4   Properties of FG-ABEET

Correctness: Let dk be the decryption key generated by KeyGen algorithm having the inputs MSK and a set of attributes γ, then
$\forall\, M \in \mathcal{M}$
$\Pr[\text{M} \leftarrow \text{Decrypt}(SK, \text{Encrypt}(PK, M, \tau))] = 1$.

Consistency: following the trapdoors generated by trapdoor algorithm and equality test algorithm, the perfect consistency holds.
$\forall\, M \in \mathcal{M}$ and $M_i = M_j$
$\Pr[1 \leftarrow \text{Test}(CT_i, td_i, CT_j, td_j)]$.

Soundness: following the trapdoors generated by trapdoor algorithm and equality test algorithm, the perfect soundness holds.
$\forall\, M \in \mathcal{M}$ and $M_i \neq M_j$
$\Pr[1 \leftarrow \text{Test}(CT_i, td_i, CT_j, td_j)]$ is negligible.

4   The Framework of FG-ABEET Scheme

In this part, we present a concrete FG-ABEET scheme which works as below.

1. **Setup:** The setup algorithm works as follows:

- Generate the pairing parameters: two groups $\mathbb{G}_1, \mathbb{G}_2$ of prime order p, and an admissible bilinear map $e : \mathbb{G}_1 \times \mathbb{G}_1 \rightarrow \mathbb{G}_2$, it chooses a random generator $g \in \mathbb{G}_1$.
- Define the lagrange coefficient $\triangle_{i,S}$ for $i \in \mathbb{Z}_p$ and a set, S, of element in $\mathbb{Z}_p : \triangle_{i,S}(x) = \prod_{(j \in S, i \neq j)} x - j / i - j$.
- Define universe set of attributes $\Omega = \{1, 2, \ldots, n\}$. For each attribute $i \in \Omega$ chooses $t_i \in \mathbb{Z}_p$ randomly.
- Randomly choose β_1, and $\beta_2 \in \mathbb{Z}_p$.

   the message space is $\mathcal{M} \in \mathbb{G}_2$. the ciphertext space $\mathcal{C} \in \mathbb{G}_2$. The public parameter PK are: $T_1 = g^{t_1}, \ldots, T_n = g^{t_n}, Y_1 = e(g,g)^{\beta_1}, Y_2 = e(g,g)^{\beta_2}$. The master secret key MSK is: $t_1, \ldots, t_n, \beta_1, \beta_2$.

2. **KeyGen**(MSK, τ): Its inputs are: a master secret key MSK and access tree τ. The algorithm works as follows:
   - First, select randomly a polynomial q_x for each node x (the leaves also are considered) in the tree τ. The polynomials are selected in a top-down manner, beginning from the root node r.
   - For each node x in the tree, select $d_x = k_x - 1$.
   - For the root node r, set $q_r(0) = \beta_1$, $q'_r(0) = \beta_2$ and select randomly d_r and q_r to satisfy the forementioned equations completely. For any other node x, set $q_x(0) = q_{\mathrm{parent}(x)}(\mathrm{index}(x))$ and select randomly d_x to define q_x completely.
   - for each leaf node x, we give the following decryption key to the user: $dk = (dk_1, dk_2) = (g^{q_x(0)/t_i}, g^{q'_x(0)/t_i})$, where $i = \mathrm{index}(att(x))$.

3. **Trapdoor**(dk): It takes as input the decryption key dk and outputs the trapdoor $td = dk_2 = g^{q'_x(0)/t_i}$.

4. **Encrypt** (PK, M, γ): It inputs the message M and a set of attributes γ, the encryption algorithm picks two random numbers s, and $r \in \mathbb{Z}_p^*$ and computes: $CT = (\gamma, C_1 = g^r, C_2 = M^r Y_2^s, C_3 = M Y_1^s, \{C_i = T_i^s\}_{i \in \gamma})$

5. **Decrypt** (CT, dk): We try to reconstruct $e(g,g)^{s.\beta_1}$ using the access structure τ and decryption key from down up to root recursively as fallows:

$$\mathrm{DecryptNode}(CT, dk, x) = \begin{cases} e(CT_i, dk_1) = e(g^{q_x(0)/t_i}, g^{s.t_i}) \\ = e(g,g)^{s.q_x(0)} \text{ if } i \in \gamma \\ \perp \text{ otherwise} \end{cases}$$

When x is a non-leaf node, the algorithm DecryptNode (CT, dk, x) runs as follows: For all nodes z that are children of x, it calls DecryptNode (CT, dk, z) and stores the output as F_z. Let S_x be an arbitrary k_x-sized set of child nodes z such that $F_z \neq \perp$. If such set doesn't exists, then the node isn't satisfied and the function returns $\perp$. Otherwise, we calculate:

$$F_x = \prod_{z \in S_x} F_z^{\Delta_{i,S'_x}(0)}, \text{where } \begin{array}{l} i=\text{index}(z) \\ S'_x=\text{index}(z):z \in S_x \end{array}$$

$$= \prod_{z \in S_x} (e(g,g)^{s \cdot q_z(0)})^{\Delta_{i,S'_x}(0)}$$

$$= \prod_{z \in S_x} (e(g,g)^{s \cdot q_{\text{parent}_z}(\text{index}(z))})^{\Delta_{i,S'_x}(0)} \quad \text{(by constr.)}$$

$$= \prod_{z \in S_x} e(g,g)^{s \cdot q_x(i) \cdot \Delta_{i,S'_x}(0)}$$

$$= e(g,g)^{s \cdot q_x(0)} \quad \text{(using polynomial interpolation)}$$

Then, return the result.

We observe that DecryptNode$(CT, dk, r) = e(g,g)^{\beta_1 s} = Y_1^s$ if and only if the ciphertext satisfies the tree. Since, $CT' = MY_1^s$. Y_1^s is divided out simply by the decryption algorithm which also recovers the message M.

6. **Test** (CT_i, td_i, CT_j, td_j): It is ran by the cloud server, takes as inputs U_i's ciphertexts CT_i, trapdoor td_i and U_j's ciphertexts CT_j , trapdoor td_j. If the set γ of attributes fulfills the access structure τ, the algorithm runs as follows:

$$\text{TestNode}(x) = \begin{cases} e(CT_i, dk_2) = e(g^{q_x(0)/t_i}, g^{s \cdot t_i}) \\ = e(g,g)^{s \cdot q_x(0)} \text{ if } i \in \gamma \\ \perp \text{ otherwise} \end{cases}$$

We now consider the recursive case when x is a non-leaf, the algorithm Test-tNode (CT_i, dk_2, x) runs as follows: For all nodes z that are children of x, it calls TesttNode (CT_i, dk_2, z) and the output F_z is stored. Let S_x be an arbitrary k_x-sized set of child nodes z such that $F_z \neq \perp$. If such set doesn't exist, then the node is not satisfied and the function outputs $\perp$. Otherwise, we calculate:

$$F_{x_i} = \prod_{z \in S_x} F_z^{\Delta_{i,S'_x}(0)}, \text{where } \begin{array}{l} i=\text{index}(z) \\ S'_x=\text{index}(z):z \in S_x \end{array}$$

$$= \prod_{z \in S_x} (e(g,g)^{s \cdot q'_z(0)})^{\Delta_{i,S'_x}(0)}$$

$$= \prod_{z \in S_x} (e(g,g)^{s \cdot q'_{\text{parent}_z}(\text{index}(z))})^{\Delta_{i,S'_x}(0)} \quad \text{(by constr.)}$$

$$= \prod_{z \in S_x} e(g,g)^{s \cdot q'_x(i) \cdot \Delta_{i,S'_x}(0)}$$

$$= e(g,g)^{s \cdot q'_x(0)} \quad \text{(using polynomial interpolation)}$$

If the ciphertext satisfies the tree, the TestNode $(CT_i, dk_2, r) = e(g,g)^{\beta_2 s} = Y_2^s$

$$X_i = \frac{C_2}{Y_2^s} = \frac{M^{r_i} \cdot Y_2^s}{Y_2^s} = M^{r_i}$$

From the previous calculation, the result of $(CT_j, dk_2, r) = e(g,g)^{\beta_2 s} = Y_2^s$

$$X_j = \frac{C_2}{Y_2^s} = \frac{M^{r_i} \cdot Y_2^s}{Y_2^s} = M^{r_j}$$

The test algorithm outputs 1 if CT_i and CT_j include same message. Otherwise, gives symbol $\perp$.

Correctness: The following equations hold, and returns $\perp$ otherwise

$$e(X_i, C_{j,1}) = e(M^{r_i, g^{r_j}}) = e(M,g)^{r_i r_j}$$
$$e(X_j, C_{i,1}) = e(M^{r_j, g^{r_i}}) = e(M,g)^{r_i r_j}$$

5 Security Analysis

Theorem 1. *The FG-ABEET scheme is selective IND-CPA security against the adversary $\mathcal{A}$ based on the assumption of the DBDH.*

Proof. Assume that $\mathcal{A}$ attacks our FG-ABEET scheme with advantage ϵ . lets create a simulator which plays the decisional BDH game with advantage $\epsilon/2$. The game runs as below:

First, the challenger $\mathcal{C}$ sets the bilinear map e for $\mathbb{G}_1$ and $\mathbb{G}_2$, and generator g. The $\mathcal{C}$ flips binary coin ς, without knowing $\mathcal{B}$. if $\varsigma = 0$, the C sets $(A, B, C, Z) = (g^a, g^b, g^c, e(g,g)^{abc})$; otherwise it sets $(A, B, C, Z) = (g^a, g^b, g^c, e(g,g)^z)$ for random a, b, c, z. The universe Ω is defined.

- **Setup.** $\mathcal{A}$ is called by the simulator $\mathcal{B}$. $\mathcal{A}$ submits the attributes set γ to be challenged. The simulator considers $Y_1(A, B) = e(g,g)^{ab}$. $\forall i \in \mathcal{U}$, also it sets T_i as: if $i \in \gamma$. The simulator selects a random $r_i \in \mathbb{Z}_p$ and considers $T_i = g^{r_i}$ (consequently, $t_i = r_i$). Otherwise, the simulator selects a random $\delta_i \in \mathbb{Z}_p$ and chooses $T_i = g^{b\delta_i} = B^{\delta_i}$ (Thus, $t_i = \delta_i$). After that, it sends the public parameters to $\mathcal{A}$.

- **Phase 1.** The key requests corresponding to τ are created by the adversory $\mathcal{A}$. Assume $\mathcal{A}$ is making a request for the decryption key corresponding to τ insuring $\tau(\gamma) = 0$. To create the decryption key, the $\mathcal{B}$ picks a polynomial Q_x of degree d_x for each node in τ. We determine two procedures: Proced1 and Proced2.

  Proced1 $(\tau_x, \gamma, \lambda_x)$: It takes as inputs τ_x including the root node x, and γ satisfying $\tau_x(\gamma) = 1$ and an integer $\lambda_x \in \mathbb{Z}_p$.
  - First, it sets degree d_x for a polynomial q_x to be one less than the value of threshold k_x of that node, which means that $d_x = k_x - 1$.
  - Concerning the root node x, it sets $q_x = \lambda_x$.
  - Then, for each child node x' of x by running Proced1 $(\tau_{x'}, \gamma, q_x(\text{index}(x')))$.
  - For each x' of x, it sets $q_{x'}(0) = q_x(\text{index}(x'))$.

  Proced2 $(\tau_x, \gamma, g^{\lambda_x})$: It takes as inputs τ_x including the root node x, γ with unsatisfied $\tau_x(\gamma) = 0$ and an integer $g^{\lambda_x} \in \mathbb{G}_1$ (where $\lambda \in \mathbb{Z}_p$).

- First, it sets degree d_x for a polynomial q_x to the node x. When $\tau_x(\gamma) = 0$, Proced2 doesn't satisfy no more d_x children of x.
- Set $h_x \leq d_x$ be the number of satisfied children of x.
- For each x' of x, Proced2 selects a random point $\gamma_x \in \mathbb{Z}_p$
- Then, it fixes $d_x - h_x$ points of q_x. We repeat the algorithm to determine polynomials for the other nodes located in the tree as the following: For each child node x' of x, the algorithm runs:
  * Proced1 $(\tau_x, \gamma, q_x(\text{index}(x')))$ if x' is a satisfied node, in this case $q_x(\text{index}(x'))$ is known.
  * Proced2 $(\tau_x, \gamma, g^{q_x(\text{index}(x'))})$ if x' is not a satisfied node, in this case only $g^{q_x(0)}$ is known. Also $q_{x'}(0) = q_x(\text{index}(x'))$.

The $\mathcal{B}$ runs Proced2 (τ, γ, A) to determine a polynomial $q_x \; \forall x \in \tau$. Let $q_r(0) = a$, the $\mathcal{B}$ define the final polynomial $Q_x(.) = bq_x(.)$. This sets $\beta_1 = Q_r(0) = ab$. For each leaf node the decryption key generation is done as below. Consider $i = index(att(x))$.

$$
dk = \begin{cases} g^{\dfrac{Q_x(0)}{t_i}} = g^{\dfrac{bq_x(0)}{r_i}} = B^{\dfrac{q_x(0)}{r_i}} & \text{if } i \in \gamma \\ = g^{\dfrac{Q_x(0)}{t_i}} = g^{\dfrac{bq_x(0)}{b\delta_i}} = g^{\dfrac{q_x(0)}{\delta_i}} & \text{otherwise} \end{cases}
$$

- **Challenge** $\mathcal{A}$ will submit two m_0, m_1 with equal lengths to $\mathcal{B}$. The $\mathcal{B}$ flips a fair binary coin v, and sends back the ciphertext of m_v. The calculation of the ciphertext is done as: $CT = (\gamma, CT' = m_v Z, \{CT_i - C^{r_i}\}_{i \in \gamma})$. The ciphertext is valid if $\mu = 0$ then $Z = e(g,g)^{abc}$. If we set $s = c$, then we have $Y^s = (e(g,g)^{ab})^c = e(g,g)^{abc}$, and $CT_i = (g^{r_i})^c = C^{r_i}$.
  Otherwise, if $\mu = 1$, then $Z = e(g,g)^z$. So we get $CT' = m_v e(g,g)^z$. Since z is random, $\mathcal{A}$ won't get information from m_v, because CT is also a random element of $\mathbb{G}_2$.
- **Phase 2.** The simulator repeats **Phase 1.**
- **Guess.** The adversary $\mathcal{A}$ outputs a guess bit v' of v. If $v' - v$ the $\mathcal{B}$ will output $\mu' = 0$ to indicate that was given the BDH-tuple, otherwise output $\mu' = 1$.

If $\mu = 1$ the $\mathcal{A}$ doesn't discover information about v. Hence, we have the next probability $\Pr[v \neq v' \mid \mu = 1] = 1/2$. Because $\mathcal{B}$ guesses $\mu' = 1$ when $v \neq v'$, we get $\Pr[\mu' = \mu \mid \mu = 1] = 1/2$.
If $\mu = 0$ the $\mathcal{A}$ discovers the ciphertext of m_v. The advantage of the adversary in this case is ϵ (according to the definition). Therefore, we obtain $\Pr[v = v' \mid \mu = 0] = 1/2 + \epsilon$. Because the $\mathcal{B}$ guesses $\mu' = 0$ when $v = v'$, we get $\Pr[\mu' = \mu \mid \mu = 0] = 1/2 + \epsilon$.
The total advantage of the $\mathcal{B}$ in the Decisional BDH game is:
$$
\frac{1}{2} \Pr[\mu' = \mu \mid \mu = 0] = \frac{1}{2} + \frac{1}{2} \Pr[\mu' = \mu \mid \mu = 1] - \frac{1}{2} = \frac{1}{2}(\frac{1}{2} + \epsilon) + \frac{1}{2}\frac{1}{2} - \frac{1}{2} = \frac{1}{2}\epsilon.
$$

6   Performance Evaluation

In this section, we estimate the performance of our proposed FG-ABEET scheme and other similar schemes in [10, 21, 26] regarding computation complexity as presented in Table 1. We conducted the experiment by choosing the Type A pairing using pairing-based cryptography (PBC) library [28], for a variety of cryptographic operations. The implementation is taken on an Intel Core i5-4460, 3.2 GHz machine with 4G RAM. To achieve a 80-bit security level, the implementation uses a 20-bit elliptic curve group based on the super singular curve $y^2 = x^3 + x$ over a 64-bit finite field and the embedding degree is 2. Let ABE-KS denotes to Attribute based encryption with keyword search, ABE-ET: Attribute based encryption with equality test, $\mathbb{P}$: denotes to be the bilinear pairing, $\mathbb{E}_1$: exponentiation in group $\mathbb{G}_1$, $\mathbb{E}_2$: exponentiation in group $\mathbb{G}_2$, n: is the number of attributes involved, s: the number of attributes in access policy, s': the number of attributes in attribute set, w_1: the number of wildcards in access policy. We consider $n = 15$, $w_1 = 2$ and $s = 5$.

The computation cost of FG-ABEET scheme and [10, 21, 26] is presented in Fig. 2. The time cost of encryption in our FG-ABEET scheme is the lowest compared with other relevant schemes. For decryption, the time in FG-ABEET

Table 1. The comparison of computational complexity.

Schemes	Encryption	Decryption	Test
ABE-KS [10]	$\mathbb{P} + (s+5)\mathbb{E}_1 + 2\mathbb{E}_2$	$2\mathbb{P} + 2s\mathbb{E}_1$	$2\mathbb{P} + 2s\mathbb{E}_1$
KP-ABE-ET [26]	$(2s' + 3)\mathbb{E}_1$	$2s'\mathbb{P} + (2s' + 2)\mathbb{E}_1$	$2s'\mathbb{P} + 2s'\mathbb{E}_1$
CP-ABE-ET [21]	$(2n + 11)\mathbb{E}_1$	$(8w_1 + 1)\mathbb{E}_1 + 4\mathbb{E}_2 + 12\mathbb{P}$	$8w_1\mathbb{E}_1 + 4\mathbb{E}_2 + 14\mathbb{P}$
FG-ABEET [our]	$(s' + 1)\mathbb{E}_1 + 4\mathbb{E}_2$	$2s'\mathbb{P} + 2s'\mathbb{E}_1$	$2s'\mathbb{P} + 2s'\mathbb{E}_1$

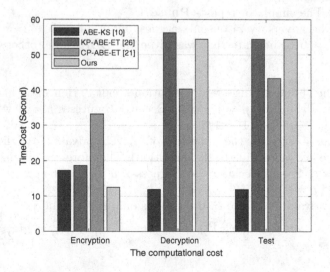

Fig. 2. Computational cost comparison

is less than scheme [26], but, it is higher than schemes [10,21]. Because the time-cost is related to the number of attributes associated with corresponding algorithms. The test algorithms in our FG-ABEET scheme and [26] is relatively costly. But, this is not an obstacle, because the test phase is done in the cloud which has large computation capacity. From Fig. 2, it can be seen that the scheme presented in [10] has the lowest cost in decryption and test. However, this scheme doesn't support equality test.

7   Conclusion

Attribute-based encryption has many uses in cloud computing. In this paper, we presented fine-grained attribute-based encryption supporting equality test (FG-ABEET), which has various traits: (1) It allows users with searching capability on ciphertexts; (2) secure fine-grained and access control in the cloud. The proposed scheme is proved to be secure under decisional Bilinear Diffie Hell-man (BDH) assumption. Additionally, we show the performance comparisons of existing ABE-ET schemes with our FG-ABE-ET scheme to explain that the proposed scheme is more efficient. The coming work focuses on a few interesting obstacles such as how we design more efficient ABE-ET scheme with authorization mechanism.

Acknowledgements. We would like to thank the anonymous reviewers for their valuable comments and suggestions. This work is supported by the National Natural Science Foundation of China (Grant No. 61872058) and Fundamental Research Funds for the Central Universities (Grant No. ZYGX2016J081)

References

1. Abdalla, M., Bellare, M., Catalano, D., Kiltz, E., Kohno, T., Lange, T., Malone-Lee, J., Neven, G., Paillier, P., Shi, H.: Searchable encryption revisited: consistency properties, relation to anonymous ibe, and extensions. J. Cryptol. **21**, 350–391 (2005)
2. Benaloh, J., Leichter, J.: Generalized secret sharing and monotone functions. In: Goldwasser, S. (ed.) CRYPTO 1988. LNCS, vol. 403, pp. 27–35. Springer, New York (1990). https://doi.org/10.1007/0-387-34799-2_3
3. Bethencourt, J., Sahai, A., Waters, B.: Ciphertext-policy attribute-based encryption. In: 2007 IEEE Symposium on Security and Privacy (SP 2007), pp. 321–334 (2007)
4. Boneh, D., Di Crescenzo, G., Ostrovsky, R., Persiano, G.: Public key encryption with keyword search. In: Cachin, C., Camenisch, J.L. (eds.) EUROCRYPT 2004. LNCS, vol. 3027, pp. 506–522. Springer, Heidelberg (2004). https://doi.org/10.1007/978-3-540-24676-3_30
5. Cheung, L., Newport, C.: Provably secure ciphertext policy ABE. In: 14th ACM Conference on Computer and Communications Security (CCS 2007), pp. 456–465 (2007)

6. Goyal, V., Pandey, O., Sahai, A., Waters, B.: Attribute-based encryption for fine-grained access control of encrypted data. In: Proceedings of the 13th ACM Conference on Computer and Communications Security, pp. 89–98. ACM (2006)
7. Li, H., Liu, D., Dai, Y., Luan, T.H., Shen, X.S.: Enabling efficient multi-keyword ranked search over encrypted mobile cloud data through blind storage. IEEE Trans. Emerg. Top. Comput. **3**(1), 127–138 (2015)
8. Li, J., Chen, X., Chow, S.S., Huang, Q., Wong, D.S., Liu, Z.: Multi-authority fine-grained access control with accountability and its application in cloud. J. Netw. Comput. Appl. **112**(C), 89–96 (2018)
9. Li, J., Li, J., Chen, X., Jia, C., Wong, D.S.: Secure outsourced attribute-based encryption. IACR Cryptology ePrint Archive, p, 635 (2012)
10. Liang, K., Susilo, W.: Searchable attribute-based mechanism with efficient data sharing for secure cloud storage. IEEE Trans. Inf. Forensics Secur. **10**(9), 1981–1992 (2015)
11. Liao, Y., Chen, H., Li, F., Jiang, S., Zhou, S., Mohammed, R.: Insecurity of a key-policy attribute based encryption scheme with equality test. IEEE Access **6**, 10189–10196 (2018)
12. Liu, Z., Luo, J., Xu, L.: A fine-grained attribute-based authentication for sensitive data stored in cloud computing. Int. J. Grid Util. Comput. **7**(4), 237–244 (2016)
13. Ma, S.: Identity-based encryption with outsourced equality test in cloud computing. Inf. Sci. **328**, 389–402 (2016)
14. Phuong, T.V.X., Yang, G., Susilo, W.: Poster: efficient ciphertext policy attribute based encryption under decisional linear assumption. In: Proceedings of the 2014 ACM SIGSAC Conference on Computer and Communications Security (CCS 2014), pp. 1490–1492 (2014)
15. Sahai, A., Waters, B.: Fuzzy identity-based encryption. In: Proceedings of the 24th Annual International Conference on Theory and Applications of Cryptographic Techniques, EUROCRYPT 2005, pp. 457–473 (2005)
16. Sebé, F., Domingo-Ferrer, J., Martinez-Balleste, A., Deswarte, Y., Quisquater, J.J.: Efficient remote data possession checking in critical information infrastructures. IEEE Trans. Knowl. Data Eng. **20**(8), 1034–1038 (2008)
17. Shah, M.A., Swaminathan, R., Baker, M.: Privacy-preserving audit and extraction of digital contents. IACR Cryptology ePrint Archive, p. 186 (2008)
18. Song, D.X., Wagner, D., Perrig, A.: Practical techniques for searches on encrypted data. In: 2000 IEEE Symposium on Security and Privacy, S&P 2000, Proceedings, pp. 44–55 (2000)
19. Tang, Q.: Towards public key encryption scheme supporting equality test with fine-grained authorization. In: Proceedings of the 16th Australasian Conference on Information Security and Privacy, (ACISP 2011), pp. 389–406 (2011)
20. Tang, Q.: Public key encryption supporting plaintext equality test and user-specified authorization. Secur. Commun. Netw. **5**(12), 1351–1362 (2012)
21. Wang, Q., Peng, L., Xiong, H., Sun, J., Qin, Z.: Ciphertext-policy attribute-based encryption with delegated equality test in cloud computing. IEEE Access **PP**, 1 (2017)
22. Wu, L., Zhang, Y., Choo, K.K.R., He, D.: Efficient and secure identity-based encryption scheme with equality test in cloud computing. Futur. Gener. Comput. Syst. **73**(C), 22–31 (2017)
23. Yang, G., Tan, C.H., Huang, Q., Wong, D.S.: Probabilistic public key encryption with equality test. In: Pieprzyk, J. (ed.) CT-RSA 2010. LNCS, vol. 5985, pp. 119–131. Springer, Heidelberg (2010). https://doi.org/10.1007/978-3-642-11925-5_9

24. Zhang, R., Ma, H., Lu, Y.: Fine-grained access control system based on fully out-sourced attribute-based encryption. J. Syst. Softw. **125**, 344–353 (2017)
25. Zheng, Q., Xu, S., Ateniese, G.: Vabks: Verifiable attribute-based keyword search over outsourced encrypted data. In: IEEE International Conference on Computer (IEEE INFOCOM 2014), pp. 522-530 (2014)
26. Zhu, H., Wang, L., Ahmad, H., Niu, X.: Key-policy attribute-based encryption with equality test in cloud computing. IEEE Access **5**, 20428–20439 (2017)
27. Zhu, S., Yang, X.: Protecting data in cloud environment with attribute-based encryption. Int. J. Grid Util. Comput. **6**(2), 91–97 (2015)
28. Lynn, B.: The pairing-based cryptography library benchmarks. http://crypto.stanford.edu/pbc/times.html

Detecting Evil-Twin Attack
with the Crowd Sensing of Landmark
in Physical Layer

Chundong Wang[1,2], Likun Zhu[1,2], Liangyi Gong[1,2(✉)], Zheli Liu[3],
Xiuliang Mo[1,2], Wenjun Yang[1,2], Min Li[3], and Zhaoyang Li[3]

[1] Key Laboratory of Computer Vision and System, Ministry of Education,
Tianjin University of Technology, Tianjin 300384, China
gongliangyi@gmail.com
[2] Tianjin Key Laboratory of Intelligence Computing and Novel Software Technology,
Ministry of Education, Tianjin University of Technology, Tianjin 300384, China
[3] Nankai University, Tianjin 300350, China

Abstract. With the popularity of mobile computing, WiFi has become
one of the essential technologies for people to access the Internet, and
WiFi security has also become a major threat for mobile computing. The
Evil-Twin attack can steal a large amount of private data by forging the
same SSID as the real Access Point. This paper proposes a passive Evil-
Twin attack detection scheme through CSI in physical layer. First of all,
we propose a location model based on the edge of landmark area. In this
model, the improved MUSIC algorithm is used to calculate each AP's
AoA by CSI phase. Secondly, it proposes an algorithm for simplifying
the generation of location model files, which is the dataset of a small
number of AoA and RSSI samples. Finally, according to location model,
attack detection algorithm combines a large number of crowd sensing
data to determine whether it is a malicious AP. Experiments show that
our attack detection system achieves a higher detection rate.

1 Introduction

WLAN (Wireless Local Area Networks) become more and more popular in many
public places. It also faces risks while having a convenient access to the Internet. What's more, smart home [20] also plays an important role in nowadays
life because of its intelligent, automation system. However, whether in a public
network or private network, Evil-Twin attacks [10] can easily forge a legal AP
(Access Point) to steal users' data and to destroy its internal network facili-
ties. The Evil-Twin AP is a fake authenticated AP, which has the same SSID
and channel as the existing AP in WLAN. It usually increases signal strength
so that users will automatically connect. Privacy and account numbers will be
stolen and smart homes will be controlled by hijacking of Evil-Twin attack.

The traditional detection algorithms are mainly divided into two categories.
The first category mainly monitors RTTs (Round Trip Time) of client packets [15], arrival times of IATs (Inter-packet Arrival Time) [19] and consecutive

© Springer Nature Switzerland AG 2018
J. Vaidya and J. Li (Eds.): ICA3PP 2018, LNCS 11337, pp. 234–248, 2018.
https://doi.org/10.1007/978-3-030-05063-4_19

ACK pairs, etc. in TCP traffic. However, such detection algorithms are often affected by the configuration of the environment and parameters. The other [6] is based on physical layer hardware information, which requires collecting all system hardware information in advance and establishing an authentication list of normal AP. The disadvantages of those detection method are that the establishment of the fingerprint library requires a lot of time. Recently, scholars [18] have proposed a system for detecting rogue APs based on RSSI (Received Signal Strength Indicator) fingerprints. Although this method can solve these problems from the physical layer to a certain extent, RSSI is not stable in time domain and their system is also based on pre-collected RSSI fingerprints.

This paper describes a novel Evil-Twin attack detection system based on crowd sensing [11], which can extract crowd mobile devices' CSI (Channel State Information) [22] from the physical layer to achieve passive detection. Primarily, we observed that the RSSI of specific areas is significantly different and can remain relatively stable. Therefore, we set these areas as landmark areas, but it is difficult to distinguish the Evil-Twin APs only through RSSI. So, first of all, different from the traditional RSSI detection methods, we also extract more stable and fine-grained CSI features of these locations. And our improved MUSIC algorithm can eliminate CSI phase offsets, which can obtain more accurate AoA (Angle of Arrival) than traditional ones. Second, based on the uniqueness of APs' AoA and RSSI in each region, a lightweight landmark locatizion model is proposed, which avoid collecting large amounts of CSI&RSSI information and reduce a large amount of error range. Finally, the attack detection system base on crowd sensing can determine whether the spatial location of the AP has moved, thereby detecting the existence of a Evil-Twin AP. Furthermore, it also can detect some users who have been affected by rouge AP, and warn others who are not connected but belong to dangerous areas. Our experiments showed that our system could achieve an average of 92.3% detection rate.

Our main contributions are summarized as follows.

1. We propose an improved MUSIC algorithm that can calculate the stable AoA of any AP and does not require professional indoor measurement equipment. Make up for the RSSI instability in the time domain.
2. We propose a location algorithm of Landmark in which each RSSI is correspond to a range of AoA. This method can avoid collecting large amounts of fingerprint datas to create the standard files.
3. We realize a completely Evil-Twin attack detection system base on crowd sensing. Without incentive, a large number of users actively upload data. It can detect a wide range of attacks and applicable to multiple WLAN.

The rest of the paper is organized as follows. In Sect. 2, we will discuss different types of Evil-Twin APs detections. We describe our observations in Sect. 3. In Sect. 4, we propose an attack detection system and discuss the key parts of the system in detail. Further, we describe the results of the experiment and performance analysis in Sect. 5, and conclusion is in Sect. 6.

2   Related Work

The existing attack detection mechanism is mainly divided into two parts and is aimed at rouge AP in public places. One is to monitor RF link signals and the other is client-based detection.

Monitor RF link signals detection methods. Desmond et al. [5] established fingerprint library which can identify unique devices only through timing analysis of 802.11 probe request frames. [2] Alotaibi et al. [1] proposed a new framework to detect the size of each beacon frame of RAP and evaluate the detection effect of its established fingerprint library on rogue AP. Elleithy et al. [6] propose a passive fingerprint technique by using one or more of its characteristics via its wireless traffic. And it can be recognized in less than 100 ms. In a word, RF link signals based detection [2,17] algorithms needs to collect a large amount of fingerprint information to build an authentication list. At the same time, the detection process requires additional detection time. A malicious AP detection method based on an authentication and data encryption server [12,13] needs to collect a large amount of device fingerprint information, and an attacker can also use the same type of device to avoid being detected. The establishment of each hardware fingerprint library also consumes a lot of time and effort.

Client-based detection detection methods. It is mainly based on data flow characteristics, which is to detect the rogue AP from the user side. Beyah et al. [3] utilizes inter-packet arrival time to detect Evil-Twin AP. Wei et al. [19] calculate the arrival time of the ACK pair in TCP traffic. And the literature [7, 15] proposed RTT to distinguish between wired and wireless networks. However, these time delays are not caused by adding devices. Attackers can use high performance bridges to reduce this delay. The literature [16] compares the time that APs are consumed by accessing DNS server, which can distinguish between rogue APs and legitimate APs. However, this detection mechanism requires the pre-collection of relevant information on the target wireless network. The attack detector [8,21] captures the TCP/IP packet by monitor mode and analyzes its hop count information to detect Evil-Twin AP. The traceroute detection [4] mechanism establishes a remote detection server that compares the response time from the client to the user to verify the existence of the Evil-Twin AP. Einstein et al. [9] analyze the interference between different channels to achieve attack detection, but cannot detect rogue APs when attackers are on the same channel. Recently, Tang et al. [18] determine the AP location based on the RSSI fingerprints established by the three normal APs in smart home, which can detect attacks from the physical layer to some extent. But the RSSI value is not stable enough in the time domain, and it takes a lot of time to collect RSSIs.

3   Observations

It is found that the location of the AP in the WLAN environment is not easily changed. At the same time, even if Evil-Twin attacker can fake channels, SSIDs, and other information, but it is difficult to forge physical layer information, such as the location of the real AP. Because Evil-Twin AP with the same physical location can be easily detected due to the size of the same device. Although the RSSI is not stable within a certain time range, the RSSI is obviously different for a specific area. When these areas are at different angles of the AP, the locations of these APs can be located by using the CSI to detect AoA. Therefore, we only need to find out these areas of significant differentiation. These areas are called landmark areas, which are prominent, recognizable geographical elements in the environment and play an anchor role in spatial perception.

Before setting the landmark area, the relationship between RSSI and it needs to be explained. In an indoor WLAN environment, there is multipath fading in the signal propagation path due to the effects of multipath effects. Therefore, the propagation path loss can be calculated by formula 1

$$PL(\text{dB}) = 10\log\frac{P_{\text{t}}}{P_{\text{r}}} = -10\log\left[\frac{G_{\text{t}}G_{\text{r}}\lambda^2}{(4\pi)^2 d^2}\right] \tag{1}$$

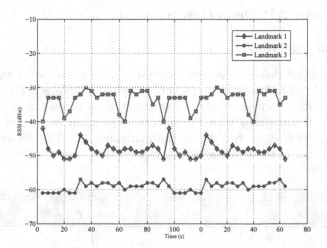

Fig. 1. RSSI of different locations

RSSI (Signal Strength Indicator Received) is the intensity of the received signal; its value can be calculated by the following formula: RSSI = Transmit Power + Antenna Gain − Path Loss. In general, since the device will not change, the sum of the transmit power and the antenna gain will not change, so the RSSI is related to the path loss, which will be a function related to the distance. Therefore, we select multiple RSSI thresholds with different radiuses as the landmark threshold. The data format initially received by the system is [SSID, Landmark$_i$, RSSI, CSI]. At the establishment stage of the landmark standard document, if the RSSI at the Landmark is set to be less than the threshold r, the system can effectively identify that the user is in the Landmark area by uploading data. The threshold r is calculated from the mean at the uploaded data. The selection of the landmark area is the location where the RSSI basically remains stable and the AoA of the AP differentiates significantly, such as near the door, the corner and the position close to the AP. As shown in the Fig. 1, it can be seen that the RSSI values are significantly different and the variation is stable within the range.

When an Evil-Twin AP exists in WLAN, some users are passively connected, because its signal strength is far stronger than that of a normal AP with the same SSID. Although these users may still be located in the landmark area, the RSSI of evil twins AP has far exceeded the threshold. In fact, in the detection stage, we deploy a reference AP in the environment. Such an AP can monitor the user's RSSI in real time. Further, it can more accurately determine whether the users are in the landmark area and also avoids forgery of the landmark value in the uploaded data. This method will be discussed in detail in Part 4.3. Based on this motivation, we can present our attack detection system of CSI and RSSI obtained at landmark.

4   Evil-Twin AP Detection System

4.1   System Overview

Our Evil-Twin AP detection system generates a location model by collecting AoA and RSSI of Landmark area. The crowd sensing module detects the users' AP channel state information in the Landmark area in real time. The crowdsourcing data is compared with the historical location data, and the attack detection algorithm is used to detect the malicious AP. The detection system overview is shown in the Fig. 2, which is divided into three modules.

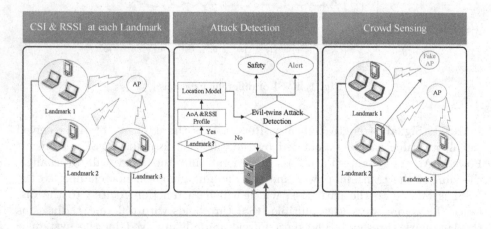

Fig. 2. Evil-Twin AP detection system overview

(1) The CSI and RSSI data files of each Landmark are established. All terminals will participate in Evil-Twin APs detection as a crowd sensing group. At the same time, we do not need to collect the channel features of all positions. And we only collect all crowd sensing mobile devices' data in the Landmark area as reference files for the location system. Therefore, each normal APs information can be collected and uploaded to the cloud server.

(2) Attack detection module. This module first determines if users are truly in the Landmark area, and then calculates its AoA and RSSI values. After that, the location model can minimize number of CSI and RSSI samples, and establish a standard location file for each Landmark areas. Based on the attack detection algorithm, the system can determine whether the connected user is being attacked or the unconnected user is in dangerous.

(3) The Crowd Sensing module. It uploads informations of APs monitored by all terminals in each landmark. When there is a Evil-Twin AP, all the attacked users will send the connected AP's CSI and RSSI to the server. Once the attack detection model finds that the associated AoA and RSSI values are inconsistent with range of normal AP calculated by the location model, system will send an alarm signal.

Mobile crowd sensing [14] is a new data acquisition model that combines crowdsourcing and mobile device awareness and is a manifestation of the Internet of Things. At the same time, it publishes awareness tasks to individuals or groups in the network to complete. The crowd sensing incentive mechanism of our detection model is that each individuals wants to ensure the security of the entire network. Therefore, after reaching the Landmark areas, they actively monitors all APs' information and uploads it according to the awareness task. Only in this way will the corresponding packet be generated, that is, users may upload data only if they pass the landmark area instead of other locations. Next we will elaborate on each part of detection system in detail.

4.2 Feature Profile

RSSI and CSI should be standardized to a file required by the system. What's more, we need to extract features based on the user's uploaded CSI to get each user's AoA of the AP. RSSI also needs to be processed at the same time.

Calculate AoA Through CSI Phase. The CSI contains the phase values of 30 sub-carriers, so AoA can be calculated by the phase difference of all 30 subcarriers on the three antennas. The traditional MUSIC algorithm assumes that there are M signals incident on N array, and $M < N$. Then received signal can be expressed as $x(t) = \sum_{k=1}^{M} a(\theta_k)s_k(t) + n(t)$, where $s_k(t)$ is the number of signals, $a(\theta_k)$ is steering vector, and $n(t)$ is an additive noise. Assuming that the sources are statistically independent, the correlation matrix of the input signal $x(t)$ can be expressed as $R = \sum\limits_{k=1}^{M} \sigma_k^2 a(\theta_k) a^H(\theta_k) + R_n$. The eigenvalue decomposition of the correlation matrix results in:

$$R = \sum_{i=1}^{M} \lambda v_i v_i{}^H + \sigma_n^2 \sum_{i=M+1}^{N} v_i v_i{}^H \tag{2}$$

The signal subspace is $v_1, v_2, \cdots, v_M$, and the noise subspace is $v_{M+1}, v_{M+2}, \cdots, v_N$. M is large eigenvalues. σ_n^2 is white noise power. We first perform SG filter filtering on the received signal, and then we can estimate $\hat{R} = \sum\limits_{L=1}^{30} xx^H$, which is the correlation matrix of 30 subcarriers. Based on the subspace projection algorithm, the MUSIC spatial spectral function is

$$P_{MUSIC} = \frac{1}{a^H(\theta) \cdot \sum\limits_{i=M+1}^{N} v_i v_i{}^H \cdot a(\theta)} \tag{3}$$

When the noise subspace is orthogonal to the signal direction of arrival, the angle is the signal angle, then the spectrum peak has the maximum value, and the AoA angle of the signal can be calculated.

However, because the traditional MUSIC algorithm is affected by the device's RF oscillator, It will cause the sampling frequency offset due to the unsynchronization of the receiver and transmitter clocks and the packet detection delay due to ADC sampling during signal processing. As a result, there is a certain offset in the CSI phase, which results in an error in the AoA. Therefore, we propose an improved MUSIC algorithm to eliminate this offset.

We assume the CSI phase offset between the antennas is $(\delta_1, \cdots, \delta_i)$, $i - 1$ is the number of antennas. Because this phase offset is a fixed value, it will only change when the device is started every time. So we traverse each combination of phase deviations to match the true AoA with its true value. In this way, the system can initially obtain a stable phase difference between the antennas and thus calculate an accurate AoA of each AP. Our pseudospectral search function is defined as follows:

$$\mu(\rho) = \frac{g_\alpha(\theta)\rho'(\theta)\mathrm{d}\theta}{(1 - g_\alpha(\theta))\rho'(\theta)\mathrm{d}\theta} \tag{4}$$

Our experiments showed that the multipath effect interference could be eliminated by improving the algorithm, and the influence of white noise on the phase change can be effectively reduced. Our system mainly detects the angle of the AP on the line of sight. In order to enhance the line-of-sight path, spatial smoothing algorithm is adapted. Once the number of receiving antennas is greater than or equal to 3, they will be grouped into new inputs. That is, if the receiving antenna receives i antenna data $x = \{x_1, x_2, \cdots, x_i\}$, the new packet data is divided into $x = \{[x_1, x_2], [x_2, x_3], \cdots, [x_{i-1}, x_i]\}$. By improving music to calculate the AoA average value of these grouped data, a stable line-of-sight AoA can be obtained.

RSSI Value Processing. Since the client is not stationary in the Landmark area, The client's walking will generate a small hop interval in the time domain for RSSI. Then, the RSSI value should be selected as a stable value in the interval. The basis for filtering the steady RSSI value is to select the change rate of the variance value in the different time window of the RSSI, and then the stable variation range of the RSSI can be obtained. RSSI value is stable through a time window of size 120. Therefore, we can get the final processed data $[SSID, Landmark_i, RSSI, AoA]$. Based on this, we can establish AP profiles of multiple Landmarks for our location model.

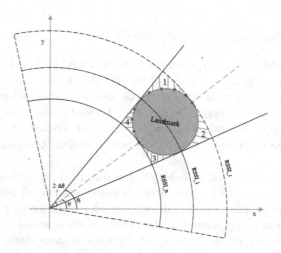

Fig. 3. Location model of each landmarks (Color figure online)

4.3   Location Model

Firstly, we standardized the Landmark area based on RSSI and AoA. The location model first establishes a standard reference file for each landmark areas. As shown in the Fig. 3, the orange area is the landmark area, and each big arc in black corresponds to a value of RSSI. AoA range of the Landmark area is between two rays, which are tangent to the landmark circle. However, the crowd sensing users can still be considered as reference data of this landmark, when they are in the four white blocks marked with red characters. Because the model only calculates the independent range of AoA and RSSI and does not take into account its relevance, the range of AoA at each individual RSSI is different. Thus these four areas will cause a lot of location errors. Therefore, in order to eliminate this kind of errors, we propose an AoA and RSSI range correlation algorithm.

Secondly, AoA and RSSI range correlation algorithm is proposed. The location point selected by the algorithm is located on the semicircle above the centerline of Landmark. In the Fig. 3, it is the red dot uniformly distributed on the circle. First, location model calculates the AoA value on the center ray of the corresponding AP for each landmark. Then, the user's $RSSI = (RSSI_1, RSSI_2, RSSI_3, \cdots)$ and AoA $= (\theta_1, \theta_2, \theta_3, \cdots)$ are sequentially collected at each red sampling point. There is only one RSSI value for each location sampling point on the landmark circle. The arc of the sample point intersects with the landmark and produces two symmetrical AoA values at the intersection. θ is the angle of the centre of the Landmark, θ_i is the angle of the detection point, then the angle of the two rays is $\Delta\theta$, that is, the range of the semicircle of the Landmark. In this way, according to $\Delta\theta = \theta_i - \theta$, we can calculate an RSSI-related AoA range based on the detection value of a certain point, which can be expressed as

$$range(AoA) = [\theta_i - 2\Delta\theta, \theta_i] \, ; profile_i = [RSSI_i; \text{range}(\text{AoA})] \tag{5}$$

The two points intersecting the centerline are the only AoA and RSSI, which are the maximum and minimum ranges of the RSSI. At the same time, when the edge of the detection point is tangent to the radiation emitted by the detection center, the point has the largest AoA range. These two files can be used as the initial file for rough determination in the detection system. The final location model adjusts the RSSI resolution to the best based on the detection accuracy of generated file.

Finally, the model is also suitable for Landmark data authentication. Once the user is in the Landmark location area, its value must be within the associated range determined by the established location file. In order to prevent the fake Landmark tag from being present in the uploaded data, when a large amount of error detection occurs in the system, it is possible to accurately verify whether the Landmark in the user-uploaded data is correct according to the reference AP. Then it is handed over to the inspection system for further processing so that the data of other APs in the Landmark area is the correct data uploaded. Finally, we set up profiles for all APs in different Landmark areas. At this point, the location system can effectively distinguish whether the user is at the Landmark area. Further, the attack detection algorithm can also distinguish whether the angle of the rouge AP is the same as that of the normal AP according to the result of this model.

4.4 Attack Detection Based on Crowd Sensing

When there are evil twin AP in the WLAN environment, attackers may initiate a Dos attack to make the original AP unable to work, forcing users to connect to evil APs. It is also possible that the attacker coexists with the original AP, and only some users are connected to the rogue AP that they create. Based on the above two conditions, the system implements different attack detection algorithms.

The Coarse-Grained Detection of Landmarks. When N crowd sensing devices are connected to the rogue AP, the system matches the user-uploaded

RSSI and CSI sampling data. And calculate its AoA by improved MUSIC algorithm. Based on this, generate the user's data set [SSID, Landmark$_i$, RSSI, AoA] and then match the landmark. It can be seen that in the current system, M users are in the landmark area. As we know, it is impossible for an attacker to build an Evil AP that is exactly the same as a normal AP. That is, the possibility that the malicious AP has the same AoA as the normal AP is slim. For example, the algorithm 1 determines whether each AoA is in the maximum range of the profile AOA. If the user AoA is within the range, the AP's angle does not change. If not, these users are connected to the rouge AP. However, if AoA is the same, we further determine whether the RSSI of the system matches the profile RSSI in the location model. If the match is satisfied, the landmark is a security. A warning is issued to inform the user that the AP of the SSID is a malicious AP. The same way to match users at other landmarks.

The Fine-Grained Detection of Rouge APs. When some crowd sensing users have not connected rogue AP but they are in the dangerous Landmark area. Not all nodes in the environment are connected to malicious AP. Evil twin attacks are only valid for some users. In response to this situation, we can determine malicious APs based on the uploaded data of other connected users and implement warnings for unconnected users. The detection system is based on the Landmark matching principle: 1. The AoA and RSSI values in the same Landmark area of the same AP must be the same as the associated range generated by the location model. 2. The generation of rouge APs will change the AoA values of Landmarks of all affected users. We sample the average time window of AoA generated by user-uploaded CSI phase, $[avg(AoA), avg(RSSI)]$. When one of users detects that the AP_i is a rogue AP in the environment, that is, after sensing the RSSI in the user matching location model, his $avg(AoA)$ is not within the AoA range corresponding to the RSSI, and the AP_i is suspected to be malicious. The system immediately sends a request to other users who have connected to APi and votes the obtained crowdsourced AoA data. If a user's detection result is different from that of most users, the rogue AP is voted as malicious. Finally, our detection system sends the detailed rouge AP information that the user connects to other users, including RSSI, AoA, and so on. Send warnings to all users. In this way, even if the user does not access the network, it can obtain information about whether the AP is a normal AP, and also avoids matching with the history profile data.

5   Experimental Evaluation

We have implemented a series of experiments in order to verify the accuracy of the AoA+RSSI evil twins attack detection system based on the crowd-sensing of Landmark. Before evaluating system accuracy, we first need to verify the stability of the location model, namely the accuracy of the AoA algorithm detection.

Our experimental environment is a conference room of approximately $60m^2$, filled with tables and tools, etc. We use a laptop equipped with an Intel 5300

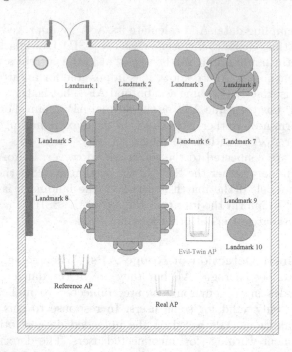

Fig. 4. Experimental environment with different landmarks

network card and successfully installed CSI tools as a receiver and ensured that the antenna height was uniform. And there are three IEEE 802.11b/g APs in the environment, one of which is an evil twin AP. The three APs are located in different locations in the room. We set up 10 Landmark areas with a radius of 1m. As shown in the Fig. 4, each Landmark center has a different AoA value for different APs. To ensure that there are no other disturbances in the environment, we use notebooks to collect 180 CSI data packets at each Landmark center. Finally, we determine the accuracy of AoA for each landmark point based on the minimum mean squared error function. As shown in the Fig. 5, it can be seen that when the data packet is less than 50, the traditional MUSIC algorithm changes drastically in the mean square error value and cannot be kept stable. However, the improved MUSIC can be maintained within the allowable range of error. With the increase of the number of data packets, the improved MUSIC algorithm proposed in this paper can provide more stable AoA measurement values, and is superior to the traditional MUSIC algorithm. The accuracy of the AoA detection algorithm is higher than 4.7°. At the same time, as shown in the Fig. 6, It can be seen that when the detection error of the improved MUSIC algorithm is 13.6°, the detection accuracy can reach 95%, while the traditional algorithm can only reach 61.8%.

This experiment is to verify the robustness of AoA detection effect at different positions. In fact, it is not necessary to select too many Landmark areas for detecting rogue APs. Generally, 2 to 3 landmark areas are sufficient. Moreover,

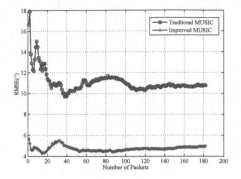

Fig. 5. AoA RMSE of different packets

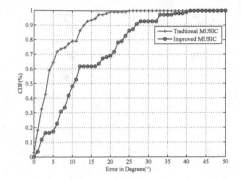

Fig. 6. CDF of different algorithms

the angles of these positions are very different, so the location detection accuracy is very high.

Discussion of Crowd-Sensing Location Model. In the next step, three specific Landmark points are selected. The radius is set to 1 m, 2 m, and 3 m. Each point collects 100 sets of upload data, including the RSSI of each SSID and the AoA calculated by the MUSIC algorithm. We use a sliding time window size of 120. When the amount of data is less than 120, the RSSI packet file is discarded. The AoA range corresponding to each user's RSSI is counted. The positioning model can show the data set's detection range for the AP as shown in the Fig. 7. It can be seen that the user's RSSI and AoA distributions are at different locations. According to the positioning algorithm, based on a large number of user perceptions, the difference between the AoA real value and the theoretical value range is small, and the system can distinguish which Landmark point the user belongs to. At the same time, we can see that as the Landmark radius increases, the detection error increases. Therefore, we set the radius to 1 m for each Landmark detection radius. Finally, we set up multiple sampling points for each landmark to establish a positioning file. As shown in the Fig. 8, as the sampling point increases, the resolution of the positioning file becomes higher and the detection error becomes smaller. Our experiments showed that the average accuracy of the RSSI combined with AoA location model based on edge detection can reach 97.5%.

The Accuracy Analysis of the Attack Detection System. The three landmarks still selected in the experiment. First, we placed the rogue APs close to three landmarks. Because of the large signal strength of malicious APs, users in the Landmark area will all be affected by malicious APs. We divided the experiment into 300 experiments, of which 150 were closed malicious APs and 150 were turned on. During the detection phase, we divided into 5 groups of users, each with 20 users, randomly accessing and leaving all detection points. We performed

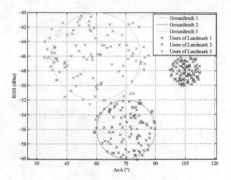

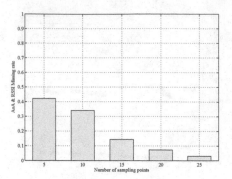

Fig. 7. RSSI & AoA measurements in different landmark areas

Fig. 8. RSSI & AoA missing rate of different samples

the experiments where the attacks occurred at different Landmark points. The test results are shown in the Fig. 9. It can be seen that the average accuracy of the detection system can reach 92.3%. RSSI based fingerprint detection algorithm is only 80.6%. With the increase in the number of crowd-sensing users in the network, the system detection accuracy is gradually improved. And the closer it is to the Landmark spot detection rate of malicious twin APs, the higher the detection rate, because it combines both AoA and RSSI. But with the increase in the number of users, the detection rate of each Landmark point is almost the same, and the average is as high as 94.7%,which is 13.5% higher than RSSI based Evil-Twin detection.

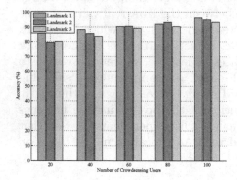

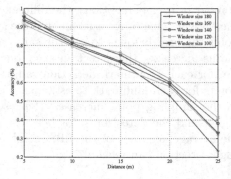

Fig. 9. Detection rate of different landmark areas

Fig. 10. Detection rate of different time windows

When a malicious AP constructed by an attacker can only affect some users at the edge of Landmark, malicious APs and normal APs coexist in the network. In the experiment, we built a malicious AP at a distance of 5 m from Landmark and located at the center of two detection points. In this way, the malicious AP can only connect the group-wise users at the edge of the landmark to their malicious APs. The scope of influence varies depending on the malicious AP. We select different malicious AP locations in different time windows to perform multiple groups of detection experiments and take the detection mean. The results in Fig. 10 show that when the time window is 120, a better detection rate can be obtained. At the same time, as the distance from the malicious AP increases, the accuracy of the detection gradually decreases. Because the malicious AP may not affect the user at a long distance, resulting in the system missed. At the same time, the error range of RSSI and AoA increases with distance, so the detection accuracy gradually decreases.

6   Conclusion

This paper proposes an improved MUSIC algorithm to obtain stable AoA from CSI phase. In order to reduce the complexity of the fingerprint collection process, we use the mechanism of crowd wisdom and propose a landmark-based location model. This model, combined with AoA and RSSI, can effectively avoid the complex fingerprint collection process and achieve high accuracy. In the end, our evil twin attack detection system can effectively combine crowd sensing users to effectively detect different kinds of attacks. Our experiments showed that our detection system could achieve a higher detection rate.

Acknowledgments. Our work was supported by the Foundation of the Educational Commission of Tianjin, China (Grant No.2013080), the General Project of Tianjin Municipal Science and Technology Commission under Grant (No.15JCYBJC15600), the Major Project of Tianjin Municipal Science and Technology Commission under Grant (No. 15ZXDSGX00030), and NSFC: The United Foundation of General Technology and Fundamental Research (No. U1536122). The authors would like to give thanks to all the pioneers in this field, and also gratefully acknowledge the helpful comments and suggestions of the reviewers, which have improved the presentation.

References

1. Alotaibi, B., Elleithy, K.: An empirical fingerprint framework to detect rogue access points. In: Systems, Applications and Technology Conference, pp. 1–7 (2015)
2. Bahl, P., et al.: Enhancing the security of corporate Wi-Fi networks using DAIR. In: International Conference on Mobile Systems, Applications, and Services, pp. 1–14 (2006)
3. Beyah, R., Kangude, S., Yu, G., Strickland, B.: Rogue access point detection using temporal traffic characteristics. In: Global Telecommunications Conference, GLOBECOM 2004, vol. 4, pp. 2271–2275. IEEE (2004)
4. Burns, A., Wu, L., Du, X., Zhu, L.: A novel traceroute-based detection scheme for Wi-Fi evil twin attacks. In: 2017 IEEE Global Communications Conference, GLOBECOM 2017 (2018)

5. Desmond, L.C.C., Yuan, C.C., Tan, C.P., Lee, R.S.: Identifying unique devices through wireless fingerprinting. In: ACM Conference on Wireless Network Security, WISEC 2008, Alexandria, VA, USA, 31 March–April, pp. 46–55 (2008)
6. Elleithy, K., Alotaibi, B.: A passive fingerprint technique to detect fake access points. In: IEEE Wireless Telecommunications Symposium (2015)
7. Han, H., Sheng, B., Tan, C.C., Li, Q., Lu, S.: A timing-based scheme for rogue ap detection. IEEE Trans. Parallel Distrib. Syst. **22**(11), 1912–1925 (2011)
8. Hsu, F.H., Wang, C.S., Hsu, Y.L., Cheng, Y.P., Hsneh, Y.H.: A client-side detection mechanism for evil twins. Comput. Electr. Eng. **59**, 76–85 (2015)
9. Jang, R.H., Kang, J., Mohaisen, A., Nyang, D.H.: Rogue access point detector using characteristics of channel overlapping in 802.11n. In: IEEE International Conference on Distributed Computing Systems, pp. 2515–2520 (2017)
10. Kaushal, P.K.: Survey on evil twin attack. Int. J. Sci. Eng. Res. **4**(4), 54–58 (2016)
11. Kremer, I., Mansour, Y., Perry, M.: Implementing the "wisdom of the crowd". In: Fourteenth ACM Conference on Electronic Commerce, pp. 605–606 (2013)
12. Li, M., Liu, Z., Li, J., Jia, C.: Format-preserving encryption for character data. J. Netw. **7**(8), 1239 (2012)
13. Liu, Z., Li, T., Li, P., Jia, C., Li, J.: Verifiable searchable encryption with aggregate keys for data sharing system. Future Gener. Comput. Syst. **78**, 778–788 (2018)
14. Liu, Z., Luo, D., Li, J., Chen, X., Jia, C.: N-Mobishare: new privacy-preserving location-sharing system for mobile online social networks. Int. J. Comput. Math. **93**(2), 384–400 (2016)
15. Mustafa, H., Xu, W.: CETAD: detecting evil twin access point attacks in wireless hotspots. In: Communications and Network Security, pp. 238–246 (2014)
16. Nivangune, M.K., Vanjale, S., Vanjale, M.: A survey on unauthorized AP detection in WLAN by measuring DNS RTT **4** (2013)
17. Jana, S., Kasera, S.K.: On fast and accurate detection of unauthorized wireless access points using clock skews. IEEE Trans. Mob. Comput. **9**(3), 449–462 (2012). Mobicom 2008
18. Tang, Z., et al.: Exploiting wireless received signal strength indicators to detect evil-twin attacks in smart homes. Mob. Inf. Syst. **2017**(4), 1–14 (2017)
19. Wei, W., Jaiswal, S., Kurose, J., Towsley, D., Suh, K., Wang, B.: Identifying 802.11 traffic from passive measurements using iterative bayesian inference. IEEE/ACM Trans. Network. **20**(2), 325–338 (2012)
20. Yan, W., Wang, Q., Gao, Z.: Smart home implementation based on internet and WiFi technology. In: Control Conference, pp. 9072–9077 (2015)
21. Yang, C., Song, Y., Gu, G.: Active user-side evil twin access point detection using statistical techniques. IEEE Trans. Inf. Forensics Secur. **7**(5), 1638–1651 (2012)
22. Yang, Z., Zhou, Z., Liu, Y.: From RSSI to CSI: Indoor localization via channel response. ACM Comput. Surv. **46**(2), 1–32 (2014)

Security Extension and Robust Upgrade of Smart-Watch Wi-Fi Controller Firmware

Wencong Han[1], Quanxin Zhang[1], Chongzhi Gao[3], Jingjing Hu[1], and Fang Yan[2(✉)]

[1] School of Computer Science and Technology, Beijing Institute of Technology,
Beijing 100081, China
[2] School of Information, Beijing Wuzi University, Beijing, China
yanfang.joy@gmail.com
[3] School of Computer Science, Guangzhou University, Guangzhou, China

Abstract. At present, smart watches are loved by users because of their convenience, high efficiency, aesthetics and practicality. Smart watches interconnect with matching smart phones instead of working individually to achieve their maximum functionality. The wireless network interface serves as an interconnection bridge between smart watches and smart phones to realize application data exchange, which introduces a risk to personal security and privacy. Therefore, improving Wi-Fi firmware security is very important. To boost the security of the wearable device, we propose a security upgrade and replacement scheme of the Wi-Fi firmware by expanding the security function of the Wi-Fi watch firmware and a reliable replacement method, which can effectively improve the security of the smart watch. We implement firmware switching and recovery at the kernel level. Data encryption module is added to the firmware to enhance data interaction security. Experiments show that our approach improves robustness of Wi-Fi firmware upgrade and data interaction security while guarantees the ordinary functionality of the Wi-Fi module.

Keywords: Smart watch · Upgrade Wi-Fi firmware · Tizen OS · Decompile

1 Introduction

At present, with the continuous improvement of the miniaturization and convenience of smart devices, smart wearable devices have become a new consumer trend. The most popular operating systems are Android wear, watchOS and Tizen [1].

The three most commonly used operating systems for smart watches correspond to different firmware. Taking Samsung Smart Watch Gear S2 as an example, the operating system is the Tizen operating system [2, 3]. In this series of smart watches, the path of the Wi-Fi firmware is */lib/firmware/wlan_net_bcm4343w.bin*. "bcm4343w" in the firmware name indicates Broadcom Wi-Fi chip. The key issue facing the watch is to upgrade the secure operation of the firmware. Since the smart watch does not have a wired port, if the Wi-Fi firmware does not work properly, the watch will be damaged and cannot be repaired. In this case, the original Wi-Fi firmware cannot be deleted or replaced, and it needs to be smoothly switched between the old and new firmware. If the new firmware

© Springer Nature Switzerland AG 2018
J. Vaidya and J. Li (Eds.): ICA3PP 2018, LNCS 11337, pp. 249–259, 2018.
https://doi.org/10.1007/978-3-030-05063-4_20

cannot be used, we need to switch the firmware of the original version. In this way, the watch can be connected to Wi-Fi for recovery or further modification.

Based on this background, we propose a security upgrade and replacement scheme to complete the firmware switching operation and recovery from the kernel level.

The contributions of this paper are as follows:

- We expand the security function of the Wi-Fi watch firmware for smart watches by experimenting and clarifying a feasible firmware upgrade method.
- We propose a firmware upgrade method for a smart watch without an external port, and implement a safe and reliable replacement program for the upgraded firmware.

2   Related Work

2.1   Get Wi-Fi Firmware and Decompile

To facilitate the operation of Samsung Gear S2 internal files, we need to obtain the root privileges of the watch [4]. The root process is actually putting the *su* file in */system/bin/* and *Superuser.apk* in the *system/app*. On this basis, we need to set */system/bin/su* to allow any user to run by getting "set uid" and "set gid" permissions. We use the loopholes in the operating system to complete the root process. In the actual experiment, connect to the computer via Wi-Fi and obtain root privileges by brushing in the root package.

After setting the firmware file directory to be read and written, we can extract the Wi-Fi firmware locally, use the IDA pro tool to decompile the obtained Wi-Fi firmware. For the role of the Wi-Fi firmware, the available function expansion positions in the firmware are searched, and the Wi-Fi firmware is upgraded with hook technology from the standpoint of security.

2.2   Modify Kernel and Load Running Upgrade Firmware

To prevent the watch from being damaged and cannot be used again, we need to propose a safe program to load and run the firmware in a safe manner [5]. Devices such as mobile phones can be connected to the shell terminal in a wired manner to implement operations such as brushing, repair, and upgrade of the mobile phone. The smart watch must be connected to the terminal device through the Wi-Fi interface to achieve the above functions. If the Wi-Fi firmware does not work properly, it cannot connect to the *shell*. Then we cannot perform any operation, and data interaction cannot be completed normally, which will result irreversible damage to the watch. Base on the mechanism of the kernel loading Wi-Fi firmware in Sect. 1, we can design a feasible solution. The original firmware and the upgraded firmware are all in the */lib/firmware* directory. The user can perform the key operation through the kernel, such as loading the upgraded Wi-Fi firmware according to the specific key operation, restarting the Wi-Fi function, and running the upgrade Wi-Fi firmware. When the upgraded firmware fails, we can always switch back to the original firmware.

The kernel of the Samsung Gear S2 watch is based on Linux 3.4. During the compilation process, the core compile command *make tizen_wc1_defconfig* indicates that the kernel is compiled against the configuration features of the Tizen system. After the kernel is compiled, we generate a new kernel image zipped file in the */arch/arm/boot* directory and place the *zImage* file in the watch's boot partition */dev/mmcblk0p6*. Then, we restart the device and the watch works under the new kernel.

3   Robust Wi-Fi Firmware Upgrade

After obtaining the native Wi-Fi firmware, it is analyzed, then we add additional functions, after that we compile and generate a new upgraded Wi-Fi firmware [6]. The new upgraded Wi-Fi firmware performs switching between the old and new firmware with the cooperation of the kernel, ensuring that the watch can still be modified using the original Wi-Fi firmware if the Wi-Fi firmware fails to be upgraded.

3.1   Decompile and Analyze Wi-Fi Firmware Structure

Get Wi-Fi firmware *wlan_net_bcm4343w.bin*, view the address, which is located at memory 0x00000000; The ROM of the controller is located at memory 0x00800000. Find the positioning key code *wlc_ioctl* [7]. The main feature of this function is to execute a command request from the host. Its function prototype is:

extern int wlc_ioctl(struct wlc_info *wlc, int cmd, void *arg, int len, struct wlc_if *wlcif)

The list of values for the cmd parameter is defined in wlioctl.h. Its meaning is to support different command types. When the host performs an ioctl request for *cmd* = *WLC_GET_MAGIC*, the firmware should return the cmd value, *WLC_GET_MAGIC* (0x14E46C77 is the hexadecimal value of the value) [8]. Finding the following location in the decompiled file through the return value 0x14E46C77. The location is:

seg001:0081ABC8   dword_81ABC8   DCD   0x14E46C77; DATA XREF: sub_819C84:loc_81A8E2

This obtains the instruction code, which is the code in the firmware that executes the *WLC_IOCTL_MAGIC* request:

```
seg001:0081A8E2        LDR        R3, =0x14E46C77
seg001:0081A8E4        MOV.W      R9, #0
seg001:0081A8E8        STR        R3, [R5]
seg001:0081A8EA        B.W        loc_81C0DA
```

The entry address of this function is shown in Fig. 1:

```
seg001:0081A2D4 x_wlc_ioctl_sub_81A2D4              ; DATA XREF: ROM:0006C3E0To
seg001:0081A2D4                 PUSH.W    {R4-R11,LR}
seg001:0081A2D8                 SUB       SP, SP, #0x16C
seg001:0081A2DA                 LDR.W     R11, [SP,#0x27C+var_EC]
seg001:0081A2DE                 MOV       R0, R1
seg001:0081A2E0                 MOV       R1, R11
seg001:0081A2E2                 MOV       R5, R2
seg001:0081A2E4                 MOV       R7, R3
seg001:0081A2E6                 MOV       R4, R0
seg001:0081A2E8                 BL        sub_881340
seg001:0081A2EC                 LDR.W     R1, [R0,#0xF8]
seg001:0081A2F0                 LDR.W     R2, [R0,#0xFC]
seg001:0081A2F4                 LDR.W     R3, [R0,#0x104]
```

Fig. 1. The address displayed in the decompiled file

The instruction of this function is a *Thumb* instruction, the address of the function is the entry address plus 1. Search for 0x0081A2D5 in the decompiled file and get:

00039170 0081A2D5 0081CA2D 00822D25 00822F79

The corresponding instruction is:

ROM:00039170 off_39170 DCD x_wlc_ioctl_sub_81A2D4 + 1

Find the corresponding program execution section, show in Fig. 2:

```
ROM:000390FC x_wlc_attach_module_sub_390FC

ROM:000390FC                 PUSH      {R0,R1,R4,LR}
ROM:000390FE                 MOVS      R3, #0
ROM:00039100                 MOV       R4, R0
ROM:00039102                 STR       R3, [SP,#0x10+var_10]
ROM:00039104                 MOV       R1, R4
ROM:00039106                 LDR       R0, [R0]
ROM:00039108                 LDR       R2, =(x_wlc_ioctl_sub_81A2D4+1)
ROM:0003910A                 BL        x_wlc_seq_cmds_attach_sub_390A8
```

Fig. 2. Wlc function to execute program sections

By viewing the decompiled process, we can see the key code and parameter information and address information of the Wi-Fi firmware, providing an important basis for the upgrade.

3.2 Wi-Fi Firmware Upgrade Process

After the firmware is upgraded and the original firmware is loaded in the firmware directory, the secure loading process of firmware is shown in Fig. 3:

The kernel loading firmware is completed by calling the function:

int request_firmware(const struct firmware **fw, char *name, struct device *device)

The function request_firmware requests the user space to provide a firmware image file named name and waits for completion. The parameter device is the device loaded by the firmware. The file content is returned to request_firmware and returns 0 if the firmware request succeeds. During the call, the user is required to locate the space and provide a firmware image to the kernel. The name parameter identifies the required firmware, usually an executable binary .bin file. Loaded successfully, returns 0, fw points to the firmware structure.

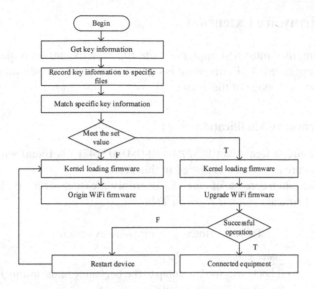

Fig. 3. Kernel loading upgrade firmware process

The firmware subsystem uses *sysfs* and hot plug mechanisms. When calling request firmware, a new directory is created with the name of the driver under /sys/class/firmware. That directory contains the following 3 attributes.

- **loading:** The initial value of this attribute in the user space process is 1, when the loading process is completed, it should be set to 0. Writing a value −1 to loading will abort the firmware loading process.
- **data:** This property receives firmware data in binary form. After loading is set, user space writes firmware data into the attribute.
- **device:** This attribute is the entry item symbol attached to the associated device in*/sys/device*.

Once the *sysfs* entry is created, the kernel creates a hot-plug event for the device. The environment passed to the hot plug handler includes a variable *FIRMWARE* which is set to the name given to *request_firmware*. This handler should locate the firmware file and copy it to the kernel using the provided attributes. If this file cannot be found, the processor should set the loading attribute to *-1*. If a firmware request is not serviced within 10 s, the kernel closes the request and returns a failed status to the driver. The timeout period can be changed by setting the *sysfs* attribute */sys/class/firmware/ timeout*. Using the *request_firmware* interface allows the user to publish the firmware of the device based on the driver. The user can correctly integrate the firmware into the hot swap mechanism and simplify the firmware loading subsystem through external loading.

The upgraded Wi-Fi firmware still needs to be stored in the */lib/firmware* directory. It obtains the key information through the kernel and obtains the flag to switch the Wi-Fi firmware version through matching with the key information. In this way, switching between the firmware of the two versions is achieved by calling the interface.

4   Wi-Fi Firmware Extension

The firmware upgrade must first implement the function expansion of the Wi-Fi firmware, then the upgraded Wi-Fi firmware is operated under the condition of security to prevent the process damage of the device [9].

4.1   Wi-Fi Firmware Modification

In the firmware file, a free area (0x00050430-0x0005142F) is found with a length of 4 KB. The firmware patch code is placed in this area.

The firmware patch consists of *entry.S* (assembly file) and *main.c* (C file) [10]. The structure of the firmware patch is show in Table 1:

Table 1. Structure of firmware extension

Offset	Statement	Purpose
0x00050430	B hook_wlc_ioctl	Jump to the beginning of the instruction
hook_wlc_ioctl	BL ex_wlc_ioctl	Call C patch code
ex_wlc_ioctl	...	Expand the firmware function according to cmd

The value of the pointer at 0x00039170 is modified to 0x00050431. After the above modification, when the host executes the *wlc_ioctl* command, it first goes to 0x00050430, jumps to *hook_wlc_ioctl*, and finally executes the *ex_wlc_ioctl()* function. The *ex_wlc_ioctl()* function completes the function expansion of the firmware. Normally, when the host executes the *WLC_GET_VERSION* command, the value of len is set to *4*, requiring the firmware to return the *magic* number.

When the function of the firmware is extended, the host executes the *WLC_GET_VERSION* command and the value of len is greater than 4. At this point, the patch code uses the memory pointed to by arg as the structure pointer of *io_cmd*, and *io_cmd* can include various extended commands and data buffers.

```
typedef struct _io_cmd {
    int cmd;
    int len;
    int para;
    unsigned char data[1];
} __attribute__((packed)) io_cmd;
```

When executing the *WLC_GET_VERSION* command or other commands, the *ex_wlc_ioctl()* function calls the original code of the firmware, that is:

```
wlc_ioctl_func wlc_ioctl = (wlc_ioctl_func)(0x81A2D4 + 1);
if (cmd == WLC_GET_VERSION && len > 4)
{
    struct _io_cmd *ic;
    ic = (struct _io_cmd *)arg;
    if (ic->cmd == 0)
    {
        ...
    }
    if (ic->cmd == 1)
    {
        ...             // crypt the data
    }
    return 0;
}
else
{
    return wlc_ioctl(r0, cmd, arg, len, wlcif);
}
```

4.2   Kernel Gets Key Data and Listens to Load Upgrade Firmware

Kernel improvement is used as the core part of firmware replacement [11]. The main goal is to acquire key data, record data, and if it is specific data, we need to change the firmware switch flag. Based on this, when the Wi-Fi is restarted, the flag data triggers the use of an upgraded version of the Wi-Fi firmware in the process of the kernel calling the. The operating flow is as follows [12]:

- Design press power button record 1 return button record 2;
- Record key data to the uptime file at the kernel level;
- Listen to the last ten digits of the uptime file and match the identification data;
- If the data matches, load the upgrade firmware after restarting the Wi-Fi function.

5   Case Evaluation

After switching to the upgraded firmware, the core issue focuses on whether it can be successfully loaded and run normally [13], the following subsections demonstrate detailed evaluations.

5.1   Program Effectiveness Assessment

We can view the enabling status of the Wi-Fi firmware through the following command and view the contents of the uptime file, as shown in Fig. 4:

```
sh-3.2# cat /proc/uptime
276.57 9.96 0000000000000000000000000000000000000000000000000000000000000000000000000000000000000000000000002
```

Fig. 4. View uptime data when no key operation

The compilation time of this version of the firmware is stored in a fixed location in the Wi-Fi firmware. We can check the firmware version running at this time and determine the version of the current Wi-Fi firmware. The Wi-Fi firmware file information course is viewed through *winhex*, and the corresponding compile time information can be seen in its designated location, as shown in Fig. 5:

```
0002D500  6F 6E 20 25 73 20 46 57   49 44 20 30 31 2D 25 78   on %s FWID 01-%x
0002D510  0A 00 53 65 70 20 20 39   20 32 30 31 35 00 31 34   Sep 9 2015 14
0002D520  3A 34 35 3A 35 30 00 77   6C 66 63 74 69 6D 65 72   :45:50 wlfctimer
```

Fig. 5. Original version Wi-Fi firmware information

By comparing the time in the log and the time displayed in *winhex*, it can be determined that the current running Wi-Fi firmware version is the original firmware of the watch, as shown in Fig. 6:

```
[ 28.886205] [0:    net-config: 502] dhdcdc_set_ioctl: SET PM to 2
[ 28.898167] [0:    net-config: 502] Firmware version = w10: Sep 9 2015 14:45:50 version 7.10.323.56.1 (A1 Station/P2P) FWID 01-63c4c065
[ 28.899043] [0:    net-config: 502] [WIFI_SEC] .wifiver.info already saved.
[ 28.900453] [0:    net-config: 502] dhd_wlfc_init(): successfully enabled bdcv2 tlv signaling, 79
```

Fig. 6. Log information shows current running firmware compile time information

By modifying the kernel and outputting the Wi-Fi firmware call path information, we can also see the firmware information called by the watch when it is turned on for the first time, as shown in Fig. 7:

```
[0:    net-config: 502] DHD: dongle ram size is set to 524288(orig 524288) at 0x0
[0:    net-config: 502] dhdsdio_download_firmware: firmware path=/lib/firmware/wlan_net_bcm4343w.bin, nvram path=/lib/firmware/nvram
[0:    mmcqd/0:    65] [drm] [off vhllr[0]dvms[0]lvm[0]
```

Fig. 7. Log information shows calling Wi-Fi firmware path

When running Wi-Fi firmware is upgraded Wi-Fi firmware. Open the file with *winhex* and check the compile time, as shown in Fig. 8:

```
0002D510  0A 00 53 65 70 20 20 39   20 32 30 31 35 00 31 33   Sep 9 2015 13
0002D520  3A 34 35 3A 35 30 00 77   6C 66 63 74 69 6D 65 72   :45:50 wlfctimer
```

Fig. 8. Update firmware compile time information

Restart the Wi-Fi firmware and view information, as shown in Figs. 9 and 10:

```
[  167.963346] [0:    net-config:  502] dhdcdc_set_ioctl: SET PM to 2
[  167.976574] [0:    net-config:  502] Firmware version = w10: Sep_9 2015 13:45:50 version 2.10.323.56.1 (A1 Station/P2P) FWID 01-63c4c065
[  167.980082] [0:    net-config:  502] [WIFI_SEC] save .wifiver.info file.
[  167.981553] [0:    net-config:  502] dhd_wlfc_init(): successfully enabled bdcv2 tlv signaling. 79
```

Fig. 9. Log shows upgrade Wi-Fi firmware compile time information

```
[0:    net-config:  502] DHD: dongle ram size is set to 524288(orig 524288) at 0x0
[0:    net-config:  502] dhdsdio_download_firmware: firmware path=/lib/firmware/wlan_net_bcm4343w.fw, nvram path=/lib/firmware/nvram_net_bcm4343w
[0:    net-config:  502] dhdsdio_write_vars: Download, Upload and compare of NVRAM succeeded.
[0:    net-config:  502] dhd_bus_init: enable 0x06, ready 0x06 (waited 0us)
```

Fig. 10. Log information shows invoking upgrade Wi-Fi firmware path

We can see that the Wi-Fi firmware can be successfully switched through a specific key sequence. The subsequent use and upgrade of the watch will not be affected [14].

5.2 Extended Function Validation

The purpose of the Wi-Fi firmware upgrade is to improve the effectiveness and security of data and information transmission [15]. In the data interaction process, the data is first encrypted, then the data is sent to a designated FTP account, and the upload encryption speed is evaluated to verify the function of the Wi-Fi firmware [16]. The feasibility and effectiveness of the expansion are evaluated in this section. We test the following key aspects.

- Test the time required to upload the specified size data to FTP using the original Wi-Fi firmware;
- Test the time required to upload the specified size data to FTP using the upgraded Wi-Fi firmware;
- Test the time required to upload the specified size data to FTP using the upgraded Wi-Fi firmware. Use the extended Wi-Fi function to encrypt data before uploading.

Comparing and collating the data to form a histogram, we can directly observe the performance and efficiency of the Wi-Fi firmware upgrade [17], as shown in Fig. 11:

In the test, the network status is the same, the upload data size is about 40 M, and it is equally to four users [18]. The blue line indicates the transmission time overhead of using the original Wi-Fi firmware. The orange line indicates the transmission time cost of using the upgraded Wi-Fi firmware. The green line indicates the total time required for uploading encrypted data using the upgraded Wi-Fi firmware. Four sets of data were tested in various situations. It can be seen from the above figure that the communication efficiency of the upgraded Wi-Fi firmware is not affected, and the transmission efficiency is basically consistent with the original version, which means that after we upgrade the Wi-Fi firmware, it does not affect the main function and data transmission.

The Wi-Fi firmware extension function is rc4 encryption customized for data, and the key length is 256 bytes [19]. The data is first encrypted by a custom encryption algorithm and then uploaded to FTP. The green line represents the time spent on uploading encrypted data. It can be seen that the time expenditure does increase but the increase is small. So that the proper extension of the function of the Wi-Fi firmware does

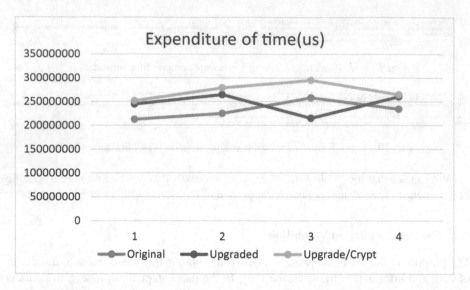

Fig. 11. Time comparison of uploading data to ftp

not substantially affect its use efficiency, and the influence on the main function and data interaction can be neglected.

In the actual test, the total size of the transmitted data is the same in the three cases. The first three users receive 10289334 bytes of data per user, and the last user receives 9699328 bytes of data. Through testing we can see that using the upgraded Wi-Fi firmware to upload data, as along with data encrypting and transmitting, has no packet loss and disruption, which ensures data integrity.

6 Conclusion

This paper expands the security features of the Wi-Fi firmware for the Samsung Smart Watch. Through in-depth research and analysis of the Wi-Fi firmware of the smart watch, we explored the core code segment and theme functions of the firmware, and added encryption modules into the data transmission of the Wi-Fi firmware to enhance its security. At the same time, we proposed a safe and recoverable replacement solution for the Wi-Fi firmware. Even if the Wi-Fi upgrade firmware fails, the original state can be restored smoothly. Experiments show that the function expansion and security replacement for the smart watch Wi-Fi firmware is feasible and effective, and its efficiency is basically the same as that of the original firmware.

We currently use Samsung Smart Watches that run Tizen operating system to evaluate our scheme. There are many smart watch brands in the market, they are different in configuration, hardware and software. At the same time, we need to modify the kernel to adopt the proposed security program. Thus, in the following studies, we will conduct a classification study and a differential analysis for more hardware platforms and propose a more general scheme to increase the security of current popular wearable devices.

Acknowledgement. This work was supported by Guangzhou scholars project for universities of Guangzhou (No. 1201561613).

References

1. Do, Q., Martini, B., Choo, K.K.R.: Is the data on your wearable device secure? An Android Wear smartwatch case study. Softw. Pract. Exp. **47**(3), 391–403 (2017)
2. Moynihan, T.: Hands-on: Samsung's gear S2 classic may be the first great smartwatch (2015)
3. Gadyatskaya, O., Massacci, F., Zhauniarovich, Y.: Security in the Firefox OS and Tizen mobile platforms. Computer **47**(6), 57–63 (2014)
4. Tan, Y.A., Xue, Y., Liang, C., et al.: A root privilege management scheme with revocable authorization for Android devices. J. Netw. Comput. Appl. **107**, 69–82 (2018)
5. Chung, C.: Baseboard management controller and method of loading firmware (2017)
6. Schulz, M., Wegemer, D., Hollick, M.: DEMO: using NexMon, the C-based Wi-Fi firmware modification framework. In: ACM Conference on Security & Privacy in Wireless and Mobile Networks, pp. 213–215. ACM (2016)
7. Raleigh, J.: Bin hook (2012)
8. Debates, S.P., et al.: Contextually updating wireless device firmware. US9307067 (2016)
9. Dai, S., Wang, H.: Design and implementation of an embedded web server based on ARM-Linux (2010)
10. Schulz, M., Wegemer, D., Hollick, M.: NexMon: a cookbook for firmware modifications on smartphones to enable monitor mode (2015)
11. Xiao-Hui, W.: The establishment of ARM-linux based cross-compiler environment. Comput. Knowl. Technol. **15**, 106 (2007)
12. Srinivasan, V., et al.: Energy-aware task and interrupt management in Linux. In: Ottawa Linux Symposium (2008)
13. Narayanaswami, C., Raghunath, M.T.: Application design for a smart watch with a high resolution display. In: International Symposium on Wearable Computers, pp. 7–14. IEEE (2000)
14. Jaygarl, H., et al.: Professional Tizen Application Development (2014)
15. Zhang, X., Tan, Y.A., Xue, Y., et al.: Cryptographic key protection against FROST for mobile devices. Cluster Comput. **20**(3), 1–10 (2017)
16. Zhong-Hua, M.A., et al.: Research on data sharing technology based on FTP protocol. Earthquake **3**, 012 (2008)
17. Kim, H.S., Seo, J.S., Seo, J.: Development of a smart wearable device for human activity and biometric data measurement. Int. J. Control Autom. **8**, 45–52 (2015)
18. Lee, S., Chou, V.Y., Lin, J.H.: Wireless data communications using FIFO for synchronization memory. US, US 6650880 B1 (2003)
19. Dey, H., Roy, U.K.: Performance analysis of encrypted data files by improved RC4 (IRC4) and original RC4. In: Satapathy, S.C., Bhateja, V., Raju, K.Srujan, Janakiramaiah, B. (eds.) Data Engineering and Intelligent Computing. AISC, vol. 542, pp. 513–519. Springer, Singapore (2018). https://doi.org/10.1007/978-981-10-3223-3_50

A Java Code Protection Scheme via Dynamic Recovering Runtime Instructions

Sun Jiajia[1], Gao Jinbao[1], Tan Yu-an[1], Zhang Yu[2,3], and Yu Xiao[4(✉)]

[1] School of Computer Science and Technology, Beijing Institute of Technology,
Beijing 100081, China
[2] School of Electrical and Information Engineering,
Beijing Key Laboratory of Intelligent Processing for Building Big Data,
Beijing University of Civil Engineering and Architecture, Beijing 100044, China
[3] State Key Laboratory in China for GeoMechanics and Deep Underground Engineering
(Beijing), China University of Mining and Technology, Beijing 100083, China
[4] Department of Computer Science and Technology, Shandong University of Technology,
Zibo 255022, Shandong, China
yuxiao8907118@163.com

Abstract. As Android operating system and applications on the device play important roles, the security requirements of Android applications increased as well. With the upgrade of Android system, Android runtime mode (*ART* mode) has gradually become the mainstream architecture of the Android operating system. *ART* introduces several improvements in Android, but it also introduces new ways to enhance malicious activities. This paper proposed a confidential finer granularity protection scheme for application programs under *ART* mode of ROOT Android devices. Taking Java method as the protection granularity, the protection scheme increased the accuracy of protecting targets. In addition, the protection scheme provided a more thorough protection for applications by combining dynamic loading technology and encryption technology in *ART* mode, and improved the security of Android applications. Experiments showed that the proposed protection scheme is effective.

Keywords: Android application protection · Android runtime mode (*ART*)
Dynamic loading · AES encryption

1 Introduction

With the steady increase of Android system's market share, a variety of applications have shown blowout development and there are over 50 billion app downloads since 2008 [1]. Moreover, as phones are utilized in some privacy-sensitive areas and commercial transactions, such as online purchases, bank accounts, and social security numbers [2], more effective protection schemes need to be adopted to prevent hacker attacks.

The existing security issues of Android devices can be classified into the following two categories. One is the lawbreakers use reverse-engineering to steal the code of applications and infringing other people's intellectual property rights; the other is malicious developers embed malicious code into Android devices to collect user information,

© Springer Nature Switzerland AG 2018
J. Vaidya and J. Li (Eds.): ICA3PP 2018, LNCS 11337, pp. 260–269, 2018.
https://doi.org/10.1007/978-3-030-05063-4_21

business information, etc. for unfair business competition, even steal other people's financial accounts [3].

In this paper, we focus on the protection of Android applications under *ART* mode to solve the above security issues. We present a novel protection scheme for anti-disassembly techniques. Based on shell technology and dynamic code loading technology, we implement the protection scheme in a finer granularity (Java method granularity). In allusion to the Java method that we want to protect in the application, the protection scheme encrypts it and stores it into a .so file that is not easily under suspicion, and then clears all the corresponding code excepting for cryptographic code in the .so file. In this way, no key code is procurable when a malicious developer decompiles this application. When the application is running on the Android system, a dynamic analysis approach for monitoring behaviors of apps is used to get the address of memory where the code is loaded [4]. In this way, when the protected Java methods are invoked, the encrypted code stored in the .so file can be decrypted and backfilled to guarantee the application running correctly.

Our main contributions are as follows:

- A protection scheme for Java methods without any modification to the Android kernel is presented.
- For Android 4.0–Android 6.0, the scheme is fully compatible with most real devices running under the *ART* mode with root privilege.
- A plug-in that can be loaded in Android system is developed, which can automatically protect the target app.

The rest of the paper is organized as follows: Sect. 2 gives the background and related works. Section 3 proposes the Android application protection scheme in *ART* mode and describes how to protect the application program at the Java method level [5]. We test and verify the feasibility and effectiveness of the proposed scheme in Sect. 4. Section 5 concludes our paper.

2   Background and Related Works

Android apps that run on *Dalvik* virtual machine are written in Java and compiled to *Dalvik* bytecode (*DEX*) before running. Android Software Development Kit (SDK) provides all the tools and *APIs* for developers to develop Android applications [6]. With Android's Native Development Kit (NDK), developers can write native code and embed them into apps [7]. The common method of invoking native code on Android is by Java Native Interface (JNI) [8].

Replacing *Dalvik*, the process virtual machine originally used by Android, Android Runtime (*ART*) applies Ahead-of-Time (*AoT*) compilation to translate the application's bytecode into native instructions that are executed by the device's runtime environment [9]. The on-device *dex2oat* tool compiles *Dalvik* bytecode to native code and produces an *OAT* file at the installation time of *APK* file. To allow preloading Java classes used in runtime, an image file called *boot.art* is created by *dex2oat*. In *ART* mode, Java methods exist in memory as an array of *ArtMethod* elements [10].

ArtMethod is declared in a class, pointed by the *declaring_class_ field*, and the structure in memory is the *OAT* Class. The index value of *ArtMethod* is stored in the *method_index_ field*. The *PtrSizedFields* structure contains pointers to the *ArtMethod*'s entry points. Pointers stored within this structure are assigned by the *ART* compiler driver at the compilation time [10].

2.1   OAT File and DEX File

The *OAT* file is the execution file of an app obtained after the Android system pre-compiles the *APK* file. For the protection scheme, we need to analyze the structure of the *OAT* file. Figure 1 shows the structure of an *OAT* file.

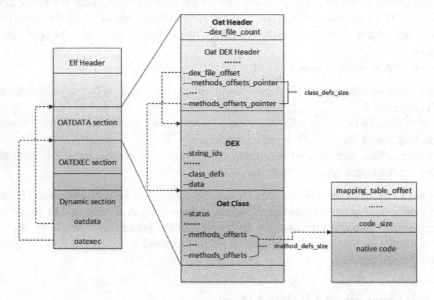

Fig. 1. The structure of the *OAT* file in *ART* mode.

The first part is the *OATDATA* section, which contains the original *DEX* file and *OAT* class; the second part is the *OATEXEC* section, which stores the native code executed when the program runs. The *OAT* Class is a list of classes in the *OAT* file that holds all the Java classes and related information used by the precompiled Android application.

The *class_def_item* is stored in the *class_def* data block and is obtained by the class_defs_off_ in the *DEX* file header structure. The related string of the class name is stored in the string table area in the *DEX* file. As can be seen that there is an index number for each data structure, which is utilized to search the data in the file. The *class_defs* field stores the structure of class_*def_item* and records the definition information of classes. The data field contains all types of data, such as the *Dalvik* bytecode. The *Dalvik* virtual machine will parse the *DEX* file when the app needs the specific data. Figure 2 is the structure of *class_def*.

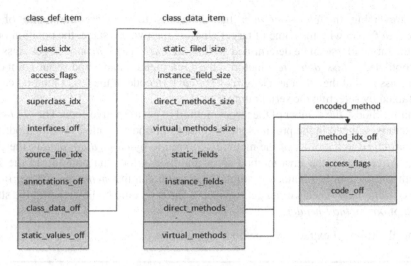

Fig. 2. The structure of *class_def*.

The *class_def* stores the data set of *class_def_item*. The *class_data_item* pointed by the *class_data_off* and the *class_def_item* are important in the *DEX* file. The *class_data_item* records the most relevant information about a class at runtime. *Direct_methods* and *virtual_methods* point to an array structure whose type is *encoded_method* where *code_off* points to the offset of the *code_item* in the *DEX* file, which holds the *Dalvik* bytecode of the Java method.

3 Confidential Finer Granularity Protection Scheme Under ART Mode

The scheme consists of three steps in execution logic: extract Java method, clear Java method, hide and restore Java method. In the following, the Java method will be called target method.

3.1 Extract Java Method

This part is to extract *Dalvik* bytecode and native code of the target method in the *OAT* file after installing the application on the device. The size and position of *Dalvik* bytecode and native code could be obtained through analyzing the *OAT* file. In Android 6.0, the *OAT* file exists in the directory of */data/app/< package >/oat/arm*. *Adb* commands can be used to pull or push the *OAT* file from the device [11].

- Firstly, parse the *OAT* file efficiently and accurately by utilizing the C/C++ language characteristics. The binary data of each file header is directly loaded into the structure by reading the binary file operation so that the members in the structure are initialized.
- Secondly, determine the class that target method exists in by class name. Class informations are included in *class_def_item*. Therefore, we can get the class information

by traversing the *class_def_item* list. It needs to compare the name of the *class_def_item* with the name of target class. If the two are same, the position order of the target class can be determined so that the *class_data_item* of target class can be obtained. *Class_data_item* includes the Java method name and serial number in the class so that the offset and length of *Dalvik* bytecode of the target method can be obtained by selecting the serial number [12].

- Finally, choose the number of the target method to get the native code. The *OAT* class structure obtained in the previous step points to all the compiled Java methods that are arranged in the order of the methods pointed to by *class_data_item* in the *DEX* file. After getting the Java method serial number, a location pointing to the Java method code can be obtained through the elements in the *methods_offsets* array of *class_data_item*. Then we can get the size of the target method by reading the structure of *oat-method-header*.

The algorithm of extract java method is as follows.

Algorithm 1 Extract Java Method

1: oatdata_offset←ParseOATFile
2: oatdexheader,dex_file_pointer←ParseOATDATA
3: **while** !process All Classes **do**
4:     list of class_def_item←dex_file_pointer
5:     **while** !class_data_item[i].name==classname **do**
6:         get class_data_item[i+1]
7:     **end while**
8:     Output(all Messages of Java Method in current Class)
9:     Input(method_id)
10:    Record(method_offset,method_size)
11:    copy codefile←method_code
12:**end while**

Where, *oatdata_offset* is the offset address of *OATDATA* section, *oatdexheader* is the header structure of the *DEX* file in the *OAT* file, *dex_file_pointer* points to the *DEX* file in the *OAT* file, *method_offset* and *method_size* are the address and size of target method.

3.2 Clear Java Method

The target method that needs to be cleared includes the native code, the *Dalvik* bytecode, and the *DEX* file in the *APK*. In Sect. 3.1, we have gotten the offset and the size of native code and the offset of the *Dalvik* bytecode. After that, "*ctypes*" standard library is used to load the *DLL* file to clear the target native code and *Dalvik* bytecode.

In addition, the *DEX* file in the *APK* also needs to be cleared. In this scheme, we uses *APK* reverse tool *APKTool* to unpack the *APK*, and then modify the *DEX* file and repackage it.

When applications runs, the *libart* library will judge whether the invoked Java method is an interpreted mode or a compiled mode. This judgment is determined by the invoke instruction of the *Dalvik* bytecode corresponding to the native code, so the invoke instruction couldn't be cleared. For native code, its starting address should be decremented by one when it is a *Thumb2* instruction. The algorithm of clear java method is as follows.

Algorithm 2 Clear Java Method

1: B1, P1←Java method location from DEX file
2: **while** !P1-B1>code_size **do**
3:     **if** read(P1)!= invoke instruction
4:         clear code
5:     P1=P1+1
6: **end while**
7: B2, P2←Java method location from OAT file
8: **if** P2/2!=0
9:     P2=P2-1
10:**while** !P2-B2>code_size **do**
11:    clear code
12:    P2=P2+1
13:**end while**

Where, *B1* and *P1* are the start address and current address of the target method's *Dalvik* code, *B2* and *P2* are the start address and current address of the target method's native code.

3.3 Hide and Restore Java Method

This scheme uses the AES256 as the encryption algorithm to encrypt the temporary file which the extracted code is stored in and makes the user enter the key [13]. The implementation of the AES256 algorithm is defined in the *DLL* file and called by the Python program. The encrypted code is hidden from the 0x10000 location of the *.so* library with the class name length and class name as identifiers at the beginning of each encrypted native code [14].

The native code of target method loaded in memory has become an all-zero zone according to the *OAT* file map when the Android application is running. The work done by the restoration is to write the target native code to the all-zero area of memory. The implementation of restoring Java method is defined in C/C++ program and is called by the *JNI* technology. Two *JNI* methods are implemented: *initPwd* and *init* [15]. The *initPwd* method is used to initialize the secret key. In this paper, we add the process of inputting the key by the user to increase the security of the Android application.

It starts to read and parse the encrypted code previously placed in the *.so* library after the user passes the authentication. Firstly open the *.so* library file with *fopen*, and set the file read/write pointer to the *0x10000* location of the *.so* library file, then read the class name, the size of the class name and the hidden data segment in turn [16]. After comparing the class name with the target class name, if they match, read the encrypted text and decrypt the text with the previously initialized key; if not, skip the encrypted area, and determine whether the next class name is the same [17].

In *JNI*, developers can get the parameter named *JNIEnv* (the Java runtime environment variable) and use it to get the memory address of the target method. The address points to an all-zero area because this part of the *OAT* file has been cleared. The decrypted target code needs to be restored to this area. Before the restoration, it is necessary to process the permission of this memory [18].

The following is the algorithm of hiding and restoring Java method.

Algorithm 3 Hide and Restore Java Method

1: **while** exist other methods **do**
2:    codefile_new←AES256Encrypt(codefile)
3:    delete codefile
4:    write codefile_new to .so file
5: **end while**
6: encrypt_method_code←.so file
7: method_code←Input(keys)
8: **while** exsit Java method **do**
9:    get method_loction of internal storage
10:   copy metgod_code to method_location
11:**end while**

Where, *codefile* stores the extracted code, the *codefile_new* is generated form encrypting *codefile*, *method_code* is the code of the target method.

4   Experiment Results

To measure the effectiveness of the protection scheme, we carried out experiment with a set of methods on Android phone with Android 6.0. One goal of the experiment is to verify that the methods can continue to be used after the restoration operation, and the other goal is to ensure that the reverse developer couldn't obtain the protected method.

4.1   Experimental Preparation

Open the *cmd* to enter the directory of the Python script file *artToolPack.py* and *DLL* file *artTool*.dll, and then start the Python executable program. In the beginning, the Python program will extract the *OAT* file and the *APK* file from the device. After waiting for a while, the Python program will output all the information of target classes on the command line and prompt users to enter the serial number of the protection method.

For example, the sequence number of a target method named *CutAndWrite* is 12. Input number 12 to extract the *CutAndWrite* method and clear it. Then enter 0 to indicate that there is no other method that needs protection. The Python program continues to run to handle other classes.

4.2 Evaluation

The protection experiment, Android application is divided into two phases. The first phase is to verify that *Dalvik* bytecode and native code of the target method are cleared, that is, whether the Java method was successfully protected. In this test, we utilize the reverse tool named *ApkTool* to decode the *APK* file and get the *smali* file disassembled from the *DEX* file. Then we can observe the *Dalvik* code of the target method through the *smali* file. Next, we use the *oatdump* tool to parses the *OAT* file to observe the native code of the target method. Take the method of *CutAndWrite* as an example and the results are as follows.

Figures 3 and 4 show that the native code of *CutAndWrite* before and after the protection. We can observe that the size of the native code is still correct, but all the instructions have become *nop*, which proves that the method is protected successfully.

```
1268917      11: void com.serenegiant.encoder.CutAndWrite.CutAndWrite(byte[]
             dex_method_idx=23402)
1268918         DEX CODE:
1268919            0x0000: 1d30                       | monitor-enter v48
1268920            0x0001: 1622 0000                  | const-wide/16 v34, #+0
1268921            0x0003: 1628 0000                  | const-wide/16 v40, #+0
1268922            0x0005: 131f 0000                  | const/16 v31, #+0
1268923            0x0007: 1321 0000                  | const/16 v33, #+0
1268924            0x0009: 1325 0000                  | const/16 v37, #+0
```

Fig. 3. The target method's native code in the *OAT* file before the protection

```
1268917      11: void com.serenegiant.encoder.CutAndWrite.CutAndWrite(byte[]
             dex_method_idx=23402)
1268918         DEX CODE:
1268919            0x0000: 0000                       | nop
1268920            0x0001: 0000                       | nop
1268921            0x0002: 0000                       | nop
1268922            0x0003: 0000                       | nop
1268923            0x0004: 0000                       | nop
1268924            0x0005: 0000                       | nop
```

Fig. 4. The target method's native code in the *OAT* file after the protection.

At the same time, we have selected five different apps to test the effectiveness of the scheme and run 20 times for each protected app and extract the corresponding *OAT* file to examine. The average running time for the protected apps and the number of instructions in the *OAT* file are shown in Table 1.

Table 1. Performances of protected apps

Application	Method	Startup time	Instructions
Notepad	CutAndWrite()	0.478 s	6656
FTPDownload	downLoadBinder()	0.235 s	1690
Calculator	getNumberBase()	0.395 s	10712
PaiPai360	creatSingleChat ()	0.415 s	3932
AndroidGo	connectToServer()	0.295 s	2760

The second phase is to verify whether the protected method can be executed correctly, *i.e.*, whether the method is correctly restored. In Notepad program, in order to verify target methods, we add some output information for verification in the source code. Start the application after this processing has been completed, we can observe that apps successfully entered.

5 Conclusions

In this paper, we proposed a confidential finer granularity protection scheme for application programs under *ART* mode of ROOT Android devices combining with shelling technology and dynamic loading technology. The experiments show that the scheme is feasible and high-efficiency.

Protection scheme of Android apps is a hot spot of research, but the research with Java method or application key as the granularity under *ART* mode is rarely mentioned. The proposed scheme can effectively protect Android applications with the Java method as a granularity, which is very meaningful for further research on protection technology of Android application.

Acknowledgement. This work was partly supported by The Fundamental Research Funds for Beijing Universities of Civil Engineering and Architecture (Response by ZhangYu), and also Excellent Teachers Development Foundation of BUCEA (Response by ZhangYu), and also National Key R&D Program of China (No. 2016YFC060090).

References

1. Operating System Market Share [EB/OL]. https://netmarketshare.com/operating-system-market-share.aspx. Accessed 01 Mar 2018/08 Apr 2018
2. Portokalidis, G., et al.: Paranoid Android: versatile protection for smartphones. In: Proceedings of the 26th Annual Computer Security Applications Conference. ACM (2010)
3. Enck, W., Ongtang, M., McDaniel, P.: Understanding android security. IEEE Secur. Priv. **7**(1), 50–57 (2009)
4. Zhang, X., Tan, Y.A., Zhang, C., Xue, Y., Li, Y., Zheng, J.: A code protection scheme by process memory relocation for android devices. Multimed. Tools Appl. (2017). http://dx.doi.org/10.1007/s11042-017-5363-9
5. Shabtai, A., et al.: Google android: a state-of-the-art review of security mechanisms. arXiv preprint arXiv:0912.5101 (2009)

6. Aycock, J., Jacobson, M.: Anti-disassembly using cryptographic hash functions. J. Comput. Virol. **2**(1), 79–85 (2006)
7. Lee, J., Kang, B., Im, E.G.: Evading anti-debugging techniques with binary substitution. Int. J. Secur. Appl. **8**, 183–192 (2014)
8. Linn, C., Debray, S.: Obfuscation of executable code to improve resistance to static disassembly. In: Proceedings of the 10th ACM Conference on Computer and Communications Security. ACM (2003)
9. Chen, Q., Jia, L.F., Zhang, W.: Research of software protection methods based on the interaction between code and shell. Comput. Eng. Sci. **12**, 011 (2006)
10. Costamagna, V., Zheng, C.: ARTDroid: a virtual-method hooking framework on android ART runtime. In: IMPS@ ESSoS, pp. 20–28 (2016)
11. Xue, Y., Tan, Y.-A., Liang, C., Li, Y., Zheng, J., Zhang, Q.: RootAgency: a digital signature-based root privilege management agency for cloud terminal devices. Inf. Sci. **444**, 36–50 (2018)
12. Enck, W., et al.: A study of android application security. In: USENIX Security Symposium, vol. 2 (2011)
13. Yang, Z., et al.: Appintent: analyzing sensitive data transmission in android for privacy leakage detection. In: Proceedings of the 2013 ACM SIGSAC Conference on Computer & Communications Security. ACM (2013)
14. Backes, M., et al.: ARTist: the android runtime instrumentation and security toolkit. In: 2017 IEEE European Symposium on Security and Privacy (EuroS&P). IEEE (2017)
15. Daemen, J., Rijmen, V.: The Design of Rijndael: AES-The Advanced Encryption Standard. Springer, Heidelberg (2013)
16. Guan, Z., Li, J., Wu, L., Zhang, Y., Wu, J., Du, X.: Achieving efficient and secure data acquisition for cloud-supported internet of things in smart grid. IEEE Internet Things J. **4**(6), 1934–1944 (2017)
17. Xiao, Y., Changyou, Z., Yuan, X., Hongfei, Z., Yuanzhang, L., Yu-an, T.: An extra-parity energy saving data layout for video surveillance. Multimed. Tools Appl. **77**, 4563–4583 (2018)
18. Sun, Z., Zhang, Q., Li, Y., Tan, Y.-A.: DPPDL: a dynamic partial-parallel data layout for green video surveillance storage. IEEE Trans. Circuits Syst. Video Technol. **28**(1), 193–205 (2018)

Verifiable Outsourced Computation
with Full Delegation

Qiang Wang[1], Fucai Zhou[1(✉)], Su Peng[2], and Zifeng Xu[1]

[1] Software College, Northeastern University, Shenyang, China
wangq3635@126.com, fczhou@mail.neu.edu.cn, dk@tnimdk.com
[2] School of Computer Science and Engineering, Northeastern University,
Shenyang, China
supeng@stumail.neu.edu.cn

Abstract. With the development of cloud computing, verifiable computation (VC) has attracted considerable attentions due to its importance. However, the existing VC schemes suffer from two substantial shortcomings that limit their usefulness: (i) they have to invest expensive computational tasks in the preprocessing stage, which has exceeded the available computation capacity of the client, and (ii) they do not support frequent updates, so that each update needs to perform the computation from scratch. To resolve these problems, we propose a novel primitive called verifiable outsourced computation with full delegation (FD-VC), which greatly reduces the computation cost of the client by delegating the preprocessing to the cloud. During this phase, the cloud cannot obtain any knowledge of the verification key. To the best of our knowledge, it is the first VC scheme not only supporting full delegation but also supporting dynamic update. The highlight of our scheme is that verification and update cost are constant and independent of the degree of the polynomial. Our scheme is provably correct and secure based on bilinear pairing and the hardness assumption of Bilinear Diffie-Hellman Exponent problem, and our analyses show that our scheme is very practical and suitable for the real world applications.

Keywords: Verifiable computing · Full delegation · Dynamic update
Bilinear pairing

1 Introduction

Cloud computing [1] provides cheap, flexible and on-demand access to its centralized pool of computing resources. One of the most attractive benefits of the cloud computing is the so-called outsourcing paradigm, where resource-limited clients can offload their heavy computation tasks to the cloud in a pay-per-use manner. As a result, the enterprises and individuals can avoid large infrastructure investment in hardware/software deployment and maintenance.

However, past real-world incidents [2] have shown that the cloud cannot be fully trusted and it may misbehave by exposing or tampering the clients' sensitive data, or forging computation results for profits. In order to tackle this

© Springer Nature Switzerland AG 2018
J. Vaidya and J. Li (Eds.): ICA3PP 2018, LNCS 11337, pp. 270–287, 2018.
https://doi.org/10.1007/978-3-030-05063-4_22

problem, Gennaro et al. [3] introduced a novel primitive called verifiable computation (VC), which enables a resource-constrained client to securely outsource some expensive computations to one or more untrusted servers with unlimited computation power and yet obtain a strong assurance that the result returned is correct. Due to the limitations of storage and computation capabilities, the key requirement is that the amount of work invested by the client must be substantially cheaper than performing the computation on its own, since otherwise the client would either not be willing to outsource the computation, or would perform the computation on its own to begin with. Although the primitive of verifiable computation has been well studied by lots of researchers in the past decades, the previous solutions still cannot be applied into practice. The main reasons are summarized as follows:

1. Expensive preprocessing: the workload of the client mainly comes from two stages: preprocessing and verification. The former is a one-time phase to generate some auxiliary information. The latter is a highly efficient phase to check the correctness of the computation. In the existing VC schemes, to the best of our knowledge, the amount of work in verification phase is substantially cheaper than that of performing the computation locally. However, in the preprocessing phase the client has to suffer from a large amount of computational task. The computational task exceeds the available computation capacity of clients' lightweight devices, such as smart phones or portable laptop. In order to solve this problem, [3] introduced an amortized model, which aimed to amortize its expensive cost over all the future executions. Obviously, it does not reduce the overhead of preprocessing at all. As a result, the client still cannot afford it. Furthermore, its workload is always greater than that of computing the function from scratch. So, it breaks the key requirement.
2. Re-executing for slight modification: in some real scenarios, the computation undergoes frequent updates with small modifications. However, the existing schemes are tailored to "static" computations, such as set and matrix. They do not support dynamic updates. If the client wants to update the outsourced function, he needs to perform the computation from the beginning. As discussed above, the overhead of preprocessing costs is much greater than that of performing the computation from scratch. So, it also breaks the key requirement.

From these points, there is a pressing need for a VC scheme that satisfies the above requirements simultaneously.

1.1   Contributions

To resolve the problems mentioned above, in this paper, we introduce a novel primitive called verifiable outsourced computation with full delegation (FD-VC), which is a privately verifiable computation protocol. In other words, only the delegator can check the integrity of computation. To offset the first challenge, we delegate the preprocessing to the cloud while the amount of work performed by the client to generate and verify the preprocessing instance is far less than performing the computation by himself. Apart from that, the cloud cannot learn any information about the verification key of the outsourced computation during outsourcing preprocessing stage. It ensures that only when the cloud performs outsourced preprocessing correctly will the client authorize the cloud to delegating the computation. Meanwhile, it allows the result recipient to check whether the computation was performed correctly, without having to keep a local copy of outsourced function. The verification efficiency of our scheme is constant. Furthermore, it achieves all that while supporting a dynamic update with constant efficiency.

1.2   Related Work

Verifiable Computation (VC) was first proposed by Gennaro et al. [3] to securely delegate computation of a function to a powerful but untrusted cloud. In this setting, the client can check whether the result returned is correct with a little cost. Due to constrains of storage and computation resource, the key requirement of VC is that the amount of work invested by the client must be far less than performing the computation by himself, since otherwise the client would either not be willing to delegate the computation, or would calculate it locally from scratch. Following Gennaro et al.'s pioneering work, lots of VC schemes [4–10,12–20] have been proposed. Existing VC schemes can be classified into two folds: generic VC and specific VC. The former can be applied into any function, and the latter is designed for specific class of functions. However, supporting dynamic update with a low cost of preprocessing is particularly challenging either in the former or in the latter. Among these works, the schemes [4–10] can delegate any generic computations, but they are highly impractical due to extremely large computation and storage costs. The schemes of [4–7] relied on probabilistically checkable proofs [11] that no one can implement in reality. [8] relies on fully homomorphic encryption (FHE) that suffers from low efficiency. Some other recent work [9,10] has improved these protocols, but efficiency remains problematic. Furthermore, these schemes do not support dynamic update so that each update need to perform the computation from the beginning. Specific function solutions [12–20] can only deal with a narrow class of computations, but they are often efficient. However, these schemes take advantage of amortized model to amortize expensive preprocessing over all the future executions. Obviously, it does not reduce the overhead of preprocessing at all. What is more, most of these schemes do not support dynamic update. As a result, each update has to perform the computation from scratch. For example, [14] designed a publicly verifiable computation from attribute-based encryption. Once the update happens, the client needs to re-execute the computation from scratch.

As discussed above, none of the existing schemes satisfy low cost of preprocessing and dynamic update simultaneously. So, it is essential to design a VC scheme supporting dynamic update with low cost preprocessing.

1.3   Paper Organization

The rest of this paper is organized as follows. Section 2 reviews some knowledge need beforehand. Section 3 formally defines our system model and its security. Section 4 proposes the detailed construction of our scheme and proves its correctness. Section 5 gives the analyses of our scheme in terms of security and computation cost. Finally, Sect. 6 concludes this paper.

2   Preliminaries

In this section, we first give some necessary definitions that are going to be used in the rest of the paper. Let λ denote the security parameter. If the function $negl(\lambda)$ is a negligible function of λ, $negl(\lambda)$ must be less than $1/poly(\lambda)$ for arbitrary polynomial $poly(\lambda)$. PPT is an abbreviation of probabilistic polynomial time. Also, we denote the set $\{0, 1, \ldots, n\}$ with $[n]$.

2.1   Bilinear Pairings

Let $\mathcal{G}_1$ and $\mathcal{G}_2$ be two cyclic multiplicative groups with a same prime order p and let g be a generator of $\mathcal{G}_1$. Let $e : \mathcal{G}_1 \times \mathcal{G}_1 \to \mathcal{G}_2$ be a bilinear map [21] which satisfies the following properties:

1. Bilinearity. $\forall u, v \in \mathcal{G}_1$ and $a, b \in \mathcal{Z}_p$, $e(u^a, v^b) = e(u, v)^{ab}$.
2. Non-degeneracy. $e(g, g) \neq 1_{\mathcal{G}_2}$.
3. Computability. $\forall u, v \in \mathcal{G}_1$, There exists an efficient algorithm to compute $e(u, v)$.

2.2   Bilinear Diffie-Hellman Exponent (BDHE) Problem [22]

Let $\mathcal{G}_1$ be a cyclic multiplicative group of prime order p and let y, u be two generators of $\mathcal{G}_1$. Given a tuple of elements $(U_0, U_1, \ldots, U_n, U_{n+2}, \ldots, U_{2n+1})$ such that $U_i = u^{\alpha^{i+1}}$, for $i = 1, \ldots, n, n + 2, \ldots, 2n + 1$ and randomly chosen $\alpha \in \mathcal{Z}_p$, calculate $e(g, U_{n+1}) = e(g, u^{\alpha^{n+2}}) \in \mathcal{G}_2$.

3   Definitions

In this section, we present the system model and security model of our scheme.

3.1   System Model

A FD-VC protocol comprises three different entities which are illustrated in Fig. 1. We describe them in the following:

1. Trusted Third Party (TTP): a fully trusted entity, who is responsible for bootstrapping the public parameter for the system.

2. Client: an honest entity with limited computing capability, who can delegate some computations to the cloud. Meanwhile, it can check the integrity of outsourced computations and update the outsourced computation.
3. Cloud: an untrusted entity with powerful computation resource, who can perform the corresponding computation outsourced by the client and return the computation result along with a witness.

Definition 1 (Verifiable Outsourced Computation with Full Delegation). *The FD-VC scheme is comprised of seven procedures:*

1. $\mathsf{Setup}(1^\lambda) \to params$. *The procedure is run by the the third trusted party (TTP). It takes as input the security parameter λ and outputs the public parameters params.*
2. $\mathsf{KeyGen}(params, \mathcal{F}) \to (\mathcal{EK}_{\mathcal{F}}, \mathcal{EK}_{pp}, \mathcal{VK}_{pp}, \mathcal{RK}_{pp})$. *The procedure is run by each client. It takes as input the public parameters params and delegated computation function $\mathcal{F}$ and outputs the corresponding evaluation keys $\mathcal{EK}_{\mathcal{F}}$ and $\mathcal{EK}_{pp}$, verification key $\mathcal{VK}_{pp}$, retrieval key $\mathcal{RK}_{pp}$. Note that these keys $\mathcal{EK}_{\mathcal{F}}, \mathcal{EK}_{pp}, \mathcal{VK}_{pp}, \mathcal{RK}_{pp}$ are used for outsourcing computation $\mathcal{F}$, outsourcing preprocessing operation, checking the integrity of delegated preprocessing and retrieving the verification key $\mathcal{VK}_{\mathcal{F}}$, respectively. The verification key $\mathcal{VK}_{\mathcal{F}}$ is defined in the following (see $\mathsf{PPVerify}$).*
3. $\mathsf{PPCompute}(params, \mathcal{EK}_{pp}) \to (\sigma_{\mathcal{VK}_{\mathcal{F}}}, \pi_{\mathcal{VK}_{\mathcal{F}}})$. *The procedure is run by the cloud. It takes as input the public parameters params and the evaluation key of preprocessing $\mathcal{EK}_{pp}$ and outputs the encoding of verification key $\sigma_{\mathcal{VK}_{\mathcal{F}}}$, the corresponding witness $\pi_{\mathcal{VK}_{\mathcal{F}}}$.*
4. $\mathsf{PPVerify}(params, \mathcal{VK}_{pp}, \sigma_{\mathcal{VK}_{\mathcal{F}}}, \pi_{\mathcal{VK}_{\mathcal{F}}}, \mathcal{RK}_{pp}) \to \{\mathcal{VK}_{\mathcal{F}}, \bot\}$. *The procedure is run by the client who prepares to delegate the computation $\mathcal{F}$ to the cloud. It takes as input the public parameters params, the verification key of preprocessing $\mathcal{VK}_{pp}$, the encoding of verification key $\sigma_{\mathcal{VK}_{\mathcal{F}}}$, the witness $\pi_{\mathcal{VK}_{\mathcal{F}}}$ and retrieval key $\mathcal{RK}_{pp}$ and outputs either the corresponding verification key $\mathcal{VK}_{\mathcal{F}}$ (valid) or $\bot$ (invalid).*
5. $\mathsf{FCompute}(\mathcal{EK}_{\mathcal{F}}, x) \to (y, \pi_y)$. *The procedure is run by the cloud. It takes as input $\mathcal{EK}_{\mathcal{F}}$ and computation request $x \in \mathsf{domain}(\mathcal{F})$ and outputs a pair (y, π_y), where $y = \mathcal{F}(x)$ is the output of the function $\mathcal{F}$ at point x, and π_y is the witness.*
6. $\mathsf{FVerify}(params, \mathcal{VK}_{\mathcal{F}}, \mathcal{RK}_{pp}, x, y, \pi_y) \to \{0, 1\}$. *The procedure is run by the client who has delegated the computation $\mathcal{F}$ to the cloud. It takes as input the public parameters params, verification key $\mathcal{VK}_{\mathcal{F}}$, retrieval key $\mathcal{RK}_{pp}$, the request x, the claimed result y and the witness π_y and outputs either 1 (valid) or 0 (invalid).*
7. $\mathsf{Update}(\mathcal{VK}_{\mathcal{F}}, \mathcal{RK}_{pp}, \mathcal{F}') \to (\mathsf{upd}, \mathcal{VK}_{\mathcal{F}'})$. *The procedure is run by the client who has delegated the computation $\mathcal{F}$ to the cloud. It takes as input the verification key $\mathcal{VK}_{\mathcal{F}}$ for the old function $\mathcal{F}$, retrieval key $\mathcal{RK}_{pp}$ and the updated function description $\mathcal{F}'$ and outputs the update information upd and the updated verification key $\mathcal{VK}_{\mathcal{F}'}$.*

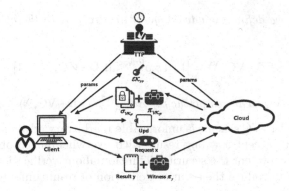

Fig. 1. Architecture of FD-VC.

3.2 Correctness and Security Definition

A FD-VC scheme should be correct, private and unforgeable. Intuitively, the FD-VC is correct if whenever its algorithms are executed honestly, a correct result will never be rejected. More formally:

Definition 2 (FD-VC Correctness). *A FD-VC scheme is correct if the following holds:*

$$\Pr \left[\begin{array}{l} \mathsf{Setup}(1^\lambda) \to params, \\ \mathsf{KeyGen}(params, \mathcal{F}) \to (\mathcal{EK}_\mathcal{F}, \mathcal{EK}_{pp}, \mathcal{VK}_{pp}, \mathcal{RK}_{pp}), \\ \mathsf{PPCompute}(params, \mathcal{EK}_{pp}) \to (\sigma_{\mathcal{VK}_\mathcal{F}}, \pi_{\mathcal{VK}_\mathcal{F}}) : \\ \mathsf{PPVerify}(params, \mathcal{VK}_{pp}, \sigma_{\mathcal{VK}_\mathcal{F}}, \pi_{\mathcal{VK}_\mathcal{F}}, \mathcal{RK}_{pp}) \to \mathcal{VK}_\mathcal{F} \end{array} \right] \geq 1 - negl(\lambda)$$

and

$$\Pr \left[\begin{array}{l} \mathsf{FCompute}(\mathcal{EK}_\mathcal{F}, x) \to (\sigma_y, \pi_y) : \\ \mathsf{FVerify}(params, \mathcal{VK}_\mathcal{F}, \mathcal{RK}_{pp}, x, y, \pi_y) \to 1 \end{array} \right] \geq 1 - negl(\lambda).$$

Intuitively, a FD-VC scheme is private if a the malicious cloud cannot get any knowledge of verification key of outsourced computation. More formally:

Definition 3 (FD-VC Privacy). *Let* FD-VC *be a verifiable outsourced computation with full delegation scheme, and let* $\mathcal{A}(\cdot) = (\mathcal{A}_0, \mathcal{A}_1)$ *be a two-tuple of PPT machine. We define security via the following experiment.*

$$\mathsf{Exp}_\mathcal{A}^{\mathsf{Privacy}}[\mathrm{FD-VC}, \lambda] :$$
$$params \leftarrow \mathsf{Setup}(1^\lambda);$$
$$(\mathcal{EK}_{\mathcal{F}_0}, \mathcal{EK}_{\mathcal{F}_1}) \leftarrow \mathcal{A}_0(params, \mathcal{F}_0, \mathcal{F}_1);$$
$$b \in_R \{0, 1\};$$
$$(\sigma_{\mathcal{VK}_{\mathcal{F}_b}}, \pi_{\mathcal{VK}_{\mathcal{F}_b}}) \leftarrow \mathsf{PPCompute}(params, \mathcal{EK}_{\mathcal{F}_b});$$
$$\hat{b} \leftarrow \mathcal{A}_1(\mathcal{EK}_{\mathcal{F}_0}, \mathcal{EK}_{\mathcal{F}_1}, \sigma_{\mathcal{VK}_{\mathcal{F}_b}}, \pi_{\mathcal{VK}_{\mathcal{F}_b}});$$
$$\text{If } b = \hat{b} :$$
$$\quad \text{output } 1;$$
$$\text{else}$$
$$\quad \text{output } 0;$$

For any $\lambda \in N$, we define the advantage of arbitrary $\mathcal{A}$ in the above experiment against FD-VC as

$$Adv_{\mathcal{A}}^{\mathsf{Privacy}}(\mathrm{FD-VC}, \lambda) = \left| \Pr[\mathsf{Exp}_{\mathcal{A}}^{\mathsf{Privacy}}[\mathrm{FD}-VC, \lambda] = 1] - 1/2 \right|$$

We say that FD-VC achieves privacy if $Adv_{\mathcal{A}}^{\mathsf{Privacy}}(\mathrm{FD-VC}, \lambda) \leq negl(\lambda)$.

Intuitively, a FD-VC scheme is unforgeable if arbitrary adversary cannot convince a verifier to accept a wrong result with overwhelming probability. In the following, we first present the security definition about verification key unforgeability and then introduce the security definition of result unforgeability.

Definition 4 (FD-VC Verification Key Unforgeability). *Let FD-VC be a verifiable outsourced computation with full delegation scheme, and let $\mathcal{A}(\cdot) = (\mathcal{A}_0, \mathcal{A}_1, \mathcal{A}_2)$ be a three-tuple of PPT machine. We define security via the following experiment.*

$$
\begin{aligned}
&\mathsf{Exp}_{\mathcal{A}}^{\mathsf{VKU}}[\mathrm{FD-VC}, \lambda] : \\
&params \leftarrow \mathsf{Setup}(1^{\lambda}); \\
&\text{For } i = 1 \text{ to } q = poly(\lambda) : \\
&\quad \mathcal{F}_i \leftarrow \mathcal{A}_0(1^{\lambda}, params); \\
&\quad (\mathcal{VK}_{pp_i}, \mathcal{RK}_{pp_i}, \mathcal{EK}_{\mathcal{F}_i}, \mathcal{EK}_{pp_i}) \leftarrow \mathsf{KeyGen}(params, \mathcal{F}_i); \\
&\quad (\sigma_{\mathcal{VK}_{\mathcal{F}_i}}, \pi_{\mathcal{VK}_{\mathcal{F}_i}}) \leftarrow \mathsf{PPCompute}(params, \mathcal{EK}_{pp_i}); \\
&\text{End For} \\
&\mathcal{EK}_{pp_i} \leftarrow \mathcal{A}_1(params, \mathcal{EK}_{pp_1}, \dots, \mathcal{EK}_{pp_q}, \\
&\qquad\qquad\qquad \sigma_{\mathcal{VK}_{\mathcal{F}_1}}, \dots, \sigma_{\mathcal{VK}_{\mathcal{F}_q}}, \pi_{\mathcal{VK}_{\mathcal{F}_1}}, \dots, \pi_{\mathcal{VK}_{\mathcal{F}_q}}); \\
&(\hat{\sigma}_{\mathcal{VK}_{\mathcal{F}_i}}, \hat{\pi}_{\mathcal{VK}_{\mathcal{F}_i}}) \leftarrow \mathcal{A}_2(params, \mathcal{EK}_{pp_i}, \sigma_{\mathcal{VK}_{\mathcal{F}_i}}, \pi_{\mathcal{VK}_{\mathcal{F}_i}}); \\
&\hat{b} \leftarrow \mathsf{PPVerify}(params, \mathcal{VK}_{pp_i}, \hat{\sigma}_{\mathcal{VK}_{\mathcal{F}_i}}^{*}, \hat{\pi}_{\mathcal{VK}_{\mathcal{F}_i}}^{*}, \mathcal{RK}_{pp_i}); \\
&\text{If } \hat{\sigma}_{\mathcal{VK}_{\mathcal{F}_i}} \neq \sigma_{\mathcal{VK}_{\mathcal{F}_i}} \text{ and } \hat{b} = \mathcal{VK}_{\mathcal{F}_i} : \\
&\quad \text{output } 1; \\
&\text{else} \\
&\quad \text{output } 0;
\end{aligned}
$$

For any $\lambda \in N$, we define the advantage of arbitrary $\mathcal{A}$ in the above experiment against FD-VC as

$$Adv_{\mathcal{A}}^{\mathsf{VKU}}(\mathrm{FD-VC}, \lambda) = \Pr[\mathsf{Exp}_{\mathcal{A}}^{\mathsf{VKU}}[\mathrm{FD-VC}, \lambda] = 1]$$

We say that FD-VC achieves verification key unforgeability if $Adv_{\mathcal{A}}^{\mathsf{VKU}}(\mathrm{FD-VC}, \lambda) \leq negl(\lambda)$.

Definition 5 (FD-VC Result Unforgeability). *Let FD-VC be a verifiable outsourced computation with full delegation scheme, and let $\mathcal{A}(\cdot) = (\mathcal{A}_0, \mathcal{A}_1)$ be a two-tuple of PPT machine. We define security via the following experiment.*

$\mathsf{Exp}_{\mathcal{A}}^{\mathsf{RU}}[\mathrm{FD\!-\!VC}, \mathcal{F}, \lambda]$:

$params \leftarrow \mathsf{Setup}(1^{\lambda})$;

$(\mathcal{RK}_{pp}, \mathcal{VK}_{pp}, \mathcal{EK}_{pp}, \mathcal{EK}_F) \leftarrow \mathsf{KeyGen}(params, \mathcal{F})$;

$(\sigma_{\mathcal{VK}_{\mathcal{F}}}, \pi_{\mathcal{VK}_{\mathcal{F}}}) \leftarrow \mathsf{PPCompute}(params, \mathcal{EK}_{pp})$;

$\mathcal{VK}_{\mathcal{F}} \leftarrow \mathsf{PPVerify}(params, \sigma_{\mathcal{VK}_{\mathcal{F}}}, \pi_{\mathcal{VK}_{\mathcal{F}}}, \mathcal{VK}_{pp}, \mathcal{RK}_{pp})$;

For $i = 1$ to $q = poly(\lambda)$:

    $(y_i, \pi_{y_i}) \leftarrow \mathsf{FCompute}(\mathcal{EK}_{\mathcal{F}}, x_i)$;

End For

$x^* \leftarrow \mathcal{A}_0(params, x_1, \ldots, x_q, y_1, \ldots, y_q, \mathcal{EK}_{\mathcal{F}})$;

$(\hat{y}^*, \hat{\pi}_y^*) \leftarrow \mathcal{A}_1(params, x^*, x_1, \ldots, x_q, y_1, \ldots, y_q, \mathcal{EK}_{\mathcal{F}})$;

$\hat{b}^* \leftarrow \mathsf{FVerify}(params, \mathcal{VK}_{\mathcal{F}}, \mathcal{RK}_{pp}, \hat{y}^*, \hat{\pi}_y^*, x^*)$;

If $\hat{y}^* \neq y^*$ and $\hat{b}^* = 1$:

    output 1;

else

    output 0;

For any $\lambda \in N$, we define the advantage of arbitrary $\mathcal{A}$ in the above experiment against FD-VC as

$$Adv_{\mathcal{A}}^{\mathsf{RU}}(\mathrm{FD\!-\!VC}, \mathcal{F}, \lambda) = \Pr[\mathsf{Exp}_{\mathcal{A}}^{\mathsf{RU}}[\mathrm{FD\!-\!VC}, \mathcal{F}, \lambda] = 1]$$

We say that FD-VC achieves result unforgeability if $Adv_{\mathcal{A}}^{\mathsf{RU}}(\mathrm{FD\!-\!VC}, \mathcal{F}, \lambda) \leq negl(\lambda)$.

4 Construction for Polynomial Computation

In this section, we first introduce a sub-protocol MExp for our construction. Next, we present our construction for polynomial evaluation. Finally, we proof its correctness property.

4.1 Building Block: Verifiable Outsourced Modular Exponentiations

In our construction, we use the verifiable outsourced multiple modular exponentiations protocol MExp as a sub-protocol to delegate preprocessing operation to the cloud. For the sake of convenience, let p be a large prime, $u_i \in \mathcal{Z}_p$ be the base and $c_i \in \mathcal{Z}_p$ be the power for $i = 0, \ldots, n$. The MExp protocol is proposed by Ding et al. [23], which has two participants, a client and an untrusted cloud. The client wants to delegate multiple modular exponentiation computation $u_0^{c_0} u_1^{c_1} \cdots u_n^{c_n} \bmod p$ to the powerful but untrusted cloud with the ability to verify the results with high checkability. For simplicity, we extract the system model from their protocol and omit all mod p operation in the following. The extracted model MExp is comprised of three procedures:

1. MExp.Setup$(u_0, \ldots, u_n, c_0, \ldots, c_n, p) \to$ (MExp.EK, MExp.VK): The procedure is run by the client to generate evaluation key MExp.EK and verification key MExp.VK both with respective to modular exponentiation computation $u_0^{c_0} u_1^{c_1} \cdots u_n^{c_n}$. The client works as follows:

   (a) Generate six blinding pairs (k_0, g^{k_0}), (k_1, g^{k_1}), (k_2, g^{k_2}), (k_3, g^{k_3}), (k_4, g^{k_4}), (k_5, g^{k_5}), and set $s_0 = g^{k_0}$, $s_1 = g^{k_1}$, $v_0 = g^{k_4}$, $v_1 = g^{k_5}$.

   (b) Generate logical division:

   $$
   \begin{aligned}
   u_0^{c_0} \cdots u_n^{c_n} &= (v_0 w_0)^{c_0} \cdots (v_0 w_n)^{c_n} \\
   &= v_0^{c_0 + c_1 + \cdots + c_n} w_0^{c_0} \cdots w_n^{c_n} \\
   &= g^{k_4(c_0 + c_1 + \cdots + c_n) - k_0 t_0 h_0} g^{k_0 t_0 h_0} \cdot (w_0 \cdots w_n)^{t_0 h_0} w_0^{b_0} \cdots w_n^{b_n} \\
   &= g^{k_2} (s_0 w_0 \cdots w_n)^{t_0 h_0} w_0^{b_0} \cdots w_n^{b_n}
   \end{aligned}
   $$

   where $w_i = u_i / v_0$ for $i = 0, \ldots, n$.

   (c) Computes b_i and $t_0 h_0$ such that $k_2 = k_4(c_0 + c_1 + \cdots + c_n) - k_0 t_0 y_0$, $c_i = b_i + t_0 h_0$, where $i = 0, \ldots, n$.

   (d) Choose a random $r \in \mathcal{Z}_p$ and transforms $(u_0^{c_0} \cdots u_n^{c_n})^r$ as follows:

   $$
   \begin{aligned}
   (u_0^{c_0} \cdots u_n^{c_n})^r &= (v_1 w_0')^{r c_0} \cdots (v_1 w_n')^{r c_n} \\
   &= v_1^{r(c_0 + c_1 + \cdots c_n)} w_0'^{c_0} \cdots w_n'^{c_n} \\
   &= g^{k_5 r(c_0 + c_1 + \cdots c_n) - k_1 t_1 h_1} g^{k_1 t_1 h_1} \cdot (w_0' \cdots w_n')^{t_0 h_0} w_0'^{b_0'} \cdots w_n'^{b_n'} \\
   &= g^{k_3} (s_1 w_0' \cdots w_n')^{t_1 h_1} w_0'^{b_0'} \cdots w_n'^{b_n'}
   \end{aligned}
   $$

   where $w_i' = u_i' / v_1$ for $i = 0, \ldots, n$.

   (e) Computes b_i' and $t_1 h_1$ such that $k_3 = k_5 r(c_0 + c_1 + \cdots + c_n) - k_1 t_1 y_1$, $r c_i = b_i' + t_1 h_1$, where $i = 0, \ldots, n$.

   (f) Set MExp.VK $= \{g^{k_2}, g^{k_3}, r, t_0, t_1\}$ and MExp.EK $= \{(h_0, s_0 w_0 \cdots w_n), (h_1, s_1 w_0' \cdots w_n'), (b_i, w_i)_{i \in [n]}, (b_i', w_i')_{i \in [n]}\}$.

2. MExp.Compute(MExp.EK) $\to$ (MExp.σ_y, MExp.π_y): The procedure is run by the cloud to generate encoding result MExp.σ_y and witness MExp.π_y. The cloud works as follows:

   (a) Parse MExp.EK as $\{(h_0, s_0 w_0 w_1 \cdots w_n), (h_1, s_1 w_0' w_1' \cdots w_n'), (b_i, w_i)_{i \in [0,n]}, (b_i', w_i')_{i \in [0,n]}\}$.

   (b) Compute $w_i^{b_i}$ and $w_i'^{b_i'}$ for $i = 0, \ldots, n$.

   (c) Set $R_0 = (s_0 w_0 w_1 \cdots w_n)^{h_0}$ and $R_1 = (s_1 w_0' w_1' \cdots w_n')^{h_1}$.

   (d) Return MExp.$\sigma_y = \{\{w_i^{b_i}\}_{i \in [n]}, R_0\}$ and MExp.$\pi_y = \{\{w_i'^{b_i'}\}_{i \in [n]}, R_1\}$.

3. MExp.Verify(MExp.VK, MExp.σ_y, MExp.π_y) $\to$ {MExp.y, $\bot$}: The procedure is run by the client to check the correctness of computation result. The client works as follows:

   (a) Parse MExp.VK, MExp.σ_y and MExp.π_y as $\{g^{k_2}, g^{k_3}, r, t_0, t_1\}$, $\{\{w_i^{b_i}\}_{i \in [n]}, R_0\}$ and $\{\{w_i'^{b_i'}\}_{i \in [n]}, R_1\}$, respectively.

(b) Check whether the following equation holds:

$$(g^{k_2} R_0^{t_0} w_0^{b_0} w_1^{b_1} \cdots w_n^{b_n})^r = g^{k_3} R_1^{t_1} w_0^{'b_0'} w_1^{'b_1'} \cdots w_n^{'b_n'}$$

If not, output $\perp$ and abort. Otherwise, recover real computation result
MExp.y as $g^{k_2} R_0^{t_0} w_0^{b_0} w_1^{b_1} \cdots w_n^{b_n}$.

The MExp protocol has the following properties:

1. **Correctness:** It ensures that the client can always output MExp.y rather than $\perp$ if the cloud is honest and follows all procedures described above.
2. **Zero-Knowledge:** It ensures that a malicious cloud who deviates from the advertised protocol cannot get any knowledge of the secret inputs (i.e. the bases and the powers) and outputs (i.e. modular exponentiation result).
3. **α-Checkability:** It ensures that a wrong result returned by a malicious cloud can be detected with the probability no less than α.

4.2 Detailed Construction

The construction of our scheme is detailed as follows:

1. Setup(1^λ) $\rightarrow$ *params*. Given a security parameter λ, the TTP first chooses two groups $\mathcal{G}_1$ and $\mathcal{G}_2$ with the same order $p \in poly(\lambda)$ along with a bilinear map $e : \mathcal{G}_1 \times \mathcal{G}_1 \rightarrow \mathcal{G}_2$. After that it picks two generators $g, u \in \mathcal{G}_1$ at random. Finally, it sets the public parameter $params = (p, g, u, \mathcal{G}_1, \mathcal{G}_2, e)$ and publishes it.
2. KeyGen($params, \mathcal{F}$) $\rightarrow$ ($\mathcal{EK}_\mathcal{F}, \mathcal{EK}_{pp}, \mathcal{VK}_{pp}, \mathcal{RK}_{pp}$). Let $\mathcal{F}(x) = \sum_{i=0}^n c_i x^i$ denote the polynomial that the client prepares to delegate. The client first sets the coefficient vector $C = \{c_0, c_1, \ldots, c_n\}$ and then chooses two random numbers $\gamma, k \in \mathcal{Z}_p$. It sets the random number k and (C, γ) as the retrieval key $\mathcal{RK}_{pp}$ and $\mathcal{EK}_\mathcal{F}$, respectively. After that it also picks a random $\alpha \in \mathcal{Z}_p$ as the PRF key and constructs a pseudo random function PRF(α, t) as follows:

$$\mathsf{PRF}(\alpha, t) = g^{k\alpha^{t+1}}.$$

Let j denote the index of modular exponentiation operation, where $j \in [2n + 1] \backslash \{n + 1\}$. For $\forall j \in [2n + 1] \backslash \{n + 1\}$, it runs modular exponentiation setup algorithm MExp.Setup(u, α^{j+1}, p) to produce corresponding evaluation key MExp.EK[j] and verification key MExp.VK[j], where u and α^{j+1} are the base and the power, respectively. When $j = 2n + 2$, it performs algorithm MExp.Setup(F, C, p) to generate corresponding evaluation key MExp.EK[j] and verification key MExp.VK[j], where $F = \{\mathsf{PRF}(\alpha, i) | i = 0, 1, \ldots, n\}$ is the base set. Next, it sets:

$$\mathcal{VK}_{pp} = \{\mathsf{MExp.VK}[j] | 0 \le j \le 2n + 2 \wedge j \ne n + 1\},$$
$$\mathcal{EK}_{pp} = \{\mathsf{MExp.EK}[j] | 0 \le j \le 2n + 2 \wedge j \ne n + 1\},$$

where $\mathsf{MExp.VK}[j] = \{g^{k_{j,2}}, g^{k_{j,3}}, r_j, t_{j,0}, t_{j,1}\}$ and $\mathsf{MExp.EK}[j] = \{(b_{j,i}, w_{j,i})_{i \in [n]}, \{(b'_{j,i}, w'_{j,i})_{i \in [n]}, (h_{j,0}, s_{j,0} w_{j,0} \cdots w_{j,n}), (h_{j,1}, s_{j,1} w'_{j,0} \cdots w'_{j,n})\}$.

Finally, it keeps PRF key α, $\mathcal{EK}_{\mathcal{F}}$, $\mathcal{VK}_{pp}$ and $\mathcal{RK}_{pp}$ private and forwards $\mathcal{EK}_{pp}$ to the cloud. Note that in this procedure the client only choose six blinding randoms for the first performing algorithm $\mathsf{MExp.Setup}$. After that the client uses same blinding randoms every time $\mathsf{MExp.Setup}$ is conducted. That is, $k_{j,i} = k_{0,i}$ for all $i \in [5]$ and $j \in [2n+2] \setminus \{n+1\}$

3. $\mathsf{PPCompute}(params, \mathcal{EK}_{pp}) \rightarrow (\sigma_{\mathcal{VK}_{\mathcal{F}}}, \pi_{\mathcal{VK}_{\mathcal{F}}})$. When the client receives the evaluation key of preprocessing $\mathcal{EK}_{pp}$, it parses $\mathcal{EK}_{pp}$ as $\{\mathsf{MExp.EK}[j] | 0 \leq j \leq 2n+2 \wedge j \neq n+1\}$. After that it runs modular exponentiation computation algorithm $\mathsf{MExp.Compute}(\mathsf{MExp.EK}[j])$ to generate corresponding encoding of result $\mathsf{MExp.}\sigma_{y[j]}$ and witness $\mathsf{MExp.}\pi_{y[j]}$ for all $0 \leq j \leq 2n+2$ and $j \neq n+1$. Next, it sets:

$$\sigma_{\mathcal{VK}_{\mathcal{F}}} = \{\mathsf{MExp.}\sigma_{y[j]} | 0 \leq j \leq 2n+2 \wedge j \neq n+1\},$$
$$\pi_{\mathcal{VK}_{\mathcal{F}}} = \{\mathsf{MExp.}\pi_{y[j]} | 0 \leq j \leq 2n+2 \wedge j \neq n+1\},$$

where $\mathsf{MExp.}\sigma_{y[j]} = \left\{\{w_{j,i}{}^{b_{j,i}}\}, R_{j,0}\right\}$ and $\mathsf{MExp.}\pi_{y[j]} = \left\{\{w'_{j,i}{}^{b'_{j,i}}\}, R_{j,1}\right\}$. Finally, it sends $\sigma_{\mathcal{VK}_{\mathcal{F}}}, \pi_{\mathcal{VK}_{\mathcal{F}}}$ to the client.

4. $\mathsf{PPVerify}(params, \mathcal{VK}_{pp}, \sigma_{\mathcal{VK}_{\mathcal{F}}}, \pi_{\mathcal{VK}_{\mathcal{F}}}, \mathcal{RK}_{pp}) \rightarrow \{\mathcal{VK}_{\mathcal{F}}, \perp\}$. The client first parse $\mathcal{VK}_{pp}, \sigma_{\mathcal{VK}_{\mathcal{F}}}, \pi_{\mathcal{VK}_{\mathcal{F}}}$ as below:

$$\mathcal{VK}_{pp} = \{\mathsf{MExp.VK}[j] | 0 \leq j \leq 2n+2 \wedge j \neq n+1\},$$
$$\sigma_{\mathcal{VK}_{\mathcal{F}}} = \{\mathsf{MExp.}\sigma_{y[j]} | 0 \leq j \leq 2n+2 \wedge j \neq n+1\},$$
$$\pi_{\mathcal{VK}_{\mathcal{F}}} = \{\mathsf{MExp.}\pi_{y[j]} | 0 \leq j \leq 2n+2 \wedge j \neq n+1\}.$$

After that it runs algorithm $\mathsf{MExp.Verify}(\mathsf{MExp.VK}, \mathsf{MExp.}\sigma_{y[j]}, \mathsf{MExp.}\pi_{y[j]})$ to generate corresponding result $\mathsf{MExp.}y[j]$ for all $0 \leq j \leq 2n+2$ and $j \neq n+1$. For the case $j \in [2n+1] \setminus \{n+1\}$, the client checks whether the following equation holds:

$$\left(g^{k_{j,2}} R_{j,0}^{t_{j,0}} w_{j,0}{}^{b_{j,0}}\right)^{r_j} = \left(g^{k_{j,3}} R_{j,1}^{t_{j,1}} w'_{j,1}{}^{b'_{j,1}}\right). \tag{1}$$

If not, the client outputs $\perp$ and aborts. Otherwise, it sets:

$$U_j = \mathsf{MExp.}y[j] = \left(g^{k_{j,2}} R_{j,0}^{t_{j,0}} w_{j,0}{}^{b_{j,0}}\right) = u^{\alpha^{j+1}}.$$

For the case $j = 2n+2$, the client checks whether the following equation holds:

$$\left(g^{k_{j,2}} R_{j,0}^{t_{j,0}} \prod_{i=0}^{n} w_{j,i}{}^{b_{j,i}}\right)^{r_j} = \left(g^{k_{j,3}} R_{j,1}^{t_{j,1}} \prod_{i=0}^{n} w'_{j,i}{}^{b'_{j,i}}\right). \tag{2}$$

If not, the client outputs $\perp$ and aborts. Otherwise, it sets:

$$\sigma_{\mathcal{F}} = g^{\gamma} \mathsf{MExp.}y[j]^{\mathcal{RK}_{pp}^{-1}} = g^{\gamma} \left(g^{k_{j,2}} R_{j,0}^{t_{j,0}} \prod_{i=0}^{n} w_{j,i}{}^{b_{j,i}}\right)^{\mathcal{RK}_{pp}^{-1}} = g^{\gamma} \prod_{i=0}^{n} g^{c_i \alpha^{i+1}}.$$

Next, it adds $\{U_j\}_{j\in[2n+1]\setminus\{n+1\}}$ to the evaluation key of outsourced computation $\mathcal{EK_F}$. It sends the updated evaluation key $\mathcal{EK_F}$ to the cloud, where $\mathcal{EK_F} = \{C, \gamma, \{U_j\}_{j\in[2n+1]\setminus\{n+1\}}\}$. Finally, it sets:

$$\mathcal{VK_F} = \left\{\sigma_\mathcal{F}, \{U_j\}_{j\in[2n+1]\setminus\{n+1\}}\right\}.$$

5. FCompute$(\mathcal{EK_F}, x) \to (y, \pi_y)$. Once the cloud with $\mathcal{EK_F}$ receives the computation request x, it first parses $\mathcal{EK_F}$ as $\{C, \gamma, \{U_i\}_{i\in[2n+1]\setminus\{n+1\}}\}$ and sets:

$$X = \left\{1, x, x^2, \ldots, x^n\right\}.$$

After that it generates the computation result y by computing:

$$y = \langle X, C \rangle = \sum_{i=0}^{n} c_i x^i.$$

Next, it generates the witness $\pi_y = \prod_{i=0}^{n} W_i^{x^i}$ by setting:

$$W_i = U_{n-i}^\gamma \cdot \prod_{j=0, j\neq i}^{n} U_{n+1+j-i}^{c_j}.$$

Finally, it sends to the client the result y along with the corresponding witness π_y.

6. FVerify$(params, \mathcal{VK_F}, \mathcal{RK}_{pp}, x, y, \pi_y) \to \{0, 1\}$. After the client receives the result y and witness π_y, the client parses $\mathcal{VK_F}$ as $\left\{\sigma_\mathcal{F}, \{U_j\}_{j\in[2n+1]\setminus\{n+1\}}\right\}$. Next, it computes $sum - \sum_{i=0}^{n} \alpha^{n-i+1} \cdot x^i$ and outputs 1 (valid) or 0 (invalid) by checking whether the following equation holds:

$$e(\sigma_\mathcal{F}, u^{sum}) = e(g, \pi_y) \cdot e(F_\alpha(0), U_n)^{y \cdot \mathcal{RK}_{pp}^{-1}} \tag{3}$$

Note that u^{sum} can be easily computed with no need to delegate it to the cloud, since $sum = \sum_{i=0}^{n} \alpha^{n-i+1} \cdot x^i$ can be easily obtained by computing $\frac{\alpha^{n+1} \cdot \left(1 - (\alpha^{-1}x)^{n+1}\right)}{1 - \alpha^{-1}x}$. As a result, this trick improves the efficiency of verification of outsourced computation.

7. Update$(\mathcal{VK_F}, \mathcal{RK}_{pp}, \mathcal{F}') \to (upd, \mathcal{VK_{F'}})$. Let $\mathcal{F}$ denote the current polynomial and $\mathcal{F}'$ be the new polynomial that corresponds to the update. Assume that $\mathcal{F}$ and $\mathcal{F}'$ differ in only one coefficient. Let $upd = (i, c, c')$, where $i \in [n]$ is the index of coefficient set C, c_i is the current corresponding coefficient, and c_i' is the updated coefficient. The procedure computes $\sigma_{\mathcal{F}'} = \sigma_\mathcal{F}\mathsf{PRF}_\alpha(i)^{(c'-c)/\mathcal{RK}_{pp}}$ and update $\mathcal{VK_F}$ to $\mathcal{VK_{F'}}$. Finally, the client updates the description of the function to $\mathcal{F}'$ and forwards the upd to the cloud.

4.3   Correctness

In the following, we will show the correctness of our construction based on Eqs. 1, 2 and 3. For the Eqs. 1 and 2, we refer the reader to [23]. For the Eq. 3, we have:

$$
e(\sigma_F, u^{sum}) = e\left(\sigma_F, u^{\sum\limits_{i=0}^{n} \alpha^{n-i+1} \cdot x^i}\right) = e\left(\sigma_F, \prod_{i=0}^{n} u^{\alpha^{n-i+1} \cdot x^i}\right) = \prod_{i=0}^{n} e(\sigma_F, U_{n-i})^{x^i},
$$

and

$$
\begin{aligned}
e\left(g, \pi_y\right) \cdot e(F_\alpha\left(0\right), U_n)^{y \cdot \mathcal{RK}_{pp}^{-1}} &= e\left(g, \prod_{i=0}^{n} W_i\right) \cdot e(F_\alpha\left(0\right), U_n)^{\mathcal{RK}_{pp}^{-1} \cdot \sum_{i=0}^{n} c_i x^i} \\
&= e\left(g, \prod_{i=0}^{n} W_i\right) \cdot e\left(F_\alpha\left(0\right)^{\mathcal{RK}_{pp}^{-1}}, \prod_{i=0}^{n} U_n^{c_i}\right)^{x^i} \\
&= \prod_{i=0}^{n} \left(e\left(g, W_i\right) \cdot e\left(g^{k\alpha \mathcal{RK}_{pp}^{-1}}, U_n^{c_i}\right)\right)^{x^i} \\
&= \prod_{i=0}^{n} \left(e\left(g, W_i\right) \cdot e\left(g^\alpha, U_n\right)^{c_i}\right)^{x^i}
\end{aligned}
$$

Due to Eq. 3, it is not hard to see that:

$$
\prod_{i=0}^{n} e(\sigma_F, U_{n-i})^{x^i} = \prod_{i=0}^{n} \left(e\left(g, W_i\right) \cdot e\left(g^\alpha, U_n\right)^{c_i}\right)^{x^i} \tag{4}
$$

Therefore, if the Eq. 3 holds, the Eq. 4 must hold. The left-hand side (LHS) of Eq. 4 can be expressed as:

$$
\begin{aligned}
LHS &= \prod_{i=0}^{n} e\left(g^\gamma \cdot \prod_{j=0}^{n} g^{c_j \alpha^{j+1}}, U_{n-i}\right)^{x^i} \\
&= \prod_{i=0}^{n} \left(e\left(g^\gamma, U_{n-i}\right) \cdot \left(e\left(\prod_{j=0, j\neq i}^{n} g^{c_j \cdot \alpha^{j+1}}, U_{n-i}\right) \cdot e\left(g^{c_i \cdot \alpha^{i+1}}, U_{n-i}\right)\right)\right)^{x^i} \\
&= \prod_{i=0}^{n} \left(e\left(g, U_{n-i}^\gamma\right) \cdot \left(e\left(g, \prod_{j=0, j\neq i}^{n} U_{n-i}^{c_j \cdot \alpha^{j+1}}\right) \cdot e\left(g^{c_i \cdot \alpha^{i+1}}, U_{n-i}\right)\right)\right)^{x^i} \\
&= \prod_{i=0}^{n} \left(e\left(g, U_{n-i}^\gamma\right) \cdot \left(e\left(g, \prod_{j=0, j\neq i}^{n} u^{\alpha^{n-i+1} \cdot c_j \cdot \alpha^{j+1}}\right) \cdot e\left(g^{c_i \cdot \alpha^{i+1}}, u^{\alpha^{n-i+1}}\right)\right)\right)^{x^i} \\
&= \prod_{i=0}^{n} \left(e\left(g, U_{n-i}^\gamma\right) \cdot \left(e\left(g, \prod_{j=0, j\neq i}^{n} u^{c_j \cdot \alpha^{n+j-i+2}}\right) \cdot e\left(g^{\alpha^{i+1}}, u^{\alpha^{n-i+1}}\right)^{c_i}\right)\right)^{x^i}
\end{aligned}
$$

Or equivalently,

$$LHS = \prod_{i=0}^{n} \left(e\left(g, U_{n-i}^{\gamma}\right) \cdot \left(e\left(g, \prod_{j=0, j\neq i}^{n} U_{n+j-i+1}^{c_j}\right) \cdot e\left(g^{\alpha}, u^{\alpha^{n+1}}\right)^{c_i} \right) \right)^{x^i}$$

$$= \prod_{i=0}^{n} \left(e\left(g, U_{n-i}^{\gamma}\right) \cdot \left(e\left(g, \prod_{j=0, j\neq i}^{n} U_{n+j-i+1}^{c_j}\right) \cdot e\left(g^{\alpha}, U_n\right)^{c_i} \right) \right)^{x^i}$$

$$= \prod_{i=0}^{n} \left(e\left(g, U_{n-i}^{\gamma} \cdot \prod_{j=0, j\neq i}^{n} U_{n+j-i+1}^{c_j}\right) \cdot e\left(g^{\alpha}, U_n\right)^{c_i} \right)^{x^i}$$

$$= \prod_{i=0}^{n} \left(e\left(g, W_i\right) \cdot e\left(g^{\alpha}, U_n\right)^{c_i} \right)^{x^i}$$

Obviously, if the TTP, the client and the cloud are honest and follow all procedures described above, the responses $(\sigma_{\mathcal{VK_F}}, \pi_{\mathcal{RK_F}})$ and (y, π_y) can always pass the client's verification. This completes the proof.

5 Analysis

In this section, we proof the security of our proposed scheme and analyze its computation overhead.

5.1 Security

Theorem 1. *If there exists a PPT adversary $\mathcal{A}$ win the privacy experiment as defined in Definition 3 with non-negligible probability $negl(\lambda)$, then adversary $\mathcal{A}$ can construct an efficient algorithm $\mathcal{B}$ to break zero-knowledge property of verifiable outsourced multiple modular exponentiation.*

The privacy property of FD-VC relies on the zero-knowledge property of MExp sub-protocol. Therefore, we refer the reader to [23] for its rigorous proof.

Theorem 2. *If there exists a PPT adversary $\mathcal{A}$ win the verifiable key unforgeability experiment as defined in Definition 4 with non-negligible probability $negl(\lambda)$, then adversary $\mathcal{A}$ can construct an efficient algorithm $\mathcal{B}$ to break α-checkability of verifiable outsourced multiple modular exponentiation.*

The verifiable key unforgeability property of FD-VC relies on the α-checkability property of MExp sub-protocol. Therefore, we also refer the reader to [23] for its rigorous proof.

Theorem 3. *If there exists a PPT adversary $\mathcal{A}$ win the result unforgeability experiment as defined in Definition 5 with non-negligible probability $negl(\lambda)$, then adversary $\mathcal{A}$ can construct an efficient algorithm $\mathcal{B}$ to solve BDHE problem with non-negligible probability.*

Proof. The adversary $\mathcal{A}$ outputs a forgery for the committed point x^*. The forgery consists of a claimed outcome $\hat{y}^*$ of the polynomial at x^*, and a witness $\hat{\pi}_{y^*}$. If the forgery is successful, the following must be true: $\hat{y}^* \neq y^*$ and FVerify $(params, \mathcal{VK}_{\mathcal{F}}, \mathcal{RK}_{pp}, x^*, \hat{y}^*, \hat{\pi}_{y^*}) = 1$. The adversary $\mathcal{A}$ will leverage this forgery to construct a method $\mathcal{B}$ to solve BDHE problem.

Specifically, let $c = \hat{y}^* - y^* \neq 0 \in \mathcal{Z}_p$, i.e., the difference between the claimed computation result and the true computation result. Since the verification succeeds, the following equation holds:

$$e(\sigma_{\mathcal{F}}, u^{sum}) = e(g, \pi_{\hat{y}^*}) \cdot e(F_\alpha(0), U_n)^{\hat{y}^* \cdot \mathcal{RK}_{pp}^{-1}} \tag{5}$$

Similarly, for a correct pair (y^*, π_{y^*}), we have:

$$e(\sigma_{\mathcal{F}}, u^{sum}) = e(g, \pi_{y^*}) \cdot e(F_\alpha(0), U_n)^{y^* \cdot \mathcal{RK}_{pp}^{-1}} \tag{6}$$

Due to Eqs. 5 and 6, it is not hard to see that:

$$e(g, \pi_{y^*}) \cdot e(F_\alpha(0), U_n)^{y^* \cdot \mathcal{RK}_{pp}^{-1}} = e(g, \pi_{\hat{y}^*}) \cdot e(F_\alpha(0), U_n)^{\hat{y}^* \cdot \mathcal{RK}_{pp}^{-1}}$$

$$e(g, \pi_{y^*}) \cdot e\left(g^{k\alpha}, u^{\alpha^{n+1}}\right)^{y^* \cdot \mathcal{RK}_{pp}^{-1}} = e(g, \pi_{\hat{y}^*}) \cdot e\left(g^{k\alpha}, u^{\alpha^{n+1}}\right)^{\hat{y}^* \cdot \mathcal{RK}_{pp}^{-1}}$$

$$e(g, \pi_{y^*}) \cdot e\left(g^{\alpha}, u^{\alpha^{n+1}}\right)^{y^*} = e(g, \pi_{\hat{y}^*}) \cdot e\left(g^{\alpha}, u^{\alpha^{n+1}}\right)^{\hat{y}^*}$$

$$e(g, \pi_{y^*}) \cdot e\left(g, u^{\alpha^{n+2}}\right)^{y^*} = e(g, \pi_{\hat{y}^*}) \cdot e\left(g, u^{\alpha^{n+2}}\right)^{\hat{y}^*}$$

$$e(g, \pi_{y^*}) \cdot e(g, U_{n+1})^{y^*} = e(g, \pi_{\hat{y}^*}) \cdot e(g, U_{n+1})^{\hat{y}^*}$$

As a result, we have:

$$e(g, U_{n+1}) = \left(\frac{e(g, \pi_{y^*})}{e(g, \pi_{\hat{y}^*})}\right)^{\frac{1}{\hat{y}^* - y^*}} = \left(\frac{e(g, \pi_{y^*})}{e(g, \pi_{\hat{y}^*})}\right)^{c^{-1}} \tag{7}$$

Therefore, it is not hard to see that the right-hand side of Eq. 7 provides an efficient method to break the BDHE assumption. This completes the proof.

5.2 Computation Complexity

In this paper, we mainly resolve the problem mentioned above: expensive preprocessing. That is, the client needs to perform a costly initialization in preprocessing phase. In order to relieve the burden of the client, we delegate this process to the cloud. So, in the following, we would compare computation complexity with the regular solution (performing computation locally without delegation). Since computation complexity is mainly dominated by bilinear pairing and exponentiation, we omit other operations and evaluate computation overhead by counting the number of such operations. The computation comparison can be summarized in Table 1. In Table 1, n, Pairing and Exp denote the degree of polynomial, time cost for bilinear pairing and exponentiation, respectively. In preprocessing phase, our FD-VC scheme need to conduct 6 exponentiations to generate six blinding pairs in KeyGen and $(2n + 2)$ exponentiations to check whether outsourced preprocessing was performed correctly in PPVerify. So, in total $(2n + 8)$ exponentiations are carried out by the client in preprocessing stage. However, the regular solution performing locally conducts $(4n+1)$ exponentiations totally, where $(2n + 1)$ exponentiations are used for generating $\{U_i\}_{i\in[2n+1]\backslash\{n+1\}}$ and another $2n$ exponentiations are used for produce $\sigma_{\mathcal{F}}$. Obviously, our scheme reduces the client's computation overhead greatly in preprocessing phase. In our FD-VC scheme, the client performs only one bilinear pairing to check the correctness of the result returned by the cloud, while the client has to conduct n exponentiations to produce the result in regular scheme. Furthermore, our FD-VC scheme supports dynamic update with constant overhead (i.e. one exponentiation). Therefore, it is especially suitable for the case that the outsourced polynomial needs frequent updates.

Table 1. Comparison of computation cost

Entity	Stage	Performing locally	Our FD-VC	
Client	Preprocessing	$(4n + 1)$·Exp	KeyGen	6·Exp
			PPVerify	$(2n + 2)$·Exp
			Total	$(2n + 8)$·Exp
	Evaluation	n Exp	FVerify	1·Paring
	Update	N/A	Update	1·Exp
Cloud	Outsourcing	N/A	PPCompute	$(2n + 1) \cdot (2n + 2)$·Exp
			FCompute	$3n$Exp

6   Conclusion

We proposed a novel primitive called verifiable outsourced computation with full delegation (FD-VC) in this paper. FD-VC reduces the computation cost of client greatly by delegating the preprocessing to cloud. During this phase, the cloud cannot obtain any knowledge of verification key. Meanwhile, FD-VC supports dynamic update with constant efficiency. The highlight of our scheme is that verification cost is constant and independent of the degree of the outsourced polynomial. We proved that our FD-VC is correct and secure, and our analyses show that our FD-VC is more efficient than other existing schemes.

Acknowledgement. We thank the anonymous reviewers and Bao Li for their fruitful suggestions. This work was supported by the Natural Science Foundation of China under Grant Nos. 61772127, 61703088 and 61472184, the National Science and Technology Major Project under Grant No. 2013ZX03002006, the Liaoning Province Science and Technology Projects under Grant No. 2013217004, the Fundamental Research Funds for the Central Universities under Grant No. N151704002.

References

1. Chen, X., Li, J., Ma, J., Tang, Q., Lou, W.: New algorithms for secure outsourcing of modular exponentiations. In: Foresti, S., Yung, M., Martinelli, F. (eds.) ESORICS 2012. LNCS, vol. 7459, pp. 541–556. Springer, Heidelberg (2012). https://doi.org/10.1007/978-3-642-33167-1_31
2. BBC-NEW: The interview: a guide to the cyber attack on Hollywood. http://www.bbc.co.uk/news/entertainment-arts-30512032
3. Gennaro, R., Gentry, C., Parno, B.: Non-interactive verifiable computing: outsourcing computation to untrusted workers. Cryptology ePrint Archive, Report 2009/547 (2009). http://eprint.iacr.org/
4. Arora, S., Safra, S.: Probabilistic checking of proofs: a new characterization of NP. J. ACM **45**(1), 70–122 (1998)
5. Kilian, J.: A note on efficient zero-knowledge proofs and arguments. In: Proceedings of the 24th Annual ACM Symposium on Theory of Computing, pp. 723-732 (1992)
6. Micali, S.: Computationally sound proofs. SIAM J. Comput. **30**(4), 1253–1298 (2000). Preliminary version appeared in FOCS 1994
7. Goldwasser, S., Kalai, Y.T., Rothblum, G.N.: Delegating computation: interactive proofs for Muggles. In: Proceedings of the ACM Symposium on the Theory of Computing (2008)
8. Chung, K.-M., Kalai, Y., Vadhan, S.: Improved delegation of computation using fully homomorphic encryption. In: Rabin, T. (ed.) CRYPTO 2010. LNCS, vol. 6223, pp. 483–501. Springer, Heidelberg (2010). https://doi.org/10.1007/978-3-642-14623-7_26
9. Parno, B., Gentry, C., Howell, J., Raykova, M.: Pinocchio: nearly practical verifiable computation. In: Proceedings of the 34th IEEE Symposium on Security and Privacy, S&P 2013, pp. 238–252 (2013)
10. Costello, C., et al.: Geppetto: versatile verifiable computation. In: Proceedings of the 36th IEEE Symposium on Security and Privacy, S&P 2015, pp. 253–270 (2015)
11. Kalai, Y.T., Raz, R.: Probabilistically checkable arguments. In: Halevi, S. (ed.) CRYPTO 2009. LNCS, vol. 5677, pp. 143–159. Springer, Heidelberg (2009). https://doi.org/10.1007/978-3-642-03356-8_9
12. Fiore, D., Gennaro, R.: Publicly verifiable delegation of large polynomials and matrix computations, with applications. ePrint 2012/281 (2012)
13. Benabbas, S., Gennaro, R., Vahlis, Y.: Verifiable delegation of computation over large datasets. In: Rogaway, P. (ed.) CRYPTO 2011. LNCS, vol. 6841, pp. 111–131. Springer, Heidelberg (2011). https://doi.org/10.1007/978-3-642-22792-9_7
14. Parno, B., Raykova, M., Vaikuntanathan, V.: How to delegate and verify in public: verifiable computation from attribute-based encryption. In: Cramer, R. (ed.) TCC 2012. LNCS, vol. 7194, pp. 422–439. Springer, Heidelberg (2012). https://doi.org/10.1007/978-3-642-28914-9_24
15. Fiore, D., Gennaro, R., Pastro, V.: Efficiently verifiable computation on encrypted data. In: Proceedings of the 21st ACM Conference on Computer and Communications Security, Scottsdale, AZ, USA, pp. 844–855 (2014)
16. Ma, H., Zhang, R., Wan, Z., Lu, Y., Lin, S.: Verifiable and exculpable outsourced attribute-based encryption for access control in cloud computing. IEEE Trans. Dependable Secur. Comput. **14**(6), 679–692 (2015)
17. Sun, W., et al.: Verifiable privacy-preserving multi-keyword text search in the cloud supporting similarity-based ranking. IEEE Trans. Parallel Distrib. Syst. **25**(11), 3025–3035 (2014)

18. Wang, Q., Zhou, F., Chen, C., Xuan, P., Wu, Q.: Secure collaborative publicly verifiable computation. IEEE Access **5**(1), 2479–2488 (2017)
19. Papamanthou, C., Shi, E., Tamassia, R.: Signatures of correct computation. In: Sahai, A. (ed.) TCC 2013. LNCS, vol. 7785, pp. 222–242. Springer, Heidelberg (2013). https://doi.org/10.1007/978-3-642-36594-2_13
20. Zhang, L.F., Safavi-Naini, R.: Batch verifiable computation of outsourced functions. J. Des. Codes Crypt. **77**, 563–585 (2015)
21. Boneh, D., Franklin, M.: Identity-based encryption from the Weil pairing. In: Kilian, J. (ed.) CRYPTO 2001. LNCS, vol. 2139, pp. 213–229. Springer, Heidelberg (2001). https://doi.org/10.1007/3-540-44647-8_13
22. Boneh, D., Boyen, X., Goh, E.-J.: Hierarchical identity based encryption with constant size ciphertext. In: Cramer, R. (ed.) EUROCRYPT 2005. LNCS, vol. 3494, pp. 440–456. Springer, Heidelberg (2005). https://doi.org/10.1007/11426639_26
23. Ding, Y., Xu, Z., Ye, J., Choo, K.: Secure outsourcing of modular exponentiations under single untrusted programme model. J. Comput. Syst. Sci. **90**, 1–17 (2016)

Keyword Searchable Encryption with Fine-Grained Forward Secrecy for Internet of Thing Data

Rang Zhou[1], Xiaosong Zhang[1](✉), Xiaofen Wang[1], Guowu Yang[1], and Wanpeng Li[2]

[1] Center for Cyber Security, School of Computer Science and Engineering, University of Electronic Science and Technology of China, Chengdu, Sichuan, China
zhour1987@sohu.com, {johnsonzxs,guowu}@uestc.edu.cn, wangxuedou@sina.com
[2] School of Computing, Mathematics and Digital Technology, Manchester Metropolitan University, Manchester M15 6BH, UK
W.Li@mmu.ac.uk

Abstract. With the incessant development and popularization of Internet of things (IoT), the amount of the data collected by IoT devices has rapidly increased. This introduces the concerns over the heavy storage overhead to such systems. In order to relief the storage burden, a popular method is to use the outsourced cloud technology. While the massive collected IoT data is outsourced to the cloud, the security and privacy of these outsourced data is therefore of critical importance, and many researches have been done in this area. In this paper, we propose a new keyword searchable encryption system with fine-grained right revocation. In the system, each IoT device's data are stored in a special document. Thus the data owner can revoke users' search rights at fine-grained document level by setting new random number in each time period. Especially, to realize search right revocation, re-encryption operations on keyword cipheretexts are not needed in our scheme. Then, we instantiate a valid construction in practical application and discuss the security properties in the construction. Our performance evaluations show that the proposed construction is efficient.

Keywords: Searchable encryption · Data sharing
Fine-grained forward secrecy · Internet of Things

1 Introduction

Internet of Things (IoT) introduces an emerging data collection paradigm that aims to obtain IoT data from pervasive things through distributed networks. The emerging paradigm creates new growth of economy, and more researchers pay close attention to the technology. In practical IoT, massive physical devices are connected with each other through wireless or wired network to collect data, such as smart homes and cities, smart vehicle networks, industrial manufacturing and

© Springer Nature Switzerland AG 2018
J. Vaidya and J. Li (Eds.): ICA3PP 2018, LNCS 11337, pp. 288–302, 2018.
https://doi.org/10.1007/978-3-030-05063-4_23

smart environment monitoring. Moreover, data analysis is essential to enhance IoT service, for example the process optimization in industrial manufacturing. Therefore, to meet the requirement of data analysis, data sharing is deployed in IoT. However, with the growth-up scale of IoT, it is not efficient to store and search data directly from each resource-constrained IoT device.

To handle the lack of computing and storage power in IoT device, cloud-assisted method is introduced. This provides an economic and practicable platform with rich computing and storage resource and low cost in data sharing. Each IoT device, which is controlled by data owner, uploads shared data to the cloud server in encrypted format. The cloud server receives a search query which is submitted by an authorized user, and does query match and responds the corresponding encrypted data to the user.

Moreover, for a practical data sharing application in IoT, the users, who are authorized to search and access data, always update their search right dynamically. Therefore, dynamical right update has become a concern in date sharing. The authorization operation can be completed easily, and most studies paid close attention to the right revocation in the cloud assisted system. Especially, to maintain the property of data forward security, the users could not search the encrypted data by the old trapdoors computed from the old secret keys if their search privileges are withdrawn.

In the past, user's right revocation in IoT data sharing scheme generally is not done at fine-grained level. Such schemes [19, 21–23] are not suitable for many cases. For example, a user transfers between different projects inside the same company. The manager might wish to reclaim the search right of project A from the staffs who have transferred to project B. Previous data sharing schemes can not meet this need, because after the search right revocation, the user is not able to search all the documents any more. To meet the requirement, search right revocation at document level is needed, where the data owner can reclaim each users' search privilege in document level.

Our Contribution. In this paper, we aim to solve the fine-grained search right revocation problem for IoT data in keyword searchable encryption system, where forward secrecy is met. We proposed a new keyword searchable encryption scheme with fine-grained search right revocation at document level. The main contributions include:

- We analyze the security requirements of public key keyword searchable encryption scheme with dynamic right revocation in an IoT data sharing system. To achieve forward secrecy for IoT data, we propose a new keyword searchable encryption scheme, which prompts a fine-grained search right revocation at document level.
- We give a concrete construction to complete the search right revocation function for IoT data sharing system. In the construction, we design an user right revocation method without re-encryption operations on keyword ciphertexts, which is more efficient.

– We analyze the performance evaluation of our scheme. The evaluation result shows that the scheme is practical for IoT applications.

1.1   Related Work

Since cloud-assisted technology is provided to improve IoT, the researchers are focus on data management stored in cloud server server. Moreover, data privacy becomes the concern in IoT data storage system. To ensure data security, the data owner needs to encrypt the data before sending it to the cloud server. In order to crease the quality of service, data manager needs to share IoT data with authorized users for data analysis. Keyword searchable encryption, which meets the requirement in data management, is proposed for secure data sharing. Therefore, the design of lightweight keyword searchable encryption construction is a challenge in IoT data sharing application.

To reduce the cost of massive key management in searchable symmetric encryption construction [1], the concept of public key encryption with keyword search (PEKS) is introduced by [2]. Moreover, multi-key searchable encryption and forward secrecy searchable encryption are presented to complete the functions of fine-grained document sharing and user right revocation in practical system.

Multi-key Searchable Encryption. The multi-key searchable encryption framework is designed by Popa et al. [5], and the first web application are built on Mylar in [6]. Only one trapdoor is provided to server, and keyword search match is completed by in different documents, which is encrypted by different keys. Moreover, an new security model for multi-owner searchable encryption are proposed by Tang [7] in this framework. Liu et al. [8] design a scheme in data sharing. Unfortunately, low performance problem is inevitable, because the trapdoor size is linear with the number of documents, in their scheme. To complete provable security, Rompay et al. [9] constructed a new scheme on proxy method. However, heavy overhead does not be ignored on proxy.

Combining with the study of [10], Cui et al. [11] proposed a new key-aggregate searchable encryption scheme, where an aggregation method on file keys is introduced to compute authorization key generation. One user generates a trapdoor to complete keyword search in all authorized file set to this user. However, Kiayias et al. [12] design two key guessing attacks to the study of [11]. Li et al. [14] and Liu et al. [15] proposed their two improved schemes to maintain data verification and multi-owner functions. However, in [14] and [15], the similar drawbacks as in [11] can be found. Kiayias et al. [12] proposed their improved scheme for the study of [11], and more communication and computation are inevitable. To reduce the computation and communication cost, [13] designs a new scheme.

Forward Secrecy Searchable Encryption. In recent studies [16–18], to achieve the function of fine-grained access control in searchable encryption, many schemes, in different scenario, are proposed based on attribute-based encryption. The study [17] implements user revocation in a practical multi-user and multi-owner scenario. In [18], a key-policy and a ciphertext-policy key searchable encryption scheme, where the data owner manages users' search right, are proposed. To meet fine-grained search right management, Shi et al. [16] proposed an attribute-based keyword searchable encryption scheme.

However, all above schemes are constructed applying attribute based encryption, and the search right revocation is achieved from the attribute revocation, where re-encryption is needed to generate new keyword ciphertexts.

To adapt to more practical application, researchers introduced the random number method in computing the keys in each discrete time period without attribute-based encryption. The first scheme [19] is constructed using BLS short signature [20], and the keyword encryption is separated two phases. The first one is completed using a corresponding complementary key maintained by the server. The other one is executed by data sender to generate keyword ciphertexts. Dong et al. [21,22] separated a search key to two parts, where one is users' secret keys and the other one is re-encryption key stored on the server. To reduce the communication and computation cost on proxy, Wang et al. [23] designed a new forward secrecy searchable encryption without proxy, which is similar with the study of [22]. However, this scheme is used in the peer-to-peer scenario. Moreover, the above constructions can not provide the user revocation in fine-grained right management at document level.

2 Preliminaries

2.1 Bilinear Pairing

Bilinear Map. Let two multiplicative cyclic groups $\mathbb{G}_1$ and $\mathbb{G}_2$ be of the same prime order p, and g, h be the generators of $\mathbb{G}_1$. A bilinear pairing e is a map $e : \mathbb{G}_1 \times \mathbb{G}_1 \to \mathbb{G}_2$ with the following properties:

1. Bilinearity: $e(g^{r_1}, h^{r_2}) = e(g, h)^{r_1 r_2}$ for all $g, h \in \mathbb{G}_1$ and $r_1, r_2 \in \mathbb{Z}_p^*$.
2. Non-degeneracy: $e(g, g) \neq 1$.
3. Computability: for any $g, h \in \mathbb{G}_1$, $e(g, h)$ can be computed efficiently.

2.2 Complexity Assumptions

Computational Diffie-Hellman (CDH) Assumption. Let $\mathbb{G}_1$ be bilinear groups of prime order p, given $g, g^{Z_1}, g^{Z_2} \in \mathbb{G}_1$ as input, it is infeasible to compute $g^{Z_1 Z_2} \in \mathbb{G}_1$, where $Z_1, Z_2 \in \mathbb{Z}_p^*$.

Variational Computational Diffie-Hellman (CDH) Assumption. Let $\mathbb{G}_1$ be bilinear groups of prime order p, given $g, g^{Z_3}, g^{Z_1 Z_5}, g^{Z_1 Z_4}, g^{Z_2 Z_4}, g^{Z_1 Z_3 Z_5} \in \mathbb{G}_1$ as input, it is infeasible to compute $g^{Z_2 Z_4 Z_5} \in \mathbb{G}_1$, where $Z_1, Z_2, Z_3, Z_4, Z_5 \in \mathbb{Z}_p^*$.

3 System Model

3.1 System Architecture

The Fig. 1 shows the system architecture, which is consisted of data owner, cloud server, user and IoT nodes. The system role of each party is described as follows.

Data Owner. The data owner is keys generator and data manager in the system. The data owner maintains a users list to generate and distribute all authorized keys to each user and encryption secret key to IoT nodes. Users' search right managements are maintained to achieve the function of fine-grain right revocation.

Cloud Server. The cloud server provides the storage and search service for IoT data management. Especially, the cloud server is "honest but curious", which completes search queries honestly and does not modify stored information maliciously. Moreover, it does not collude with other parties to guess the keyword information from ciphertexts and search queries.

Users. The users are registered in the data owner's list and receive authorized keys from the data owner. The users can generate query trapdoor to search the data on the cloud server.

IoT Nodes. The IoT nodes are data collection nodes for a IoT system. Real-time data to the cloud server for data storage are handled and sent to the cloud server by the IoT nodes. To maintain the data privacy, the IoT nodes achieve the function of encryption for collection data. Moreover, in most actual scenes, encryption operations are executed in resource constrained IoT nodes. Therefore, designed scheme is focus on less computation cost in the system for IoT nodes.

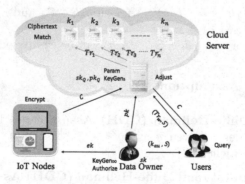

Fig. 1. The fine-grained revocation searchable encryption system

3.2   System Definition

Definition 1. *As shown in Fig. 1, the keyword searchable encryption system definition with revocation capability in data sharing consists of the following eight algorithms:*

- **Param**(ξ): *The algorithm takes security parameter ξ as input, and generates system global parameter $\mathcal{GP}$.*
- **KeyGen$_S$**$(\mathcal{GP})$: *The cloud server takes system parameter $\mathcal{GP}$ as input, and outputs server's public and secret key pair (pk_Q, sk_Q).*
- **KeyGen$_{DO}$**$(\mathcal{GP}, \tau)$: *The data owner takes system parameter $\mathcal{GP}$, time period τ_b as input, and outputs his/her public and secret key pair (pk, sk) and IoT node secret key ek.*
- **Authorize**$(\mathcal{GP}, \tau, sk, S)$: *The data owner takes the system parameter $\mathcal{GP}$, time period τ_b, data owner's private key sk and authorized document set S as input, and outputs authorization key k_{au}. The data owner sends (k_{au}, S) to each corresponding user through a secure channel.*
- **Encrypt**$(\mathcal{GP}, F_i, pk_Q, ek, w)$: *For a document F_i $(i \in \{1, \cdots, n\})$, IoT node takes system parameter $\mathcal{GP}$, IoT node secret key ek, server's public key pk_Q, the document number F_i, keywords w as input, and generates ciphertexts C.*
- **Query**$(\mathcal{GP}, \tau, k_{au}, pk, sk_Q, w)$: *An authorized user takes system parameter $\mathcal{GP}$, time period τ, authorization key k_{au}, data owner's public key pk, server's public key pk_Q, a keyword w as input, and generates query trapdoor Tr_w.*
- **Adjust**$(\mathcal{GP}, \tau, pk, S, Tr_w)$: *The cloud server takes system parameter $\mathcal{GP}$, data owner's public key PK, authorized document set S, query trapdoor $Tr_w =$ Query$(\mathcal{GP}, k_{au}, w)$ as input, and outputs each adjust trapdoor Tr_i for each F_i in S.*
- **Match**$(\mathcal{GP}, \tau, pk, sk_Q, S, Tr_i, C)$: *A deterministic algorithm runs by the cloud server, which takes system parameter $\mathcal{GP}$, time period τ, data owner's public key pk, server's private key sk_Q, authorized document set S, an adjust trapdoor $Tr_i =$ Adjust$(\mathcal{GP}, pk, S, Tr_w)$, a ciphertext $C =$ Encrypt$(\mathcal{GP}, F_i, pk_Q, sk, w)$ as input, and outputs a symbol "True" if C contains w; Otherwise, "False".*

3.3   Security Requirement

To maintain the security of keyword searchable encryption system, keyword confidentiality and trapdoor privacy must be considered. Further, a keyword searchable encryption construction with user search right revocation function has the ability to distinguish the unrevoked users and revoked users. The correctness is satisfied for unrevoked users and the forward secrecy is maintained for revoked user.

Correctness. A keyword searchable encryption system is correct if it satisfies that each authorized user who has the authorized key can perform a successful keyword search.

Keyword Confidentiality. A keyword searchable encryption system maintains keyword confidentiality if it satisfies that only the authorized users can complete the keyword search, and unauthorized users are incapable of learning the privacy information of the stored keyword ciphertexts.

Query Privacy. A keyword searchable encryption system maintains query privacy if it satisfies that only the authorized users can generate a trapdoor from a keyword, and unauthorized users and the honest-but-curious cloud server are incapable to determine a keyword from the submitted query trapdoor.

Forward Secrecy. A keyword searchable encryption system is forward secrecy if it satisfies that the data owner can delete a user and revoke his ability from the system. Moreover, for each revoked user, the data owner can support more fine-grained search right revocation, which is corresponding to every document.

4   The Designed Scheme and Security Analysis

4.1   The Designed Scheme

Param(ξ). The algorithm works as follows:

1. Take the security parameter ξ as input and generate a bilinear group parameters $(p, \mathbb{G}_1, \mathbb{G}_2, e)$;
2. Set the maximum number of documents as n for a data owner and the keyword space as m.
3. Choose a generator $g \in \mathbb{G}_1$ and a collision resistant hash function $H : \{0,1\}^* \to \mathbb{Z}_p^*$.

The system parameters are published as $(p, \mathbb{G}_1, \mathbb{G}_2, e, g, n, m, H : \{0,1\}^* \to \mathbb{Z}_p^*)$.

KeyGen$_S$. The cloud server randomly chooses a random secret key $\beta_1 \in \mathbb{Z}_p^*$ and computes $u = g^{\beta_1} \in \mathbb{G}_1$. The server's private key and public key are $(sk_Q, pk_Q) = (\beta_1, u)$.

KeyGen$_{DO}(\mathcal{GP})$. At time period τ_b $(b = 1, \cdots, \rho)$, the data owner randomly chooses $d_b \in \mathbb{Z}_q^*$. The algorithm performs the following steps:

1. Randomly choose an element $\alpha \in \mathbb{Z}_p^*$, and compute secret keys $g_i = g^{(\alpha)^i} \in \mathbb{G}_1$ for $i = (1, 2, \ldots, n)$.
2. Randomly choose secret keys $\beta_2, \gamma_1, \gamma_2 \in \mathbb{Z}_p^*$, and compute the public parameters $v = g^{\beta_2} \in \mathbb{G}_1$, $h_{1,i,b} = g_i^{\gamma_1 \cdot d_b} \in \mathbb{G}_1$ for $i = (1, 2, \ldots, n)$, and $h_{2,i,b} = g_i^{\gamma_2 \cdot d_b} \in \mathbb{G}_1$ for $i = (1, 2, \ldots, n, n+1, \ldots, 2n)$.
3. Compute IoT node secret key $ek = (ek_1, ek_2) = (u^{\gamma_1}, v^{\gamma_1})$.
4. Destroy α.

The data owner's private key $sk = (\beta_2, \gamma_1, \gamma_2, \{g_i\}_{i=1,2,\ldots,n})$ is kept secretly and public key $pk = (v, \{h_{1,i,b}\}_{i=1,2,\ldots,n}, \{h_{2,i,b}\}_{i=1,2,\ldots,n,n+1,\ldots,2n})$ is stored on cloud server, respectively. Moreover, the data owner distributes the secret key ek to each IoT node.

Authorize(sk, S). The data owner takes document subset $S \subseteq \{1, \ldots, n\}$ as input, computes the authorized key: $k_{au,b} = \prod_{j \in S} g_{n+1-j}^{\beta_2 \cdot d_b}$. The data owner securely sends $(k_{au,b}, S)$ to users.

Encrypt(pk_Q, pk, ek, F_i, l). Each encryption node encrypts keyword w_l, $(l \in \{1, \ldots, m\})$ to the corresponding document F_i, $(i \in \{1, \ldots, n\})$, and uploads the ciphertexts to the cloud server. The encrypt node randomly chooses $t_{i,l} \in \mathbb{Z}_p^*$ and computes ciphertext C as:

$$
\begin{aligned}
C &= (c_{1,i,l}, c_{2,i,l}, c_{3,i,w_l}) \\
&= (ek_1^{t_{i,l}}, ek_2^{t_{i,l}}, (v^{H(w_l)} h_{2,i})^{t_{i,l}}) \\
&= (g^{\gamma_1 \beta_1 t_{i,l}}, g^{\beta_2 \gamma_1 t_{i,l}}, (g^{\beta_2 H(w_l)} g_i^{\gamma_2})^{t_{i,l}})
\end{aligned}
$$

Query$(k_{au,b}, u, v, w_l)$. User chooses a random $x \in \mathbb{Z}_p^*$, and generates query trapdoor $Tr_b = (Tr_{1,b}, Tr_2) = (k_{au,b}^{H(w_l)} v^x, u^x)$. The user sends (Tr_b, S) to the cloud server.

Adjust(pk, i, S, Tr). The cloud server runs the adjust algorithm to compute the discrete trapdoors $Tr_{1,i}$ for each document F_i as:

$$
Tr_{1,i,b} = Tr_{1,b} \cdot \prod_{j \in S, j \neq i} h_{2,(n+1-j+i),b} = Tr_{1,b} \cdot \prod_{j \in S, j \neq i} g_{n+1-j+i}^{\gamma_2 \cdot d_b}.
$$

Match$(Tr_{1,i,b}, Tr_2, S, pk, sk_Q, C)$. The cloud server does keyword search match as follows:

1. Compute $pub_b = \prod_{j \in S} h_{1,(n+1-j),b} = \prod_{j \in S} g_{n+1-j}^{\gamma_1 \cdot d_b}$ for the subset S;
2. Check the equation:

$$
\frac{e(pub_b, c_{3,i,w_l})^{\beta_1} \cdot e(c_{2,i,l}, Tr_2)}{e(Tr_{1,i,b}, c_{1,i,l})} \stackrel{?}{=} e(h_{2,n+1,b}, c_{1,i,l})
$$

If the result holds, outputs "True". Otherwise, "False".

If only one document F_j is authorized in S, $k_{au} = g_j^{\beta_2 d_b}$. The cloud server does not run the **Adjust** algorithm.

4.2   Security Analysis

Assuming that the public cloud server is "honest-but-curious" and does not colludes with the the revoked users. We analyze the security properties of our scheme including correctness, keyword confidentiality, query privacy and forward secrecy.

Theorem 1. Correctness: *Each authorized user is able to retrieve the encrypted documents, which are authorized to search.*

Proof. We show the correctness of our construction in the time period τ_b ($b = 1, \cdots, \rho$) as

$$
\frac{e(pub_b, c_{3,i,w_l})^{\beta_1} \cdot e(c_{2,i,l}, Tr_2)}{e(Tr_{1,i,b}, c_{1,i,l})}
$$

$$
= \frac{e(\prod_{j \in S} g_{n+1-j}^{\gamma_1 \cdot d_b}, (g^{\beta_2 H(w_l)} \cdot g_i^{\gamma_2})^{t_{i,l}})^{\beta_1} \cdot e(g^{\beta_2 \gamma_1 t_{i,l}}, g^{\beta_1 x})}{e(Tr_{1,b} \cdot \prod_{j \in S, j \neq i} g_{n+1-j+i}^{\gamma_2 \cdot d_b}, g^{\gamma_1 \beta_1 t_{i,l}})}
$$

$$
= \frac{e(\prod_{j \in S} g_{n+1-j}^{\gamma_1 \cdot d_b}, g^{\beta_2 H(w_l) \beta_1 t_{i,l}}) \cdot e(\prod_{j \in S} g_{n+1-j}^{\gamma_1 \cdot d_b}, g_i^{\gamma_2 \beta_1 t_{i,l}}) \cdot e(g^{\beta_2 \gamma_1 t_{i,l}}, g^{\beta_1 x})}{e((\prod_{j \in S} g_{n+1-j}^{\beta_2 \cdot d_b})^{H(w_l)} \cdot v^x \cdot \prod_{j \in S, j \neq i} g_{n+1-j+i}^{\gamma_2 \cdot d_b}, g^{\gamma_1 \beta_1 t_{i,l}})}
$$

$$
= \frac{e(\prod_{j \in S} g_{n+1-j}^{\gamma_1 \cdot d_b}, g^{\beta_2 H(w_l) \beta_1 t_{i,l}}) \cdot e(\prod_{j \in S} g_{n+1-j}^{\gamma_1 \cdot d_b}, g_i^{\gamma_2 \beta_1 t_{i,l}}) \cdot e(g^{\beta_2 \gamma_1 t_{i,l}}, g^{\beta_1 x})}{e((\prod_{j \in S} g_{n+1-j}^{\beta_2 \cdot d_b})^{H(w_l)}, g^{\gamma_1 \beta_1 t_{i,l}}) \cdot e(g^{\beta_2 x}, g^{\gamma_1 \beta_1 t_{i,l}}) \cdot e(\prod_{j \in S, j \neq i} g_{n+1-j+i}^{\gamma_2 \cdot d_b}, g^{\gamma_1 \beta_1 t_{i,l}})}
$$

$$
= \frac{e(\prod_{j \in S} g_{n+1-j+i}, g)^{\gamma_1 \cdot d_b \gamma_2 \beta_1 t_{i,l}}}{e(\prod_{j \in S, j \neq i} g_{n+1-j+i}, g)^{\gamma_2 \cdot d_b \gamma_1 \beta_1 t_{i,l}}}
$$

$$
= e(g_{n+1}, g)^{\gamma_1 \gamma_2 \cdot d_b \beta_1 t_{i,l}}
$$

$$
= e(g_{n+1}^{\gamma_2 \cdot d_b}, g^{\gamma_1 \beta_1 t_{i,l}})
$$

$$
= e(h_{2,n+1,b}, c_{1,i,l}).
$$

Theorem 2. Keyword Confidentiality: *The proposed scheme is security on keyword confidentiality to resist the attack from unauthorized users.*

Proof. The unauthorized users are curious to the keyword in keyword ciphertexts C and become attacker A_1. It may obtain some information to launch an attack. A_1 can obtain the stored information including public parameters, other documents search keys $k_j (i \neq j)$, keyword ciphertexts C.

Assuming that the unauthorized users want to guess the keyword w_θ from keyword ciphertexts $C = (c_{1,i,\theta}, c_{2,i,\theta}, c_{3,i,w_\theta}) = (u^{\gamma_1 t_{i,\theta}}, g^{\beta_2 \gamma_1 t_{i,\theta}}, (g^{\beta_2 H(w_\theta)} g_i^{\gamma_2})^{t_{i,\theta}})$ of document F_i.

- A_1 retrieves the partial number $(g_i^{\gamma_2})^{t_{i,\theta}}$ from C. A_1 maintains $u^{t_{i,\theta} \gamma_1}, v^{t_{i,\theta} \gamma_1}$, $u, v, g_i^{\gamma_2}, g_i^{\gamma_1}$ and wants to obtain $g_i^{\gamma_2 t_{i,\theta}}$. $u, v, g_i \in \mathbb{G}_1$ and $v = u^{z_1}, g_i = u^{z_2}$, where $z_1, z_2 \in \mathbb{Z}_p^*$. A_1 maintains $u^{t_{i,\theta} \gamma_1}, u^{z_1 t_{i,\theta} \gamma_1}, u, u^{z_1}, u^{z_2 \gamma_2}, u^{z_2 \gamma_1}$ and wants to obtain $u^{z_2 \gamma_2 t_{i,\theta}}$. Therefore, if A_1 can obtain the value of $g_i^{\gamma_2 t_{i,\theta}}$ in this case, A_1 can solve Variational Computational Diffie-Hellman problem.
- A_1 retrieves the partial number $(g^{\beta_2 H(w_\theta)})^{t_{i,\theta}} = (g^{\beta_2 t_{i,\theta}})^{H(w_\theta)}$ from C. A_1 needs the value of $g^{\beta_2 t_{i,\theta}} = v^{t_{i,\theta}}$. A_1 maintains $v^{t_{i,\theta} \gamma_1}, v$ and wants to obtain $v^{t_{i,\theta}}$. $v \in \mathbb{G}_1$ and $v = z^{\gamma_1^{-1}}$, where $z \in \mathbb{G}_1$. A_1 maintains $z^{t_{i,\theta}}, z^{\gamma_1^{-1}}$ and wants to obtain $z^{t_{i,\theta} \gamma_1^{-1}}$. Therefore, if A_1 can obtain the value of $v^{t_{i,\theta}}$ in this case, A_1 can solve Computational Diffie-Hellman problem.

Therefore, the attacker A_1 does not distinguish w_θ to achieve the attack goal.

Theorem 3. Query Privacy: *The proposed scheme is security on query trapdoor privacy to resist the attack from honest-but-curious cloud server and unauthorized users, who do not have search right of attacked document F_i.*

Proof. (1) The honest-but-curious cloud server is curious to the keyword information in query trapdoor and becomes an attacker A_2. It may obtain some information to launch an attack. A_2 can obtain the stored information including public parameters, server secret key β_1, other documents search keys $k_j (i \neq j)$, submitted query trapdoor Tr_b.

Assuming that the server wants to guess the keyword w_θ from trapdoor $Tr_b = (Tr_{1,b}, Tr_2) = (k_{au,b}{}^{H(w_\theta)} v^x, u^x)$, where S is the authorized search set and $F_i \in S$, and becomes a attacker A_2. A_2 does the guess attacks as following:

- A_2 retrieve the partial number v^x from the Tr_b. A_2 maintains u, u^x, v and wants to obtain v^x. $u, v \in \mathbb{G}_1$ and $v = u^z$, where $z \in \mathbb{Z}_p^*$. A_1 maintains u, u^x, u^z and wants to obtain u^{xz}. Therefore, if A_2 can obtain the value of v^x in this case, A_2 can solve Computational Diffie-Hellman problem.
- A_2 computes the $k_{au,b}{}^{H(w_\theta)}$ from the secret key $g_{n+1-i}^{\beta_2 \cdot d_b}$. However, for F_i, A_2 only has a negligible probability to get the secret search key $g_{n+1-i}^{\beta_2 \cdot d_b}$, and the data owner's private keys $\beta_2, \gamma_1, \gamma_2$. Moreover, A_2 computes $Tr_{1,i,b} = Tr_{1,b} \cdot \prod_{j \in S, j \neq i} h_{2,(n+1-j+i),b}$, and get the discrete trapdoor $Tr_{1,i,b}$ for the file F_i. The computation is executed by the cloud server and leak no any information to A_2 to determine w_θ in the query trapdoor.

Therefore, A_2 does not distinguish w_θ to achieve the attack goal.

(2) The unauthorized users are curious to the keyword in submitted trapdoor and become attacker A_1. It may obtain some information to launch an attack. A_1 can obtain the stored information including public parameters, other documents search keys $k_j (i \neq j)$, submitted query trapdoor Tr_b.

Comparing with A_2, A_1 has weak capability because of the lack of server secret key. Therefore, A_1 does not achieve the attack goal.

Theorem 4. Forward Secrecy: *To maintain the fine-grained forward secrecy, the system manages the search right for each document. Each revoked user can not retrieve the special encrypted documents, which are revoked from his search right.*

Proof. In the time period τ_{bb}, the revoked users could not get the new short time authorized key from our scheme. Therefore, he only has the ability to generate and send the old trapdoor $Tr_b = (Tr_{1,b}, Tr_2)$ from the old short time authorized key in time period τ_b ($b \neq bb$). The server does the adjust and match algorithms as follows:

1. Compute $Tr'_{1,i,bb} = Tr_{1,b} \cdot \prod_{j \in S, j \neq i} h_{2,(n+1-j+i),bb} = Tr_{1,b} \cdot \prod_{j \in S, j \neq i} g_{n+1-j+i}^{\gamma_2 \cdot d_{bb}}$
2. Compute the $pub_{bb} = \prod_{j \in S} h_{1,(n+1-j),bb} = \prod_{j \in S} g_{n+1-j}^{\gamma_1 \cdot d_{bb}}$ based on subset S.
3. Test the equation:

$$\frac{e(pub_{bb}, c_{3,i,w_l})^{\beta_1} \cdot e(c_{2,i,l}, Tr_2)}{e(Tr'_{1,i,bb}, c_{1,i,l})} \overset{?}{=} e(h_{2,n+1,bb}, c_{1,i,l})$$

Due to $Tr'_{1,i,bb} \neq Tr_{1,i,bb}$, the test equation does not hold.

From the above analysis, we show that the revoked users could not search the specific encrypted document by submitting the trapdoor generated from an old short time authorized key. Therefore, the forward secrecy is achieved in our scheme.

5　Performance Analysis

5.1　Implementation Details

The performance is constructed by the basic cryptographic operations in pairing computation. Two different settings are considered: one is in JAVA on smart phone, which has a 64-bit 8 core CPU processor (4 core processor runs at 1.5 GHz and 4 core processors runs at 1.2 GHz), 3 GB RAM with Android 5.1.1. The other is in C on computer, which has Intel Core i3-2120 CPU @3.30 GHz, 4.00 GB RAM with windows7 64-bits operation system. JPBC and PBC library [3] are used to implement the cryptographic operations for smart phone and computer, respectively. We choose the type A elliptic curve, which is shown as $E : y^2 = x^3 + x$. To maintain the security and efficiency, our experiment is conducted as $|Z_p| = 160$ bits, $|\mathbb{G}_1| = 1024$ bits and $|\mathbb{G}_2| = 1024$ bits. Some useful experiment results [4] about pair computation are shown in Table 1.

Table 1. The computation time on different platforms (ms)

Computation	Smart phone	Computer
Bilinear pairing $\mathbb{G}_1 \times \mathbb{G}_1 \rightarrow \mathbb{G}_2$	195.11	18.03
Exponentiation on group $\mathbb{G}_1$	90.12	9.18
Exponentiation on group $\mathbb{G}_2$	33.4	2.78

5.2　Experiment Evaluation

In the IoT data sharing system simulation, the cloud server is considered as computer. Moreover, two different simulations are implemented for data owners on smart phone and computer. Smart phone and computer are instantiated on user, encryption node and data owner. **Param**, **KeyGen$_S$**, **Adjust** and **Match** run on the cloud server. **KeyGen$_{DO}$** and **Authorize** run on the data owner and **Encrypt** runs on encryption node. **Query** runs on user. Next, we discuss the performance evaluation of our construction on cloud server, data owner, encryption node and user.

The simulation results show in Fig. 2. The time cost of algorithms on cloud server, data owner, encryption node and user are matched to the Fig. 2(a)–(d), Fig. 2(e) and (f), Fig. 2(g) and Fig. 2(h), respectively. The evaluation analysis is shown as follows:

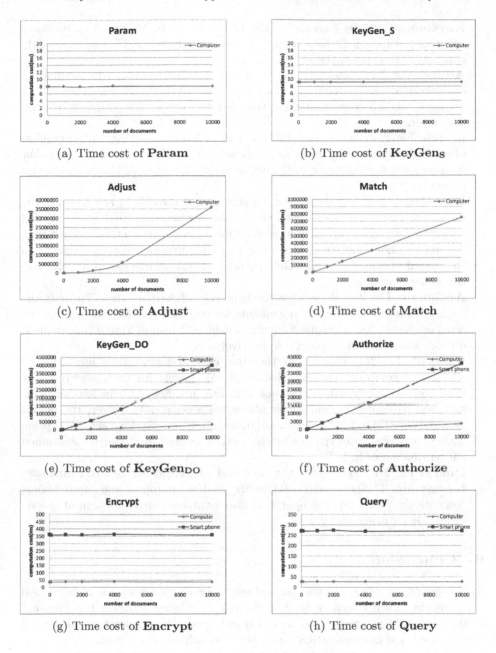

Fig. 2. The execution time of the algorithm in the system

- **Param:** Fig. 2(a) shows that the time cost of **Param** is a constant size. Moreover, the operations are consisted of bilinear group generation and hash function setting.

- **KeyGen$_S$:** Fig. 2(b) shows that the time cost of **KeyGen$_S$** is a constant size. For instance, 9.22 ms is used on computer. Moreover, the operation only contains once exponentiation on group $\mathbb{G}_1$.
- **Adjust:** Fig. 2(c) shows that the time cost of **Adjust** is linear in the number of authorized search documents for one submitted keyword search query. For instance, when S contains 1000 authorized documents, 359640 ms is used on computer.
- **Match:** Fig. 2(d) shows that the time cost of **Match** is linear in the number of authorized search documents for one submitted keyword search query. For instance, when S contains 1000 authorized documents, 77360 ms is used on computer.
- **KeyGen$_{DO}$:** Fig. 2(e) shows that the time cost of **KeyGen$_{DO}$** is linear in the maximum number of documents. For instance, when $n = 1000$, 28067 ms and 283620 ms are used on computer and smart phone, respectively. Therefore, the smart phone and computer meet the computation cost requirement in the system, because the **KeyGen$_{DO}$** runs in system idle excepting the first key generation phase.
- **Authorzie:** Fig. 2(f) shows that the time cost of **Authorzie** is linear in the number of authorized search documents for one user. For instance, when the set S contains 1000 authorized documents, 368.82 ms and 4186.02 ms are used on computer and smart phone, respectively.
- **Encrypt:** Fig. 2(g) shows that the time cost of **Encrypt** is linear in the number of keywords for each document. Moreover, for each keyword, the time cost of **Encrypt** is a constant size. For instance, 37.5 ms and 360.4 ms are used on computer and smart phone, respectively. Moreover, the operation only contains fourth exponentiations on group $\mathbb{G}_1$ for each encryption node. Therefore, **Encrypt** can be efficiently executed by resource constrained encryption nodes in IoT.
- **Query:** Fig. 2(h) shows that the time cost of **Trapdoor** is a constant size. For instance, 27.39 ms and 271.03 ms are used on computer and smart phone, respectively. Moreover, the operation only contains third exponentiations on group $\mathbb{G}_1$ for every query.

6   Conclusion

In this paper, we propose a fine-grained search privilege revocation construction to maintain forward secrecy for IoT data. Our scheme achieves the proposal of user search right revocation at document level. We implement a practical construction and our evaluation shows that our scheme is efficient.

Acknowledgement. This work is supported by the National Key Research and Development Program under Grant 2017YFB0802300, National Natural Science Foundation of China under grant No. 61502086 and 61572115; the Sichuan Provincial Major Frontier Issues (2016JY0007); the Guangxi Key Laboratory of Trusted Software (No. PF16116X); the foundation from Guangxi Colleges and Universities Key Laboratory of Cloud Computing and Complex Systems (No. YF16202).

References

1. Song, D.X., Wagner, D., Perrig, A.: Practical techniques for searches on encrypted data. In: 2000 IEEE Symposium on Security and Privacy, pp. 44–55. IEEE Computer Society Press, May 2000
2. Boneh, D., Di Crescenzo, G., Ostrovsky, R., Persiano, G.: Public key encryption with keyword search. In: Cachin, C., Camenisch, J.L. (eds.) EUROCRYPT 2004. LNCS, vol. 3027, pp. 506–522. Springer, Heidelberg (2004). https://doi.org/10.1007/978-3-540-24676-3_30
3. PBC library. https://crypto.stanford.edu/pbc/
4. Yang, Y., Liu, X., Deng, R.H., Li, Y.: Lightweight sharable and traceable secure mobile health system. IEEE Trans. Dependable Secur. Comput. **99**, 1–1 (2017)
5. Popa, R.A., Zeldovich, N.: Multi-key searchable encryption, Cryptology ePrint Archive, Report 2013/508 (2013)
6. Popa, R.A., Stark, E., Valdez, S., Helfer, J., Zeldovich, N., Balakrishnan, H.: Building web applications on top of encrypted data using Mylar. In: Proceedings of the 11th USENIX Symposium on Networked Systems Design and Implementation, NSDI 2014, pp. 157-172 (2014)
7. Tang, Q.: Nothing is for free: security in searching shared and encrypted data. IEEE Trans. Inf. Forensics Secur. **9**(11), 1943–1952 (2014)
8. Liu, Z., Li, J., Chen, X., Yang, J., Jia, C.: TMDS: thin-model data sharing scheme supporting keyword search in cloud storage. In: Susilo, W., Mu, Y. (eds.) ACISP 2014. LNCS, vol. 8544, pp. 115–130. Springer, Cham (2014). https://doi.org/10.1007/978-3-319-08344-5_8
9. Van Rompay, C., Molva, R., Önen, M.: Multi-user searchable encryption in the cloud. In: Lopez, J., Mitchell, C.J. (eds.) ISC 2015. LNCS, vol. 9290, pp. 299–316. Springer, Cham (2015). https://doi.org/10.1007/978-3-319-23318-5_17
10. Chu, C.-K., Chow, S.S.M., Tzeng, W.-G., Zhou, J., Deng, R.H.: Key-aggregate cryptosystem for scalable data sharing in cloud storage. IEEE Trans. Parallel Distrib. Syst. **25**(2), 468–477 (2014)
11. Cui, B., Liu, Z., Wang, L.: Key-aggregate searchable encryption for group data sharing via cloud storage. IEEE Trans. Comput. **65**(8), 2374–2385 (2016)
12. Kiayias, A., Oksuz, O., Russell, A., Tang, Q., Wang, B.: Efficient encrypted keyword search for multi-user data sharing. In: Askoxylakis, I., Ioannidis, S., Katsikas, S., Meadows, C. (eds.) ESORICS 2016. LNCS, vol. 9878, pp. 173–195. Springer, Cham (2016). https://doi.org/10.1007/978-3-319-45744-4_9
13. Zhou, R., Zhang, X., Du, X., Wang, X., Yang, G., Mohsen, G.: File-centric multi-key aggregate keyword searchable encryption for industrial internet of things. IEEE Trans. Ind. Inform. **14**(8), 3648–3658 (2018)
14. Li, T., Liu, Z., Li, P., Jia, C., Jiang, Z.L., Li, J.: Verifiable searchable encryption with aggregate keys for data sharing in outsourcing storage. In: Liu, J.K., Steinfeld, R. (eds.) ACISP 2016. LNCS, vol. 9723, pp. 153–169. Springer, Cham (2016). https://doi.org/10.1007/978-3-319-40367-0_10
15. Liu, Z., Li, T., Li, P., Jia, C., Li, J.: Verifiable searchable encryption with aggregate keys for data sharing system. Future Gener. Comput. Syst. **78**, 778–788 (2018)
16. Shi, J., Lai, J., Li, Y., Deng, R.H., Weng, J.: Authorized keyword search on encrypted data. In: Kutyłowski, M., Vaidya, J. (eds.) ESORICS 2014. LNCS, vol. 8712, pp. 419–435. Springer, Cham (2014). https://doi.org/10.1007/978-3-319-11203-9_24

17. Sun, W., Yu, S., Lou, W., Hou, Y.T.: Protecting your right: verifiable attribute-based keyword search with fine-grained owner-enforced search authorization in the cloud. IEEE Trans. Parallel Distrib. Syst. **27**(4), 1187–1198 (2016)
18. Zheng, Q., Shouhuai, X., Ateniese, G.: VABKS: verifiable attribute-based keyword search over outsourced encrypted data. In: 2014 Proceedings IEEE, INFOCOM, pp. 522–530 (2014)
19. Bao, F., Deng, R.H., Ding, X., Yang, Y.: Private query on encrypted data in multi-user settings. In: Chen, L., Mu, Y., Susilo, W. (eds.) ISPEC 2008. LNCS, vol. 4991, pp. 71–85. Springer, Heidelberg (2008). https://doi.org/10.1007/978-3-540-79104-1_6
20. Boneh, D., Lynn, B., Shacham, H.: Short signatures from the weil pairing. In: Boyd, C. (ed.) ASIACRYPT 2001. LNCS, vol. 2248, pp. 514–532. Springer, Heidelberg (2001). https://doi.org/10.1007/3-540-45682-1_30
21. Dong, C., Russello, G., Dulay, N.: Shared and searchable encrypted data for untrusted servers. In: Atluri, V. (ed.) DBSec 2008. LNCS, vol. 5094, pp. 127–143. Springer, Heidelberg (2008). https://doi.org/10.1007/978-3-540-70567-3_10
22. Dong, C., Russello, G., Dulay, N.: Shared and searchable encrypted data for untrusted servers. J. Comput. Secur. **19**(3), 367–397 (2011)
23. Wang, X., Mu, Y., Chen, R., Zhang, X.: Secure channel free ID-based searchable encryption for peer-to-peer group. J. Comput. Sci. Technol. **31**(5), 1012–1027 (2016)

IoT-SDNPP: A Method for Privacy-Preserving in Smart City with Software Defined Networking

Mehdi Gheisari[1], Guojun Wang[1(✉)], Shuhong Chen[1],
and Hamidreza Ghorbani[2]

[1] School of Computer Science and Technology, Guangzhou University,
Guangzhou 510006, China
csgjwang@gzhu.edu.cn
[2] Department of Electrical Engineering and Information Technology,
Azad University of Tehran-Electronic Branch, Tehran, Iran

Abstract. Internet of Things (IoT) era appeared to connect all the digital and non-digital devices around the globe through the Internet. Based on predictions, billions of devices will be connected with each other by 2050 with the aim of providing high-level and humanized services. One application of IoT is a smart city that means IT-enabled cities running by themselves without human interventions. These large number of devices, especially in a smart city environment, may sense sensitive and personal data which makes the system vulnerable. We have to protect private information so that unwanted parties would not be able to find original data, which is a part of privacy-preserving. Meanwhile, a new networking paradigm evolved called Software Defined Networking (SDN) that aimed to separate the Control Plane and the Data Plane of the network results in much more flexibility to manage the network. Most of the existing works are deficient in flexibility or very tedious. In this paper, we facilitated IoT-based smart city with SDN paradigm to leverage the benefits of SDN. Then, based on the environment, we propose IoT-SDN Privacy-Preserving, IoT-SDNPP, to keep private data safe. We have done extensive experiments, and the experimental results have demonstrated the effectiveness of our approach.

Keywords: Privacy-preserving · Software Defined Networking
Smart city · Privacy rules · Internet of Things

1 Introduction

IoT is a network of things that are connected through the Internet. Objects in IoT have variety of kinds including computers, sensors, equipped humans, and machines. They must be accessible at any place and at any time [32]. IoT provides a virtual image of all connected physical devices that are connected to the Internet. Each connected device has to have a Unique Identifier (ID) such as IP and be identifiable [2].

Based on predictions, more than half of world population will inhabit in cities by 2050 [27]. A smart city is an application of IoT with the aim of managing cities in an automatic manner, without human intervention. Smart city aim is increasing the quality

© Springer Nature Switzerland AG 2018
J. Vaidya and J. Li (Eds.): ICA3PP 2018, LNCS 11337, pp. 303–312, 2018.
https://doi.org/10.1007/978-3-030-05063-4_24

of services while minimizing administrative overhead through more efficient resource management. Smart city plays dominant role when population of cities are high. In detail, it aims to monitor critical infrastructures, optimizing resources, planning maintenance, and offering services to citizens [6]. With the usage of IoT in smart cities, we will have seamless integration between the physical world and cyberspace. Security flaws not only have a negative effect in cyberspace but also have a bad effect on the physical world [30].

Due to a high number of connected devices in smart cities and each one produces data, we entered Big Data era [12]. With the big data, we can discover various kinds of value-added knowledge for citizens, companies, government, and organizations in order to provide high-level services. Although we can gain benefits from produced data by IoT device in smart city, regretfully, it has critical drawbacks too. One drawback is that the produced data can be sensitive. It means that the data provider do not want to disclose this data to unwanted third parties. If sensitive data discloses, the environment maybe face with harm and vulnerability, privacy-preserving challenge. We can not manage this large amount of data manually so we need agile paradigms in order to accommodate increasing amount of data and process them while keep private data safe.

Recently, a new network paradigm emerged that tries to provide flexibility for network management, called Software Defined Networking (SDN). SDN can cause more efficient system management. In SDN, Control plane and Data plane are separated [16]. Data Plane is about the actions that devices take to forward data. In SDN, Data plane consists of dumb switches. Each switch is plain hardware with a little capability to be programmed. The rests will be the Control plane. In SDN, switches are different from traditional networks, OpenFlow switches [19]. All OpenFlow switches are controlled by SDN controller/controllers. With a small amount of threshold, in SDN, smartness from switches, hardware domain, transfers to SDN controller, non-hardware domain. SDN controller is able to manage the network such as routing of data packets by software commands. With the leverage of this basic advantage, we can achieve striking benefits in networking of devices, smart city, such as flexibility and centralized management [29]. We can also send IoT devices' data to Cloud environment, for further analysis or archival aim, without disclosing sensitive information with the help of SDN paradigm in IoT-based smart city environment [23].

The major contributions of this paper are mainly three-folded:

1. We integrate smart city environment with SDN paradigm. Thus, we are able to leverage capabilities of both IoT-based smart city and flexibility of SDN paradigm.
2. We offer a solution for achieving an efficient IoT-based smart city while preventing privacy breaching, preserving the privacy. We do not assume any predefined principle behaviors/rules in IoT-SDNPP so that it can be applied to other applications such as social networks.
3. Finally, we validate IoT-SDNPP in extensive simulations. We have found that IoT-SDNPP achieves a superior performance in terms of communication cost. The evaluation results demonstrate overload of the system is acceptable in a highly-dynamic environment such as smart city. We will also show that IoT-SDNPP can be widely used in IoT-based smart city.

This paper is organized as follows; Sect. 2 describes background information. In Sect. 3, we focus on related work. Section 4 indicates our IoT-SDNPP solution that preserves private data safe in smart city space with the help of SDN paradigm. Finally, Sect. 5, end of this paper, concludes the paper and also presents future works.

2   Background

In this section, some background information are described such as comparison between traditional networks and SDN. Then, we pay attention to the privacy-preserving issue.

2.1   Traditional Networks vs. Software Defined Networking

Traditional networks, typical systems, have some characteristics that are:

- Traditional systems are made up of switches with integrated control and data-forwarding planes. Thus, each part needs to be programmed and managed separately. For a minor change, we have to make changes manually that is very tedious and tough task.
- Switches do not have the capability of dynamic programming. Thus, the rules cannot be changed dynamically as per our wish [7].
- The possibility of path clog is high and may cause the current services to get cut [3].

The entire system applies one static privacy rule in typical networks. This can cause unacceptable penetration rate [31]. Even their penetration rates are acceptable but later attackers can penetrate the system easily due to the system is static.

SDN is a network paradigm that is created by Stanford university with the aim of separating a network into two Control Plane for managing network and Data Plane for traffic flows in order to address many challenges such as privacy-preserving [3, 22]. SDN can satisfy the situations that have the following characteristics:

- High demand for resources.
- Unpredictable traffic patterns.
- Rapid network reconfiguration.

For example, in SDN, we have less path clog in comparison to traditional networks. When the path is clogged, the controller can send the appropriate command to the congested switch in order to take the alternative path or rerouting packets [9].

Specifically, although current technologies, future technological innovations as well, can deliver enormous benefits, they bring more urgent to address various concerns over personal data, privacy breaches [15]. Data privacy is concerned with the ways IoT devices handle the sensed information such as how they are collecting, processing, sharing, storing, and using them [10]. Personal data encompasses any information which can identify a living person such as addresses, IDentity card numbers, number of alive person in a sensitive building, medical records, employment records, and credit card reports [25].

Based on the United Nation Global Cyberlaw Tracker (UNCTAD) report [4], around 60 developing countries do not have fully baseline protection laws and around 35 only have draft legislation. From another perspective, based on the DLA Piper 2017 survey, an awareness report, a multinational law firm, about General Data Protection Regulations (GDPR) that is widely acceptable, levels of maturity to meet the new standards are low, less than 50% of all business sectors [1]. Nearly, all in charge organizations have significant work to do to address data protection challenge. In other words, this shows a large amount of effort is needed to be done to provide data privacy of human rights.

3   Related Work

IoT aims is connecting all devices all over the world. This connection should be available at any demanding place and time. SDN is a paradigm to design, manage and build a network so that it results in the network to become flexible and agile. This section pays attention to the literature that has done in order to preserve privacy of devices in IoT-SDN environment. To the best of our knowledge, there are few researches that took heed of security and privacy in IoT-SDN environment. Here, we pay attention to those literature that try to keep privacy in IoT environment with the help of SDN paradigm.

Authors in [26] proposed a novel authentication scheme for IoT environment based on identity identification and SDN paradigm. They also implemented a trusted certificate authority on the SDN controller. They also proposed a security protocol for authentication so that each device can authenticate itself securely. The problem is that they did not deploy and evaluate their method. So there is not any performance analysis of their method. Thus, we cannot compare their method with other solutions.

Nobakht et al. in [20] proposed a framework for intrusion detection in IoT-SDN integration domain. They tried to find and address attacks against a specific host. Authors, in addition, tried to minimize communicational and computational costs through paying attention to the activity and traffic of the target host. They also considered the diversity of network devices. Their method called IoT-IDM discovers suspicious activities in the network and tries to extract features of them based on the network flow data. In addition, they used machine learning for malicious traffic detection. In detail, they used Support Vector Machine (SVM) for detecting abnormal hosts situations by classifying data [10]. They tried to reduce attack effects by loading required traffic rules on switches and hubs. They also tried to select features of the current attack. They used heuristic methods to extract features based on learned signature patterns of known attacks. One of the drawbacks of their method is that feature selection is extracted in a static mode without any flexibility so distinguishing malicious flows of all kinds of attacks are impossible.

Bull et al. in [5] proposed a security approach based on data flow with the help of SDN gateway. Their method monitors traffic flows to find abnormal behaviors. They tried to enhance the amount of availability of the system by resisting against Distributed Denial of Service (DDOS) attacks [11]. As promoter, they used IoT gateways in the SDN paradigm environment. Unfortunately, they only provided simulation result for ICMP and TCP [18]. Their solution is needed to be evaluated from more different dimensions such as modern DDOS kind of attacks.

A secure solution for IoT-SDN environment is proposed in [8]. They extended SDN domain to multiple domains. Each SDN controller focuses solely to policies of its domain area. The communications among different domains would be done through the domain controller. Thus, each domain is independent in case of failure so the system is somehow fault tolerant, we do not have issue of single-point failure. One of its disadvantages is that there is not any simulation test or even experimental test of their solution.

We facilitate smart city networking paradigm with SDN paradigm. So we are able to leverage advantages of SDN such as flexibility, more convenient management of the network and so on. After combination, we propose and evaluate a solution on top of it in order to enhance privacy-preserving level.

4 IoT-SDN Privacy-Preserving (IoT-SDNPP)

In this section, at first, we focus on system overview, IoT-SDN integration in smart city environment. Then, we will introduce an SDN-based solution in the environment that can preserve privacy along with it brings the flexibility to network management, IoT-SDNPP.

4.1 System Overview

We should consider the following requirements in the design of solutions. At first, the designed solution should be able to provide privacy-preserving services locally or even remotely and the end users of IoT devices should not burden with heavy tasks. Typical IoT devices' users of smart devices often lack enough expertise and vigilance to provide a secure and privacy-aware of the network, which hugely pose heterogeneous architectures and varying degrees of security and privacy properties [13].

The second main design objective is the efficiency of the solution; the solution should incur low communication and computation overheads in order to be applicable. To this end, we consider the application-specific environment to design our solution. This can cause the limitation of the amount of the network traffic that is one criterion to lower overload, fewer data is needed to be analyzed. For instance, if the SDN controller requires investigating the traffic of a particular IoT device and application in smart city space, the appropriate approach must be considered to reduce the volume of overall traffic [17].

In addition, the solution should be able to block the network traffic of a specific IoT device to reduce the amount of data transferred and preserve the privacy of device. For example, if SDN controller finds privacy breach, it should be able to clog the path and block data in order to preserve-privacy and resisting attacks. This feature will be added as a new feature in our future work [28].

On the other hand, new IoT devices are emerging in our lives and pushing in the smart city environment at a fast manner from diverse manufacturers. Novel technologies are integrated into these emerging devices to provide a wide variety of capabilities. This trend ends up with a great degree of heterogeneity in their structures. It can also create different types of challenges such as security and privacy, disclosing sensitive data. The proposed solution should support the new coming devices and technologies in the smart city on a large scale. In short, the solution should consider the scalability challenge in order to provide a more secure environment [11].

Beyond addressing above mentioned challenges in designing an efficient smart city, we employ SDN technology due to it can provide the possibility for remote management. Therefore, a third party, which has security and privacy skill is able to take responsibility for security and privacy management on behalf of end users, Privacy as a Service (PaaS) [14].

Figure 1 compares traditional smart city with smart city-SDN integration environment. In our smart city scenario, smart buildings, are connected to each other through OpenFlow switches [21]. These OpenFlow switches are connected to SDN controller in direct access mode. And, SDN controller is connected to the Cloud environment for future analyses.

As Fig. 1(a) shows in a traditional smart city, each smart building sends its data directly to Cloud space for further processing and analysis. However, when we use SDN paradigm in the smart city, IoT devices are connected to each other and send their data to OpenFlow switches, in our scenario smart buildings. These switches, then, are connected to SDN controller in wired/wireless mode. These switches are controlled and managed by SDN controller and the SDN controller is connected to Cloud environment, Fig. 1(b). With this smart city architecture, we can leverage the advantages of SDN architecture (e.g. flexibility, remote management and centralized management) while privacy of data is pre-served. The SDN controller has a two mutual connection to Cloud environment. It denotes that SDN controller can get commands from cloud environment and pose them to IoT devices, mutual relation.

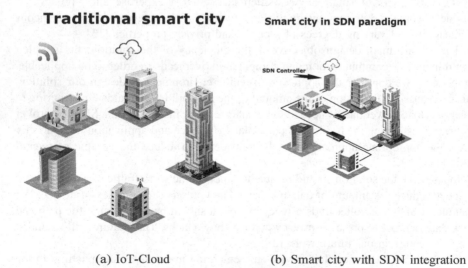

Traditional smart city   Smart city in SDN paradigm

(a) IoT-Cloud   (b) Smart city with SDN integration

Fig. 1. Traditional smart city vs. smart city with SDN paradigm

Evaluation Metrics for Privacy Solutions. Evaluation parameters that can be used for measurement of different solutions that are trying to solve privacy-preserving issues are:

1. Accuracy: Amount of information loss.
2. Completeness and Consistency: Degree of unused and non-important data in the original dataset.
3. Scalability: Increase rate of performance when the number of IoT devices are increased.
4. Penetration rate: Number of successful attacks.
5. Overload: The amount of computational cost and overload.

4.2 IoT-SDNPP Flow Chart

Figure 2 shows our proposed algorithm step by step in flowchart mode.
The proposed algorithm is iterative.

1. SDN controller divides its under control IoT devices into two classes that is done through clustering methods [24].
2. Controller sends privacy class label of each device to it.
3. Based on the privacy class label that can be 1 or 2.
4. If privacy tag is 1:
   (a) Controller sends the encryption method IoT device should use.
   (b) The IoT device applies the corresponding encryption method as its privacy-preservation method.

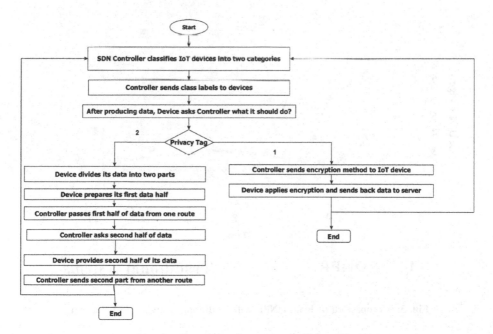

Fig. 2. Flowchart of our proposed algorithm

5. If its privacy tag is 2 then:
   (a) IoT device divides its data into two parts.
   (b) IoT device prepares its first-half data.
   (c) Controller transfers first half of data from one route.
   (d) Controller asks second half of divided data.
   (e) Device prepares second half of its data.
   (f) Controller sends second part of IoT device data from different route.

4.3 Simulation and Discussion

We integrated SDN paradigm with the smart city domain. Due to the smart city is a highly dynamic environment, with the help of SDN, we gained many advantages. We simulated our method with the help of Visual studio.Net CSharp version 2018.

We evaluate IoT-SDNPP from computational cost aspect.

Computational Cost. From the computational cost aspect, our proposed method posed utmost 9.0% overload to the system. Figure 3 shows a comparison of the computational cost of IoT-SDNPP compared with time that we do not use SDN architecture, plain smart city:

As Fig. 3 indicates, IoT-SDNPP in the smart city environment does not impose much pressure on the whole system utmost 9.0%. So most of IoT devices can afford IoT-SDNPP. However, preferably, it would be better to use IoT-SDNPP for IoT devices that are not energy-constrained especially in smart city environment due to large number of devices.

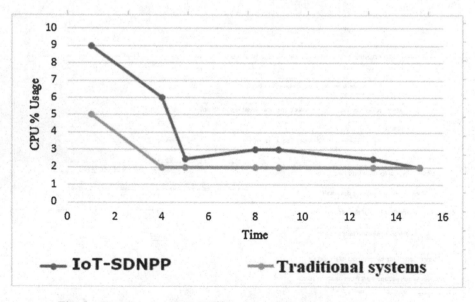

Fig. 3. Comparison of IoT-SDNPP with traditional networking paradigm

5   Conclusion and Future Work

With the emergence of both IoT and SDN paradigm, we are able to leverage benefits of both of them at the same time. SDN striking advantages are flexibility and centralized management. The managing network easier, the greater achievements. In this paper, we used the advantage of SDN paradigm in the IoT-based smart city for data privacy-preserving and proposed a novel method on top of it called IoT-SDNPP in order to preserve privacy of IoT devices' data. We preserved privacy in the smart city through changing the privacy behavior of the IoT devices dynamically. We evaluated IoT-SDNPP based on the computational cost. We showed the advantages and drawbacks of the IoT-SDNPP. There are many future works that can be done in smart city-SDN integration environment for privacy-preserving such as proposing a method that is also fault-tolerant. We can also extend IoT-SDNPP through proposing clustering IoT devices more accurately and so on.

Acknowledgment. This work is supported in part by the National Natural Science Foundation of China under Grants 61632009 and 61472451, in part by the Guangdong Provincial Natural Science Foundation under Grant 2017A030308006, and High-Level Talents Program of Higher Education in Guangdong Province under Grant 2016ZJ01.

References

1. Dataprotection. Technical report, DLA piper (2017). https://www.dlapiperdataprotection.com/index.html?t=about&c=BR
2. Alinani, K., Alinani, A., Narejo, D.H., Wang, G.: Aggregating author profiles from multiple publisher networks to build a list of potential collaborators. IEEE Access **6**, 20298–20308 (2018)
3. Arif, M., Wang, G., Balas, V.E.: Secure vanets: trusted communication scheme between vehicles and infrastructure based on fog computing. Stud. Inform. Control **27**(2), 235–246 (2018)
4. Broadhurst, R.: Developments in the global law enforcement of cyber-crime. Polic. Int. J. Police Strat. Manag. **29**(3), 408–433 (2006)
5. Bull, P., Austin, R., Popov, E., Sharma, M., Watson, R.: Flow based security for IoT devices using an SDN gateway. In: 2016 IEEE 4th International Conference on Future Internet of Things and Cloud (FiCloud), pp. 157–163. IEEE (2016)
6. Chase, J.: The evolution of the internet of things. Texas Instruments, pp. 1–5 (2013)
7. Dai, Y., Wang, G., Li, K.C.: Conceptual alignment deep neural networks. J. Intell. Fuzzy Syst. **34**(3), 1631–1642 (2018)
8. Flauzac, O., Gonzlez, C., Hachani, A., Nolot, F.: SDN based architecture for IoT and improvement of the security. In: 2015 IEEE 29th International Conference on Advanced Information Networking and Applications Workshops, pp. 688–693 (2015)
9. GhadakSaz, E., Amini, M.R., Porkar, P., Gheisari, M.: Design, implement and compare two proposed sensor datas storages named SemHD and SSW. From Editor in Chief, p. 78 (2012)
10. Gheisari, M.: The effectiveness of schema therapy integrated with neurological rehabilitation on reducing early maladaptive schemas and symptoms of depression in patients with chronic depressive disorder. Health Sci. J. **10**(4) (2016)

11. Gheisari, M., Baloochi, H., Gharghi, M., Khajehyousefi, M.: An evaluation of two proposed systems of sensor datas storage in total data parameter. Int. Geoinformatics Res. Dev. J. (2012)
12. Higginbotham, S.: Ericsson CEO predicts 50 billion internet connected devices by 2020. Ericsson (2011). http://gigaom.com/2010/04/14/ericsson-sees-the-internet-of-things-by-2020
13. Hunt, T., Song, C., Shokri, R., Shmatikov, V., Witchel, E.: Chiron: privacy- preserving machine learning as a service. arXiv preprint arXiv:1803.05961 (2018)
14. Itani, W., Kayssi, A., Chehab, A.: Privacy as a service: privacy-aware data storage and processing in cloud computing architectures. In: DASC 2009, pp. 711–716. IEEE (2009)
15. Karim, A., Shah, S.A.A., Salleh, R.B., Arif, M., Noor, R.M., Shamshirband, S.: Mobile botnet attacks-an emerging threat: classification, review and open issues. TIIS 9(4), 1471–1492 (2015)
16. Liu, Q., Guo, Y., Wu, J., Wang, G.: Effective query grouping strategy in clouds. J. Comput. Sci. Technol. 32(6), 1231–1249 (2017)
17. Low, Y., Gonzalez, J.E., Kyrola, A., Bickson, D., Guestrin, C.E., Hellerstein, J.: GraphLab: a new framework for parallel machine learning. arXiv preprint arXiv:1408.2041 (2014)
18. Gheisari, M., Esnaashari, M.: Data storages in wireless sensor networks to deal with disaster management. In: Emergency and Disaster Management: Concepts, Methodologies, Tools, and Applications, pp. 655–682. IGI Global (2019)
19. Mekky, H., Hao, F., Mukherjee, S., Zhang, Z.L., Lakshman, T.: Application-aware data plane processing in SDN. In: Proceedings of the Third Workshop on Hot Topics in Software Defined Networking, pp. 13–18. ACM (2014)
20. Nobakht, M., Sivaraman, V., Boreli, R.: A host-based intrusion detection and mitigation framework for smart home IoT using OpenFlow. In: ARES, pp. 147–156, August 2016
21. Porkar, P., Gheisari, M., Bazyari, G.H., Kaviyanjahromi, Z.: A comparison with two sensor data storagesin energy. In: ICCCI. ASME Press (2011)
22. Raza, M., Chowdhury, S., Robertson, W.: SDN based emulation of an academic networking testbed. In: CCECE, pp. 1–6. IEEE (2016)
23. Rezaeiye, P.P., Gheisari, M.: Performance analysis of two sensor data storages. In: Proceedings of 2nd International Conference on Circuits, Systems, Communications & Computers (CSCC), pp. 133–136 (2011)
24. Rezaeiye, P.P., Rezaeiye, P.P., Karbalayi, E., Gheisari, M.: Statistical method used for doing better corneal junction operation. In: Material and Manufacturing Technology III. Advanced Materials Research, vol. 548, pp. 762–766. Trans Tech Publications, September 2012
25. Rezaeiye, P.P., et al.: Agent programming with object oriented (c ++). In: ICECCT, pp. 1–10. IEEE (2017)
26. Salman, O., Abdallah, S., Elhajj, I.H., Chehab, A., Kayssi, A.: Identity-based authentication scheme for the internet of things. In: ISCC, pp. 1109–1111. IEEE (2016)
27. Shanahan, D., et al.: Variation in experiences of nature across gradients of tree cover in compact and sprawling cities. Landsc. Urban Plann. 157, 231–238 (2017)
28. Sicari, S., Rizzardi, A., Grieco, L.A., Coen-Porisini, A.: Security, privacy and trust in internet of things: the road ahead. Comput. Netw. 76, 146–164 (2015)
29. Wang, F., Jiang, W., Li, X., Wang, G.: Maximizing positive influence spread in online social networks via fluid dynamics. Future Gener. Comput. Syst. 86, 1491–1502 (2018)
30. Wang, T., Li, Y., Wang, G., Cao, J., Bhuiyan, M.Z.A., Jia, W.: Sustainable and efficient data collection from WSNs to cloud. IEEE Trans. Sustain. Comput. 1 (2018)
31. Zhang, Q., Liu, Q., Wang, G.: PRMS: a personalized mobile search over encrypted outsourced data. IEEE Access 6, 31541–31552 (2018)
32. Zhang, S., Wang, G., Liu, Q.: A dual privacy preserving scheme in continuous location-based services. In: 2017 IEEE Trustcom/BigDataSE/ICESS, pp. 402–408, August 2017

User Password Intelligence Enhancement by Dynamic Generation Based on Markov Model

Zhendong Wu$^{(\boxtimes)}$ ⬤ and Yihang Xia

School of Cyberspace, Hangzhou Dianzi University, Zhejiang, China
wzd@hdu.edu.cn, j123jt@126.com

Abstract. The use of passwords in daily life has become more and more widespread, which has become an indispensable part of life. However, there are still some security risks when using passwords. These security risks occupy a large part due to users using low strength password because of the very limited memory ability of human beings. It makes verbal guessing based on human memory habits achieve good attack effectiveness. In order to improve the security of network password system, this paper proposes a password enhancement method combining Markov model intelligent prediction and dynamic password enhanced technology. This method can greatly increase the password strength by more than 80% without increasing the memory burden of the user. At the same time, it does not need to store complex keys in the system, which can significantly improve the security of the network password system.

Keywords: Password security enhancement · Markov model
Dynamical password generation

1 Introduction

Today, identity authentication is an important part of communicating and exchanging people from one person to another. In many authentication systems, password authentication system is the dominant system of today's identity authentication system because of its convenience to be used. Compared with other identity authentication systems, the deployment of the password authentication system does not depend on any hardware device at all, the operation is simple and convenient, and the maintenance cost is not high. It can be said that in the foreseeable future, passwords are still an important part of identity authentication [1,2]. However, the drawback is that the password authentication system has numerous security and availability issues. Because the status of the

Supported by National Natural Science Foundation of China (No. 61772162), Joint fund of National Natural Science Fund of China (No. U1709220), National Key R&D Program of China (No. 2016YFB0800201), Zhejiang Natural Science Foundation of China (No. LY16F020016).

© Springer Nature Switzerland AG 2018
J. Vaidya and J. Li (Eds.): ICA3PP 2018, LNCS 11337, pp. 313–325, 2018.
https://doi.org/10.1007/978-3-030-05063-4_25

password authentication system cannot be replaced in a short time, it needs paying more attention to the repair and improvement of the problems exposed by the password authentication system.

Researchers studied the security of password system from the perspective of password set distribution, password guessing and security enhancement. Castelluccia et al. [3] and Batagelj et al. [4] studied the habits of people's password setting and found that when personal information is used in passwords, most people prefer to use personal family information such as name, birthday, address, zip code, or mobile number. And this personal information is not used in a mix. Bonneau [5] studied the statistical and guessing characteristics of the corpus of 70 million Yahoo passwords, tried various mathematical metrics of password safety and found that there was some uncertainty when simply using an attack algorithm to evaluate the security of a password, and different attack algorithms may give a large difference with the same password. Ma et al. [6] studied some probabilistic password models. They showed that probability model had important advantages over guess-number graphs, and found that, Markov models perform significantly better than other models, such as Probabilistic Context-Free Grammar model (PCFG). Kelley et al. [7] studied the password strength of different password-composition policies using 12,000 collected passwords, and found that password-composition policies requiring long passwords could provide good resistance to guessing. Komanduri et al. [8] presented a large-scale study on password strength of different password-composition policies by calculating their entropy. Narayanan et al. [9] studied the dictionary attacks through time-space tradeoff technology using the weakness of the human memory password, and found that the distribution of letters in human passwords was likely to be similar to the distribution of letters in the user's native language.

The researchers proposed some password probability models for more accurate measurement of password security. Weir et al. [10] proposed the Probabilistic Context-Free Grammar model (PCFG) to predict user passwords in large-scale password sets. Weir et al. [11] studied the validity of some password creation policies, especially the NIST SP800-63. Weir et al. found that most common password creation policies remained vulnerable to online attack. Castelluccia et al. [12] studied the Markov models for enhancing password security. Sparsity was a very low probability state in the Markov model calculation process. These low-probability states could greatly affect overall efficiency. Through grouping the uppercase letters and special characters in the password, paper [12] improved the sparsity of Markov models. de Carnavalet et al. [13] studied the differences in password strengths reported by different models, and found that the same password could be judged completely differently with different models, from weak to strong. Dürmuth et al. [14] proposed a new Markov model-based password cracker that generated password candidates according to their occurrence probabilities.

There is always a problem with security in password systems that relying on human memory entirely. Therefore, various new technologies [15–17] and theories [18–20] are being introduced to understand the overall operating rules of the password system more deeply, and to enhance the security and ease of use. This paper proposes a new password security enhancement method (Password Dynamic Markov Enhancement, named PDME) combined with software and probability model, which allows the user to memorize weak passwords. However, the system can dynamically enhance the user passwords so that the passwords reach the ideal intensity while maintaining the readability of the passwords, which makes it difficult to be read. The attacker perceives and thus upgrades the attack strength.

This paper is organized as following: Sect. 2 introduces the password probability model which we used. Section 3 proposes the password security enhancement method, Password Dynamic Markov Enhancement, named PDME. Section 4 presents the experimental processes and results. Section 5 summarizes the paper and puts research forward.

2   Models

According to recent research, there are some obvious common setup habits for human groups to set up passwords independently, which makes the space of password guessing be greatly reduced. Markov chain is considered as an effective guessing model, which is in line with the basic habit of the people's password setting, that is, the selection of the latter character is closely related to the selection of the previous characters. There are several successful password cracking tools that use the Markov model to guess passwords. This paper considers that the Markov model can not only be used for password guessing, but also be used for password enhancement, and the enhanced password can be memorized by a little effort, thus helping people to improve the password setting habits and enhance the password strength. The specific method is as follows.

2.1   The Password Prediction Markov Model

Password sequence is expressed as:

$$X_n = X(n), n = 0, 1, 2, ...$$

The sequence of passwords is regarded as a combination of password characters, each character is described with a random variable, and a Markov chain is regarded as a sequence of random variables of a password character, $X_1, X_2, ...$ The set of values for each variable X_n is called the "state space" at that location. The password character Markov chain satisfies the following hypothesis:

The probability distribution of the nth character is only related to the distribution of the preceding m characters, but not to the rest of the character distribution, the m generally takes 1 to 3.

The probability prediction formula for the nth character is:

$$P(x_n|x_{n-1}...x_1) = P(x_n|x_{n-1}...x_{n-m}) \tag{1}$$

Then the probability prediction for the entire password is:

$$
\begin{aligned}
P(X_n) &= P(x_1 x_2...x_n) \\
&= P(x_1) \cdot P(x_2|x_1) \cdot ... \cdot P(x_n|x_{n-1}...x_1) \\
&= P(x_1) \cdot P(x_2|x_1) \cdot ... \cdot P(x_n|x_{n-1}...x_{n-m})
\end{aligned} \tag{2}
$$

The probability prediction of the password can be calculated as follows:

$$
P(x_n|x_{n-1}x_{n-2}...x_{n-m}) = \frac{count(x_n x_{n-1}...x_{n-m})}{count(x_{n-1}...x_{n-m})} \tag{3}
$$

Where the $count()$ function is a statistical function of the number of samples. In order to increase the generalization ability of the formula, we smoothed the formula (3) and adjusted it to

$$
P(x_n|x_{n-1}x_{n-2}...x_{n-m}) = \frac{count(x_n x_{n-1}...x_{n-m})+1}{count(x_{n-1}...x_{n-m})+k} \tag{4}
$$

Where k is the size of a single character set.

2.2 User Password Enhancement Model Based on Markov (UPEM)

The Markov model is generally used for guessing passwords or detecting password strengths. However, for the password system security, only reminding the user of the weak password is not enough to protect the password system security, because the user still selects the weaker password for memory because of the convenience of memory. The password system needs to improve the strength of the user's password as a whole, and at the same time the password's memory needs to accord with the user's memory capacity, so that the user can use it conveniently. This paper proposes a user password enhancement model based on the Markov model, which can obtain high-intensity new passwords based on the user's preset passwords with minor changes. The user can easily remember the new password through proper exercises. The key idea of the model is to add a random item to the existing password prediction Markov model. The item can well expand the entropy space of the password while still maintaining the Markov nature of the password, which is consistent with the habit of people's password generation.

We consider the Markov model formed by the password system as a set of state transitions. The state transition probability at a certain moment determines the entropy value at that moment. By appropriately increasing the probability of random transitions between different states, the overall entropy of the set can be significantly increased. Assume that the combination of consecutive m characters at any position of the user's password forms a set of password Markov states. State transition probability between state sets is denoted by $P_{ij}, i, j \in \{state\_sets\}$, and each state is set by a probability score $PR(i)$. In the general password Markov model, the state transition matrix is sparse, and many states are not experienced when people set a password. The new user password enhancement model adds a random roll-out probability value for each state, as follows:

1. Calculating the probability score for each state

$$PR(i) = \alpha \sum_{j \in S(i)} \frac{PR(j)}{l(j)} + \frac{(1-\alpha)}{N} \tag{5}$$

Where $S(i)$ is a collection of all states that have outgoing links to the i state, $l(j)$ is the number of outgoing chains of the j state, N is the total number of states, $(1 - \alpha)$ is a randomization factor, generally 0.1–0.3.

2. Extending a single probability score to a Markov matrix

According to the prior-period probability, set the state node transition probability initial matrix P_s without random factor option:

$$P_s = \begin{bmatrix} 0 & S(2,1) & ... & S(N,1) \\ S(1,2) & 0 & ... & S(N,2) \\ ... & ... & ... & ... \\ S(1,N) & S(2,N) & ... & 0 \end{bmatrix} \tag{6}$$

Where $S(i,j)$ represents the initial transition probability from i to j, the prior-period probability is obtained from the initial training sample by statistical calculation. Add a random factor entry to the P_s matrix. The extended matrix is P_A

$$P_A = \alpha P_s + \frac{(1-\alpha)}{N} e e^T \tag{7}$$

Where e is a column vector where all components are 1.

3. Iteratively calculates the $PR(i)$ value until it converges

We use the following formula to iteratively calculate the PR value:

$$PR_{n+1} = P_A \cdot PR_n \tag{8}$$

PR_n is a column vector consisting of $PR(i)$, $1 \leq i \leq N$, and n is denoted as the nth iteration. The model continuously iterates the PR value until it converges or approaches convergence:

$$|PR_{n+1} - PR_n| < \varepsilon \tag{9}$$

According to the Markov process convergence conditions, the P_A matrix meets the convergence conditions. Through the calculation of steps 1, 2, and 3, the proposed Markov enhancement model can give a high probability of password prediction and a high entropy password recommendation, according to different sorting and selection methods of PR values.

3   The Password Dynamic Markov Enhancement (PDME)

Password strength is related to the length of the password, the disorder of the password, and the unpredictability of the password. In essence, the strength of the password is related to these three parameters. Therefore, enhancing password strength only needs to start with these three aspects. However, in fact, simply passing these three aspects of the password change will make the password appear an extremely complex structure, and do not have the possibility of being remembered by the user. Therefore, the ultimate goal of the PDME algorithm is to increase the password strength while making the password still look like a user-defined password and still have the possibility of being remembered. This requires the dependence on the UPEM model mentioned in Sect. 2.2 above. The PDME algorithm framework is shown in Fig. 1.

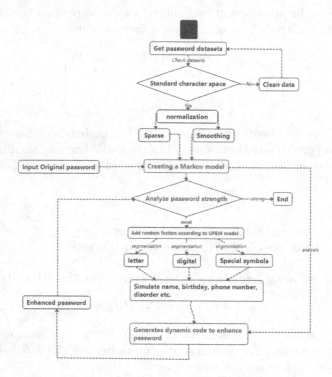

Fig. 1. The PDME algorithm framework

The PDME algorithm is mainly composed of 3 steps:

Step 1. Creating a Markov model to analyze the strength of users' original input passwords;
Step 2. Increasing the user's original password strength according to the UPEM model;
Step 3. According to the enhanced password obtained in step 2, generates dynamic code to support the automatic conversion of the original user password to the enhanced password.

3.1 Password Strength Analysis

The detection of the security strength of the password has many indicators, such as information entropy, minimum entropy, guess entropy, and the like. In PDME, we evaluated the strength of the password by building a Markov model. The main steps in establishing the Markov model were cleaning datasets, normalization, sparseness handling, model establishing. The purpose of cleaning the datasets was to remove some insignificant characters, increase the effectiveness of the Markov model, and prevent the occurrence of some characters that are unlikely to occur under normal conditions in the analysis process. The main purpose of normalization was to ensure that the sum of the total probability of the Markov model is 1. In this paper, we use the ending character z normalization proposed by Ma et al. [6]. The higher-order Markov model is characterized by overfitting and sparsity. Sparseness indicates that there are some very low probability states during password probability calculation. And it is not known whether the state of this small probability is the noise that appears when the Markov model is established. To solve the sparsity, this article uses Grouping method [12]. That is, uppercase letters and special characters in the password are represented by Y and Z, respectively. In the process of splitting the state, all uppercase letters are represented by Y, and all special characters are represented by Z. We construct the Markov model by the method described in Sect. 2.1.

3.2 Password Strength Enhancement

We divided the password sequence into several parts: uppercase letters, lowercase letters, numbers, special symbols, and targeted enhancements for each part. Targeted measures included sequence growth, sequence randomization, sequence disorder and so on.

Password Length Extension. According to statistics, most of the passwords are generally concentrated at 6-11 digits, and it is usually difficult to achieve high-intensity passwords under such a length. Therefore, in order to increase the password strength, it is needed to increase the length of the password. A character is selected in each type of character according to the PR values coming from the UPEM model. We randomly select the characters whose PR values are in the middle range, because such characters are not too unpopular, but at the same time they are not used regularly.

Password Disorder. After the length of the password is extended, the order of the characters in the password needs to be disturbed, which makes the password more disorderly. However, in order to be able to guarantee the memorable ability of the password, it is necessary to keep the password in a certain structure while scrambling the order of the password so that the password appears to be memorable. According to social engineering knowledge, passwords containing personal information are generally longer in length, but are relatively more memorable.

Therefore, while maintaining this structure, the irregular characters appear to be understandable even if the password is out of order (especially when the first letter of each word in certain sentences is used).

Some studies have shown that when personal information is used in passwords, most people prefer to use personal family information such as names, birthdays, addresses, zip codes, and cell phone numbers. And this personal information is generally not used in a mix (you do not choose to insert your mobile phone number between the initials), and when special characters are used, several special characters are usually inserted between the two messages. Therefore, if you want to masquerade as a password containing personal information, you only have to use the structure of such a password. The PDME algorithm mainly adopts several modes including name mode, birthday mode, cell phone mode, license plate mode, and sentence mode. Each character is categorized into uppercase letters, lowercase letters, numbers, and special symbols. Then use these completed grouped characters to operate.

In order to make the out-of-order characters in this part look more like passwords that can be memorized, when using the UPEM model, it is necessary to select some states with intermediate probability as the criteria for out-of-order. The remaining characters such as the probability of the transition state, select the medium probability transition state, as a new prefix character, and remove the character in the remaining characters. Then, continue to try the transition state probabilities for all remaining characters with the new prefix character, select a medium-probability transition state, and remove the character from the remaining characters. Repeat the above operation until the latest prefix character contains all remaining characters.

3.3   Generates Dynamic Code to Enhance Password Security

After completing the above operations, the password enhancement has been completed. Although such a password can seem to be remembered, in fact, the user cannot remember this password very well because the password does not contain real personal information. Therefore, this article chooses to feedback each user's specific enhancement process in the form of a dynamic code list to the user. This article chooses a combination of JavaScript scripting and plugin Tampermonkey. After completing the password enhancement for the user, the system will provide the relevant JavaScript script for the password to the user for download. After the user downloads the JavaScript script, the script is added to the plugin Tampermonkey. Tampermonkey can automatically execute the corresponding scripts to login the web domain. According to different user input, the dynamic code differences between similar passwords can be large.

4   Experiment Results

This article used publicly leaked database to carry out the testing, with more than 1 million records. We extracted the passwords used by all users from the database, and did some cleaning of the data, to ensure that all passwords use 95 visible characters as a password character space.

4.1   The Effect of Using UPEM Model

In order to confirm the effectiveness of using the enhanced Markov model (UPEM) and analyze the security of passwords, this paper compares the strength of the password analyzed by the UPEM model with the commonly used password analysis website results. We randomly selected 1000 sets of password data, and used the Markov model and password analysis website to analyze the password. The specific results are shown in Table 1.

Table 1. The comparison between different password strength tests

Password strength	Enhanced Markov model (UPEM) (%)	Website1 (%)	Website2 (%)
Strong	11.5	31.2	28.7
Normal	42.8	35.6	32.1
Weak	11.5	33.2	39.2

By comparison, it can be found that most of the passwords are biased toward 'Normal' and 'weak' when the password strength is analyzed using the UPEM model, and the distribution of passwords of the three strengths in the password analysis website is relatively uniform. It can be found that most of the password strengths are not high. Therefore, we can find that the analysis of password security through the UPEM model is more effective.

Notes: The address of the Website1 is http://www.passwordmeter.com/ and the Website2 is http://password-checker.online-domain-tools.com/.

4.2   The Effect of PDME Algorithm

We then compared the password strengths of several groups of passwords before and after enhancement. First, several passwords before and after enhancement was compared in Table 2, in which illustrated how the password enhancement algorithm improved the password strength.

Figure 2 below compares the strengths before and after password enhancement using the two methods of PDME and PCFG. PCFG is one of the most common methods of password strength enhancement.

We randomly selected 1000 groups of passwords to participate in the comparison and recorded the average information entropy before and after password enhancement when using PDME and PCFG as evaluation methods. Due to different methods of evaluation, the entropy of information obtained by the two

Table 2. The comparison before and after password enhancement

Password	Enhanced password	Information entropy (original)	Information entropy (enhanced)
123456	wD!1658243ani	5.110	79.284
password	8540@Xpdawsoms	10.882	85.815
ipajv2bvp7	PJP_271198bai4n	39.822	78.421
qazwsx271744045	qxw*170524ass474	46.221	85.753

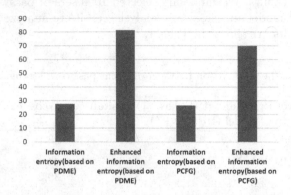

Fig. 2. The comparison of password strength statistics

methods was different. However, from the above figure, it can be seen that the password strength has been increased with certain strength after the enhancement algorithm. The PDME enhancement algorithm also has certain flaws. It can be found that the enhanced password strength is difficult to be increased to a very high intensity. In order to make the password look like a password using personal information, a certain degree of disorder is sacrificed in the process of enhancing the password, which makes the enhanced password difficult to approach in a random manner.

4.3   Password Anti-guessing Test

In order to increase persuasiveness, we also used the famous password attack software JtR (John the Ripper) to perform a certain degree of anti-guess ability testing on passwords. JtR tools contain a large number of actual password dictionaries, guessing attack effect is recognized. The specific results are shown in Fig. 3. It can be found that passwords are significantly more resistant to speculative attacks after being enhanced (27% Vs 0%, test time is 30 min for the single machine). In a random selection of 1000 passwords, JtR can crack some of the unenhanced passwords, but it cannot crack the enhanced passwords (of course, within a limited time. If given unlimited time JtR can crack all the passwords). And most dictionaries do not include the enhanced password. Therefore, after the password is enhanced by PDME, it is more resistant to guessing attacks and dictionary attacks.

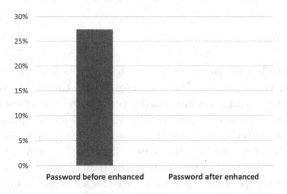

Fig. 3. The password anti-guess ability test before and after enhancement

4.4   PDME Algorithm Randomness Test

At the same time, we also performed a random test on the final results of the PDME algorithm. We performed 1,000,000 enhancement tests on the same password and collected all enhanced passwords. We used the NIST randomness evaluation kit to randomize these passwords, and made a test. The results are shown in Table 3.

Table 3. The password enhancement algorithm randomness test results

Type of test	P-value
Frequency	0.020329
Block Frequency	0.126125
Cumulative Sums	0.114866
Runs	0.080723
Longest Run of Ones	0.008372
Nonperiodic Template Matchings	0.007534
Overlapping Template Matchings	0.010365
Universal Statistical	0.057803
Approximate Entropy	0.116740
Serial	0.063261
Linear Complexity	0.064093

From Table 3, it can be found that the index of $P < 0.05$ is over 50%, and the index of $P < 0.10$ is over 70%. It can be seen that the enhanced password shows a great degree of randomness, but at the same time, because the password selection is designed, it is still some indicators show some non-randomness, for example 'Block Frequency', 'Approximate Entropy', and so on.

5   Conclusions

The use of passwords has now become part of people's lives. Regardless of ordinary social life or economic activities, passwords are the key to our response to these behaviors. Increasing the password strength used by oneself can not only improve the security of the account used by itself, reduce the possibility of being attacked, but also indirectly improve the security of the password authentication system. The method proposed in this paper effectively improves the security of a single password, while taking into account the ease of use, so that the password does not look like the password generated by the software, users can remember such passwords with a small amount of effort, which can effectively increase the overall security of the password system.

References

1. Dell Amico, M., Michiardi, P., Roudier, Y.F.: Password strength: an empirical analysis. In: 2010 Proceedings IEEE INFOCOM, San Diego, CA, USA, pp. 1–9 (2010)
2. Wang, P., Wang, D., Huang, X.: Advances in password security. J. Comput. Res. Dev. **53**(10), 2173–2188 (2016)
3. Vu, K.P.L., Proctor, R.W., Bhargav-Spantzel, A., et al.: Improving password security and memorability to protect personal and organi-zational information. Int. J. Hum.-Comput. Stud. **65**(8), 744–757 (2007)
4. Castelluccia, C., Chaabane, A., Dürmuth, M., et al.: When privacy meets security: leveraging personal information for password cracking. Computer Science (2013)
5. Bonneau, J.: The science of guessing: analyzing an anonymized corpus of 70 million passwords. In: 2012 IEEE Symposium on Security and Privacy (SP), pp. 538–552. IEEE (2012)
6. Ma, J., Yang, W., Luo, M., et al.: A study of probabilistic password models. In: 2014 IEEE Symposium on Security and Privacy (SP), pp. 689–704. IEEE (2014)
7. Kelley, P.G., Komanduri, S., Mazurek, M.L., et al.: Guess again (and again and again): measuring password strength by simulating password-cracking algorithms. In: 2012 IEEE Symposium on Security and Privacy (SP), pp. 523–537. IEEE (2012)
8. Komanduri, S., Shay, R., Kelley, P.G., et al.: Of passwords and people: measuring the effect of password-composition policies. In: Proceedings of the SIGCHI Conference on Human Factors in Computing Systems, pp. 2595–2604. ACM (2011)
9. Narayanan, A., Shmatikov, V.: Fast dictionary attacks on passwords using time-space tradeoff. In: Proceedings of the 12th ACM Conference on Computer and Communications Security, pp. 364–372. ACM (2005)
10. Weir, M., Aggarwal, S., de Medeiros, B., Glodek, B.: Password cracking using probabilistic context-free grammars. In: Proceedings of the 30th IEEE Symposium on Security and Privacy, pp. 391–405. IEEE (2009)

11. Weir, M., Aggarwal, S., Collins, M., et al.: Testing metrics for password creation policies by attacking large sets of re-vealed passwords. In: Proceedings of the 17th ACM Conference on Computer and Communications Security, pp. 162–175. ACM (2010)
12. Castelluccia, C., Dürmuth, M., Perito, D.: Adaptive password-strength meters from markov models. In: The Network and Distributed System Security Symposium (NDSS 2012) (2012)
13. de Carnavalet, X.D.C., Mannan, M.: From very weak to very strong: analyzing password-strength meters. In: The Network and Distributed System Security Symposium (NDSS 2014) (2014)
14. Dürmuth, M., Angelstorf, F., Castelluccia, C., Perito, D., Chaabane, A.: OMEN: faster password guessing using an ordered markov enumerator. In: International Symposium on Engineering Secure Software and Systems, Mar 2015, Milan, Italy (2015)
15. Batagelj, V., Brandes, U.: Efficient generation of large random networks. Phys. Rev. E **71**(3), 036113 (2005)
16. Zhendong, W., Liang, B., You, L., Jian, Z., Li, J.: High-dimension space projection-based biometric encryption for fingerprint with fuzzy minutia. Soft Comput. **20**(12), 4907–4918 (2016)
17. Zhendong, W., Tian, L., Li, P., Ting, W., Jiang, M., Wu, C.: Generating stable biometric keys for flexible cloud computing authentication using finger vein. Inf. Sci. **433**, 431–447 (2018)
18. Li, J., Sun, L., Yan, Q., Li, Z., Witawas, S., Ye, H.: Significant permission identification for machine learning based android mal-waredetection. IEEE Trans. Ind. Inform. 1–12 (2018). https://doi.org/10.1109/TII.2017.2789219
19. Liu, Z., Wu, Z., Li, T., Li, J., Shen, C.: GMM and CNN hybrid method for short utterance speaker recognition. IEEE Trans. Ind. Inform. 1–10 (2018). https://doi.org/10.1109/TII.2018.2799928
20. Melicher, W., et al.: Fast, lean, and accurate: modeling password guessability using neural networks. In: Proceedings of the 25th USENIX Security Symposium, 10 12 August, Austin, TX (2016)

The BLE Fingerprint Map Fast Construction Method for Indoor Localization

Haojun Ai[1,3,4], Weiyi Huang[2(✉)], Yuhong Yang[2,4], and Liang Liao[5,6]

[1] School of Cyber Science and Engineering, Wuhan University,
Hubei, China
aihj@whu.edu.cn
[2] National Engineering Research Center for Multimedia Software,
School of Computer Science, Wuhan University, Hubei, China
hwy2017@whu.edu.cn
[3] Key Laboratory of Aerospace Information Security and Trusted Computing,
Ministry of Education, Wuhan, China
[4] Collaborative Innovation Center of Geospatial Technology, Wuhan, China
[5] ChangZhou Municipal Public Security Bureau, Changzhou, China
[6] Key Laboratory of Police Geographic Information Technology,
Ministry of Public Security, Nanjing, China

Abstract. Radio fingerprinting-based localization is one of the most promising indoor localization techniques. It has great potential because of the ubiquitous smartphones and the cheapness of Bluetooth and WiFi infrastructures. However, the acquisition and maintenance of fingerprints require a lot of labor, which is a major obstacle in site survey. In this paper, we propose a radio map fast construction mechanism for Bluetooth low energy (BLE) fingerprint localization. The advertising interval of BLE beacon and the way of smartphones scanning BLE packets are different from WiFi. The lower interval of BLE packets and the mode of smartphone returning packets instantly both signify more refined fingerprints. Firstly, we reproduce the walking path based on pedestrian dead reckoning (PDR) and sensor landmarks and then map BLE signals to the path finely, which helps the collection process. Then we develop a detection rule according to the probability of smartphone scanning BLE beacons in a short period of time, avoiding accidental BLE signals. Finally, BLE signals associated with estimated collection coordinates are used to predict fingerprints on untouched places by Gaussian process regression. Experiments demonstrate that our method has an average localization accuracy of 2.129 m under the premise of reducing the time overhead greatly.

Keywords: Indoor localization · BLE fingerprint · Gaussian process regression
Radio map

1 Introduction

Indoor location is a support technology for extending Location Based Service (LBS) from outdoor to indoor. Due to the lack of indoor infrastructure such as Global Navigation Satellite System (GNSS) of outdoor localization, various indoor

© Springer Nature Switzerland AG 2018
J. Vaidya and J. Li (Eds.): ICA3PP 2018, LNCS 11337, pp. 326–340, 2018.
https://doi.org/10.1007/978-3-030-05063-4_26

localization solutions adoptable to the smart phones have been proposed. They can make full use of sensing and computing capabilities provided by smart phone to achieve tracking and provide LBS without special infrastructure. One of the major locating schemes is utilizing location-dependent radio frequency (RF) signal features to estimate position by generating or decision patterns. It is the same as other supervised learning methods, divided into two phases, offline and position estimation phase. In the offline phase, database called fingerprint map (FM) is constructed by recording received signals strength (RSS) at given positions as fingerprints for a period of time in the target area. In the position estimation phase, the smartphone scans radio signals in real time and compares the similarities with the stored fingerprints to estimate location. This algorithm achieves average accuracy of 1–5 m, depending on different implementation details of algorithm and test conditions [2–5].

During the offline phase, acquiring fingerprints is the most critical. However, the process is heavy, time-consuming and ineffective especially when constructing a FM for a large area. For example, it takes 390 min to construct a FM covering 500 m^2 by collecting WiFi RSS at 338 points with known locations [9]. Therefore, seeking a convenient and efficient FM construction method has important practical significance for the widespread use of the indoor positioning system. Although crowdsourcing and simultaneous localization and mapping (SLAM) [12–14] reduce the cost of data collection to some extent, unreliable data, unpredictable performance and insufficient coverage still plague the realization. There are some WiFi fingerprint localization systems easing the burden by reducing the sampling time of each point [1], or by walking along paths to collect sensor and signal data in the offline phase [8, 9, 24, 25]. But, for Bluetooth fingerprint, there is little related research.

Bluetooth Low Energy (BLE), a low power version of Bluetooth, was originally used as a proximity sensor for Far and Near by Apple. The frequency of beacon sending BLE signals and the mode of smartphone capturing BLE signals are significantly different from WiFi. Faragher et al. show the unique nature of BLE compared with WiFi and the impact of beacon parameters on localization performance [21]. Therefore, the fast construction method for WiFi can't be applied to BLE directly and designing the method for BLE is necessary. BLE protocol defines the mode of broadcasting advertisement messages and the minimum transmission interval [3, 21]. When beacon is battery-powered, power consumption can be reduced by increasing the transmission interval. Besides, the BLE scanning driver in mobile receive an advertisement packet and return to the application at once, which reduces the delay.

Our proposed fast FM construction method is based on the generation and reception mechanism of BLE signals. Comparing with the existing methods, the mapping of BLE signals to spatial locations is more refined than of step events. Meanwhile, we design a detection rule for accidental BLE signals to optimizes localization results. We train Gaussian process regression (GPR) model to form a FM outside the walking path. It is shown in test result that walking on the predefined path to collect data is more efficient than the static sampling collection and the removal of abnormal BLE packets improves fingerprint localization accuracy.

The main contribution of this paper is listed as follows:

1. We combine PDR and sensor landmarks to obtain movement sequences in the area. Then we put BLE packets on the path according to the time relationship of step events and them, which has smaller interval for fingerprints and reduces collection time greatly.
2. We design a detection rule based on the probability of beacon being captured, which can improve the effect of FM construction and localization.
3. We train GPR model for each beacon with the fingerprints on the walking path. RSS from different BLE beacons are merged to generate a FM outside the walking path.

This article is organized as follows: In Sect. 2, we review and summarize related work. In Sect. 3, we present the overall structure of the system. In Sect. 4, we detail each part of our proposed algorithms. We evaluate the validity of the algorithm in the real scenes in Sect. 5 and conclude the full paper in Sect. 6.

2   Related Work

For recent years, fingerprint localization has received continuous attention. And radio signals have been widely used among them, mainly WiFi and Bluetooth. The pioneering work of fingerprint localization is RADAR proposed in 2000 [11]. RADAR uses WiFi signal as location fingerprint and designs a prototype method of fingerprint localization. Since then, a large number of indoor localization systems optimize algorithms and improve performance on the basis of RADAR from all aspects [5, 7, 12, 23]. With the increasing types of smartphone sensors, more abundant sensor information are added to location fingerprints such as background sounds, magnetic fields and multiple fusions [15–17], but the construction of all FMs still needs fingerprint collection as the first step. This process often requires professionals to use specialized equipment, which is time-consuming, high cost, labor-intensive and even sensitive to environmental changes. This is the biggest bottleneck in the practical application of fingerprint localization.

The broadcast and receive mechanisms between BLE and WiFi signals are different, which are listed below [21]. Each AP uses a particular radio channel (of width at least 20 MHz) mainly concentrated on 2.4 GHz or 5 GHz bands and the transmission rate can reach 54 Mbps. While BLE signals operate on the three advertising channels (of width 2 MHz) concentrated on 2.4 GHz band. In addition, we get smartphone capture mode from the develop manual for Android. One scanning returns a list of captured WiFi signals but a BLE signal is captured and then returned to the Application instantly.

Currently, there are some Bluetooth fingerprint localization studies: Considering that the RSS value and noise of different broadcast channels of BLE beacons are different, Zhuang et al. uses three fingerprint maps and regression models respectively [3]. A time-variant multi-phase fingerprint map is proposed [10]. It automatically adopts the most suitable FM according to the time period and overcomes the instability of RSS. [2] IW-KNN algorithm combines Euclidean distance and Cosine similarity to measure the similarity of two RSSI vectors. The RSSI measurements and the prior information from a motion model are fused by Bayesian fusion method [8]. They all focus on improving localization accuracy and system stability but pay little attention to the cost problem of FM construction. The algorithm we proposed is collecting BLE signals while walking on the path and it reduces FM construction burden.

Some main methods applied to the fast Radio Map construction are analyzed as follows.

2.1 Dead-Reckoning Based on Built-in Sensor

Sensors in smartphones have been used to understand the locations of user. The smartphone performs a scan and records the scanned RSS and SSID of surrounding APs in every step [9, 18, 25, 31]. Inertial sensor and the map are used for producing the coordinates of the sampling points, which takes much less time than traditional method. Three collection method, static sampling (SS), moving sampling (MS) and stepped MS (SMS) are listed and experiments show that MS and SMS are comparable to SS in terms of RSS value and positioning accuracy [24].

2.2 Propagation Model for Signal Interpolation

Propagation models establish the relationship between RSS and distance. The most common is the lognormal shadowing model [19, 20]. The WiFi signals follow the Log-distance path loss model [29], so we make more WiFi fingerprints with the model. The Gaussian regression model also provides a flexible train. The first one [6] adopts GPR and establishes the posterior mean and variance of each location, which can not only predict RSS mean but also infer fluctuation. Horus [7] makes the RSS at each location obey a Gaussian distribution. [9, 26] RF signals are collected sparsely at first and used to train the GP model. Then, GPR is used to build a dense FM in the area to be localized. For some areas not accessible, Zuo et al. adopt kriging interpolation which depends on the spatial autocorrelation of the RSSI [10].

2.3 Crowdsource and SLAM

Some crowdsource methods [23, 27] build multi-modal RF signal maps easily. Zhuang et al. propose two crowdsourcing-based WiFi positioning systems which needs no floor plan or GPS and suits for not only specific environments [28]. A fraud detection mechanism is proposed to detect the forgery accurately and improve indoor localization accuracy in MobiBee [30]. Zee [12] estimates location with the help of an indoor map and particle filtering then back propagate to improve the accuracy in the past. Although these methods have not any additional effort from the testers, localization accuracy and coverage are not guaranteed.

3 System Framework

Figure 1 represents the overview of the smartphone-based BLE fingerprint map fast construction method. The smartphone is used to measure sensing data from its built-in sensors and signal data.

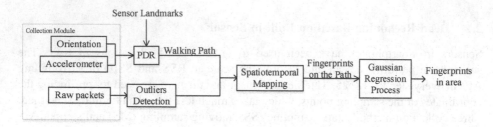

Fig. 1. System overview of our position system

1. Data collection: Collector walks along a predetermined path and the application in the smartphone records sensor messages $sr = (a_x, a_y, a_z, ori, t)$ and signal data $sl = (s, t')$, where a_x, a_y, a_z are acceleration of three direction x, y, z respectively, ori is angle around the z-axis, a BLE advertisement packet s contains MAC of beacon and RSS, and t, t' are timestamps of each message in sr, sl.
2. Simulation of the walking path: We identify sensor landmarks according to orientation and each identified point is fixed by the coordinate of landmark. Then step detection is done and steps are placed on the straight line between the landmarks to determine the position and timestamp of each step happened.
3. Outlier detection of BLE packets: We design a detection rule based on the probability of BLE packets being captured to avoid that accidental packets deteriorate the localization results.
4. Spatiotemporal mapping: We utilize time relationship of packets between starting and stopping point of each step to determine the packets' coordinates and get fingerprints on the walking path.
5. GPR model training: The fingerprints on the walking path is used as a training set to establish the signal variation models for BLE beacons by GPR and integrates RSS of beacons to form a FM in the target area.

4 Algorithm Description

4.1 Trajectory Estimation

In order to achieve fast and reliable fingerprint collection, we need to set a walking path in advance so collector can walk along the path with the mobile phone collecting sr and sl.

PDR is a pedestrian movement trajectory estimation method that relies on built-in sensors of smartphone. Based on the step frequency, walking trajectory is reckoned by the walking direction and step length. The work [22] summarizes implementation of

PDR from all aspects, in which we choose a simple and efficient method, containing two parts, step detection and sensor landmark match.

Step Detection. Step detection is the peak detection of acceleration. Furthermore, we take step frequency and peak magnitude of people as a threshold to eliminate false peak points.

Acceleration a_i of each sample i can be calculated as:

$$a_i = \sqrt{a_{xi}^2 + a_{yi}^2 + a_{zi}^2}. \tag{1}$$

and we obtain peak sequence $\langle mag_i, t_i \rangle$ after a low pass filter being applied to a_i. The minimum time per step spend is denoted by δ_t, and the minimum of acceleration magnitude of per step is denoted by a', then the set of valid steps among the peak sequence $\langle mag_i, t_i \rangle$ is:

$$\{t_i - t_{i-1} > \delta_t, mag_i > a'\} \tag{2}$$

we set $\delta_t = \frac{1}{3}$ s, $a' = 2\,\text{m/s}^2$.

We clip acceleration a' duration 10 s where the sampling frequency is 20 Hz in Fig. 2. Most of the original high-frequency noise is eliminated by using the low-pass filtering, making step detection more accurate. We can observe that there are 18 steps within this time window.

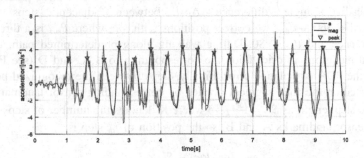

Fig. 2. Example of step detection. The red line represents the raw acceleration a'. The blue inverted triangles indicate all valid steps satisfying set (2). (Color figure online)

We select a rectangular path in an underground parking, about 38 m length and 14 m width and experiments in this paper are all based on the path (see Fig. 3). Acceleration with timestamp is collected while walking along A → B → C → D A and we walk 10 rounds repeatedly with Google Nexus 5. The average accuracy of step detection can achieve 99.80% as shown in Table 1.

Table 1. Accuracy of step detection

Ture value	145	146	147	145	147	148	147	147	148	149
Calculated value	145	146	147	147	147	148	147	147	148	150
Error rate (%)	0	0	0	1.38	0	0	0	0	0	0.67

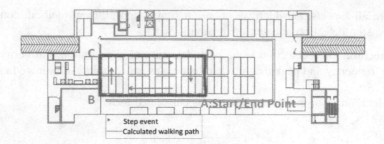

Fig. 3. The walking path calculated from inertial sensor data. It is basically consistent with our predetermined path.

Sensor Landmark Match. In indoor environment, it is easy to list sensor landmarks sensitive to inertial sensors such as elevators, stairs, and corners [23]. Matching sensor landmarks can fix the current position while passing through them, thereby overcoming the cumulative error of PDR and improving estimation accuracy. In this paper, we select several sensor landmarks based on the orientation from the walking path. This kind of landmarks matching is suitable for the same floor and it's better that the walking direction is not changeable frequently and mobile phone is hold in a relatively stable condition.

We set the points with obvious change in direction as landmarks on the path, such as point B, C and D in Fig. 3, and assume the coordinates *loc* of these points known. When heading angle difference Δori between adjacent steps satisfies $\theta_{ori} < |\Delta ori| < 360 - \theta_{ori}$, we correct positions with *loc*, where θ_{ori} is a threshold of angle difference and $\theta_{ori} = 80$. During walking along predetermined path, the three recognized mutations in orientation are corresponding to B, C and D (see Fig. 4) to minimize the PDR cumulative error. Finally, steps between the recognized points are evenly placed on the road segment divided by corresponding sensor landmarks. Note we assume step length as $SL = \frac{loc_B - loc_A}{K}$ where K denotes the number of steps between adjacent sensor landmarks A and B, so the position of j_{th} step is

$$l_j = loc_A + SL \times j \tag{3}$$

The moment of j_{th} step happening can be extracted from the peak sequence $\langle mag_i, t_i \rangle$.

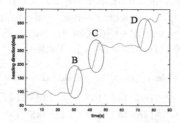

Fig. 4. Landmark matching based on orientation

4.2   Outlies Detection of BLE Advertisement Packet

According to the BLE protocol, a BLE beacon periodically broadcasts advertisement packets s which are separated at least 20 ms and there are three channels 38/39/40 out of 40 channels for broadcasting packets. In the localization method based on the BLE, smartphone capturing BLE packets s are used to triangulation method or radio fingerprint localization method, which is similar with WiFi localization.

The BLE beacon usually operates on 2.4 GHz band and RSS attenuates with the increasing of distance. Meanwhile, the probability that BLE packets are captured has an inverse relationship with distance [3, 4]. The research [5] models the probability of packets being captured as a quadratic function to estimate position. Along the walking path, we set the beacon advertising interval as 500 ms, in fact, Nexus 5 receives about 50 packets in 1 s. We stand at the sampling point to collect BLE packets for 5 s and could observe that RSS does have decline as the distance increases in Fig. 5. During the same time, we also find an inverse correlation among the distance and the number of packets captured and that smartphone scans the beacons far from the sampling point hardly in Fig. 6. If probability of receiving packets from a beacon is low at a sampling point and these packets are directly used to build a FM, they are still hard to be captured in the localization process at the same point, which may cause deterioration for location estimation results. Therefore, we consider removing packets with low captured probability.

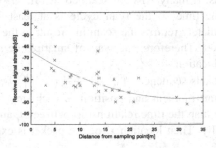

Fig. 5. The mean RSS from each iBeacons at a sampling point during 5 s vs. the distances between each of those scanned beacons and sampling point. one discrete point means one beacon.

We propose a simple and reasonable detection rule to eliminate the accidental packets and optimize the localization result. The packets satisfied $fre^j \geq \theta_{fre}$ are reserved, where θ_{fre} is the frequency threshold and fre^j is the number of packets from Mac_j within a short time T. Let $\theta_{fre} = 3$, it can be seen that there are total 278 packets received from 30 beacons during this time window, 23 BLE packets received from each of 2 beacons and one packet received from each of 5 beacons in Fig. 7. Thus, 5 of 278 BLE packets from 5 beacons are removed after the detection rule, accounting for 1.80% of the total packets number and having negligible impact on the original data. We compare the localization results of two FMs constructed by original packets and packets after elimination in Sect. 5 and prove that the latter has better localization performance. So, the rule is both used for the BLE packets collected from the offline stage and the test packets during the localization stage.

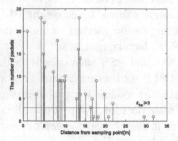
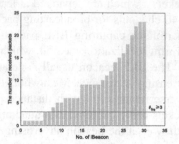

Fig. 6. The number of packets captured from different iBeacons during 5 s vs. the distance between iBeacon and sampling point

Fig. 7. The number of packets captured from 30 iBeacons during 5 s

4.3 Spatiotemporal Mapping of BLE Signals

Taking the path calculated by PDR and sensor landmarks, we can establish the spatial-temporal mapping for the captured BLE packets to determine the locations of packets. When scanning WiFi on Android, the underlying driver returns the scan results after scanning all the channels. If many APs are scanned, RSSI, MAC, SSID of many APs are returned at the same time so the scan cycle is at least 200 ms. Whereas, the underlying driver immediately returns the scanning result to the application layer after scanning one BLE packet. Therefore, the way of smartphone scanning BLE packets can get a more refined location.

We get the BLE packets sequence $\langle (s_0, t'_0), \cdots, (s_n, t'_n) \rangle$ between adjacent sensor landmarks. Under the start moment and position of each step (t_i, l_i) known, for BLE packet captured at t'_i, we map the time relationship between t'_i and j_{th} step to the spatial relationship proportionally. Then location x_i of the packet is expressed as

$$x_i = l_j + \frac{t'_i - t_j}{t_{j+1} - t_j} \times SL \tag{4}$$

where $t_j \leq t'_i \leq t_{j+1}$. For example, a step with start time t_1 and end time t_7 as shown in Fig. 8. We can see that five packets are captured in one step and location of the packet captured at t_4 is $l_1 + \frac{t_4 - t_1}{t_7 - t_1} \times SL$ by (4).

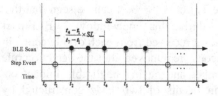

Fig. 8. BLE signals locations determination from temporal to spatial

4.4   Fingerprint Prediction Outside the Walk Path

The Gaussian regression model fits RSS to a Gaussian distribution [6, 7, 9, 26]. We get BLE fingerprints with location tags on the walking path $F = \{(x_1, f_1), (x_2, f_2), \cdots, (x_n, f_n)\}$, where $f_i = \langle f_i^{Mac_0}, f_i^{Mac_1}, \cdots \rangle$ and $f_i^{Mac_j}$ denotes mean RSS value from Mac_j captured at location i. However, F is incomplete for constructing a FM in space now and it doesn't have sufficient coverage area for the entire target area. The problem we have to solve is to predict f for larger coverage by gaussian model on the basis of F and additional location input x.

Assuming that RSS from different beacons are independent, we train Gaussian process model for each beacon. First, we extract BLE packets of one beacon from F and establish the set $\langle x, f \rangle$, where x is location of a BLE packet being captured, f is RSS of the packet. For the establishment of GPR model, we specify arguments as listed in Table 2. Form of the covariance function ardmatern32 is Matern kernel with parameter 3/2 and a separate length scale per predictor. It is defined as

$$k(x_i, x_j | \theta) = \sigma_f^2 \left(1 + \sqrt{3}r\right) exp\left(-\sqrt{3}r\right) \tag{5}$$

where $r = \sqrt{\sum_{m=1}^{d} \frac{(x_{im} - x_{jm})^2}{\sigma_m^2}}$. The method used to estimate parameters of the GPR model and make predictions is both sd which selects subset of data as the activeset and uses exact methods to estimate GPR parameters in the activeset. We set initial value for the noise standard deviation of the model as 2 and set 'Standardize' as 1, then the software centers and scales each column of the predictor data, by the column mean and standard deviation, respectively.

Table 2. Name-value pair arguments

Argument name	Argument value
KernelFunction	ardmatern32
FitMethod	subset of data (sd)
PredictMethod	sd
Sigma	2
Standardize	1

Then we use GPR model to predict RSS of the iBeacon at any point in the target area. We select N points at regular intervals and input the coordinates X of these points, then RSS of the iBeacon at these points are output through GPR model. Figure 9 shows predicted RSS distribution of an iBeacon in the parking lot.

In the same way, GPR is applied to all iBeacons in turn and signal variation model is established for each iBeacon. We integrate RSS of all iBeacons and put them on the N selected corresponding coordinates. A FM covering the entire target area what we initially need is formed $FP = \{(X_1, RSS_1), (X_2, RSS_2), \cdots, (X_N, RSS_N)\}$, where $RSS_i = \langle rss_i^1, \cdots, rss_i^{80} \rangle$ and 80 beacons are scanned along the walking path.

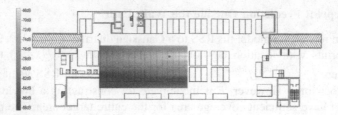

Fig. 9. RSS distribution prediction in the target area. Blue solid circle indicates the location of the iBeacon. (Color figure online)

5   Field Experiments

5.1   Experimental Setup

We develop an app called "SenBleScanner" on Nexus 5 to monitor the sensors and Bluetooth interface, thus creating the following log, $sr = (a_x, a_y, a_z, ori, t)$ and $sl = (s, t')$. Tester held the Nexus 5 steadily and walked along predetermined path for 7 rounds, indicated by a dotted line, which took about 13 min for 7 rounds. Each set of data is collected from walking in a round.

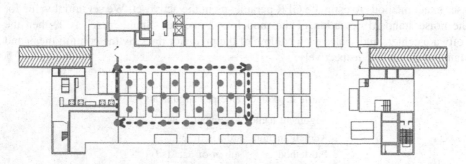

Fig. 10. Two kind of collection approaches

Firstly, we rebuild the walking trajectory and get start moment and position of each step (t_i, l_i). Then, we get coordinate of each captured packet through spatiotemporal mapping. Finally, we divide the target area into numerous grids size of $0.28\,\mathrm{m} \times 0.31\,\mathrm{m}$ and GPR is used to establish the signal distribution model of each iBeacon in space. The total number of vertices of all grids is 6000. RSS of all iBeacons constitute a vector at each point and form a FM size of 6000×82 which means 6000 fingerprints and each fingerprint contains RSS from 80 iBeacons and corresponding coordinate X.

5.2   Performance Evaluation

In the following, we compare the localization results of the FMs made by the original packets *sl* and the "filtered" packets, and describe the localization performance using the FM generated by proposed algorithm in the real scenario.

We select 11 test points with known locations from the target environment. Researcher holds Nexus 5 at each test point and collects BLE packets for 3 s. Then we calculate the mean RSS from different beacons after the abnormal packets being removed. A total of 542 test fingerprints are generated, then match with each fingerprint in the FM in turn. The research [1] points out that the stronger the RSS value is, the higher the iBeacon's response rate is, so we take 10 iBeacons with strongest RSS in a test fingerprints to reduce computation and calculate the Euclidean distances *dist* from FM.

We choose a simple algorithm KNN to evaluate the performance [2, 21, 32]. That is, the K fingerprints in the FM having the smallest Euclidean distances from a test fingerprint are selected and the mean value of their coordinates is output as localization result.

$$X_{pr} = \frac{\sum_{j=1}^{K} X_j | \arg\ min \sum_{j=1}^{K} dist_j}{K} \tag{6}$$

Figure 11 shows cumulative distribution function (CDF) of error for two FMs. One is the collected BLE packets, and the other is the packets that obey the detection rule. The result indicates that the average error of the FM constructed by the latter is 2.129 m, which is better than the median error of the fingerprint database constructed by the former of 2.444 m. Figure 12 illustrates the trajectories of the true path and the proposed algorithm. Although this error is larger than the average error of using traditional fingerprint method, it is comparable to many of the latest localization methods.

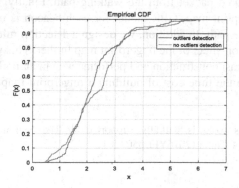

Fig. 11. CDF of position estimation errors of FM built by two sets of packets

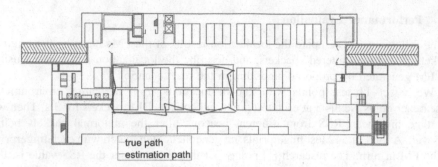

Fig. 12. Estimated trajectory using the proposed algorithm

Besides, 33 sampling points are selected in the target area and the interval between adjacent sampling points is about 6 m, represented by solid dots as shown in Fig. 10. Each sampling point takes at least one minute by traditional fingerprint collection method, it takes $33 \times 1 = 33$ min but our rapid collection method takes about 13 min, which significantly shortens the site survey time. Furthermore, the positions of sensor landmarks are relatively fixed. It can be considered that this construction method is stable and easy to implement. In addition, increasing FM size helps to improve the localization accuracy and using GPR can form a dense FM.

6 Conclusion

This paper proposes a fast fingerprint map construction method based on the characteristics of BLE signal. Location and moment of each step during walking is determined by sensors data and landmarks and time relationship between step and packet is obtained. Then we map the relationship from temporal to spatial to estimate the location of each captured packet from the walking path. Finally, to establish a larger and more fined fingerprint map, GPR model for each beacon is trained to predict the fingerprints outside the path. In addition, we design a detection rule for BLE packets to optimize the localization effect of the fingerprint map further. This work fills the gap for BLE fingerprint map fast construction and performs well in an underground parking: it can effectively reduce the time cost of building a fingerprint map and maintain localization accuracy.

Acknowledgment. This work is partially supported by The National Key Research and Development Program of China (2016YFB0502201).

References

1. Yang, S., Dessai, P., Verma, M., Gerla, M.: FreeLoc: calibration-free crowdsourced indoor localization. In: 2013 Proceedings of IEEE INFOCOM, pp. 2481–2489. IEEE (2013)
2. Peng, Y., Fan, W., Dong, X., Zhang, X.: An iterative weighted KNN (IW-KNN) based indoor localization method in Bluetooth low energy (BLE) environment. In: 2016 International IEEE Conferences on Ubiquitous Intelligence and Computing, Advanced and Trusted Computing, Scalable Computing and Communications, Cloud and Big Data Computing, Internet of People, and Smart World Congress (UIC/ATC/ScalCom/CBDCom/IoP/SmartWorld), pp. 794–800. IEEE (2016)
3. Zhuang, Y., Yang, J., Li, Y., Qi, L., El-Sheimy, N.: Smartphone-based indoor localization with bluetooth low energy beacons. Sensors 16(5), 596 (2016)
4. Radhakrishnan, M., Misra, A., Balan, R.K., Lee, Y.: Smartphones & BLE services: empirical insights. In: 2015 IEEE 12th International Conference on Mobile Ad Hoc and Sensor Systems (MASS), pp. 226–234. IEEE (2015)
5. De, S., Chowdhary, S., Shirke, A., Lo, Y.L., Kravets, R., Sundaram, H.: Finding by counting: a probabilistic packet count model for indoor localization in BLE environments. arXiv preprint arXiv:1708.08144 (2017)
6. Kumar, S., Hegde, R.M., Trigoni, N.: Gaussian process regression for fingerprinting based localization. Ad Hoc Netw. 51, 1–10 (2016)
7. Youssef, M., Agrawala, A.: The horus WLAN location determination system. In: Proceedings of the 3rd International Conference on Mobile Systems, Applications, and Services. pp. 205–218. ACM (2005)
8. Chen, L., Pei, L., Kuusniemi, H., Chen, Y., Kröger, T., Chen, R.: Bayesian fusion for indoor positioning using Bluetooth fingerprints. Wirel. Pers. Commun. 70(4), 1735–1745 (2013)
9. Li, C., Xu, Q., Gong, Z., Zheng, R.: TuRF: fast data collection for fingerprint-based indoor localization. In: 2017 International Conference on Indoor Positioning and Indoor Navigation (IPIN), pp. 1–8. IEEE (2017)
10. Zuo, J., Liu, S., Xia, H., Qiao, Y.: Multi-phase fingerprint map based on interpolation for indoor localization using iBeacons. IEEE Sens. J. 18, 3351–3359 (2018)
11. Bahl, P., Padmanabhan, V.N.: RADAR: an in-building RF-based user location and tracking system. In: IEEE Proceedings of the Nineteenth Annual Joint Conference of the IEEE Computer and Communications Societies, INFOCOM 2000, vol. 2, pp. 775–784. IEEE (2000)
12. Rai, A., Chintalapudi, K.K., Padmanabhan, V.N., Sen, R.: Zee: zero-effort crowdsourcing for indoor localization. In: Proceedings of the 18th Annual International Conference on Mobile Computing and Networking, pp. 293–304. ACM (2012)
13. Yang, Z., Wu, C., Liu, Y.: Locating in fingerprint space: wireless indoor localization with little human intervention. In: Proceedings of the 18th Annual International Conference on Mobile Computing and Networking, pp. 269–280. ACM (2012)
14. Shen, G., Chen, Z., Zhang, P., Moscibroda, T., Zhang, Y.: Walkie-Markie: indoor pathway mapping made easy. In: Proceedings of the 10th USENIX Conference on Networked Systems Design and Implementation, pp. 85–98. USENIX Association (2013)
15. Tarzia, S.P., Dinda, P.A., Dick, R.P., Memik, G.: Indoor localization without infrastructure using the acoustic background spectrum. In: Proceedings of the 9th International Conference on Mobile Systems, Applications, and Services, pp. 155–168. ACM (2011)
16. Chung, J., Donahoe, M., Schmandt, C., Kim, I.J., Razavai, P., Wiseman, M.: Indoor location sensing using geo-magnetism. In: Proceedings of the 9th International Conference on Mobile Systems, Applications, and Services, pp. 141–154. ACM (2011)

17. Azizyan, M., Constandache, I., Roy Choudhury, R.: SurroundSense: mobile phone localization via ambience fingerprinting. In: Proceedings of the 15th Annual International Conference on Mobile Computing and Networking, pp. 261–272. ACM (2009)
18. Liu, H.H., Liao, C.W., Lo, W.H.: The fast collection of radio fingerprint for WiFi-based indoor positioning system. In: 2015 11th International Conference on Heterogeneous Networking for Quality, Reliability, Security and Robustness (QSHINE), pp. 427–432. IEEE (2015)
19. Wang, B., Zhou, S., Liu, W., Mo, Y.: Indoor localization based on curve fitting and location search using received signal strength. IEEE Trans. Ind. Electron. 62(1), 572–582 (2015)
20. Mazuelas, S., et al.: Robust indoor positioning provided by real-time RSSI values in unmodified WLAN networks. IEEE J. Sel. Top. Signal Process 3(5), 821–831 (2009)
21. Faragher, R., Harle, R.: Location fingerprinting with Bluetooth low energy beacons. IEEE J. Sel. Areas Commun. 33(11), 2418–2428 (2015)
22. Harle, R.: A survey of indoor inertial positioning systems for pedestrians. IEEE Commun. Surv. Tutor. 15(3), 1281–1293 (2013)
23. Wang, H., Sen, S., Elgohary, A., Farid, M., Youssef, M., Choudhury, R.R.: No need to war-drive unsupervised indoor localization. In: Proceedings of the 10th International Conference on Mobile Systems, Applications, and Services, pp. 197–210. ACM (2012)
24. Liu, H.H., Liu, C.: Implementation of Wi-Fi signal sampling on an android smartphone for indoor positioning systems. Sensors 18(1), 3 (2017)
25. Liu, H.H.: The quick radio fingerprint collection method for a WiFi-based indoor positioning system. Mob. Netw. Appl. 22(1), 61–71 (2017)
26. Yiu, S., Yang, K.: Gaussian process assisted fingerprinting localization. IEEE Internet Things J. 3(5), 683–690 (2016)
27. Mirowski, P., Ho, T.K., Yi, S., MacDonald, M.: SignalSLAM: Simultaneous localization and mapping with mixed WiFi, Bluetooth, LTE and magnetic signals. In: 2013 International Conference on Indoor Positioning and Indoor Navigation (IPIN), pp. 1–10. IEEE (2013)
28. Zhuang, Y., Syed, Z., Li, Y., El-Sheimy, N.: Evaluation of two WiFi positioning systems based on autonomous crowdsourcing of handheld devices for indoor navigation. IEEE Trans. Mob. Comput. 15(8), 1982–1995 (2016)
29. Jung, S., Lee, C.o., Han, D.: Wi-Fi fingerprint-based approaches following log-distance path loss model for indoor positioning. In: 2011 IEEE MTT-S International Microwave Workshop Series on Intelligent Radio for Future Personal Terminals (IMWS-IRFPT), pp. 1–2. IEEE (2011)
30. Xu, Q., Zheng, R.: MobiBee: a mobile treasure hunt game for location-dependent fingerprint collection. In: Proceedings of the 2016 ACM International Joint Conference on Pervasive and Ubiquitous Computing: Adjunct, pp. 1472–1477. ACM (2016)
31. Guimaraes, V., et al.: A motion tracking solution for indoor localization using smartphones. In: 2016 International Conference on Indoor Positioning and Indoor Navigation (IPIN), pp. 1–8. IEEE (2016)
32. Luo, X., O'Brien, W.J., Julien, C.L.: Comparative evaluation of received signal-strength index (RSSI) based indoor localization techniques for construction jobsites. Adv. Eng. Inform. 25(2), 355–363 (2011)

VISU: A Simple and Efficient Cache Coherence Protocol Based on Self-updating

Ximing He[1,2], Sheng Ma[2(✉)], Wenjie Liu[2], Sijiang Fan[2], Libo Huang[2], Zhiying Wang[2], and Zhanyong Zhou[1]

[1] Bejing Aerospace Command Control Centre, Beijing, China
[2] The State Key Laboratory of High Performance Computing,
National University of Defense Technology, Changsha, China
{heximing15,masheng,liuwenjie15,fansijiang15,libohuang,zywang}nudt@edu.cn

Abstract. Existing cache coherence protocols incur high overheads to shared memory systems and significantly reduce the system efficiency. For example, the widely used snooping protocol broadcasts messages at the expense of high network bandwidth overheads, and the directory protocol requires massive storage spaces to keep track of sharers. Furthermore, these coherence protocols have numerous transient states to cover various races, which increase the difficulty of implementation and verification. To mitigate these issues, this paper proposes a simple and efficient, two-state (Valid and Invalid) cache coherence protocol, VISU, for data-race-free programs. We adopt two distinct schemes for the private and shared data to simplify the design. Since the private data does not need to maintain coherence, we apply a simple write-back policy. For shared data, we leverage a write-through policy to make the last-level cache always hold the up-to-date data. A self-updating mechanism is deployed at synchronization points to update stale copies in L1 caches; this obviates the need for the broadcast communication or the directory.

Experimental results show that the VISU protocol achieves a significant reduction (31.0%) in the area overhead and obtains a better performance (2.9%) comparing with the sophisticated MESI directory protocol.

Keywords: Shared memory · Cache coherence · Self-updating · VISU

1 Introduction

The shared memory model is arguably the most widely used parallel programming model. Over the last few years, there has been an increasing demand for larger and more powerful high-performance shared memory systems. Cache coherence protocols are essential to provide a coherent memory view among different cores in shared memory systems. But the complexity and overhead of current coherence protocols hinder the establishment of efficient, low power and scalable systems.

© Springer Nature Switzerland AG 2018
J. Vaidya and J. Li (Eds.): ICA3PP 2018, LNCS 11337, pp. 341–357, 2018.
https://doi.org/10.1007/978-3-030-05063-4_27

In order to maintain coherence, cache coherence protocols must respond to write operations immediately and invalidate all stale copies in other caches. Specifically, the directory protocols track sharers with the directory which causes high storage overheads. The snooping protocols broadcast coherence requests which consumes significant network bandwidth. In addition, current protocols add extra stable states, such as the Exclusive and Owned states, to improve performance, and induce a number of transient states to cover various races. All these states cause an explosion in state transitions. For example, the MESI directory protocol implemented in gem5 [1] has up to 15 states and 55 state transitions in the L1 cache, as shown in Fig. 1.

Most of the complexities and overheads, including the broadcast, directory and state bits, of the widely used protocols stem from the effort to make the cache coherence maintenance *invisible* even to the strongest memory consistency model. We observe that releasing this stringent requirement can significantly simplify the design of efficient coherence protocols. In particular, we make full use of the characteristics of the data-race-free (DRF) [2] model to reduce the complexity and overheads for cache coherence protocols. The data-race-free model as a relaxed memory model is strong enough to keep the safety and security of programs and week enough to allow standard compiler and hardware optimizations. DRF programs are the most pervasive and important type of parallel programs since multithreaded programming languages prohibit or discourage data races. Moreover, current memory models of the Java and C++ guarantee sequential consistency (SC) for DRF programs [3,4].

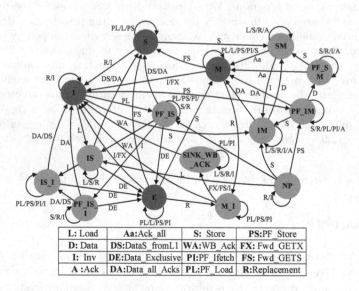

L: Load	Aa: Ack_all	S: Store	PS: PF_Store
D: Data	DS: DataS_fromL1	WA: WB_Ack	FX: Fwd_GETX
I: Inv	DE: Data_Exclusive	PI: PF_Ifetch	FS: Fwd_GETS
A: Ack	DA: Data_all_Acks	PL: PF_Load	R: Replacement

Fig. 1. The state transition graph of a MESI protocol. There are 4 stable states (red vertexes) and 11 transient states (blue vertexes). (Color figure online)

Besides, we notice that most of data used by parallel programs is only accessed by one core [5]. These private data causes no coherence issues. This feature can be leveraged to optimize coherence protocols, such as filtering requests [6] or reducing storage overheads [7]. We exploit this feature to propose a simple and efficient coherence protocol, the Valid/Invalid, Self-Updating (VISU) protocol. The VISU protocol deploys distinct schemes for the private and shared data. It applies a write-back policy for the private data since these data do not need the coherence maintenance. The VISU protocol maintains coherence for the shared data. It applies a write-through policy for the shared data to make the last level cache (LLC) always hold the latest data. At synchronization points, cores conduct self-updating to update the possible stale copies in their own L1 caches from the LLC. This maintains coherence for shared data in DRF programs.

The VISU protocol only has two stable states, valid and invalid; this significantly simplify the complexity of implementations and verifications. The self-updating mechanism eliminates the needs for directories or broadcast communication; this significantly reduces the storage or on-chip bandwidth overheads. Our evaluation results show that, compared with a sophisticated MESI directory protocol, the VISU achieves a significant reduction (31.0%) of the area overhead and gains a better performance (2.9%). In summary, this paper makes the following main contributions:

– Proposes a novel coherence protocol for DRF programs. This protocol has only two state states, which significantly reduces complexities and overheads.
– Combines a write-through policy and a self-updating mechanism at synchronization points to provide coherence for the shared data. This obviates the need for the directory or the broadcast communication.

2   VISU Protocol

This section first introduces the definition of cache coherence, and then presents the design of VISU protocol.

2.1   The Definition of Cache Coherence

Sorin, Hill and Wood [8] define the cache coherence with two invariants, the Single-Writer/Multiple-Reader (SWMR) invariant and the Data-Value invariant.

SWMR Invariant: For any memory location A, at any given (logic) time, there exists only a single core that may write to A (and can also read it) or some number of cores that may only read A.

Data-Value Invariant: The value of the memory location at the start of an epoch is the same as the value of the memory location at the end of its last read-write epoch.

Current coherence protocols induce significant overheads to maintain these two invariants. In contrast, benefiting from its simplified design, our proposed

VISU protocol can easily hold these invariants. The following section describes the design of VISU protocol with emphasis on its maintenance of these invariants.

2.2   Coherence for Data-Race-Free Programs

We design cache coherence protocols for DRF programs. A data race occurs when two threads access the same memory location, at least one of the accesses is a write, and there are no intervening synchronization operations. Since data races are the culprits of many problems existing in parallel programs, mainstream multithreaded programming languages deploy memory models that prohibit or discourage data races. Thus, most parallel programs are DRF programs. Choi et al. [9, 10] believe that DRF programs enable a fundamental rethinking of shared-memory hardware. We leverage the property of DRF programs to design a simple and efficient cache coherence protocol, the Valid/Invalid, Self-Updating (VISU) protocol.

The VISU deploys distinct schemes for the private and shared data to simplify protocols. The private data is only accessed by one core; it does not need to maintain coherence. Only the shared data needs to maintain coherence. Without loss of generality, we demonstrate the VISU protocol in a typical multicore cache hierarchy with private L1 caches and a shared Last-Level-Cache (LLC).

The Private Data Scheme. The VISU protocol adopts a write-back policy for the private data. Figure 2 shows the read (Rd), write (Wrt) and write-back (WB) transactions for private data. When read (Rd) or write (Wrt) misses take place, as shown in Fig. 2(a) and (b), the L1 cache controller sends GetS or GetX requests to the LLC. Then the LLC responds the data. These transactions involve no indirect messages because other L1 caches have no copies for private data. When a private cache line is evicted, the L1 cache writes the dirty data to the LLC and awaits the Ack response, as shown in Fig. 2(c).

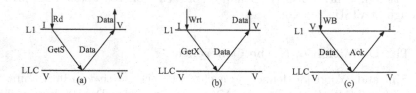

Fig. 2. VISU: Read (Rd), Write (Wrt), Write-back (WB) transactions for private lines.

Figure 3 shows the state transitions in the L1 cache and LLC. The state transition from I via IV to V in Fig. 3(a) shows the behaviours of L1 cache to handle the read (Rd) misses and write (Wrt) misses. When a read or write miss happens, the L1 cache controller sends GetS/GetX to the LLC and then awaits the data. The state transition from V via VI to I is the eviction of a L1 cache line. The L1 cache initials the WB transaction by sending the dirty data to the

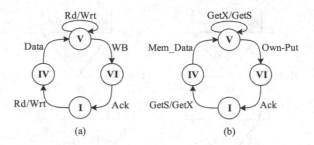

Fig. 3. VISU: Transitions between states in the L1 cache and LLC.

LLC and changes the state from V to VI. When it receives the Ack response, the L1 cache controller goes into the state I.

Figure 3(b) is the state transitions in the LLC. When the LLC controller receives GetS/GetX requests from the L1 cache, it issues a request to fetch data from the main memory if the data misses; it changes the state from I to IV. Once receiving the memory data, the LLC controller completes the transition from IV to V. The right side of Fig. 3(b) shows the eviction of a LLC line. The LLC controller writes dirty data (Own-Put message) into the main memory and transitions the state from V to VI. Once receiving the Ack, it goes into the state I. The protocol of private cache line only contains two stable states (V and I) and two transient states (VI and IV) for both the L1 cache and the LLC.

The Shared Data Scheme. The shared data needs coherence maintenance. The VISU protocol combines a write-through policy and a self-updating mechanism for the shared data. The write-through policy always keeps the latest data in the LLC. Thus, the LLC can response requests directly as the owner. The self-updating mechanism updates stale copies; it obviates indirect invalidations or broadcast communications.

Figure 4 shows read (Rd), write (Wrt), write-through (WT-timeout) and synchronization (Sync) transactions for shared data. Similar to the private data scheme, all these transactions are handled in a strict request-reply manner. We do not add extra states in this shared data scheme. In Fig. 4(a) and (b), when read or write misses occur, the L1 cache sends GetS or GetX requests. After it receives the data from the LLC, the L1 cache sets the state into V. In order to reduce the amount of packets generated by the write-through policy, the VISU protocol uses a delayed write-through (WT-timeout) scheme to merge multiple writes of the same cache line, as shown in Fig. 4(c). In addition, the VISU protocol identifies synchronization points in DRF programs and adopts the self-updating (SelfU) to update stale copies, as shown in Fig. 4(d). The L1 cache control issues the SelfU requests and gets the latest data from LLC.

The self-updating and write-through policy not only eliminate the indirect invalidation and directories but also simplify the VISU protocol to only four states (V, I, VI, IV).

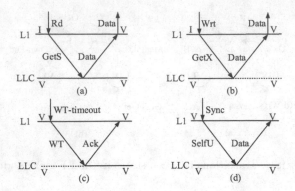

Fig. 4. VISU: Read(Rd),Write(Wrt),Write-back(WB) transactions for shared lines.

Coherence of VISU Protocols. Both the private and shared schemes of VISU maintain the SWMR and data value invariants. First, since the private data is accessed by a single core, the private data scheme of VISU protocol does not violate the SWMR and data value invariants. Second, the shared data scheme of VISU protocol leverages the DRF property of memory consistency models. The DRF maintains the SWMR invariant itself. A simple write-through policy and the self-updating mechanism maintain the data-value invariant by updating the L1 cache from LLC (the data owner) at synchronization points. Overall, the whole VISU protocol maintains the two coherence invariants and greatly simplifies the design of cache coherence protocols.

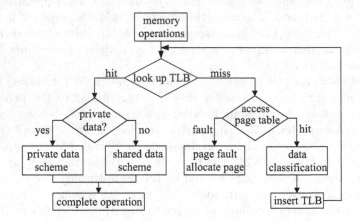

Fig. 5. The block diagram of the actions for memory accesses.

3   Implementation

Figure 5 depicts the main actions for memory accesses in the VISU protocol. The VISU protocol applies different schemes for the private and shared data. The data type classification information is stored in the TLB entry and page table entry (PTE). So during a memory access operation, the core first accesses the TLB to find out the data type of current accessed cache line, and then applies the corresponding coherence maintenance schemes. If a TLB miss occurs, the page table is accessed, and the appropriate data type is inserted into the PTE and TLB entry. The key implementation issues of VISU protocol include the classification of the shared data and private data, the data type transition and the supporting for synchronization. We delve into these issues in following sections.

3.1   Data Classification

The classification of private and shared data has aroused lots of concerns in the design of coherence protocols [5,7]. In this paper, we leverage the OS to distinguish private and shared pages, similar to the method discussed in [5].

As shown in Fig. 6, the TLB entry and PTE consist of the virtual address, the physical address and attributes of the page. Since the TLB entry and PTE often contain some reserved bits that are not used, we add a private bit (P) in the TLB entry as well as PTE and a keeper field (keeper) in PTE without extra dedicated hardware. The private bit (P) is used to differentiate private and shared pages. The keeper field (keeper) indicates the core that first accesses the page.

Once a page fault occurs, the OS allocates a new PTE and set the page private (P = 1) if the entry has not been cached in any TLB yet. Then, the OS will set the core that first accesses the allocated page as the page keeper. The fields in the PTE need no update if a core accesses a shared page or a private page that it has already kept. Otherwise, the OS will trigger a transition of page from private to shared. Finally, a new entry with the P and keeper will be inserted into TLB to complete the data classification, as shown in Fig. 5.

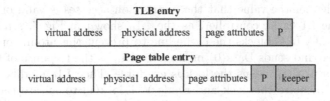

Fig. 6. TLB entry and page table entry format

3.2 Transition Mechanism

When a core accesses a private page kept by another core, the page needs to be changed into the shared type. The page type transition is achieved with inter-processor interrupts (IPI), a feature that is available in many architectures. The current accessing core sends an interrupt to the keeper which is recorded in the PTE. When the keeper receives the interrupt message, it updates the TLB entry of the relevant page by setting the page as shared ($P = 0$) and writing all dirty data within this page from the L1 cache to the LLC. As a result, all data within this page are latest in the LLC. Then, the keeper sends a reply to the current accessing core. Finally, the current accessing core can access the data correctly.

3.3 Synchronization with L1 Cache Bypassing

Synchronization mechanisms are typically built with user-level software routines that rely on hardware-supplied synchronization instructions. The key to implement synchronization is to use hardware primitives, such as Test&Set or Compare&Swap, to atomically read-modify-write (RMW) a memory location. A core tests or compares a condition to see whether it is met or not. If the condition is met, this core will atomically RMW the memory location to acquire a lock. Otherwise, the core spins on the copy in its L1 cache until the copy is changed by another core.

Without indirect messages, the VISU protocol cannot signal the changed condition to other spinning cores when a core releases a lock. The waiting cores cannot acquire the released lock. In order to support synchronization operations, the VISU protocol performs the read-modify-write operation by bypassing the L1 cache. When the core executes an atomic instruction, it bypasses the L1 cache and sends a GetX to the LLC directly. Then, the LLC controller sends the data back as the response. If the lock is acquired by another core, the current core will spin the data in LLC. When the lock is released, the spinning core performs the RMW operation and acquires this lock. Thus, bypassing the L1 cache and always reading the lock data from the LLC make spinning cores be aware of the released lock.

Figure 7 shows a simple lock where the value 0 indicates that the lock is free and 1 indicates that the lock is unavailable. For RMW atomic instruction, regardless whether the value that the instruction accesses is valid or invalid in L1 cache, the L1 cache controller, as the $L1_0$ shown in Fig. 7, sends a GetX message to LLC. LLC blocks the cache line to prevent this atomic operation to be interrupted and sends Data(0) message to $L1_0$ as the response of GetX. $L1_0$ gets the Data(0) that means the lock is available. Then $L1_0$ modifies this data to value 1 to acquire this lock and sends WT_lock(1) to release cache line in LLC. After that, program can get into the short critical section until the lock is released. When other cores perform RMW operations, L1 cache controller, as $L1_1$ shown in Fig. 7, sends a GetX message and finds that LLC is blocked. Then the GetX request enters the queue to wait the line to be unblocked. When LLC line is unblock, $L1_1$ gets Data(1) that the lock is unavailable and $L1_1$

spins. After $L1_0$ releases the lock by sending WT_unlock(0), $L1_1$ can get value 0 and acquire the lock. Bypassing L1 cache and reading the lock data from LLC certainly cause some performance loss, but synchronization operation in the entire parallel program is rare and the loss is still accepted, which can see from the evaluation in Sect. 4.

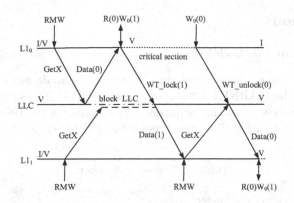

Fig. 7. Atomic RMW transactions for shared lines

By this mechanism, the VISU protocol can support synchronization correctly. Existing designs apply similar mechanisms [11].

3.4   Other Implementation Issues

Write-Through at the Word Granularity. VISU protocols maintain coherence based on the DRF property of parallel programs. The software keeps DRF at the word granularity instead of the cache-line granularity. When two concurrent threads write different words of the same cache line at the same time, these two writes do not violate the DRF in software and there is no synchronization operation between them. But these two writes cause data race at the cache line granularity; they overwrite the same cache line in LLC simultaneously. The solution in this paper is to perform the write-through at the word or less granularity. We add dirty bits for each word in the L1 cache line. When different cores write different words of the same cache line with the write-through policy, they can only update their modified words in the LLC and won't overwrite other words.

Supporting for the DMA. The Direct Memory Access (DMA) is essential for modern processors; cache coherence protocols must offer supporting for DMA operations. The DMA directly uses physical addresses to access data without accessing TLBs for address translation. A DMA operation that reads memory should find the up-to-date data. Similarly, a DMA operation that writes memory needs to invalidate all stale copies of the data.

Therefore, the VISU protocol broadcasts the DMA requests to support these operations. Specifically, when the LLC receive a request from the DMA controller, whether read or write request, the LLC broadcasts this request to all L1 caches. L1 caches invalidate stale copies and write the dirty data into the LLC as the response. After that, the DMA accesses the data from the LLC correctly.

4   Evaluation

4.1   Evaluation Methodology

To evaluate performance, we carry out a full-system simulation using the gem5 simulator with the GARNET [12] network model. This infrastructure provides a detailed memory system timing model. We simulate a tiled 8-core processor running on linux 2.6.22 with parameters given in Table 1.

Table 1. System parameters

Memory parameter	
Processor frequency	1 GHz
Cache block size/Page size	64bytes/4 KB
Split L1 I&D caches	32 KB, 8-way
Shared L2 cache	4 MB, 512 KB/tile, 8-way
Delay timeout	500 cycles (write-though)
Network parameter	
Topology	2-dimensional mesh (4 * 2)
Routing technique	Deterministic X-Y
Garnet-network	Fixed

We use CACTI 6.5 [13] with a 32 nm technology process to evaluate the overhead of caches. Our workloads include FFT (64K complex doubles), LU (LU-contiguous_block, 512 * 512 matrix), LU-Non (LU-non_contiguous_block, 512 * 512 matrix) and Water-Nsq (Water-nsquared, 512 molecules) from the SPLASH-2 benchmark [14].

We identify synchronization operations (locks, fence, barriers and interrupt) in both the OS and benchmarks so that the hardware can appropriately perform self-updating. We evaluate the VISU protocol with two other protocols.

The first one is a MESI directory-based protocol. The second one is the VIPS-M (VIPS for short) proposed by Ros [11]. Table 2 summarizes the characteristics of the three evaluated protocols, including the invalidation manner, the indirection transaction, the write policy, L1 cache states and tag area of LLC.

MESI directory-based protocols use a directory to keep tracking of the status for all cache blocks; the status of each block include in which cache coherence state that block is, and which nodes are sharing that block at that time. When a write occurs, in order to obtain the exclusive access, MESI protocols will send the write request to the directory node and then the directory node sends the invalidation messages to all sharers by the way of using multicast. Besides, MESI protocols adopt the write-back policy and have a series of transient states as shown in Table 2.

As for VIPS and VISU protocols, they both adopt two distinct schemes for the private and shared data. They apply the write-through policy for shared data and apply the write-back policy for private data. Dynamic write policies simplify the complex coherent states to only 4 states in L1 cache. Moreover, VIPS protocols implement a self-invalidation mechanism to make processors invalidate the local shared copies by themselves at the synchronization point instead of the indirect invalidation. The combination of self-invalidation and write-through policy can eliminate the directory and indirect invalidation. Different from VIPS protocols, VISU protocols propose a self-updating mechanism to update the shared copies. The self-updating mechanism not only removes the directory and indirect invalidation like the self-invalidation mechanism, but also improves the cache miss rate since the shared data is updated and is valid in L1 cache after synchronization points. Due to the self-updating mechanism, VISU protocols will get better performance than VIPS protocols if the shared data is repeatedly accessed by cores after the synchronization.

Table 2. The characteristics of three evaluated protocols.

Protocol	Directory	Invalidation	Indirection	Write policy	L1 stable/transient states	LLC tag area
MESI	Full-map	Multicast	Yes	WB	4/11	0.1363 mm^2
VIPS	None	Self-invalidation	No	WB&WT	2/2	0.0941 mm^2
VISU	None	Self-updating	No	WB&WT	2/2	0.0941 mm^2

4.2 Data Classification

The VISU protocol dynamically identifies the private and shared data in parallel programs. Figure 8 divides memory access requests into four classes: the instruction fetch (Ifetch) requests, the private requests, the shared requests and the synchronization (synch) requests. Ifetch requests access the read-only data. The read-only data, like the private data, adopts the write-back policy and obviates self-updating in the VISU protocol even it is accessed by two or more cores. Therefore, requests applying the private data scheme (including Ifetch and private requests) account for 77.2% of all requests. The proportions of synchronization requests are tiny; in the FFT, LU, LU-Non and Water-Nsp, they are 0.11%, 0.10%, 0.08% and 0.22%, respectively (0.14% on average).

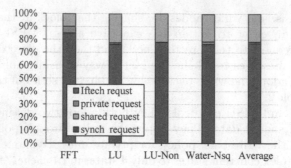

Fig. 8. The fraction of different requests in parallel programs.

4.3   Performance Results

Figure 9 shows the application runtime of the three protocols. The results are normalized to the runtime of the MESI protocol. On average, the VISU protocol with two stable states obtains a better performance (2.9%) to that of the MESI protocol with four stable states, even the MESI protocol uses the directory. In FFT, the simple VISU protocol obtains a 14.3% performance improvement compared with the MESI due to its massive private data and rare synchronizations. In Water-Nsp, the VISU protocol gets performance loss compared with the MESI protocol because of frequent synchronizations. Compared with performing self-invalidation at synchronization points, performing self-updating can reduce the number of cache misses. On average, the VISU protocol performs 3.2% better than the VIPS protocol.

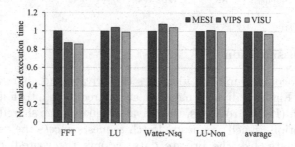

Fig. 9. Normalized execution time w.r.t. MESI.

4.4   Overhead

Figure 10 shows the basic directory entry for MESI protocols in a system with N nodes. The MESI protocol uses a full-map directory with two major storage overheads: the owner field and the sharer lists. These two fields induce extra $\log_2 N$ and N bits to each data block, respectively. These storage costs seriously limit the scalability of directory protocols. We use CACTI 6.5 with a 32 nm technology process to evaluate the area overhead of the LLC tag with parameters given in Table 3. In MESI protocols, the LLC tag size is 58 bits since the directory entry, as shown in Fig. 10, was stored in the LLC tag. The VIPS and VISU protocols have no directories and the tag is 45 bits; so they get a 31.0% reduction in the area overhead of the tag of the LLC compared with MESI protocols as shown in Table 2.

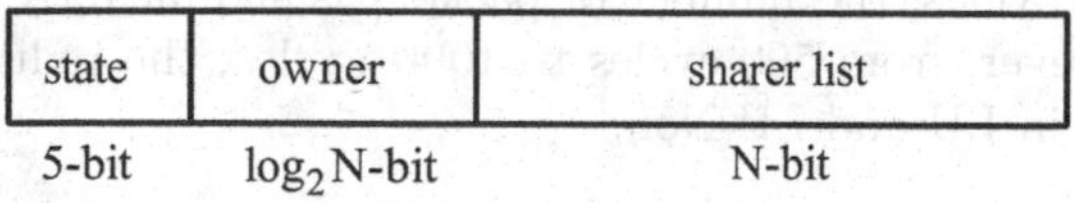

state	owner	sharer list
5-bit	$\log_2 N$-bit	N-bit

Fig. 10. Directory entry for a block in a system with N nodes.

Table 3. CACTI 6.5 parameters

LLC parameter	
Technology	32 nm
Cache block size/page size	64 bytes/4 KB
Associativity	8
Read write ports	1
Physical address	52 bits
MESI tag	58 bits
VIPS/VISU tag	48 bits

The verification for protocols with numerous states and races faces great challenges [15]. The VISU and VIPS protocols use the self-updating and self-invalidation to handle stale copies. Both protocols perform in a strict request-response manner with no indirections. However, the MESI directory protocol uses directories to multicast invalidations as shown in Table 2. Our VISU protocol is divided into two independent parts for the shared data and the private data. These two parts can be verified separately. At the same time, the VISU protocol only has two stable states (V/I) and two transient states (IV/VI) in the L1 cache. Compared with the MESI protocol, which has 4 stable and 11 transient states and numerous races, the VISU protocol is simple and significantly easily to be verified.

4.5 Sensitivity Analysis

Delay Time of Write-Through Policy. Both VISU and VIPS protocols apply the delayed write-though policy to merge several neighbouring write requests. On the one hand, the delayed write-though policy reduces the packets in NoC and improve the performance of system by reducing the amount of write-through operations. On the other hand, this policy delays writing the new data to LLC. When the data are accessed by the RWM requests, the delayed write-though policy will make the spinning core spend more time to get new data and cause some performance loss.

Figure 11 collects the amount of NoC packets when configuring the delay time as 100 cycles, 500 cycles and 1000 cycles. When the delay time increases from 100 cycles to 500 cycles, the number of packets is significantly reduced (30.7% on average). However, from 500 cycles to 1000 cycles, the reduction of packets is rare, especially in LU and LU-Non.

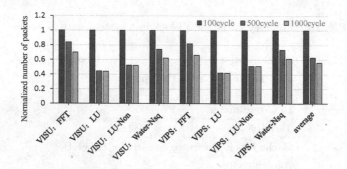

Fig. 11. Number of packets in the VISU and VIPS.

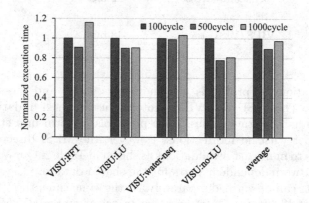

Fig. 12. Runtime with the different delay time in VISU.

Figure 12 shows the application execution time in the VISU protocol when setting the delay time at 100 cycles, 500 cycles and 1000 cycles. The results are normalized to the performance when the delay time is 100 cycles. As shown in Fig. 12, VISU protocols get best performance at 500 cycles and the performance at 500 cycles obtains 11.9% and 9.2% improvement on average comparing with the performance at 100 cycles and 1000 cycles.

The Cache Miss Rate of VISU and VIPS. When a synchronization point occurs, the VISU uses self-updating to update the shared data within L1 cache while the VIPS uses self-invalidation to invalidate shared data. Due to the spatial locality, the shared data is generally repeatedly accessed by some cores; the self-updating mechanism can significantly reduce the number of L1 cache misses compared with the self-invalidation mechanism. Figure 13 depicts the L1 cache miss rate of the VISU protocol normalized with the VIPS protocol. Compared with the VIPS, VISU reduces the L1 cache miss rate by an average of 5.2%.

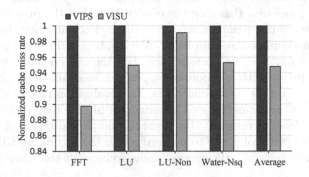

Fig. 13. Normalized cache miss rate

5 Related Work

There is a vast body of existing work on coherence protocols [5,7,11,16,17]. We just discuss the work mostly close to ours. The POPS design [5] adopts the data classification to optimize both private and shared data. The design provides localized data and metadata access for shared data and private data through delegation and controlled local migration. The POPS proposes specific optimizations for sharing and access pattern but adds the complexity of protocols. The VIPS-M protocol [11] uses the data classification to perform a dynamic write-policy (write-back for private data, write-through for shared data) and adopts self-invalidation at synchronization points. Unavoidably, the self-invalidation incurs extra cache misses. Unlike their work, our VISU protocol uses self-updating to reduce the cache misses. In addition, the recent SARC coherence protocol [7] also exploits the DRF programming model. They adopt self-invalidation for read-only tear-off cache blocks to eliminate invalidation traffic and the write prediction to eliminate directory indirection. But the SARC protocol still requires the directory to store the sharer list and does not reduce the protocol complexity.

Other efforts focus on disciplined parallelism [9,10,18]. For example, the DeNovo [9] exploits language-level annotations designed for coherence and focus on deterministic codes. They require programmers to assign every object field or array element to a named region and the applications must define the memory regions of the certain read/write behaviour. The DeNovo eliminates directory storage, write invalidation and transient states. But its performance heavily relies on the characteristics of applications.

6   Conclusion and Future Work

Inspired by efforts to simplify the complexity and reduce the overhead for existing coherence protocols, we propose a simple and efficient two-state VISU protocol for DRF programs. Based on the observation that the private data do not need the coherence maintenance, we apply distinct schemes for the private and shared data to simplify the complexity. We apply a write-back policy for the private data to improve the performance. For the shared data, we combine a write-through policy with a simple self-updating mechanism. It does not need broadcast or indirection communications. The evaluation results show that the VISU protocol outperforms the sophisticated MESI directory while significantly reduces the hardware overheads. Moreover, the simplification of coherence states makes the VISU protocol easily to be verified. In the future, we will extend the VISU protocol to hierarchical clustered cache to improve the scalability of VISU protocols.

Acknowledgments. This work is supported by the National Natural Science Foundation of China(No.61672526,61572508,61472435) and Research Project of NUDT(ZK17-03-06).

References

1. Binkert, N.L., et al.: The gem5 simulator. SIGARCH Comput. Arch. News **39**(2), 1–7 (2011)
2. Adve, S.V., Hill, M.D.: Weak ordering-a new definition. In: International Symposium on Computer Architecture, vol. 18, no. 3, pp. 2–14 (1990)
3. Manson, J., Pugh, W., Adve, S.V.: The Java memory model. In: POPL (2005)
4. Boehm, H.-J., Adve, S.V.: Foundations of the C++ concurrency memory model. In: PLDI (2008)
5. Cuesta, B., et al.: Increasing the effectiveness of directory caches by avoiding the tracking of noncoherent memory blocks. IEEE Trans. Comput. **62**(3), 482–495 (2013)
6. Kim, D., et al.: Subspace snooping: filtering snoops with operating system support. In: PACT (2010)
7. Hossain, H., Dwarkadas, S., Huang, M.C.: POPS: coherence protocol optimization for both private and shared data. In: PACT (2011)
8. Sorin, D.J., Hill, M.D., Wood, D.A.: A Primer on Memory Consistency and Cache Coherence. Morgan & Claypool Publishers (2011)
9. Choi, B., et al. DeNovo: rethinking the memory hierarchy for disciplined parallelism. In: PACT (2011)
10. Sung, H., Komuravelli, R., Adve, S.V.: DeNovoND: efficient hardware support for disciplined non-determinism. In: ASPLOS (2013)

11. Ros, A., Kaxiras, S.: Complexity-effective multicore coherence. In: PACT (2012)
12. Agarwal, N., et al.: GARNET: a detailed on-chip network model inside a full-system simulator. In: ISPASS (2009)
13. Muralimanohar, N., Balasubramonian, R., Jouppi, N.P.: Architecting efficient interconnects for large caches with CACTI6.0. IEEE Micro 28(1), 69–79 (2008)
14. Woo, S.C., et al.: The splash-2 programs: characterization and methodological considerations. In: ISCA 1995, pp. 24–36 (1995)
15. Nanda, A.K., Bhuyan, L.N.: A formal specification and verification technique for cache coherence protocols. In: ICPP (1992)
16. Kaxiras, S., Keramidas, G.: SARC coherence: scaling directory cache coherence in performance and power. IEEE Micro 30(5), 54–65 (2010)
17. Ros, A., et al.: Efficient self-invalidation/self-downgrade for critical sections with relaxed semantics. IEEE Trans. Parallel Distrib. Syst. 28(12), 3413–3425 (2017)
18. Sung, H., Komuravelli, R., Adve, S.V.: Denovond: efficient hardware for disciplined nondeterminism. IEEE Micro 34(3), 138–148 (2014)

PPLDEM: A Fast Anomaly Detection Algorithm with Privacy Preserving

Ao Yin[1], Chunkai Zhang[1(✉)], Zoe L. Jiang[1(✉)], Yulin Wu[1], Xing Zhang[2], Keli Zhang[2], and Xuan Wang[1]

[1] Department of Computer Science and Technology, Harbin Institute of Technology, Shenzhen, China
yinaoyn@126.com, ckzhang812@gmail.com, zoeljiang@hit.edu.cn, {yulinwu,wangxuan}@cs.hitsz.edu.cn
[2] National Engineering Laboratory for Big Data Collaborative Security Technology, Beijing, China
{zhangxing,zhangkeli}@cecgw.cn

Abstract. In this paper, we first propose a fast anomaly detection algorithm LDEM. The key insight of LDEM is a fast local density estimator, which estimates the local density of instances by the average density of all features. The local density of each feature can be estimated by the defined mapping function. Furthermore, we propose an efficient scheme PPLDEM to detect anomaly instances with considering privacy protection in the case of multi-party participation, based on the proposed scheme and homomorphic encryption. Compare with existing schemes with privacy preserving, our scheme needs less communication cost and less calculation. From security analysis, it can prove that our scheme will not leak any privacy information of participants. And experiments results show that our proposed scheme PPLDEM can detect anomaly instances effectively and efficiently.

Keywords: Anomaly detection · Local density · Privacy preserving

1 Introduction

Anomaly detection is to find the instances that have different data characteristics from the most instances. There are many literatures that define the notion of "different data characteristics". For example, in cluster-based anomaly detection algorithms [4,8], anomaly instances are the instances that do not lie in any large clusters. In distance-based algorithms [11,20,22], anomaly instances are the instances that are distant with most of instances. In density-based anomaly detection algorithms [3,5,7,21,25], anomaly instances are the instances with lower local density, and most of these algorithms obtain the local density of instances by counting the number of near neighbors. In this paper, we focus on the research of density-based algorithms, and propose a fast local density estimation method LDEM. Different with the existing algorithms to calculate

© Springer Nature Switzerland AG 2018
J. Vaidya and J. Li (Eds.): ICA3PP 2018, LNCS 11337, pp. 358–373, 2018.
https://doi.org/10.1007/978-3-030-05063-4_28

directly the local density of instances, LDEM estimate the density of instances by the average density of all features. And compare with the existing algorithms to obtain neighbors by calculating euclidean distance of instances, LDEM obtains the neighbors of each feature by the defined mapping function. And the time complexity of our algorithm only needs $O(N)$.

What's more, we adopt our algorithm to the case of the data distributed in multiple parties. But due to the growing awareness of data privacy, it is important to consider privacy protection in the case of multi-party anomaly detection. There are some existing anomaly detection algorithms [9,13,14,24], which have taken privacy protection into considering. But most of these algorithms not only need many addition and multiplication on ciphertexts, but also need multiple communications between data owners. Even some algorithms only can be used among two parties [13]. In order to solve these disadvantages, we propose a simple and security anomaly detection scheme with privacy preserving based on our proposed anomaly detection algorithm LDEM and homomorphic encryption scheme BCP [1,6,17–19]. Compare with the existing scheme, our scheme only needs outsource the sketch tables and each data owner only need constant communication times, which can reduce most communication cost. Furthermore, our scheme only needs linear addition operations on ciphertexts. From security analysis, it can easily prove that our scheme does not leak out any privacy information. And experiments results show that our algorithm can detect anomaly instances correctly with multi-party participation without leaking out any privacy information.

This paper is organized as follows. In Sect. 2, we analysis the background used in our work. In Sect. 3, we introduce the proposed local density estimation in detail. In Sect. 4, we present the system model and introduce the proposed anomaly detection with privacy preserving in detail. In Sect. 5, we analyze the security of our scheme. In Sect. 6, we perform some empirical experiments to illustrate the effectiveness of our algorithm. Lastly, our work is concluded in Sect. 7.

2 Preliminary

In this section, we will analysis the existing density-based anomaly detection algorithm, and introduce homomorphic encryption scheme BCP used in this paper.

2.1 Local Density Estimation

There are many density-based anomaly detection algorithms, such as [3,5,7,21] et.al. These density-based anomaly detection algorithms can be divided into two categories, distance-based [3,5,7], kernel-based [21]. Most of these algorithms obtain the local density of data by counting the number of near neighbors, and these near neighbors are determined by euclidean distance. The algorithm, in [21], also uses the Euclidean Distance in the Gaussian-Kernel. So distanced-based and kernel-based algorithms all contain the distance calculation operations, and this distance is the sum of distance of all features (seen in Eq.(1)). But in high dimensional data, the euclidean distance is indistinguishable. So the effect of these algorithms always can not obtain the good results. In addition, it is difficult to extend these algorithms to parallel versions.

$$Dist(x, y) = \sum_{i=1}^{d} (x_i - y_i)^2 \tag{1}$$

From Eq. (1), we can find that each feature of an instance has a distance with this feature of other instances. So based on the independence assumption of Naive Bayes, we can estimate the local density of each feature, and then determine the density of this instance. Compare with existing algorithms, our algorithm does not need any distance calculation, since we define a mapping function, which can map any similar value into the same key. We count the number of data points with same key to get the local density of each feature.

2.2 Homomorphic Encryption

The homomorphic encryption scheme used in our work is BCP cryptosystem, which is variant of the ElGamal cryptosystem [6] proposed by Bresson, Catalano and Pointcheval [2]. BCP has the property of additive homomorphic (seen Eq. (2)), and it can be competent at the computations on ciphers encrypted by different keys. Since BCP cryptosystem has two independent decryption mechanisms. First, a given ciphertext is decrypted by the corresponding private key. Second, any given ciphertext can be decrypted by the master key. The detail of BCP can be seen in [2,6].

$$Enc_{pk}(x + y) = Enc_{pk}(x) * Enc_{pk}(u) \tag{2}$$

2.3 Security Protocol

There are two security protocols used in our scheme. One is *ProbKey* protocol that can transform the ciphertexts encrypted by different pk_i into the ciphertexts encrypted by the same public key pk. pk belongs to server C. The other is the reverse operation of the previous protocol. This security protocol is called *TransDec*, which can transform the ciphertexts encrypted by pk into the ciphertexts encrypted by pk_i. Both of these two security protocols are used between the server C and the server S.

ProdKey: Given a message x encrypted by pk_i, $[x]_{pk_i}$. The steps of transforming this ciphertext into the ciphertext encrypted by pk as below.

(1) Server C picks a random number $r \in \mathbb{Z}_N$, and encrypts it to get the cipher $[r]_{pk_i}$. So we can get $[x+r]_{pk_i} = [x]_{pk_i} * [r]_{pk_i}$, and send $[x+r]_{pk_i}$ to server S.

(2) Server S decrypt cipher $[x+r]_{pk_i}$ by the master key, and encrypt the plain text by pk. So we can get $[x+r]_{pk}$, and send $[x+r]_{pk}$ and pk to server C.

(3) Server C encrypt the $-r$ by pk, so it can get $[-r]_{pk}$. Then, it can get the raw plaintext encrypted by pk, as $[x]_{pk} = [x+r-r]_{pk} = [x+r]_{pk} * [-r]_{pk}$.

TransDec: The process of this protocol is similar to the process of the *Prod-Key*. At here, we will not repeat this description. Given a cipher $[x]_{pk}$, this protocol can transform it back to the cipher $[x]_{pk_i}$.

3 The Proposed Local Density Estimation Method: LDEM

3.1 Local Density Estimation Method: LDEM

Compare with other algorithms [3,5,7,21], our method can achieve linear time and liner space complexity. What's more, our method more easily extends to parallel version. Before introducing the details of our method, we will present the symbolics used in our work (seen Table 1) and the proposed two definitions.

Table 1. The description of symbolic.

Symbolic	Description
X	A data set
X_j	A vector of jth feature in X
X_i	A vector of ith instance in X
X_{ij}	The value of jth feature in X_i
N	The length of data set X
d	The number of features in X
M	The number of components

Definition 1. *Mapping Function is used to map similar values in X_j to the same key. The mapping function is defined as Eq. (3). In this function, v denotes the value of one feature, r and w are generated randomly in our work.*

$$f(v) = \lfloor \frac{v+r}{w} \rfloor \tag{3}$$

Definition 2. *Sketch Table is composed of keys and corresponding times (seen Eq. (4)). In which each k_i denotes an output value of mapping function, and t_i is the corresponding times. The $|sketchtable| = q$ is the number of function output values in X_j. (Note: the length of sketch table in different features may be not same.)*

$$sketchtable = \{(k_1, t_1), (k_2, t_2), ..., (k_q, t_q)\} \tag{4}$$

Local Density Estimation: The key insight of estimating the density of instances is to estimate the density of each feature of instances. In our method, we define some mapping functions that can map similar values into the same key. So we only need count the instance number with the same key on each feature, and this number denotes the local density of the corresponding feature. Now, we will show the process steps in detail.

(1) First, initialize d mapping functions. Randomly select global parameter w from the range $(1/ln(N), 1-1/ln(N))$. Generate a vector, $r = \{r_1, r_2, ..., r_d\}$, with length d, in which each r_j is selected uniformly at the range $(0, w)$. So, we can get the d mapping functions as

$$f(X_{ij}) = \lfloor \frac{X_{ij} + r_j}{w} \rfloor \tag{5}$$

(2) Normalize each X_j in data set X as Eq. (6), in which u_j is the mean value of jth feature in X and std_j is the standard deviation of jth in X.

$$X_{ij} = \frac{X_{ij} - u_j}{std_j} \tag{6}$$

(3) Then, we can take the Eq. (5) to map the value of each feature in data set X. So we will get d sketch table as Eq. (7). (Note: the length of $sketchtable_j$ in d features may be different.)

$$sketchtable_j = \{(k_{1j}, t_{1j}), (k_{2j}, t_{2j}), ..., (k_{qj}, t_{qj})\} \quad j \in [1, d] \tag{7}$$

(4) After we have built up these sketch tables, we can do estimate the local density of each instance X_i, as Eq. (8). In which, $sketchtable_j[f(X_{ij})]$ denotes the value of t_{qj} with $k_{qj} = f(X_{ij})$. If no k_{qj} is equal to $f(X_{ij})$, the value of $sketchtable_j[f(X_{ij})]$ will be set to zero. Then, we will get the local density of instance X_i by calculating the average value of $sketchtable_j[f(X_{ij})], j = \{1, 2, ..., d\}$. Obviously, this process only need scan data set X once, so our algorithm only needs $O(N)$ time complexity.

$$density(X_i) = \frac{1}{d} \sum_{j=1}^{d} sketchtable_j[f_j(X_{ij})] \tag{8}$$

Same as other density-based algorithms, the smaller value $density(X_i)$ is, the more likely abnormal X_i is.

Ensemble: Since the mapping function for each feature is generated randomly, the keys mapped by one mapping function in each feature may be biased. In order to ensure to obtain unbiased local density estimation for each feature, we will randomly generate M different mapping functions for getting M different sketch tables of each feature. Therefore, we will get M components, in which each component is composed of d sketch tables. Each sketch table summaries the information of each feature. Then, at the feature density estimation stage, each feature will be estimated M times. Hence, the final estimated local density of any instance X_i is the average of M estimation results, as Eq.(9). After considering the ensemble, the time complexity of our algorithm will become $O(MN)$. But $O(M)$ is a constant, so the final time complexity is also linear.

$$
\begin{aligned}
Density(X_i) &= \frac{1}{M} \sum_{m=1}^{M} density_m(X_i) \\
&= \frac{1}{dM} \sum_{m=1}^{M} \sum_{j=1}^{d} sketchtable_{mj}[f_{mj}(X_{ij})]
\end{aligned}
\tag{9}
$$

4   The Proposed Anomaly Detection Algorithm with Privacy Preserving: PPLDEM

In this section, we will introduce the system model used in this paper, and describe the proposed anomaly detection scheme with privacy preserving PPL-DEM in detail.

4.1   System Model

In our scheme, system model is composed of data owners and a cloud. This system model can be seen Fig. 1. The cloud consists of two servers. One is called as server S, which is responsible for initializing system parameters, including public parameters of BCP and parameters of our anomaly detection algorithm LDEM. Since this server has the master key, it is also in charge of conversion ciphers encrypted one public key into ciphers encrypted by other public key. This server only communicates with server C. The other server is called as server C, which is responsible for integrate the sketch tables (seen *Definition* 2) received from all data owners. In the cloud, the server S is a trusted server and the server C is a untrusted server. Data owners can be also called the participant parties. Our scheme can apply to the case with multiple participants (two or more). Different with existing schemes, our scheme does not need for data owners to outsource the original data set. Data owners only need sent their sketch tables to server C, and then server C will return integrated sketch tables encrypted by pk to data owners. These sketch tables contain all information of data owners contained in server C. Except requesting parameters, data owners can do any anomaly detection tasks by only communicating with server C.

4.2   Anomaly Detection with Privacy Preserving

It is noticed easily that the key of detecting anomaly data is the sketch table in LDEM. So it is very important to protect the sketch tables of each participant, when there are many participants to do anomaly detection mining together. Protecting the information of sketch tables from being leaked means hiding the real keys and times in sketch tables. In our method, the crucial technologies of hiding these information are random disturbance and homomorphic encryption.

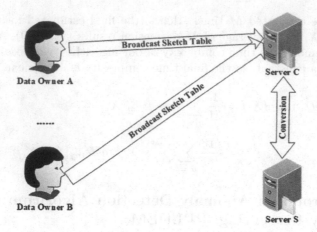

Fig. 1. System model of our scheme (Data owner A has pk_a, sk_a. Data owner B has pk_b, sk_b and server S has pk and sk)

- **Random Disturbance.** Random Disturbance means adding fictitious items in sketch tables. Each fictitious item is a tuple $(key, 0)$, in which key can be any integer in the digital space that does not appear in the original sketch table, and 0 is used to mark fictitious key. For example, Table 2 is the original sketch table, and Table 3 shows the sketch table after adding some fictitious items in Table 2 and these fictitious items are marked in color red. The purpose of adding fictitious items is to ensure that nobody can guess whether this key is a real key. Because the keys after adding fictitious items are still plain texts. To better hiding the real keys, we propose a adding fictitious items method. Since each feature data has been normalized by the Eq. (6), the normalized data is distributed in two sides of *zero* and the size in two sides are equal approximately. So we can add some fictitious keys to ensure that the keys sent to server C also have this characteristic. For example, in Table 3 we add the fictitious items $(-4, 0)$, $(-3, 0)$, $(0, 0)$ and $(2, 0)$ to ensure the keys on both sides of 0 are symmetrical. In order to better privacy protection, we advise that each data owner can set the keys in each sketch table be the all digits in the range of -1000 to 1000, since the value of Eq. (5) is almost impossible to beyond this range.
- **Homomorphic Encryption.** After adding some fictitious items in sketch table, we need to do other operations to achieve the aim that the real keys and the fictitious keys are indistinguishable. So we need select a encryption system to encrypt the *times* that can distinguish the real keys and the fictitious keys. In order to ensure the addition operations on ciphertexts encrypted by different public key, we select a semi-homomorphic encryption system, BCP [2,6,17,19], which supports homomorphism addition. Assume party A has a sketch table (Table 2). And the public key of party A is pk_a. Then, after

Table 2. Original sketch table.

key	−2	−1	1	3	4
times	23	43	2	2	2

Table 3. Sketch table after random disturbance.

key	−4	−3	−2	−1	0	1	2	3	4
times	0	0	23	43	0	2	0	2	2

random disturbance and homomorphic encryption operations, this table can be seen as Table 4.

Table 4. Sketch table after random disturbance and homomorphic encryption.

key	−4	−3	−2	−1	0	1	2	3	4
times	$Enc_a(0)^a$	$Enc_a(0)$	$Enc_a(23)$	$Enc_a(43)$	$Enc_a(0)$	$Enc_a(2)$	$Enc_a(0)$	$Enc_a(2)$	$Enc_a(2)$

^{a} $Enc(.)$ is the encryption function of BCP.

Then, we will introduce our scheme in detail, based on these two crucial technologies and the proposed anomaly detection algorithm. In our scheme, an anomaly detection task will be divided into two steps. One is the preprocessing step, and the other is the step of calculating anomaly scores of data.

Preprocessing: In this step, data owners will initialize encryption system and LDEM. For encryption system, data owners will request *public parameters* from server S, which are used to generate *public key* and *secret key*. For LDEM, data owners will request the number of component M and dM mapping functions from server S. Then, each data owner will do the follow operations.

(1) Transform the data in their own database into sketch tables by the mapping functions requested from server C, as the description in Sect. 3.
(2) Add fictitious items in each sketch table. Then, encrypt the times of each key in their sketch table by their public key pk_i, and they can send their sketch tables to server C.

After server C received sketch tables sent by data owners, it will transform these sketch table encrypted by different pk_i using the *ProdKey* security protocol, and then merge these sketch tables.

Detection Stage: Assume there is a data owner (participant) A, and his public key is pk_a and his secret key is sk_a. If he wants to do anomaly detection tasks, he will firstly request the merged sketch tables encrypted by the public key pk of server C. Then, he will transform the data in each feature by the corresponding mapping function. The data in each feature will be represented by the output value (key) of mapping function, and he can query the local density of each feature in the corresponding sketch table. After getting the local densities of all features of each instance, the final local density of each feature will be obtained. But now, the final local densities are encrypted by pk. To get the plain density values, data owner A needs to send these ciphertexts to server

C, and server C will transform these ciphertexts encrypted by pk_a using the *TransDes* security protocol. And then, data owner A can get the plain density values through these ciphertexts by sk_a. Lastly, data owner A can determine which instances are more likely to be anomaly instances, according to the local density ranking. The all process of this stage in data owner A can be seen in Algorithm 1.

Algorithm 1. PPLEDM:Anomaly Detection With Privacy Preserving.

Input: Data set X
Output: The local density *Density*.

1 // Request *Table* from server C;
2 $\hat{X} \leftarrow mapping(X);$ // Preprocessing data set X;
3 $Density \leftarrow \emptyset;$
4 **for** $\hat{x}$ *in* $\hat{X}$ **do**
5      $density_x = 0;$
6   **for** $j = 1$ *to* d **do**
7          $density_x = density_x + Table[j][\hat{x}];$
8   **end**
9      $Density \leftarrow [Density, density_x];$
10 **end**
11 $Density \leftarrow TransDec(Density);$
12 **return** *Density*;

---

5 Security Analysis

Our anomaly detection scheme with privacy preserving is based on semi-honest model. In semi-honest model, all participants will comply with the security protocols, but they may collect the received information (inputs, outputs, calculated results) to look for some privacy information [19]. In our scheme, we assume that all participants, including server C, server S and data owners, will do anomaly detection tasks on the basis of the proposed protocols.

5.1 Security Under the Cloud's Attack

(1) The Security Under Server C. In our scheme, server C is responsible for two things, merging sketch tables received from different data owners and transforming the densities encrypted by pk into ciphertexts encrypted by pk_i. For the first thing, server C may do the keys attack on the basis of the received sketch tables. But in our scheme, the keys in these sketch tables are composed of real keys and fictitious keys, and these two type keys are marked by the times encrypted by the pk_i. Since any two times ciphertexts are indistinguishable based on the security of BCP encryption system [19], server C can not distinguish the true and false of any two keys, such as $(k_i, Enc(0))$ and $(k_j, Enc(1))$. It only can know the frequencies of any received key, but it can not infer the true times of these keys in there original sketch tables. For the other thing, all operations in server C are based on ciphertexts. Any information will not be leaked in this thing, since cracking BCP is difficult NP problem. From the above analysis, it can be determined that our scheme will not leak any information of data owners in server C.

(2) The Security Under Server S. Server S is a trusted server, so it can do initialize public parameter of BCP, and generate the parameters of LDEM. What's more, it is responsible for transforming ciphertexts with server C together. In the process of transforming ciphertexts, it only receives encrypted digits, but it do not know the meaning of these digits, and these digits are the disturbed digits. Therefore, there is no more than one-half probability to guess the original true digit, and with random perturbation can achieve indistinguishable.

5.2 Security Under the Data Owner's Attack

It is security about the original data set of any data owner, since there is no any communication about original data set among data owners in our scheme. For each data owner, they may do the key's times attack. For example, data owner A has finished an anomaly detection task with the sketch tables received from server C, and obtain the density $Density(x)$ of an instance x. He may try to guess the times in others sketch table by subtracting the $density(x)$ obtained from his own sketch table. Assume the received sketch tables of data owner A are combined with Q data owners, and then he can only get the sum density of others, $Density(x) - density(x) = \sum_{q=1}^{Q-1} density_q(x)$. Analysis the value $Density(x) - density(x)$, he only can know whether there are other participants, and can not defer any other privacy information with more than one-half probability. Therefore, for any data owners, they only can know their own data set and the density value of their data set in our scheme.

6   Experimental Evaluation

In this section, we evaluate the proposed anomaly detection algorithm in terms of AUC value and running time. First, we demonstrate the utility of our proposed detection algorithm with all original databases under single-party participation. Then, we will analyze the performance of our algorithm by encrypted data with multiple parties participation.

For comparability, we implemented all experiments on our workstation with 2.5 GHz, 64 bits operation system, 4 cores CPU and 16 GB RAM, and the algorithms codes are built in Python 2.7.

6.1 Evaluation Metrics and Experimental Setup

Metics: In our experiment, we use Area Under Curve (AUC) as the evaluation metric with other classic anomaly detection algorithms. AUC denotes the area under of Receiver Operating Characteristic (ROC) curve, and it illustrates the diagnostic ability of a binary classifier system. AUC is created by plotting the true positive rate against the false positive rate at various threshold settings[1]. The anomaly detection algorithms with larger AUC value have the better accuracy, otherwise, the anomaly detection algorithms are less effective.

Experimental Setup: There are two experiments. In the first experiment, we compare our proposed algorithm LDEM with other state-of-art algorithms. These compared algorithms contain RS-Forest [23], LOF [3], ABOD [12], iForest [15,16], HiCS [10] and RDOS [21]. RS-Forest is rapid density estimator for streaming and static anomaly detection. iForest detects anomaly instances based on the average path of instances in isolation forest. ABOD determines anomaly instances based on the angle among instances. RDOS determines anomaly instances according to the local density distribution. The parameters of these algorithms are set to the value suggested in the original paper. And all the above algorithms are executed on the data sets from UCI Repository[2], and these data sets are summarized in Table 5. Since many of these data sets contain more than two class labels, it needs some preprocessing operations to obtain the data sets which are suitable for anomaly detection. We preprocess these data sets according to some of the commonly used principles in the literature. In the second experiment, we evaluate the performance of our algorithm under the multiple parties participation. We assume each data set in Table 5 is the sum of all participants. We can randomly sample a part of each data set in Table 5, as the data set of data owner A. Then, we will compare the detection accuracy on the whole data sets and the data set A.

6.2 Performance Efficiency of LDEM

In this section, we will analysis the performance in terms of AUC value and running time, and we will analysis the impact of the number of components on the results of our algorithm.

Accuracy Analysis: For fairness, we build up our algorithm and reproduce all compared algorithms in Python Language. All algorithms are executed many times to obtain stable results on all data sets in Table 5. The experiment results are shown in Table 6. The column LDEM* is the results of our algorithm, and the other columns are the results of other algorithms. It is clear that the AUC value of our algorithm has a great improvement than all compared algorithms on eight out of ten data sets, and there is an approximate AUC value with the best algorithms on the other two data sets. LDEM has the largest improvement of 46% on the breast data set. Our algorithm can achieve the 0.7 or even larger AUC

---

[1] https://en.wikipedia.org/wiki/Receiver_operating_characteristic.
[2] http://archive.ics.uci.edu/ml/datasets.html.

Table 5. Data sets information

Data set	Instances	Attribute	Anomaly ratio (%)
Breast	569	30	37.3
Ann_thyroid	7200	6	7.4
Waveform	1727	21	4.6
Ecoli	336	7	2.7
Optdigits	3823	64	9.8
Arrhythmia	452	272	14.6
Pima	768	8	34.9
Satellite	6435	36	31.6
Shuttle	14500	9	6.0
Epileptic	11500	178	20.0

value on most of these data sets, while each of the all compared algorithms have extremely poor performance on one or more data sets. What's more, although some of these data sets are high dimensional data sets (*Arrhythmia, Epileptic*), our algorithm also can get the good detection results. This illustrates that it is significant to estimate the density of instance based on the densities of all features, and these AUC values prove the effectiveness of our algorithm.

Table 6. AUC comparion of different anomaly detection algorithms on many benchmark data sets. And the best results are in bold font.

Data set	LDEM*	LOF	iForest	HiCS	ABOD	RS-Forest	RDOS
Breast	**0.913**	0.629	0.84	0.593	0.759	0.71	0.512
Ann_thyroid	**0.953**	0.72	0.81	0.951	0.506	0.68	0.716
Waveform	**0.841**	0.611	0.725	0.626	0.589	0.785	0.61
Ecoli	0.849	0.863	0.854	0.737	0.847	**0.866**	0.756
Optdigits	**0.825**	0.615	0.727	0.391	0.721	0.683	0.5
Arrhythmia	**0.789**	0.69	0.80	0.623	0.808	0.695	0.746
Pima	**0.697**	0.513	0.67	0.581	0.531	0.49	0.513
Satellite	**0.837**	0.52	0.71	0.529	0.725	0.7	0.517
Shuttle	0.991	0.55	**1.00**	0.586	0.542	**0.998**	0.623
Epileptic	**0.981**	0.57	0.98	0.668	0.988	0.88	0.585

Running Time Analysis: To illustrate that our algorithm not only gets good detection results, but also needs less running time. We do an experiment to compare the running time of all aforementioned algorithms on the selected four data sets with different size from Table 5. The results of this experiment are shown in Fig. 2. From this Fig, it can be easily seen that the running time of our algorithm is larger than RS-Forest, but less than LOF, FastABOD and RDOS, since these three algorithms all need two much distance calculation. Compare with these three algorithms, LDEM takes distances into account by the mapping function, so it does not need any distance calculation. What's more, our algorithm LDEM only need $O(N)$ time complexity.

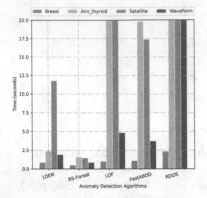

Fig. 2. Running time of these algorithms on four of the data sets.

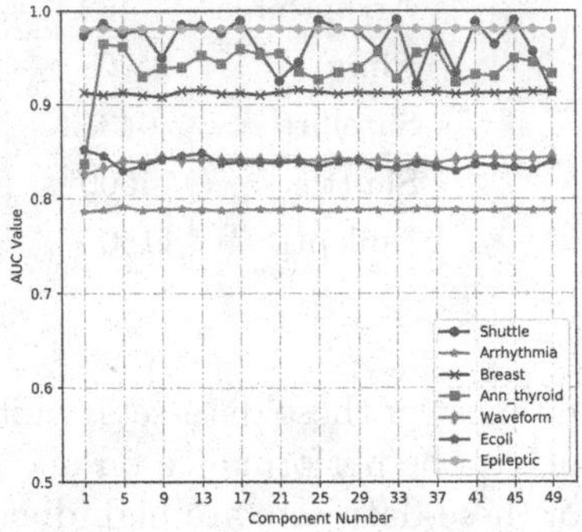

Fig. 3. Sensitive analysis of the parameter M.

Sensitivity Analysis: In our algorithm, there is only one parameters, the number of components M, which can affect the detection accuracy. In this experiment, we will record the AUC value of these ten data sets, when the range of this number is from 1 to 50. The results are shown in Fig. 3. From this fig, we can notice that our algorithm is not sensitive on most of these data sets. The AUC value of over half of data sets has not any fluctuation. Only a few data sets have small fluctuations in their values. As a result, this experiment can illustrate that our algorithm is insensitive to parameter M.

6.3   Performance Efficiency of PPLDEM

In this section, we will present the improvement of our algorithm under multiple participants. In this experiment, we assume each data set in Table 5 is composed of the corresponding data sets of all data owners, and assume that there is a data owner A who wants to do an anomaly detection task. We will randomly sample a part of the original data sets in Table 5, as the data set of data owner A. The sample size of all data sets are summarized in second column of Table 7. Then, we will calculate the AUC value of these data sets based on the sketch tables obtained from the data set of data set A and the sketch tables obtained from the data sets of all participants. The results based on the sketch tables obtained from the data set of data owner A are recorded in the third column *STDSA* of

Table 7, and the results based on the sketch tables obtained from the data sets of all participants are recorded in the fourth column $STDSAP$ of Table 7. Since data sets of data owner A are sampled randomly, the results in Table 7 are the average values of executing 50 times this experiments. Compare the results of these two columns, it can be seen that the column $STDSAP$ has a better AUC value on most of all data sets. Hence, from this experiment, it can prove that our algorithm is effective under multiple participants.

Table 7. AUC value on different sketch tables. STDSA denotes the sketch table obtained from only data owner A, and STDSAP denotes the sketch tables from all participants.

Data set	Sample size	STDSA	STDSAP
Breast	227	0.8239	**0.8762**
Ann_thyroid	2160	**0.95**	**0.95**
Waveform	800	0.8351	**0.8365**
Ecoli	134	0.83	**0.9159**
Optdigits	1146	0.7103	**0.7125**
Arrhythmia	135	0.8087	**0.8094**
Pima	230	0.679	**0.685**
Satellite	1930	0.8135	**0.8141**
Shuttle	4350	**0.9873**	**0.9873**
Epileptic	3450	0.9812	**0.9813**

7   Conclusions

In this paper, we first propose a fast local density estimation method LDEM, which can be used in anomaly detection. Then, we extend this algorithm to the case of multi-party participants, and we propose an efficient scheme PPLDEM to detect anomaly instances with considering privacy protection under multi-party participants. LDEM obtains the local density of instances by calculating the average local density of all features, and the local density of each feature can be estimated by the defined mapping function. Compare with the existing density-based algorithms, LDEM does not any distance calculation, and it only need $O(N)$ time complexity. PPLDEM is finished with the aid of a cloud, and this cloud is composed of two servers, server S and server C. In our scheme, the detection stage of PPLDEM are executed in each participant own, based on the sketch tables requested from server C. So compare with the existing anomaly detection algorithms with privacy preserving, our scheme need less communication cost and less calculation, under the premise of ensuring safety and detection accuracy. And experiments and theoretical analysis show that our proposed scheme PPLDEM can detect anomaly instances effectively and efficiently.

Acknowledgment. This study was supported by the Shenzhen Research Council (Grant No. JSGG20170822160842949, JCYJ20170307151518535).

References

1. Bendlin, R., Damgård, I., Orlandi, C., Zakarias, S.: Semi-homomorphic encryption and multiparty computation. In: Paterson, K.G. (ed.) EUROCRYPT 2011. LNCS, vol. 6632, pp. 169–188. Springer, Heidelberg (2011). https://doi.org/10.1007/978-3-642-20465-4_11
2. Bresson, E., Catalano, D., Pointcheval, D.: A simple public-key cryptosystem with a double trapdoor decryption mechanism and its applications. In: Laih, C.-S. (ed.) ASIACRYPT 2003. LNCS, vol. 2894, pp. 37–54. Springer, Heidelberg (2003). https://doi.org/10.1007/978-3-540-40061-5_3
3. Breunig, M.M., Kriegel, H.P., Ng, R.T., Sander, J.: LOF: identifying density-based local outliers, vol. 29, no. 2, pp. 93–104 (2000)
4. Chen, Z., Fu, A.W.-C., Tang, J.: On complementarity of cluster and outlier detection schemes. In: Kambayashi, Y., Mohania, M., Wöß, W. (eds.) DaWaK 2003. LNCS, vol. 2737, pp. 234–243. Springer, Heidelberg (2003). https://doi.org/10.1007/978-3-540-45228-7_24
5. Duan, L., Xiong, D., Lee, J., Guo, F.: A local density based spatial clustering algorithm with noise. In: IEEE International Conference on Systems, Man and Cybernetics, pp. 978–986 (2007)
6. ElGamal, T.: A public key cryptosystem and a signature scheme based on discrete logarithms. IEEE Trans. Inf. Theor. **31**(4), 469–472 (1985)
7. Gao, J., Hu, W., Zhang, Z.M., Zhang, X., Wu, O.: RKOF: robust kernel-based local outlier detection. In: Huang, J.Z., Cao, L., Srivastava, J. (eds.) PAKDD 2011. LNCS (LNAI), vol. 6635, pp. 270–283. Springer, Heidelberg (2011). https://doi.org/10.1007/978-3-642-20847-8_23
8. He, Z., Xu, X., Deng, S.: Discovering cluster-based local outliers. Pattern Recogn. Lett. **24**(9–10), 1641–1650 (2003)
9. Kantarcıoğlu, M., Clifton, C.: Privately computing a distributed k-nn classifier. In: Boulicaut, J.-F., Esposito, F., Giannotti, F., Pedreschi, D. (eds.) PKDD 2004. LNCS (LNAI), vol. 3202, pp. 279–290. Springer, Heidelberg (2004). https://doi.org/10.1007/978-3-540-30116-5_27
10. Keller, F., Muller, E., Bohm, K.: HiCS: high contrast subspaces for density-based outlier ranking. In: IEEE International Conference on Data Engineering, pp. 1037–1048 (2012)
11. Knorr, E.M., Ng, R.T.: Algorithms for mining distance-based outliers in large datasets. In: International Conference on Very Large Data Bases, pp. 392–403 (1998)
12. Kriegel, H.P., S Hubert, M., Zimek, A.: Angle-based outlier detection in high-dimensional data, pp. 444–452 (2008). Dbs.ifi.lmu.de
13. Li, L., Huang, L., Yang, W., Yao, X., Liu, A.: Privacy-preserving LOF outlier detection. Knowl. Inf. Syst. **42**(3), 579–597 (2015)
14. Lin, X., Clifton, C., Zhu, M.: Privacy-preserving clustering with distributed EM mixture modeling. Knowl. Inf. Syst. **8**(1), 68–81 (2005)

15. Liu, F.T., Kai, M.T., Zhou, Z.H.: Isolation-based anomaly detection. ACM Trans. Knowl. Discov. Data **6**(1), 1–39 (2012)
16. Liu, F.T., Ting, K.M., Zhou, Z.H.: Isolation forest. In: 2008 Eighth IEEE International Conference on Data Mining, ICDM 2008, pp. 413–422. IEEE (2008)
17. Liu, X., Deng, R.H., Choo, K.K.R., Weng, J.: An efficient privacy-preserving outsourced calculation toolkit with multiple keys. IEEE Trans. Inf. Forensics Secur. **11**(11), 2401–2414 (2016)
18. Damgård, I., Pastro, V., Smart, N., Zakarias, S.: Multiparty computation from somewhat homomorphic encryption. In: Safavi-Naini, R., Canetti, R. (eds.) CRYPTO 2012. LNCS, vol. 7417, pp. 643–662. Springer, Heidelberg (2012). https://doi.org/10.1007/978-3-642-32009-5_38
19. Peter, A., Tews, E., Katzenbeisser, S.: Efficiently outsourcing multiparty computation under multiple keys. IEEE Trans. Inf. Forensics Secur. **8**(12), 2046–2058 (2013)
20. Sugiyama, M., Borgwardt, K.M.: Rapid distance-based outlier detection via sampling. In: Advances in Neural Information Processing Systems, pp. 467–475 (2013)
21. Tang, B., He, H.: A local density-based approach for outlier detection. Neurocomputing **241**, 171–180 (2017)
22. Wang, X., Wang, X.L., Wilkes, M.: A fast distance-based outlier detection technique. In: Poster and Workshop Proceedings of Industrial Conference Advances in Data Mining, ICDM 2008, Leipzig, Germany, 2008 July, pp. 25–44 (2008)
23. Wu, K., Zhang, K., Fan, W., Edwards, A., Yu, P.S.: RS-forest: a rapid density estimator for streaming anomaly detection 2014, pp. 600–609 (2014)
24. Zhang, C., Liu, H., Yin, A.: Research of detection algorithm for time series abnormal subsequence. In: Zou, B., Li, M., Wang, H., Song, X., Xie, W., Lu, Z. (eds.) ICPCSEE 2017. CCIS, vol. 727, pp. 12–26. Springer, Singapore (2017). https://doi.org/10.1007/978-981-10-6385-5_2
25. Zhang, C., Yin, A., Deng, Y., Tian, P., Wang, X., Dong, L.: A novel anomaly detection algorithm based on trident tree. In: Luo, M., Zhang, L.-J. (eds.) CLOUD 2018. LNCS, vol. 10967, pp. 295–306. Springer, Cham (2018). https://doi.org/10.1007/978-3-319-94295-7_20

Towards Secure Cloud Data Similarity Retrieval: Privacy Preserving Near-Duplicate Image Data Detection

Yulin Wu[1], Xuan Wang[1], Zoe L. Jiang[1(✉)], Xuan Li[2], Jin Li[3], S. M. Yiu[4],
Zechao Liu[1], Hainan Zhao[1], and Chunkai Zhang[1]

[1] School of Computer Science and Technology, Harbin Institute of Technology
(Shenzhen), Shenzhen, China
{yulinwu,wangxuan,liuzechao}@cs.hitsz.edu.cn, zoeljiang@hit.edu.cn,
hainan.hh@gmail.com, ckzhang812@gmail.com

[2] College of mathematics and informatics, Fujian Normal University, Fuzhou, China
jessieli24@163.com

[3] School of Computational Science and Education Software, Guangzhou University,
Guangzhou, China
jinli71@gmail.com

[4] The University of Hong Kong, Pok Fu Lam, Hong Kong SAR, China
smyiu@cs.hku.hk

Abstract. As the development of cloud computing technology, cloud storage service has been widely used these years. People upload most of their data files to the cloud for saving local storage space and making data sharing available everywhere. Except for storage service, data similarity retrieval is another basic service that cloud provides, especially for image data. As demand for near-duplicate image detection increases, it has been an attracted research topic in cloud image data similarity retrieval in resent years. However, due to some image data (like medical images and face recognition images) contains important privacy information, it is preferred to support privacy protection in cloud image data similarity retrieval. In this paper, focusing on image data stored in the cloud, we propose a privacy preserving near-duplicate image data detection scheme based on the LSH algorithm. In particular, users would use their own image data to generate image-feature LSH metadata vector using LSH algorithm and would store both the ciphertexts of image data and image-feature LSH metadata vector in cloud. When the inquirer queries the near-duplicate image data, he would generate the image-feature query token LSH metadata vector using LSH algorithm and send it to cloud. With the query token, cloud will execute the privacy-preserving near-duplicate image data detection and return the encrypted result to inquirer. Then the inquirer would decrypt the ciphertext and get the final result. Our security and performance analysis shows that the proposed scheme achieves the goals of privacy preserving and lightweight.

Keywords: Near-duplicate · Privacy preserving
LSH algorithm · Cloud image data · Lightweight

J. Vaidya and J. Li (Eds.): ICA3PP 2018, LNCS 11337, pp. 374–388, 2018.
https://doi.org/10.1007/978-3-030-05063-4_29

1 Introduction

On the basis of IDC report [1], the total global data will be more than 40ZB by 2020 (equivalent to 40 trillion gigabytes). Cloud storage services has been one of the most crucial part in cloud computing for users' daily cloud life. One of the biggest advantages for users is to save the local storage space and access data at anytime and anywhere. Given the fact that people perform same task on different devices, cloud storage services can provide a convenient, high-efficient, real-time way for users to store, access and synchronize data from multiple different devices.

Further, in order to reduce the consumption of storage resources and network bandwidth for both users and cloud storage servers, the cloud services providers can resort to cross-user deduplication scheme, that is, if one user wants to upload the same file that has already been stored in the cloud, cloud services provider will detect the fact that this particular file has already been uploaded by some other user previously, and then it will remain store only one copy in cloud storage and save users' data upload costs at the same time. This is the initial idea for using deduplicate detection scheme to save storage and bandwidth.

When it comes to the problem of data privacy, cryptography algorithms should be considered to meet the privacy needs. There have been lots of schemes working on this issue through the Convergent Encryption (CE) [2]. This promises to realize file deduplication with considering ensure the privacy of user data. It first encrypts the file with a convergent key which is derived from the hash value of the data content itself. The user uploads the ciphertext of data file to the cloud. As the encryption is deterministic, identical data file copies will generate the same corresponding convergent key and ciphertext, thus the cloud services provider will detect the duplication on the ciphertexts. Also, when the users want to download, the encrypted data file can only be decrypted by the data file owner, no matter whether he is the original uploader or not. Later, Bellare et. al proposed message-locked encryption (MLE) in [3], in which they not only provided security analysis for CE, but also define a primitive message-locked encryption (MLE) for secure deduplication. CE is a particular MLE scheme in which the convergent key is derived by hashing the data file itself. However, The previous work only considered the duplicate files which means that only when the two files are complete same or exact duplicate, the above cryptography algorithms can work.

However, there are many near-duplicate data files exist in data storage setting. This kind of files not only contains the duplicates of text data also some image data files that have been transformed by scaling, rotation, cropping and contrast & bright changes. People would like to detect these near-duplicate files and store some of them to represent all of these near-duplicate images to save storage space and realize efficient image data management. At the same time, they also want privacy protection to against some ulterior motives attackers. But the traditional secure data deduplication scheme cannot be applied to construct secure near-duplicate data detection scheme directly as we explained above.

In this paper, for secure cloud data similarity retrieval, we propose a near-duplicate image data detection scheme, inspired by Wang et.al's work [4]. We allow the cloud services provider to return the near-duplicate image data file to users who queries that.

To summarize, we make the following contributions:

Based on the LSH algorithm and symmetric encryption, we design the near-duplicate image data detection scheme, which realizes near-duplicate feature matching and privacy protection. With the security and performance analysis, it proves that we achieve the following design goals: privacy preserving, query correctness and lightweight.

The rest of this paper is organized as follows: We give some related work on this topic in Sect. 2. Problem statement including the system model, threat model and design goals is presented in Sect. 3. Then we introduce several preliminaries in Sect. 4. Detailed design is presented in Sect. 5. The security analysis and performance evaluation of our mechanism are shown in Sect. 6. Finally, we conclude this paper in Sect. 7.

2 Related Work

Harnik et al. [5] proposed several attacks caused by client-side data deduplicion. The most important one is that the adversary can get knowledge of whether the data file exists in the cloud by guessing the hash value of the predictable messages. In [6,7] the schemes called Proofs of Ownership (PoW) are proposed to against the above attack. PoW is derivated from the Proof of Retrievalbility (PoR) and Proof of Data Possession (PDP) to enable the user to prove that he himself truly possesses the outsourced file. In [7], Halevi et al. proposed a Merkle tree PoW scheme which had better performance on construction and verification of PoW. But this scheme does not consider any kind of leakage setting. Later Xu et al. [8] followed [7] and proposed client-side deduplication in a waker leakage setting. Di Pietro et al. [6] reduced the communication complexity of [7], but introduced additional server computation cost. In [2], Douceur et al. proposed the convergent encryption (CE) which ensures data privacy during the deduplication process. It is the determinisitic encryption in which the encryption key is derived from message itself. But this encryption only provide confidentiality for unpredictable messages and is not semantically secure. Later, Bellare et al. formalized above primitive as message-locked encryption in [3]. Tan et al. [9] proposed SAM for cloud backup service to achieve an optimal trade-off between efficiency and overhead of deduplication. Fu et al. [10] proposed AA-Dedupe devote a lot in reducing the computational overhead, increasing transfer efficiency and throughput. Xu et al. [11] proposed SHHC which focuses on improving efficiency on fingerprint storage and search mechanism. Li et al. [12] focused on key-management issue on block-level secure data deduplication. With aid of Ramp secret sharing scheme (RSSS), they distributed the key across serveral key server. In [13], Li et al. proposed a hybrid cloud architecture to design the authorized data deduplication scheme. And they also improved the reliability of the distributed privacy-preserving deduplication system in [14]. Bellare et al. [15] focused on deduplicated-data confidentiality and proposed a system called DupLESS, which resorts to the Convergent Encryption(CE)-type base Message Locked Encryption(MLE) scheme to support secure deduplication and against brute-force attacks. Stanek et al. [16] proposed deduplication scheme which provides different security levels for two-class data: popular and unpopular data, and achieves a better trade-off between security and efficiency. In their scheme, the traditional convergent encryption is applied to the popular data which is not sensitive enough and the two-layered encryption scheme is applied to unpopular data for stronger secure guarantee.

Near-duplicate detection mainly consists of two phases: near-duplicate feature extraction and near-duplicate feature match. Considering the combination with cryptography, we focus on the data independent algorithm to generate the index structure. As known, the locality-sensitive hashing (LSH) [17] has been widely used in near-duplicate image detection. The main idea of LSH algorithm is to hash the input points into different buckets with a set of particular hash functions. Thus, in a certain range of adjacent data points in original data space will be mapped to the same bucket with high probability and the non-adjacent data in a certain range will be mapped to the same bucket with quite low probability. Note that each image feature can be represented as a point in the high-dimensional space. The LSH-based near-duplicate image detection schemes often consist of two stages. At the first stage, the scheme uses LSH to efficiently find the near-duplicate candidates set. While for the second stage, the scheme search the candidates set for exhaustive final results. Ke et al. [18] first used LSH in near-duplicate image detection scheme and proposed a system focusing on detecting copyright violations and foraged images based on near-duplicate detection and sub-image retrieval scheme. Qamra et al. [19] worked hard on the similarity distance functions and scalability in near-duplicate image recognition. Chum et al. [20] focused on the large image and video databases and propose two near duplicate detection for both image and video-shot. Hu et al. [21] used the examplar near-duplicates to learn a distance measure metric and incorporate it into the locality-sensitive hash for retrieval. However, all above works are in the plaintext domain.

In these years, some near-duplicate detection schemes have already shifted their attention on the ciphertext domain. In [22], Kuzu et al. achieved similarity search on encrypted data by using the LSH and secure index they built. But the scheme incurs a waste of index space. In [23], Cui et al. based on the SIFT features built a secure cloud-assisted mobile image sharing system. Yuan et al. [24] proposed a low latency similarity index scheme. In [25], Cui et al. combined LSH algorithm with multi-key searchable encryption to design an effective and secure near-duplicate detection system in encrypted in-network storage environment. In [26], Yuan et al.worked hard on searching similarity joins in ciphertext domain with LSH algorithm and searchable encryption, but did not focus on the image data.

It is easy to think of using encryption techniques to strengthen the protection of data privacy, but it is hard to come up with ideas on addressing privacy-preserving problems on near-duplicate image data detection in cloud.

3   Problem Statement

In this section, we first illustrate the system model contains three entities: the cloud storage server, the content providers and the inquirers. Second, we define the two types of attackers: the inside and outside ones. At last, we elaborate our design goals.

3.1   System Model

Our system involves three entities: the cloud storage server, the content providers and the inquirers, as shown in Fig. 1. Their roles are described below:

- The cloud storage server: It is managed by the cloud service provider to mainly provide data storage service for content providers. At the same time, it can provide the near-duplicate file query service for the inquirers.
- The content providers: They outsource the encrypted file to the cloud storage server, as well as the encrypted image feature LSH metadata vector for near-duplicate file detection.
- The inquirers: They have the requirements to query the one file's near-duplicate version, and send the query token to the cloud storage server.

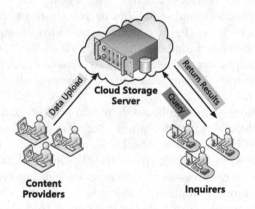

Fig. 1. System model of near-duplicate detection

3.2   Threat Model

Our threat model considers two types of attackers which are described below:

- Outside Attackers: They may intercept some valuable knowledge (eg. the encrypted image feature LSH metadata) via the public channel, and can pretend to be the real inquirers to query the near-duplicate file stored in the cloud storage server.
- Inside Attackers: They are semi-honest, which means that they may have partial knowledge of the whole cloud database for inferring the content providers' plaintext data contents. But they will follow the protocol strictly. The inside attacker refers to the cloud storage server in our system.

3.3   Design Goals

- Query Correctness: to ensure that the content providers can return correct near-duplicate file to the inquirer.
- Privacy Preserving: to ensure that the semi-honest cloud storage server cannot derive or infer any data of content providers from information which it can collect during the content providers' uploading phase.
- Lightweight: to ensure that the cloud can inform near-duplicate detection with the minimum communication and computation cost.

4   Preliminaries

In this section, we briefly introduce some preliminaries including symmetric encryption, bilinear map, and locality-sensitive hashing. The first cryptography tool is to protect user's data privacy efficiently. And the last two are the basis of constructing near-duplicate detection scheme. Note that the property of bilinear map is the key point to design detection algorithm.

4.1   Symmetric Encryption

Symmetric encryption realizes messages encryption and decryption with a common secret key k. A symmetric encryption scheme is a tuple of probabilistic polynomial-time algorithms (Gen, Enc, Dec) such that:

(1) The key-generation algorithm $Gen(1^n) \to k$: takes as input 1^n and outputs a key k. Note that 1^n is the security parameter written in unary, and assume that without loss of generality any key k output by this algorithm satisfies $\mid k \mid \geq n$.

(2) The encryption algorithm $Enc_k(m) \to c$: takes as input a key k and a plaintext message $m \in 0,1^*$, then outputs a ciphertext c. Note that Enc may be randomized if it needs.

(3) The decryption algorithm $Dec_k(c) := m$: takes as input a key k and a ciphertext c, then outputs a message m or an error. Denote that a generic error by the symbol $\perp$, and assume that Dec is deterministic.

4.2 Bilinear Map

Let $\mathbb{G}_1$, $\mathbb{G}_2$, and $\mathbb{G}_T$ be multiplicative cyclic groups of prime order p. Bilinear map e is a map: $\mathbb{G}_1 \times \mathbb{G}_2 \to \mathbb{G}_T$ with following properties:

(1) Computable: for computing map e, there exists an efficient algorithm.
(2) Bilinear: for all $u \in \mathbb{G}_1$, $v \in \mathbb{G}_2$ and $a, b \in \mathbb{Z}_p$, there exists $e(u^a, v^b) = e(u, v)^{ab}$.
(3) Nondegenerate: there exists $e(g_1, g_2) \neq 1$, where g_1 and g_2 are generators of G_1 and G_2 , respectively.

4.3 Locality-Sensitive Hashing

Locality-sensitive Hashing(LSH) aims to solve the $(R, c) - NN$ problem by mapping similar items into the same buckets with high probability, while mapping the dissimilar items into the same buckets with low probability. LSH is based on the definition of LSH family, which is a hash function family with the property to realize that similar items collide with higher probability than dissimilar items. Denote $B(o, r) = \{q \mid d(o, q) \leq r\}$ as a sphere with center o and radius r. Denote W as the points set domain. The LSH family is defined as follows:

The hash family $H = \{h : S \to U\}$ is $(r_1, r_2, p_1, p_2) - sensitive$ for any points $w, n \in W$,

- if $w \in B(n, r_1)$ then $Pr_H[h(n) = h(w)] \geq p_1$
- if $w \notin B(n, r_2)$ then $Pr_H[h(n) = h(w)] \leq p_2$

Note that the parameter r_1, r_2, p_1, p_2 should satisfy $p_1 > p_2$ and $r_1 < r_2$

With aid of [27], we can solve the $(R, c) - NN$ problem as follows: On the basis of above definition, denote $r_1 = R$ and $r_2 = c \cdot R$. Define a hash family $G = \{g_i : S \to U\}$ such that $g_i(v) = (h_1(v), \ldots, h_k(v))$, where $h_i \in H$, and uniformly at random choose L hash functions $g_1, \ldots, g_L$ from G, and process every input point w in the bucket $g_i(w)$, where $i = 1, ..., L$. Later, for querying a point q, the enquirer checks all the buckets $g_1(q), \ldots, g_L(q)$. For every point v_i that encounters in the same bucket, check if $v_i \in B(n, r_2)$, if so return YES and the point v_i, else return NO.

5 Privacy Preserving Near-Duplicate Image Data Detection Scheme

In this section, we first give a brief description of the scheme and divide the process into five phases. And then we illustrate it in construction details with the aid of symmetric encryption, bilinear map, and locality-sensitive hashing.

5.1   Brief Description

The general process of the scheme is that the content provider will upload files to the cloud storage server for storage service. We assume that the cloud storage server is semi-honest, which means that it will operate correctly on the scheme and intend to infer much information from the stored data. When an inquirer send the query to find the near-duplicate file sets of some file, the cloud storage server will execute the near-duplicate detection algorithm and return the final result removed some false positive candidate results. Specifically, this scheme contains five phases:

1. **Setup Phase:** The content provider generates the system parameters consist of public and private parameters.
2. **Data Upload Phase:** The content provider processes image data file with fingerprint techniques to generate image-feature metadata vector, and with the aid of LSH algorithm to generate the image-feature LSH metadata vector, and then encrypt the image-feature LSH metadata vector. Finally, the content provider uploads the encrypted data file and the encrypted image-feature LSH metadata vector to the cloud storage server.
3. **Query Token Upload Phase:** The inquirer generates the image-feature query token metadata vector with fingerprint techniques from the queried image data file, and utilizes LSH algorithm to generate image-feature query token LSH metadata vector, and then generates the challenge message and related parameters calculated from the image-feature query token LSH metadata vector. Finally, the user uploads the challenge message and corresponding parameters to the cloud storage server.
4. **Near-duplicate Detection Phase:** The cloud storage server utilizes a matching equation to match the queried image data file with all the image data files stored in the cloud storage server previously, and get the candidate near-duplicate results.
5. **False Positives Reduce Phase:** The cloud storage server uses Yao's garbled circuits to get more accurate results based on the candidate set.

5.2   Detailed Description

Setup Phase: Denote $\mathbb{G}_1$, $\mathbb{G}_2$ and $\mathbb{G}_T$ as multiplicative cyclic groups of prime order p, and define the bilinear map $e : \mathbb{G}_1 \times \mathbb{G}_2 \to \mathbb{G}_T$, where g is the generator of $\mathbb{G}_2$. Define two hash functions $H(\cdot) : \{0,1\}^* \to \mathbb{G}_1$(i.e. uniformly maps arbitrary strings to $\mathbb{G}_1$), also define $h(\cdot) : \mathbb{G}_T \to \mathbb{Z}_p$ (i.e. uniformly maps group element of $\mathbb{G}_T$ to $\mathbb{Z}_p$). The content provider(abbr. CP) then takes KeyGen algorithm to generate the system public and secret parameters as follows: (1) The CP of group j is distriputed a random group signing key pair (spk_j, ssk_j), a random parameter $\alpha_j \leftarrow \mathbb{Z}_p$ and another random parameter $\beta \leftarrow \mathbb{G}_1$; (2) The CP computes $\gamma \leftarrow g^{\alpha_j}$; (3) The CP sets the system secret and public parameter as $SK_j = (\alpha_j, ssk_j)$ and $PK = (spk_j, \gamma, g, \beta, e(\beta, \gamma))$ respectively. Note that we assume a group consist of content providers and inquirers has the same group signing key and secret key(i.e. the users of group j G_j all have the same signing key pair (spk_j, ssk_j) and the same secret key SK_j).

Data Upload Phase: As for an image data file I that the content provider (abbr. CP) wants to upload to cloud storage server, the CP processes the image data file as follows: (1) The CP utilizes fingerprint techniques to generate the image-feature metadata vector $F_I = \{f_{I,1}, f_{I,2}, \ldots, f_{I,l}\}$; (2) The CP uses the LSH algorithm to generate the image-feature LSH metadata vector that is $W_I = \{w_{I,1}, w_{I,2}, \ldots, w_{I,l}\}$ from image-feature metadata vector $F_I = \{f_{I,1}, f_{I,2}, \ldots, f_{I,l}\}$; (3) The CP encrypts every $w_{I,i} \in W_I$ with sk_j to generate encrypted image-feature LSH metadata vector $C_I = \{c_{I,1}, c_{I,2}, \cdots, c_{I,l}\}$, by $c_{I,i} \leftarrow (H(t_i) \cdot \beta^{w_i})^{\alpha_j} \in \mathbb{G}_1, i \in [1, l]$. Here, $t_i = GID \| i$, where GID is the identifier of the group that the CP belongs to and is uniformly chosen from group Z_p ; (4) The CP also computes $T_I = GID \| Sig_{ssk_j}(GID)$ as the group identifier for group j, where $Sig_{ssk_j}(GID)$ is the signature with the CP's private group j signing key ssk_j; (5) The CP sends the encrypted image data file I', the encrypted image-feature LSH metadata vector $C_I = \{c_{I,1}, c_{I,2}, \cdots, c_{I,l}\}$, and the group tag $T_I = GID \| Sig_{ssk_j}(GID)$ together as (I_E, C_I, T_I) to the cloud storage server, and deletes local copy from the local storage system.

Query Token Upload Phase: For the queried image data file Q, the inquirer processes the query image data file as follows: (1) The inquirer uses the fingerprint techniques to generate the image-feature query token metadata vector $F_Q = \{f_{Q,1}, f_{Q,2}, \ldots, f_{Q,l}\}$ of the queried image data file Q; (2) The inquirer uses the LSH algorithm to generate the image-feature query token LSH metadata vector $W_Q = \{w_{Q,1}, w_{Q,2}, \cdots, w_{Q,l}\}$; (3) The inquirer generates the challenge message *"chal"* for the cloud storage server to efficiently match the query in the subsequent phase. To generate the challenge message *"chal"*, the inquirer randomly chooses a value v_i for each element $i \in [1, l]$ which means the i-th position element of the image-feature query token LSH metadata vector $W_Q = \{w_{Q,1}, w_{Q,2}, \cdots, w_{Q,l}\}$, defined as $chal = \{(i, ch_i)\}_{i \in [1,l]}$; (4) The inquirer randomly chooses a value $k \leftarrow \mathbb{Z}_p$, and then calculates $K = e(\beta, \gamma)^k \in \mathbb{G}_T$; (5) The inquirer defines $x = \sum_{i \in [1,l]}(ch_i w_{Q,i})$ as the linear combination of i-th element specified in $chal = \{(i, ch_i)\}_{i \in [1,l]}$; (6) The inquirer blinds x with mask k to generate $X = k + \kappa x \mod p$, where $\kappa = h(K) \in \mathbb{Z}_p$; (7) The inquirer sends the challenge message $chal = \{(i, ch_i)\}_{i \in [1,l]}$, $X = k + \kappa x \mod p$ and the value $K = e(\beta, \gamma)^k \in \mathbb{G}_T$ as $(chal, X, K)$ to the cloud storage server.

Near-duplicate Detection Phase: Inspired by Wang et.al's work [4], we design that upon receiving the encrypted image-feature LSH metadata vector $C_I = \{c_{I,1}, c_{I,2}, \cdots, c_{I,l}\}$ and the group tag $T_I = GID \| Sig_{ssk_j}(GID)$ from the user, and the challenge message $chal = \{(i, ch_i)\}_{i \in [1,l]}$, X and K from the inquirer, the cloud storage server: (1)Verifies the signature $Sig_{ssk_j}(GID)$ with spk_j. If the verification fails, the cloud storage server outputs FALSE, else continues; (2) Computes an aggregated value based on the encrypted image-feature LSH metadata vector $C_{I'} = \{c_{I',1}, c_{I',2}, \cdots, c_{I',l}\}$ for each image data file I' stored in the cloud storage server: $\sigma = \prod_{i \in [1,l]}(c_{I',i})^{ch_i} \in \mathbb{G}_1$, where $c_{I',i}$ is the i-th element of the encrypted image-feature LSH metadata vector $C_{I'} = \{c_{I',1}, c_{I',2}, \ldots, c_{I',l}\}$; (3) Computes $\kappa = h(K)$; (4) Checks the matching Eq. (1) for the queried image data file Q and all the stored image data file I' with the corresponding parameters. If the equation holds, then the checked image data file I' can be returned as one of the candidate results; Else, the image data file I' will be ruled out, and comes to match the next image data file I' with the Eq. (1) in the cloud storage system until all the stored image data file I' have been checked.

$$K \cdot e(\sigma^\kappa, g) \overset{?}{=} e((\prod_{i \in I}(H(t_i)^{ch_i}))^\kappa \cdot \beta^X, \gamma) \tag{1}$$

False Positives Reduce Phase: In this phase, we work hard on eliminating the false positives of above initial detection results. The main idea is to let the cloud storage server check whether the distances between the fingerprints of candidates and the queried one are within a pre-set threshold. We resort to the scheme proposed in [25], to achieve the above goal with the security considerations. Here, we simply describe the main steps of the scheme. For more details, we suggest you to read [25]. The main steps are as follows: (1) Let the garbled-circuit generator to generate the encryption key pair (pk, sk), and deploy the circuit to the cloud storage server; (2) The inquirer and the cloud storage server both use the pk to encrypt feature fingerprint f_Q of queried image data file and every single feature fingerprints f_I of near-duplicate candidate image data file, and get the ciphertext $[f_Q], [f_I]$ respectively; (3) The circuit takes the $\widetilde{[f_Q]}, \widetilde{[f_I]}, \widetilde{sk}, \widetilde{\epsilon}$ as garbled inputs, where ϵ is the pre-set distance threshold. (4) The evaluator inside the circuit decrypts $[f_Q], [f_I]$ with sk, and executes the distance function $Dist(f_Q, f_I)$, and verifies if $Dist(f_Q, f_I)$ is within ϵ. If it is passed, then the circuit comes to the next candidate. Otherwise excludes this candidate. The circuit will stop working until all the candidates are checked, and finally the cloud storage server output the truly results(i.e. after reducing false positives) to the inquirer. Then the inquirer would decrypt the corresponding ciphertexts I_{ES} with the same group secret key SK_j to get the final near-duplicate plaintext results.

6 Evaluation

In this section, we evaluate our scheme from two perspectives: security and performance. In the security analysis, we mainly focus on the correctness and privacy of the scheme. And in the performance analysis, we analyze the cost on storage, communication and computation in comparison with [25].

6.1 Security Analysis

Query Correctness: This property should guarantee the correctness of matching, where the correctness of Eq. (1) is the key point. We give the proof for privacy preserving near-duplicate image data detection scheme as follows:

$$K \cdot e(\sigma^{\kappa}, g) \stackrel{?}{=} e((\prod_{i \in I}(H(t_i)^{ch_i}))^{\kappa} \cdot \beta^{X}, \gamma) \tag{2}$$

$$
\begin{aligned}
K \cdot e(\sigma^{\kappa}, g) &= e(\beta, \gamma)^k \cdot e((\prod_{i \in I}(H(t_i) \cdot \beta^{w_i})^{\alpha_j \cdot ch_i})^{\kappa}, g) \\
&= e(\beta^k, \gamma) \cdot e((\prod_{i \in I}(H(t_i)^{ch_i} \cdot \beta^{ch_i w_i})^{\kappa}, g)^{\alpha_j} \\
&= e(\beta^k, \gamma) \cdot e((\prod_{i \in I}(H(t_i)^{ch_i})^{\kappa} \cdot \beta^{x\kappa}, \gamma) \\
&= e((\prod_{i \in I}H(t_i)^{ch_i})^{\kappa} \cdot \beta^{k+x\kappa}, \gamma) \\
&= e((\prod_{i \in I}H(t_i)^{ch_i})^{\kappa} \cdot \beta^{X}, \gamma)
\end{aligned}
$$

Privacy Perserving: With the help of symmetric encryption, we guarantee the privacy of content provider's data. Also, resort to the random masking technique, the adversary cannot get the information of what the inquirer has queried. According to the $X = k + \kappa x \mod p$, where $\kappa = h(K) \in \mathbb{Z}_p$, even if the adversary captures the l $\{X, K\}$s to construct the l linear equations, he still cannot work out the x which is the linear combination of the queried image-feature LSH metadata vector $W_I = \{w_{I,1}, w_{I,2}, \ldots, w_{I,l}\}$, as the random parameter k is not transmitted on any channel.

6.2 Performance Analysis

From these three parts of performance analysis compared to [25], we show that although our scheme has a little more cost in storage, but it really improves efficiency especially in computation.

Storage Overhead. Our scheme incurs little storage at user side which consists of content providers and inquirers. For content providers, the main data that they need to store is the private group j signing key ssk_j and the private group j encryption key SK_j ; For inquirers nothing is needed to be stored. In our scheme, most data is needed to be stored on the cloud server side, to be exactly, they are (1) public system parameter $PK = (spk_j, \gamma, g, \beta, e(\beta, \gamma))$; (2) encrypted image data file I', encrypted image-feature LSH metadata vector $C_I = \{c_{I,1}, c_{I,2}, \cdots, c_{I,l}\}$ and group tag $T_I = GID||Sig_{ssk_j}(GID)$ sent from CPs; (3) challenge message $chal = \{(i, ch_i)\}_{i \in [1,l]}$, $X = k + \kappa x \mod p$ and the value $K = e(\beta, \gamma)^k \in \mathbb{G}_T$ sent from inquirers. Compared to [25], the extra data should be stored in our scheme is the challenge message, which is the key point to improve efficiency with sacrificing storage overhead.

Communication Cost. Except for the cost of negotiating the consistent group system parameter (PK, SK), there are three components: (1) content messages (I_E, C_I, T_I) sent from CPs to cloud; (2) the challenge corresponding messages $(chal, X, K)$ sent from inquirer to cloud storage server; (3) the near-duplicate results sent from cloud to the inquirer. Compared to [25], this part is almost the same with three communication rounds: one between CP and cloud, and two between the inquirer and cloud.

Computation Cost. The total computation cost consist of three parts: the content provider side, the inquirer side, and the cloud storage server side. And we estimate the cost based on the basic calculation operations showed in Table 1.

Table 1. Defination of calculation operations

$Hash_G^t$	hash t values into the group G
$Mult_G^t$	t multiplications in group G
Exp_G^t	t exponentiations g^{a_i}, for $g \in G, |a_i| = l$
$m - MultExp_G^t$	t m-term exponentiations $\prod_{i=1}^m g^{a_i}$
$Pair_{G_1,G_2}^t$	t pairings $e(v_i, g_i)$, where $v_i \in G_1, g_i \in G_2$
$m - MultPair_{G_1,G_2}^t$	t m-term pairings $\prod_{i=1}^m e(v_i, g_i)$
Add_G^t	t additions in group G
$m - addDB$	m operations for adding data to database

(1) The content provider side. The computation cost includes key generation $KeyGen()$, the image feature extraction(not mainly talked about), The main parts consist of (1) the LSII feature metadata vector generation: $Hash_G^l$; (2)the feature metadata vector encryption $Encrypt()$: $Hash_G^l + Mult_G^l + Exp_G^{2l}$ (Ref. $C_I = \{c_{I,1}, c_{I,2}, \cdots, c_{I,l}\}$, by $c_{I,i} \leftarrow (H(t_i) \cdot \beta^{w_i})^{\alpha_j} \in \mathbb{G}_1, i \in [1, l]$). In total, the cost is that $Hash_G^{2l} + Mult_G^l + Exp_G^{2l}$. Compared to [25], for the content provider, it needs to do the operations: $Hash_G^{3l} + Pair_{G_1,G_2}^l + Exp_G^l$. Thus, both schemes are almost the same considering the number of operations. They both need $5l$ operations.

(2) The inquirer side. The mainly computation cost includes: (1) query token image feature extraction; (2) LSH feature metadata vector generation: $Hash_G^l$; (3) generate random element: $Pair_{G_1,G_2}^1 + Exp_G^1$ (Ref.$K = e(\beta, \gamma)^k \in G_T$); (4) calculate the blinded linear combination of random-ized sampled data block: $Add_G^l + Mult_G^l$. (Ref.$X = k + \kappa x \bmod p$, where $\kappa = h(K) \in Z_p$, $x = \sum_{i \in [1,l]}(ch_i w_{Q,i})$). In total, the cost is that $Hash_G^l + Pair_{G_1,G_2}^1 + Exp_G^1 + Add_G^l + Mult_G^{1+l}$. Compared to [25], the cost is $Hash_G^{2l} + Exp_G^l + l - addDB$. As to the number of operations that our scheme has is $3l + 3$ operations which is less than [25]'s $4l$.

(3) The cloud storage server side. For each file stored in the cloud storage server: (1) computes the aggregated parameter (according to the number of stored files):$l - MultPair^1_{G_1,G_2}$ (Ref. $\sigma = \Pi_{i \in I}(c_{I',i})^{ch_i} \in G_1$); (2) computes the parameter (only once for one query): $Hash^1_G$ (Ref. $\kappa = h(K) \in Z_p$); (3) checks whether the match equation holds (only once for one query): $Mult^2_G + Pair^2_{G_1,G_2} + Exp^3_G + l - MultExp^1_G$ (Ref. the Eq. (1)). In total, the cost is that $Mult^2_G + Pair^2_{G_1,G_2} + Exp^3_G + 2l - MultExp^1_G + Hash^{l+1}_G$. Compared to [25], the cost is that $Mult^1_G + Pair^l_{G_1,G_2} + Exp^1_G + Hash^l_G + 2l - addDB$, which has $4l + 2$ operations more than our $3l + 9$ operations.

7   Conclusion

In this work, we propose a secure near-duplicate image data detection scheme for cloud data similarity retrieval. We combine the symmetric encryption and LSH algorithm to make cloud provide privacy preserving near-duplicate image data detection service for cloud users. Our security and performance analysis shows that our scheme achieves the design goals: query correctness, privacy preserving and lightweight. As future work, we will focus on the advanced similarity retrieval algorithms and searchable encryption to further provide secure schemes beyond cloud image data.

Acknowledgments. This work is supported by Basic Reasearch Project of Shenzhen of China (No. JCYJ20160318094015947, JCYJ20170307151518535), National Key Research and Development Program of China (No. 2017YFB0803002), The Natural Science Foundation of Fujian Province, China (No. 2017J05099), and National Natural Science Foundation of China (No. 61472091).

References

1. Gantz, J., Reinsel, D.: The digital universe in 2020: big data, bigger digital shadows, and biggest growth in the far east. IDC iView: IDC Anal. Future **2007**(2012), 1–16 (2012)
2. Douceur, J.R., Adya, A., Bolosky, W.J., Simon, P., Theimer, M.: Reclaiming space from duplicate files in a serverless distributed file system. In: Proceedings of the 22nd International Conference on Distributed Computing Systems, pp. 617–624. IEEE (2002)
3. Bellare, M., Keelveedhi, S., Ristenpart, T.: Message-locked encryption and secure deduplication. In: Johansson, T., Nguyen, P.Q. (eds.) EUROCRYPT 2013. LNCS, vol. 7881, pp. 296–312. Springer, Heidelberg (2013). https://doi.org/10.1007/978-3-642-38348-9_18
4. Wang, C., Chow, S.S.M., Wang, Q., Ren, K., Lou, W.: Privacy-preserving public auditing for secure cloud storage. IEEE Trans. Comput. **62**(2), 362–375 (2013)
5. Harnik, D., Pinkas, B., Shulman-Peleg, A.: Side channels in cloud services: deduplication in cloud storage. IEEE Secur. Priv. 8(6), 40–47 (2010)
6. Di Pietro, R., Sorniotti, A.: Boosting efficiency and security in proof of ownership for deduplication. In: Proceedings of the 7th ACM Symposium on Information, Computer and Communications Security, pp. 81–82. ACM (2012)

7. Halevi, S., Harnik, D., Pinkas, B., Shulman-Peleg, A.: Proofs of ownership in remote storage systems. In: Proceedings of the 18th ACM Conference on Computer and Communications Security, pp. 491–500. ACM (2011)
8. Xu, J., Chang, E.-C., Zhou, J.: Weak leakage-resilient client-side deduplication of encrypted data in cloud storage. In: Proceedings of the 8th ACM SIGSAC Symposium on Information, Computer and Communications Security, pp. 195–206. ACM (2013)
9. Tan, Y., Jiang, H., Feng, D., Tian, L., Yan, Z., Zhou, G.: Sam: a semantic-aware multi-tiered source de-duplication framework for cloud backup. In: The 39th International Conference on Parallel Processing (ICPP), pp. 614–623. IEEE (2010)
10. Fu, Y., Jiang, H., Xiao, N., Tian, L., Liu, F.: AA-Dedupe: an application-aware source deduplication approach for cloud backup services in the personal computing environment. In: IEEE International Conference on Cluster Computing (CLUSTER), pp. 112–120. IEEE (2011)
11. Xu, L., Hu, J., Mkandawire, S., Jiang, H.: SHHC: a scalable hybrid hash cluster for cloud backup services in data centers. In: The 31st International Conference on Distributed Computing Systems Workshops (ICDCSW), pp. 61–65. IEEE (2011)
12. Li, J., Chen, X., Li, M., Li, J., Lee, P.P., Lou, W.: Secure deduplication with efficient and reliable convergent key management. IEEE Trans. Parallel Distrib. Syst. 25(6), 1615–1625 (2014)
13. Li, J., Li, Y.K., Chen, X., Lee, P.P., Lou, W.: A hybrid cloud approach for secure authorized deduplication. IEEE Trans. Parallel Distrib. Syst. 26(5), 1206–1216 (2015)
14. Li, J., et al.: Secure distributed deduplication systems with improved reliability. IEEE Trans. Comput. 64(12), 3569–3579 (2015)
15. Bellare, M., Keelveedhi, S., Ristenpart, T.: DupLESS: server-aided encryption for deduplicated storage. IACR Cryptology ePrint Archive 2013/429 (2013)
16. Stanek, J., Sorniotti, A., Androulaki, E., Kencl, L.: A secure data deduplication scheme for cloud storage. In: Christin, N., Safavi-Naini, R. (eds.) FC 2014. LNCS, vol. 8437, pp. 99–118. Springer, Heidelberg (2014). https://doi.org/10.1007/978-3-662-45472-5_8
17. Andoni, A., Indyk, P.: Near-optimal hashing algorithms for approximate nearest neighbor in high dimensions. In: The 47th Annual IEEE Symposium on Foundations of Computer Science, pp. 459–468. IEEE (2006)
18. Ke, Y., Sukthankar, R., Huston, L., Ke, Y., Sukthankar, R.: Efficient near-duplicate detection and sub-image retrieval. In: ACM Multimedia, vol. 4, p. 5. Citeseer (2004)
19. Qamra, A., Meng, Y., Chang, E.Y.: Enhanced perceptual distance functions and indexing for image replica recognition. IEEE Trans. Pattern Anal. Mach. Intell. 27(3), 379–391 (2005)
20. Chum, O., Philbin, J., Isard, M., Zisserman, A.: Scalable near identical image and shot detection. In: Proceedings of the 6th ACM International Conference on Image and Video Retrieval, pp. 549–556. ACM (2007)
21. Hu, Y., Li, M., Yu, N.: Efficient near-duplicate image detection by learning from examples. In: 2008 IEEE International Conference on Multimedia and Expo, pp. 657–660. IEEE (2008)
22. Kuzu, M., Islam, M.S., Kantarcioglu, M.: Efficient similarity search over encrypted data. In: The 28th International Conference on Data Engineering (ICDE), pp. 1156–1167. IEEE (2012)
23. Cui, H., Yuan, X., Wang, C.: Harnessing encrypted data in cloud for secure and efficient image sharing from mobile devices. In: 2015 IEEE International Conference on Computer Communications, pp. 2659–2667. IEEE (2015)

24. Yuan, X., Wang, X., Wang, C., Weng, J., Ren, K.: Enabling secure and fast index-ing for privacy-assured healthcare monitoring via compressive sensing. IEEE Trans. Multimed. **18**(10), 2002–2014 (2016)
25. Cui, H., Yuan, X., Zheng, Y., Wang, C.: Enabling secure and effective near-duplicate detection over encrypted in-network storage. In: The 35th Annual IEEE International Conference on Computer Communications, pp. 1–9. IEEE (2016)
26. Yuan, X., Wang, X., Wang, C., Chenyun, Y., Nutanong, S.: Privacy-preserving similarity joins over encrypted data. IEEE Trans. Inf. Forensics Secur. **12**(11), 2763–2775 (2017)
27. Datar, M., Immorlica, N., Indyk, P., Mirrokni, V.S.: Locality-sensitive hashing scheme based on P-stable distributions. In: Proceedings of the 20th annual Symposium on Computational Geometry, pp. 253–262. ACM (2004)

An Efficient Multi-keyword Searchable Encryption Supporting Multi-user Access Control

Chuxin Wu[1], Peng Zhang[1(✉)], Hongwei Liu[1,2], Zehong Chen[1], and Zoe L. Jiang[3]

[1] ATR Key Laboratory of National Defense Technology, College of Information Engineering, Shenzhen University, Shenzhen 518060, Guangdong, China
wuchuxin2016@email.szu.edu.cn, {zhangp,zhchen}@szu.edu.cn
[2] Shenzhen Technology University, Shenzhen 518118, Guangdong, China
liuhongwei@sztu.edu.cn
[3] Harbin Institute of Technology, Shenzhen 518055, Guangdong, China
zoeljiang@hit.edu.cn

Abstract. Due to the strong storage capacity and calculating power of cloud computing, more and more users outsource their data to the cloud. To avoid users' data exposed to cloud, searchable encryption which can search over the encrypted data is studied. In this paper, based on the multi-keyword searchable encryption proposed by Cash et al., through enforcing access control for users, we present an efficient multi-keyword searchable encryption supporting multi-user access control(MMSE). MMSE supports multi-user scenarios, and only the users whose attributes satisfy the policy can generate the search token, no matter the data owner is online or not. The security and performance analysis shows that the proposed MMSE is secure and efficient.

Keywords: Searchable encryption · Multi-keyword search
Multi-user search · Access control

1 Introduction

With the increasing popularity and great convenience of cloud computing [7,14], people tend to outsource some of their data to the cloud. However, outsourcing sensitive data (e.g., health data, finance statements, customer relationship) may bring a series of privacy problems. Once the data is uploaded, the data owner loses control of it. The cloud service provider (CSP) could access the user's data without authorization. Encrypting data before uploading it to the cloud is the general way to protect the user's privacy from leakage. But how to search over the encrypted data becomes a critical problem.

Song et al. [9] first proposed searchable encryption(SE), which can search over the encrypted data and has less computing overhead. Subsequently, many SE schemes were proposed [4,8]. In 2013, Cash et al. [3] proposed a SE scheme,

© Springer Nature Switzerland AG 2018
J. Vaidya and J. Li (Eds.): ICA3PP 2018, LNCS 11337, pp. 389–398, 2018.
https://doi.org/10.1007/978-3-030-05063-4_30

which achieves efficient multi-keyword search through allowing users to estimate the least frequent keyword in the conjunctive search. However, due to using symmetric key in database encryption and token generation, this scheme is limited to a single user model. If other users want to search on data which is encrypted and uploaded by data owner, they must request the symmetric key or search token from data owner, who need be online at all time.

To address the drawback of the single-user model, multi-user model was proposed, which allows multiple users to search the encrypted data without the data owner online at all times. Access control restricts users by setting a series of access conditions, and only the user who satisfies the access conditions can decrypt. Based on [3], Sun et al. [10] used ciphertext-policy attribute-based encryption (CP-ABE) to extend it to support multi-user, which reduces the communication overhead and eliminates the need of the data owner to provide the online services. As each document identity is encrypted repeatedly by CP-ABE, the computation cost is high.

1.1   Contribution

In this paper, we discuss the searchable encryption in the cloud computing, and propose an efficient multi-keyword searchable encryption supporting multi-user access control(MMSE). Based on the multi-keyword scheme of Cash et al. [3], this paper solves the following problems: multi-user search and fast search.

In MMSE, the data owner sets the corresponding access policy for the search key, and only the user whose attribute set satisfies this policy can decrypt and obtain the search key. In this situation, no matter whether the data owner is online or not, the users with access authority could search. Therefore, multi-user search is supported. To achieve fast search, we use a computational structure which is similar to Cash et al. [3] to design the search scheme. Compared with the scheme in [10], our MMSE scheme reduces the number of search keys and is more efficient.

1.2   Related Work

Multi-keyword Searchable Encryption. Cash et al. [3] proposed a multi-keyword SE scheme, which uses inverted index and estimates the least frequent keyword in the conjunctive search to construct a fast search algorithm. Based on [3], Li et al. [5] proposed an efficient multi-keyword search scheme that estimates the least frequent keyword in the conjunctive search to improve the search efficiency, and use blind storage to hide access pattern. Similarly, based on [3], Sun et al. [10] proposed a SE scheme with multi-keyword search, which reduces the number of interactions between the data owner and users in cash et al.'s scheme. Xia et al. [13] proposed a multi-keyword ranked search scheme, which used a keyword banlanced binary tree to construct index, and proposed a "Greedy Depth-first Search" algorithm to achieve fast search.

Multi-user Searchable Encryption. Wang et al. [12] proposed a CP-ABE scheme that supports keyword search. Only those users whose attributes satisfy the access policy can obtain the encrypted data via keyword search. Sun et al. [11] proposed a SE scheme for multi-user scenario that uses CP-ABE to encrypt the index of each file to realize multi-user senario. The SE scheme proposed by Li et al. [6], which uses symmetric encryption to encrypt the index and encrypt documents with ABE that only users satisfy the policy can decrypt the ciphertext.

1.3 Organization

The remainder of the paper is organized as follows. The preliminary is introduced in Sect. 2. In Sect. 3, the MMSE scheme is proposed. In Sects. 4 and 5, the security and performance of MMSE are analyzed. The whole paper is concluded in Sect. 6.

2 Preliminary

2.1 Bilinear Maps

Let $\mathbb{G}_0$ and $\mathbb{G}_T$ be two groups of prime order p. g is the generator of $\mathbb{G}_0$. A bilinear mapping $e : \mathbb{G}_0 \times \mathbb{G}_0 \to \mathbb{G}_T$ satisfies the following properties [1]:

1. Bilinearity: For any $u, v \in \mathbb{G}_0$ and $a, b \in \mathbb{Z}_p$, it has $e(u^a, v^b) = e(u, v)^{ab}$.
2. Non-degeneracy: There exists $u, v \in \mathbb{G}_0$ such that $e(u, v) \neq 1$.
3. Computability: For all $u, v \in \mathbb{G}_0$, there is an efficient algorithm to compute $e(u, v)$.

2.2 Hardness Problem

Let $\mathbb{G}$ be a cyclic group of prime order p. Decision Diffie-Hellman (DDH) problem [2] is to distinguish the ensembles $\{(g, g^a, g^b, g^{ab})\}$ from $\{(g, g^a, g^b, g^z)\}$, where the elements $g \in \mathbb{G}$ and $a, b, z \in \mathbb{Z}_p$ are chosen uniformly at random. Formally, the advantage for any probabilistic polynomial time (PPT) distinguisher D is defined as:

$$Adv_{D,\mathbb{G}}^{DDH}(\lambda) = |\Pr[D(g, g^a, g^b, g^{ab}) = 1] - \Pr[D(g, g^a, g^b, g^z) = 1]|$$

We say that the DDH problem holds if for any PPT distinguisher D, its advantage $Adv_{D,\mathbb{G}}^{DDH}(\lambda)$ is negligible in λ.

2.3 PRF Definition

Let $F : \{0,1\}^\lambda \times X \to Y$ be a function defined from $\{0,1\}^\lambda \times X$ to Y [3]. We say F is a pseudorandom function (PRF) if for all efficient adversaries A, its advantage $Adv_{F,A}^{prf}(\lambda)$ defined as:

$$Adv_{F,A}^{prf}(\lambda) = |\Pr[A^{F(K,\cdot)}(1^\lambda)] - \Pr[A^{f(\cdot)}(1^\lambda)]|$$

is negligible in λ, where $K\{0,1\}^\lambda$ and f is a random function from X to Y.

3   Multi-user and Multi-keyword Searchable Encryption

Based on the SE algorithm $\Pi = (EDBSetup, TokenGen, Search, Retrieve)$ proposed in [3] and the CP-ABE algorithm $\sum = (Setup, Encrypt, KeyGen, Decrypt)$ proposed in [1], we propose an efficient multi-keyword searchable encryption supporting multi-user access control(MMSE). Some notations used in MMSE are shown in Table 1.

Table 1. Notations

Notation	Description
λ	Security parameter
$\mathbb{G}$	A bilinear group with prime order p and a generator g
Γ	Access policy
$N = \{a_1, a_2, \cdots, a_n\}$	Attribute set
S	User's attribute set, $S \subseteq N$
$\{0,1\}^{\lambda}$	Consists of 0,1 sequences of length λ
$\{0,1\}^*$	Consists of 0,1 sequences of indefinite length
id_i	Identity $id_i \in \{0,1\}^{\lambda}$
W_i	Keyword $W_i \subseteq \{0,1\}^*$
$DB = (id_i, W_i)_{i=1}^{d}$	A list of identity/keyword set pairs
$W = \bigcup_{i=1}^{d} W_i$	Keywords set
m	Number of documents
$Doc = \{f_1, f_2, \cdots, f_m\}$	Document set
$R = \{r_1, r_2, \cdots, r_m\}$	Symmetric key set
$\bar{W} = (w_1, w_2, \cdots, w_n)$	Keyword set in a search query
xterm	Other queried term in a search query

Choose any symmetric encryption algorithm $\Phi = (Encrypt, Decrypt)$. Define $PRF\ F : \{0,1\}^{\lambda} \times \{0,1\}^{\lambda} \to \{0,1\}^{\lambda}$ and $PRP\ P : \{0,1\}^{\lambda} \times \{0,1\}^{\lambda} \to \{0,1\}^{\lambda}$. Input a security parameter λ and an attribute set N. PKG runs $\sum .Setup(1^{\lambda}, N)$ to obtain public key PK and master secret key MSK. The data owner encrypts document f_i with symmetric key r_i to obtain the ciphertext ct_i as $ct_i \leftarrow \Phi.Encrypt(r_i, f_i)$ $(i = 1, 2, \cdots, m)$, and uploads the encrypted documents to CSP. To encrypt the index and the search key, the data owner runs Algorithm 1 as follows, and uploads the output including the encrypted index and the encrypted search key to CSP.

Algorithm 1. EDBSetup Algorithm

Input: DB
Output: $EDB, XSet, EK, Stags[\|W\|]$
  function $EDBSetup(DB)$
  - Select search key k for PRF F and parse DB as $(id_i, W_i)_{i=1}^d$.
  - Initialize T to an empty array indexed by keywords from W.
  - Initialize $XSet$ to an empty set.
  - Initialize $Stags[\|W\|]$ to an empty set.
  - For each $w \in \mathsf{W}$,build the tuple list $T[stag_w]$ and $XSet$ elements as follows:
    - Initialize t to be an empty list, compute $stag_w \leftarrow F(k, w)$ and add $stag_w$ to store in $Stags[\|W\|]$.
      - Compute $k_1 \leftarrow F(k, 1\|w)$.
      - for all $id_i \in DB(w)$ in random order, initialize a counter $c \leftarrow 0$, then:
        - Compute $rind \leftarrow P(k, id_i\|r_i)$, $z \leftarrow P(k_1, c)$, $y \leftarrow rind \cdot z^{-1}$.
        - Append $(rind, y)$ to t.
        - Compute $xtag \leftarrow g^{k_1 \cdot rind}$ and add $xtag$ to $XSet$.
        - $c \leftarrow c + 1$.
      - $T[stag_w] \leftarrow t$.
  - Encrypted search key $EK \leftarrow \sum.Encrypt(PK, k, \Gamma)$.
  - Output $(EDB = T, XSet, EK, Stags[\|W\|])$.
  end function

If a user with attribute set S wants to search for a keyword set $\bar{W} = (w_1, w_2, \cdots, w_n)$, where w_1 is assumed to be the least frequent keyword in $\bar{W}$, he submits a search request to CSP, and then obtains the corresponding encrypted search key EK. PKG runs $\sum.KeyGen(MSK, S)$ and returns the secret key SK to the user. The user sends search token to CSP, which is the output of the following $TokenGen$ algorithm.

Algorithm 2. Token generation Algorithm

Input: $EK, SK, \bar{W} = (w_1, w_2, \cdots, w_n)$
Output: $stag, (xtoken[1], xtoken[2], \ldots)$
  function $TokenGen(EK, SK, \bar{W})$
  - The user runs $\sum.Decrypt(EK, SK)$ algorithm. If his attribute set S satisfies the database's access policy Γ, he decrypts and obtains the search key k; otherwise, obtains $null$.
  - The message $(stag, (xtoken[1], xtoken[2], \ldots))$ sent to CSP is defined as:
    - $stag \leftarrow F(k, w_1)$.
    - $k_1 \leftarrow F(k, 1\|w_1)$.
    - For $c = 1, 2, \ldots$ and until CSP sends stop
      - For $i = 2, \ldots, n$, set $xtoken[c, i] \leftarrow g^{P(k_1, c) \cdot F(k, 1\|w_i)}$.
      - Set $xtoken[c] = xtoken[c, 2], \ldots, xtoken[c, n]$.
  end function

To response the search token $(stag, (xtoken[1], xtoken[2], \cdots))$ from the user, CSP runs the $Search$ algorithm and outputs the document identity set ID, which is described as follows.

Algorithm 3. Search Algorithm

Input: $stag, (xtoken[1], xtoken[2], \ldots), EDB, XSet, Stags[\|W\|]$
Output: ID
  function $Search(stag, (xtoken[1], xtoken[2], \ldots), EDB, XSet, Stags[\|W\|])$
  - Search process is as follow.
    - Initialize ID to an empty set.
    - Initialize t to an empty list.
    - Verify that whether the equation $stag_w = stag$ holds, where $stag_w \in Stags[\|W\|]$. If so, output $t = T[stag_w]$; otherwise, return $null$.
    - For $c = 1, 2, \ldots, |t|$
      - retrieve $(rind, y)$ from the c-th tuple in t.
      - if $\forall i = 2, \ldots, n : xtoken[c, i]^y \in XSet$ then set $ID \leftarrow ID \bigcup rind$.
    - When last tuple in t is reached, return ID.
  end function

The user performs the *Retrieve* algorithm, which is described as follows.

Algorithm 4. Retrieve Algorithm

Input: ID, k
Output: $\{f_i\}$
  function $Retrieve(ID, k)$
    • The user decrypts the search result ID with the search key k, obtains the document identity id_i and the corresponding key r_i.
      - For $rind \in ID$
        - Compute $(id_i \| r_i) \leftarrow P^{-1}(k, rind)$.
      - Return $\{(id_i, r_i)\}$.
    • The user sends $\{id_i\}$ to the CSP, the CSP returns $\{ct_i\}$. For each ct_i, the user decrypts the document $f_i = \Phi.Decrypt(ct_i, r_i)$ with the corresponding symmetric key r_i. Then the user obtains the document set $\{f_i\}$.
  end function

---

4   Security Analysis

The definition of semantic security for searchable encryption we use is similar to [3].

Theorem 1. *L is defined as a leakage function. The scheme we proposed is L-semantic security under non-adaptive attacks, assuming that DDH assumption holds in $\mathbb{G}$, and F and P are secure PRFs, and that CP-ABE is a CPA secure attribute-based encryption.*

Proof. The proof for above theorem we use is similar to [3]. A series of games $G_0, G_1, \cdots, G_8$ and simulator S are described. In each game, A provides the database DB and quires q as Initialize input, and the game outputs a bit to A. G_0 has the same distribution as $Real_A^\Pi$ (assuming no false positives). The difference between the distribution of each game and the distribution of previous games is negligible, and it can be proved that the simulator S satisfies the definition, thus proving this theorem. We did not use $TSet$ in our algorithm design, so we don't have a game equivalent to G_6.

Game$_0$: In order to make the analysis easier, the game has slightly changed from the real game. The game first runs Initialize, same as $EDBSetup$ in Algorithm 1 except that $XSet$ is separated as a single function $XSetSetup$, helps to see changes in the following games. Before initializes the $GenTrans$ function to generate the transcript, an array stags used in the game is calculated. Specifically, for each $i = 1, 2, \cdots, Q$, $stags[i] \leftarrow F(k, s[i])$. Computes the transcript array t, for each $i = 1, 2, \cdots, Q$, let $t[i] = GenTrans(EDB; EK; s[i]; x[i]; stag[i])$. The difference between $GenTrans$ and actual game is that it calculates the $ResInds$ array in a different way: $GenTrans$ does not decrypt the ciphertext returned by $ResInds$, but instead looks for the rind value corresponding to the result. We also made the following changes: record the order of document identifiers used by each keyword w in array $WPerms[w]$. The order is chosen to be randomized to match the real game. By design, G_0 is exactly $Real_A^\Pi(\lambda)$ (assuming no false positives). So, assuming F_p is a secure PRF, we have

$$\Pr\left[Game_0 = 1\right] \leq \Pr\left[Real_A^\Pi(\lambda) = 1\right] + \text{neg}(\lambda)$$

$Game_1$: This game is almost the same as the last game. More specifically, instead of recomputing them, we record the value of $stag$ in the first computation in this game: for each $t \in T$, compute $query\_stag \leftarrow stags[s[t]]$. The calculation of $stags$ in the $GenTrans$ algorithm makes it easy to see that the distribution of the two games are same. We have

$$\Pr[Game_1 = 1] = \Pr[Game_0 = 1]$$

$Game_2$: G_2 is the same as G_1 except that $PRFF$ and $PRFP$ are replaced by random functions. $F(k, \cdot)$, $P(k, \cdot)$ and $P(k_1, \cdot)$ are replaced by f_k, p_k and p_{k_1}, respectively. By a standard hybrid argument, it is show that there are valid adversaries $B_{2,1}$ and $B_{2,2}$. We have

$$\Pr[Game_2 = 1] - \Pr[Game_1 = 1] \leq Adv_{F,B_{2,1}}^{prf}(\lambda) + 2Adv_{P,B_{2,2}}^{prf}(\lambda)$$

$Game_3$: G_3 is similar to G_2. The difference is that the encryption of the document identity is replaced by the constant string 0^λ, such as $ploy(\lambda)$. Through a standard hybrid argument, we can show that there is a valid adversary B_3, so

$$\Pr[Game_3 = 1] - \Pr[Game_2 = 1] \leq ploy(\lambda) \cdot Adv_{\Sigma,B_3}^{prf}(\lambda)$$

$Game_4$: The only difference from G_3 is that $XSet$ and $xtoken$ are generated differently. In short, all possible values $XSET\_ELEM(w, id) = g^{f_k(1||w) \cdot p_k(id)}$ are pre-computed and stored in the array H. In addition, the $xtoken$ generated in transcripts that do not match are stored in another array Y.

In G_4, we have $H[id; w] \in XSet$. In addition, if the value of $xtoken$ are the same in both games, the $GenTrans$ will returns the same output as the previous game. Therefore, we only focus on the following $xtoken$ array generation. Specifically, $xtoken$ value $xtoken[\alpha, c]$ is set to $p_{k_1}(c) \cdot f_k(1||w_i)$ for each $xterm$ $x_t[\alpha]$, $c \in [T_c]$. In this game, $xtoken$ is generated as follows. First, $GenTrans$ looks for $(id_1, id_2, \cdots, id_{T_s}) \leftarrow DB[s_t]$ and $\sigma \leftarrow WPerms[s_t]$. For each $x_t[\alpha]$, it uses the query_stag to search $T[stag] = (rind, y)$, where $y = p_k(id_i||r_i) \cdot p_{k_1}(c)^{-1}$. And when $c \in [T_s]$, set $xtoken[\alpha, c] = Y[s_t, x_t[\alpha], c]$; when $c \in [T_c]\backslash[T_s]$, set $xtoken[\alpha, c] = H[id_{\sigma[c]}, x_t[\alpha]]^{1/y}$. We can see that for each $x_t[\alpha]$ and $c \in [T_c]$, $xtoken[\alpha, c] = p_{k_1}(c) \cdot f_k(1||w_i)$. This indicates that the $xtoken$ value will be the same in the both games. So we have

$$\Pr[Game4 = 1] = \Pr[Game3 = 1]$$

$Game_5$: This game is almost the same as G_4 except that y is chosen randomly from $\mathbb{Z}_p^*$. During Initialize, $p_{k_1}(c)$ is only computed in one location. In addition, $y = rind \cdot z^{-1}$ depends on the random value of p_{k_1}, so it is not change the distribution. Therefore, setting y to random does not affect the game. So we have

$$\Pr[Game5 = 1] = \Pr[Game4 = 1]$$

$Game_6$: G_6 is almost the same as G_5 except that H and Y are randomly chosen from $\mathbb{G}$, denoted as $H[id, w] \xleftarrow{\$} \mathbb{G}$ and $Y[w, u, c] \xleftarrow{\$} \mathbb{G}$. The values used in H and Y are randomly chosen from $\mathbb{G}$. By DDH problem, we have $\Pr[Game_6 = 1] - \Pr[Game_5 = 1] \le Adv_{G, B_6}^{DDH}(\lambda)$. The values of X array are g^a. The values of X rise to the power of $rind$ when calculating H, and rise to the power of $p_{k_1}(c)$ when Y is calculated, so $rind$ and $p_{k_1}(c)$ will be the b values. In G_5, the form of H and Y are g^{ab}, and in G_6 they are replaced by random values. These distinctions are DDH issues.

$Game_7$: This game modifies $XSetSetup$ to only include the members of H that can be tested multiple times. Array H is only used in functions $XSetSetup$ and $GenTrans$. Obviously, for $(id; W)$ of H, just check whether it will be accessed by $GenTrans$. $GenTrans$ accesses H only for locations where t and α satisfy $id \in DB[s_t]$ and $w = x_t[\alpha]$. For other locations, the corresponding element can not be distinguished from the random choices. Therefore, the changes will not change the distribution of the game. We have

$$\Pr[Game7 = 1] = \Pr[Game6 = 1]$$

$Game_8$: In $XSetSetup$, $XSet$ members H must be used by $GenTrans$ and tested by the first if statement. In different queries t_1 and t_2, the same member in $GenTrans$ may be used twice. The current query number is passed in as a parameter t_1, and the second if statement checks if other queries t_2 will also uses the same element of H. If none of these conditions apply, then $xtoken$ is randomly chosen from $\mathbb{G}$. Since all repeating H values are still used, we have

$$\Pr[Game8 = 1] = \Pr[Game7 = 1]$$

The simulator S will input leakage $L(DB; s; x) = (N; s; SP; RP; SRP; IP; XT)$ and output EDB, $XSet$ and array t. By proving that the simulator produces the same distribution with G_8, we can show that simulator S satisfies the theorem. Our simulator works is similar to [3].

5   Performance Analysis

We analyze and compare Sun et al.'s scheme [11] and our scheme MMSE in terms of performance. The notations used in the analysis are described in Table 2. Table 3 summarizes the performance comparisons between Sun et al.'s scheme and MMSE. Since hash and pseudo-random function operations are not time-consuming operation, we do not include them in efficiency comparison.

In Table 3, we theoretically analyze the costs of $EDBSetup$, $TokenGen$, and $Search$ in two schemes. In $EDBSetup$, the computational overhead of Sun et al.'s scheme is significantly larger than MMSE, since it requires CP-ABE encryption multiple times. In $TokenGen$ and $Search$, the costs of MMSE are similar to Sun et al.'s. The size of search key in MMSE is C_k, which is $4C_k$ in Sun et al.'s. Therefore, the MMSE is more efficient than Sun et al.'s scheme.

Table 2. Notation definition

Notation	Description
E	Exponential operation
P	Pairing operation
M	Multiplication operation
C_k	Bit size of search key in $EDBSetup'$
s	$\sum_{i=1}^{d} |DB[w_i]|$
l	Number of attributes in policy
d	Total number of keywords
n	Number of search keyword
c	Number of files corresponding to the least frequent keyword in n
a	Number of attributes of user

Table 3. Performance comparisons

Scheme	Sun et al.'s scheme	MMSE
$EDBSetup$	$(2sl + 3s)E + sP + 2sM$	$(2l + s + 1)E + P + 2sM$
$TokenGen$	$(3cn - 3c + 4)E + (cn - c)M$	$(cn - c + 1)E + (2a + 1)P$
$Search$	$c(n - 1)E$	$c(n - 1)E$
Search key size	$4C_k$	C_k

6   Conclusion

In this paper, we presented an efficient multi-keyword searchable encryption supporting multi-user access control(MMSE), which achieved multi-keyword search and can be well applied in databases. At the same time, MMSE used CP-ABE as access control to achieve multi-user scenarios. The security of scheme is secure against non-adaptive attacks. The performance analysis confirms that our scheme is efficient and practical.

Acknowledgements. This work was supported by the National Natural Science Foundation of China (61702342), the Science and Technology Innovation Projects of Shenzhen (JCYJ20170302151321095, JCYJ20160318094015947) and Tencent "Rhinoceros Birds" - Scientific Research Foundation for Young Teachers of Shenzhen University.

References

1. Bethencourt, J., Sahai, A., Waters, B.: Ciphertext-policy attribute-based encryption. In: 7th IEEE Symposium on Security and Privacy, pp. 321–334. IEEE Computer Society (2007)
2. Boneh, D.: The decision Diffie-Hellman problem. In: Buhler, J.P. (ed.) Algorithmic Number Theory, pp. 48–63. Springer, Heidelberg (1998). https://doi.org/10.1007/BFb0054851

3. Cash, D., Jarecki, S., Jutla, C.-S., Krawczyk, H., Rosu, M., Steiner, M.: Highly-scalable searchable symmetric encryption with support for boolean queries. Advances in Cryptology-CRYPTO, pp. 353–373. Springer, Berlin, Heidelberg (2013). https://doi.org/10.1007/978-3-642-40041-4_20

4. Huang, M., Xie, W., Zhang, P.: Efficient fuzzy keyword search over encrypted medical and health data in hybrid cloud. J. Med. Imaging Health Inform. **7**(4), 867–874 (2017)

5. Li, H., Liu, D., Dai, Y., Luan, T.-H., Shen, X.-S.: Enabling efficient multi-keyword ranked search over encrypted mobile cloud data through blind storage. IEEE Trans. Emerg. Top. Comput. **3**(1), 127–138 (2015)

6. Li, H., Yang, Y., Dai, Y., Bai, J., Yu, S., Xiang, Y.: Achieving secure and efficient dynamic searchable symmetric encryption over medical cloud data. IEEE Trans. Cloud Comput. **99**, 1–1 (2017)

7. Li, J., Chen, X., Chow, S.-S.-M., Huang, Q., Wong, D.-S., Liu, Z.: Multi-authority fine-grained access control with accountability and its application in cloud. J. Netw. Comput. Appl. **112**, 89–96 (2018)

8. Li, J., Wang, Q., Wang, C., Cao, N., Ren, K., Lou, W.: Fuzzy keyword search over encrypted data in cloud computing. In: 29th IEEE International Conference on Computer Communications, pp. 441–445. IEEE, San Diego (2010)

9. Song, D.-X., Wagner, D.-A., Perrig, A.: Practical techniques for searches on encrypted data. In: IEEE Symposium on Security and Privacy, pp. 44–55. IEEE Computer Society (2000)

10. Sun, S.-F., Liu, J.K., Sakzad, A., Steinfeld, R., Yuen, T.H.: An efficient non-interactive multi-client searchable encryption with support for boolean queries. In: Askoxylakis, I., Ioannidis, S., Katsikas, S., Meadows, C. (eds.) ESORICS 2016. LNCS, vol. 9878, pp. 154–172. Springer, Cham (2016). https://doi.org/10.1007/978-3-319-45744-4_8

11. Sun, W., Yu, S., Lou, W., Hou, Y.T., Li, H.: Protecting your right: verifiable attribute-based keyword search with fine-grained owner-enforced search authorization in the cloud. IEEE Trans. parallel Distrib. Syst. **27**(4), 1187–1198 (2016)

12. Wang, C., Li, W., Li, Y., Xu, X.: A ciphertext-policy attribute-based encryption scheme supporting keyword search function. In: Wang, G., Ray, I., Feng, D., Rajarajan, M. (eds.) CSS 2013. LNCS, vol. 8300, pp. 377–386. Springer, Cham (2013). https://doi.org/10.1007/978-3-319-03584-0_28

13. Xia, Z., Wang, X., Sun, X., Wang, Q.: A secure and dynamic multi-keyword ranked search scheme over encrypted cloud data. IEEE Trans. parallel Distrib. Syst. **27**(2), 340–352 (2016)

14. Zhang, P., Chen, Z., Liang, K., Wang, S., Wang, T.: A cloud-based access control scheme with user revocation and attribute update. In: 21st Australasian Information Security and Privacy, pp. 525–540. Springer, Berlin, Heidelberg (2016). https://doi.org/10.1007/978-3-319-40253-6_32

Android Malware Detection Using Category-Based Permission Vectors

Xu Li, Guojun Wang[✉], Saqib Ali, and QiLin He

School of Computer Science and Technology, Guangzhou University,
Guangzhou 510006, People's Republic of China
csgjwang@gzhu.edu.cn

Abstract. With the drastic increase of smartphone adoption, malware attacks on smartphones have emerged as serious privacy and security threat. Kaspersky Labs detected and intercepted a total of 5,730,916 malicious installation packages in 2017. To curb this problem, researchers and various security laboratories have developed numerous malware analysis models. In Android based smartphones, permissions have been an inherent part of such models. Permission request patterns can be used to detect behavior of different applications. As applications with similar functionalities should use permission requests in similar ways, they can be used to distinguish different types of apps. However, when analysis models are trained on permission vectors extracted from a mixture of applications without maintaining any differences that naturally exist among different application categories, aggregated results can miss details and this can result in errors. In this paper, we propose a permission analysis model for android applications which includes a classification module and a malware detection module based on application permission vectors to deal with Android malware detection problem. We mine the benign application permission vector set into 32 categories by mining the similarity of permission vectors, and input malicious application permission vector sets into the model to obtain class labels, then extract sensitive features from different classes. Finally, sensitive features of each class are respectively input into the machine learning algorithm to obtain a classification model of malicious and benign applications. Our experimental results show that our model can achieve 93.66% accuracy of detecting malware instances.

Keywords: Clustering · Permission vectors · Malware detection
k-means

1 Introduction

The latest Android system security report released by Google in March 2018 [1] states that there are 2 billion Android smart devices currently. To serve the functional needs of users bearing these devices, many Android application markets such as Google Play, Android Market, and Huawei App Store have been established. Users can download various applications from these App stores which meet their operational and functional requirements. As of now, the gaming applications in Google Play store, they have been downloaded nearly 65 billion times in over 3 million total applications [2]. While these stores provide the convenience of application distribution to the developers and ease of

© Springer Nature Switzerland AG 2018
J. Vaidya and J. Li (Eds.): ICA3PP 2018, LNCS 11337, pp. 399–414, 2018.
https://doi.org/10.1007/978-3-030-05063-4_31

download to the users, they can also contribute to spreading malware applications, if they do not have effective malware detection controls. Due to the popularity of the Android-based smart devices, they are become the main target of malicious software attacks. A recent study conducted by the company Qihoo360 [3], shows that in the first quarter of 2017, their software intercepted a total of 2.228 million new malicious applications developed to target Android platform. Thus, on the average 25,000 mobile phone malicious samples were intercepted each day. Kaspersky Labs detected and intercepted a total of 5,730,916 malicious installation packages in 2017 [4]. According to the type of attacks, these malware can be divided into trojans, worms, vulnerabilities and viruses [5]. In order to evade security and satisfy interest changes, they have seen different variants. This makes the development and design of detecting procedures more challenging.

Android platform has undergone many security updates and evolved over time. Google has strengthened the security of the Android platform release after release [6]. Much research needs to be done to detect security threats such as malwares from entering application stores, spreading to Android devices and damaging user trust. Mainly, there are two ways to detect malwares detection i.e. static approach and dynamic approach [7]. Normally, static detection methods typically use large-scale training to extract application-sensitive features such as the permissions requested by the applications [8–12] or the usage of specified API functions [13–16]. Different tools have been developed to employ these techniques. Such as [16], uses kernel-based exploits and API-level rewriting. The feature analysis of the large and chaotic training set, and the classification results are only benign or malicious. Moreover, the extracted sensitive features are only valid for a part of applications. Thus, these tools do not effectively provide detection against malicious applications.

It has been discovered that a vast majority of newly discovered malware samples are variations of existing malware. This provides an opportunity to observe and analyze group behaviors of such malware and later use this learning to detect malware [17, 18]. One of such behaviors is an application pattern of requesting permissions in Android. It is important to note that in Android, default capabilities of applications are very limited and they need to request user permissions to access data and resources on the device to perform different functions. As such permissions specify which data and resources an application is accessing, machine learning and data mining techniques can be used how different types of applications use such permissions. For example [7] extracts normal and dangerous permission pairs based on Google Store category, then predicts the application's risk level based upon risk scores and detects abnormal applications. Their experimental results show that the model can achieve high detection accuracy by permission combination score. However, a large number of possible permission pairs lead to increased modeling complexity, while the number of malicious pair occurrences may be just a little. Furthermore, it is very difficult to give a valid score for each combination. So, we need a more reasonable solution for malware app detection problem. Previously, different studies have identified certain widely used and dangerous permission and termed them as sensitive permissions due to their potential impact on user data privacy and security [19]. Such sensitive permissions are used to determine application behavior and malware detection. But they have not considered application behavior categories.

In this paper, we propose a solution which establishes a clustering model based on similarities of benign application permissions using vector distance. Consequently, we input the malicious application's permission vector into that model to get the classification results. Next, we extract sensitive permission features based on categories. Afterward, we effectively detect malwares using supervised learning algorithms as shown in Fig. 1. Finally, for the unknown applications, we first extract permission vector and calculate the distance with different class centroids to classify them accordingly. Then we extract the sensitive permissions of every class and then detect the malicious or benign behavior as shown in Fig. 2.

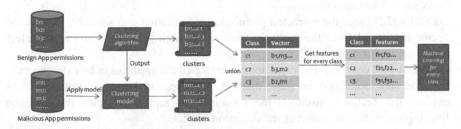

Fig. 1. Proposed framework (training phase)

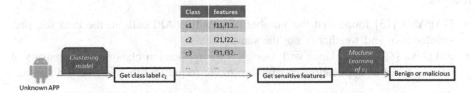

Fig. 2. Proposed framework (malware detection phase)

Rest of the paper is organized as follows. In Sect. 2, describes the research and progress on malicious application detection of Android related to permission requests and API call. Section 3 introduces our dataset, the design of the clustering model, and the extraction of sensitive features. Section 4, we verify and discuss the effective of the model through experiments and comparisons. Finally, Sect. 5 concludes the paper.

2 Related Work

As we all know, with the rapid increase in the number of devices equipped with Android, Android security issues are getting worse. Many security companies, researchers, and third-party system developers are investigating the detection of malicious applications.

We have found that all detection tools preprocess the dataset, and then extract the sensitive features directly, at last use machine learning algorithms to analyze and eventually obtain the detection model.

- In the latest research progress, SIGPID [9] filters sensitive permissions by mining permission data, finally determines 10 most important permissions that can effectively distinguish between benign and malicious applications, then classify malware and benign applications based on machine learning-based classification methods. It is similar with Wang et al. [20], they proposed three approaches, namely, mutual information, CorrCoef, and T-test for analysis of the permissions ranking, to reflect the danger and sensitivity of the permissions.
- Permlyzer [21] compares the permissions information of the application with the calling method to remove redundant permissions and detect the mapping relationship between the permissions components in the malware and trusted software to establish a detection model.
- DREBIN [22] maps the extracted permission information and sensitive API to the vector space and finds the malware patterns through machine learning to detect unknown applications.
- DAPASA [13] describes the suspicious behavior of the application by extracting the sensitive subgraph from the static method call graph of the application, and then extracts five features based on the sensitive subgraph and inputs the machine learning algorithm to construct the detection model.

However, the differences in application functions, the resources used in training applications are very different. This has a great influence on the extraction of sensitive features.

- DAPASA [13] found that the number of sensitive API calls in the data set, personalization, and weather is not the same.
- Sokolova [8] in accordance with Google's 35 application classification analysis of various types of applications permission mode found that they are very different.

Different from the previous analysis scheme, in this paper, we cluster benign applications and malicious applications according to similarity before extracting sensitive features, and then extraction sensitive feature for each class.

3 Proposed Model: Android Malware Detection Using Category-Based Permission Vectors

In this section, we will introduce training sets, classification model, and the extraction of sensitive features. The classification model will be completed in three steps: Step 1, the classification model will be obtained by clustering the benign applications; Step 2, the malicious applications will be classified based on the model, and Step 3, the same category of data will be combined to form the new data set.

3.1 Datasets for Benign and Malicious Android Applications

In the proposed framework, we used two datasets. One dataset consists of 13,382 benign apps downloaded from official Android application market i.e., Google App Store [23], Huawei App Store [24], and Xiao MI App Store [25] by using *android-*

market-api [26, 30]. The second dataset is of 13,588 malicious applications. This dataset is available on VirusShare [27]. The VirusShare is a repository of 30,677,508 samples of malware applications which provide an excellent opportunity to security researchers, incident responders, and forensic analysts, to carry out their research and analysis.

Data Extraction Phase: In order to obtain the app permission information, we decompiled the *.apk* file using Androguard package [28, 31]. Afterward, the permission vector of each app is extracted from its specific *AndroidManifest.xml* file.

After extracting the permissions of every app, we pre-processed the datasets by removing the apps which are using three or less permissions. Similarly, we filtered the applications using custom or misspelled permissions. Finally, we get 13,099 malicious and 12,925 benign application permission vectors. Note that the permission vectors are based on Android 4.4 SDK which contains 122 system permissions.

3.2 Clustering

Most of the researchers directly extract sensitive feature permissions in various ways. But, can they extract effective sensitive features? No, the effectiveness and applicability of sensitive features are often low due to factors such as the finiteness, complexity, and reliability of the training set. The results of DAPASA [13] show that sensitive features show different sensitivities for each category in the App store. So feature extraction for different classes is necessary and it can improve detection efficiency. However, App store classifies every application by businesses which cannot reflect the similarity of request resources. Therefore, in this proposed approach we classify the applications on the basis of requested permissions and establish a classification model.

Normally, a malicious application adds additional malicious behavior when it completes a similar function to a benign application. Therefore, we classify malicious applications by clustering benign applications and obtaining clustering models to achieve the same class of malicious applications and benign applications with similar basic functions.

We will complete the functional clustering of training apps in third steps. In order to better understand the details of the clustering module, we introduce some symbols.

p_m: It is permission. $p_m = 1$ is means that request, $p_m = 0$ is means that have not, and $1 < m < 122$.

$\vec{v_i}$:   It is permission vector for an app, each dimension p_m represents permission. $\vec{v_i} = (p_1, p_2, \cdots, p_{122})$

V: Set of all permission vectors, $V = \{\vec{v_i} | 1 \le i \le n\}$

$\vec{s_x}$:   The centroids for class x, $\vec{s_x} \in V$

C: Set of all centroids, $C = \{\vec{s_x} | 1 \le x \le k\}$

Clu_x: Set of class x, $1 \le x \le k$.

Step 1: Cluster benign applications.
Output: Clustering model and a class tag for each benign application.
We used an unsupervised learning algorithm, because for any application, we didn't know its category at first. We need to cluster by comparing the similarities between applications. In other words, we compare the similarity between the unknown object and the object of center. This is a centroid models, k-means is the good choice. The core of k-means consists of two steps.

Step 1: For C, we randomly acquire $\vec{s_x}$ from V, and assign each $\vec{v_i} \in V$ to the cluster whose mean has the least distance with $\vec{s_x}$, this is intuitively the "nearest" mean. Exactly, each $\vec{v_i} \in V$ is assigned to one Clu_x as shown in Eq. 1.

$$Clu_x = \min\left[\sum\nolimits_{x=1}^{k} dist\left(\vec{v_i}, \vec{s_x}\right)\right] \quad \forall \vec{v_i} \in V \tag{1}$$

Step 2: Get the new $\vec{s_x} = (p_1, p_2, \cdots, p_{122})$ in Clu_x and iterate step 1 (p_m of $\vec{s_x}$ is the average of all vectors in Clu_x). If the $\vec{s_x}$ no longer change, the algorithm has converged and the algorithm terminates.

After the 2 steps, we got Clu_x and C. The degree of similarity of $\vec{v_i}$ in each class is very high. It is means that applications in each class use similar system resources. Figure 3 shows the algorithm flow chart.

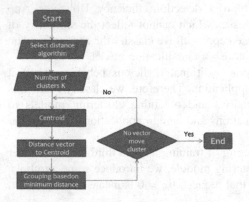

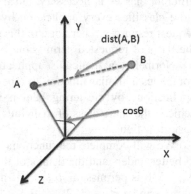

Fig. 3. K-means algorithm flow chart

Fig. 4. Cosine similarity

Distance calculation – In our model, $dist\left(\vec{v_i}, \vec{s_x}\right)$ is means that the degree of similarity of $\vec{v_i}$ and $\vec{s_x}$. This is the most important parameter for the classifier. It directly determines the validity of the classification result. Compared to the distance metrics, the cosine similarity focuses more on the difference in direction of the two vectors than the distance or length. Cosine similarity uses the cosine of the angle between two vectors in vector space as the measure of the difference between two individuals. It is $\cos\theta$ not $dist(A, B)$ as shown in Fig. 4. Cosine Similarity not only reflects the number of same permissions, but also reflects the relationship between two permission vectors.

The $\text{dist}(\overrightarrow{v_i}, \overrightarrow{s_x})$ basic with Cosine similarity:

$$\text{dist}(\overrightarrow{v_i}, \overrightarrow{s_x}) = \frac{\sum_1^{122}(\overrightarrow{v_i} \times \overrightarrow{s_x})}{\sqrt{\sum_1^{122}(\overrightarrow{v_i})^2} \times \sqrt{\sum_1^{122}(\overrightarrow{s_x})^2}} \tag{2}$$

The number of clusters is also a very important parameter and the appropriate number of classifications determines the effectiveness of the extraction of sensitive feature permissions. If the number of clusters is small, the distance within the cluster is large and the cohesion is low, which may lead to the same sensitive feature permissions as the classification. A large number of classifications will result in a high degree of similarity between groups, the distances of permission vectors are almost equal to the centroid and can not classify effectively. Google Store classify the applications into 35 categories, we tried different values of k ranging from 10 to 42. The Davies–Bouldin index [32, 33] is calculated for each value of k and the results are summarized in Fig. 5 with concluding value of k is 32.

The Davies-Bouldin index is the most important parameter to measure the clustering model. It reflects the intra-class cohesion and inter-class repulsive force by calculating the ratio of the sum of infraclass distances to extraterrestrial distances in the computed classification results. The smaller the value is, the higher the degree of similarity within the class is, and the lower the degree of similarity between classes is, the better the clustering effect is.

For step 1, we input the permission vector in the benign application set into the clustering algorithm, through n iterations, the algorithm tends to converge. All trusted application vectors are divided into 32 classes from Cluster_0 to Cluster_31 and a clustering model is obtained include C.

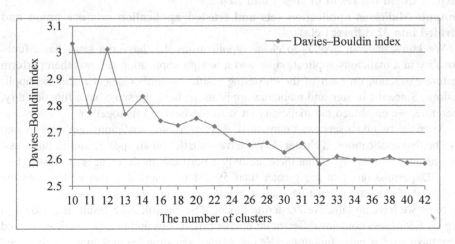

Fig. 5. Davies–Bouldin index for k

Step 2: Classification of malicious applications based on the clustering model.
Output: Add a class tag for each malicious application.

The permissions requested by the malicious applications not only need to complete basic functions, but also need to complete malicious behaviors, so their permission vector is not "trustworthy". In order to effectively classify, we calculated the similarity between the malicious application permission vector and the centroid vector in the clustering model to predict the basic functions of malicious applications and classify them.

Because of the high dimension of the permission vector, we use the 4-dimensional vector as an example in Table 1. For the malicious application M_1, the similarity is confirmed by calculating the cosine distances from different centroids respectively, the boldface words represent the number of dimensions of the same value, and the application is then classified into the class with the highest similarity.

For step 2, we input the permission vector of the malicious applications into the clustering model which classify by comparing the cosine similarity of each vector with the centroid.

Table 1. A simple example of classification

	C_1: 0110	C_2: 1001	
M_1: 0010	0.71 **2**	0 **1**	C_1
M_2: 0100	0.58 **3**	0 **1**	C_1
M_3: 1101	0.41 **1**	0.82 **3**	C_2
M_4: 1011	0.41 **1**	0.82 **3**	C_2

Step 3: Union the result of step 1 and step 2.
Output: Malicious application sets and trusted application sets are union and divided into 32 different classes.

We know that our goal is to cluster applications that have the same basic functionality in a malicious application set and a benign application set, and then perform feature extraction on each of the clustering results to further detect malicious applications. Since the benign and malicious applications have the same basic functionality, therefore, we combined the malicious set with the benign sets together.

After the two data sets were combined, there were 465 malicious applications and 445 benign applications in cluster_1. We have statistics on all applications in this class. The results show in Fig. 6 that there are only 8 permissions differences in cluster_1 of the 122 permissions that are greater than 5%. It is means that this will reduce the difficulty of extracting sensitive features while improving the effectiveness.

Now we have an effective clustering model. The classification results are shown in Fig. 7. Each class contains different numbers of malicious and benign applications and they have similar basic functions. We can extract sensitive features more easily based on the classification results, and it is very effective.

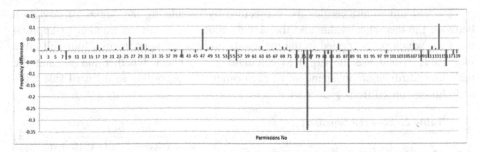

Fig. 6. Per-permissions frequency difference between malware and benign app in cluster_1

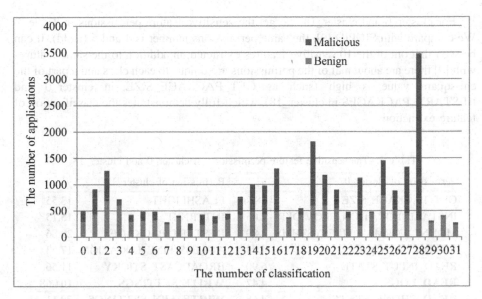

Fig. 7. Malicious apps and benign apps classification results

3.3 Feature Extraction Module

After the classification of permission vector set, the similarity of vectors in same class is high. Therefore, we do not need to use a very complicated method to filter the classification extraction. A lot of researchers use chi-square test to extract sensitive features because its sensitivity to single features is very good, but due to the problem of correlation between features, it has not achieved very good results. However, with vector clustering, a high degree of similarity within a class means that a high degree of relevance has a high number of occurrences in the class and does not become a sensitive feature. Therefore, we choose chi-square test [34, 35] to extract sensitive features.

The chi-square test verifies the conjecture by calculating the degree of deviation between the theoretical value and the actual value. We count the number of applications for which p_m is applied in the malicious and benign apps, form a four-cell table like Table 2, and use the Eq. 3 to calculate χ^2, to check whether the p_m and the malicious attribute are independent of each other. We according to the card side table and choose top 10 from $\chi^2 > 3.84$.

Table 2. Four-cell table for p_m

	$p_m = 1$	$p_m = 0$
Malware	a	b
Benign	c	d

$$\chi_m^2 = \frac{(ad - bc)^2 * N}{(a+b)(c+d)(a+c)(b+d)} \quad (3)$$

$$N = a+b+c+d \quad (4)$$

For cluster_0 and cluster_18, we get the sensitive feature permissions in Table 3. We compare with SIGPID [9], the same permissions number is 4 and 5 (Bold). It can be seen that out of the 10 sensitive features extracted, in addition to the same features with [9] there are about half of the permissions are unique to each class and a part of the chi-square value is high (such as GET_PACKAGE_SIZE in cluster_0 and RESTART_PACKAGES in cluster_18), which fully demonstrates the classification of feature extraction.

Table 3. The sensitive feature permissions of cluster_0 and cluster_18

Permission of cluster_0	χ^2	Permission of cluster_18	χ^2
GET_PACKAGE_SIZE	18.74	FLASHLIGHT	13.55
INSTALL_LOCATION_PROVIDER	7.05	INTERNET	13.15
MOUNT_FORMAT_FILESYSTEMS	4.89	RESTART_PACKAGES	29.86
READ_CALENDAR	4.78	ACCESS_FINE_LOCATION	17.53
READ_INPUT_STATE	6.90	BROADCAST_STICKY	11.56
READ_LOGS	**4.47**	**WRITE_SETTINGS**	**104.68**
READ_PHONE_STATE	**4.68**	**WRITE_APN_SETTINGS**	**39.11**
VIBRATE	**4.16**	**SYSTEM_ALERT_WINDOW**	**12.71**
WRITE_SMS	**212.17**	READ_HISTORY_BOOKMARKS	12.16
		READ_SMS	15.67

4   Results and Discussion

We verified the validity of the model and the accuracy of the detection through experiments. The results showed that the detection rate reached 93.66%. In this part we describe and analyze the details and results of the experiment, Sect. 4.1 introduce the dataset and the metrics. Section 4.2 compared the detection results by different machine learning algorithms to select an algorithm with high detection efficiency for this model. Section 4.3 compared detection results with other models.

4.1   Dataset and Metrics

In order to obtain more effective test results, we set up two training sets. One is randomly selecting 7581 permission vectors from malicious and benign sets; the other one is 263 android malware applications were downloaded from another malware sharing site named contagion mobile [29], which is widely used as a benchmark dataset for malware detection.

The metrics used to measure our detection results are shown in Table 4 from [13].

Table 4. The metrics of performance

Abbr (Term)	Definition	Abbr (Term)	Definition
TP (True Positive)	Malicious apps classified as malicious apps	Acc (Accuracy)	TP + TN/ (TP + TN + FN + FP)
TN (True Negative)	Benign apps classified as benign apps	TPR (True Positive Rate)	TP/(TP + FN)
FN (False Negative)	Malicious apps classified as benign apps	FPR (False Positive Rate)	FP/(FP + FN)
FP (False Positive)	Benign apps classified as benign apps		

4.2   Detection Performances with Six Machine Learning Algorithms

Mainly to get the better performance of machine learning algorithm, six common machine learning algorithms, Neural networks, Deep learning, k-NN, Naive Bayes, Decision Tree and Random Forest. The choice of algorithm requires a lot of data for testing and statistics so we chose all of the sets data and get ACC FPR TPR in Table 5. After classification, the performance of the six algorithms can achieve a high Acc and a low FPR. In particular, the result shows that Neural networks algorithm not only has highest ACC TPR but also low FPR. Therefore, in this work, Neural networks is selected as the classifier in subsequent experiments.

Table 5. Performance detection of six algorithms

	Neural networks	Deep learning	k-NN	Naive Bayes	Decision tree	Random forest
Acc	94.02% (1)	84.83%	89.66%	85.52%	86.21%	82.99%
FPR	3.80% (2)	22.78%	0.00%	6.33%	13.92%	5.91%
TPR	91.41% (2)	93.94%	77.27%	75.76%	86.36%	69.70%

4.3   Comparison with Other Approaches

In this section, we use cross-validation to test our dataset based on Neural networks, we show that 9 of these test results are analyzed in Fig. 7. The Acc for data set detection results is 93.66%. Next, we compared and analyzed the design and results of state-of-the-art malicious app detection tools.

SIGPID [9] is a scheme for realizing the extraction of sensitive features through the three-layer pruning scheme of the data matrix permission matrix to optimize the feature extraction process and finally obtain 10 sensitive permissions. Then use the support vector machine and decision tree algorithm to retrain the training set, and finally get the detection model. However, because of the limited training set, the authority is extracted and the unknown software is detected.

Wang et al. [20] ranks permissions by analyzing permissions, and then re-determines 40 dangerous permissions. However, due to the small number of malicious software in the training set, the analysis results are not good, especially the false positive rate.

The other 10 comparison objects are the existing anti-virus scanners described in [9] (Table 6).

Table 6. Detection rates of this model and anti-virus scanners

This model	Mutual information [20]	SIGPID [9]	AV1	AV2	AV3	AV4
93.66%	86.4%	93.62%	96.41%	93.71%	84.66%	84.54%
AV5	AV6	AV7	AV8	AV9	AV10	
78.38%	64.16%	48.50%	48.34%	9.84%	3.99%	

The results show that we have the same classification effect with SIGPID [9]. The extraction scheme is very good. But in fact, he only extracted 10 features based on the training set. Although the training set has high test results, the number of applications in the training set is limited, and the applicability of the extracted features to unknown applications is also limited. Need to improve. In the following work, we will try to use the model's feature extraction scheme in our 32 classes and expect to be able to extract detection efficiency.

The test results of the 10 commercial detection tools on the test set show that one of them is 3% points higher than ours, another one is similar to ours, and the other 8 are very poor. The reason is that most of the current detection tools rely on the matching of malicious code bases and malware signature libraries to detect them, but they are affected by changes in the attack methods, limitations on the number of samples, and regional conditions (Fig. 8).

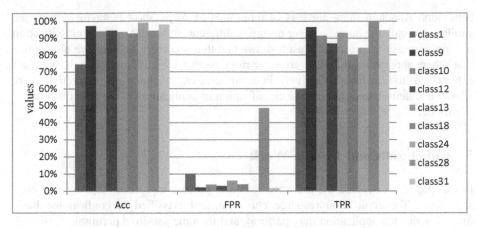

Fig. 8. Cross-validation results

In other wise, 263 android malware applications were downloaded from another malware sharing site named contagion mobile [29], the results show that 237 apps have been detect, detection rate for unknown software is 90.11% (Fig. 9).

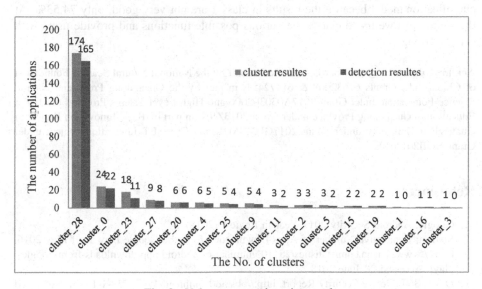

Fig. 9. Unknown apps detection results

4.4 Discussion

The experiments show that our approach achieves good performance with Acc of 93.66%. We analysis the result of our work to other approaches that permission classifier, and found that our plan is more reasonable. First, in order to complete the target function, App will call a set of resources of the system to implement a set of behaviors. Although there are tens of thousands of Apps, most behavior groups are similar, and only the business layer design is different, so we can achieve classification of App permission vector. The result shows that this is correct. Second, we also notice that others approaches that only consider risky permissions, it's not enough, we can't extract sensitive features effectively in a big dataset. In one word, extracting more effective features based on accurate classification of applications is the core outcome of our model.

5   Conclusion and Future Work

In this paper, we divided the malware detection process into three steps by two classifications. The application resource cluster is first classified to confirm the basic functions that the application may perform, and then the sensitive permissions of such applications are extracted. Finally, the extracted sensitive rights are utilized to detect whether the application is a malicious application using a machine learning algorithm. The detection result is superior to most of the detection tools, and we only analyze the permission information with a low complexity and the detection scheme is logically designed. Through this scheme, the extraction of sensitive features is more accurate and precise, improving the detection performance. In the future, we will optimize the classification model because the results in class 1 are not very good, only 74.53%. At the same time, we try to clarify the various possible functions and provide users with early warning.

Acknowledgments. This work is supported in part by the National Natural Science Foundation of China under Grants 61632009 & 61472451, in part by the Guangdong Provincial Natural Science Foundation under Grant 2017A030308006 and High-Level Talents Program of Higher Education in Guangdong Province under Grant 2016ZJ01, in part by Basic Innovation Project of Guangzhou University under Grant 2017GDJC-M18 and CERNET Innovation Project under Grant NGII20170102.

References

1. Google: Android Security 2017 Year in Review (2018)
2. Statista: Cumulative Number of Apps Downloaded from the Google Play as of May 2016. https://www.statista.com/statistics/281106/number-of-android-app-downloads-from-google-play/. Accessed 20 June 2018
3. Qihoo 360: Mobile Security Report. http://bbs.360.cn/thread-14972358-1-1.html. Accessed 20 June 2018
4. Kaspersky Labs: Mobile Malware Evolution (2017). https://securelist.com/mobile-Malware-review-2017/84139/. Accessed 20 June 2018
5. Symantec: Latest Intelligence for March 2016. In: Symantec Official Blog (2016)
6. Drake, J., Lanier, Z., Mulliner, C., et al.: Android Hacker's Handbook. Wiley, Hoboken (2014)
7. Faruki, P., et al.: Android security: a survey of issues, malware penetration, and defenses. IEEE Commun. Surv. Tutors. **17**, 998–1022 (2015)

8. Sokolova, K., Perez, C., Lemercier, M.: Android application classification and anomaly detection with graph-based permission patterns. Decis. Support Syst. **93**, 62–76 (2017)
9. Li, J., Sun, L., Yan, Q., Li, Z., Srisa-an, W., Ye, H.: Android malware detection. IEEE Trans. Ind. Inform. **14**(7), 3216–3225 (2018)
10. Felt, A., Chin, E., Hanna, S.: Android permissions demystified. In: Proceedings of 18th ACM Conference on Computer and Communications Security - CCS 2011, pp. 627–636 (2011)
11. Peng, H., et al.: Using probabilistic generative models for ranking risks of Android apps. In: Proceedings of 2012 ACM Conference on Computer and Communications Security - CCS 2012, p. 241 (2012)
12. Enck, W., Ongtang, M., McDaniel, P.: On lightweight mobile phone application certification. In: Proceedings of 16th ACM Computer and Communications Security. - CCS 2009, p. 235 (2009)
13. Fan, M., Liu, J., Wang, W., Li, H., Tian, Z., Liu, T.: DAPASA: detecting android piggybacked apps through sensitive subgraph analysis. IEEE Trans. Inf. Forensics Secur. **12**, 1772–1785 (2017)
14. Grace, M., Zhou, Y., Zhang, Q., Zou, S., Jiang, X.: RiskRanker: scalable and accurate zero-day android malware detection. In: 10th International Conference on Mobile Systems, Applications, and Services, pp. 281–294 (2012)
15. Zhou, Y., Wang, Z., Zhou, W., Jiang, X.: Hey, you, get off of my market: detecting malicious apps in official and alternative android markets. In: Proceedings of 19th Annual Network and Distributed System Security Symposium, pp. 5–8 (2012)
16. Hao, H., Singh, V., Du, W.: On the effectiveness of API-level access control using bytecode rewriting in Android. In: Proceedings of 8th ACM SIGSAC Symposium on Information, Computer and Communications Security - ASIA CCS 2013, p. 25 (2013)
17. Bu, K., Xu, M., Liu, X., Luo, J., Zhang, S., Weng, M.: Deterministic detection of cloning attacks for anonymous RFID systems. IEEE Trans. Ind. Inform. **11**, 1255–1266 (2015)
18. Cruz, T., et al.: A cybersecurity detection framework for supervisory control and data acquisition systems. IEEE Trans. Ind. Inform. **1**, 1–10 (2016)
19. G. Android: Requesting permissions. https://developer.android.google.cn/guide/topics/permissions/overview#normal-dangerous
20. Wang, W., Wang, X., Feng, D., Liu, J., Han, Z., Zhang, X.: Exploring permission-induced risk in android applications for malicious application detection. IEEE Trans. Inf. Forensics Secur. **9**, 1869–1882 (2014)
21. Xu, W., Zhang, F., Zhu, S.: Permlyzer: analyzing permission usage in Android applications. In: 2013 IEEE 24th International Symposium on Software Reliability Engineering, ISSRE 2013, pp. 400–410 (2013)
22. Arp, D., Spreitzenbarth, M., Hübner, M., Gascon, H., Rieck, K.: Drebin: effective and explainable detection of android malware in your pocket. In: Proceedings of 2014 Network and Distributed System Security Symposium (2014)
23. Google Play Homepage. https://play.google.com/store. Accessed 19 June 2018
24. Huawei App Store Homepage. http://appstore.huawei.com/soft/list. Accessed 20 June 2018
25. Xiao MI App Store Homepage. http://app.mi.com/. Accessed 20 June 2018
26. Application Details Query Interface. http://code.google.com/p/android-market-api/. Accessed 19 May 2018
27. Malicious App Sharing Site. https://virusshare.com/. Accessed 20 June 2018
28. Application Analyzing Tool. http://code.google.com/p/androguard/. Accessed 25 Apr 2018
29. Android Malicious Application Sharing. https://contagiominidump.blogspot.com/. Accessed 20 June 2018

30. Ali, S., Wang, G., Cottrell, R.L., Anwar, T.: Detecting anomalies from end-to-end internet performance measurements (PingER) using cluster based local outlier factor. In: 2017 IEEE ISPA/IUCC, pp. 982–989 (2017)

31. Fuchs, A.P., Chaudhuri, A., Foster, J.: SCanDroid : automated security certification of android applications. Read, vol. **10**, p. 328 (2010)

32. Ali, S., Wang, G., Xing, X., Cottrell, R.L.: Substituting missing values in end-to-end internet performance measurements using k-nearest neighbors. In: 2018 IEEE 16th International Conference on Dependable, Autonomic and Secure Computing, 16th International Conference on Pervasive Intelligence and Computing, 4th International Conference on Big Data Intelligence and Computing and Cyber Science and Technology Congress (DASC/PiCom/DataCom/CyberSciTech), pp. 919–926. IEEE, August 2018

33. Davies, D.L., Bouldin, D.W.: A cluster separation measure. IEEE Trans. Pattern Anal. Mach. Intell. **PAMI-1**, 224–227 (1979)

34. Fornasini, P.: The Uncertainty in Physical Measurements (2008)

35. Ali, S., Wang, G., Cottrell, R.L., Masood, S.: Internet performance analysis of South Asian countries using end-to-end internet performance measurements. In: 2017 IEEE ISPA/IUCC, pp. 1319–1326 (2017)

Outsourced Privacy Preserving SVM with Multiple Keys

Wenli Sun[1], Zoe L. Jiang[1(✉)], Jun Zhang[2], S. M. Yiu[2], Yulin Wu[1],
Hainan Zhao[1], Xuan Wang[1], and Peng Zhang[3]

[1] Harbin Institute of Technology (Shenzhen), Shenzhen 518055, China
{sunwenli,yulinwu,wangxuan}@cs.hitsz.edu.cn,
zoeljiang@hit.edu.cn, hainan.hh@gmail.com
[2] The University of Hong Kong, Pok Fu Lam, Hong Kong
{jzhang3,smyiu}@cs.hku.hk
[3] Shenzhen University, Shenzhen, China
zhangp@szu.edu.cn

Abstract. With the development of cloud computing, more and more people choose to upload their own data to cloud for storage outsourcing and computing outsourcing. Because cloud is not completely trusted, the uploading data is encrypted by user's own public key. However, many of the current secure computing methods only apply to single-key encrypted data. Therefore, it is a challenge to efficiently handle multiple key-encrypted data on cloud. On the other hand, the Demand for data classification is also growing. In particular, using support vector machine (SVM) algorithm to classify data. But currently there is no good way to utilize SVM for ciphertext especially the ciphertext is encrypted by multiple key. Therefore, it is also a challenge to efficiently classify data encrypted by multiple keys using SVM. In order to solve the above challenges, in this paper we propose a scheme that allows the SVM algorithm to perform classification processing on the outsourced data encrypted by multi-key without jeopardizing the privacy of the user's original data, intermediate calculation results and final classification result. In addition, we also verified the safety and correctness of our designed protocol.

Keywords: Support vector machine · Multiple keys
Privacy preserving · Outsourced computation and storage
Homomorphic encryption

1 Introduction

The development of Internet technology has made it easy to obtain massive amounts of information. Along with the advancement of Internet technology, the number of medical data is also growing exponentially. At present, data mining technology based on machine learning can effectively help people convert huge data resources into useful knowledge and information resources, which in turn can help people make scientific decisions. So we can use data mining in

© Springer Nature Switzerland AG 2018
J. Vaidya and J. Li (Eds.): ICA3PP 2018, LNCS 11337, pp. 415–430, 2018.
https://doi.org/10.1007/978-3-030-05063-4_32

the medical field to help doctors diagnose. However, in order to analyze more accurately, it is necessary to collect data from multiple medical units. Also due to local storage restrictions, data should be stored and also calculated on cloud. But there are many problems in the process of data mining.

First, the disclosure of the patient's private information is a problem. Because the cloud is provided by a third party, it is not entirely trustworthy.

Second, the calculation on ciphertext is also a problem. Since data mining is performed on cloud, how to perform data mining on the ciphertext stored on cloud without revealing data privacy is also a problem.

Third, it is a problem to calculate on the ciphertext after multikey encryption. Because each unit's data is encrypted with its own public key. Therefore, the cloud stores ciphertexts encrypted by multiple different key. However, the homomorphic encryption protocol can only support the computation on the same public key encrypted data. So this is also a problem.

Finally, Choosing a data mining algorithm is a problem. Nowadays, with the increasing complexity of medical data mining objects, people have put forward new requirements for the efficiency and accuracy of data mining algorithms. Therefore, choosing an efficient data mining algorithm is a problem.

In summary, this paper will focus on how to solve the above problems. The specific solutions are as follows. First, the solution to the first problem is that these medical data need to be encrypted before uploading to cloud. Second, the solution to the second problem is to design the protocol based on the semi-homomorphic encryption protocol so that it can support various kinds of machine learning calculations. Next, the solution to the third problem is to redesign the protocol so that it can satisfy the various computing of the machine learning algorithm on the multikey encrypted data. Finally, the solution to the last problem is to choose SVM algorithm, because SVM algorithm has a strong generalization ability, can handle high-dimensional data sets and can solve nonlinear problems very well without local minima problems.

1.1   Our Contribution

In this paper, we focus on how to use SVM for privacy preserving data mining on horizontal, vertical and arbitrary data distribution. In addition, we also discuss how to use kernel functions to complete data classification tasks when data is linearly inseparable.

Because we use SVM for data classification, in order to enable SVM to perform calculations on ciphertext, we analyzed that the main calculation of SVM is dot product, and dot product can be divided into addition after multiplication. Therefore, we designed a secure addition protocol and a secure multiplication protocol that can be calculated on ciphertext for SVM. And these two protocols can also be applied to other machine learning models.

In addition, because the storage outsourcing and computing outsourcing are used in this paper, the cloud stores ciphertext encrypted by each medical unit's public key. Therefore, in order to achieve the calculation of multikey encrypted data, we refer to the efficient privacy preserving outsourced calculation framework with multiple keys protocol when designing the solution.

Finally, in order to improve the security of the system, in this model, adversaries can eavesdrop on data exchanged between different participants. And we allow adversaries to collude with users or one of two clouds without allowing them to collude with those challenge users. In addition, in order to prevent the abuse of data, we have increased the control of the authority of the research institutions.

1.2 Paper Organization

The rest of this paper is organized as follows. In Sect. 2, we briefly discuss the related work. In Sect. 3, Some notations, including efficient privacy preserving outsourced calculation framework with multiple keys, and support vector machine will be described. In Sect. 4, we formalize the system model and introduce the attacker model. we describe the details of our outsourced privacy preserving SVM with multiple keys scheme in Sect. 5. Sections 6 and 7 show the security and performance analysis of the proposed system respectively. we conclude this paper in Sect. 8.

2 Related Work

We will introduce related work from three aspects: privacy-preserving data mining on distributed data, privacy-preserving data mining based on computational outsourcing, and privacy-preserving data mining based on computation outsourcing and storage outsourcing.

2.1 Distributed Privacy Preserving Data Mining Method

The distributed privacy preserving data classification method mainly considers the privacy issues of distributed computing on the data stored in each participant. There are three kind of data distribution: horizontal distribution, vertical distribution and arbitrary distribution. In 2006, Yu et al. [1] proposed a privacy preserving solution for SVM classification based on nonlinear kernel functions. This scheme builds a global SVM classification model for horizontally distributed data set which is distributed on various parties. In the same year, they also proposed a SVM classification model for vertically distributed data sets without leaking data privacy [2]. In 2008, Vaidya et al. [3] presented a privacy-preserving SVM classification model, which can be applied to arbitrarily distributed data sets in addition to horizontally and vertically distributed data. In 2010, Hu et al. [4] proposed a privacy-preserved SVM classification scheme based on arbitrarily distributed data, and the SVM classification scheme will not reveal the privacy of data even if it is published.

2.2   Computing Outsourcing Privacy Preserving Data Mining Method

Computing outsourcing is mainly based on the cloud computing technology. It outsources the calculations of each participant to cloud, which greatly reduces the computing load of each participant. In recent years, there are few researches for computing outsourcing privacy preserving data mining, which mainly include: in 2015, Liu et al. [5] proposed a two-party computational outsourcing privacy preserving K-means method for single-key homomorphic encryption. In 2016, Zhang et al. [6] proposed a computing outsourcing privacy preserving deep learning model.

2.3   Storage and Computing Outsourcing Privacy Preserving Data Mining Method

Because in the process of computing outsourcing, users and the cloud need to conduct a large amount of data communication, thus limiting the efficiency of the entire system. To solve this problem, the methods of storage and computing outsourcing can be adopted. In 2015, Liu et al. [8] proposed a privacy-preserved storage and computing outsourcing SVM classification scheme based on the fully homomorphic encryption protocol for the vertically distributed data. However, this solution is not efficient due to the use of the fully homomorphic encryption scheme. Moreover, the user needs to participate in some calculations during the calculation process. In 2017, Li et al. [16] proposed a scheme based on BCP cryptosystem [11] and fully homomorphic encryption protocol that can support the use of deep learning to privacy preserving data mining on the data encrypted by multiple keys. In the same year they designed a privacy preserving framework that can be used for classification outsourcing based on the fully homomorphic encryption protocol [17]. And Zhang et al. [9] proposed a SVM classification scheme supporting data outsourcing and calculation outsourcing based on the integer vector encryption protocol. In this scheme, two users negotiate a key-switching matrix to achieve the purpose of ciphertext conversion, thus completing the computation on multikey encrypted data. At the same year, Zhang et al. [10] designed a SVM classification scheme based on BCP cryptosystem [11] and multiplicative homomorphism protocol for the vertically distributed data set, and introduced two clouds in the scheme. The comparison results of using SVM for privacy preserving data mining works are shown in Table 1.

Through the analysis of the above-mentioned related work, we found that there is still a lot of work to be done for privacy preserving data mining using SVM. Therefore, this paper will focus on how to use SVM for data mining on multikey encrypted data based on storage outsourcing and computation outsourcing. The distribution of the data is horizontal, vertical or arbitrary. In addition, we will also discuss how to use SVM for privacy preserving data mining on linearly inseparable data.

Table 1. The characteristic comparison among different schemes.

Scheme	Horizontal distribution	Vertical distribution	Arbitrary distribution	Computing outsourcing	Computing and storage outsourcing	Users online
[1]	✓	×	×	✓	×	✓
[2]	×	✓	×	×	×	✓
[3, 4]	✓	✓	✓	×	×	✓
[8]	×	✓	×	×	✓	✓
[10]	×	✓	×	×	✓	×

3   Preliminaries

In this section we will introduce a cryptographic algorithm that supports multiple key calculations and an optimized SVM classification model that will be used in the following scenarios.

3.1   Efficient Privacy Preserving Outsourced Calculation Framework with Multiple Keys (EPOM)

Liu et al. [12] proposed the EPOM, which we utilize for our privacy preserving SVM algorithm. Liu's Scheme is as follows:

$Setup(k)$: Given a security parameter k and two large prime numbers p, q (i.e., $p = 2p' + 1$ and $q = 2q' + 1$ for distinct primes p' and q', respectively). Both the length of p, q are k. We then compute $N = pq$ and choose a random element $g \in Z_{N^2}^*$ of order $2p'q'$ (this can be achieved by selecting a random number $a \in Z_{N^2}^*$ and computing g as $g = -a^{2N}$). The algorithm outputs public parameter $PP = (N, k, g)$ and master secret $MK = lcm(p-1, q-1)$. Then the KGC sends the PP to each user, and splits the MK into two parts $MK^{(1)}, MK^{(2)}$.

$KeyGen(P, P)$: Each user selects a random $a_i \in Z_{N^2}$ and $a_i \in [1, N/4]$, then Computes $h_i = g^{a_i} \bmod N^2$ and outputs public key $pk_i = (N, g, h_i)$, secrete key $sk_i = a_i$.

$Enc_{pk_i}(m)$: Given a message $m \in Z_N$, then choose a random number $r \in [1, N/4]$. The ciphertext under pk_i can be generated as $Enc_{pk_i}(m) = (A, B)$, where $A = g^r \bmod N^2$, $B = h_i^r(1 + mN) \bmod N^2$.

$Dec_{sk_i}(A_i, B_i)$: Given a ciphertext (A_i, B_i) and secrete key $sk_i = a_i$, output the plaintext m as:

$$m = \frac{B_i/(A_i^{a_i}) - 1 \bmod N^2}{N} \tag{1}$$

$MKs(MK)$: The master key MK can be randomly split into two parts $MK^{(1)} = k_1, MK^{(2)} = k_2$, s.t., $k_1 + k_2 \equiv 0 \bmod MK$ and $k_1 + k_2 \equiv 1 \bmod N^2$.

$PSDec1(A_i, B_i)$: Once a ciphertext (A_i, B_i) is received, The key $MK^{(1)}, MK^{(2)}$ can be used consecutively to decrypt the ciphertext as follows:

$$C_i^{(1)} = PSDec1(A_i, B_i) = g^{r a_i k_1}(1 + mNk_1) \ mod \ N^2 \tag{2}$$

$PSDec2(A_i, B_i, C_i^{(1)})$: Once the $C_i^{(1)}$ and the ciphertext (A_i, B_i) are received, then the ciphertext can be partially decrypted by $MK^{(2)}$ as follows:

$$C_i^{(2)} = B_i^{k_2} = g^{r a_i k_2}(1 + mNk_2) \ mod \ N^2 \tag{3}$$

After decryption using $MK^{(1)}, MK^{(2)}$, the plaintext m can be calculated as:

$$C_i = C_i^{(1)} \cdot C_i^{(2)}, \ m = PSDec2(A_i, B_i, C_i) = \frac{C_i - 1}{N} \ mod \ N^2 \tag{4}$$

If given a ciphertext (A_i, B_i) encrypted with the joint public key pk_{Σ_p} (i.e., $pk_{\Sigma_p} = (N, g, h_{\Sigma_p} = g^{a_p + \Sigma_{j=1, \cdots, n} a_j})$) which associates with user $j(j = 1, \cdots, n)$ and user p, the decryption of this ciphertext can be divided into two steps and implemented by the following calculation.

$PWDec1$: Once ciphertext (A_i, B_i) is received, the partial weak decrypted ciphertext WT^i can be calculated with partial private key $sk_i = a_i$ as follows:

$$WT^i = A_i{}^{a_i} = g^{r a_i} \ mod \ N^2 \tag{5}$$

$PWDec2$: Once ciphertext$(A_i, B_i), WT^{(1)}, WT^{(2)}, \cdots, WT^{(n)}$ are received, the $PWDec2$ algorithm can be run as follows:

By virtue of partial private key $sk_p = a_p$, the partial weak decrypted ciphertext $WT^{(p)}$ can be calculated as:

$$WT^{(p)} = (A_i)^{a_p} = g^{r a_p} \ mod \ N^2 \tag{6}$$

Then the plaintext m can be calculated as:

$$WT = \Pi_{i=1}^{n} WT^{(i)} \cdot WT^{(p)}, \ m = \frac{\frac{B_i}{WT} \ mod \ N^2 - 1}{N}. \tag{7}$$

In addition, when given $C_1 = Enc_{pk}(m_1)$ and $C_2 = Enc_{pk}(m_2)$ encrypted with the same key, it can be verified by the following calculation that the algorithm satisfies additive homomorphism properties.

$$C_1 \cdot C_2 = Enc_{pk}(m_1 + m_2), \ [Enc_{pk}(m)]^{N-1} = Enc_{pk}(-m) \tag{8}$$

3.2 Support Vector Machine

Support vector machines are mainly used to classify data. The classification process can be divided into two steps: training and classification, as follows:

Training: Given a training data set $\{(x_i, y_i)\}_{i=1}^n$, where the training set sample $x_i \in R^m$ and the corresponding class lable $y_i \in \{+1, -1\}$. We first consider the case of linear separability. For the problem of linear inseparability, we can solve it with the aid of a kernel function. When linearly separable, the mechanism of the SVM is to find a hyperplane ($w^T x - b = 0$) to divide data into two categories based on the labels, where $w \in R^m$ is a weight vector and b is a bias item. The distance from the sample point of the support vectors to the hyperplane is $\frac{1}{||w||}$. In order to better divide the sample we need to maximize this distance. For the purpose of dealing with noise and increased fault tolerance, we use soft margin in practice, of which ξ denotes the slack variable to allow error. To minimize errors while maximizing the margin, the standard solution of SVM is written as follows.

$$min \frac{1}{2}||w||^2 + C\sum_{i=1}^n \xi_i \tag{9}$$

$$s.t. \ y_i(w^T x_i + b) \geq 1 - \xi_i, \ and \ \xi_i \geq 0, \ i = 1, \cdots, n$$

where C is a penalty factor used to balance the margin size and the error. The primal form of SVM is often solved in its dual form.

$$\max_\alpha \sum_{i=1}^n \alpha_i - \frac{1}{2} \sum_{i,j=1}^n \alpha_i \alpha_j y_i y_j < x_i, x_j > \tag{10}$$

$$s.t. \ 0 \leq \alpha_i \leq C, i = 1, \cdots, n$$

When linearly inseparable, the kernel function can then be used as

$$\max_\alpha \sum_{i=1}^n \alpha_i - \frac{1}{2} \sum_{i,j=1}^n \alpha_i \alpha_j y_i y_j K(x_i, y_j) \tag{11}$$

$$s.t. \ 0 \leq \alpha_i \leq C, \ i = 1, \cdots, n$$

where $\alpha \in R^n$ and $K(x_i, x_j)$ is called a kernel. The kernel matrix $K \in R^{n \times n}$ contains the kernel values for every pair of training samples. For linear SVM, K is called gram matrix computed as $K(x_i, x_j) = x_i^T x_j$. The main calculation in the training process shown above is dot product calculation. It is very difficult and time consuming to solve the quadratic programming problem of Eq. (11) directly. Therefore, we introduce an sequential minimal optimization (SMO) algorithm, which can help us to solve the optimal value of α faster. The specific approach is to perform the following two steps until convergence as follows:

(1) Select a pair of variables α_i and α_j that need to be updated;
(2) Fix the parameters other than α_i and α_j, solve the dual form of the SVM algorithm and get the updated α_i and α_j.

After we get α by solving the above formula (11), we can further compute w as:

$$w = \sum_{i=1}^n \alpha_i x_i y_i \tag{12}$$

Noting that for any support vector (x_l, y_l) satisfies $y_l * (w^T x_l + b) = 1$ $(l = 1, 2, \cdots, m)$, then b can be solved according to the following formula for computational robustness.

$$b = \frac{1}{m} \sum_{l \in m} (y_l - w^T x_l) \tag{13}$$

Finally, the separating plane is $w^T x - b = 0$.

Classification: When there is a new data X, in order to predict the category of X, X can be substituted into the above-calculated model, and the category of X is predicted by calculating the value of $W^T X - b$:

(1) If $W^T X - b \geq 1$, then the category of X is $+1$;
(2) If $W^T X - b < 1$ then the category of X is -1.

4   System Model and Privacy Requirement

Next we will introduce our scheme from two aspects: system model and attack model.

4.1   System Model

In this paper, in order to classify data on multikey encrypted medical data without leaking data privacy, we propose a classification model with outsourced SVM. As shown in Fig. 1, the involved parties are cloud server (S_1), cloud server (S_2), key generation center (KGC), data owners (DO) and request users (RU).

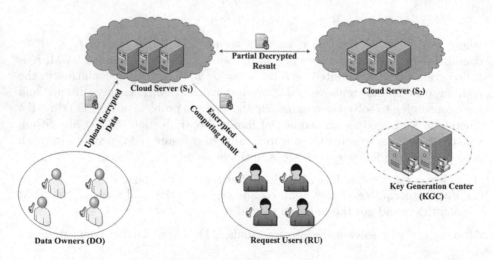

Fig. 1. The system model.

- KGC: The main function of the KGC in this article is to generate public parameters and distribute them to users for generating public and private keys. The other is to generate a master key and divide the master key into two separate parts for the two clouds S_1 and S_2.
- S_1: S_1 can store the encrypted data, and perform multiplication and addition on the multikey encrypted data together with S_2. In addition, S_1 need encrypt the calculation result and return it to RU.
- S_2: S_2 can perform multiplication and addition calculations on multikey encrypted data together with S_1.
- DO: When uploading it's data to cloud, DO needs to use it's own public key to encrypt the data.
- RU: RU is mainly a researcher or research institute for data mining on encrypted medical data. After completing the calculation, RU can decrypt the final calculation result with the help of DO.

In our model, each DO needs to use its own public key to encrypt the data and upload it to cloud S_1. Then RU can send the request for data mining to cloud with the consent of DO. Through the introduction of SVM in the previous, we know that the calculation of SVM mainly includes the calculation of dot product which can be divided into multiplication calculation first and then addition calculation, so at this time the cloud S_1 and S_2 can work together to calculate on the ciphertext based on the secure addition and the secure multiplication protocol. After the calculation is completed, the calculation result is encrypted and sent to RU. At this time, RU can decrypt and get the result with the help of DO.

4.2 Attack Model

We believe that KGC is a trusted entity, while S_1, S_2, DO, and RU are semi-honest entities. They strictly follow the process of implementing the protocol, but also record intermediate calculation results during protocol execution and try to guess the raw data of other entities. In addition, in order to further analyze security, we also introduced a malicious adversary A. Its main purpose is to obtain the original data of DO and the plaintext information corresponding to the final result. The capabilities of the adversary are as follows:

(1) A can eavesdrop on interactions between entities of the model.
(2) A can collaborate with S_1 (or S_2) to guess the plaintext information corresponding to the ciphertext data sented to S_1 (or S_2). It should be noted that the adversary A can only conspire with one of S_1 and S_2, and cannot simultaneously collude with S_1 and S_2.
(3) A can collaborate with one or more RU and DO to guess the ciphertext of challenge RU or challenge DO, but the adversary cannot collude with challenge RU or challenge DO.

5   Privacy Preserving SVM Protocol with Multiple Keys

Because the data to be processed in this paper is encrypted with multiple keys, the basic homomorphic encryption algorithm can only support calculation on single-key encrypted data. Therefore we need to design protocols to support the calculation of addition and multiplication on multikey encrypted data. The specific scheme is as follows.

5.1   Outsourced Privacy Preserving SVM with Multiple Keys

According to the previous introduction of the EPOM algorithm and the optimized SVM algorithm, we will specifically describe our model based on the horizontally distributed data set.

Initialization: First, with the help of KGC the medical unit DO_1, DO_2 and the research institution RU use the $KeyGen()$ algorithms to generate their own public key $pk_i = (N, g, h_i)$ and private key $sk_i = a_i$ $(i = 1, 2, 3)$, respectively, and the two cloud S_1, S_2 running $KeyGen()$ and $Mks()$ algorithms to obtain their own partial master keys k_1 and k_2, respectively.

Data Uploading: DO_1 and DO_2 have n_1 data and n_2 data respectively, where $n = n_1 + n_2$. Then DO_1 and DO_2 use their own public key to encrypt data and obtain ciphertext (A_i, B_i), then upload the ciphertext to the cloud S_1. In addition, they also need to upload their own public key pk_i and the ciphertext corresponding to data class labels which are $+1$ or -1 to S_1.

Training: When S_1 receives the ciphertext data (A_i, B_i), then RU can initiate a calculation request to S_1 after obtaining the agreement of DO_1 and DO_2. Then, S_1 and S_2 calculate together on the ciphertext data to solve the hyperplane $wx + b = 0$ which can divide these data.

According to the previous introduction to SVM, it can be known that when the Lagrange factor α is introduced, the naive SVM model can be converted into a dual form and then use SMO algorithm to find the optimal Lagrangian factor α. In the process of solving, the calculation of the dot product is mainly involved. In order to calculate the dot product of ciphertext, the dot product can be divided into a multiplication calculation and an addition calculation. When the could S_1 stores ciphertexts $Enc_{pk_1}(m_1)$ and $Enc_{pk_2}(m_2)$, the specific product calculation of m_1 and m_2 is as follows:

First, S_1 selects 4 random numbers $r_1, r_2, R_1, R_2 \in Z_n$ and calculates the following ciphertexts based on the homomorphic addition properties:

$$
\begin{aligned}
C_1 &= Enc_{pk_1}(m_1) \cdot Enc_{pk_1}(r_1) = Enc_{pk_1}(m_1 + r_1) \\
C_2 &= Enc_{pk_2}(m_2) \cdot Enc_{pk_2}(r_2) = Enc_{pk_2}(m_2 + r_2) \\
C_3 &= Enc_{pk_1}(R_1) \cdot [Enc_{pk_1}(m_1)]^{N-r_2} = Enc_{pk_1}(R_1 - m_1 \cdot r_2) \\
C_4 &= Enc_{pk_2}(R_2) \cdot [Enc_{pk_2}(m_2)]^{N-r_1} = Enc_{pk_2}(R_2 - m_2 \cdot r_1)
\end{aligned}
\tag{14}
$$

Next S_1 calculates C_1', C_2', C_3' and C_4' according to the above result and the partial master key k_1 as follows:

$$C_1' = PSDec1_{k_1}(C_1), \ C_2' = PSDec1_{k_1}(C_2)$$
$$C_3' = PSDec1_{k_1}(C_3), \ C_4' = PSDec1_{k_1}(C_4) \tag{15}$$

Finally S_1 sends the calculated result $C_1, C_2, C_3, C_4, C_1', C_2', C_3', C_4'$ to S_2.

When S_2 receives the ciphertext, it uses k_2 to complete the following calculations.

$$C_5 = PSDec2_{k_2}(C_1, C_1') \cdot PSDec2_{k_2}(C_2, C_2')$$
$$C_6 = PSDec2_{k_2}(C_3, C_3'), \ C_7 = PSDec2_{k_2}(C_4, C_4') \tag{16}$$

Next, S_2 encrypts the above calculation result with the public key $pk_{\Sigma} = (N, \ g, \ g^{a_1+a_2+a_3})$ to get $C_5' = Enc_{pk_{\Sigma}}(C_5), \ C_6' = Enc_{pk_{\Sigma}}(C_6), \ C_7' = Enc_{pk_{\Sigma}}(C_7)$ and sends $C_5', \ C_6', \ C_7'$ to S_1.

Next, S_1 encrypts the previously selected random number using k_1, and calculates $m_1 \cdot m_2$ according to the ciphertext data sent from S_2.

$$CR_1 = [Enc_{pk_{\Sigma}}(r_1 \cdot r_2)]^{N-1}, \ CR_2 = [Enc_{pk_{\Sigma}}(R_1)]^{N-1}$$
$$CR_3 = [Enc_{pk_{\Sigma}}(R_2)]^{N-1} \tag{17}$$
$$Enc_{pk_{\Sigma}}(m_1 \cdot m_2) = C_5' \cdot C_6' \cdot C_7' \cdot CR_1 \cdot CR_2 \cdot CR_3$$

After the above calculation, S_1 can get $Enc_{pk_{\Sigma}}(m_1 \cdot m_2)$ according to ciphertext $Enc_{pk_1}(m_1)$ and $Enc_{pk_2}(m_2)$. In order to calculate the sum of m_1 and m_2, the cloud S_1 and S_2 can perform the following interactions:

First, S_1 selects two random numbers $r_1, r_2 \in Z_N$ and performs the following calculations.

$$C_1 = (A_1, B_1) = Enc_{pk_1}(m_1) \cdot Enc_{pk_1}(r_1) = Enc_{pk_1}(m_1 + r_1)$$
$$C_2 = (A_2, B_2) = Enc_{pk_2}(m_2) \cdot Enc_{pk_2}(r_2) = Enc_{pk_2}(m_2 + r_2) \tag{18}$$

Next S_1 computes $C_1' = PSDec1_{k_1}(C_1)$ and $C_2' = PSDec1_{k_1}(C_2)$ using k_1 and sends C_1, C_1', C_2, and C_2' to S_2. Then S_2 uses partial master key k_2 to calculate $C_1'' = PSDec2_{k_2}(C_1, C_1')$ and $C_2'' = PSDec2_{k_2}(C_2, C_2')$. Finally S_2 sends the calculated result $C = Enc_{pk_{\Sigma}}(C_1'' + C_2'')$ to S_1.

After S_1 receives the ciphertext data, it calculates $Enc_{pk_{\Sigma}}(m_1 + m_2)$ as follows:

$$Enc_{pk_{\Sigma}}(m_1 + m_2) = C \cdot [Enc_{pk_{\Sigma}}(r_1 + r_2)]^{(N-1)} \tag{19}$$

By the above calculation, we can get $Enc_{pk_{\Sigma}}(m_1 + m_2)$ under the public key pk_{Σ}. Combining the SMO algorithm with the above-mentioned secure multiplication and addition, the optimal value α can be obtained. Substituting the value of α into Eq. (12) to calculate the parameter w of the hyperplane. Noting that for any support vector (x, y) satisfy $y * (wx + b) = 1$, so b can be solved according to formula (13) for the sake of computational robustness. Since both w and b are encrypted by the public key pk_{Σ}, then S_1 can send the ciphertext data corresponding to w and b to DO_1, DO_2, and RU. Then DO_1 and DO_2 send the result of the calculation to RU by running the $PWDec1$ protocol. Next, RU

can use its own private key sk_3 to get the values of w and b by running the $PWDec2$ protocol, and then obtain the prediction model $wx + b = 0$ for the medical unit DO_1 and DO_2.

Classification: When DO_1 has new medical data X, it can use the previously trained model to predict the categories of X with the help of RU. DO_1 first encrypts X using its own public key pk_1 and uploads it to S_1. The cloud then substitutes $Enc_{pk_1}(X)$ into the model and sends the calculated results to DO_1 and RU respectively after calculation. Then RU runs the $PWDec1$ protocol and sends the result to DO_1. After that, DO_1 runs the $PWDec2$ protocol based on the data sent from S_1 and RU to get the decrypted calculation result.

If the decrypted result is greater than or equal to 1, the final category of X is $+1$, otherwise the category is -1, so the medical unit can get the category of new data X according to the specific meaning represented by $+1$ and -1.

We explained above based on horizontally distributed datasets, because when different users use different public keys to encrypt data, all ciphertexts will eventually be converted into ciphertexts encrypted with pk_Σ. At this time, the ciphertext has nothing to do with the users and the distribution of data, so our solution is also applicable to both vertically and arbitrarily distributed data sets. In addition, when the data cannot be linearly separable, an appropriate kernel function can be selected in the SVM model, and the data can be mapped into a high-dimensional data set to be divided by the kernel function. A general kernel function can be approximated by Taylor or Maclaurin series if it is not linear. Therefore, our solution is also applicable to linearly indivisible data.

Through the above operations, the SVM algorithm can be used to help the medical unit to perform disease prediction and other related research.

6   Security Analysis

Theorem 1. *The double trapdoor scheme described in Sect. 3 is semantically secure, based on the assumed intractability of the DDH assumption over $Z_{N^2}^*$.*

Proof. Our solution uses a double trapdoor decryption cryptosystem, so the security of our solution is based on the security of this double trapdoor decryption cryptosystem, because this double trapdoor decryption cryptosystem has been proved to be semantically secure under the standard model based on the complexity of DDH assumptions on $Z_{N^2}^*$ [11]. The security of the master key splitting into two parts can also be guaranteed by Shamir's secret sharing [13] that is information theoretic secure.

Theorem 2. *The secure addition and multiplication algorithm described in Sect. 5 can separately calculate the sum and product of multikey encrypted data in the presence of semi-honest adversaries.*

Proof. First analyze the secure addition algorithm, assuming there are 4 adversaries A_{DO_1}, A_{DO_2}, A_{S_1}, and A_{S_2} who collude with DO_1, DO_2, S_1, and S_2, respectively. Next we build four simulators, Sim_{DO_1}, Sim_{DO_2}, Sim_{S_1}, and Sim_{S_2}.

Sim_{DO_1} chooses m_1 as input and simulates A_{DO_1} as follows: It encryptes m_1 with pk_1 and sends $Enc_{pk_1}(m_1)$ to A_{DO_1}, then outputs the entire view of A_{DO_1}. The views of A_{DO_1} in both real and ideal executions are indistinguishable for the semantic security of double trapdoor decryption cryptosystem. In addition Sim_{DO_2} works analogously to sim_{DO_1}.

Sim_{S_1} simulates A_{S_1} as follows: it uses pk_1 and pk_2 to encrypt two randomly selected messages m_1, m_2, and obtains $Enc_{pk_1}(m_1 + r_1)$ and $Enc_{pk_2}(m_2 + r_2)$, where r_1, $r_2 \in Z_N$. Based on the $PWDec1(\cdot, \cdot)$ algorithm, it calculates $Enc_{pk_1}(m_1 + r_1)$ and $Enc_{pk_2}(m_2 + r_2)$ to get c_1 and c_2 respectively. After that, Sim_{S_1} sends $Enc_{pk_1}(m_1 + r_1)$, $Enc_{pk_2}(m_2 + r_2)$, c_1, and c_2 to A_{S_1}. If A_{S_1} replies with $\perp$, then Sim_{S_1} returns $\perp$. In both real and the ideal executions, it get the output of the $Enc_{pk_1}(m_1 + r_1)$, $Enc_{pk_2}(m_2 + r_2)$, c_1, and c_2. In the real world, it is supported by the fact that DOs are honest and the semantic security of double trapdoor decryption cryptosystem. The A_{S_1}'s views in the real and ideal executions are indistinguishable.

Finally, we analyze Sim_{S_2} as follows: It uses pk_Σ to encrypt randomly selected messages M and sends $Enc_{pk_\Sigma}(M)$ to A_{S_2}. If A_{S_2} replies with $\perp$, then Sim_{S_2} outputs $\perp$. The view of A_{S_2} consists of the encrypted data it creates. In the real world, it is guaranteed by the semantic security of double trapoor decryption cryptosystem. The A_{S_2}'s views are indistinguishable in the real and the ideal executions.

The proof process of secure multiplication algorithm is similar to the above secure addition algorithm, which is not described in detail here.

Through the above introduction, we next analyze the security of the protocol interaction process in the scheme.

If there is an interaction between participants DOs, RUs, S_1, and S_2 in the process of adversary A eavesdropping, A will obtain the corresponding ciphertext. When A colludes with S_1, A can get the ciphertext uploaded by the challenge DO. But because the master key has been divided into two parts and placed on two clouds respectively, the adversary cannot also decrypt the challenge ciphertext at this time. Based on blinded technology [7], if the adversary A colludes with S_2 then the adversary can decrypt to get the corresponding plaintext, but the plaintext is the result of the blinding, so the adversary must not have the original data at this time. Based on the analysis of Li [14], we found that when an authentication protocol is added between two clouds, even if the adversary collude with RU and S_1 to launch a "bypass" attack, the original data of challenge DOs cannot be obtained. In addition, through the analysis of the $PWDec1$ and $PWDec2$ algorithms, it can be found that the final calculation result can only be calculated by the cooperation of challenge DOs and challenge RUs, so this can also be seen as a control over the decryption authority of the final calculation result.

7 Performance Analysis

In the following, we will analyze the performance of our scheme from both computation overhead and communication overhead.

7.1 Computation and Communication Overhead

Assuming one exponentiation calculation with an exponent of length $|N|$ requires $1.5|N|$ multiplications [15]. For our double trapdoor decryption scheme, Enc algorithm requires $3|N|$ multiplications, Dec algorithm requires $1.5|N|$ multiplications, $PWDec1$ costs $1.5|N|$ multiplications and $PWDec2$ requires $1.5N + k$ multiplications. In addition, $PSDec1$ and $PSDec2$ rquires $4.5|N|$ multiplications to decrypte ciphertext respectively. For the addition operation of our scheme, it needs $21|N|$ multiplications for S_1 and $12|N|$ for S_2. For the multiplication, it requires $45|N|$ mulitplications for S_1 and $27|N|$ multiplications for S_2.

The ciphertext of our scheme requires $4|N|$ bits to transmit. For the secure addition and multiplication, they costs $16|N|$ bits and $36|N|$ bits to transmit respectively.

7.2 Comparative Summary

Our scheme is similar to the works of [10]. Both of these schemes introduce two clouds. Our scheme supports horizontal, vertical and arbitrary data distribution. However, the scheme of [10] only considers the vertical distribution data and does not consider the horizontal and arbitrarily distributed data. In the scheme of [10], a homomorphism addition and a homomorphism multiplication protocol was also introduced to calculate the dot product. However, this homomorphic multiplication protocol can only support the computation on the data encrypted by single key. Moreover, this scheme is mainly aimed at two users instead multiple users and supports multikey homomorphic addition operations at the expense of escalating space and communication overhead in ciphertext. Our solution can support multiplication and addition calculations on multikey encrypted data. In the scheme of [8], a fully homomorphic algorithm is used to design the SVM algorithm for privacy preserving data mining. However, the efficiency of the fully homomorphic algorithm is low. And compared to our solution, this scheme can only be applied to vertically distributed data and requires users to participate in calculations online.

8 Conclusion and Future Work

In this paper we propose an outsourced privacy preserving SVM with multiple keys scheme which allows different medical units to outsource data to cloud without revealing data privacy and use the SVM algorithm to calculate a classification model for patient records. The medical unit can use the calculated classification model to classify the new disease data to help doctors diagnose.

In addition, we are now mainly considering integer data. In the following, we need to research other data types and try to use zero-knowledge proofs and commitments to solve the problem of malicious adversaries.

Acknowledgement. This work is supported by National Key Research and Development Program of China (No. 2017YFB0803002), Basic Reasearch Project of Shenzhen of China (No. JCYJ20160318094015947), Key Technology Program of Shenzhen of China (No. JSGG20160427185010977), National Natural Science Foundation of China (No. 61702342).

References

1. Yu, H., Jiang, X., Vaidya, J.: Privacy-preserving SVM using nonlinear kernels on horizontally partitioned data. In: Proceedings of the 2006 ACM Symposium on Applied Computing, pp. 603–610. ACM (2006)
2. Yu, H., Vaidya, J., Jiang, X.: Privacy-preserving SVM classification on vertically partitioned data. In: Ng, W.-K., Kitsuregawa, M., Li, J., Chang, K. (eds.) PAKDD 2006. LNCS (LNAI), vol. 3918, pp. 647–656. Springer, Heidelberg (2006). https://doi.org/10.1007/11731139_74
3. Vaidya, J., Yu, H., Jiang, X.: Privacy-preserving SVM classification. Knowl. Inf. Syst. **14**(2), 161–178 (2008)
4. Hu, Y., He, G., Fang, L., et al.: Privacy-preserving SVM classification on arbitrarily partitioned data. In: IEEE International Conference on Progress in Informatics and Computing, pp. 543–546 (2010)
5. Liu, X., Jiang, Z.L., Yiu, S.M., et al.: Outsourcing two-party privacy preserving k-means clustering protocol in wireless sensor networks. In: 2015 11th International Conference on Mobile Ad-hoc and Sensor Networks (MSN), pp. 124–133. IEEE (2015)
6. Zhang, Q., Yang, L.T., Chen, Z.: Privacy preserving deep computation model on cloud for big data feature learning. IEEE Trans. Comput. **65**(5), 1351–1362 (2016)
7. Peter, A., Tews, E., Katzenbeisser, S.: Efficiently outsourcing multiparty computation under multiple keys. IEEE Trans. Inf. Forensics Secur. **8**(12), 2046–2058 (2013)
8. Liu, F., Ng, W.K., Zhang, W.: Encrypted SVM for outsourced data mining. In: 2015 IEEE 8th International Conference on Cloud Computing (CLOUD), pp. 1085–1092. IEEE (2015)
9. Zhang, J., Wang, X., Yiu, S.M., et al.: Secure dot product of outsourced encrypted vectors and its application to SVM. In: Proceedings of the Fifth ACM International Workshop on Security in Cloud Computing, pp. 75–82. ACM (2017)
10. Zhang, J., He, M., Yiu, S.-M.: Privacy-preserving elastic net for data encrypted by different keys - with an application on biomarker discovery. In: Livraga, G., Zhu, S. (eds.) DBSec 2017. LNCS, vol. 10359, pp. 185–204. Springer, Cham (2017). https://doi.org/10.1007/978-3-319-61176-1_10
11. Bresson, E., Catalano, D., Pointcheval, D.: A simple public-key cryptosystem with a double trapdoor decryption mechanism and its applications. In: Laih, C.-S. (ed.) ASIACRYPT 2003. LNCS, vol. 2894, pp. 37–54. Springer, Heidelberg (2003). https://doi.org/10.1007/978-3-540-40061-5_3
12. Liu, X., Deng, R.H., Choo, K.K.R., et al.: An efficient privacy-preserving outsourced calculation toolkit with multiple keys. IEEE Trans. Inf. Forensics Secur. **11**(11), 2401–2414 (2016)

13. Shamir, A.: How to share a secret. Commun. ACM **22**(11), 612–613 (1979)
14. Li, C., Ma, W.: Comments on "an efficient privacy-preserving outsourced calculation toolkit with multiple keys". IEEE Trans. Inf. Forensics Secur. **13**(10), 2668–2669 (2018)
15. Knuth, D.E.: The Art of Computer Programming: Seminumerical Algorithms, vol. 2, Addison Wesley, Boston (1981)
16. Li, P., Li, J., Huang, Z., et al.: Multi-key privacy-preserving deep learning in cloud computing. Future Gen. Comput. Syst. **74**, 76–85 (2017)
17. Li, P., Li, J., Huang, Z., et al.: Privacy-preserving outsourced classification in cloud computing. Cluster Comput. **21**, 1–10 (2017)

Privacy-Preserving Task Allocation for Edge Computing Enhanced Mobile Crowdsensing

Yujia Hu[1], Hang Shen[1,2(✉)] (iD), Guangwei Bai[1], and Tianjing Wang[1] (iD)

[1] College of Computer Science and Technology, Nanjing Tech University,
Nanjing 211816, China
hshen@njtech.edu.cn
[2] Department of Electrical and Computer Engineering, University of Waterloo,
Waterloo N2L 3G1, Canada

Abstract. In traditional mobile crowdsensing (MCS) applications, the crowdsensing server (CS-server) need mobile users' precise locations for optimal task allocation, which raises privacy concerns. This work proposes a framework P2TA to optimize task acceptance rate while protecting users' privacy. Specifically, edge nodes are introduced as an anonymous server and a task allocation agent to prevent CS-server from directly obtaining user data and dispersing privacy risks. On this basis, a genetic algorithm that performed on edge nodes is designed to choose an initial obfuscation strategy. Furthermore, a privacy game model is used to optimize user/adversary objectives against each other to obtain a final obfuscation strategy which can be immune to posterior inference. Finally, edge nodes take user acceptance rate and task allocation rate into account comprehensively, focusing on maximizing the expected accepted task number under the constraint of differential privacy and distortion privacy. The effectiveness and superiority of P2TA to the exiting MCS task allocation schemes are validated via extensive simulations on the synthetic data, as well as the measured data collected by ourselves.

Keywords: Mobile crowdsensing · Edge computing
Privacy preserving

1 Introduction

With the rapid expansion of sensing, computing and communicating technologies, mobile crowdsensing (referred as MCS) [1,2] can leverage millions of indi-

The authors gratefully acknowledge the support and financial assistance provided by the National Natural Science Foundation of China under Grant Nos. 61502230, 61501224 and 61073197, the Natural Science Foundation of Jiangsu Province under Grant No. BK20150960, the Natural Science Foundation of the Jiangsu Higher Education Institutions of China under Grant No. 15KJB520015, and Nangjing Municipal Science and Technology Plan Project under Grant No. 201608009.

© Springer Nature Switzerland AG 2018
J. Vaidya and J. Li (Eds.): ICA3PP 2018, LNCS 11337, pp. 431–446, 2018.
https://doi.org/10.1007/978-3-030-05063-4_33

vidual mobile devices to sense, collect and analyze data without deploying thousands of static sensors [3]. While MCS has become a cheap and fast sensing paradigm, it also brings contradiction between privacy and efficiency.

On a typical MCS system, mobile users are registered as candidate workers. When new tasks come, the crowdsensing server (referred as CS-server) selects a user to complete a task by paying some incentives. The shorter the user's travel distance, the higher his or her acceptance of the task. Therefore, a natural solution for CS-servers to improve user acceptance rate is to assign nearest task to each user based on user's precise location. Nevertheless, due to privacy leakage, this solution actually reduces users' willingness to participate in MCS.

Fortunately, the emergence of edge computing makes it possible to decrease travel distance while reducing privacy risks. The basic idea of edge computing enhanced mobile crowdsensing is to perform computations at the edge of network as an anonymous server and a task allocation agent [4]. By introducing edge computing, a user's real location can be replaced by an obfuscated location, and the task assignment is based on the obfuscated location. Therefore, it is promising to reduce user's travel distance while cutting off user's real location from the CS-server. Nevertheless, due to the lack of comprehensive consideration of different influencing factors, achieving an optimal task allocation is still a challenging issue.

While some works [5–7] take travel distance into account, they assume that users' locations are known to CS-server. The lack of consideration of privacy may make users get discouraged and leave the MCS platform. Some of studies [8–10], though support privacy-preserving, but they are not applicable in the actual scene. Shokri et al. [9] propose to generalize the precise location of users into a confused area which protects the location privacy, but according to such a generalized area to allocate task is no difference with random allocation. Haze [8] supports the task assignment based on statistical information, providing privacy protection under k-anonymous guarantee. Yet, its task allocation efficiency is limited by precision. In SPOON [11], sensing tasks are protected by utilizing proxy reencryption and BBS+ signature. The task submission are anonymized, which prevents privacy leaks. However, anonymous task submission makes the incentive mechanism difficult to run.

Although both user's privacy and travel distance are taken into account, [12–15] fail to achieve optimal task allocation efficiency. Fo-SDD [12] uses edge nodes to assist task allocate which provide a more accurate and secure task allocation for mobile users. Even so, it ignores task allocation rate, which limits the upper limit of efficiency. The work in [13] generates obfuscated locations for each user and increases user acceptance rate by minimizing the expected overall travel distance of all users. Nevertheless, in some scenarios, less overall travel distance is not equivalent to a high task allocation efficiency. References [14,15] also fail to balance user acceptance rate and task allocation rate while protecting user privacy and improving task allocation efficiency.

In this paper, a privacy-preserving task allocation framework P2TA is proposed for edge computing enhanced mobile crowdsensing, focusing on maximizing the number of task accepted while considering privacy, travel distance and task allocation efficiency. The main contributions can be concluded as follows:

1. To begin with, the influence of user acceptance rate and task allocation rate on task allocation efficiency is analyzed, based on which edge nodes are introduced to protect user's privacy and allocate tasks. Under such an edge enhanced MCS framework, an optimal task allocation problem regarding privacy, travel distance and task allocation efficiency is formulated.
2. To reduce computational complexity, the optimal task allocation problem is decomposed to find an optimal obfuscation strategy and an optimal task allocation strategy respectively. A stackerberg privacy game is established to choose the optimal obfuscation strategy against inference attacks. A linear programming is built to calculate the optimal task allocation strategy, which can maximize the number of accepted task subject to task allocation constraints.
3. Through extensive simulations, we demonstrate that P2TA outperforms typical task allocation mechanism in terms of privacy protection level and task allocation efficiency. Our results indicate that when inference error is 1 km and differential privacy budget is 0.3, the task acceptance rate reaches its maximum under an appropriate privacy level.

The remainder of this paper is organized as follows. The motivation and system framework are described in Sects. 2 and 3. Section 4 defines the task allocation process for edge nodes and the specific strategies and metrics involved in each step. Section 5 formulates an optimal task allocation problem and decompose the problem into two sub-problems to be solved, followed by performance evaluation in Sect. 6. Concluding remarks and the research prospect are illustrated at the end.

2   Motivation

The success of a MCS task allocation depends on how many MCS tasks are accepted. Thus, task allocation efficiency is equal to the number of tasks accepted, which makes the goal of a task allocation become to maximize the number of accepted tasks A, as defined below

$$A = \sum_{r_t \in R_t} a_t \tag{1}$$

where a_t is affected by user acceptance rate whose definition will be presented in Sect. 4, indicating whether to accept a task with target region t.

2.1   Effect of User Acceptance Rate on Task Acceptance Rate

The introduction of edge computing cuts off the chance of the CS-server to acquire users' real location directly, while dispersing the risk of privacy exposure.

After obtaining the privacy guarantee by edge computing, users tend to accept tasks with smaller travel distance. Hence, a user-centric task allocation strategy is naturally presented to allocate nearest task to each user. However, such a strategy may lead to some tasks not allocated to any user. Take Fig. 1(a) as an example to illustrate an unreasonable allocation caused by only pursuing user acceptance rate. In this scenario, with a user-centric task allocation strategy, User A and User B both assign Task A. Although the distance from User B to Task B is only a little farther than to Task A, Task B is still not allocated to anyone. In this allocation, user acceptance rate is 100%, but since only one task is assigned, the number of tasks accepted is only 1. This motivates to study the impact of task allocation rate whose definition will be presented in Sect. 4.

2.2 Effect of Task Allocation Rate on Task Acceptance Rate

A task-centric allocation strategy naturally emerge to improve task allocation rate. In the scenario shown in Fig. 1(b), with the task-centric allocation strategy, a common approach is to select the nearest user for each task. So, Task A is allocated to User A. Then, the nearest user from Task B is still User A, but each user can only assign one task. A straightforward way is to assign the sub-nearest User B to Task B. However, the distance between User B and Task B is 3, which is likely to be rejected. This leads to all tasks are assigned but only 1 task accepted, indicating that simply increasing user acceptance rate or task allocation rate doesn't apply to all scenes. This motivates us to consider both user acceptance rate and task allocation rate.

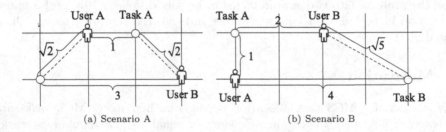

(a) Scenario A   (b) Scenario B

Fig. 1. Task allocation examples.

3   System Framework

Figure 2 gives the overall framework of P2TA, consisting of three parties:

1. **CS-server** transforms MCS requirements into MCS tasks and releases them to corresponding edge nodes based on location. It is also responsible for receiving and processing task data uploaded by mobile users.

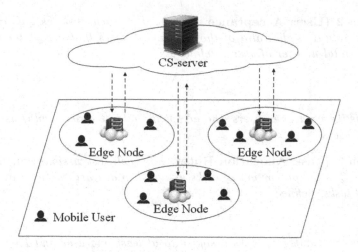

Fig. 2. System framework.

2. **Edge Nodes** are in charge of the specific privacy protection and task allocation, concerning (1) creating an obfuscated region for each user, and (2) allocating nearer task to user based on obfuscated region.
3. **Mobile Users** include users with smart phones, automotive sensing devices and smart wearable devices. Upon receiving a task, they choose to accept or reject it. Once a user has accepted a task, he or she reports an obfuscated region and the accepted task's id to CS-server. After that, the user goes to the task's target region and uses his or her sensing device to collect data.

4 Definitions

The success of a task assignment depends on the task acceptance rate.

Definition 1 (Task Acceptance Rate). *For each task assignment, task acceptance rate η is the proportion of accepted task out of the total task number, defined as*

$$\eta = \frac{A}{T} \tag{2}$$

where A is the number of accepted tasks, T is the total number of tasks determined by MCS perception requirements.

There are two factors that determine the η of a task assignment, concerning:

(1) user acceptance rate α which determines how many users will accept tasks;
(2) task allocation rate β which determines the upper limit of η.

Definition 2 (User Acceptance Rate). *For each task assignment, user acceptance rate α is the ratio of the number of users that accept the assigned task to the total number of users, defined as*

$$\alpha = \frac{X}{U} \tag{3}$$

where X is the number of users who accept the allocated task and U is the total number of users.

Definition 3 (Task Allocation Rate). *For each task assignment, task allocation rate β is the proportion of tasks assigned to at least one user in the total number of tasks, defined as*

$$\beta = \frac{C}{T} \tag{4}$$

where C is the number of tasks assigned to at least one user and T is the total number of tasks.

This work uses region instead of the specific location. When these region's size is small enough, it can meet users' precision requirement. Figure 3 gives the task allocation process.

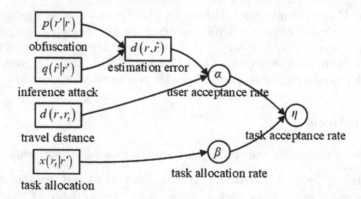

Fig. 3. Task allocation process. The purpose of task allocation is to maximize η via improving α and β. There are two strategies in this process for improving α, concerning: (1) protecting users' privacy through an obfuscation strategy p, and the error between the estimated region $\hat{r}$ and the real region r is ensured under the attack strategy q; (2) reducing travel distance between r and assigned task target region r_t. To constrain the lower bound of β, an obfuscated region r'-based task allocation strategy x is proposed.

4.1 Obfuscation Mechanism

Assume that the CS-server is an adversary aiming at finding users' real region r. To increase α, each user only exposes an obfuscated region r' to CS-server in

P2TA. Thus, an edge node produces a general obfuscation location, in which the observed r' is sampled according to the probability distribution p below.

$$p(r'|r) = \Pr\{R = r'|R_u = r\} \tag{5}$$

The indiscernibility degree of obfuscated regions, reflects the effectiveness of the obfuscation mechanism, which is captured by differential privacy [16].

4.2 Differential Privacy Metric

The basic idea behind differential privacy is that suppose the obfuscated region is r', for any two regions r_1 and r_2, their probability of being mapped to r' are similar. Then, if the CS-server observes a user u in r', it cannot distinguish whether u is in r_1 or r_2, even if the CS-server knows obfuscation probability distribution p. Differential privacy formally shows such similarity between any two regions r_1, r_2 for arbitrary r'.

Definition 4 (Differential Privacy). *An obfuscation mechanism satisfies – differential-privacy, if*

$$p(r'|r_1) \le e^{\varepsilon d(r_1,r_2)} p(r'|r_2)\ \forall r_1, r_2, r' \in R \tag{6}$$

where p is the probability of obfuscating r to r', ε is the privacy budget and the smaller ε, the higher privacy. $d(r_1, r_2)$ is the distance between r_1 and r_2 which reflects the intuition that if r_1 and r_2 are close to each other, they should be more indistinguishable.

4.3 Inference Attack

When the CS-server owns complete background knowledge, it can use the Bayesian attack [17] to calculate the probability of r with r'.

$$q(\hat{r}|r') = \frac{p(r'|\hat{r})\,\pi(\hat{r})}{\sum\limits_{r\in R} \pi(r)\cdot p(r'|r)} \tag{7}$$

Confronted with Bayesian attack, the obfuscation mechanism will reorient the probability distribution p to ensure user's privacy level. This motivates the CS-server to design an adaptive inference attack mechanism. For any observation r', the CS-server determines an adaptive inference probability distribution q.

$$q(\hat{r}|r') = \Pr\{R_u = \hat{r}|R = r'\} \tag{8}$$

The adaptive inference q estimates the real region r is $\hat{r}$ by inverting a given obfuscation p. The estimation error of $\hat{r}$ to r reflects the effectiveness of inference, which is measured by distortion privacy [18].

4.4   Distortion Privacy Metric

Once r' is observed by CS-server, it will estimate the original region r and get an estimate value $\hat{r}$ though q. The distance between r and $\hat{r}$, i.e., $d(r, \hat{r})$, is defined as the distortion privacy. The longer the distortion privacy, the lower the attack effect.

Definition 5 (Distortion Privacy). *The distortion privacy is the expected error of an attacker*

$$p\left(r'\left|r_1\right.\right) \le e^{\varepsilon d(r_1, r_2)} p\left(r'\left|r_2\right.\right) \forall r_1, r_2, r' \in R \tag{9}$$

where p is the obfuscation probability distribution, q is the inference probability distribution and $d(r, \hat{r})$ is the Euclidean distance between r and $\hat{r}$.

With users' region distribution $\pi(r)$, the expected distortion privacy can be computed by

$$\sum_{r_i \in R} \pi\left(r_i\right) \sum_{r' \in R} p\left(r'\left|r\right.\right) \sum_{\hat{r} \in R} q\left(\hat{r}\left|r'\right.\right) \cdot d\left(r, \hat{r}\right) \tag{10}$$

4.5   Travel Distance

The travel distance $d(r, r_t)$ is the Euclidean distance between a user's real region r and his or her assigned task region r_t.

For users, if travel distance is too long, he or she will probably be unwilling to conduct the task. For task organizers, long travel distance may lead to unsatisfactory conditions such as high incentive to pay and large sensing delay.

Consequently, assuming users have no privacy concerns, the travel distance is inversely proportional to the user acceptance rate, i.e.,

$$\alpha = \frac{k}{d\left(r, r_t\right)} \tag{11}$$

where k is a constant obtained by investigation.

4.6   Task Allocation

The assignment of task with target region r_t follows probability distribution x, expressed as

$$x\left(r_t\left|r'\right.\right) = \Pr\left\{R_t = r_t \left|R_u = r'\right.\right\} \tag{12}$$

where r' is an obfuscated region of user. The allocation is based on obfuscated region to ensure that the CS-server cannot infer user's real region through x.

The upper limit of η is determined by β. A natural way to improve β is to constrain x, such that each task is allocated to at least one user can be guaranteed.

$$\sum_{r' \in R} x\left(r_t\left|r'\right.\right) \cdot U \ge 1, r_t \in R_t \tag{13}$$

For a determined allocation probability distribution x, the expected travel distance of a user in r, denoted by d_r, is expressed as

$$d_r = \sum_{r' \in R} \sum_{r_t \in R} p\left(r' \,|\, r\right) x\left(r_t \,|\, r'\right) d\left(r, r_t\right) \tag{14}$$

which can be calculated before task assignment.

5   Privacy-Preserving Task Allocation

The optimal task allocation aims to maximize η, which is equivalent to maximizing the number of accepted tasks. Suppose a concerned area involves a set of regions R and a user region set R_u distributed in R, given a task at r_t. Whether the task is accepted, denoted by a_t, is defined as

$$a_t = \begin{cases} 1, if \sum_{r \in R_u} \sum_{r' \in R} p\left(r' \,|\, r\right) x\left(r_t \,|\, r'\right) d\left(r_t \,|\, r\right) \le d_u \\ 0, otherwise \end{cases} \tag{15}$$

where d_u represents the acceptable travel distance of the user u. If one has accepted the task at r_t, a_t is set to 1, otherwise 0.

The Optimal Task Allocation (OTA) problem can be mathematically formalized as:

$$\text{Maximize} : A = \sum_{r_t \in R_t} a_t \tag{16}$$
$$ {}_{p,x}$$

$$s.t. \quad p\left(r' \,|\, r\right) \ge 0, \sum_{r' \in R} p\left(r' \,|\, r\right) = 1, \forall r \in R_u, \forall r' \in R \tag{17}$$

$$p\left(r' \,|\, r_1\right) \le e^{\varepsilon d(r_1, r_2)} p\left(r' \,|\, r_2\right), \forall r_1, r_2 \in R_u, \forall r' \in R \tag{18}$$

$$\sum_{r \in R_u} \pi\left(r\right) p\left(r' \,|\, r\right) = \pi\left(r'\right) \tag{19}$$

$$q\left(\hat{r} \,|\, r'\right) \ge 0, \sum_{\hat{r} \in R} q\left(\hat{r} \,|\, r'\right) = 1, \forall r', \hat{r} \in R \tag{20}$$

$$\sum_{r' \in R} p\left(r' \,|\, r\right) \sum_{\hat{r} \in R} q\left(\hat{r} \,|\, r'\right) \cdot d\left(r, \hat{r}\right) \ge d_m \tag{21}$$

$$x\left(r_t \,|\, r'\right) \ge 0, \sum_{r_t \in R_t} x\left(r_t \,|\, r'\right) = 1, \forall r_t \in R_t, \forall r' \in R \tag{22}$$

$$\sum_{r' \in R} x\left(r_t \,|\, r'\right) \cdot U \ge 1, r_t \in R_t \tag{23}$$

Before task allocation, an edge node can get a task region set (i.e. R_t) from the CS-server. Then, the edge node attempts to maximize the objective function (16) i.e., the number of tasks accepted, while obfuscation probability distribution p, inference probability distribution q and task allocation probability distribution x satisfying following constraints. Constraints (17), (20) and (22) are general probability constraints. Constraint (18) guarantees user's differential privacy. Constraint (19) ensures that P2TA does not change the overall region distribution of users. Constraint (21) guarantees user's distortion privacy. Constraint (23) ensures that any task is assigned at least once, where U is the number of users in R_u.

There is a complex dependence among p, q and x. It is very difficult to solve OTA problem directly because the computational complexity of enumerating all p, q and x is $O(n^4)$. A natural step is to decompose the problem and solve the different unknowns separately.

5.1 $p\&q$-Subproblem

This work extracts obfuscation probability distribution p and inference probability distribution q from OTA problem to form a $p\&q$-subproblem. Because p and q are with opposite objectives, the $p\&q$-subproblem can be formalized as a privacy game problem.

Stackerberg Privacy Game. The privacy game can be regarded as a kind of stackerberg game [19] where one player, an edge node, commits to a strategy p first, and the other players, the CS-server, selfishly chooses its best response strategy q considering the edge node's strategy p.

In our game, the strategic space of the edge node is the obfuscation probability distribution p, which is defined as:

$$p_i = p\left(\cdot \left|r_i\right.\right) = \{p\left(r_1' \left|r_i\right.\right), p\left(r_2' \left|r_i\right.\right), \ldots, p\left(r_n' \left|r_i\right.\right)\}$$

$$p\left(r' \left|r\right.\right) \geq 0, \sum_{r' \in R} p\left(r' \left|r\right.\right) = 1, \forall r \in R_u, \forall r' \in R \tag{24}$$

The optimal strategy for edge node is to maximize the expected inference error of CS-server. This correspond to the following formulas

$$p^* = \arg\max_p \sum_{r' \in R} p\left(r' \left|r\right.\right) \sum_{\hat{r} \in R} q^*\left(\hat{r} \left|r'\right.\right) \cdot d\left(r, \hat{r}\right) \tag{25}$$

$$s.t. \quad p\left(r' \left|r\right.\right) \geq 0, \sum_{r' \in R} p\left(r' \left|r\right.\right) = 1 \forall r \in R_u, \forall r' \in R \tag{26}$$

$$p\left(r' \left|r_1\right.\right) \leq e^{\varepsilon d\left(r_1, r_2\right)} p\left(r' \left|r_2\right.\right) \forall r_1, r_2 \in R_u, \forall r' \in R \tag{27}$$

$$\sum_{r \in R_u} \pi\left(r\right) p\left(r' \left|r\right.\right) = \pi\left(r'\right) \tag{28}$$

$$\sum_{r', \hat{r} \in R} \pi\left(r\right) \cdot p^*\left(r' \left|r\right.\right) \cdot q\left(\hat{r} \left|r'\right.\right) \cdot d\left(r, \hat{r}\right) \geq d_m \tag{29}$$

Similarly, as an attacker, CS-server's strategic space is the inference probability distribution q, defined as:

$$q_i = q\left(\cdot \left|r_i'\right.\right) = \{q\left(\hat{r}_1 \left|r_i'\right.\right), q\left(\hat{r}_2 \left|r_i'\right.\right), \ldots, q\left(\hat{r}_n \left|r_i'\right.\right)\}$$
$$q\left(\hat{r} \left|r'\right.\right) \geq 0, \sum_{\hat{r} \in R} q\left(\hat{r} \left|r'\right.\right) = 1, \forall r', \hat{r} \in R \tag{30}$$

The optimal strategy for CS-server is to minimize error of the inference, hence the problem formulated as

$$q^* = \arg\max_q \sum_{r, r', \hat{r} \in R} \pi\left(r\right) p^*\left(r' \left|r\right.\right) \cdot q\left(\hat{r} \left|r'\right.\right) \cdot d\left(r, \hat{r}\right) \tag{31}$$

$$s.t. \quad q\left(\hat{r} \left|r'\right.\right) \geq 0, \sum_{\hat{r} \in R} q\left(\hat{r} \left|r'\right.\right) = 1, \forall r', \hat{r} \in R \tag{32}$$

$$\sum_{r', \hat{r} \in R} \pi\left(r\right) \cdot p^*\left(r' \left|r\right.\right) \cdot q\left(\hat{r} \left|r'\right.\right) \cdot d\left(r, \hat{r}\right) \geq d_m \tag{33}$$

The computational complexity of enumerating p and q is still $O(n^3)$. When n is large enough, $p\&q$-subproblem is not suitable for enumerating. To reduce the complexity, an iteration algorithm is proposed to find the optimal p and q. The basic idea is that the solution of p (or q) can be seen as the input of q (or p), and the p and q are alternatively solved until convergence (or the iteration times exceed a given threshold).

Genetic Algorithm Based Initialization. To start the iteration of solving p and q, we need to set an initial p, denoted as p_0. As using our iteration algorithm often leads to the local optima, the selection of the initial value p_0 affects how good the local optimal can achieve.

To address this issue, Genetic Algorithm (GA) [20] is used to select the initial values. The key idea behind GA is to generate a potential solution for utility testing from existing solutions by using either Mutation or Crossover methods under a given probability. The Mutation and Crossover processes are designed according to $p\&q$-subproblem as follows (examples in Fig. 4).

Mutation: given a previous obtained p_0, a region pair $(r_1, r_2) \in \{(r', r)|\forall r', r \in R\}$. Then, a new p_1 is constructed by setting $p_1(r_1, r_2) = p_0(r_1, r_2)/2$, $p_1(r_3, r_2) = p_0(r_3, r_2) + p_0(r_1, r_2)/2$, and rest value same as p_0.

Crossover: given the parents p_0^1 and p_0^2, the crossover function is used to generate two children p_1^1 and p_1^2 by row exchange. More specifically, edge node randomly select a region r and then set $p_1^1\left(:, r\right) = p_0^2\left(:, r\right)$ and $p_1^2\left(:, r\right) = p_0^1\left(:, r\right)$; for the rest values, $p_1^1 = p_0^1$ and $p_1^2 = p_0^2$.

5.2   x-Subproblem

The solution to $p\&q$-subproblem (i.e. the optimal strategy for p and q) can be brought into the OTA problem. This translates OTA problem into a x-subproblem of finding an obfuscated region based task allocation strategy x

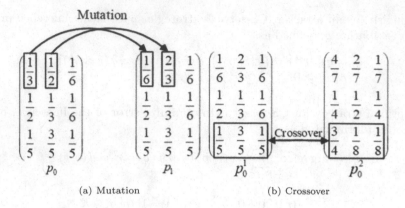

(a) Mutation   (b) Crossover

Fig. 4. Examples of mutation and crossover

which can maximize the number of tasks accepted. Accordingly, x-subproblem can be formulated as

$$\text{Maximize}_{x} A = \sum_{r_t \in R_t} a_{r_t} \tag{34}$$

$$s.t. \quad \sum_{r' \in R} x\left(r_t \,|r'\right) \cdot U \geq 1, \forall r_t \in R_t \tag{35}$$

$$x\left(r_t \,|r'\right) \geq 0, \sum_{r_t \in R_t} x\left(r_t \,|r'\right) = 1, \forall r_t \in R_t, \forall r' \in R \tag{36}$$

In doing so, the x-subproblem is transformed into a simple 0-1 programming problem with only one group of unknowns x, which can be efficiently solved with off-the-shelf linear optimization software.

6   Performance Evaluation

This section assesses the effectiveness of our proposed framework in terms of the privacy constraints and the number of users.

In our simulation, an edge node covered area is divided into n regions, the collection of which forms the whole region set R. Each region is set to $500\,\text{m} \times 500\,\text{m}$. The basic parameter settings are detailed in Table 1. Evaluation metrics includes privacy satisfaction rate μ, task acceptance rate η, user acceptance rate α and task allocation rate β.

For comparison, a typical differential obfuscation task allocation mechanism [13] is chosen as a baseline, where the focus is on minimizing users' total travel distance based on differential privacy constraints. We also introduce a No-Privacy scheme which is P2TA without privacy constraints.

Table 1. Key parameters in simulation.

Notation	Default	Description
n	36	Region number
U	30	User number
T	10	Task number
ϵ	0.3	Differential privacy level
d_m	1	Distortion privacy level
π	Uniform	User spatial distribution
τ	Uniform	Task spatial distribution

6.1 Impact of Privacy Constraints

Experiment I examines the impacts of different privacy constraints.

Figure 5(a) compares η and α in the three-different strict of privacy constraint under P2TA. It can be observed that the weakest privacy level ($d_m = 1.5$, $\varepsilon = 0.1$)'s η and α is the worst performers. This is because users refuse to participate in the MCS with a low privacy level. The strictest privacy level ($d_m = 0.5$, $\varepsilon = 0.5$) for η is concentrated on 60%–85%, because the excessive expectation error of distortion privacy is contradictory to the constraint of differential privacy. It can be observed that when $d_m = 1$, $\varepsilon = 0.3$, a relatively better η (most of which is over 90%) is achieved.

Figure 5(b) shows the impact of privacy on travel distance. With the increase of privacy satisfaction rate, the median travel distance becomes longer and the distribution range tends to become enlarged. This is because the higher the privacy satisfaction rate is, the stricter the privacy constraint is. Tighter privacy constraints increase the randomness of task assignments, making unreasonable assignments more likely. Therefore, choosing the constraint strength of 85% μ may result in a higher α than 100% μ.

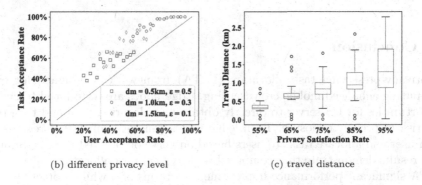

(b) different privacy level   (c) travel distance

Fig. 5. Impact of privacy constraints (Experiment I)

6.2   Impact of User Number

Experiment II looks at the effect of user number on user acceptance rate and task acceptance rate.

Turning to Fig. 6(a), the variation of the α in different number of users by each algorithm. When the number of users is low, baseline's α is even higher than a non-privacy scheme based on P2TA. The reason for this lies in the P2TA's task allocation constraint, which allows P2TA to assign non-nearest tasks to users. The purpose of this allocation strategy is to increase the β to improve η. When the number of users increased, the α of Baseline begans to be lower than that of P2TA. This is because when the number of users is large enough, the probability that the overall travel distance does not reflect η will increase.

According to Fig. 6(b), task acceptance rate under the number of users with respect to different allocation schemes shows an increase when the user number changes from 10 to 40. P2TA can provide higher η than baseline. It is comparable to the optimum No-Privacy schemes after the user number is exceeds 30. This is because P2TA considers the α and β comprehensively, while baseline only optimizes the overall travel distance.

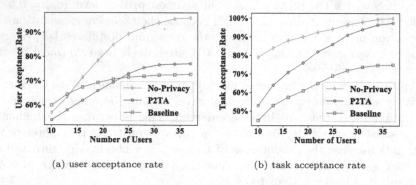

(a) user acceptance rate   (b) task acceptance rate

Fig. 6. Impact of user number (Experiment II)

7   Conclusion

A privacy-preserving task allocation (P2TA) framework is designed for edge computing enhanced mobile crowdsensing. Edge nodes are introduced to cut off opportunities for CS-server to directly obtain user' location data and to spread the risk of privacy exposure. Then, edge nodes generate obfuscated regions for each user and allocate tasks to users based on these obfuscated regions. Simulation results demonstrate that compared with typical task allocation mechanism, P2TA significant performance improvement in terms of η while protect the privacy and reduce travel distance.

Finally, there is still room for improvement in future research. Follow-up work includes: (1) The current user model is relatively simple, and all users are only willing to accept short travel distance tasks. Future research can consider user models that are closer to reality so that each user can accept different travel distance tasks based on probability. (2) Another research direction is how to maximize the task acceptance rate and protect the user's trajectory privacy in the scenario of user continuously accept and complete the task.

References

1. Alsheikh, M.A., Jiao, Y.: The accuracy-privacy trade-off of mobile crowdsensing. IEEE Commun. Mag. **55**(6), 132–139 (2017)
2. Ma, H., Zhao, D.: Opportunities in mobile crowd sensing. IEEE Commun. Mag. **52**(8), 29–35 (2014)
3. Yang, D., Xue, G., Fang, X.: Incentive mechanisms for crowdsensing: crowdsourcing with smartphones. IEEE/ACM Trans. Netw. **24**(3), 1732–1744 (2016)
4. Shi, W., Cao, J., Zhang, Q.: Edge computing: vision and challenges. IEEE Internet Things J. **3**(5), 637–646 (2016)
5. Guo, B., Liu, Y., Wang, L., Li, V.O.K.: Task allocation in spatial crowdsourcing: current state and future directions. IEEE Internet Things J. **PP**(99), 1 (2018)
6. Guo, B., Liu, Y., Wu, W.: ActiveCrowd: a framework for optimized multitask allocation in mobile crowdsensing systems. IEEE Trans. Hum.-Mach. Syst. **47**(3), 392–403 (2017)
7. Wang, L., Zhang, D., Yang, D.: Differential location privacy for sparse mobile crowdsensing. In: Proceedings of IEEE ICDM (2017)
8. He, S., Shin, D.H., Zhang, J.: Toward optimal allocation of location dependent tasks in crowdsensing. In: Proceedings of IEEE INFOCOM, pp. 745–753 (2014)
9. Shokri, R., Theodorakopoulos, G., Troncoso, C.: Protecting location privacy: optimal strategy against localization attacks. In: Proceedings of ACM CCS, pp. 617–627 (2016)
10. Brown, J.W.S., Ohrimenko, O.: Haze: privacy-preserving real-time traffic statistics. In: Proceedings of ACM GIS, pp. 540–543 (2017)
11. Ni, J., Zhang, K., Xia, Q., Lin, X., Shen, X.: Enabling strong privacy preservation and accurate task allocation for mobile crowdsensing. arXiv preprint arXiv:1806.04057 (2018)
12. Ni, J., Zhang, K., Yu, Y., Lin, X.: Providing task allocation and secure deduplication for mobile crowdsensing via fog computing. IEEE Trans. Depend. Secure Comput. **PP**(99), 1 (2018)
13. Wang, L., Yang, D., Han, X.: Location privacy-preserving task allocation for mobile crowdsensing with differential geo-obfuscation. In: Proceedings of ACM WWW, pp. 627–636 (2017)
14. Xiong, H., Zhang, D., Chen, G.: iCrowd: Near-optimal task allocation for piggyback crowdsensing. IEEE Trans. Mob. Comput. **15**(8), 2010–2022 (2016)
15. Wang, J., Wang, Y.: Multi-task allocation in mobile crowd sensing with individual task quality assurance. IEEE Trans. Mob. Comput. **PP**(99), 1 (2018)
16. Bordenabe, N., Chatzikokolakis, K.: Optimal geo-indistinguishable mechanisms for location privacy. In: Proceedings of ACM CCS, pp. 251–262 (2014)
17. Zhang, X., Gui, X.: Privacy quantification model based on the bayes conditional risk in location-based services. Tsinghua Sci. Technol. **19**(5), 452–462 (2014)

18. Shokri, R., Freudiger, J.: A distortion-based metric for location privacy. In: ACM Workshop on Privacy in the Electronic Society, pp. 21–30 (2009)
19. Shokri, R.: Privacy games: optimal user-centric data obfuscation. Proc. Priv. Enhanc. Technol. **2015**(2), 299–315 (2014)
20. Mitchell, M.: Genetic algorithms: an overview. Complexity **1**(1), 31–39 (2013)

Efficient Two-Party Privacy Preserving Collaborative k-means Clustering Protocol Supporting both Storage and Computation Outsourcing

Zoe L. Jiang[1], Ning Guo[1], Yabin Jin[1], Jiazhuo Lv[1], Yulin Wu[1], Yating Yu[1], Xuan Wang[1], S. M. Yiu[2], and Junbin Fang[3(✉)]

[1] Harbin Institute of Technology (Shenzhen), Shenzhen 518055, China
zoeljiang@hit.edu.cn,{guoning,yulinwu,wangxuan}@cs.hitsz.edu.cn,
lvjiazhuo@hotmail.com,yuyating18@gmail.com
[2] The University of Hong Kong, Hong Kong, China
smyiu@cs.hku.hk
[3] Jinan University, Guangzhou, China
junbinfang@gmail.com

Abstract. Privacy preserving collaborative data mining aims to extract useful knowledge from distributed databases owned by multiple parties while keeping the privacy of both data and mining result. Nowadays, more and more companies reply on cloud to store data and handle with data. In this context, privacy preserving collaborative k-means clustering framework was proposed to support both storage and computation outsourcing for two parties. However, the computing cost and communication overhead are too high to practical. In this paper, we propose to encrypt each party's data once and then store them in cloud. Privacy preserving k-means collaborative clustering protocol is executed mainly at cloud side, with total $O(k(m + n))$-round interactions among the two parties and the cloud. Here, m and n means that the total numbers of records for the two parties, respectively. The protocol is secure in the semi-honest security model and especially secure in the malicious model supporting only one party corrupted during k centroids re-computation. We also implement it in real cloud environment using e-health data as the testing data.

Keywords: Privacy-preserving data mining · k-means clustering
Storage outsourcing · Computation outsourcing
Secure multiparty computation

1 Introduction

The active research area of privacy preserving data mining aims to gain much useful information from multiple sources without sharing their data. Clustering can be considered as a very useful method in data mining and it is widely used in

© Springer Nature Switzerland AG 2018
J. Vaidya and J. Li (Eds.): ICA3PP 2018, LNCS 11337, pp. 447–460, 2018.
https://doi.org/10.1007/978-3-030-05063-4_34

pattern recognition, marketing analysis, image processing and so on. It is well-known that clustering models become better as the data grows bigger, so it is getting more common for collaboration on data which is owned by different parties or stored in different locations. But collaboration on data will cause problem of privacy data leakage. In this case, we propose outsourcing two-party privacy preserving k-means clustering protocol in cloud in malicious model. Cloud server computes k-means on two-party data without disclosing privacy of data owners. In this paper, we use cloud computing power and hand most of computation to cloud server to solve data owners' problem of weaking computing power.

The first works of privacy preserving data mining were given by [1,2] for the ID3 decision trees classification on horizontally partitioned data using different models of privacy. Lindell's work [1] allows two-party collaborate in the extraction of knowledge without any of the cooperating parties having to reveal their privacy data items to each other or any other parties, while Agrawal [2] allows one party to outsource mining task to the other party without the party (delegatee) having to reveal its private data items to the other delegated party (delegator).

The first multi-party privacy preserving k-means clustering on vertically partitioned data was proposed by Vaidya [3]. In the proposed protocol, the data items of each party are kept confidential by introducing the secure permutation and the homomorphic encryption, supporting secure distance computation and comparison. Jha [4] present two two-party privacy preserving protocols for WAP (Weighted Average Problem). The first protocol is based on oblivious polynomial evaluation and the second on homomorphic encryption. The experiment based on the homomorphic encryption can cluster the data set containing 5687 samples and 12 features in approximately 66 seconds. Doganay et al. [5] proposed a new protocol for privacy preserving k-means clustering, however, the approach in [5] must use Trusted Third Party (TTP) to achieve privacy. After that, [8,10] proposed many schemes in the malicious model, but they are not efficient. Mohassel et al. [15] proposed a fast and secure three-party computation scheme supporting one malicious party based on garbled circuits [16].

Liu et al. [9], following the former framework in [2], proposed outsourcing one-party privacy preserving k-means clustering to the cloud, while keeping both data items and mining result private to the cloud or any other party. Liu etc. [11] extended the framework of [9] to two parties with cloud, where most of the storage and computation is outsourced to cloud. However the cost of computation and interaction between each party and cloud is high. Other data mining protocols can be found in [14,18,19]. The detailed comparison can be found in Table 1.

1.1   Our Contribution

Our main result is to design an efficient two-party privacy preserving collaborative k-means clustering protocol with the following properties.

1. Each party's database is stored in cloud in encrypted form to keep data privacy from the cloud or any other party.
2. K-means clustering protocol is executed on the joint encrypted database in cloud with some interactions to each party.

Table 1. Comparison of the existing privacy preserving data mining protocols

Protocol	Partition model	Security model	Number of parties n	Number of cloud R	Cryptographic techniques
LP00 [1]	Horizontal	Semi-honest	2	0	Oblivious transfer Randomizing function
AS00 [2]	Horizontal	Semi-honest	1	1	Data perturbation Oblivious evaluation of polynomialsOblivious circuit evaluation A protocol for computing $x\ln x$
VC03 [3]	Vertical	Semi-honest	>2	0	Secure permutation Paillier encryption Yao's evaluation circuit
JKM05 [4]	Horizontal	Semi-honest	2	0	Oblivious polynomial evaluation (OPE) Homomoprhic (DPE)
DPS08 [5]	Vertical	Semi-honest	>3	0	Additive secret sharing
UMS10 [6]	Arbitrary	Semi-honest	>1	>2	Secret sharing
PGJ12 [7]	Horizontal	Semi-honest	>1	0	Shamir's secret sharing
PJ13 [8]	Horizontal or vertical	Malicious	>1	0	Zero knowledge proof Verifiable secret sharing
PPJ13 [8]	Horizontal	Malicious	>1	0	Shamir's secret sharing Code-based zero knowledge identification
LBY13 [9]	Horizontal	Semi-honest	1	1	Homomorphic encryption
PSJ14 [10]	Horizontal or vertical	Malicious	>1	0	Verifiable secret sharing Homomorphic commitments
LJY15 [11]	Horizontal	Semi-honest	2	1	Liu's encryption, Paillier encryption PPWAP
SRB14 [12]	Horizontal	Semi-honest	>1	2	Secure squared order-preserving Euclidean distance Secure minimum out of k numbers Secure evaluation of termination condition

3. The clustering result in encrypted from is sent to each party for decryption, so as to keep it private from the cloud or any other party.

To achieve the above properties, the underlying encryption algorithm has to support some specific operations simultaneously, including encrypted distance computation, encrypted distance comparison, as well as encrypted centroids recomputation. Unfortunately, no existing half-homomorphic encryption itself can support all the above operations, while fully homomorphic encryption is too slow to be used. In this paper, we use Paillier encryption as the primitive encryption algorithm and extend it to support various operations.

The rest of the paper is organized as follows. In Sect. 2, we review the relevant techniques, followed by presenting our privacy-preserving collaborative k-means clustering protocol in Sect. 3. In Sect. 4, we discuss the efficiency and privacy of our protocol. Then concludes the paper in Sect. 5.

Protocol 1: $\mathsf{SM}(\mathsf{E}(x), \mathsf{E}(y)) \rightarrow \mathsf{E}(xy)$

Require: C has $\mathsf{E}(x)$ and $\mathsf{E}(y)$; P has sk
1. C: (a) Pick any two different numbers $r_x, r_y \in Z_N$
    (b) $x' \leftarrow \mathsf{E}(x)\mathsf{E}(r_x)$, $y' \leftarrow \mathsf{E}(y)\mathsf{E}(r_y)$
    (c) Send x', y' to P
2. P: (a) $h_x \leftarrow D(x')$, $h_y \leftarrow D(y')$, $h \leftarrow h_x h_y \bmod N$, $h' \leftarrow \mathsf{E}(h)$
    (b) Send h' to C
3. C: (a) $s \leftarrow h' \mathsf{E}(x)^{N-r_y}$, $s' \leftarrow s\mathsf{E}(y)^{N-r_x}$
    (b) $\mathsf{E}(xy) \leftarrow s' \mathsf{E}(r_x r_y)^{N-1}$

Protocol 2: $\mathsf{SSED}([X], [Y]) \rightarrow \mathsf{E}_{pk}(|X - Y|^2)$

Require: C has $[X]$ and $[Y]$; P has sk
1. C: **for** $1 \leq i \leq \ell$ **do:** $\mathsf{E}(x_i - y_i) = \mathsf{E}(x_i)\mathsf{E}(y_i)^{N-1}$
2. C and P: **for** $1 \leq i \leq \ell$ **do:**
    Call $\mathsf{SM}(\mathsf{E}(x_i - y_i), \mathsf{E}(x_i - y_i))$ to compute $\mathsf{E}((x_i - y_i)^2)$
3: C: Compute $\mathsf{E}(|X - Y|^2) = \prod_{i=1}^{\ell} \mathsf{E}((x_i - y_i)^2)$

Protocol 3: $\mathsf{SMIN}_2([u], [v])) \rightarrow [\min(u, v)]$

Require: C has $[u]$ and $[v]$, where $0 \leq u, v \leq 2^{\alpha} - 1$; P has sk
1. C: (a) Randomly choose the functionality F
    (b) **for** $i = 1$ to α **do:** $\mathsf{E}(u_i v_i) \leftarrow \mathsf{SM}(\mathsf{E}(u_i), \mathsf{E}(v_i))$
        if F: $u > v$ **then:**
            $W_i \leftarrow \mathsf{E}(u_i)\mathsf{E}(u_i v_i)^{N-1}$, $\Gamma_i \leftarrow \mathsf{E}(v_i - u_i)\mathsf{E}(\hat{r}_i); \hat{r}_i \in Z_N$
        else
            $W_i \leftarrow \mathsf{E}(v_i)\mathsf{E}(u_i v_i)^{N-1}$
            $\Gamma_i \leftarrow \mathsf{E}(u_i - v_i)\mathsf{E}(\hat{r}_i); \hat{r}_i \in Z_N$
            $G_i \leftarrow \mathsf{E}(u_i \oplus v_i)$, $H_i \leftarrow H_{i-1}^{r_i} G_i; r_i \in_R Z_N$ and $H_0 = \mathsf{E}(0)$
            $\Phi_i \leftarrow \mathsf{E}(-1)H_i$, $L_i \leftarrow W_i \Phi_i^{r_i'}; r_i' \in Z_N$
    (c) $\Gamma' \leftarrow \pi_1(\Gamma)$, $L' \leftarrow \pi_2(L)$
    (d) Send Γ' and L' to P
2. P: (a) $M_i \leftarrow D(L_i')$, for $1 \leq i \leq \alpha$
    (b) **if** $\exists j$ such that $M_j = 1$ **then** $\lambda \leftarrow 1$
        else $\lambda \leftarrow 0$
    (c) $M_i' \leftarrow \Gamma_i'^{\lambda}$, for $1 \leq i \leq \alpha$
    (d) Send M' and $\mathsf{E}_{pk}(\lambda)$ to C
3. C: (a) $\widetilde{M} \leftarrow \pi_1^{-1}(M')$
    (b) **for** $i = 1$ to l **do:** $\theta_i \leftarrow \widetilde{M}_i \mathsf{E}(\alpha)^{N-\hat{r}_i}$
        if F: $u > v$ **then** $\mathsf{E}(\min(u, v)_i) \leftarrow \mathsf{E}(u_i)\theta_i$
        else $\mathsf{E}(\min(u, v)_i) \leftarrow \mathsf{E}(v_i)\theta_i$
    (c) According to $\mathsf{E}(\min(u, v)_i)$, C can get $\mathsf{E}(\min(u, v))$

Protocol 4: $\mathsf{SMIN}_k([d_1], \cdots, [d_k]) \rightarrow [d_{min}]$

Require: C has $([d_1], \cdots, [d_k])$; P has sk

1. C: $[d'_i] \leftarrow [d_i]$, for $1 \leq i \leq k$, $num \leftarrow k$
2. C and P: (a) **for** $i = 1$ to $\lceil \log_2 k \rceil$:
   for $1 \leq j \leq \lfloor \frac{num}{2} \rfloor$:
   if $i = 1$ **then**: $[d'_{2j-1}] \leftarrow \mathsf{SMIN}_2([d'_{2j-1}], [d'_{2j}])$, $[d'_{2j}] \leftarrow 0$
   else $[d'_{2i(j-1)+1}] \leftarrow \mathsf{SMIN}_2([d'_{2i(j-1)+1}], [d'_{2ij-1}])$, $[d'_{2ij-1}] \leftarrow 0$
   (b) $num \leftarrow \lceil \frac{num}{2} \rceil$
3. C: Set $[d_{min}]$ to $[d'_1]$

Protocol 5: $\mathsf{SC}(x_1, x_2, x_3^*) \rightarrow y$

Require: P_1 has x_1, P_2 has x_2 and C has x_3^*

1. C: (a) Sampling a common random string, can also be expressed as crs for the commitment scheme and randomly secret-shares his input x_3^* as $x_3^* = x_3 \oplus x_4$.
   (b) Send x_3 to P_1 and x_4 to P_2 and broadcast common random string to both parties.
2. P_1: Choose random pseudo-random function seed $r \leftarrow \{0,1\}^k$ and send it to P_2.
3. P_1 and P_2: (a) Garble the function f' via $\mathsf{Gb}^i(1^\lambda, f') \rightarrow (F, e, d)$
   (b) Commit to all $4m$ input wire labels in the following way. Sample $b \leftarrow \{0,1\}^{4m}$. Then for all $j \in [4m]$ and generate the following commitments:

$$(C_j^a, \sigma_j^a) \longleftarrow Com_{crs}(e[j, b[j] \oplus a])$$

   (c) Both P_1 and P_2 send the following values to C:

$$(b[2m+1...4m], F, \{C_j^a\}_{j,a})$$

4. C: Abort if P_1 and P_2 report different values for these items.
5. P_1 and P_2. (a) P_1 sends decommitment $\sigma_j^{x_1[j] \oplus b[j]}$ and $\sigma_{2m+j}^{x_3[j] \oplus b[2m+j]}$ to C
   (b) P_2 sends decommitment $\sigma_{m+j}^{x_2[j] \oplus b[m+j]}$ and $\sigma_{3m+j}^{x_4[j] \oplus b[3m+j]}$ to C
6. C: (a) For $j \in [4m]$, compute $X[j] = \mathsf{Chk}_{crs}(C_j^{o[j]}, \sigma_j^{o[j]})$, for the appropriate $o[j]$. If any call to Chk returns $\perp$, then abort. Similarly, C knows the values $b[2m+1, \cdots, 4m]$, and aborts if P_1 or P_2 did not open the "expected" commitments $\sigma_{2m+j}^{x_1[j] \oplus b[2m+j]}$ and $\sigma_{3m+j}^{x_1[j] \oplus b[3m+j]}$ corresponding to the garbled encodings of x_3 and x_4
   (b) Run $Y \longleftarrow \mathsf{Ev}(F, X)$ and broadcast Y to P_1 and P_2
7. P_1 and P_2: Compute $y = \mathsf{De}(d, Y)$. If $y \neq \perp$, then output y. Otherwise, abort

---

2 Preliminaries

In this section, we give a brief overview of k-means clustering algorithm, homomorphic encryption, some cryptographic primitives, as well as the data partition.

Table 2. K-means clustering algorithm

---
1. Select k centroids $M = \{\mu_c \in R^\ell | 1 \le c \le k\}$ randomly.
2. Repeat the following algorithm to converge {
    For each i, compute the nearest cluster center
      $C_c := \mathsf{argmin}_c ||x_i - \mu_c||^2$ where $1 \le c \le k$
    For every class c, recompute the centroid $\mu_c := \frac{sum}{|C_c|}$, where $sum = \sum\limits_{x_i \in C_c} x_i$ }

---
* $|| \cdot ||$ denotes the Euclidean distance.

2.1 Overview of k-means Clustering Algorithm

K-means clustering algorithm is a classical clustering algorithm based on distance. We denote the training sample by $\{x_i \in R^\ell | 1 \le m \le \ell\}$, and the algorithm could be illustrated in Table 2:

2.2 Homomorphic Encryption

The homomorohic encryption we use is Paillier encryption [13] which is a probabilistic asymmetric 3-tuple encryption algorithm denoted by $\mathsf{Enc}_{P_a} = \{\mathsf{K}, \mathsf{E}, \mathsf{D}\}$.

- $\mathsf{K}(1^\kappa) \to (pk, sk)$:
  (1) Choose two large prime numbers p and q which satisfy that $\gcd(pq, (p-1)(q-1)) = 1$.
  (2) Calculate $n = pq$ and $\lambda = \mathsf{lcm}(p-1, q-1)$.
  (3) Randomly choose an integer $g \in Z_{n^2}$.
  (4) Check whether there exists $u = (\mathsf{L}(g^\lambda \bmod n^2))^{-1} \bmod n$ where function L is $\mathsf{L}(\mu) = (\mu - 1)/n$. Then pk is (n, g) and sk is (λ, μ).

- $\mathsf{E}_{pk}(x, r) \to c$:
  Select a random $r \in Z_n^*$ for the message x and the ciphertext is $c = g^x r^n \bmod n^2$.

- $\mathsf{D}_{sk}(c) \to x$:
  Decrypt the message by $x = \mathsf{L}(c^\lambda \bmod n^2)\mu \bmod n$.

In the case of no ambiguity, we remove the subscripts pk of E_{pk} and sk of D_{sk}. Then, the additive homomorphic properties of Paillier encryption are:

$$\mathsf{E}(x)\mathsf{E}(y) = \mathsf{E}(x + y), \mathsf{E}(x)^y = \mathsf{E}(xy).$$

2.3 Basic Cryptographic Primitives

In this section, we propose a group of cryptographic primitives that will be known to toolkits when producing our presented protocol. In particular, the Paillier's public key pk will be used to public and secret key sk will only be used to P.

(1) Secure Multiplication (SM) Protocol (**Protocol 1**):
    This protocol denotes C with inputs $(E(x), E(y))$ and the corresponding output $E(xy)$ to C with the help of P. P has public key pk is created as public, and the secret key sk generated by Paillier encryption.

(2) Secure Squared Euclidean Distance (SSED) Protocol (**Protocol 2**): Let $X = (x_1, \cdots, x_\ell)$ and $Y = (y_1, \cdots, y_\ell)$ denote the two ℓ-dimension vectors, and $[X] = (E(x_1), \cdots, E(x_\ell))$ and $[Y] = (E(y_1), \cdots, E(y_\ell))$ means the sets of the encrypted components of X and Y. C with input $([X], [Y])$ and P calculate the corresponding encryption value of the squared Euclidean distance. In the end of the protocol, the final output $E(|X - Y|^2) = \prod_{i=1}^{\ell} E_{pk}((x_i - y_i)^2)$ is known only to C.

(3) Secure Minimum out of 2 Numbers (SMIN$_2$) Protocol (**Protocol 3**):
    Let $u \in \{0,1\}^\alpha$ and $v \in \{0,1\}^\alpha$ are two α-length bit strings, where u_i and v_i $(1 \le i \le \alpha)$ denote each bits of u and v, respectively. Therefore, we have $0 \le u, v \le 2^\alpha - 1$. Let $[u] = (E(u_1), \cdots, E(u_\alpha))$ and $[v] = (E(v_1), \cdots, E(v_\alpha))$ mean that the encrypted the following bits. (u_1, u_α) and (v_1, v_α) are the most and least significant bits of u and v, respectively.

(4) Secure Minimum out of k Numbers (SMIN$_k$) Protocol (**Protocol 4**):
    Let $d_i \in \{0,1\}^\alpha (1 \le i \le k)$ denotes the α-length of the bits, where $d_{i,j} \in \{0,1\}, 1 \le j \le \alpha$ denotes each bit of d_i. So, $0 \le d_i \le 2^\alpha - 1$. Let $[d_i] = (E(d_{i,1}), \cdots, E(d_{i,\alpha}))(1 \le i \le k)$ denotes the encrypted vector to encrypt d_i bit by bit. $d_{i,1}$ and $d_{i,\alpha}$ are the most and least significant bits of d_i. C has k encrypted vectors $([d_1], \cdots, [d_k])$ and P has sk. At the end, no information is revealed to any party.

(5) Secure Circuit (SC) Protocol (**Protocol 5**):
    We symbolize the three parties in the protocol by P_1, P_2 and C, their respective inputs by x_1, x_2 or x_3^* and their collective output by y. They aim to compute the following function securely, $y = f(x_1, x_2, x_3^*) - \frac{x_1 + x_2}{x_3^*}$. To simplify the problem, we assume that $|x_i| = |y| = m$. In the following we suppose that P_1 and P_2 can learn the same output y. C can not get the output y with these garbled values. This protocol use a scheme of garbling, a four-tuple algorithm $\delta = (Gb, En, De, Ev)$, as the underlying algorithm. Gb is a randomized garbling algorithm that transforms. En and De are encoding and decoding algorithms, respectively. Ev is the algorithm that derive garbled output on the basis of garbled input and garbled circuit. Chk is the algorithm that can verify commitments.

2.4   Horizontal Data Partition

Here we review the concept of horizontal data partition for two parties. Assume the two parties, P_1 and P_2, each has a dataset, $D_x = \{x_1, x_2, \cdots, x_m\}$ and $D_y = \{y_1, y_2, \cdots, y_n\}$. Both record $x_i = \{x_{i,1}, x_{i,2}, \cdots, x_{i,\ell}\}$ and $y_i = \{y_{i,1}, y_{i,2}, \cdots, y_{i,\ell}\}$ are ℓ-dimension vectors. We say the total $m + n$ records form a joint data set $D = \{x_1, x_2, \cdots, x_m, y_1, y_2, \cdots, y_n\}$, only if the ℓ attributes in D_x are same and in the exact sequence as those in D_y. Then the mining algorithm will executes on the joint data set D. In this case, we say the data partition of D is horizontal.

Besides the horizontal data partition, please refer to [3] for the vertical data partition and refer to [23] for arbitrary data partition.

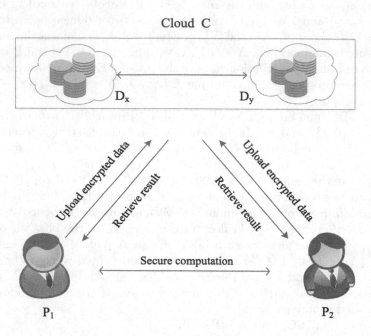

Fig. 1. Framework of privacy preserving collaborative k-means clustering protocol

3 Two-Party Privacy Preserving Collaborative k-means Clustering Protocol

3.1 Security Model

During the first 4 steps described in Sect. 3.2, P_1 and P_2 interact with C, respectively, with no interactions between P_1 and P_2 or among P_1, P_2 and C. Specifically, P_1 and P_2 outsource the encrypted distance computation and comparison to C. Since traditional Paillier encryption cannot support the above two operations at the same time, P_1 and P_2's help is required which introduces the extra interactions between P_1 and C, P_2 and C. Therefore, the security underlying is essentially secure computation outsourcing. In semi-honest model, the honest-but-curious cloud will honestly execute the outsourced computation protocols while being motivated to learn any information of P_1 and P_2's raw data or the computation result for financial gains (Fig. 1).

In the last step, where $F(x_1, x_2, x_3^*) = \frac{x_1 + x_2}{x_3^*}$ is required with each input x_1, x_2, x_3^* of P_1, P_2 and C, it is indeed three-party secure computation. We adapt the model of 1-out-of-3 active security where C is actively corrupt [15].

3.2   Details of the Privacy Preserving Collaborative k-means Clustering Protocol

Step 1. P_1 and P_2 upload encrypted data

P_1 and P_2 encrypt their data D_x and D_y to C_x and C_y, and upload to the cloud C, respectively.

$C_x = \{C_{x_i}|1 \leq i \leq m\}$, where $C_{x_i} = \{C_{x_{ij}} = \mathsf{E}_{pk_1}(x_{ij})|1 \leq j \leq \ell\}$

$C_y = \{C_{y_i}|1 \leq i \leq n\}$, where $C_{y_i} = \{C_{y_{ij}} = \mathsf{E}_{pk_2}(y_{ij})|1 \leq j \leq \ell\}$

Step 2. Cloud C randomly chooses k centroids for k clusters

C randomly chooses the set of k centroids $\Phi = \{\mu_c|1 \leq c \leq k\}$, where each $\mu_c = \{u_{cj}|1 \leq j \leq \ell\}$. Encrypt it using P_1 and $P_2's$ public keys, pk_1 and pk_2, respectively, and store as C_μ^1 and C_μ^2.

$C_\mu^1 = \{C_{\mu_c}^1|1 \leq c \leq k\}$, where $C_{\mu_c}^1 = \{C_{\mu_{cj}}^1 = \mathsf{E}_{pk_1}(\mu_{cj})|1 \leq j \leq \ell\}$

$C_\mu^2 = \{C_{\mu_c}^2|1 \leq c \leq k\}$, where $C_{\mu_c}^2 = \{C_{\mu_{cj}}^2 = \mathsf{E}_{pk_2}(\mu_{cj})|1 \leq j \leq \ell\}$

C_μ^1 and C_μ^2 are sent to P_1 and P_2, respectively. After decryption, Φ is stored by P_1 and P_2, respectively for comparison use later in Step 5.

Step 3. Cloud C computes distances

C computes all encrypted distances between each record C_{x_i} and each centroid $C_{\mu_c}^1$, and distances between each record C_{y_i} and $C_{\mu_c}^2$, as follows.

$$CD^1 = \{CD_i^1 = \{cd_{ic}^1 = \mathsf{SSED}(C_{x_i}, C_{\mu_c}^1)|1 \leq c \leq k\}|1 \leq i \leq m\}$$

$$CD^2 = \{CD_i^2 = \{cd_{ic}^2 = \mathsf{SSED}(C_{x_i}, C_{\mu_c}^2)|1 \leq c \leq k\}|1 \leq i \leq m\}$$

Specifically, C and P_1 run SSED to compute the distance between each x_i and μ_c in encrypted form, denoted by cd_{id}^1. Similarly, C and P_2 run SSED to compute the distance between each y_i and μ_c in encrypted form, denoted by cd_{ic}^2. All distances from x_i to μ_c are stored in CD_i^1, and those from y_i to μ_c are stored in CD_i^2.

Step 4. Cloud C clusters records to k clusters for P_1 and P_2

By comparing the distances in CD_i^1 and CD_i^2, x_i and y_i will be clustered to the cth cluster if and only if cd_{ic}^1 and cd_{ic}^2 are the smallest distance in CD_i^1 and CD_i^2, respectively. For encrypted distance comparison, C runs $\mathsf{SMIN}_k(CD_i^1)$ with P_1 and $\mathsf{SMIN}_k(CD_i^2)$ with P_2, as follows. Then, C_{x_i} and C_{y_i} will be assigned to CL_c^1 and CL_c^2, respectively. As the result, each CL_c^1 stores the encrypted data C_{x_i} whose distance to the cth centroid μ_c is the shortest among all the k centroids. In other words, x_i belongs to the cth cluster. The same as CL_c^2.

$$CL1 = \{CL_c^1 = \{C_{x_i}|cd_{ic}^1 = min(CD_i^1) = \mathsf{SMIN}_k(CD_i^1)\}|1 \leq c \leq k\}$$

$$CL2 = \{CL_c^2 = \{C_{x_i}|cd_{ic}^2 = min(CD_i^2) = \mathsf{SMIN}_k(CD_i^2)\}|1 \leq c \leq k\}$$

Step 5. Cloud C, P_1 and P_2 jointly re-compute k centroids

Now, C is required to find the new centroid within each cluster given all the data in the cluster. Note that there are two sub-clusters in each cluster CL_c^1 and CL_c^2 as the data in those two sub-clusters are encrypted by different public keys pk_1 and pk_2. Therefore, the computation of $\mu'_{cj} = \frac{\sum_{i,\text{s.t.},C_{x_i} \in CL^1_c} x_{ij} + \sum_{i,\text{s.t.},C_{y_i} \in CL^2_c} y_{ij}}{|CL^1_c| + |CL^2_c|}$ in not straightforward. Our idea is to send CL^1_c and CL^2_c to P_1 and P_2 for decryption first. Let L^1_c and L^2_c denote the decrypted data in the cth cluster owned by P_1 and P_2, respectively. Then we have

$$L^1_c = \{x_i = \{x_{ij} = D_{sk_1}(C_{x_{ij}}) | 1 \le j \le \ell\} | C_{x_i} \in CL^1_c\}$$

$$L^2_c = \{y_i = \{y_{ij} = D_{sk_2}(C_{y_{ij}}) | 1 \le j \le \ell\} | C_{y_i} \in CL^2_c\}$$

Then, P_1, P_2 and C jointly run $\text{SC}(\sum_{i,\text{s.t.},C_{x_i} \in CL^1_c} x_{ij}, \sum_{i,\text{s.t.},C_{y_i} \in CL^2_c} y_{ij}, A|L^1_c| + |L^1_c|)$ to calculate each component of the c-th centroid μ'_{cj}. SC guarantees both P_1 and P_2 can get all the new k centroids in plaintext. Let $\Phi' = \{\mu'_c | 1 \le c \le k\}$, where $\mu'_c = \{\mu'_{cj} | 1 \le j \le \ell\}$. Denote $\Phi - \Phi' = \{|\mu_c = \mu'_c| | 1 \le c \le k\}$ the distance set of the newly generated k centroids to the previous k centroids, where $|\mu_c = \mu'_c| = \sum_{j=1}^{i}(|\mu_{cj} - \mu'_{cj}|)$.

Once $|\mu_c = \mu'_c| \le \tau_c$ for each c, P_1 and P_2 request C for the clustered records CL_1 and CL_2 for decryption, respectively. Then the protocol ends. Otherwise, P_1 and P_2 encrypt the new k centroids by their public keys and upldad to C. Then go to Step 3 and iterate.

3.3 Security Analysis

As for the Paillier encryption, we can't decrypt the ciphertext without the private key. So each date owner encrypts the data they own and the Cloud or any party can't decrypt. For the SBD protocol and $SMIN_k$ protocol, we can ensure safety by using Zero-Knowledge proof technology.

We can proof the safety of SC protocol that can against a single malicious party as follows:

First, when the situation that P_1 is corrupted. We know that the ideal and real models can not be distinguished by all environment. The simulator takes the role as honest P_2 and C obtaining their inputs x_2 and x_{3*} on their behalf. Then the simulator sends a random value r_{crs} a random share r_{x_3} to P_1 in step(1); it can be aborted in step(5) if P_1 has changed the binging any commitment; otherwise it extracts $x_1 = o \oplus b[1...m]$ and sends it to the ideal functionality F_f. It receives y, and in step(5) sends Y to P_1. We can get the $View_{real}^{env} = \{crs, x_3, Y, y\}$ and $View_{ideal}^{env} = \{r_{crs}, r_{x_3}, Y, y\}$. Because crs and x_3 are pseudorandom number and r_{crs} and r_{x_3} are random number, all environments can't distinguish them with non-negligible probability.

Next, we consider a corrupt C: The simulator takes the role as both honest P_1 and P_2. It extracts $x_3^* = x_3 \oplus x_4$ in step(1) and send it to F_f, obtaining the output y in return. Then it produces a simulated garbled circuit/input(F,X) using y. We can get the $View_{real}^{env} = \{C_j^{o[j]}, o, y\}$ and $View_{ideal}^{env} = \{C_j^{r_o[j]}, r_o, y\}$. Because o are pseudorandom number and r_{crs} and r_o are random number, all environments can't distinguish them with non-negligible probability.

Therefore, SC protocol that can against a single malicious party.

4 Performance Analysis

4.1 Theoretical Analysis

In the paper, we consider that cloud C owns strong ability of calculation and ignore computing time in it. For each data owner, they do not need to store the ciphertext, and just encrypt the message with the public key and decrypt the ciphertext with the private key.

Every iteration, data owners will private some information and these information will be computed in each iteration, and P_1, P_2 and C will recalculated the cluster. We assume t is the time of iteration, so $O((m+n) * \ell * t)$ is the time complexity.

In each iteration, firstly, each data owner will execute SBD protocol and $SMIN_k$ protocol with Cloud. There are two interactions in SBD protocol and $2k$ interactions in $SMIN_k$ protocol. Then, P_1, P_2 and C will execute 6 times interactions in SC protocol. Finally, each data owner will execute 1 times interactions when they upload new centroids to Cloud. We assume t is the time of iteration, so the communication is mostly $O(k * t)$.

4.2 Experimental Analysis

In this section, the performance of our scheme will be calculated. Our implementation was written in Java with Paillier library. The experiments were conducted on cloud computing instance and personal computer. C runs on the cloud computing instance and P_1 or P_2 runs on the personal computer. Cloud computing instance is running 64-bit Centos7.1 with 228 GB memory, and 144 1.87 GHz Intel cores totally. The personal computer that stands for P_1 or P_2 is running 64-bit Windows7 with 8 Gb memory, and a 3.2 GHz Intel core.

In our experiment, P_1 and P_2 chose a 512-bit key as Paillier's key. The running time is affected by iterations, so we compute the time of one iterator. We implemented multi-group experiments because the size of data can bring different times. We considered the number of the data points as the size of data and the ciphertext of 10000 data points with 15 dimensions is about 100 MB. We repeated our experiments 30 times for each size of data, and we took the average values as our experimental results.

Table 3 shows the encryption time of data in different dimensions. Table 4 shows the decryption time of data in different dimensions. Obviously, with the increase of data size and dimension, time is increasing.

At the end, to examine the effect of the cloud computing on the performance, we disable it and run the some experiments. The results are shown in Table 6. And Table 6 shows the time of each participant in one iteration. C undertakes the most of computing time, and P_1 and P_2 undertake little computing time in one iteration. What's more, with the increase of data size, the time of C changes slightly. Table 5 shows the time comparison between ciphertext and plaintext. With the increase of data size, the proportion of time of encryption and time of no encryption decreases from 4000 to 800. All of this is obvious, the cloud

Table 3. Time of encryption

Data size	3-dimension(ms)	7-dimension(ms)
500	1730	4227
1000	3603	8330
2000	7504	16287
5000	17690	35917
10000	34929	80543

Table 4. Time of decryption

Data size	3-dimension(ms)	7-dimension(ms)
500	3575	8354
1000	7533	16786
2000	14676	32786
5000	35128	70351
10000	69456	161583

Table 5. Time comparison in one iteration

Data size	Encryption(ms)	No encryption(ms)
500	23872	6
1000	25095	7
2000	25572	9
5000	32640	24
10000	42746	50

Table 6. Time of each participant in one iteration

Data size	C(ms)	P_1(ms)	P_2(ms)
500	20923	385	354
1000	23296	747	691
2000	24381	1501	1328
5000	24639	3564	3276
10000	31618	6301	6247

computing plays a very important role for computing, and makes the scheme more efficient as we expected.

At the same time, we got the same experiment results when we ran this scheme based ciphertext and k-means algorithm based plaintext on the same dataset.

5   Conclusion

In this paper, we first present the method of two-party privacy-preserving k-means clustering with Cloud in malicious model. We achieve security in the malicious model with zero-knowledge and secure circuit. Since most of the operations are performed on the Cloud, any two parties with weak computing power are able to run the protocol to achieve privay-preserving k-means clustering. In the future work, we will utilize multi-key fully homomorphic encryption in [17] to decrease communication cost to make k-means algorithm more efficient. And we will reduce the risk of primate key leakage and private key management cost of work [21] in a multi-key setting. Moreover, we will securely outsource the storing and processing of rational numbers and floatint point numbers to cloud server which is not considered in [20, 22].

Acknowledgement. This work is supported by Basic Reasearch Project of Shenzhen of China (No. JCYJ20160318094015947), National Key Research and Development Program of China (No. 2017YFB0803002), National Natural Science Foundation of China (No. 61771222), Key Technology Program of Shenzhen, China (No. JSGG20160427185010977).

References

1. Lindell, Y., Pinkas, B.: Privacy preserving data mining. In: Bellare, M. (ed.) CRYPTO 2000. LNCS, vol. 1880, pp. 36–54. Springer, Heidelberg (2000). https://doi.org/10.1007/3-540-44598-6_3
2. Agrawal, R., Srikant, R.: Privacy preserving data mining. ACM Sigmod **29**(2), 439–450 (2000)
3. Vaidya, J., Clifton, C.: Privacy-preserving K-means clustering over vertically partitioned data. In: ACM SIGKDD International Conference on Knowledge Discovery and Data Mining, pp. 206–215. ACM (2003)
4. Jha, S., Kruger, L., McDaniel, P.: Privacy preserving clustering. In: di Vimercati, S.C., Syverson, P., Gollmann, D. (eds.) ESORICS 2005. LNCS, vol. 3679, pp. 397–417. Springer, Heidelberg (2005). https://doi.org/10.1007/11555827_23
5. Doganay, M.C., Pedersen, T.B., Saygin, Y., et al.: Distributed privacy preserving k-means clustering with additive secret sharing. In: International workshop on Privacy and Anonymity in Information Society 2008, pp. 3–11. ACM (2008)
6. Upmanyu, M., Namboodiri, A.M., Srinathan, K., Jawahar, C.V.: Efficient privacy preserving K-means clustering. In: Chen, H., Chau, M., Li, S., Urs, S., Srinivasa, S., Wang, G.A. (eds.) PAISI 2010. LNCS, vol. 6122, pp. 154–166. Springer, Heidelberg (2010). https://doi.org/10.1007/978-3-642-13601-6_17
7. Patel, S., Garasia, S., Jinwala, D.: An efficient approach for privacy preserving distributed K-means clustering based on Shamir's secret sharing scheme. In: Dimitrakos, T., Moona, R., Patel, D., McKnight, D.H. (eds.) IFIPTM 2012. IAICT, vol. 374, pp. 129–141. Springer, Heidelberg (2012). https://doi.org/10.1007/978-3-642-29852-3_9
8. Patel, S., Patel, V., Jinwala, D.: Privacy preserving distributed K-means clustering in Malicious model using zero knowledge proof. In: Hota, C., Srimani, P.K. (eds.) ICDCIT 2013. LNCS, vol. 7753, pp. 420–431. Springer, Heidelberg (2013). https://doi.org/10.1007/978-3-642-36071-8_33

9. Liu, D., Bertino, E., Yi, X.: Privacy of outsourced k-means clustering. In: ACM Symposium on Information, Computer and Communications Security 2014, pp. 123–134. ACM (2014)

10. Patel, S., Sonar, M., Jinwala, D.C.: Privacy preserving distributed K-means clustering in Malicious model using verifiable secret sharing scheme. Int. J. Distrib. Syst. Technol. (IJDST) 5(2), 44–70 (2014)

11. Liu, X., Jiang, Z.L., Yiu, S.M., et al.: Outsourcing two-party privacy preserving K-means clustering protocol in wireless sensor networks. In: 2015 11th International Conference on Mobile Ad-hoc and Sensor Networks (MSN) 2015, pp. 124–133. IEEE (2015)

12. Samanthula, B.K., Rao, F.Y., Bertino, E., et al.: Privacy-preserving and outsourced multi-user k-means clustering. In: IEEE Conference on Collaboration and Internet Computing 2015, pp. 80–90. IEEE (2015)

13. Paillier, P.: Public-key cryptosystems based on composite degree residuosity classes. In: Stern, J. (ed.) EUROCRYPT 1999. LNCS, vol. 1592, pp. 223–238. Springer, Heidelberg (1999). https://doi.org/10.1007/3-540-48910-X_16

14. Xu, L., Jiang, C., Wang, J., et al.: Information security in big data: privacy and data mining. IEEE Access 2014(2), 1–28 (2014)

15. Mohassel, P., Rosulek, M., Zhang, Y.: Fast and secure three-party computation: the garbled circuit approach. In: ACM SIGSAC Conference on Computer and Communications Security, pp. 591–602. ACM (2015)

16. Bellare, M., Hoang, V.T., Rogaway, P.: Foundations of garbled circuits. In: ACM Conference on Computer and Communications Security 2012, pp. 784–796. ACM (2012)

17. López-Alt, A., Tromer, E., Vaikuntanathan, V.: On-the-fly multiparty computation on the cloud via multikey fully homomorphic encryption. In: ACM Symposium on Theory of Computing 2012, pp. 1219–1234. ACM (2012)

18. Li, P., Li, J., Huang, Z., et al.: Privacy-preserving outsourced classification in cloud computing. Cluster Comput. 1–10 (2017)

19. Li, P., Li, J., Huang, Z., et al.: Multi-key privacy-preserving deep learning in cloud computing. Future Gener. Comput. Syst. 74, 76–85 (2017)

20. Liu, X., Choo, R., Deng, R., et al.: Efficient and privacy-preserving outsourced calculation of rational numbers. IEEE Trans. Dependable Secure Comput. 15, 27–39 (2016)

21. Liu, X., Deng, R.H., Choo, K.K.R., et al.: An efficient privacy-preserving outsourced calculation toolkit with multiple keys. IEEE Trans. Inf. Forensics Secur. 11(11), 2401 (2016)

22. Liu, X., Deng, R.H., Ding, W., et al.: Privacy-preserving outsourced calculation on floating point numbers. IEEE Trans. Inf. Forensics Secur. 11(11), 2513–2527 (2016)

23. Jagannathan, G., Wright, R.N.: Privacy-preserving distributed K-means clustering over arbitrarily partitioned data. In: ACM SIGKDD International Conference on Knowledge Discovery in Data Mining 2005, pp. 593–599. ACM (2005)

Identity-Based Proofs of Storage with Enhanced Privacy

Miaomiao Tian[1,2,3], Shibei Ye[1,3], Hong Zhong[1,2,3](✉), Lingyan Wang[1,3], Fei Chen[4], and Jie Cui[1,2,3]

[1] School of Computer Science and Technology, Anhui University, Hefei, China
zhongh@ahu.edu.cn
[2] Institute of Physical Science and Information Technology, Anhui University, Hefei, China
[3] Anhui Engineering Laboratory of IoT Security, Anhui University, Hefei, China
[4] College of Computer Science and Engineering, Shenzhen University, Shenzhen, China

Abstract. Proofs of storage (PoS) refer to an effective solution for checking the integrity of large files stored in clouds, such as provable data possession and proofs of retrievability. Traditional PoS schemes are mostly designed in the public key infrastructure setting, thus they will inevitably suffer from the complex certificate management problem when deployed. Identity-based PoS (IBPoS) is a lightweight variant of traditional PoS that eliminates the certificate management problem via identity-based cryptographic technology. Although there are several IBPoS schemes in the literature, all of them cannot simultaneously protect both identity privacy and data privacy against a third-party verifier that is pervasive in IBPoS systems. To fill this gap, in this paper we propose a new IBPoS scheme, from which a verifier is able to confirm the integrity of the files stored in clouds but cannot get the files or the identity information of their owners. We prove our scheme is secure in the random oracle model under a standard assumption. Finally, we also conduct a series of experiments to evaluate its performance.

Keywords: Proof of storage · Identity-based cryptography
Identity privacy · Data privacy

1 Introduction

Cloud computing is attracting widespread attentions from both academia and industry since clouds are able to offer many kinds of economical services for users. One of the services is cloud storage, by which users could outsource a mass of files into a cloud. Later, these users may access their outsourced data at anytime and anywhere via any network-connectable devices. Cloud storage services benefit users greatly, they however also bring severe security risks to users, e.g. the cloud may delete some rarely-used outsourced data for storage saving (see [4] for more

© Springer Nature Switzerland AG 2018
J. Vaidya and J. Li (Eds.): ICA3PP 2018, LNCS 11337, pp. 461–480, 2018.
https://doi.org/10.1007/978-3-030-05063-4_35

examples). Therefore, checking the integrity of outsourced data is indispensable for cloud storage.

A crude approach for checking integrity of cloud data is downloading the entire data from the cloud and then detecting its integrity. Obviously, it will incur a huge communication and computation overhead. In order to address this problem, researchers suggest to make use of proofs of storage (PoS) schemes such as provable data possession [1] and proofs of retrievability [17]. Roughly speaking, a PoS scheme first divides a file into many blocks and calculates all block tags, then outsources the file together with the tags into a cloud. The tags are authenticators of blocks and can be aggregated into one authenticator on any linear combination of blocks. As a result, to prove the integrity of an outsourced file, the cloud only needs to give a linear combination of blocks and a corresponding authenticator. In this way, PoS schemes reduce the communication and computation overhead of cloud data integrity checking to be small and independent with the scale of outsourced data.

The first PoS schemes were concurrently proposed by Ateniese et al. [1] and by Juels and Kaliski [17] in 2007; from then on, many new PoS schemes have been published, e.g., [2,3,10,13–16,21,22,24–27,31–33,37,38] among many others. We note that most of the schemes enjoy the favorable feature of public verifiability, which enables any third-party verifier to check the integrity of outsourced data. Publicly-verifiable PoS schemes usually produce block tags using a variant of some digital signature scheme and most of the underlying signature schemes rely on the public key infrastructure (PKI). Therefore, in those PoS schemes digital certificates are necessary for the authenticity of public keys; otherwise, the integrity of outsourced files cannot be verified. In other words, those PKI-based PoS schemes will inevitably suffer from the certificate management problem when deployed.

To remove digital certificates from PoS schemes, researchers resort to identity-based cryptography [23] and present several identity-based PoS (IBPoS) schemes, e.g. [18,28–30,34–36], where each user's public key is simply its identity and the corresponding secret key is generated by a trusted private key generator (PKG). These IBPoS schemes can be divided into two categories—one includes [28–30] and the other involves [18,34–36]—according to whether they need new secret keys to produce block tags or not. The IBPoS schemes in [28–30] are highly compact since they produce block tags directly using the secret keys generated by the PKG via the Schnorr signature scheme [20]. Contrastly, those in [18,34–36] use a new secret key to generate block tags and then bind the secret key with an identity via a secure signature scheme like [9].

Motivation. We notice that Wang et al. [29] recently introduced an efficient anonymous IBPoS scheme upon the anonymous PKI-based PoS in [24,25], which enables the identity of any file owner to be unavailable for a third-party verifier. In a nutshell, their construction was based on the Schnorr signature [20], the ring signature in [8] and the compact publicly-verifiable PoS scheme due to Shacham and Waters [21,22]. Very recently, Yu et al. [34] designed a new IBPoS scheme achieving zero knowledge data privacy, hence a third-party verifier cannot get any outsourced file from the scheme. Unfortunately, the two IBPoS schemes both fail to protect identity privacy and data privacy simultaneously. That is, for an outsourced file the third-party verifier either can recognize the identity of its owner or is able to acquire the whole file when executing these schemes. Clearly, the knowledge obtained by the verifier from these IBPoS schemes exceeds what we expect. It's even insufferable in some scenes such as the outsourced files are private and their owners refuse to disclose whether or not they have deposited them in the cloud.

Our Results. In this paper, we put forward the concept of privacy-enhanced IBPoS as well as an efficient realization, from which the third-party verifier can only confirm the integrity of outsourced files while cannot get the files or the identity information of their owners. We formally prove that our scheme is secure in the random oracle model under the divisible computational Diffie-Hellman assumption (as shown in [5], this assumption is equivalent to the well-known computational Diffie-Hellman assumption [12]). Experimental results also demonstrate the efficiency of our scheme.

Technically, our scheme combines some classic cryptographic techniques in a secure way. Specifically, we first use the Schnorr signature scheme [20] to generate the secret key corresponding to an identity, then load the ring signature of [8] into the compact publicly-verifiable PoS scheme of [21,22] for preserving the identity privacy of file owners, and finally complete the whole design by supporting data privacy using the data mask method of [26,27]. At first glance, one may suppose that the scheme in [29] and ours are similar. However, we would like to stress that there exist subtle yet essential differences between the two schemes because our scheme is provably secure while the other is not. More precisely, the IBPoS scheme in [29] is not unconditionally anonymous as claimed. Recall that in [29] the tag for a file consists of a value obtained by hashing the file owner's signature on the file. An unbounded adversary could simply break the anonymity and find the identity of the file owner by first calculating all signatures on the file and then checking their hashes one-by-one. It implies the security proof in [29] is also faulty. We remark that giving proper security proofs for complex schemes is not an easy task. We address this problem using a slightly weak security model, called semi-adaptive attack model, to prove security of our scheme.

Moreover, we also solve the problem that all the IBPoS schemes in [28–30] are not totally identity-based. Observe that in those schemes the secret key corresponding to an identity is a Schnorr signature (R, s) on the identity, where R is a random element picked from some large set Σ. The random R will later be heavily used by the verifier for data verification. However, the verifier doesn't know the right R to which an identity corresponds, since all R's are independent of identities. Therefore, in [28–30] R is set to a part of a user's public key while it violates the principle of identity-based cryptography. To fix this problem, in this paper we introduce a public function f, which is prepared by the PKG in the beginning by choosing unique R's for identities such that for any inputted identity f will always output the right R.

Paper Organization. The rest of this paper is organized as follows. Section 2 reviews related works. Section 3 introduces the system and security models of IBPoS. Section 4 recalls cryptographic background to be used in this work. Our IBPoS scheme and its security proofs are given in Sect. 5. In Sect. 6, we evaluate the performance of our scheme. Finally, Sect. 7 concludes this paper.

2   Related Work

The first PoS scheme presented by Ateniese et al. [1] named provable data possession and the scheme by Juels and Kaliski [17] called proofs of retrievability. The main difference between the two notions is that proofs of retrievability could provide stronger security guarantees than provable data possession does. Ateniese et al.'s scheme works under the famous RSA assumption [19] and supports public verifiability, while the Juels-Kaliski scheme only provides private verifiability. Shacham and Waters [21] later designed two more efficient PoS schemes, one of which is publicly-verifiable and secure under the well-known computational Diffie-Hellman (CDH) assumption [12]. After that, many other PoS schemes are also proposed, including data privacy preserving PoS [26,27], identity privacy preserving PoS [24,25], dynamic PoS [2,14,15,31–33,37], PoS for multicloud storage [38], and so on. However, they mostly rely on PKI and thus will inevitably suffer from the certificate management problem when deployed.

Wang et al. [30] and Yu et al. [36] independently proposed two IBPoS schemes for removing the certificate management problem in PKI-based PoS schemes. Subsequently, anonymous IBPoS and IBPoS for multicloud storage are also presented respectively in [29] and [28]. As mentioned before, the IBPoS in [29] is not unconditionally anonymous. Liu et al. [18] recently have pointed out that the IBPoS in [28] is insecure and they also gave a remedy that is secure under the CDH assumption. As an alternative, Yu et al. [35] built an IBPoS scheme under the RSA assumption. Very recently, Yu et al. [34] designed a new IBPoS scheme that achieves zero knowledge data privacy. However, we remark that the schemes in [18,34–36] are less efficient than their counterparts in [28–30] for the same situation since they all employ new secret keys and will need additional signatures to bind the secret keys with the associated identities. Unfortunately, all the schemes in [28–30] are not totally identity-based. In addition, we also remark that there is still no IBPoS in the literature that could simultaneously protect both identity privacy and data privacy.

3   Problem Formulation

3.1   System Model

The system considered in this work is illustrated in Fig. 1. The system involves four types of entities namely users, PKG, cloud, and verifier. Users are data owners; each of them produces a large file and wants to outsource it into the cloud. Every file in our system has a distinct identifier, which is public among all participants. Each user also has a unique identity, e.g. its email address, which will serve as its public key. All users' private keys are generated by the PKG according to their identities. For distributing these private keys securely, we assume secure channels already exist between the PKG and all users. The cloud is the provider of data storage services who owns significant storage space and computation resources. Similarly, we assume that there exists a secure channel between the cloud and each user; hence every user could upload its file into cloud in a secure and guaranteed way. To check the integrity of the outsourced files, a third-party verifier, who is authorized by all users, is activated. The verifier is a professional unit that can effectively check the integrity of massive data stored in the cloud via an IBPoS scheme.

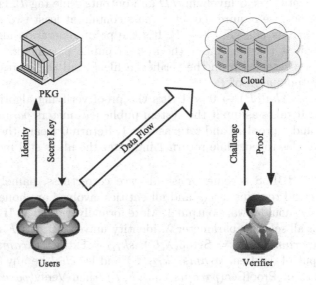

Fig. 1. The system model of IBPoS.

Generally, in an IBPoS scheme, a user first splits a file to be stored into several blocks and computes a file tag using its secret key. Then the user uploads the file as well as the file tag to the cloud, and then deletes them locally. To check the integrity of the file stored in the cloud, the verifier picks a random challenge and sends it to the cloud. After receiving the challenge, the cloud accesses the file and the corresponding file tag, then calculates and returns a proof of the challenge. Finally, the verifier checks the validity of the proof. If the proof is invalid then the verifier can confirm that the file in the cloud has been destroyed. Otherwise, it must still be intact. The verifier may report the check results upon users' requests.

The following is the formal definition of IBPoS, where we also take enhanced privacy into consideration.

Definition 1 (IBPoS). *An IBPoS scheme is composed by five algorithms* Setup, Extract, TagGen, ProofGen *and* Verify, *where:*

- Setup $(\lambda, U) \rightarrow (params, msk)$. It's a system setup algorithm run by the PKG. It takes as input a security parameter λ and the universe U of identities, and outputs the system public parameters $params$ and the PKG's master secret key msk.
- Extract $(params, msk, ID) \rightarrow sk_{ID}$. It's the private-key extraction algorithm also run by the PKG. It takes as input the system public parameters $params$, the master secret key msk, a user's identity $ID \in U$, and outputs the user's private key sk_{ID}.
- TagGen $(params, sk_{ID}, F) \rightarrow T$. It's the tag generation algorithm run by the user who owns a file F and an identity $ID \in U$. It takes as input the system public parameters $params$, the user's secret key sk_{ID} and a file F, the user selects an identity set S involving ID and outputs a file tag T. For achieving identity privacy, we require the set S must contain at least two identities.
- ProofGen $(params, chal, F, T) \rightarrow P$. It's the proof generation algorithm run by the cloud. It takes as input the system public parameters $params$, the challenge $chal$ received from the verifier, a file F and the corresponding file tag T. It outputs a proof P.
- Verify $(params, chal, P) \rightarrow 0$ *or* 1: It's the proof verifying algorithm run by the verifier. It takes as input the system public parameters $params$, the challenge $chal$ and a proof P, and returns 0 or 1. Return 0 means the outsourced file has been destroyed while return 1 indicates the file is still intact.

Correctness. All IBPoS schemes must observe correctness, namely if the file stored in the cloud remains intact and all entities involved are honest, then the algorithm Verify should always output 1. More formally, we say an IBPoS scheme is correct if for all security parameter λ, identity universe U, file F and identity $ID \in U$, let $(params, msk) = \mathsf{Setup}(\lambda, U)$, $sk_{ID} = \mathsf{Extract}(params, msk, ID)$, T be the output of $\mathsf{TagGen}(params, sk_{ID}, F)$ and let $chal$ be any challenge, if P is the output of $\mathsf{ProofGen}(params, chal, F, T)$, then $\mathsf{Verify}(params, chal, P)$ should always output 1.

3.2   Security Model

Similar to the security models of other IBPoS schemes (e.g. [18,28–30,34–36]), in this work we assume all users are honest while the verifier is semi-honest, i.e., it will honestly follow the predefined procedures but may seek to obtain some additional knowledge such as a file stored in the cloud and the identity of its owner. In addition, the cloud may be malicious in some cases, e.g. it may delete some rarely used file blocks for economic reasons. Therefore, we require an IBPoS scheme to possess the following security and privacy characters.

The primary one is soundness, which models the character that in a secure IBPoS scheme the proofs generated by the cloud could pass the verifier's checking only with a negligible probability when the outsourced data has been damaged. Moreover, we enforce our IBPoS scheme to provide enhanced privacy, i.e., it should protect both identity privacy and data privacy against the verifier simultaneously. Identity privacy requires that in an IBPoS scheme the verifier cannot link a stored file to the identity of its owner, and data privacy declares that the verifier cannot acquire the outsourced file when executing the scheme.

The formal definitions of soundness, identity privacy and data privacy are respectively given below. Our security definition for soundness is inspired by the definition of unforgeability of ring signature against chosen-subring attacks [7], and we call it soundness against semi-adaptive chosen identity and subring attacks.

Definition 2 (Soundness). *We say an IBPoS scheme is sound under the semi-adaptive chosen identity and subring attacks if for any probabilistic polynomial time (PPT) adversary $\mathcal{A}$ the probability that $\mathcal{A}$ wins the following game played between a challenger $\mathcal{C}$ and the adversary $\mathcal{A}$ is negligible.*

- **Setup.** The challenger $\mathcal{C}$ runs the algorithm $\mathsf{Setup}(\lambda, U)$ to obtain the system parameters *params* and the master secret key *msk*. It sends *params* to the adversary $\mathcal{A}$, while keeps *msk* confidential.
- **Queries.** The adversary $\mathcal{A}$ could semi-adaptively make the following types of queries to the challenger $\mathcal{C}$. More specifically, $\mathcal{A}$ can make TagGen queries when all Extract queries end.
    - **Extract Queries.** The adversary $\mathcal{A}$ can make such a query to get the private key associated with an identity. The challenger $\mathcal{C}$ will maintain a set S_E of extracted identities to record all such queries. For a query on identity ID, the challenger $\mathcal{C}$ first adds ID into S_E, then obtains the private key sk_{ID} by running the algorithm $\mathsf{Extract}\,(params, msk, ID)$ and finally forwards sk_{ID} to $\mathcal{A}$.
    - **TagGen Queries.** The adversary $\mathcal{A}$ can get the tag of any file F by issuing (ID, F) to this query, where ID denotes the owner identity of the file F. The challenger $\mathcal{C}$ runs $\mathsf{TagGen}\,(params, \mathsf{Extract}\,(params, msk, ID), F)$ to get the file tag T and then forwards it to $\mathcal{A}$. Note that in generating T, the challenger $\mathcal{C}$ will select an identity set S satisfying $ID \in S$ to achieve identity privacy.
- **Proof.** In this phase, the challenger $\mathcal{C}$ behaves as the verifier and the adversary $\mathcal{A}$ serves as the cloud. For an outsourced file F and the corresponding tag T, the challenger $\mathcal{C}$ generates a random challenge *chal* and requests the adversary $\mathcal{A}$ to return a proof. After receiving the request, $\mathcal{A}$ runs the algorithm $\mathsf{ProofGen}\,(params, chal, F, T)$ to get a proof and forwards it to $\mathcal{C}$.
- **Forgery.** When the above process ends, the adversary $\mathcal{A}$ outputs a proof P of some challenge *chal* on an outsourced file F. We say $\mathcal{A}$ wins the game if $\mathsf{Verify}\,(params, chal, P) = 1$, F has been broken and $\mathcal{A}$ does't make any Extract query on identities in S, where S is the identity set used in TagGen.

Definition 3 (Identity Privacy). *We say an IBPoS scheme achieves identity privacy if for any PPT adversary $\mathcal{A}$ its advantage in the following game is negligible. This game is also played between a challenger $\mathcal{C}$ and the adversary $\mathcal{A}$.*

- **Setup.** The adversary $\mathcal{A}$ runs the algorithm $\mathsf{Setup}(\lambda, U)$ to obtain the system public parameters *params* and the master secret key *msk*. It sends both *params* and *msk* to the challenger $\mathcal{C}$.

- **Challenge.** The adversary $\mathcal{A}$ outputs a tuple (ID_1, ID_2, F). Upon receiving the tuple, the challenger $\mathcal{C}$ picks a random b from $\{1,2\}$, runs the algorithm TagGen($params$, Extract $(params, msk, ID_b)$, F) to output a file tag T_b for $\mathcal{A}$. Here, we require the identity set S used in the algorithm TagGen for producing T_b must include $\{ID_1, ID_2\}$.
- **Guess.** The adversary $\mathcal{A}$ outputs a guess $b' \in \{1,2\}$.
  We define $\mathcal{A}$'s advantage in this game as $|\Pr[b' = b] - \frac{1}{2}|$.

Similarly, we can define a stronger notion of identity privacy called *unconditional identity privacy*, that is for any adversary $\mathcal{A}$ (who may have unbounded computational resources) the probability $\Pr[b' = b]$ in the above game is no more than $1/2$.

Unconditional identity privacy means that from a set of file tags even an unbounded adversary cannot uncover the identity information of the data owner. Our IBPoS scheme presented in this paper will fulfill the stronger definition.

Definition 4 (Data Privacy). *We say an IBPoS scheme achieves data privacy if there exists a polynomial time simulator such that the distributions of the following two conversations are computationally indistinguishable.*

- *C1. This conversation is the real conversation between the cloud and the verifier.*
- *C2. This conversation is the simulated conversation between the simulator and the verifier, in which the simulator behaves as the cloud but cannot access to any file stored in the cloud.*

Definition 5. *We say an IBPoS scheme is secure and provides enhanced privacy if it achieves soundness, identity privacy and data privacy.*

4   Cryptographic Background

In this section we give some cryptographic background involved in this paper.

Definition 6 (Bilinear Pairing). *Let $\mathbb{G}_1$ and $\mathbb{G}_2$ be two cyclic groups with the same prime order p. A map $e : \mathbb{G}_1 \times \mathbb{G}_1 \to \mathbb{G}_2$ is called a bilinear map if it satisfies three properties listed as below.*

1. *Bilinearity: For all $a, b \in \mathbb{Z}$ and $u, v \in \mathbb{G}_1$, we have $e(u^a, v^b) = e(u,v)^{ab}$.*
2. *Non-degeneracy: Let g be a generator of $\mathbb{G}_1$ and $1_{\mathbb{G}_2}$ denote the identity element of group $\mathbb{G}_2$, then we have $e(g,g) \neq 1_{\mathbb{G}_2}$.*
3. *Computability: There exists an efficient algorithm to compute the map e.*

The divisible computational Diffie-Hellman (DCDH) assumption is as follows.

Definition 7 (DCDH Assumption). *Given a cyclic group $\mathbb{G}$ of order p and a generator $g \in \mathbb{G}$, for random $g^a, g^{ab} \in \mathbb{G}$, it's intractable to output g^b.*

Bao et al. [5] have shown that this assumption is equivalent to the CDH one.

5   Our Scheme

Throughout the paper, we will work in the group $\mathbb{Z}_p$ for some large prime p. When we work in the bilinear setting, the group $\mathbb{Z}_p$ is the support of the group $\mathbb{G}_1$. We denote the number of elements in a set S by $|S|$ and for a positive integer k, we let $[1, k] = \{1, \ldots, k\}$.

5.1   Construction

- Setup(λ, U). Given a security parameter λ and the universe U of identities in the system, the algorithm outputs a prime $p > 2^\lambda$, two cyclic groups $\mathbb{G}_1$ and $\mathbb{G}_2$ of order p, a generator g of $\mathbb{G}_1$, a bilinear map $e : \mathbb{G}_1 \times \mathbb{G}_1 \to \mathbb{G}_2$, three hash functions $H_1 : \{0, 1\}^* \to \mathbb{Z}_p, H_2 : \{0, 1\}^* \to \mathbb{G}_1$ and $H_3 : \{0, 1\}^* \to \mathbb{Z}_p$, and a secure identity-based ring signature scheme RSig. The PKG chooses $|U|$ elements $r_1, \cdots, r_{|U|}$ from $\mathbb{Z}_p$ uniformly at random, calculates $R_i = g^{r_i}$ for all $i \in [1, |U|]$, and finally releases a public function $f : U \to \Sigma = \{R_i | i \in [1, |U|]\}$ to map each identity to an unique element in Σ. In addition, the PKG also selects random x from $\mathbb{Z}_p$ and sets $pub = g^x$ as its public key. The system public parameters $params = (p, \mathbb{G}_1, \mathbb{G}_2, g, e, H_1, H_2, H_3, RSig, \Sigma, f, pub)$ and the master secret key $msk = (x, r_1, \cdots, r_{|U|})$.
- Extract$(params, msk, ID_i)$. Given an identity ID_i of a user, the PKG first gets $R_i = f(ID_i)$ and r_i corresponding to R_i, then computes $sk_i = r_i + xH_1(ID_i, R_i)$. The PKG distributes sk_i to the user as its private key by a secure channel. Let $v_i = R_i \cdot (pub)^{H_1(ID_i, R_i)}$. The user can check the validity of sk_i by verifying whether $g^{sk_i} = v_i$ (note that $R_i = f(ID_i)$ can be calculated by any user). If so, the user accepts sk_i and rejects otherwise.
- TagGen$(params, sk_d, F)$. Given a private key sk_d and a file F of the user with identity ID_d, the user does as follows:
  1. Encode F into n blocks, i.e., $F = (m_1, \ldots, m_n) \in (\mathbb{Z}_p)^n$.
  2. Select a random $name$ from $\mathbb{Z}_p$ and set it as the identifier of the file F.
  3. Pick a random $u \in \mathbb{G}_1$ and a random subset S of U satisfying $ID_d \in S$. Without loss of generality, we may assume $S = \{ID_1, \cdots, ID_{|S|}\}$.
  4. For all $ID_i \in S$, calculate $R_i = f(ID_i)$ and $v_i = R_i \cdot (pub)^{H_1(ID_i, R_i)}$.
  5. Sign the message $name||u||S||n$ using RSig and get a ring signature sig related to S, where "$||$" refers to a string concatenation operation. Let $t = \text{sig}||name||u||S||n$. We stress that sig can be independently produced by an identity-based ring signature scheme under new secret keys.
  6. For each identity $ID_j \in S \setminus \{ID_d\}$, pick random $a_{i,j}$ for all $i \in [1, n]$ from $\mathbb{Z}_p$ and compute $\sigma_{i,j} = g^{a_{i,j}}$.
  7. For the identity ID_d and all $i \in [1, n]$, calculate

$$\sigma_{i,d} = \left(\frac{H_2(name, S, i) \cdot u^{m_i}}{\prod_{j \in [1, |S|] \setminus \{d\}} v_j^{a_{i,j}}} \right)^{1/sk_d}.$$

  8. Set the tag for block m_i as $\sigma_i = (\sigma_{i,1}, \ldots, \sigma_{i,|S|})$ where $i \in [1, n]$, and let $T = (t, \sigma_1, \ldots, \sigma_n)$ be the tag of the file F.

9. Upload the file F together with the file tag T to the cloud, and then delete them locally.

- ProofGen$(params, chal, F, T)$. To check the integrity of file F, the verifier picks a random $I = \{(i, c_i)\}$ where $i \in [1, n]$ and $c_i \in \mathbb{Z}_p$, and issues a challenge $chal = (name, I)$ to the cloud. After receiving the challenge, the cloud first finds a matched file $F = (m_1, \ldots, m_n)$ and file tag $T = (t, \sigma_1, \ldots, \sigma_n)$ by inspecting t. Then the cloud computes $\beta_j = \prod_{(i,c_i) \in I} (\sigma_{i,j})^{c_i}$ for each $j \in [1, |S|]$, chooses a random $\tau \in \mathbb{Z}_p$, calculates $\alpha = e(u, g)^{\tau}$, $\mu = \sum_{(i,c_i) \in I} c_i m_i + \tau \cdot H_3(\alpha, \beta)$, where $\beta = (\beta_1, \ldots, \beta_{|S|})$. Finally, the cloud returns a proof $P = (t, \alpha, \beta, \mu)$ to the verifier.

- Verify$(params, chal, P)$. Given a challenge $chal = (name, I)$ and a proof $P = (t, \alpha, \beta, \mu)$, the verifier first parses t and checks the validity of the ring signature sig on the message $name||u||S||n$. If it's invalid, the algorithm outputs 0 and terminates. Otherwise, the verifier goes on to check whether

$$e\Big(\prod_{(i,c_i) \in I} H_2(name, S, i)^{c_i} \cdot u^{\mu}, g\Big) = B \cdot \alpha^{H_3(\alpha, \beta)},$$

where $B = \prod_{i \in [1, |S|]} e(\beta_i, v_i)$. If so, output 1, and 0 otherwise.

Correctness. If all entities are honest, then for all proofs produced by the cloud using the algorithm ProofGen, the algorithm Verify will always return 1 because the ring signature sig will always be valid and

$$B = \prod_{j=1}^{|S|} e(\beta_j, v_j)$$

$$= \prod_{j=1}^{|S|} e\Big(\prod_{(i,c_i) \in I} (\sigma_{i,j})^{c_i}, v_j\Big)$$

$$= \prod_{j=1, j \neq d}^{|S|} e\Big(\prod_{(i,c_i) \in I} (\sigma_{i,j})^{c_i}, v_j\Big) \cdot e\Big(\prod_{(i,c_i) \in I} (\sigma_{i,d})^{c_i}, v_d\Big)$$

$$= \prod_{j=1, j \neq d}^{|S|} e\Big(\prod_{(i,c_i) \in I} (v_j)^{c_i a_{i,j}}, g\Big) \cdot e\Big(\frac{\prod_{(i,c_i) \in I} (H_2(name, S, i) \cdot u^{m_i})^{c_i}}{\prod_{(i,c_i) \in I} \prod_{j=1, j \neq d}^{|S|} v_j^{c_i a_{i,j}}}, g\Big)$$

$$= e\Big(\prod_{(i,c_i) \in I} H_2(name, S, i)^{c_i} \cdot u^{\sum_{(i,c_i) \in I} m_i c_i}, g\Big).$$

As a result, we know

$$B \cdot \alpha^{H_3(\alpha, \beta)}$$

$$= e\Big(\prod_{(i,c_i) \in I} H_2(name, S, i)^{c_i} \cdot u^{\sum_{(i,c_i) \in I} m_i c_i}, g\Big) \cdot e\big(u^{\tau H_3(\alpha, \beta)}, g\big)$$

$$= e\Big(\prod_{(i,c_i) \in I} H_2(name, S, i)^{c_i} \cdot u^{\mu}, g\Big).$$

5.2 Security

Theorem 1. *If the identity-based ring signature scheme RSig is secure and the DCDH assumption holds in bilinear groups, then the IBPoS scheme above is secure and achieves enhanced privacy in the random oracle model.*

We prove the theorem using the following three lemmas.

Lemma 1. *If the identity-based ring signature scheme RSig is secure and the DCDH assumption holds in bilinear groups, then in the random oracle model no PPT adversary could break the soundness of our IBPoS scheme under the semi-adaptive chosen identity and subring attacks with non-negligible probability.*

Proof. According to Definition 2, we will prove that if there exists a PPT adversary $\mathcal{A}$ who breaks the soundness of the above IBPoS scheme with non-negligible probability, then we can construct a polynomial time algorithm $\mathcal{B}$ that uses the adversary $\mathcal{A}$ as a subroutine to solve a DCDH problem with non-negligible probability too. Algorithm $\mathcal{B}$ does so by interacting with $\mathcal{A}$ as follows.

Setup: Given a security parameter λ and the universe U of identities in the system, the algorithm $\mathcal{B}$ selects a prime $p > 2^\lambda$, two cyclic groups $\mathbb{G}_1$ and $\mathbb{G}_2$ of order p, a generator g of $\mathbb{G}_1$, a bilinear map $e : \mathbb{G}_1 \times \mathbb{G}_1 \to \mathbb{G}_2$, an identity-based ring signature scheme RSig, and three hash functions $H_1 : \{0,1\}^* \to \mathbb{Z}_p, H_2 : \{0,1\}^* \to \mathbb{G}_1$ and $H_3 : \{0,1\}^* \to \mathbb{Z}_p$. In this proof, all the hash functions will be viewed as random oracles controlled by $\mathcal{B}$. Additionally, the algorithm $\mathcal{B}$ also chooses $2|U|$ elements $r_1, \cdots, r_{|U|}$ and $s_1, \cdots, s_{|U|}$ from $\mathbb{Z}_p$ uniformly at random.

Suppose the input of the DCDH problem is (g, g^a, g^{ab}). Let $g_1 = g^a$. Then $\mathcal{B}$ sets the PKG's public key *pub* as g_1. In addition, $\mathcal{B}$ will maintain a list of tuples in the form of (ID_k, R_k, b, r_k, s_k). The list is initially empty and we denote it as the Setup-list. For each identity $ID_i \in U$, $\mathcal{B}$ flips a coin that shows $b = 0$ with probability ζ (it will be determined later) and $b = 1$ with probability $1 - \zeta$. If $b = 0$, $\mathcal{B}$ sets $v_i = g^{s_i}$. Otherwise, $\mathcal{B}$ sets $v_i = g_1^{s_i}$. For both cases, $\mathcal{B}$ calculates $R_i = v_i/g_1^{r_i}$, programs $H_1(ID_i, R_i) = r_i$ and stores (ID_i, R_i, b, r_i, s_i) in the Setup-list. Finally, $\mathcal{B}$ releases a public function $f : U \to \Sigma = \{R_i | i \in [1, |U|]\}$ that maps each identity ID_i to R_i. The system public parameters *params* = $(p, \mathbb{G}_1, \mathbb{G}_2, g, e, H_1, H_2, H_3, RSig, \Sigma, f, pub)$.

Hash Queries: The adversary $\mathcal{A}$ could make the following types of hash queries adaptively.

- To get the value $H_1(ID_i, R_i)$, the adversary $\mathcal{A}$ issues an H_1 query on (ID_i, R_i). Upon receiving the query, $\mathcal{B}$ looks up a matched tuple (ID_i, R_i, b, r_i, s_i) in the Setup-list and responds with r_i.
- To get the value $H_2(name, S, i)$, the adversary $\mathcal{A}$ would issue an H_2 query on $(name, S, i)$. In response to such queries, the algorithm $\mathcal{B}$ will maintain a list of tuples. We refer to the list as H_2-list that is initially empty with each tuple like $(name, S, k, y_k, h_k)$. When $\mathcal{B}$ receives an H_2 query on $(name, S, i)$, $\mathcal{B}$ first looks up it in the H_2-list. If a matched tuple is found, $\mathcal{B}$ just responds with h_i. Otherwise, $\mathcal{B}$ selects random $y_i \in \mathbb{Z}_p$, retrieves the file $F = (m_1, \ldots, m_n)$ and u matched with the identifier *name*, and then confirms whether $S \subseteq S_E$ (S_E will be described later). If so, $\mathcal{B}$ calculates $h_i = g^{y_i}/u^{m_i}$ and $h_i = g_1^{y_i}/u^{m_i}$ otherwise. For both cases, $\mathcal{B}$ finally stores $(name, S, i, y_i, h_i)$ in the H_2-list and returns h_i to $\mathcal{A}$. (Notice that y_i should also be related with *name* and S, but for notation simplicity we omit them.)

- To get the value $H_3(\alpha, \beta)$, the adversary $\mathcal{A}$ would issue an H_3 query on (α, β). Similarly, the algorithm $\mathcal{B}$ will maintain a list of tuples with each tuple like (α, β, w). We refer to the list as H_3-list that is initially empty. When $\mathcal{B}$ receives an H_3 query on (α, β), $\mathcal{B}$ first looks up it in the H_3-list. If a matched tuple is found, $\mathcal{B}$ simply responds with w. Otherwise, $\mathcal{B}$ selects random $w \in \mathbb{Z}_p$, stores (α, β, w) in the H_3-list and returns w to $\mathcal{A}$.

Extract Queries: The adversary $\mathcal{A}$ could make such queries adaptively to get the secret keys of users. To record the queries, the algorithm $\mathcal{B}$ will maintain an initially empty set S_E. For a query on the identity ID_i, $\mathcal{B}$ first updates $S_E = S_E \bigcup \{ID_i\}$ and then looks up a matched tuple (ID_i, R_i, b, r_i, s_i) in the Setup-list. If $b = 0$, $\mathcal{B}$ returns s_i. Otherwise, $\mathcal{B}$ aborts. Suppose $\mathcal{A}$ issues at most q_E such queries on identities, then we know the probability that $\mathcal{B}$ doesn't abort is not less than ζ^{q_E}.

By construction, we know that for all s_i's returned from $\mathcal{B}$ we have $g^{s_i} = v_i = R_i \cdot g_1^{r_i} = R_i \cdot (pub)^{H_1(ID_i, R_i)}$. Therefore, s_i is a valid secret key of the identity ID_i.

TagGen Queries: When the above extract queries end, the adversary $\mathcal{A}$ is able to make this type of queries for getting file tags. Assume $\mathcal{A}$ issues such a query on file F and identity $ID_d \in U$, the algorithm $\mathcal{B}$ first encodes F into n blocks such that $F = (m_1, \ldots, m_n) \in (\mathbb{Z}_p)^n$ and selects a random file identifier $name$ for F from $\mathbb{Z}_p$. Then $\mathcal{B}$ responds in the following two ways according to whether $ID_d \in S_E$.

Case 1. When $ID_d \in S_E$, then $\mathcal{B}$ knows the secret key associated with ID_d. So, $\mathcal{B}$ could pick a random set $S \subseteq S_E$ satisfying $ID_d \in S$, and simply runs the algorithm TagGen in Sect. 5.1 and returns a file tag T to $\mathcal{A}$. Here $\mathcal{B}$ will also store (F, T) in its local memory.

Case 2. If $ID_d \notin S_E$, $\mathcal{B}$ will pick a random set $S \subseteq U \backslash S_E$ so that $ID_d \in S$. We require that $v_i = g_1^{s_i}$ for any identity $ID_i \in S$. (This happens with probability $(1 - \zeta)^{|S|}$.) Then $\mathcal{B}$ does as follows.

1. Let $u = g^{ab}$. Get a signature sig associated with S and message $name||u||S||n$ using RSig. Then set $t = \text{sig}||name||u||S||n$. Without loss of generality we let $S = \{ID_1, \cdots, ID_{|S|}\}$.
2. For each identity $ID_j \in S \setminus \{ID_d\}$, pick random $a_{i,j}$ from $\mathbb{Z}_p$ for all $i \in [1, n]$ and compute $\sigma_{i,j} = g_1^{a_{i,j}}$.
3. For the identity ID_d and all $i \in [1, n]$, retrieve y_i matched with $(name, S, i)$ in the H_2-list and all s_j's matched with $ID_j \in S$ in the Setup-list, then calculate $a_{i,d} = (y_i - \sum_{j \in [1,|S|] \backslash \{d\}} s_j \cdot a_{i,j})/s_d$ and $\sigma_{i,d} = g^{a_{i,d}}$.
   Observe that $H_2(name, S, i) \cdot u^{m_i} = g_1^{y_i}$ for all $i \in [1, n]$ by construction. Furthermore, we have

$$g_1^{a_{i,d} \cdot s_d} \cdot \prod_{j=1, j \neq d}^{|S|} v_j^{a_{i,j}} = g_1^{a_{i,d} \cdot s_d} \cdot \prod_{j=1, j \neq d}^{|S|} g_1^{s_j \cdot a_{i,j}} = g_1^{y_i}.$$

Thus, the tag $\sigma_i = (\sigma_{i,1}, \ldots, \sigma_{i,|S|})$ for block m_i generated as the above is indistinguishable from the real one.

4. Finally, $\mathcal{B}$ returns the file tag T to $\mathcal{A}$ but also stores (F, T) in its local memory, where $T = (t, \sigma_1, \ldots, \sigma_n)$.

We can see that in the simulation $\mathcal{B}$ does not abort with probability at least $\zeta^{q_E} \cdot (1 - \zeta)^{|S|}$, which is maximized when $\zeta = q_E/(q_E + |S|)$.

Proof. To check whether the file F stored in the cloud with identifier $name$ remains intact or not, $\mathcal{B}$ picks a random set $I = \{(i, c_i)\}$ where $i \in [1, n]$ and $c_i \in \mathbb{Z}_p$, and issues a challenge $chal = (name, I)$ to the adversary $\mathcal{A}$. After receiving the challenge, $\mathcal{A}$ does the same as the algorithm ProofGen in Sect. 5.1 and then returns a proof to $\mathcal{B}$.

Forgery. Finally, $\mathcal{A}$ with non-negligible probability outputs a proof $P = (t, \alpha, \beta, \mu)$ of a challenge $I = \{(i, c_i)\}$ on a file F with identifier $name$. Let $t = \mathsf{sig}||name||u||S||n$, $\beta = (\beta_1, \ldots, \beta_{|S|})$. According to Definition 2, we know that F has been broken, $S \subseteq U \backslash S_E$, the ring signature sig on the message $name||u||S||n$ is valid, and

$$e\Big(\prod_{(i,c_i) \in I} H_2(name, S, i)^{c_i} \cdot u^\mu, g\Big) = B \cdot \alpha^w, \tag{1}$$

where $B = \prod_{i \in [1, |S|]} e(\beta_i, v_i)$, $w = H_3(\alpha, \beta)$.

Since the identity-based ring signature scheme RSig is secure, we know t must always be invariable for the same file F.

Now, the algorithm $\mathcal{B}$ reruns the adversary $\mathcal{A}$ with the same random tape but different responses of H_3 queries. By the general forking lemma [6], $\mathcal{B}$ with non-negligible probability will obtain another valid proof $P' = (t, \alpha, \beta, \mu')$ of the challenge I on the file F. Let w' be the output of $H_3(\alpha, \beta)$ at this time. Therefore, we have

$$e\Big(\prod_{(i,c_i) \in I} H_2(name, S, i)^{c_i} \cdot u^{\mu'}, g\Big) = B \cdot \alpha^{w'}, \tag{2}$$

where $B = \prod_{i \in [1, |S|]} e(\beta_i, v_i)$.

Dividing Eq. (1) by Eq. (2), we obtain

$$e(u^{\mu - \mu'}, g) = \alpha^{w - w'}.$$

Let $\Delta\mu = \mu - \mu'$, $\Delta w = w - w'$. We have

$$\alpha = e(u, g)^{\frac{\Delta\mu}{\Delta w}}. \tag{3}$$

Substituting α in Eq. (1) with Eq. (3) yields

$$e\Big(\prod_{(i,c_i) \in I} H_2(name, S, i)^{c_i} \cdot u^\mu, g\Big) = B \cdot e(u, g)^{\frac{w \cdot \Delta\mu}{\Delta w}}. \tag{4}$$

Recall that $\mathcal{B}$ has stored the original (F, T) in its local memory, hence $\mathcal{B}$ could calculate $\beta_j^* = \prod_{(i,c_i)\in I}(\sigma_{i,j})^{c_i}$ for all $j \in [1, |S|]$ and $\mu^* = \sum_{(i,c_i)\in I} c_i m_i$, satisfying

$$e\left(\prod_{(i,c_i)\in I} H_2(name, S, i)^{c_i} \cdot u^{\mu^*}, g\right) = \prod_{i\in[1,|S|]} e(\beta_i^*, v_i). \tag{5}$$

Dividing Eq. (5) by Eq. (4) and then rearranging terms, we obtain

$$e\left(u^{\mu^* - \mu + \frac{w\cdot\Delta\mu}{\Delta w}}, g\right) = \prod_{i\in[1,|S|]} e(\beta_i^* \cdot \beta_i^{-1}, v_i). \tag{6}$$

Since $v_i = g_1^{s_i}$ for all $i \in [1, |S|]$, $u = g^{ab}$ and $\mu^* - \mu + \frac{w\cdot\Delta\mu}{\Delta w}$ is nonzero with a large probability, we found the solution to the DCDH problem

$$g^b = \left(\prod_{i\in[1,|S|]} (\beta_i^* \cdot \beta_i^{-1})^{s_i}\right)^{1/(\mu^* - \mu + \frac{w\cdot\Delta\mu}{\Delta w})}.$$

This concludes the proof.

Lemma 2. *For any adversary its advantage in the game of Definition 3 is negligible.*

Proof. We prove that for any $F = (m_1, \ldots, m_n)$ and any two identities ID_1, ID_2, the distributions of $\mathsf{TagGen}(params, \mathsf{Extract}\,(params, msk, ID_b), F)$ are identical. Here $b \in \{1, 2\}$ and $S = \{ID_1, ID_2\}$. Therefore, in our scheme anyone (except the file owner himself and the cloud) cannot acquire the identity information of the file owner from the file tag and/or its combinations.

Observe that in our scheme the file tag for file F is $T = (t, \sigma_1, \ldots, \sigma_n)$ where $t = \mathsf{sig}||name||u||S||n$, $S = \{ID_1, ID_2\}$, sig is a ring signature and $\sigma_i = (\sigma_{i,1}, \sigma_{i,2})$ is the tag for block m_i. By our construction, we know $(\sigma_{i,1})^{sk_1} \cdot (\sigma_{i,2})^{sk_2} = H_2\,(name\,||i||\,S) \cdot u^{m_i}$ for any block m_i $(i \in [1, n])$, where sk_1 (resp. sk_2) is the private key of ID_1 (resp. ID_2). In addition, for any $b \in \{1, 2\}$ and any $h \in \mathbb{G}_1$, we know the distribution $\{g^{a_1}, g^{a_2} : a_j \in \mathbb{Z}_p\ (j = 1 + b \mod 2)$, select a_b such that $(g^{a_j})^{sk_j} \cdot (g^{a_b})^{sk_b} = h\}$ is the same as the distribution $\{g^{a_1}, g^{a_2} : a_1, a_2 \in \mathbb{Z}_p$ such that $(g^{a_1})^{sk_1} \cdot (g^{a_2})^{sk_2} = h\}$. That is, the distribution of file tags for file F generated using no matter which identity is always the same. As a result, even an unbounded adversary cannot win the game of Definition 3 with non-negligible advantage. So, our IBPoS scheme enjoys identity privacy.

Lemma 3. *Our IBPoS scheme provides data privacy.*

Proof. We show below that a simulator without accessing to any file stored in the cloud can produce valid proofs for the verifier. Let the system public parameters $params = (p, \mathbb{G}_1, \mathbb{G}_2, g, e, H_1, H_2, H_3, RSig, \Sigma, f, pub)$. For a challenged file F, let $T = (t, \sigma_1, \ldots, \sigma_n)$ be the tag of F and $\sigma_i = (\sigma_{i,1}, \ldots, \sigma_{i,|S|})$ be the tag of the i-th file block. Here S is an identity set used to produce T. Suppose the random challenge selected by the verifier is $I = \{(i, c_i)\}$ where $i \in [1, n]$ and $c_i \in \mathbb{Z}_p$. According to Definition 4, we just need to show the simulator without F could produce a proof for the challenge that is indistinguishable from the real one. The simulator does the following. (Here we treat H_3 as a random oracle controlled by the simulator.)

1. Pick $\mu, z \in \mathbb{Z}_p$ uniformly at random.
2. Set $R_i = f(ID_i)$ and $v_i = R_i \cdot (pub)^{H_1(ID_i, R_i)}$ for all identities $ID_i \in S$.
3. For each $j \in [1, |S|]$, let $\beta_j = \Pi_{(i, c_i) \in I}(\sigma_{i,j})^{c_i}$.
4. Calculate $A = e(\prod_{(i,c_i) \in I} H_2(name, S, i)^{c_i} \cdot u^\mu, g)$, $B = \prod_{i \in [1, |S|]} e(\beta_i, v_i)$, and $\alpha = (\frac{A}{B})^{1/z}$.
5. Program $H_3(\alpha, \beta) = z$, where $\beta = (\beta_1, \ldots, \beta_{|S|})$.

The proof of the challenge I generated by the simulator is $P = (t, \alpha, \beta, \mu)$. We can easily check that $A = B \cdot \alpha^{H_3(\alpha, \beta)}$. And the simulated proof is clearly indistinguishable from the real one generated by the cloud, as required.

6   Performance Evaluation

In this section, we conduct experiments to evaluate the performance of our IBPoS scheme. We also implement the recent IBPoS schemes in [29, 34] for comparison (yet we stress that the two schemes don't provide enhanced privacy as defined in this work). In the following, we will denote Wang et al.'s scheme [29] by A-IBPoS and refer to Yu et al.'s scheme [34] as PP-IBPoS.

6.1   Experiment Setup

The simulations are implemented on a Windows 7 system using Intel Core i5-4590 CPU at 3.30 GHz and the memory is 8.00 GB. The system security parameter is set to be 80 bits. All experiments utilize JPBC library of version 2.0.0 and the type A elliptic curve. The file F we choose is of size 1 GB and its total number of blocks may change from 1000 to 10000. All simulation results represent the mean of 10 trials. We apply the identity-based ring signature scheme of [11] in our scheme to sign the message $name||u||S||n$ and employ the short signature scheme of [9] in A-IBPoS to sign the file F. We construct the pseudorandom functions used in A-IBPoS from a linear congruential generator.

According to the results of [1], we know that to detect misbehavior of the cloud with success probabilities up to 99% and 95%, one just needs to respectively select the challenge blocks in I with the numbers of 460 and 300. We also notice that the strength of identity privacy in our IBPoS scheme is proportional to the size of the identity set S used in generating file tags. More users are involved in S, then the strength of identity privacy will be higher. For most practical applications, 10 users may be enough.

6.2   Computation Cost

User Side. We first evaluate the computation overhead of the user side. On the user side, the essential computation overhead comes from the cost of generating tag for a file, which depends on the total number of file blocks (and the size of the identity set S in our scheme and in A-IBPoS). First, we fill 10 users in S and range the file blocks from 1000 to 10000. Figure 2(a) illustrates that the computation costs of tag generation of all three schemes are linearly increasing with the total number of file blocks. And the cost for our scheme is slightly worse than that for A-IBPoS. PP-IBPoS is the most efficient one. Then we fix the file block number to be 5000, and set the number of identities in S to be ranged from 2 to 20. Figure 2(b) shows that the tag generation times of our scheme and A-IBPoS are both larger than that of PP-IBPoS. And our scheme is also slightly less efficient than A-IBPoS.

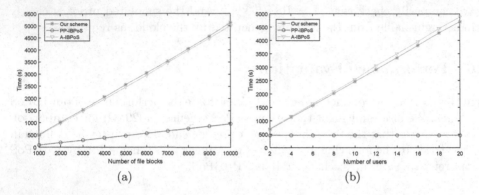

Fig. 2. Computation cost. (a) Tag generation times for various numbers of file blocks. (b) Tag generation times for various numbers of users.

Cloud Side. The computation overhead of the cloud is mainly from the cost of generating proof for the challenge picked by the verifier. It depends on the number of challenged blocks and the size of S. First, we fill 10 users in S and range the number of selected blocks in a challenge from 100 to 1000. Figure 3(a) illustrates that the computation times of all three schemes are linearly increasing with the number of selected blocks, but ours is lower than that of A-IBPoS. The computation cost of PP-IBPoS is the lowest one. Then we set the number of challenge blocks to be 460 and range the size of S from 2 to 20. Figure 3(b) shows that the proof generation times of our scheme and A-IBPoS are linearly increasing with the size of S, and ours is slightly lower than that of A-IBPoS. The proof computation time of PP-IBPoS is the lowest and has nothing to do with the size of S.

Verifier Side. The computation overhead of the verifier is mainly from the cost of verifying proof sent from the cloud, which depends on the challenge size and the size of S. First, we set the size of S as 10 and range the number of selected blocks in a challenge from 100 to 1000. Figure 4(a) illustrates that the proof verification time in our scheme is less than that of A-IBPoS, and the computation time for PP-IBPoS is the highest one. Then we set the number of challenge blocks to be 460 and range the size of S from 2 to 20. Figure 4(b) shows that the proof verification time of our scheme is the least among all the three schemes and PP-IBPoS needs the most time.

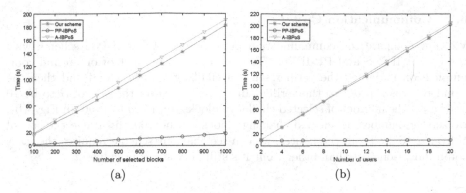

Fig. 3. Computation cost. (a) Proof generation times for various numbers of selected blocks. (b) Proof generation times for various numbers of users.

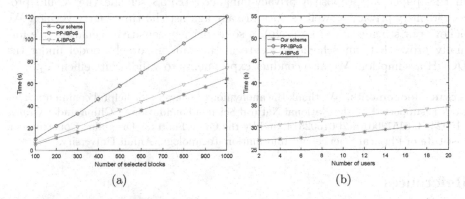

Fig. 4. Computation cost. (a) Proof verification times for various numbers of selected blocks. (b) Proof verification times for various numbers of users.

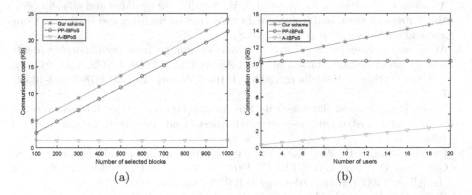

Fig. 5. Communication cost. (a) Communication overhead for various numbers of selected blocks. (b) Communication overhead for various numbers of users.

6.3   Communication Cost

We now compare the communication performance of our IBPoS scheme with those of A-IBPoS and PP-IBPoS. The communication cost of one-round communication is due to the verifier sends a challenge to the cloud and then the cloud returns a proof to the verifier. In Fig. 5(a), we fix the size of S to be 10 and range the number of selected challenge blocks from 100 to 1000. In Fig. 5(b), we set the number of selected challenge blocks to be 460 and range the size of S from 2 to 20. From the figures, we can see that our scheme requires the most communication cost than others, but it's still very small in value.

7   Conclusion

In this paper we propose a privacy-enhanced IBPoS scheme that could protect identity privacy as well as data privacy against the third-party verifier. We believe our scheme would be useful in some privacy-sensitive scenarios. We formally prove that our scheme is secure in the random oracle model under the DCDH assumption. We also conduct experiments to validate its efficiency.

Acknowledgements. We thank the anonymous reviewers for helpful comments. This work is supported by the National Natural Science Foundation of China under Grants 61502443, 61572001 and 61502314, and by the Open Fund for Discipline Construction, Institute of Physical Science and Information Technology, Anhui University.

References

1. Ateniese, G., et al.: Provable data possession at untrusted stores. In: ACM Conference on Computer and Communications Security, pp. 598–609. ACM (2007)
2. Ateniese, G., Di Pietro, R., Mancini, L.V., Tsudik, G.: Scalable and efficient provable data possession. In: International Conference on Security and Privacy in Communication Networks, p. 9. ACM (2008)
3. Ateniese, G., Kamara, S., Katz, J.: Proofs of storage from homomorphic identification protocols. In: Matsui, M. (ed.) ASIACRYPT 2009. LNCS, vol. 5912, pp. 319–333. Springer, Heidelberg (2009). https://doi.org/10.1007/978-3-642-10366-7_19
4. Babcock, C.: 9 worst cloud security threats (2014). http://www.informationweek.com/cloud/infrastructure-as-a-service/9-worst-cloud-security-threats/d/d-id/1114085
5. Bao, F., Deng, R.H., Zhu, H.F.: Variations of diffie-hellman problem. In: Qing, S., Gollmann, D., Zhou, J. (eds.) ICICS 2003. LNCS, vol. 2836, pp. 301–312. Springer, Heidelberg (2003). https://doi.org/10.1007/978-3-540-39927-8_28
6. Bellare, M., Neven, G.: Multi-signatures in the plain public-key model and a general forking lemma. In: ACM Conference on Computer and Communications Security, pp. 390–399. ACM (2006)
7. Bender, A., Katz, J., Morselli, R.: Ring signatures: stronger definitions, and constructions without random oracles. J. Cryptol. **22**(1), 114–138 (2009)

8. Boneh, D., Gentry, C., Lynn, B., Shacham, H.: Aggregate and verifiably encrypted signatures from bilinear maps. In: Biham, E. (ed.) EUROCRYPT 2003. LNCS, vol. 2656, pp. 416–432. Springer, Heidelberg (2003). https://doi.org/10.1007/3-540-39200-9_26

9. Boneh, D., Lynn, B., Shacham, H.: Short signatures from the weil pairing. J. Cryptol. **17**(4), 297–319 (2004)

10. Chen, F., Xiang, T., Yang, Y., Chow, S.S.M.: Secure cloud storage meets with secure network coding. IEEE Trans. Comput. **65**(6), 1936–1948 (2016)

11. Chow, S.S.M., Yiu, S.-M., Hui, L.C.K.: Efficient identity based ring signature. In: Ioannidis, J., Keromytis, A., Yung, M. (eds.) ACNS 2005. LNCS, vol. 3531, pp. 499–512. Springer, Heidelberg (2005). https://doi.org/10.1007/11496137_34

12. Diffie, W., Hellman, M.: New directions in cryptography. IEEE Trans. Inf. Theory **22**(6), 644–654 (1976)

13. Dodis, Y., Vadhan, S., Wichs, D.: Proofs of retrievability via hardness amplification. In: Reingold, O. (ed.) TCC 2009. LNCS, vol. 5444, pp. 109–127. Springer, Heidelberg (2009). https://doi.org/10.1007/978-3-642-00457-5_8

14. Erway, C., Küpçü, A., Papamanthou, C., Tamassia, R.: Dynamic provable data possession. In: ACM Conference on Computer and Communications Security, pp. 213–222. ACM (2009)

15. Erway, C., Küpçü, A., Papamanthou, C., Tamassia, R.: Dynamic provable data possession. ACM Trans. Inf. Syst. Secur. **17**(4), 15 (2015)

16. Guan, C., Ren, K., Zhang, F., Kerschbaum, F., Yu, J.: Symmetric-key based proofs of retrievability supporting public verification. In: Pernul, G., Ryan, P.Y.A., Weippl, E. (eds.) ESORICS 2015. LNCS, vol. 9326, pp. 203–223. Springer, Cham (2015). https://doi.org/10.1007/978-3-319-24174-6_11

17. Juels, A., Kaliski, Jr., B.S.: PORs: proofs of retrievability for large files. In: ACM Conference on Computer and Communications Security, pp. 584–597. ACM (2007)

18. Liu, H., et al.: Identity-based provable data possession revisited: security analysis and generic construction. Comput. Stand. Interfaces **54**, 10–19 (2017)

19. Rivest, R.L., Shamir, A., Adleman, L.: A method for obtaining digital signatures and public-key cryptosystems. Commun. ACM **21**(2), 120–126 (1978)

20. Schnorr, C.-P.: Efficient signature generation by smart cards. J. Cryptol. **4**(3), 161–174 (1991)

21. Shacham, H., Waters, B.: Compact proofs of retrievability. In: Pieprzyk, J. (ed.) ASIACRYPT 2008. LNCS, vol. 5350, pp. 90–107. Springer, Heidelberg (2008). https://doi.org/10.1007/978-3-540-89255-7_7

22. Shacham, H., Waters, B.: Compact proofs of retrievability. J. Cryptol. **26**(3), 442–483 (2013)

23. Shamir, A.: Identity-based cryptosystems and signature schemes. In: Blakley, G.R., Chaum, D. (eds.) CRYPTO 1984. LNCS, vol. 196, pp. 47–53. Springer, Heidelberg (1985). https://doi.org/10.1007/3-540-39568-7_5

24. Wang, B., Li, B., Li, H.: Oruta: privacy-preserving public auditing for shared data in the cloud. In: IEEE International Conference on Cloud Computing, pp. 295–302. IEEE (2012)

25. Wang, B., Li, B., Li, H.: Oruta: privacy-preserving public auditing for shared data in the cloud. IEEE Trans. Cloud Comput. **2**(1), 43–56 (2014)

26. Wang, C., Chow, S.S.M., Wang, Q., Ren, K., Lou, W.: Privacy-preserving public auditing for secure cloud storage. IEEE Trans. Comput. **62**(2), 362–375 (2013)

27. Wang, C., Wang, Q., Ren, K., Lou, W.: Privacy-preserving public auditing for data storage security in cloud computing. In: IEEE International Conference on Computer Communications, pp. 1–9. IEEE (2010)

28. Wang, H.: Identity-based distributed provable data possession in multicloud storage. IEEE Trans. Serv. Comput. **8**(2), 328–340 (2015)
29. Wang, H., He, D., Yu, J., Wang, Z.: Incentive and unconditionally anonymous identity-based public provable data possession. IEEE Trans. Serv. Comput. https://doi.org/10.1109/TSC.2016.2633260
30. Wang, H., Qianhong, W., Qin, B., Domingo-Ferrer, J.: Identity-based remote data possession checking in public clouds. IET Inf. Secur. **8**(2), 114–121 (2014)
31. Wang, Q., Wang, C., Li, J., Ren, K., Lou, W.: Enabling public verifiability and data dynamics for storage security in cloud computing. In: Backes, M., Ning, P. (eds.) ESORICS 2009. LNCS, vol. 5789, pp. 355–370. Springer, Heidelberg (2009). https://doi.org/10.1007/978-3-642-04444-1_22
32. Wang, Q., Wang, C., Ren, K., Lou, W., Li, J.: Enabling public auditability and data dynamics for storage security in cloud computing. IEEE Trans. Parallel Distrib. Syst. **22**(5), 847–859 (2011)
33. Yang, K., Jia, X.: An efficient and secure dynamic auditing protocol for data storage in cloud computing. IEEE Trans. Parallel Distrib. Syst. **24**(9), 1717–1726 (2013)
34. Yu, Y., et al.: Identity-based remote data integrity checking with perfect data privacy preserving for cloud storage. IEEE Trans. Inf. Forensics Secur. **12**(4), 767–778 (2017)
35. Yu, Y., et al.: Cloud data integrity checking with an identity-based auditing mechanism from RSA. Future Gen. Comput. Syst. **62**, 85–91 (2016)
36. Yu, Y., Zhang, Y., Mu, Y., Susilo, W., Liu, H.: Provably secure identity based provable data possession. In: Au, M.-H., Miyaji, A. (eds.) ProvSec 2015. LNCS, vol. 9451, pp. 310–325. Springer, Cham (2015). https://doi.org/10.1007/978-3-319-26059-4_17
37. Zhang, J., Yang, Y., Chen, Y., Chen, F.: A secure cloud storage system based on discrete logarithm problem. In: IEEE/ACM International Symposium on Quality of Service, pp. 1–10. IEEE (2017)
38. Zhu, Y., Hu, H., Ahn, G.J., Yu, M.: Cooperative provable data possession for integrity verification in multicloud storage. IEEE Trans. Parallel Distrib. Syst. **23**(12), 2231–2244 (2012)

Evaluating the Impact of Intrusion Sensitivity on Securing Collaborative Intrusion Detection Networks Against SOOA

David Madsen[1], Wenjuan Li[1,2], Weizhi Meng[1], and Yu Wang[3(✉)]

[1] Department of Applied Mathematics and Computer Science, Technical University of Denmark, Kongens Lyngby, Denmark
weme@dtu.dk
[2] Department of Computer Science, City University of Hong Kong, Kowloon Tong, Hong Kong
[3] School of Computer Science, Guangzhou University, Guangzhou, China
yuwang@gzhu.edu.cn

Abstract. Cyber attacks are greatly expanding in both size and complexity. To handle this issue, research has been focused on collaborative intrusion detection networks (CIDNs), which can improve the detection accuracy of a single IDS by allowing various nodes to communicate with each other. While such collaborative system or network is vulnerable to insider attacks, which can significantly reduce the advantages of a detector. To protect CIDNs against insider attacks, one potential way is to enhance the trust evaluation among IDS nodes, i.e., by emphasizing the impact of expert nodes. In this work, we adopt the notion of intrusion sensitivity that assigns different values of detection capability relating to particular attacks, and evaluate its impact on defending against a special On-Off attack (SOOA). In the evaluation, we investigate the impact of intrusion sensitivity in a simulated CIDN environment, and experimental results demonstrate that the use of intrusion sensitivity can help enhance the security of CIDNs under adversarial scenarios, like SOOA.

Keywords: Intrusion detection · Collaborative network
Insider attack · Intrusion sensitivity · Challenge-based trust mechanism

1 Introduction

To help identify and handle various threats, an intrusion detection system (IDS) is often deployed in different security-sensitive environments [31,34]. Generally, there are two types of detection systems according to the deployment: host-based IDS (HIDS) and network-based IDS (NIDS). Each kind of IDS can utilize two detection approaches: *signature-based detection* and *anomaly-based detection*. A

W. Meng—The author was previously known as Yuxin Meng.

J. Vaidya and J. Li (Eds.): ICA3PP 2018, LNCS 11337, pp. 481–494, 2018.
https://doi.org/10.1007/978-3-030-05063-4_36

signature (or rule) is a kind of description on known threat or exploit, in which a signature-based IDS can compare its signatures with incoming events [33, 39]. By contrast, anomaly-based detection discovers malicious events by building a normal profile [8, 38]. An alarm will be notified, if an accurate match is identified or the deviation between the normal profile and current profile exceeds a threshold.

Nowadays, cyber attacks have become much more complicated; thus, a single detector could be easily compromised and ineffective in detecting advanced attacks. To improve the detection performance, collaborative IDS (CIDS) or collaborative intrusion detection network (CIDN) is developed, which allows a set of IDS nodes to communicate with each other and exchange environmental information [40]. In practical setup, a CIDS or CIDN would be vulnerable to insider attacks, where an attacker can perform suspicious actions within a system or a network environment [2]. To address this issue, designing more effective trust evaluation is one promising solution, like challenge-based trust mechanisms, which compute the trustworthiness of a node by sending challenges in a periodic way [6]. However, such trust mechanisms could be compromised by some advanced attacks, i.e., Li *et al.* [18] developed an advanced collusion attack, a Special On-Off Attack, named *SOOA*, which can keep giving truthful responses to one node while providing untruthful answers to other nodes.

Contributions. An alternative way of improving the trust evaluation is to emphasize the impact of expert nodes. Li *et al.* [13, 16] identified that different IDS nodes may have different levels of sensitivity in detecting particular intrusions. Then, they introduced a notion of *intrusion sensitivity* that measures the detection sensitivity of an IDS in detecting different kinds of intrusions. As an example, if a signature-based detector owns more signatures (or rules) in detecting DoS attacks, then it should be more powerful in detecting such specific kind of attack as compared to other nodes, which have relatively fewer signatures. In this work, we attempt to evaluate the impact of intrusion sensitivity on identifying an advanced insider attack, named special On-Off attack (SOOA). The contributions of this work can be summarized as below:

- We first introduce the notion of intrusion sensitivity and explain how to compute trust values of different CIDN nodes. In this work, we focus on a specific kind of advanced insider attack, called special On-Off attack (SOOA), which can maintain the reputation by responding normally to one node while acting abnormally to another node.
- In the evaluation, we investigate the impact of intrusion sensitivity on detecting SOOA in a simulated CIDN environment. Experimental results demonstrate that intrusion sensitivity can be used to improve the security of CIDNs by highlighting the impact of expert nodes in identifying malicious nodes, i.e., it can help decrease the reputation of SOOA nodes faster.

The remaining sections are organized as follows. Section 2 reviews related studies on distributed and collaborative intrusion detection and introduces the background of challenge-based CIDNs. In Sect. 3, we introduce how SOOA works with two attacking scenarios. Section 4 describes the notion of intrusion sensitivity and evaluates its impact on defending against SOOA in a simulated network environment. Finally, we conclude the work in Sect. 5.

2 Related Work and Background

This section first introduces related work on intrusion detection, especially collaborative intrusion detection, and then describes the background of challenge-based trust mechanism for CIDNs.

2.1 Related Work

In a real-world application, a single IDS usually has no information about the protected environment where it is deployed, hence the detector is very easy to be bypassed under some advanced attacks [40]. To address this issue, one effective solution is to construct a distributed or collaborative detection network. Some previously developed distributed systems can be classified as below. (1) *Centralized/Hierarchical systems*: Emerald [32] and DIDS [35]; (2) *Publish/subscribe systems*: COSSACK [30] and DOMINO [41]; and (3) *P2P Querying-based systems*: Netbait [1] and PIER [11].

Generally, collaborative or distributed intrusion detection networks enable an IDS node to achieve more accurate detection by collecting and communicating information from/with other IDS nodes. However, it is well-recognized by the literature that existing collaborative networks are vulnerable to insider attacks. The previous work [12] figured out that most distributed intrusion detection systems (DIDS) relied on centralized fusion, or distributed fusion with unscalable communication mechanisms. Then they gave a solution by designing a distributed detection system based on the decentralized location and routing infrastructure. However, their system is vulnerable to insider attacks, as they assume that all peers are trusted. Li *et al.* [18] developed an advanced collusion attack, a Special On-Off Attack, named *SOOA*, which can keep giving truthful responses to one node while providing untruthful answers to other nodes. They further developed an advanced collusion attack, called *passive message fingerprint attack (PMFA)* [17], which can compromise the challenge mechanism through passively collecting messages and distinguishing normal requests. As such, malicious nodes can maintain their trust values by giving false information to only normal request while providing truthful feedback to other messages.

To protect distributed systems against insider attacks, building appropriate trust models is one of the promising solutions. For instance, Duma *et al.* [3] proposed a P2P-based overlay IDS to examine traffic by designing a trust-aware engine for handling alerts and an adaptive scheme for managing reputation among different nodes. The former is capable of reducing warnings sent by untrusted or low quality peers, while the latter attempts to predict their trustworthiness by evaluating their past experiences. Tuan [37] then utilized game theory to model and analyze the processes of reporting and exclusion in a P2P network. They identified that if a reputation system was not incentive compatible, the more numbers of peers in the system, the less likely that anyone will report about a malicious peer. Fung *et al.* initialized a type of challenge-based CIDNs, in which the reputation level of a node depends mainly on the received answers to the challenges. In the beginning, they focus on host-based detection (HIDS) and proposed a host-based collaboration framework that enables each node to evaluate the trustworthiness of others based on its own experience and a forgetting factor [6]. The forgetting factor is used to highlight the recent experience of peers, in order to judge the reputation more effectively.

The concept of *intrusion sensitivity* was proposed by Li *et al.* [13], in which they identified that different IDS nodes may have distinct capability or sensitivity in detecting particular types of attacks. Based on the notion, they further developed a trust management model for CIDNs through allocating *intrusion sensitivity* via machine learning techniques in an automatic way [14]. This concept can help detect intrusions and correlate alarms by emphasizing the impact of an *expert IDS*. They also studied how to apply *intrusion sensitivity* for aggregating alarms and defending against pollution attacks, in which a group of malicious peers collaborate together by providing false alarm rankings [15]. Some other related work regarding how to enhance the performance of IDSs can be referred to [4,5,9,10,19–29].

2.2 Background on Challenge-Based CIDNs

The goal of developing challenge-based trust mechanisms is to help protect CIDNs against insider threats through sending challenges in a periodic manner. Figure 1 depicts the typical architecture of a challenge-based CIDN. In addition to an IDS module, a CIDN node often contains three major components: *trust management component, collaboration component* and *P2P communication* [17].

– *Trust management component* is responsible for evaluating the reputation of other nodes via a specific trust approach. Challenge-based mechanism is a kind of trust approach that computes the trust values through comparing the received feedback with the expected answers. Each node can send out either normal requests or challenges for alert ranking (consultation). To further protect challenges, the original work [6] assumed that challenges should be sent out in a random manner and in a way that makes them difficult to be distinguished from a normal alarm ranking request.
– *Collaboration component* is mainly responsible for assisting a node in computing the trust values of another node by sending out *normal requests* or *challenges*, and receiving the relevant *feedback*. This component can help a tested node deliver its feedback when receiving a request or challenge. For instance, Fig. 1 shows that when node *A* sends a *request* or *challenge* to node *B*, it can receive relevant feedback.
– *P2P communication.* This component is responsible for connecting with other IDS nodes and providing network organization, management and communication among IDS nodes.

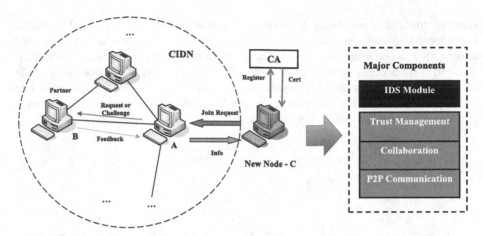

Fig. 1. The typical high-level architecture of a challenge-based CIDN with its major components.

Network Interactions. In a CIDN, each node can choose its partners based on its own policies and experience, and maintain a list of collaborated nodes, called *partner list*. This list is customizable and stores the relevant information of other nodes like current trust values. Before a node asks for joining the network, A node has to obtain its unique proof of identity (e.g., a public key and a private key) by registering to a trusted certificate authority (*CA*). As depicted in Fig. 1, if node *C* asks for joining the network, it has to send a request to a CIDN node, say node *A*. Then, node *A* makes a decision and sends back an initial *partner list*, if node *C* is accepted. A CIDN node can typically send two types of messages: *challenge* and *normal request*.

- A *challenge* mainly contains a set of IDS alarms, where a testing node can send these alarms to the tested nodes for labeling alarm severity. Because the testing node knows the severity of these alarms in advance, it can judge and compute the satisfaction level for the tested node, based on the received feedback.
- A *normal request* is sent by a node for alarm aggregation, which is an important feature of collaborative networks in improving the detection performance of a single detector. The aggregation process usually only considers the feedback from highly trusted nodes. As a response, an IDS node should send back alarm ranking information as their feedback.

3   Special On-Off Attack

Previous work has identified that challenge-based trust mechanism may be still vulnerable to advanced insider attacks, like a special On-Off attack (*SOOA*) [18], where a malicious node can keep sending truthful responses to one node, but sending malicious responses to another. This attack has a potential to affect the effectiveness of trust computation for a third node (target node). Here, we accept that a challenge can be sent in a random manner and cannot be distinguished from normal messages in an effective way. Figure 2 describes an example of $SOOA$: suppose node D is malicious and node A is the attack target, while node B and node C are two partner nodes for node A. Two attacking scenarios can be considered as below [18].

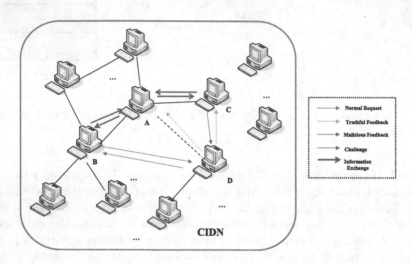

Fig. 2. A special On-Off attack (SOOA) on challenge-based CIDNs.

- **Scenario 1: node D is not a partner node for node A.** Under this condition, node D keeps sending truthful response to node C while sending malicious feedback to node B. Figure 2 shows that node A has to communicate and collect data from its partner nodes B and C. Subsequently, node A may receive different (or even opposite) reports on node D. This scenario often occurs under a hierarchical network structure, in which a central server has to collect information from other nodes and compute the trustworthiness.
- **Scenario 2: node D is a partner node for node A.** Under this condition, node D keeps sending truthful information to node A, if they are partner nodes. In a challenge-based CIDNs, node A has to judge the trustworthiness of node D through both its own trust computation and the judgement from other nodes. As a result, this special attack can maintain the reputation of node D over the threshold regarding node A.

To summarize, $SOOA$ nodes can keep providing truthful feedback to several nodes, while responding maliciously to others. In this case, it may influence the trust computation of certain nodes and maintain its trust values over the threshold. Malicious nodes thus have a good chance to make a negative impact on alarm aggregation of testing node without decreasing their trust values. In this work, we mainly focus on *Scenario 2*, since a CIDN node usually aggregates alarms by collecting relevant information from its partner nodes.

4   The Impact of Intrusion Sensitivity

In this section, we first detail the notion of intrusion sensitivity, and then introduce how to setup a CIDN and compute trust values (satisfaction levels).

4.1   Intrusion Sensitivity

The previous work [13] found that each IDS should have different sensitivity levels in detecting particular kinds of intrusions and introduced a concept of *intrusion sensitivity* as below.

- Intrusion sensitivity describes different levels of detection capability (or accuracy) for IDS nodes in detecting particular kinds of attacks or anomalies. Let I_s denote the detection sensitivity of a node and t denote a time period. For two IDS nodes A and B, we can say $I_s^A > I_s^B$ if A has a stronger detection capability within this time period.

Obviously, it is time consuming to assign the values manually in a large network. To automate the allocation of *intrusion sensitivity*, we can apply machine learning technique. In this work, we adopt a KNN classifier for value allocation based on the following reasons [16]:

- It is easy to implement a KNN algorithm, which classifies objects based on the closest training examples in the feature space. That is, an object can be classified in terms of its distances to the nearest cluster.
- This classifier can also achieve a faster speed with lower computational burden than other classifiers like neural networks in the phases of both training and classification. These properties are desirable when a classifier is deployed in a resource-constrained platform like an *IDS node*.

It is worth noting that how to objectively allocate the value is still an open challenge, as experts may give different scores for an IDS node, based on their own experience. A potential solutions is to make appropriate specifications and criterion, but it is out of the scope of this paper. To train this classifier, there are generally two steps as follows:

- We first build a classifier model by obtaining the intrusion sensitivity scores for some nodes based on expert knowledge, i.e., some scores given by different security administrators or experts regarding existing nodes.
- When evaluating the intrusion sensitivity of a target node i, we use the KNN classifier to assign a value to node i as I_s^i by running the established model.

4.2 CIDN Settings

In this experiment, we constructed a simulated CIDN environment with 50 nodes, which were randomly distributed in a 10 × 10 grid region. Each IDS node adopted Snort [36] as IDS plugin. All nodes can communicate with each other and build an initial *partner list*. The trust values of all nodes in the *partner list* were initialized as $T_s = 0.5$ based on the results in [6]. According to [16], we set the number of alarms to 40 in either a normal request or a challenge, in order to achieve good classification accuracy.

To evaluate the trustworthiness of partner nodes, each node can send out challenges randomly to its partners with an average rate of ε. There are two levels of request frequency: ε_l and ε_h. The request frequency is low for a highly trusted or highly untrusted node, as it should be very confident about their feedback. On the other hand, the request frequency should be high for other nodes whose trust values are close to the threshold. To facilitate comparisons, all the settings can be referred to similar studies [6,14,18]. The detailed parameters are shown in Table 1.

Table 1. Simulation parameters in the experiment.

Parameters	Value	Description
λ	0.9	Forgetting factor
ε_l	10/day	Low request frequency
ε_h	20/day	High request frequency
r	0.8	Trust threshold
T_s	0.5	Trust value for newcomers
m	10	Lower limit of received feedback
d	0.3	Severity of punishment

Node Expertise. This work adopted three expertise levels for an IDS node as: low (0.1), medium (0.5) and high (0.95). A beta function was utilized to model the expertise of an IDS:

$$f(p'|\alpha, \beta) = \frac{1}{B(\alpha, \beta)} p'^{\alpha-1}(1 - p')^{\beta-1}$$
$$B(\alpha, \beta) = \int_0^1 t^{\alpha-1}(1 - t)^{\beta-1} dt$$

(1)

where $p'(\in [0, 1])$ is the probability of intrusion examined by the IDS. $f(p'|\alpha, \beta)$ indicates the probability that a node with expertise level l responses with a value of p' to an intrusion examination of difficulty level $d(\in [0, 1])$. A higher value of l indicates a higher probability of correctly identifying an intrusion, while a higher value of d indicates that an intrusion is harder to figure out. In particular, α and β can be defined as below [7]:

$$\alpha = 1 + \frac{l(1-d)}{d(1-l)}r$$

$$\beta = 1 + \frac{l(1-d)}{d(1-l)}(1-r)$$

(2)

where $r \in \{0, 1\}$ is the expected detection output. For a fixed difficulty level, the node with a higher level of expertise can achieve a higher probability of correctly identifying an attack. For instance, a node with expertise level of 1 can accurately identify an intrusion with guarantee if the difficulty level is 0.

Trust Evaluation at Nodes. To calculate the trust value of a CIDN node, a testing node can send a *challenge* to the target node via a random generation process, and then compute its satisfaction level by comparing the received feedback with the expected answers. Based on [6], we can evaluate the trustworthiness of a node i according to node j in the following manner:

$$T_i^j = (w_s \frac{\sum_{k=0}^n F_k^{j,i} \lambda^{tk}}{\sum_{k=0}^n \lambda^{tk}} - T_s)(1-x)^d I_s^i + T_s$$

(3)

where $F_k^{j,i} \in [0, 1]$ is the score of the received feedback k and n is the total number of feedback. λ is a *forgetting factor* that assigns less weight to older feedback. w_s is a *significant weight* relying on the total number of received feedback, if there is only a few received feedback under a certain minimum m, then $w_s = \frac{\sum_{k=0}^n \lambda^{tk}}{m}$; otherwise $w_s = 1$. x is the percentage of "don't know" answers for a period of time (e.g., from $t0$ to tn). d is a positive incentive parameter to control the severity of punishment to "don't know" answers. $I_s^i (\in [0, 1])$ is the intrusion sensitivity of node i.

Satisfaction Evaluation. Suppose there are two factors: an expected feedback ($e \in [0, 1]$) and an actual received feedback ($r \in [0, 1]$). Then, this work used a function F ($\in [0, 1]$) to reflect the satisfaction level by measuring the difference between the received answer and the expected answer as below [7].

$$F = 1 - (\frac{e-r}{max(c_1 e, 1-e)})^{c_2} \quad e > r$$

(4)

$$F = 1 - (\frac{c_1(r-e)}{max(c_1 e, 1-e)})^{c_2} \quad e \leq r$$

(5)

where c_1 controls the degree of penalty for wrong estimates and c_2 controls satisfaction sensitivity. Based on the work [7], we set $c_1 = 1.5$ and $c_2 = 1$.

4.3   Experimental Results

In this experiment, we aim to evaluate the impact of intrusion sensitivity on the security of CIDNs. Figure 3 illustrates the convergence of trust values regarding different expert nodes with three expertise levels: low ($I = 0.1$), medium

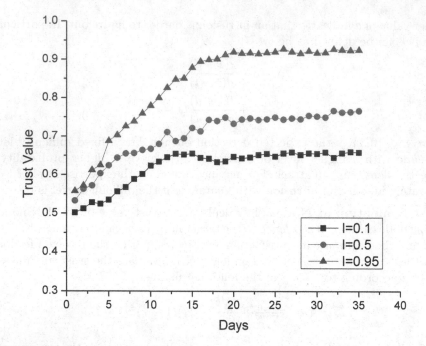

Fig. 3. Convergence of trust values of IDS nodes regarding three expertise levels.

($I = 0.5$) and high ($I = 0.95$). It is found that the nodes with higher expertise can achieve higher reputation levels. In this simulated environment, all nodes' reputation levels turned stable after around 20 days, since challenge-based trust mechanism requires a long time for establishing a high trust value.

The Impact of SOOA. According to Fig. 2, we suppose node A has seven partner nodes and node D is a partner node for node A. Similar to [18], we assume that node D keeps sending truthful feedback to several partner nodes of node A, while sending untruthful answers to the rest partner nodes. We randomly selected one expert node ($I = 0.95$) as malicious (say node D), which conducted the special attack of SOOA from Day 45. For a scenario of 4T2U, node D can send truthful feedback to four partner nodes of node A but sent untruthful feedback to the remaining two partner nodes. Figure 4 depicts the trust value of node D under this condition. It is found that the trust value of node D computed by node A could gradually decrease closer to the threshold during the first ten days, because two partner nodes could report malicious actions regarding node D to node A. Afterwards, the trust value was maintained in the range from 0.82 to 0.83 at most cases, as there are still four partner nodes reported that node D is normal. As the trust value is higher than the threshold 0.8, node D still has an impact on node A and its alarm aggregation.

The Impact of Intrusion Sensitivity. In the same CIDN environment, we assume that under 4T2U, node D keeps sending untruthful feedback to two partner nodes, which are expert nodes. Figure 4 shows the impact of intrusion sensitivity on the detection of malicious SOOA nodes. It is found that the reputation levels of malicious node steadily decreased below the threshold of 0.8 (i.e., within several days). This is because the use of intrusion sensitivity can give more weights on the feedback from expert nodes. The result demonstrated that this notion could help improve the robustness of CIDNs by reducing the reputation levels of malicious nodes under SOOA in a fast manner.

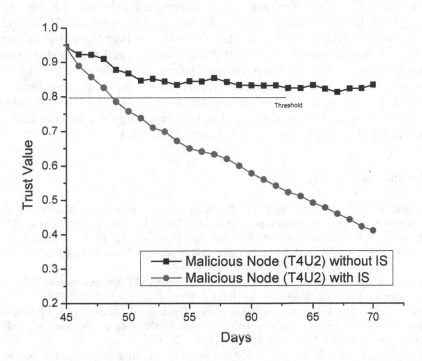

Fig. 4. Trust values of malicious nodes with and without intrusion sensitivity (IS).

4.4 Discussion

In this work, we investigate the impact of intrusion sensitivity on securing CIDNs against SOOA, whereas some challenges still remain for future work.

- *Additional measurement.* In challenge-based CIDNs, the trustworthiness of a node is mainly determined by challenges, whereas it may still leave a chance for attackers. To further increase the robustness of CIDNs, additional measures can be used to calculate the trust values of a node, like packet-level trust [26].
- *Scalability.* In this work, we explored the influence under a simulated environment, but we did not perform a particular experiment to investigate the scalability issue. This is an interesting topic for our future work.
- *Advanced insider attacks.* In this work, we mainly focus on SOOA, an advanced collusion attack for challenge-based CIDNs. In the literature, there are many kinds of advanced insider attacks like FPMA [17]. It is an important topic to examine the influence on other attacks.

5   Conclusion

As a CIDS or CIDN allows a set of IDS nodes to communicate with each other, it can enhance the detection performance of a single detector. However, such system or network is vulnerable to insider attacks, where an attacker can behave maliciously within a system or a network environment. In this work, we adopt the notion of intrusion sensitivity that assigns different values of detection capability relating to particular attacks, and evaluate its impact on securing CIDNs against a special insider attack, SOOA. In the evaluation, we investigate the impact of intrusion sensitivity in a simulated CIDN environment, and the obtained results demonstrate that intrusion sensitivity can help enhance the security of CIDNs under adversarial scenarios, through emphasizing the input from expert nodes. Our work attempts to stimulate more research in designing more secure CIDNs in real-world scenarios. Future work could include exploring the impact of intrusion sensitivity on defending other insider attacks like PMFA.

References

1. Chun, B., Lee, J., Weatherspoon, H., Chun, B.N.: Netbait: a distributed worm detection service. Technical report IRB-TR-03-033, Intel Research Berkeley (2003)
2. Douceur, J.R.: The sybil attack. In: Druschel, P., Kaashoek, F., Rowstron, A. (eds.) IPTPS 2002. LNCS, vol. 2429, pp. 251–260. Springer, Heidelberg (2002). https://doi.org/10.1007/3-540-45748-8_24
3. Duma, C., Karresand, M., Shahmehri, N., Caronni, G.: A trust-aware, P2P-based overlay for intrusion detection. In: DEXA Workshop, pp. 692–697 (2006)
4. Fadlullah, Z.M., Taleb, T., Vasilakos, A.V., Guizani, M., Kato, N.: DTRAB: combating against attacks on encrypted protocols through traffic-feature analysis. IEEE/ACM Trans. Netw. **18**(4), 1234–1247 (2010)
5. Friedberg, I., Skopik, F., Settanni, G., Fiedler, R.: Combating advanced persistent threats: from network event correlation to incident detection. Comput. Secur. **48**, 35–47 (2015)
6. Fung, C.J., Baysal, O., Zhang, J., Aib, I., Boutaba, R.: Trust management for host-based collaborative intrusion detection. In: De Turck, F., Kellerer, W., Kormentzas, G. (eds.) DSOM 2008. LNCS, vol. 5273, pp. 109–122. Springer, Heidelberg (2008). https://doi.org/10.1007/978-3-540-87353-2_9
7. Fung, C.J., Zhang, J., Aib, I., Boutaba, R.: Robust and scalable trust management for collaborative intrusion detection. In: Proceedings of the 11th IFIP/IEEE International Conference on Symposium on Integrated Network Management (IM), pp. 33–40 (2009)
8. Ghosh, A.K., Wanken, J., Charron, F.: Detecting anomalous and unknown intrusions against programs. In: Proceedings of Annual Computer Security Applications Conference (ACSAC), pp. 259–267 (1998)
9. Gong, F.: Next Generation Intrusion Detection Systems (IDS). McAfee Network Security Technologies Group (2003)
10. Gou, Z., Ahmadon, M.A.B., Yamaguchi, S., Gupta, B.B.: A Petri net-based framework of intrusion detection systems. In: Proceedings of the 4th IEEE Global Conference on Consumer Electronics, pp. 579–583 (2015)

11. Huebsch, R., et al.: The architecture of PIER: an internet-scale query processor. In: Proceedings of the 2005 Conference on Innovative Data Systems Research (CIDR), pp. 28–43 (2005)
12. Li, Z., Chen, Y., Beach, A.: Towards scalable and robust distributed intrusion alert fusion with good load balancing. In: Proceedings of the 2006 SIGCOMM Workshop on Large-Scale Attack Defense (LSAD), pp. 115–122 (2006)
13. Li, W., Meng, Y., Kwok, L.-F.: Enhancing trust evaluation using intrusion sensitivity in collaborative intrusion detection networks: feasibility and challenges. In: Proceedings of the 9th International Conference on Computational Intelligence and Security (CIS), pp. 518–522. IEEE (2013)
14. Li, W., Meng, W., Kwok, L.-F.: Design of intrusion sensitivity-based trust management model for collaborative intrusion detection networks. In: Zhou, J., Gal-Oz, N., Zhang, J., Gudes, E. (eds.) IFIPTM 2014. IAICT, vol. 430, pp. 61–76. Springer, Heidelberg (2014). https://doi.org/10.1007/978-3-662-43813-8_5
15. Li, W., Meng, W.: Enhancing collaborative intrusion detection networks using intrusion sensitivity in detecting pollution attacks. Inf. Comput. Secur. **24**(3), 265–276 (2016)
16. Li, W., Meng, W., Kwok, L.-F., Ip, H.H.S.: Enhancing collaborative intrusion detection networks against insider attacks using supervised intrusion sensitivity-based trust management model. J. Netw. Comput. Appl. **77**, 135–145 (2017)
17. Li, W., Meng, W., Kwok, L.-F., Ip, H.H.S.: PMFA: toward passive message fingerprint attacks on challenge-based collaborative intrusion detection networks. In: Chen, J., Piuri, V., Su, C., Yung, M. (eds.) NSS 2016. LNCS, vol. 9955, pp. 433–449. Springer, Cham (2016). https://doi.org/10.1007/978-3-319-46298-1_28
18. Li, W., Meng, W., Kwok, L.-F.: SOOA: exploring special on-off attacks on challenge-based collaborative intrusion detection networks. In: Au, M.H.A., Castiglione, A., Choo, K.-K.R., Palmieri, F., Li, K.-C. (eds.) GPC 2017. LNCS, vol. 10232, pp. 402–415. Springer, Cham (2017). https://doi.org/10.1007/978-3-319-57186-7_30
19. Meng, Y., Kwok, L.F.: Enhancing false alarm reduction using voted ensemble selection in intrusion detection. Int. J. Comput. Intell. Syst. **6**(4), 626–638 (2013)
20. Meng, Y., Li, W., Kwok, L.F.: Towards adaptive character frequency-based exclusive signature matching scheme and its applications in distributed intrusion detection. Comput. Netw. **57**(17), 3630–3640 (2013)
21. Meng, W., Li, W., Kwok, L.-F.: An evaluation of single character frequency-based exclusive signature matching in distinct IDS environments. In: Chow, S.S.M., Camenisch, J., Hui, L.C.K., Yiu, S.M. (eds.) ISC 2014. LNCS, vol. 8783, pp. 465–476. Springer, Cham (2014). https://doi.org/10.1007/978-3-319-13257-0_29
22. Meng, W., Li, W., Kwok, L.-F.: EFM: enhancing the performance of signature-based network intrusion detection systems using enhanced filter mechanism. Comput. Secur. **43**, 189–204 (2014)
23. Meng, W., Li, W., Kwok, L.-F.: Design of intelligent KNN-based alarm filter using knowledge-based alert verification in intrusion detection. Secur. Commun. Netw. **8**(18), 3883–3895 (2015)
24. Meng, W., Au, M.H.: Towards statistical trust computation for medical smartphone networks based on behavioral profiling. In: Steghöfer, J.-P., Esfandiari, B. (eds.) IFIPTM 2017. IAICT, vol. 505, pp. 152–159. Springer, Cham (2017). https://doi.org/10.1007/978-3-319-59171-1_12
25. Meng, W., Li, W., Xiang, Y., Choo, K.K.R.: A Bayesian inference-based detection mechanism to defend medical smartphone networks against insider attacks. J. Netw. Comput. Appl. **78**, 162–169 (2017)

26. Meng, W., Li, W., Kwok, L.-F.: Towards effective trust-based packet filtering in collaborative network environments. IEEE Trans. Netw. Serv. Manag. **14**(1), 233–245 (2017)
27. Meng, W., Wang, Y., Li, W., Liu, Z., Li, J., Probst, C.W.: Enhancing intelligent alarm reduction for distributed intrusion detection systems via edge computing. In: Susilo, W., Yang, G. (eds.) ACISP 2018. LNCS, vol. 10946, pp. 759–767. Springer, Cham (2018). https://doi.org/10.1007/978-3-319-93638-3_44
28. Meng, W., Li, W., Wang, Y., Au, M.H.: Detecting insider attacks in medical cyber-physical networks based on behavioral profiling. Future Gener. Comput. Syst. (2018, in press). Elsevier
29. Mishra, A., Gupta, B.B., Joshi, R.C.: A comparative study of distributed denial of service attacks, intrusion tolerance and mitigation techniques. In: Proceedings of the 2011 European Intelligence and Security Informatics Conference, pp. 286–289 (2011)
30. Papadopoulos, C., Lindell, R., Mehringer, J., Hussain, A., Govindan, R.: COS-SACK: coordinated suppression of simultaneous attacks. In: Proceedings of the 2003 DARPA Information Survivability Conference and Exposition (DISCEX), pp. 94–96 (2003)
31. Paxson, V.: Bro: a system for detecting network intruders in real-time. Comput. Netw. **31**(23–24), 2435–2463 (1999)
32. Porras, P.A., Neumann, P.G.: Emerald: event monitoring enabling responses to anomalous live disturbances. In: Proceedings of the 20th National Information Systems Security Conference, pp. 353–365 (1997)
33. Roesch, M.: Snort: lightweight intrusion detection for networks. In: Proceedings of USENIX Lisa Conference, pp. 229–238 (1999)
34. Scarfone, K., Mell, P.: Guide to Intrusion Detection and Prevention Systems (IDPS). NIST Special Publication 800–94 (2007)
35. Snapp, S.R., et al.: DIDS (Distributed Intrusion Detection System) - motivation, architecture, and an early prototype. In: Proceedings of the 14th National Computer Security Conference, pp. 167–176 (1991)
36. Snort: An open source network intrusion prevention and detection system (IDS/IPS). http://www.snort.org/
37. Tuan, T.A.: A game-theoretic analysis of trust management in P2P systems. In: Proceedings of ICCE, pp. 130–134 (2006)
38. Valdes, A., Anderson, D.: Statistical methods for computer usage anomaly detection using NIDES. Technical report, SRI International, January 1995
39. Vigna, G., Kemmerer, R.A.: NetSTAT: a network-based intrusion detection approach. In: Proceedings of Annual Computer Security Applications Conference (ACSAC), pp. 25–34 (1998)
40. Wu, Y.-S., Foo, B., Mei, Y., Bagchi, S.: Collaborative intrusion detection system (CIDS): a framework for accurate and efficient IDS. In: Proceedings of the 2003 Annual Computer Security Applications Conference (ACSAC), pp. 234–244 (2003)
41. Yegneswaran, V., Barford, P., Jha, S.: Global intrusion detection in the DOMINO overlay system. In: Proceedings of the 2004 Network and Distributed System Security Symposium (NDSS), pp. 1–17 (2004)

Roundtable Gossip Algorithm: A Novel Sparse Trust Mining Method for Large-Scale Recommendation Systems

Mengdi Liu[1], Guangquan Xu[1(✉)], Jun Zhang[2],
Rajan Shankaran[3], Gang Luo[3], Xi Zheng[3], and Zonghua Zhang[4]

[1] Tianjin Key Laboratory of Advanced Networking (TANK),
School of Computer Science and Technology,
Tianjin University, Tianjin 300350, China
losin@tju.edu.cn
[2] School of Software and Electrical Engineering,
Swinburne University of Technology, Melbourne, Australia
[3] Department of Computing, Macquarie University, Sydney, Australia
[4] IMT Lille Douai, Douai, France

Abstract. Cold Start (CS) and sparse evaluation problems dramatically degrade recommendation performance in large-scale recommendation systems such as Taobao and eBay. We name this degradation as the sparse trust problem, which will cause the decrease of the recommendation accuracy rate. To address this problem we propose a novel sparse trust mining method, which is based on the Roundtable Gossip Algorithm (RGA). First, we define the relevant representation of sparse trust, which provides a research idea to solve the problem of sparse evidence in the large-scale recommendation system. Based on which the RGA is proposed for mining latent sparse trust relationships between entities in large-scale recommendation systems. Second, we propose an efficient and simple anti-sparsification method, which overcomes the disadvantages of random trust relationship propagation and Grade Inflation caused by different users have different standard for item rating. Finally, the experimental results show that our method can effectively mine new trust relationships and mitigate the sparse trust problem.

Keywords: Sparse trust relationship · Anti-sparsification
Recommendation system

1 Introduction

With the increasing availability of online business interaction and the rapid development of the Internet, we face an enormous amount of digital information. The Big Data Age has already arrived and has profoundly affected people's daily lives. The rapid growth of commodity types also meets the different needs of users. However, the Taobao index [1] shows that each commodity has just a few buyers and fewer effective

© Springer Nature Switzerland AG 2018
J. Vaidya and J. Li (Eds.): ICA3PP 2018, LNCS 11337, pp. 495–510, 2018.
https://doi.org/10.1007/978-3-030-05063-4_37

comments. Searching for useful information from an enormous amount of data is similar to looking for a needle in a haystack. Large-scale recommendation systems are sought after by electronic commerce websites, identity authentication & security systems, search engines and other big data applications [2, 3]. However, large-scale recommendation systems face sparse trust problem where there is significant lack of trust evidence.

The recommendation system is the typical application scenario of trust theory. The sparse trust problem is caused by CS problem and sparse trust evaluation. Cold start which consists of user CS and item CS, means that the system accumulates too little data to build trust relationship between users. And sparse trust evaluation is the sparsity of the user's original trust relationship. Therefore, substantial research efforts are focused on the sparsity of user evaluation data [4] and the CS problem. In the context of big data, the amount of available social information is far beyond the range of what individuals or systems can afford or handle, and use effectively, which is called information overload. The recommendation system solves this problem by filtering out noise to find the information that the user desires. Moreover, it can predict whether the user wants the information supplied by the recommendation system. Some existing trust models, such as the Personalized trust model [5], VoteTrust model [6], Active-Trust model [7], swift trust model [8], and STAR: Semiring Trust Inference for Trust-Aware Social Recommenders [9], take advantage of overall ratings to assess the sellers' performance and ignore some latent information in textual reviews [10]. The Textual Reputation Model [11] improves upon the traditional model by calculating a comprehensive reputation score of the seller based on users' reviews [12, 13]. However, the recommendations that are made by these recommendation systems for inactive or new users are inaccurate, and sometimes no recommendation can be made. This is because the user evaluates or interacts with very few (or no) items [14].

Taobao is the most popular online shopping platform in China and has nearly 500 million registered users, more than 60 million visitors every day, and more than 800 million online products [15]. Therefore, the User-Item matrix size of Taobao's recommendation system is 60 million * 800 million. It is very difficult and ineffective to use Spark (Apache Spark is a fast and universal computing engine designed for large-scale data processing) to calculate such a huge matrix. The lack of trust evidence due to CS and sparse trust evaluation further aggravates the difficulty in computing the matrix. Thus, the sparse evaluation and CS problems of recommendation systems are ultimately challenging due to the sparsity of data or information [16].

In this paper, a method of sparse trust mining is proposed to implement the anti-sparsification to improve the accuracy of recommendation system. The main contributions of this paper are as follows:

- defining the concept of sparse trust;
- providing a unified formal description of sparse trust;
- proposing a novel RGA for mitigating the sparse trust problem.

The sparse trust theory provides a research idea to solve the problem of sparse evidence in the large-scale recommendation system. Accordingly, research on sparse trust representation, evaluation, reasoning and prediction will greatly promote the development and evolution of trust theory and help improve the accuracy of recommendation system. Experiments show that the proposed method can extract latent trust relationships more efficiently and mitigate sparse trust problems at lower cost.

The remainder of the paper is organized as follows: Sect. 2 introduces the related work on the sparsity problem in the recommendation system. Section 3 describes the preliminaries regarding the relevant representation of sparse trust. Section 4 presents the RGA for the sparse trust mining method. Section 5 describes the evaluation metrics and provides performance analysis and comparative experiment studies. Section 6 presents the conclusions and future work.

2 Related Work

Typically, scholars use the trust relationship method to overcome the sparsity to obtain the consensus of most people. Guo et al. [17] incorporated the trust relationship into the SVD++ model, but this work relied only on explicit and implicit influences of social trust relationships. Real-world users are often reluctant to disclose information due to privacy concerns [18]. Zhong et al. [19] proposed a computational dynamic trust model for user authorization to infer the latent trust relationship. Yao et al. [20] considered the influence of the user's dual identity as a trustor and a trusted person on trust perception recommendation to obtain latent association rules.

Some trust propagation methods have also been proposed to solve the sparse trust problem. Konstas [21] used a Random Walk with Restart to model the friendship and social annotations of a music tracking recommendation system. Chen [22] recommended communities through potential Latent Dirichlet Allocation (LDA) and association rule mining techniques. In [23], conceptual typology and trust-building antecedents were proposed in cloud computing.

Some of the existing trust models that are listed above have different advantages. However, none of the existing works fully solve the problem of data sparsity due to CS and sparse trust evaluation. In particular, many current proposals are unable to achieve anti-sparsification over highly sparse datasets and as a result, this problem becomes all the more prominent and acute in the big data environment. Moreover, there is no guarantee of prediction accuracy in such case. The experiments conducted in this paper indicates that, compared with current trust methods, RGA's trust prediction of anti-sparsification is more accurate for all users and CS environment, especially for highly sparse dataset. This is a reliable anti-sparsification method. Moreover, the results indicate that this algorithm has a certain degree of advantage in terms of stability.

3 Preliminaries

To better investigate the sparse trust problem, it is necessary to define the relevant representation of sparse trust. Generally, the sparsity of ratings for CS items is higher than 85% [24], where sparsity represents the proportion of unknown relationships.

Definition 1 (trust): Trust is an emotional tendency which the subject believes that the object is responsible and honest, and when the subject adopts the behavior of the object, it will bring him positive feedback. It is often described in the form of probability, and it is highly time-dependent and space-dependent.

Definition 2 (sparse trust): In the era of big data, the probability of direct contact between the two entities is getting smaller. Sparse trust refers to the divisible trust relationship that is masked by data sparsity. A relationship that includes ambiguous information or data noise masking evidence is known as sparse trust.

The degree of trust is reflected by the emotional intensity and described by probability function [25]. Furthermore, the emotional intensity is proportional to the probability description. We denote the trust value by P_{AB}, which is between 0 and 1 and indicates the degree of trust that entity A has in entity B. A formal description of sparse trust is ternary form. For example: [beer, diapers, 0.73]. There are many more zero elements of the sparse trust matrix than non-zero elements, and ternary vectors are used to store sparse trust relationships, which can save storage space.

4 Round-Table Gossip Algorithm (RGA)

In this section, we describe the RGA. In roundtable gossip, the final trust value of the two unassociated entities is given by the sum of multiple mining paths, where each path computes intermediate entities of the transferred trust relationship by iteration. All related entities are from the same virtual community and interrelated. In Sect. 4.1, we describe the underlying principles governing the RGA. In Sect. 4.2, we describe the RGA algorithm for mining the trust relationships.

4.1 Round-Table Gossip

Normalizing Sparse Trust. The roundtable algorithm [26] was used to determine the attack attributes for the attack decision process of a combat game. It abstracts possible event state sets into a round table, which is the origin of the round table algorithm. The trust value of each entity on the round table does not attenuate, which truly reflects the subject's emotional tendencies toward the object. Inspired by the roundtable algorithm, we proposed the RGA.

Entities used for trust mining have different degrees of trust in the same network community. Furthermore, different users have different criteria for item rating. For example, some people like to award higher or lower ratings than the target deserves while some tend to rate within a small range of values. This phenomenon is commonly known as Grade Inflation in data mining area [27]. In order to place all entities on a round table to eliminate the impact of Grade Inflating, it is necessary to normalize them. We utilize the improved softmax function [28] G_{ij} to normalize sparse trust:

$$G_{ij} = \begin{cases} \frac{e^{P_{ij}}}{\sum_{j \in I} e^{P_{ij}}}, & \text{if } e^{P_{ij}} \neq 1 \\ 0, & \text{otherwise} \end{cases} \tag{1}$$

where variable I stands for the network community. This function ensures that the sum of the trust values after normalization will be 1. Notice that if $e^{P_{ij}} = 1$, this trust value is 0, which indicates distrust. This is known as the sparseness of trust. In our work, we define the value of G_{ij} in this case as zero, which is used to mine the trust value.

The normalized sparse trust values do not distinguish between an object with which subject did not interact at all or an object with which subject has had a reasonable degree of interaction. Moreover, if $G_{ij} = G_{ik}$, we know that entity i to entity j and entity k has the same sparse trust value, but we do not know if both of them are highly trustworthy, or if both suffer from low trust values. Maybe these two trust values come from different network communities, and different communities have different evaluation criteria. That is, these normalized sparse trust values are relative, but there is no absolute interpretation. After the normalization of the trust value, the relativity of it can still be subtly reflected. This manner of normalizing sparse trust values has been chosen because it allows us to perform computations without re-normalizing the sparse trust values at each iteration (which is prohibitively costly in the trust transitive process) as shown below. This also eliminates the impact of Grade Inflation and leads to an elegant algorithmic model. This calculation method is shown in Algorithm 1 lines 2–17.

Transitiveness. RGA is based on a trust transitive mechanism and aims at finding target entities' acquaintances (have relation both with entity i and entity k, such as entity j in formula (2)). It makes sense to weight their opinions according to the trust that the subject places on them:

$$t_{ik} = \sum_{j \in I} g_{ij} g_{jk} \tag{2}$$

where t_{ik} represents the trust that entity i places in entity k, which is determined by polling their acquaintances. Note that there exists a straightforward probabilistic interpretation of this method of gossip transitive, which is similar to the Random Surfer model of user behavior based on browsing web pages [29].

The intermediate entities transfer the trust value for two entities that do not have a trust relationship. In our algorithm, each entity variable contains two quantities of information: an adjacency list of nodes that have a trust relationship with the entity node, which is denoted as $Trustlist(i)$, and a set of their trust values, which is denoted as $Data\_set(g_{ij})$. We use depth-first search to find intermediate entities. The searched entities are marked and stored in the stack. This calculation method is shown in Algorithm 1 lines 18–21.

Latent Trust Mining. Generally, social relationships are divided into single modal and multi modal relationships. Many scholars solve the sparsity problem of trust by referring to other sources of information (such as an inactive user's relationships with his or her friends). In our work, we consider the issue of latent trust relationship mining in multiple network communities (refers to the online communication space including BBS/forum, post bar, bulletin board, personal knowledge release, group discussion, personal space, wireless value-added service and so on). Mining latent trust relationships for entities from the same community is known as homogenous association rule mining, and mining of entities in different communities is referred to as heterogeneous association rule mining. In practice, users often cannot interact with all of other entities in community. If system want to build the trust relationship between two users in community A, it is general and meaningful to reference their social relations in community B.

Next, we will discuss how to aggregate the trust relationships from different communities. The first thing that needs to be clarified is the way in which the relationship of trust is expressed. For each complete path from an entity i to an entity k, the sparse trust value is calculated according to Formula (2) and stored in the corresponding matrix $T_{ik}^{(r)}$, where r represents the number of intermediate entities. The calculation method of latent trust mining is shown in Algorithm 1 lines 22–26.

4.2 Overview of Roundtable Gossip Algorithm

Here we describe the anti-sparsification method to compute the sparse trust values based on roundtable gossip algorithm. The homogenous entity association method between subjects and the heterogeneous entity association method between subject and object are used to solve the problem of multi-social relation data sparsity. In some cases, an entity may have an inter community association with another entity that resides in a different community. The algorithm aggregates multiple trust paths and each path involves gossip with multiple entities. An overview of RGA is shown in Algorithm 1. We initialize self-confidence value of entities in step 1 (line 3) before normalizing the sparse trust to mine more trust relationships. The trust value on the diagonal of the square trust matrix represents the self-confidence of the entity. We specify that the entity fully trusts itself, that is, for any entity i, the trust value i to i is equal to 1 ($p_{ii} = 1$).

Algorithm 1: Roundtable Gossip Algorithm

Input: Ternary Form P: $[i, j, p_{ij}]$;

Definitions: Sparse Matrix: S_Matrix ; Number of nonzero elements: Num_{nz} ; Number of Entities: m; Trust value of entity i in entity k when gossiping through r intermediate entities: $t_{ik}^{(r)}$;

Output: Trust Matrix T .

1: **Initial:** $S\_Matrix(i, j) \leftarrow P_{ij}$;

2: **for** $i \leftarrow 1$ to m **do**

3: $\quad S\_Matrix(i, i) \leftarrow 1$;   //Initialize Self-Confidence

4: $\quad$ **for** $j \leftarrow 1$ to m **do**

5: $\quad\quad$ **if** $e^{p_{ij}} \neq 1$ **then**

6: $\quad\quad\quad p_{i.} \leftarrow e^{p_{ij}}$;   //Sum of Trust Values for Each Row

7: $\quad\quad$ **end if**

8: $\quad$ **end for**

9: **end for**

10: **for** $i \leftarrow 1$ to m **do**

11: $\quad$ **for** $j \leftarrow 1$ to m **do**

12: $\quad\quad$ **if** $e^{p_{ij}} \neq 1$ **then**

13: $\quad\quad\quad g_{ij} \leftarrow e^{p_{ij}} / p_{i.}$; //Compute Normalized Sparse Trust

14: $\quad\quad$ **else** $g_{ij} \leftarrow 0$;

15: $\quad\quad$ **end if**

16: $\quad$ **end for**

17: **end for**

18: $t_{ik}^{(0)} = g_{ij}$;

19: **repeat**

20: $\quad t_{ik}^{(r+1)} \leftarrow g_{i1} t_{1k}^{(r)} + g_{i2} t_{2k}^{(r)} + \cdots + g_{ij} t_{jk}^{(r)}$; //Transitiveness

21: **Until** $\left| Num_{nz}^{(r+1)} - Num_{nz}^{(r)} \right| < \varepsilon$;

22: **for** $j \leftarrow 1$ to $r-1$ **do**

23: $\quad t_{ik} \leftarrow t_{ik}^{(r)}$; //Aggregate the Mining Trust Relationship

24: **end for**

25: $T_{ik} \leftarrow t_{ik} / r$;

26: **return** T_{ik} ;

---

5 Experiments

In this section, we will assess the performance of our algorithm in mining trust relationships, which target large-scale recommendation system. We conduct extensive experiments with synthetic and real-world datasets. The anti-sparsification ability of the RGA is achieved by calculating trust matrices of various sparsity degrees.

5.1 Dataset

The experimental datasets are mainly divided into two parts: The first part consists of real data from CiaoDVDs [31] and is used to evaluate our algorithm vertically in terms of updateability, validity and stability (Sects. 5.3). The second part consists of two representative datasets, which are taken from popular social networking websites, including Douban (www.douban.com) [32] and Epinions (www.epinions.com) [30], and is used to sufficiently validate the performance of our proposed methods. The statistics of the three datasets are presented in Table 1.

Table 1. Datasets statistics from popular social networking websites

Statistics	CiaoDVDs	Douban	Epinions
Num. Users	7,375	129,490	49,289
Num. Items	99,746	58,541	139,738
Num. Ratings	278,483	16,830,939	664,823
(Sparsity degree)	0.0379%	0.2220%	0.0097%
Friends/User	15.16	13.22	9.88

The acquisition of a matrix with a different sparsity degree is very important for simulation purposes. We need to use a random function to determine whether all nonzero trust values are valid to better simulate trust matrices with different sparsity degrees (valid trust values are unchanged and invalid trust values are set to zero). In other words, the sparsity degree of the original dataset that we used is uniquely identified. We consider simulating big data matrices of different sparse degree, where a big data matrix is used to infer the trust relationship.

The number of nonzero elements in the initial dataset is relative (not absolute; the error range of sparsity degree is 0.0005%). In the processing of data, eight random function values for eight sparsity degrees were obtained through repeated experimental comparisons. The sparsity degree with corresponding random function values are shown in Fig. 1.

5.2 Evaluation Metrics

In our experiment, we use two metrics, namely, the Mean Absolute Error (MAE) and the Root Mean Square Error (RMSE) [33], to measure the prediction quality of our proposed approach in comparison with other representative trust propagation methods. MAE and RMSE are used to measure the deviation between the predicted values and the original values, and the smaller the values of them, the better the algorithm.

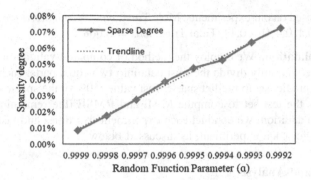

Fig. 1. Graph depicting of sparsity degree and random function. In the processing of data, eight random function values for eight sparsity degrees were obtained through repeated experimental comparisons.

The metric MAE is defined as:

$$MAE = \frac{\sum_{ij} |t_{ij} - \hat{t}_{ij}|}{N} \tag{3}$$

The metric RMSE is defined as:

$$RMSE = \sqrt{\frac{\sum_{ij} \left(t_{ij} - \hat{t}_{ij}\right)^2}{N}} \tag{4}$$

where t_{ij} denotes the original trust value that entity i gave to entity j, $\hat{t}_{ij}$ denotes the predict trust value that entity i gave to entity j, as predicted by a method, and N denotes the number of tested trust values.

5.3 Comparative Experimental Studies

In this section, to evaluate the performance improvement of our RGA approach, we compare our method with the following approaches:

Comparison Methods. To comparatively evaluate the performances of our proposed methods, we select three representative trust propagation methods as competitors: Mole Trust (MT), Propagation of trust (PT), and Tidal Trust (TT).

MT is able to propagate trust over the trust network and is capable of estimating a trust weight that can be used in place of the similarity weight [30]. PT develops a framework of trust propagation schemes [34]. TT presents two sets of algorithms for calculating trust inferences: one for networks with binary trust ratings, and one for continuous ratings [35]. All these methods use the trust transfer mechanism to predict trust relationship. The anti-sparsification accuracy of these methods and RGA are verified by comparing experiments in all users and CS environment. To focus on verification and fair comparison, for all methods, we set the optimal parameters for each method according to their corresponding references or based on our experiments: Mole Trust: $mpd = Num.iterations$; Propagation of trust: $\alpha = (0.4, 0.4, 0.1, 0.1)$; Tidal Trust: $max = 0.008$.

Compared-Validation. We employ the method of compared-validation for predicting and testing. We randomly divide the trust data into two equal parts: each time, we use one part as the predict set to predict sparse trust value (50% of the sparse trust data) and another part as the test set to compute MAE and RMSE (the remaining 50% of the sparse data). In addition, we conduct each experiment five times and take the mean as the final result for each experiment, as discussed below.

5.4   Results and Analysis

The anti-sparsification accuracy of the proposed RGA algorithm is verified by comparing the experimental results on the two datasets with those of the competing methods. Here, three algorithms are considered: Mole Trust (MT), Propagation of trust (PT), Tidal Trust (TT). MAE and RMSE, which are two benchmark error evaluation metrics, are used here. Tables 2 and 3 respectively show the results of MAE and RMSE on testing of all users and on testing of CS, which were computed based on the user's predictions. In addition, Figs. 2 and 3 show the performance comparison histogram of the experiments.

Table 2. Experimental results on testing of all users

Datasets	Measure	MT	PT	TT	RGA
Douban	MAE	0.9309	0.6525	0.8703	0.1267
	(Improve)	86.390%	80.582%	85.442%	-
	RMSE	0.9582	0.5139	1.6258	0.0922
	(Improve)	90.378%	82.059%	94.329%	-
Epinions	MAE	2.1507	2.6023	0.0700	0.0474
	(Improve)	97.796%	98.179%	32.286%	-
	RMSE	16.9959	17.7774	0.1286	0.0480
	(Improve)	99.718%	99.730%	62.675%	-

Validation on All Users. RGA outperforms other approaches in terms of both MAE and RMSE on two datasets. PT method achieves the second-best performance on the two datasets in terms of MAE, except dataset Epinions. Because the trust data of Epinions is extremely sparse (sparsity degree of 0.0097%), the traditional proposed methods, namely, TT, performs much worse than the proposed methods, namely, PT and MT. However, when the trust data are relatively dense, such as in the Douban (density of 0.2220%), PT shows a comparable, and sometimes better, performance. Finally, for Epinions, which contains directed trust networks, TT is more accurate than PT or MT. However, for Douban, which contain undirected friend networks, the performance of MT is similar to that of TT. Hence, the recommendation quality improvement that results from their combination is limited. Based on the above points, PT performs optimally on these series.

Furthermore, the improvements against respective competitors on testing of all users, which are given in the Table 2, show that our methods can significantly improve the quality of recommendations, especially for Epinions, which is a highly sparse dataset as described above in Sect. 5.1. Experimental result on testing all users proves that on the testing of all users RGA can be implemented anti-sparsification. This is a reliable anti-sparsification method, and according to several experiments, this algorithm has a certain degree of advantage in terms of stability.

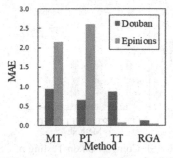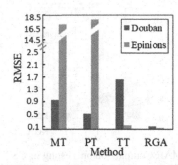

(a)MAE Comparison on Testing of All Users   (b)RMSE Comparison on Testing of All Users

Fig. 2. Performance comparison on testing of all users. Instructions: In order to improve the display effect of the data (the numerical gap is large), the truncation diagram is adopted in (b).

Validation on CS Users. As mentioned in Introduction, The CS problem becomes more severe and frequent in the large-scale recommendation system environment, which results in the sparse trust problem.

Table 3. Experimental results on testing CS user

Datasets	Measure	MT	PT	TT	RGA
Douban	MAE	0.9412	0.6742	0.9016	0.1495
	(Improve)	84.12%	77.83%	83.42%	-
	RMSE	0.9603	0.6539	1.6473	0.1103
	(Improve)	88.51%	83.13%	93.30%	-
Epinions	MAE	2.1705	2.7183	0.0918	0.0714
	(Improve)	96.71%	97.37%	22.22%	-
	RMSE	17.1202	17.97474	0.1416	0.0606
	(Improve)	99.65%	99.66%	57.20%	-

For this, we also evaluated the accurate performance of the RGA's anti-sparsification of trust relationship in CS environment. Generally, we define the users who have fewer than five trust relationships as CS user. Compared-validation is still used in the test but we only care about the accuracy of predictions for CS users (with five or fewer trust relationships) at this moment. Table 3 shows that RGA still have the best performance on dataset Douban and Epinions, especially for highly sparse dataset Epinions, which proves that RGA can be implemented accuracy anti-sparsification on the testing of CS.

The experiment indicates that, compared with current trust methods, RGA's trust prediction of anti-sparsification is more accurate in all users and CS environment.

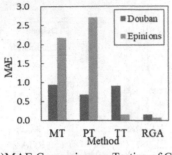
(a)MAE Comparison on Testing of CS

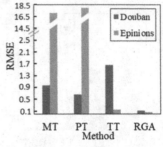
(b)RMSE Comparison on Testing of CS

Fig. 3. Performance comparison on testing of CS. Instructions: In order to improve the display effect of the data (the numerical gap is large), the truncation diagram is adopted in (b).

5.5 Performance Analysis

We experimented with datasets of different sparsity degrees and compared the updateability, validity and stability of the algorithm in four different cases. The dataset describes the subject and object in ternary. A sparse matrix has a huge number of zero elements in a big data environment, so the use of ternary form $[i, j, p_{ij}]$ to store sparse matrices reduces spatial overhead and results in better trust delivery. The processing performed by the algorithm on matrices varies with different initial sparsity degree values. The processing ability of the algorithm is evaluated in terms of the following:

Updateability: The diagonal of a sparse trust matrix indicates the self-confidence of the entity that interacts in the recommendation system. In our scheme, we assume every entity has a self-confidence relationship and the value is equal 1 ($p_{ii} = 1$), that is, the diagonal value of the sparse trust matrix is 1 (as shown in Algorithm 1 line 3). Obviously, this initialization of the self-confidence is helpful for anti-sparsification. Furthermore, even though the nonzero elements of the matrix reveal the relationship of the interacting entities, the role of the zero elements cannot be ignored. Our algorithm can establish a new relation, update the existing trust relationship, and provide more information for further association rule mining.

Validity: In this paper, experiments on 8 kinds of sparse matrices with different sparsity degrees are conducted to investigate the effectiveness of the proposed algorithm. The sparsity degrees (the proportion of nonzero elements to total elements) of the 8 matrices are as follows: 0.009%, 0.018%, 0.028%, 0.039%, 0.048%, 0.052%, 0.064%, and 0.072%. Obviously, these are sparse matrices [24]. Based on the probability

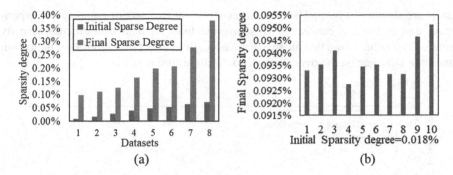

Fig. 4. (a) Column chart of datasets of 8 different sparsity degrees, compared after anti-sparsification operations. (b) Column chart of 10 datasets' sparsity degrees after anti-sparsification operations, which have the same initial sparsity degree of 0.018%.

description $t_{ik} = \sum_{j \in I} g_{ij}g_{jk}$ of the trust transitive mechanism, the intermediate entities transfer the trust value for two entities that do not have a trust relationship. In addition, the sum of multiple mining paths is expressed as the final trust, where each path computes intermediate entities of the transferred trust relationship by iteration. Figure 4 (a) gives a histogram that illustrates the anti-sparsification situation and each dataset corresponds to a sparse trust matrix with a different sparsity degree. The experimental data in Fig. 4(a) are the average values over many experiments, because each experimental result is influenced by many factors and single experiments are unreproducible (the error range of the sparsity degree is 0.0005%). Obviously, the algorithm can achieve anti-sparsification. In particular, the more is the evidence provided initially the greater the effect of the anti-sparsity. However, the sparse matrix itself can provide little evidence, which is a challenge for the experimental algorithms. Another challenge is the distribution of nonzero elements. We performed many experiments on trust matrices with the same sparsity degree and then selected ten representative experimental data with sparsity degree of 0.018%. As shown in Fig. 4(b), each column represents the residual $|Sparse'_v - Sparse_v|$ of the sparsity degree. The results of the ten sets of experimental data are not the same because the different nonzero element locations lead to different anti-sparsification results. This is because the nonzero element locations determine the number of intermediate entities and the number of mining paths. However, for any initial sparse matrix, the RGA can maximize the anti-sparsity.

Stability: Algorithm validity is affected by the locations of sparse nodes, but an overall impact is minimal or negligible. The anti-sparsification algorithm is affected by two major challenges: One is the sparsity of trust matrix evidence, and the other is the different anti-sparsity effects of different sparse node locations with same sparsity degree. The latter will affect algorithm validity (as shown in Fig. 5). For example, a trust relationship is communicated by intermediate entities and the locations of nonzero elements determine the route of trust transmission, which directly affects sparse trust value computation by the RGA. By aiming to target this problem, we design a corresponding contrast experiment. We select two datasets in our contrast experiment, each of which contains 28 kinds of trust matrices with different sparsity degrees. The experimental results are shown in Fig. 5. The two curves represent two sets of comparative experiments, and each group consists of 28 sparse residuals for data with different sparsity degrees. The result shows that the sparse node locations affect the algorithm validity, but have little influence on the overall trend, so the algorithm is stable.

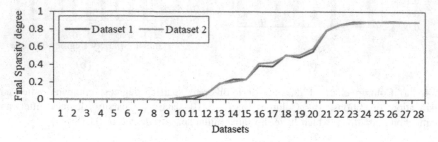

Fig. 5. Residuals of anti-sparsity

6 Conclusions and Future Work

In this paper, we presented a novel method for mining and predicting sparse trust relationships in a large-scale recommendation system. Our proposed sparse trust mining method achieves anti-sparsification for sparse trust relationship, which is mainly based on RGA. Thus, by taking into account the trust transfer relationship, we also show how to carry out the computations in a big data environment. Sparsity degree measurement is used to analyze the anti-sparsification performance. In addition, this method updates the trust relationship in an effective and scalable way. However, the sparsity degree of the data that are processed in the experiments may exceed the requirement that it should be less than one millionth [21], and although the trust relationship accuracy has been preliminarily measured by MAE and RMSE, we can also mine the hidden semantics to improve the prediction accuracy and effectiveness. These problems need to be considered in future work.

Acknowledgement. This work has been partially sponsored by the National Science Foundation of China (No. 61572355, U1736115), the Tianjin Research Program of Application Foundation and Advanced Technology (No. 15JCYBJC15700), and the Fundamental Research of Xinjiang Corps (No. 2016AC015).

References

1. Taobao index. https://shu.taobao.com/industry. Accessed 14 Apr 2017
2. Zhang, Z.: RADAR: a reputation-driven anomaly detection system for wireless mesh networks. Wirel. Netw. **16**(8), 2221–2236 (2010)
3. Saini, R.: Jammer-assisted resource allocation in secure OFDMA with untrusted users. IEEE Trans. Inf. Forensics Secur. **11**(5), 1055–1070 (2016)

4. Guo, X.: Eliminating the hardware-software boundary: a proof-carrying approach for trust evaluation on computer systems. IEEE Trans. Inf. Forensics Secur. **12**(2), 405–417 (2017)
5. Zhang, J.: Evaluating the trustworthiness of advice about seller agents in e-marketplaces: a personalized approach. Electron. Commer. Res. Appl. **7**(3), 330–340 (2008)
6. Yang, Z.: VoteTrust: leveraging friend invitation graph to defend against social network sybils. IEEE Trans. Dependable Secure Comput. **13**(4), 488–501 (2016)
7. Liu, Y.: ActiveTrust: secure and trustable routing in wireless sensor networks. IEEE Trans. Inf. Forensics Secur. **11**(9), 2013–2027 (2016)
8. Xu, G.: Swift trust in a virtual temporary system: a model based on the Dempster-Shafer theory of belief functions. Int. J. Electron. Commer. **12**(1), 93–126 (2007)
9. Gao, P.: STAR: semiring trust inference for trust-aware social recommenders. In: Proceedings of the 10th ACM Conference on Recommender Systems, Boston, Massachusetts, pp. 301–308 (2016)
10. Guo, G.: From ratings to trust: an empirical study of implicit trust in recommender systems. In: Proceedings of the 29th Annual ACM Symposium on Applied Computing, Gyeongju, Republic of Korea, pp. 248–253 (2014)
11. Xu, G.: TRM: computing reputation score by mining reviews. In: AAAI Workshop: Incentives and Trust in Electronic Communities, Phoenix, Arizona (2016)
12. Zhu, C.: An authenticated trust and reputation calculation and management system for cloud and sensor networks integration. IEEE Trans. Inf. Forensics Secur. **10**(1), 118–131 (2015)
13. Zhou, P.: Toward energy-efficient trust system through watchdog optimization for WSNs. IEEE Trans. Inf. Forensics Secur. **10**(3), 613–625 (2015)
14. Guo, G.: A novel recommendation model regularized with user trust and item ratings. IEEE Trans. Knowl. Data Eng. **28**(7), 1607–1620 (2016)
15. Cho, J.H.: A survey on trust modeling. ACM Comput. Surv. **48**(2), 1–40 (2015)
16. Jiang, W.: Understanding graph-based trust evaluation in online social networks: methodologies and challenges. ACM Comput. Surv. **49**(1), 1–35 (2016)
17. Guo, G.: TrustSVD: collaborative filtering with both the explicit and implicit influence of user trust and of item ratings. In: Twenty-Ninth AAAI Conference on Artificial Intelligence, Austin, Texas, pp. 123–129 (2015)
18. Guo, L.: A trust-based privacy-preserving friend recommendation scheme for online social networks. IEEE Trans. Dependable Secure Comput. **12**(4), 413–427 (2015)
19. Zhong, Y.: A computational dynamic trust model for user authorization. IEEE Trans. Dependable Secure Comput. **12**(1), 1–15 (2015)
20. Yao, W.: Modeling dual role preferences for trust-aware recommendation. In: Proceedings of the 37th International ACM SIGIR Conference on Research and Development in Information Retrieval, Gold Coast, Queensland, pp. 975–978 (2014)
21. Konstas, I.: On social networks and collaborative recommendation. In: Proceedings of the 32nd International ACM SIGIR Conference on Research and Development in Information Retrieval, Boston, MA, pp. 195–202 (2009)
22. Chen, W.: Collaborative filtering for Orkut communities: discovery of user latent behavior. In: Proceedings of the 18th International Conference on World Wide Web, Madrid, Spain, pp. 681–690 (2009)
23. Lansing, J.: Trust in cloud computing: conceptual typology and trust-building antecedents. database: the DATABASE for advances. Inf. Syst. **47**(2), 58–96 (2016)
24. Zhang, D.: Cold-start recommendation using bi-clustering and fusion for large-scale social recommender systems. IEEE Trans. Emerg. Top. Comput. **2**(2), 239–250 (2017)
25. Kamvae, S.D.: The Eigentrust algorithm for reputation management in P2P networks. In: Proceedings of the 12th International Conference on World Wide Web, Budapest, Hungary, pp. 640–651 (2003)

26. Roundtable Algorithm. http://www.top-news.top/news-12840672.html. Accessed 12 Apr 2017

27. Ron, Z.: A Programmer's Guide to Data Mining: The Ancient Art of the Numerati, 1st edn. The People's Posts and Telecommunications Press, Beijing (2015)

28. Ling, G.: Ratings meet reviews, a combined approach to recommend. In: Proceedings of the 8th ACM Conference on Recommender Systems, pp. 105–112. ACM, Foster City (2014)

29. Zhao, D.: A distributed and adaptive trust evaluation algorithm for MANET. In: Proceedings of the 12th ACM Symposium on QoS and Security for Wireless and Mobile Networks, pp. 47–54. ACM, New York (2016)

30. Massa, P.: Trust-aware recommender systems. In: Proceedings of the 2007 ACM Conference on Recommender Systems, pp. 17–24. ACM, Malta (2007)

31. Guo, G.: ETAF: an extended trust antecedents framework for trust prediction. In: Proceedings of the 2014 International Conference on Advances in Social Networks Analysis and Mining (ASONAM), China, pp. 540–547 (2014)

32. Ma, H.: Recommender systems with social regularization. In: Proceedings of the Fourth ACM International Conference on Web Search and Data Mining, pp. 287–296. ACM, Hong Kong (2011)

33. Ma, H.: Learning to recommend with social trust ensemble. In: Proceedings of the 32nd International ACM SIGIR Conference on Research and Development in Information Retrieval, Boston, MA, USA, pp. 203–210 (2009)

34. Guha, R.: Propagation of trust and distrust. In: Proceedings of the 13th International Conference on World Wide Web, pp. 403–412. ACM, New York (2004)

35. Golbeck, J.A.: Computing and Applying Trust in Web-Based Social Networks. University of Maryland, College Park (2005)

An Associated Deletion Scheme
for Multi-copy in Cloud Storage

Dulin[1], Zhiwei Zhang[1]([✉]), Shichong Tan[1], Jianfeng Wang[1],
and Xiaoling Tao[2,3]

[1] State Key Laboratory of Integrated Services Networks (ISN), Xidian University,
Xi'an, China
dulin@stu.xidian.edu.cn, {zwzhang,jfwang}@xidian.edu.cn,
sctan@mail.xidian.edu.cn
[2] Guangxi Cooperative Innovation Center of Cloud Computing and Big Data,
Guilin University of Electronic Technology, Guilin, China
[3] Guangxi Colleges and Universities Key Laboratory of Cloud Computing and
Complex Systems, Guilin University of Electronic Technology, Guilin, China
txl@guet.edu.cn

Abstract. Cloud storage reduces the cost of data storage and brings
great convenience for data backup, therefore in order to improve data
availability, more and more users choose to outsource personal data for
multiple copies instead of storing them locally. However, multi-copy storage brings the difficulty in associating all the copies to store, increases the
number of keys for encrypting every single copy and makes the integrity
and the verifiable deletion of copies hard to be guaranteed, all of these
issues introduce more threatens to the security of user data. In this paper,
we present a cryptographic solution called ADM to solve above problems. To reduce management cost, we outsource data keys encrypted by
blinded RSA to the third party, and not only to guarantee the integrity
of multi-copy but also to give the verifiable evidence for deletion operation of the copies, we propose a multi-copy associated deleting solution
based on pre-deleting sequence and Merkle hash tree. Finally, a proof-of-
concept implementation of ADM is presented to demonstrate its practical feasibility, and we compare our scheme with other typical schemes
in functionalities and conduct the security analysis and empirical performance of the prototype.

Keywords: Cloud storage · Multi-copy storage · Associated deletion
Pre-deleting sequence

This work is supported by National Natural Science Foundation of China (No.
61572382, No. 61702401 and No. 61772405), Key Project of Natural Science Basic
Research Plan in Shaanxi Province of China (No. 2016JZ021), China 111 Project (No.
B16037), Guangxi Cooperative Innovation Center of Cloud Computing and Big Data
(No. YD17X07), and Guangxi Colleges and Universities Key Laboratory of Cloud Com-
puting and Complex Systems (No. YF17103).

J. Vaidya and J. Li (Eds.): ICA3PP 2018, LNCS 11337, pp. 511–526, 2018.
https://doi.org/10.1007/978-3-030-05063-4_38

1 Introduction

With the rapid development of information technology, cloud computing increasingly attracts not only individuals but enterprises for its convenient and distributed service model in a pay-as-you-go way [2], of which cloud storage is a representative technique. With the dual drive of user demand and enterprise service, cloud storage has gained wide attention in academia and industry.

Although cloud storage provides a client with great convenience to outsource data, it still faces many new problems and challenges in the cloud environment, especially on the security and availability.

First of all, due to factors such as natural disasters and uncertain faults of cloud storage equipment, more and more users choose to upload multiple backups for data to cloud in order to improve data availability. Besides, from the perspective of a cloud service provider, it is also essential to provide the non-destructive and continuously available multiple replica storage service in order to boost the reputation and social recognition of himself. Both users and service providers need a practical multi-copy associated storage solution of outsourced data.

Secondly, the ownership and the management of outsourced data in the cloud are separated, so the data owner loses physical control over the data, which leads to many security risks such as data loss, data tampering, data disclosure and data remanence [16]. Most of the existing secure storage solutions use cryptography to protect the outsourced data, that is, owners encrypt the data by the specific symmetric key before uploading data. If a data owner encrypts all data to be uploaded with a single key, the risk of data leakage will increase with a high probability, so she should use different keys to encrypt different data to achieve greater security, but this will also result in the management issue of a large number of encryption keys for her.

In addition, data secure deletion is also a major concern in cloud storage. After having the multiple copies of data stored in the cloud, a data owner also has the demand for the cloud service provider to perform the deletion of the replicas to prevent him from leaking the data or using them illegally for interest. The traditional deletion schemes for cloud service are almost based on one-bit-return protocol [11], that is, only the result of the deletion request, success or failure, rather than the corresponding deletion evidence is returned to the data owner by the cloud service provider. And most implementations of these schemes are based on current cryptographic technologies, whose goal is to ensure that the data outsourced to cloud is unreadable and unrecoverable for now, but the ciphertext is still stored in the cloud. With the rapid development of different technologies and fast updating of softwares and hardwares, there is no guarantee that the data remaining in the cloud will not be cracked and broken through within polynomial-time complexity in the future. Consequently, a data owner requires the cloud service provider to perform a thorough, verifiable and accountable deletion operation and provide the corresponding deletion evidence when she proposes a deletion request.

However, these are not all the problems faced by cloud storage, and there are also many related researches in academia, such as outsourced data auditing [12,21,24], secure data deduplication [13,15,25], searchable encryption [26,27] and secure outsourcing computation [4,30]. But there are few researches on associated deletion for multi-copy, our paper focuses on solving the problem.

1.1 Contributions

In order to make it more efficient to manage outsourced data and more transparent for users to know where her data exactly are, we adopt an address-based multi-copy associated storage method, which uniquely locates a copy through physical and logical addresses. Besides, we apply an effective key management method for multi-copy, which only needs one more round of interaction than usual but greatly saves the storage cost. In addition, we also propose an integrity verification and associated deletion method for multi-copy based on the pre-deleting sequence and Merkle hash tree. In this way, when a data owner no longer needs the outsourced data and makes a deletion request, the cloud service provider will provide the integrity verification and deleting evidence for her data in the cloud, that is, the evidence can not only verify the integrity of data but also verify the deletion execution. If the service provider does not execute or erroneously executes the deletion operation, the data owner will know and can use the provided evidence for further accountability.

1.2 Related Works

Traditional data deletion methods can be roughly divided into two types [19]. One is to redirect or remove the system pointer linked to data, or to overwrite the area where the data to be deleted stores, while the other is to apply cryptographic solutions to make the data unreadable or unrecoverable but they are still stored. Existing cryptography-based secure deletion schemes can be divided into the following three categories [18,28]:

Secure Deletion Based on a Trusted Execution Environment. The core idea of these schemes is to combine hardware with software to build a secure execution environment for secure deletion. Hao *et al.* [11] propose a publicly verifiable cloud data deletion scheme by using a TPM as the trusted hardware foundation combined with Diffie-Hellman integrated encryption algorithm [1] and non-interactive Chaum-Pedersen zero-knowledge proof scheme [7]. The trusted computing technology is still under developing and probing, although these solutions can solve the problem of data remanence and deletion in a trusted execution environment, they cannot be promoted and widely used. In addition, the schemes do not solve the problem of secure deletion for data multi-copy.

Secure Deletion Based on Key Management. The core idea of such schemes is to outsource the ciphertext of data and then to find ways to manage encryption keys rather than the data itself, and after the keys expire, they are safely deleted in specific solutions based on different schemes. Tang *et al.* [23] protect different data with different access control policies and control keys for secure deletion, and then build a secure overlay cloud storage system based on the existing cloud computing infrastructure. Geambasu *et al.* [8] propose a data self-destruction scheme for the first time, which divides data encryption keys into many pieces through Shamir's (k, n) threshold secret sharing scheme [20] and distributes them into a large-scale decentralized distributed hash table (DHT) network. The DHT nodes periodically clear and update stored data, thus deleting the secret information. However, the scheme is faced with the risk of hopping and sniffing attacks and the lifetime of keys is short and out of control. Zhang *et al.* [31] define an RAO object which integrates the physical address, logical address, unique ID, replica directory, and replica metadata of each piece of data, and on this basis propose a muti-replica associated deletion scheme. Yang *et al.* [29] combine digital signatures, Merkle hash trees and blockchain techniques, and provide the deletion evidence, which are stored in the node of the private chain of the cloud service server without any trusted party, it provides a novel idea for publicly verifiable data deletion.

Secure Deletion Based on Access Control. The main point of these schemes is based on different access control policies to set trigger conditions for different data for secure deletion, and when all the conditions are satisfied, the deletion operation is performed. Cachin *et al.* [3] present the first formal model and a related security definition for encryption-based secure deletion, and construct a secure deletion scheme based on strategy and graph theory.

In the above schemes, only Zhang *et al.* [31] scheme considers the problem of multi-copy associated deletion, and only Yang *et al.* [29] scheme provides publicly verifiable deletion evidence. Other solutions rarely consider these two issues, and they only focus on the deletion process of the encryption keys but ignore the deletion of the outsourced data itself and the evidence of the deletion operation, and few solutions solve the problems of secure storage, multi-copy association of the outsourced data, and verifiable deletion of them at the same time. In this paper, we present such a scheme to adapt to the scenarios.

2   Preliminaries

In this section, we explain two relevant cryptographic primitives: the blinded RSA algorithm and the Merkle hash tree.

2.1   Blinded RSA Algorithm

The blinded RSA algorithm [14, 22] is a common symmetric encryption method for hiding the message from the key provider when the encryptor is not the key provider himself and the message decryption operation is outsourced to the key provider. The specific encryption and decryption process is as follows: The key provider B randomly generates two secret large prime numbers p and q, and calculates $n := pq$, $\varphi(n) := (p-1)(q-1)$, then selects a large integer e, which satisfies $1 < e < \varphi(n)$, and $gcd(\varphi(n), e) = 1$, and computes d which satisfies $de \equiv 1 \pmod{\varphi(n)}$, that is, (e, n) is a public key, (d, n) is the relevant private key. During encryption, the data encryptor A encrypts the message m blinded by the random large integer r with the public key e to obtain $c := m^e r^e \pmod{n} \equiv (mr)^e \pmod{n}$ and sends it to B. During decryption, B calculates $mr \equiv c^d \pmod{n} \equiv (mr)^{ed} \pmod{n}$ with the private key and sends it to A. Then A calculates $m \equiv (mr)r^{-1} \pmod{n}$ to restore the message m. Thus ensuring that B cannot get the message m even if he could do the decryption operation and get mr.

2.2 Merkle Hash Tree

Merkle hash tree [17] is a fantastic data structure for authenticating data integrity based on a one-way cryptographic hash function with low overhead. Merkle hash tree is widely used as a binary tree, but it can also be a multi-way tree. The content of every node of Merkle hash tree is a hash value computed by certain hash function such as SHA-256. For each leaf node, the hash value is computed with the input of the specific data related to the node. For each internal node, we should first concatenate the hash values of its left child and right child, and then the hash value is computed with the input of the concatenation. Merkle hash tree is generally used to ensure that data blocks received from others are undamaged and unreplaced, in our scheme we also apply the efficient property.

3 ADM Scheme Design

In this section, we first introduce the framework, threat model and security assumptions and then present our ADM scheme.

3.1 Framework of ADM

In our ADM scheme, there are three participants: the data owner, the cloud service provider and the third party. The architecture of our scheme is shown in Fig. 1.

Data Owner. The data owner is the entity who outsources her copies of original files and uses the derivative services provided by the cloud service provider, and also asks the third party to do some reasonable verification operations and few storage operations for managing the control keys to reduce her burden.

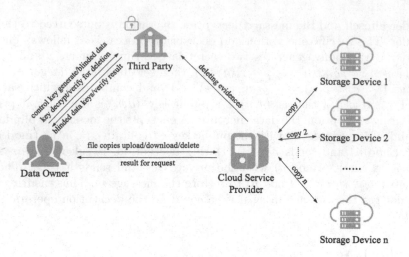

Fig. 1. System model

Cloud Service Provider. The cloud service provider maintains the copies of files and creates an address-based multi-copy associated table for each data owner, and when the data owner sends a deletion request for the specific file, he should perform the delete operation and provide the corresponding evidences.

Third Party. The third party maintains the control keys for each data owner and verifies whether the deleting evidence is genuine or not.

We use DO, CSP and TP to respectively represent the data owner, the cloud service provider and the third party in the next parts.

3.2   Threat Model and Security Assumptions

In our scheme, there are maybe different attack conditions from the three entities. Thus, we make some assumptions as follows.

Assumption One. TP is honest-but-curious [9]. TP stores the control keys for DO without tampering them but tries to learn the information of the control keys, and he honestly responds to every request and returns the result.

Assumption Two. CSP is lazy-but-honest [10], which means that CSP returns to every request from DO and TP as if he performs as rules made in our scheme but the execution results may be fake. After DO outsourcing the copies of files, CSP is responsible for the security and integrity of the data, but out of the storage cost, he may not store the copies as the negotiated number. And when DO wants to delete the file, CSP may still keep the certain copy for benefits and return fake results.

Table 1. Notations and meanings

Notations	Meaning
$UserID$	The identifier of DO
F	The original file to outsource by DO
F_{id}	The identifier of F (generated by hash filename of F)
F_{mate}	The metadata of F used for CSP to estimate the number of copies of F to create
(e_{id}, n_{id})	The RSA public control key for F
(d_{id}, n_{id})	The RSA private control key for F
n	The number of copies of F
$addr_i$	The address to store copy number i of F
$(copy\ address,\ deletion\ number)$	The item of pre-deleting sequence for the copy to be stored in $copy\ address$
$Del_{sequence}$	The pre-deleting sequence for F
K	The master data key for file F
K_i	The concrete data key generated from K for copy number i
num_i	The random number used for deleting control for copy number i
$Uhash_{F_{addr_i}}$	The integrity and deletion evidence for copy number i of F generated by DO
$Uroot_{F_{id}}$	The integral pre-deleting evidence of F generated by DO
R	The random number used for blinded RSA
$Chash_{F_{addr_i}}$	The integrity and deletion evidence for copy number i of F generated by CSP
$Croot_{F_{id}}$	The integral deleting evidence of F generated by CSP

Assumption Three. TP and CSP do not conspire with each other.

Assumption Four. DO is trusted, she does not disclose any information of her file or trap CSP or TP.

3.3 ADM Scheme Construction

Our ADM scheme consists of the following five steps, and in this part, we present the design of it in detail. The main notations used in our scheme are summarized in Table 1.

Setup. First, DO, TP and CSP respectively generate an ECDSA key pair, which is used for authentication during the interaction by signing the hash of the content to be sent, three key pairs (PK_O, SK_O), (PK_S, SK_S) and (PK_T, SK_T) are respectively for DO, CSP and TP.

Then, the three parties negotiate the session keys with each other using the Diffie-Hellman protocol [6], the session keys $K_{UserID-CSP}$, $K_{UserID-TP}$ and K_{TP-CSP} are respectively for DO and CSP, DO and TP, CSP and TP, which are used to not only authenticate one's identity but also protect the conversations from other malicious attackers by encrypting the content of conversations. The encryption algorithm here can be any symmetric encryption algorithm. Throughout the whole scheme, each DO only has to save two session keys locally, and both TP and CSP need to maintain a list of session keys corresponding to different DO and a list of session keys between themselves.

The working principle of the session key is also relatively simple: the sender encrypts the message by the specific session key negotiated with the receiver beforehand. And after receiving the message, the sender can decrypt the message with the negotiated session key to obtain the correct information so that they can confirm each other's identity – only if one uses the real session key attached to his identity can he decrypt and gain the information correctly, otherwise the identity of each other is invalid and he cannot get the correct information either.

In the next steps, if there is no special circumstance, we will take signatures for authentication and session keys for protecting the dialog during the interaction of the three parties, so no more similar details will be given.

Upload. Upload stage contains five sub-operations as follows.

- **Generate control key.** DO sends her $UserID$ and F_{id} of F to TP. After receiving them, TP generates a corresponding RSA public key (e_{id}, n_{id}) and private key (d_{id}, n_{id}), then takes the key pair as the control key of F and sends the public key (e_{id}, n_{id}) to DO. The purpose of the control key is to encrypt data key by an asymmetric encryption algorithm, here we adopt RSA. Because the overhead is quite huge for DO to maintain data keys for every file locally, DO first encrypts the file by a data key and encrypts the data key by control key for the file generated by TP, then outsources the control key to TP in order to reduce her overhead of computation and storage. Besides, for each DO, TP constructs a meta-info list to record all F_{id} of her files and relative information of control keys.
- **Set the number of copies and create a multi-copy associated table.** DO sends $UserID$, F_{id} and F_{mate} of F to CSP, which includes file size, file type, file creation time, etc. After evaluating the metadata, CSP sets the number n of copies under the premise of availability of F. And CSP picks n exact addresses in which the n copies of F will be stored. Generally, although storage devices of CSP are distributed in different geographical areas, a copy can be uniquely identified by an exact address of a storage device in the cloud, which is always composed of a physical address and a logical address.

CSP returns n and n MAC addresses, denoted as $addr_1, addr_2, \cdots, addr_n$ to DO. At the same time, CSP maintains a multi-copy associated table for DO, which records $UserID$, F_{id}, n and $addr$.

- **Generate pre-deleting sequence.** After receiving n and $addr_1$, $addr_2$, $\cdots$, $addr_n$, DO first randomly generates n unequal numbers used to control the deletion order of copies of F and the order of generating the evidence. DO randomly binds the n $addr$s and the n numbers to n pairs, whose form is like $(copy\ address,\ deletion\ number)$. And then DO sorts n pairs by the size of deletion control numbers in ascending order. The sorted sequence is expressed as $(addr_1, num_1), (addr_2, num_2), \cdots, (addr_n, num_n)$, at this time, the subscript order of each $addr$ is rearranged and may be totally different from that sent by CSP. Finally, DO concatenates the sequence and generates the result denoted as $Del_{sequence}$, i.e., pre-deleting sequence. Note that $Del_{sequence}$ is generated and prescribed before uploading F, that is why we call it pre-deleting sequence.

- **Encrypt and upload copies.** DO randomly generates a master key K, then does continuous hash operation on it to generate n data keys, which are used for encrypting each copy, denoted as $K_1, K_2, \cdots, K_n$. If DO encrypts each copy with one data key, CSP may store only one copy but lie to store n copies, so DO encrypts F for n times respectively by $K_1, K_2, \cdots, K_n$ and gets $\{F\}_{K_1}, \{F\}_{K_2}, \cdots, \{F\}_{K_n}$. And DO encrypts $Del_{sequence}$ by K and K by the control key (e_{id}, n_{id}) from TP and obtains $K^{e_{id}}$. Now DO gets n encrypted copies to be upload that includes the following information: F_{id}, $addr_i$, $K^{e_{id}}$, $\{F\}_{K_i}$, $\{Del_{sequence}\}_K$, $(i \in N\ and\ i \leq n)$. DO sends n ciphertexts of copies to CSP, and CSP stores each copy in the specific storage device according to each address information $addr_i$ but he doesn't know the corresponding deletion number num_i bound to $addr_i$, which is known until a deletion request is sent.

- **Pre-generate and upload copy integrity evidence and file deletion evidence.** DO first does $H(F_{id}\|(addr_i, num_i)\|K^{e_{id}}\|\{F\}_{K_i}\|\{Del_{sequence}\}_K)$ on each copy entry and obtains n hash values and sorts the values according to the pre-deleting random sequence $Del_{sequence}$, and then obtains the n integrity evidences of copies, i.e., the sorted values denoted as $Uhash_{F_{addr_1}}$, $Uhash_{F_{addr_2}}, \cdots, Uhash_{F_{addr_n}}$. DO creates a Merkle hash tree by using the sorted values as leaf nodes and finally calculates the value of root node as the pre-deleting evidence of F denoted as $Uroot_{F_{id}}$. After $Uroot_{F_{id}}$ has been calculated, DO signs $Uhash_{F_{addr_1}}$, $Uhash_{F_{addr_2}}, \cdots, Uhash_{F_{addr_n}}$ and $Uroot_{F_{id}}$ respectively and sends $UserID$ and the signatures to TP, TP stores them and binds these evidences to F_{id} for later verification. And the detailed procedure of generating this Merkle hash tree is shown in Fig. 2.

Download. Because there are n encrypted copies of F whose identifier is F_{id}, DO only needs to download any one of copies so that she can recover the plaintext of the original file F. First, DO sends $UserID$, F_{id} and a request to CSP to ask for downloading the F with F_{id}. CSP randomly selects a copy among

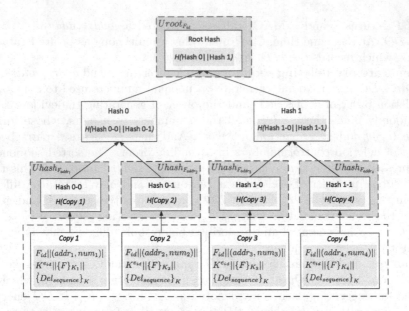

Fig. 2. Merkle hash tree of evidences

the stored copies and sends it to DO, assuming that the content of the copy is $F_{id}, addr_i, K^{e_{id}}, \{F\}_{K_i}, \{Del_{sequence}\}_K$. Second, after receiving the copy, DO generates a secret random number R as an RSA blinding factor to protect the data key from TP. DO encrypts R with e_{id}, the control key, and gets $R^{e_{id}}$, then multiplies it by $K^{e_{id}}$ to get $(KR)^{e_{id}}$. Third, DO sends $UserID$, F_{id} and $(KR)^{e_{id}}$ to TP. TP decrypts $(KR)^{e_{id}}$ by d_{id} and returns the result to DO. Finally, after DO receives KR, she removes R to recover K and hashes K properly to get K_i, then decrypts the encrypted copy by K_i to get the plaintext.

Delete. Before deleting, DO first checks whether the content of F still needs to be stored in the cloud or not. If needn't, a deletion request will be sent. First, DO sends $UserID$, F_{id} and a request for deletion to CSP. The previous steps are the same as the process of downloading a copy, after a few steps of interaction, DO recovers $Del_{sequence}$. Then DO sends $Del_{sequence}$ to CSP. CSP sequentially deletes n corresponding copies of F_{id} in different $addr$ according to the order stipulated in $Del_{sequence}$ and respectively calculates $H(F_{id}\|(addr_i, num_i)\|K^{e_{id}}\|\{F\}_{K_i}\|\{Del_{sequence}\}_K)$ to obtain the integrity evidences, i.e., the hash values of each copy. And we denote them as $Chash_{F_{addr_1}}$, $Chash_{F_{addr_2}}$, $\cdots$, $Chash_{F_{addr_n}}$, and then constructs a Merkle hash tree using the values and denotes the root of the tree as $Croot_{F_{id}}$, which is the whole evidence of all copies of F. And CSP respectively signs $Chash_{F_{addr_1}}$, $Chash_{F_{addr_2}}$, $\cdots$, $Chash_{F_{addr_n}}$ and $Croot_{F_{id}}$ and sends $UserID$, F_{id} and signatures to TP. Since CSP cannot get $Del_{sequence}$ in advance and can only obtain it when DO proposes a deletion request, CSP cannot fake evidences of deletion. Because any copy of F contains enough information to construct the Merkle tree, if the file is so important that DO worries about disclosure from CSP, when she deletes the F, she can store a copy locally for further accountability. CSP should take certain efficient overwrite method [5] to complete the deletion operation.

Verify. After TP receives the corresponding information from CSP, he first finds the deletion and integrity evidence information of F which is recorded in the last step of $Upload$ stage from DO. First, TP checks the validity of the signatures for the pre-deleting evidences from DO and the ones for the deleting evidences from CSP. Second, TP compares each $Uhash_{F_{addr_i}}$ with $Chash_{F_{addr_i}}$, if the two values of each copy are equal, it means that CSP complies with the storage rules, otherwise he does not follow the rules to store n copies completely. Third, TP further compares $Uroot_{F_{id}}$ with $Croot_{F_{id}}$, if the two values are equal, it is determined that CSP correctly performs the deletion operation and stores the copies of F intact, otherwise CSP does not delete the file correctly. Finally, TP sends the notarized result of the verification to DO so that DO is informed and can take it as a proof to make CSP be held accountable. Why the evidence can be used for accountability is explained in the next section.

4   Evaluation

4.1   Security Analysis

In this section, we analyze the security of our proposed ADM scheme from three aspects, which are correctness, confidentiality and accountability.

Correctness. Assume that each entity operates according to the protocol in ADM. Here we mainly analyze the correctness of the evidence verification results. We take a certain file F as an example. In $Upload$ stage, DO combines the pre-deleting sequence $Del_{sequence}$ with each copy ciphertext of F to generate the pre-deleting integrity evidences $Uhash_{F_{addr_i}}, (i \in N \ and \ i \leq n)$ for each copy of F, and then DO uses the evidences as the leaf nodes to construct a Merkle tree and generate the overall pre-deleting integrity evidence $Uroot_{F_{id}}$ of F. During $Delete$ stage, DO gets the pre-deleting sequence and sends it to CSP. Because DO is trusted, the pre-deleting sequence will not be tampered. CSP performs the deletion operation according to the sequence and generates the $Chash_{F_{addr_i}}, (i \in N \ and \ i \leq n)$ and $Croot_{F_{id}}$. In $Verify$ stage, CSP is also assumed to be trusted, the calculations of both $Chash_{F_{addr_i}}, (i \in N \ and \ i \leq n)$ and $Croot_{F_{id}}$ are always correct. Consequently, the equations $Uhash_{F_{addr_i}} = Chash_{F_{addr_i}}, (i \in N \ and \ i \leq n)$ and $Uroot_{F_{id}} = Croot_{F_{id}}$ always hold.

Confidentiality. The requirement for confidentiality is that only the sender and the appointed receiver can understand the content of the transmitted message, even if the eavesdropper can intercept the encrypted communication message, he cannot restore the original message anyway. In our scheme, every two of the communication entities, DO, CSP and TP, should negotiate the session keys through the Diffie-Hellman protocol, namely $K_{UserID-CSP}$, $K_{UserID-TP}$, K_{TP-CSP}, and use any symmetric encryption algorithm with the specific session key to encrypt the communication content, thus ensuring the confidentiality of the dialogues. For the outsourced file F of DO, we encrypt the n copies of it by any symmetric encryption algorithm with the data key K_i, $(i \in N \; and \; i \leq n)$ to ensure the confidentiality of copies, and use the control key (e_{id}, n_{id}) to encrypt the data keys to ensure the confidentiality. And to prevent TP from decrypting the user data keys and getting them, we use the blind factor R to confuse him in the course of the interaction. Hence our scheme ensures confidentiality from different aspects.

Accountability. After DO sending a deletion request for F, if CSP does not delete it and even leak $\{F\}_K$ out and somehow DO finds it out somewhere, DO has the right to claim compensation against CSP by providing the deleting evidence signed by CSP and the original contents reserved locally for constructing the Merkle tree. Since the hash function is unidirectional, it is a difficult problem to recover the original phase from the hash value. So if the complete original phase content can be provided, we can determine CSP did not delete the file and carried out the leakage, thus our scheme guarantees accountability.

4.2   Function Comparison

We compare the functionalities with different representative cryptography based secure deletion schemes, the comparison details are shown in Table 2. We explain four important aspects here.

No Need for Users to Manage Keys. Most schemes take the form that user is in charge of the generation and management of encryption keys to protect them from being obtained by the adversary. However, mismanagement of keys for users may also result in the loss or forgetting them, thereby failing to decrypt the ciphertext and get the original data. In our scheme, for encryption keys, a user only needs to generate but not to manage, i.e., a user does not have to record the keys locally. In this way, the data owner reduces extra cost and burden for management of keys.

Data Multi-copy Storage. Existing deletion schemes rarely consider multi-copy storage of data, but it is an important and effective way to improve data availability and is also one of the actual needs for the sake of users.

Secure Deletion for Ciphertext. Existing solutions seldom or never take into account the problem of secure deletion for ciphertext because they assume that encrypted ciphertext cannot be cracked, thus ensuring absolute security

Table 2. Function comparison among different schemes

Scheme category	TPM based		Key management based				Access control based
Specific scheme	Hao [11]	Yang [29]	Tang [23]	Geambasu [8]	Zhang [31]	Our scheme	Cachin [3]
No need for users to manage keys	×	×	√	√	×	√	×
Data outsourcing after encryption	√	√	√	√	√	√	√
Data multi-copy storage	×	×	×	×	√	√	×
Secure deletion for keys	√	√	√	√	√	√	√
Secure deletion for ciphertext	×	√	×	×	√	√	×
Key deletion verifiability	√	√	×	×	×	√	×
Ciphertext deletion verifiability	×	√	×	×	×	√	×

of data. However, with the development of computer technologies, it is difficult to ensure that ciphertext encrypted by the present fixed-digit key cannot be effectively cracked in the near future. Therefore, it is also important to delete the ciphertext itself.

Ciphertext Deletion Verifiability. Similar to the encryption keys, it is also required for the deletion executor to provide corresponding deletion evidence for ciphertext to prevent the data from being cracked or illegally used. However, most schemes ignore this point.

Our scheme implements the seven functions in a direct or indirect way, and it is a full-cycle management solution for user data in the cloud.

4.3 Performance Evaluation

We implemented a prototype of our scheme in Java and based on it we analyze the performance of the scheme. The implementation of basic cryptographic primitives used in our system is based on Java Cryptography Architecture (JCA). Our experiments are performed on the workstation with 8 core Inter Xeon (R) CPU E5-1620 v3 @ 3.50 GHz, and installed with Ubuntu 14.04 LTS.

Run Time Overhead. The time overhead of each stage is indicated in Fig. 3. The independent variable and the dependent variable is respectively the size of the file to upload and the time overhead. We repeat all the procedures for 100 times and then take the average of the computational results. In the process of implementation, we take 8 as the number of copies n, AES for all encryption operation, SHA-256 for generating the evidence Merkle tree and MD5 for other hash operations.

During the whole process, the main time cost for TP is to perform some traditional operations which are also asked in most schemes, i.e., generation and management of control keys and verification of deleting evidences. And that for DO is to do the encryption and decryption, as well as the generation of pre-deleting evidence of outsourced data. Our scheme does not introduce extra long-running operations. The overall time overhead is more efficient and acceptable to each entity under ordinary circumstances.

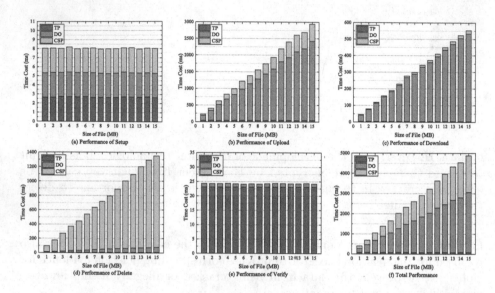

Fig. 3. Performance evaluation graphs of our ADM scheme

Storage Space Overhead. For DO, only two session keys and an ECDSA key pair need to be saved locally before *Delete*, and taking the accountability into account, DO needs to store only one copy of the vital and confidential file after *Delete*, thus greatly reducing the storage overhead. For TP, he needs to store an ECDSA key pair, session keys with CSP and different DO, control key associated tables and pre-deleting evidences for different DO. Because the number of copies of each file for guaranteeing the availability is usually a single digit number, so the space overhead for the pre-deleting evidences will not be too much. For CSP, he is the storage service provider, so storage overhead for him should not be taken into consideration.

5   Conclusion

In this paper, based on the Merkle hash tree, pre-deleting sequence and some basic cryptography techniques, we propose a scheme of integrity verification and associated deletion for multi-copy in the cloud. Our ADM scheme provides users with the integrity verification of the multi-copy of the outsourced data and the corresponding deleting evidence for the data. When cloud service providers fail to operate in accordance with the agreement, users can take the evidence provided for further accountability.

References

1. Abdalla, M., Bellare, M., Rogaway, P.: The Oracle Diffie-Hellman assumptions and an analysis of DHIES. In: Naccache, D. (ed.) CT-RSA 2001. LNCS, vol. 2020, pp. 143–158. Springer, Heidelberg (2001). https://doi.org/10.1007/3-540-45353-9_12
2. Armbrust, M., et al.: Above the clouds: a Berkeley view of cloud computing. Technical report UCB/EECS-2009-28, EECS Department, University of California, Berkeley, February 2009. http://www2.eecs.berkeley.edu/Pubs/TechRpts/2009/EECS-2009-28.html
3. Cachin, C., Haralambiev, K., Hsiao, H., Sorniotti, A.: Policy-based secure deletion. In: 2013 ACM SIGSAC Conference on Computer and Communications Security, CCS 2013, 4–8 November 2013, Berlin, Germany, pp. 259–270 (2013)
4. Chen, X., Li, J., Ma, J., Tang, Q., Lou, W.: New algorithms for secure outsourcing of modular exponentiations. IEEE Trans. Parallel Distrib. Syst. $25(9)$, 2386–2396 (2014)
5. Diesburg, S.M., Wang, A.A.: A survey of confidential data storage and deletion methods. ACM Comput. Surv. (CSUR) $43(1)$, 2:1–2:37 (2010)
6. Diffie, W., Hellman, M.E.: New directions in cryptography. IEEE Trans. Inf. Theory $22(6)$, 644–654 (1976)
7. Fiat, A., Shamir, A.: How to prove yourself: practical solutions to identification and signature problems. In: Odlyzko, A.M. (ed.) CRYPTO 1986. LNCS, vol. 263, pp. 186–194. Springer, Heidelberg (1987). https://doi.org/10.1007/3-540-47721-7_12
8. Geambasu, R., Kohno, T., Levy, A.A., Levy, H.M.: Vanish: increasing data privacy with self-destructing data. In: Proceedings of 18th USENIX Security Symposium, 10–14 August 2009, Montreal, Canada, pp. 299–316 (2009)
9. Goldreich, O.: Foundations of Cryptography: Volume 2, Basic Applications. Cambridge University Press, Cambridge (2009)
10. Golle, P., Mironov, I.: Uncheatable distributed computations. In: Naccache, D. (ed.) CT-RSA 2001. LNCS, vol. 2020, pp. 425–440. Springer, Heidelberg (2001). https://doi.org/10.1007/3-540-45353-9_31
11. Hao, F., Clarke, D., Zorzo, A.F.: Deleting secret data with public verifiability. IEEE Trans. Dependable Secure Comput. $13(6)$, 617–629 (2016)
12. Jiang, T., Chen, X., Ma, J.: Public integrity auditing for shared dynamic cloud data with group user revocation. IEEE Trans. Comput. $65(8)$, 2363–2373 (2016)
13. Jiang, T., Chen, X., Wu, Q., Ma, J., Susilo, W., Lou, W.: Secure and efficient cloud data deduplication with randomized tag. IEEE Trans. Inf. Forensics Secur. $12(3)$, 532–543 (2017)
14. Katz, J., Lindell, Y.: Introduction to Modern Cryptography, 2nd edn. CRC Press, Boca Raton (2014)
15. Li, J., et al.: Secure distributed deduplication systems with improved reliability. IEEE Trans. Comput. $64(12)$, 3569–3579 (2015)
16. Liu, J., Ma, J., Wu, W., Chen, X., Huang, X., Xu, L.: Protecting mobile health records in cloud computing: a secure, efficient, and anonymous design. ACM Trans. Embed. Comput. Syst. (TECS) $16(2)$, 57:1–57:20 (2017)

17. Merkle, R.C.: Protocols for public key cryptosystems. In: Proceedings of the 1980 IEEE Symposium on Security and Privacy, 14–16 April 1980, Oakland, California, USA, pp. 122–134 (1980)
18. Reardon, J.: Secure Data Deletion. Information Security and Cryptography. Springer, Cham (2016). https://doi.org/10.1007/978-3-319-28778-2
19. Reardon, J., Basin, D.A., Capkun, S.: SoK: secure data deletion. In: 2013 IEEE Symposium on Security and Privacy, SP 2013, 19–22 May 2013, Berkeley, CA, USA, pp. 301–315 (2013)
20. Shamir, A.: How to share a secret. Commun. ACM **22**(11), 612–613 (1979)
21. Shen, J., Shen, J., Chen, X., Huang, X., Susilo, W.: An efficient public auditing protocol with novel dynamic structure for cloud data. IEEE Trans. Inf. Forensics Secur. **12**(10), 2402–2415 (2017)
22. Stallings, W.: Cryptography and Network Security - Principles and Practice, 3rd edn. Prentice Hall, Upper Saddle River (2003)
23. Tang, Y., Lee, P.P.C., Lui, J.C.S., Perlman, R.J.: Secure overlay cloud storage with access control and assured deletion. IEEE Trans. Dependable Secure Comput. **9**(6), 903–916 (2012)
24. Wang, J., Chen, X., Huang, X., You, I., Xiang, Y.: Verifiable auditing for outsourced database in cloud computing. IEEE Trans. Comput. **64**(11), 3293–3303 (2015)
25. Wang, J., Chen, X., Li, J., Kluczniak, K., Kutylowski, M.: TrDup: enhancing secure data deduplication with user traceability in cloud computing. Int. J. Web Grid Serv. **13**(3), 270–289 (2017)
26. Wang, J., Chen, X., Li, J., Zhao, J., Shen, J.: Towards achieving flexible and verifiable search for outsourced database in cloud computing. Futur. Gener. Comput. Syst. **67**, 266–275 (2017)
27. Wang, J., Miao, M., Gao, Y., Chen, X.: Enabling efficient approximate nearest neighbor search for outsourced database in cloud computing. Soft Comput. **20**(11), 4487–4495 (2016)
28. Xiong, J., Li, F., Wang, Y., Ma, J., Yao, Z.: Research progress on cloud data assured deletion based on cryptography. J. Commun. **37**(8), 167–184 (2016)
29. Yang, C., Chen, X., Xiang, Y.: Blockchain-based publicly verifiable data deletion scheme for cloud storage. J. Netw. Comput. Appl. **103**, 185–193 (2018)
30. Zhang, X., Jiang, T., Li, K.C., Castiglione, A., Chen, X.: New publicly verifiable computation for batch matrix multiplication. Inf. Sci. (2017). https://doi.org/10.1016/j.ins.2017.11.063
31. Zhang, Y., Xiong, J., Li, X., Jin, B., Li, S., Wang, X.A.: A multi-replica associated deleting scheme in cloud. In: 10th International Conference on Complex, Intelligent, and Software Intensive Systems, CISIS 2016, 6–8 July 2016, Fukuoka, Japan, pp. 444–448 (2016)

InterestFence: Countering Interest Flooding Attacks by Using Hash-Based Security Labels

Jiaqing Dong[1], Kai Wang[1,2]($\boxtimes$), Yongqiang Lyu[1], Libo Jiao[1], and Hao Yin[1]

[1] Tsinghua University, Beijing, China
wangkai.phd@outlook.com
[2] Yantai University, Yantai, China

Abstract. Interest Flooding Attack (IFA) has been one of the biggest threats for the Named Data Networking (NDN) paradigm, while it is very easy to launch but very difficult to mitigate. In this paper, we propose the InterestFence, which is a simple, direct, lightweight yet efficient IFA countermeasure, and the first one to achieve fast detection meanwhile accurate and efficient attacking traffic filtering without harming any legitimate Interests. InterestFence detects IFA based on content servers rather than routers to guarantee accurate detection. All content items with the same prefix within a content server have a hash-based security label (HSL) to claim their existence, and a HSL verification method is securely transmitted to related routers to help filtering and cleaning IFA traffic in transit networks accurately and efficiently. Performance analysis demonstrates the effectiveness of InterestFence on mitigating IFA and its lightweight feature due to the limited overhead involved.

Keywords: Interest Flooding Attack · Named Data Networking Security

1 Introduction

Named Data Networking (NDN) [6] has been proposed to evolve Internet from today's host-based IP networks to data-centric inter-networking paradigms by changing the network-layer protocols to place the content-distribution problem at its root [8], and has attracted wide research attentions.

As NDN gradually develops, security concerns become increasingly critical and important, and it may significantly thwart the real-world deployment of NDN if not given enough attention [9]. Although NDN aims at "security by design"[6] and successfully reduces the impact of the notorious Distributed Denial-of-Service (DDoS) attacks [7] by its receiver-driven data retrieval model, the Pending Interest Table (PIT) component of each NDN router opens up a way for a new type of NDN-specific DDoS attacks - Interest Flooding Attack (IFA), which has become one of the most dangerous threats for NDN [12].

© Springer Nature Switzerland AG 2018
J. Vaidya and J. Li (Eds.): ICA3PP 2018, LNCS 11337, pp. 527–537, 2018.
https://doi.org/10.1007/978-3-030-05063-4_39

What is IFA: PIT is one of the fundamental components of every NDN router. It records all the ongoing communication status as its entries, where the names as well as the incoming interfaces of each pending Interest packet are cached until the requested data packets are returned from corresponding content servers. IFA attacks exhaust PIT table by continuously requesting non-existing contents, whose related PIT entry would not be deleted until the Time-To-Live (TTL) of the recorded Interest packet expires. As the fake Interest packets neither leak any information about the requester's identifier nor contain any security property for each content name [3,5], the attackers are free to exclude from the IFA detection or tracing, and accurate IFA detection and attacking traffic filtering is very hard to achieve.

Why Does IFA Hurt: In contrast to the convenience of launching such an attack, it is very hard to mitigate IFA: Firstly, *attacking traffic cannot be filtered before they arrive at victim content servers*, as there is no difference between legitimate and fake Interest packets of IFA except for the existence of their requested content, which can only be exactly confirmed by the content servers rather than routers. Secondly, *interest packets contain no information on the security property of the content name*, which makes accurate detection or traffic filtering very difficult to achieve. Finally, *attackers cannot be easily identified or traced to achieve punishment*, since Interest packets in NDN do not carry any identification information about the content requesters, which makes attackers very easy to exclude from the IFA detection or tracing.

Although the effectiveness and advantage of our previous work on countering IFA has been validated by other parties [2], we aim at a further step to a more secure NDN. In this paper, we propose InterestFence, a simple yet efficient IFA countermeasure, which protects NDN from IFA by employing both *accurate IFA detection at content servers* and *efficient IFA mitigation by filtering almost all the malicious traffic at intermediary routers*. InterestFence filters malicious Interest requests based on the Hash-based Security Label (HSL) received from content servers, which can accurately identify whether an Interest packet carries a fake name or not. Each InterestFence-enabled content server has a HSL computation component, designed for generating content name corresponds to a certain HSL based on some algorithms for security concerns. When IFA happens, InterestFence-enabled content server detects illegitimate Interest requests and figure out which naming prefix is under attack (denoted as m_{pref}, meaning fake Interests with this prefix match no data within content servers). In responding to IFA, InterestFence-enabled content server transmits the m_{pref} and corresponding HSL algorithm parameters to the involved routers through an encrypted message. Involved routers thus is enabled to detect whether an Interest request with specific m_{pref} comes from IFA attacker or legitimate users and take corresponding actions, i.e., to drop or forward to next hop.

2   InterestFence

This section provides details of InterestFence's design. First we describe the overall system architecture and introduce high-level workflow of InterestFence. Afterwards we propose details of how each key component works.

2.1   System Architecture

Figure 1 shows the high-level architecture of InterestFence, consisting of three key functional entities: InterestFence-enabled router, InterestFence-enabled content server and the communication between them.

Firstly, for each content server, InterestFence adds a m_{pref} *identification component* and a *HSL generation component* for generating self-prove content name. Every content name generated by InterestFence-enabled content server contains a certain HSL as suffix generated by the *HSL generation component*, based on some hash algorithms with a secret token for security concerns. The m_{pref} *identification component* takes in charge of IFA detection by monitoring the requesting statistics of every content prefix periodically. Whenever m_{pref} is identified as under attack, the alarm message is sent to notify involved routers, to enable HSL validation for all the Interest packets with content name corresponding to the m_{pref}.

Secondly, from the perspective of each router, InterestFence introduces a malicious list $(m - list)$ module recording prefixes under IFA attack as well as their TTLs, known as m_{pref} (e.g., $/M_{pref}[1]$ with TTL_1 and $/M_{pref}[2]$ with TTL_2), and corresponding validation tokens conveyed back by the alarm message from any InterestFence-enabled content server into its *HSL verification* component. Moreover, the TTL is refreshed whenever a fake Interest is identified by the HSL verification in the router. In addition, the specifical HSL rules are also recorded in the HSL verification component, including the HSL verifying results (e.g., *HSL Unmatched* or *HSL matched* or *no HSL needed*), the security property of the incoming Interest (e.g., *Fake* or *Legitimate*) and the suggested actions on an incoming Interest packet (e.g., *Forwarded* or *Dropped*).

Finally, between content servers and routers involved in IFA traffic-travelling path, InterestFence has a channel for transmitting alarm messages for IFA notification between content servers and routers. The alarm message is a special type of Data packet used for IFA countering propose, which carries secure information (e.g., cryptographic information containing $\{m_{pref}, h, k\}$ in Fig. 1) used to verify the content name with the m_{pref} of every incoming Interest packet. In current design, InterestFence takes advantage of the NACK packets [4] to pig-back messages to the involved routers.

The basic workflow of InterestFence can be described at a high-level as following:

(1) **HSL computation** for every content name in content servers in case IFA may launch: InterestFence-enabled content servers generate legal content names following HSL generating algorithms known only by its provider, then

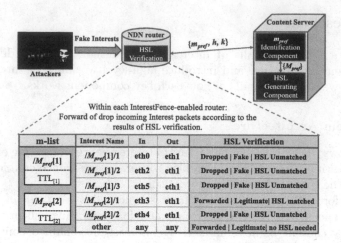

Fig. 1. System architecture of InterestFence.

sign and publish these names to the public. The HSL generating algorithms ensure that the algorithm cannot be reversely inferred so that attackers cannot fake legal names.

(2) **Identification of malicious prefix** when abnormal number of Interests requesting for non-exist content emerges: InterestFence-enabled content servers can easily detect whether itself is under IFA attack by checking whether request objects exist with the help of its m_{pref} *identification component* (see Fig. 1). Afterwards they periodically update m_{pref} under IFA attack at designated intervals.

(3) **Secure HSL transmission** from content servers to involved routers which locate along the attacking path: After each prefix identified as the m_{pref} under IFA attack, the InterestFence-enabled content servers convey corresponding HSL validating algorithms and secret tokens (e.g., $\{m_{pref}, h, k\}$) back to involved routers along the path, via a encrypted manner.

(4) **IFA Traffic filtering** based on the HSL verification component in involved routers: By comparing Interest name against the m-list via HSL verification, routers know whether a request with m_{pref} is exactly fake or not, and then make decision to forward or drop accordingly.

2.2   Malicious Prefix Identification

Whenever a content server suffers an IFA aiming at exhausting its critical resource by flooding excessive fake Interest packets, the malicious content prefix is figured out based on simple operation over all the prefixes of the unsatisfied Interest packets. Given the set of prefixes which are used in HSL computation as H_{pref}, the m_{pref} is extracted from the H_{pref} (that is, $m_{pref} \subset H_{pref}$) following the longest matching rules against Interest names, whenever there are two many fake Interest packets requesting for none-existing contents in this server within a certain duration t_{decay}.

Content names are in the form of "$/ns\_0/ns\_1/ns\_2/\ldots/ns\_k/id$". Different level of prefix indicates different level of namespaces. The content server computes the malicious prefix m_{pref} for Interest packets starting with each different root prefix.

Specifically, for each root namespace, if a content server receives n Interest packets with fake content names $N_1 = $ "$/ns\_0/ns\_1/fake$", $N_2 = $ "$/ns\_0/ns\_1/ns\_2/ekaf$" and $N_3 = $ "$/ns\_0/ns\_1/ns\_2/ns\_3/attack$" within the given pre-defined timescale t_{decay}, the m_{pref} can be computed and created as following:

$$m_{pref} = /ns\_0/ns\_1 \in H_{pref} = N_1 \cap N_2 \cap N_3 \in H_{pref} \tag{1}$$

In this case, $m_{pref} = /ns\_0/ns\_1$ is the detected malicious prefix that will be transmitted back to involved routers through an encrypted way (e.g., asymmetric cryptography technologies). Noting that the overhead caused by encrypted operations is limited (see Fig. 4, at order of milliseconds and depending on the hardware), because it only needs one cycle of such operation to finish the HSL transmission before IFA is finished.

2.3   HSL Generation and Verification

HSL is in fact a wildcard mechanism to validate whether an Interest packet contains a fake name. An Interest packet is treated as fake if its content name cannot match HSL validation.

Basic idea behind HSL is similar to that of digital signature: the message signed with a private-key can be easily validated with the corresponding public-key. In our scenario, as the adversary does not know the private-key of content servers, they cannot easily fake a name which can pass the validation with the public-key from the provider.

However, considering the frequent usage of content names in NDN network, using standard digital signature techniques without hardware support *brings high overhead to involved routers and servers*. Consequently, a simple yet efficient enough method, namely HSL, is designed for IFA detect in this paper.

For generating HSL, a certain hash algorithm will be executed over the chosen bits from the origin name. Afterwards the suffix will be treated as a signature and used for verifying whether the name is legitimate. We describe the detailed methodology as follows:

- For each content name $n \in N$, a certain hash algorithm $h(n, k) \in H$ is selected to generate its HSL m to append to n, where k indicates the bits used for hash computing and $m = h(n, k)$, to construct a new content name n', that is, $n' = g(n, m)$, where $g(x, y)$ is used to append y to x;
- To provide content service, a content server publish its content name n' to public, and content consumers use the content name n' to retrieve what they want;

- Whenever a prefix is detected as suffering IFA, the content server transmits the m_{pref} and the $h(n, k)$ to the involved routers in a secure manner (e.g., via an encrypted channel); for every prefix, the secured HSL transmission is only once, which only brings in limited overhead;
- Whenever the router receives an Interest packet, the content name prefix is checked against the m_{pref}: if matching, the HSL computation is performed based on the $h(n, k)$, which generates a verifying HSL m' for this Interest packet; and then the m' is compared with the m that is originated contained in this Interest packet; in fact, m are the last bits which has the same length with m' in the content name: if $m' \neq m$, this Interest packet is fake, otherwise it is legitimate.

Noting that attackers know neither the $h(n, k)$ nor the k, thus they cannot construct the right m, and the legitimate content name containing the matching rules between n' and n.

Even if the HSL parameters are acquired by attackers, new H_{pref} for certain prefix can also be generated on demand, which in fact consumes limited computing resource and time to finish (see overhead results in Sect. 3.3). After re-generating, all the names of this prefix should be re-registered into some name resolution system [1], to update their accessibility to any one in Internet.

3   Performance Analysis

In this section, we provide an in-depth performance analysis of our Interest flooding attack detection and mitigation method. We develop a simulation platform with sender, router and server, each with configurable parameters such as sending rate of senders, capacity and delay of links, capacity of routers, capacity of content servers and so on. We setup standard congestion control in the simulation platform.

In our experiments, we assume that legitimate users send Interest requests at a constant average rate with randomized gap between two consecutive ones, where length of gaps follow a uniform distribution. For malicious traffics, we assume that all the attackers send fake Interests as fast as they can. We vary percentage of attackers in the network to study the performance of different IFA mitigation methods.

We simulate and analyze our detection and filtering mechanism with a simple multiple sender one router one server topology instead of other complex topologies. The simple many-to-one topology is sufficient for analysis of our mechanism in that the HSL is a deterministic validation method. All involved routers get the same m_{pref} and corresponding HSL parameters from the content server and will make the same decision. As soon as the first involved router along the path detects a malicious Interest request, it will drop the Interest and thus all posterior routers will not need to check the request any more.

Existing IFA countermeasures can be categorized into two types: rate-limit based mechanisms and PIT-decouple based mechanisms. Both of these existing mechanisms detects IFA attacks based on observed statistics, for instance, satisfaction ratio of interfaces in [10], reputation of interfaces collected from coordinator [11]. For clarity, we use the same detection mechanism based on satisfaction ratio of interfaces for both mechanisms. In the uniform detection algorithm, a threshold T_r is set, interfaces with unsatisfied ratio larger than T_r will be regarded as occupied by attackers in a calculation period T. The calculation period T is derived from RTT between the router and the server. Larger T brings more accurate satisfaction ratio calculation, however in the meantime it will burden the router when attack happens in that more malicious Interest will be inserted into PIT before satisfaction ratio indicates that attack is taking place. In our experiment, T is set equal to one RTT. In addition, we implement a simple but reasonable rate-limit algorithm in our simulations, with the threshold T_r set equal to that of DPE [13]. Whenever IFA attack is detected, a pushback message will be sent downstream from this congested interface to notify corresponding routers or clients to decrease its Interest sending rate by half, forcely. Otherwise, the Interest sending rate would be increased by half.

We evaluate InterestFence mechanism from three aspects. First of all, we evaluate the efficiency of HSL. Afterwards, we investigate HSL from the perspective of quality of user experience.

3.1 Efficiency

In this experiment, our goal is to compare HSL with both rate-limit-based and PIT-decouple-based solutions in terms of efficiency. We choose the *percentage of malicious Interests reaching content server (PMR)* as the metric for evaluating efficiency. Higher percentage of malicious Interests reaching content servers results in severer computation resource consumption, indicating poor efficiency of a IFA mitigation mechanism.

Experiment Setup: for both rate-limit-based and PIT-decouple-based solutions, we set the detection parameter T_r equals to 0.8, i.e., unsatisfaction ratio larger than 80% will be regarded as under attack. The throughput capacity of router and server is set to 1 Gbps, which will limit the total sending rate of users and attackers with the help of standard congestion control. During the experiment, we vary the percentage of attackers from 10% to 70% in the network and collect statistics at the server side to calculate percentage of malicious Interests succesfully pass through the router.

In Fig. 2, we vary the percentage of attackers and compare the PMR value in steady state during attack happens. As shown in Fig. 2, HSL always keeps PMR to 0, while DPE always keep PMR to 100% and rate-limit solution gets higher PMR value as percentage of attackers in the network increases. That is the HSL of InterestFence successfully filters and cleans attackint traffic before causing further damage.

These two experiment demonstrates that HSL is quite efficient in filtering malicious traffics and protecting the routers and content servers from IFA attacks.

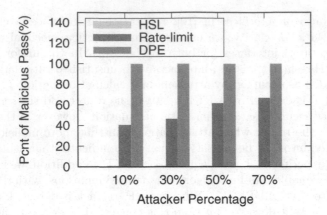

Fig. 2. Comparison of malicious Interest pass pcnt of different mechanism under various attack burden

3.2   Quality of Experience

In terms of quality of experience, we choose the *percentage of satisfied Intesets (PSI)* for legitimate users as the metric. This metric quantifies the quality of service experienced by legitimate users when the network is under attack. For two different methods A and B, if legitimate users of the network equipped with method A achieve a higher percentage of user-satisfied Interests while the network is under attack than that of the network equipped with method B, then one can conclude that method A is more effective than method B at mitigating the IFA attack.

Experiment Setup: experiment setup is the same as in previous experiment. During the experiment, we collect statistics at the sender side to calculate the percentage of satisfied Interests of legitimate users.

In Fig. 3, we vary the percentage of attackers and compare the PSI value in steady state during attack happens. As shown in Fig. 3, HSL always keeps PSI to nearly 100%. Rate-limit solution gets smaller PSI value as percentage of attackers in the network increases. An interesting result is that, while DPE keeps PSI nearly 100% when attack burden is not very high, when percentage of attackers gets extremely high, DPE starts to perform even worse than rate-limit solutions. This is because high load malicious Interest reaching the server begin exhausting computation resource at the server.

These experiments proves that HSL can ensure user experience during IFA attack significantly better than existing works. DPE is poorer than HSL in that all malicious are forwarded to content servers and the server takes more computation resource to fight against the attack. DPE performs better than rate-limit solution because intermediary routers are set free from malicious Interest in DPE.

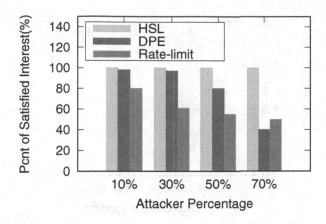

Fig. 3. Comparison of Interest satisfied pcnt of different mechanism under various attack burden

3.3   Overhead

Considering the high frequent usage of validation in network scenario, a trade-off is required between the overhead and security level. HSL shares a similar idea with digital signature mechanism, while it is much simpler in terms of computation complexity. In this experiment, we compare HSL with typical digital signature technique, asymmetric RSA signature, from the aspect of both overhead and security.

This experiment requires no network setup, but comparing the computation resource consumption. We choose *time per-signature* and *time per-validation* as the two metrics to evaluate the overhead. Higher time per-signature or per-validation all stand for higher overhead. In terms of security, we use *false positive* and *false negative* to measure security.

Dataset used in this experiment is 100,000 URLs we crawled from Sina of China, one of the top content providers in China. We classify these URLs based on their sub-domains and transform them into the form of a Interest name in NDN.

During the experiment, we setup a single thread with adequate memory resource. We read into a thousand URLs into the memory one time and sign the URLs one by one separately with RSA and HSL, and then we calculate the average per-signature time of RSA and HSL. Similarly, we get the average per-validation time of RSA and HSL, correspondingly.

The result is shown in Fig. 4. As we see, RSA takes as much as 30X longer time in signature and 5X more time in validation than HSL, indicating that RSA consumes much times more computation resource.

Then we compare RSA and HSL in terms of security. For the 100,000 URLs, we randomly generates names for each prefix as the fake name for attackers. We want to figureout the percentage of fake names that can pass HSL validation.

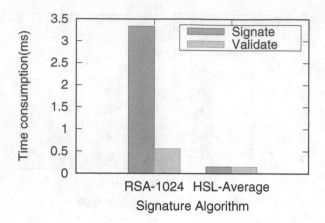

Fig. 4. Trade-off between overhead and security.

In our experiment, we see that HSL has a possibility of 1% to mistakenly treat a randomly generated fake name as a legal one. In other words, HSL trades a false positive rate of 1% for a several tens of performance increase. We do not claim that HSL provides as security guarantee as provided by RSA and other complex signature mechanisms. But we state that it is worthwhile to make a sacrifice for performance by using comparatively simple hashing algorithm. If a system has a very strict requirement for security concern, RSA and similar complex but securer algorithms should be used instead of our simple hashing algorithm.

4   Conclusion

We presented InterestFence, the first IFA mitigation framework that can accurately identify and filter IFA traffic in an efficient manner. InterestFence is based on two key contributions: *(i)* a fast and accurate HSL generating algorithm at content servers; and *(ii)* a lightweight and accurate name verification algorithm at routers.

We performed extensive evaluations of InterestFence using practical functional component simulations on real trace data, and gives comprehensive analysis on the results, which indicate that InterestFence is efficient in both detecting and mitigating Interest flooding attacks. InterestFence can filter out all malicious traffic and achieves almost 100% legitimate Interest satisfaction ratio with very low overhead.

Acknowledgment. This work is supported by China Postdoctoral Science Foundation (No. 2017M620786), Shandong Provincial Natural Science Foundation, China (No. ZR2017BF018), National Natural Science Foundation of China (NSFC) (No. 61702439, 61502410, 61602399, 61672318, 61631013), Shandong Province Higher Educational Science and Technology Program (No. J16LN17) and National Key Research and Development Program (No. 2016YFB1000102).

References

1. Afanasyev, A., et al.: NDNS: a DNS-like name service for NDN. In: Proceedings of the 26th International Conference on Computer Communications and Networks (ICCCN), Vancouver, BC, Canada, pp. 1–9, July 2017
2. Al-Sheikh, S., Wählisch, M., Schmidt, T.C.: Revisiting countermeasures against NDN interest flooding, San Francisco, CA, USA, pp. 195–196, September 2015
3. Compagno, A., Conti, M., Gasti, P., Tsudik, G.: Poseidon: mitigating interest flooding DDoS attacks in named data networking, Sydney, NSW, Australia, pp. 630–638, October 2013
4. Compagno, A., Conti, M., Ghali, C., Tsudik, G.: To NACK or not to NACK? Negative acknowledgments in information-centric networking, Las Vegas, NV, USA, pp. 1–10, August 2015
5. Gasti, P., Tsudik, G., Uzun, E., Zhang, L.: DoS and DDoS in named data networking. In: Proceedings of 22nd International Conference on Computer Communication and Networks (ICCCN), Nassau, Bahamas, pp. 1–7, October 2013
6. Jacobson, V., Smetters, D.K., Thornton, J.D., Plass, M., Briggs, N., Braynard, R.: Networking named content. Commun. ACM **55**(1), 117–124 (2012)
7. Liu, X., Yang, X., Xia, Y.: NetFence: preventing internet denial of service from inside out. In: Proceedings of ACM SIGCOMM, New Delhi, India, pp. 255–266, August 2010
8. Mangili, M., Martignon, F., Capone, A.: Performance analysis of content-centric and content-delivery networks with evolving object popularity. Comput. Netw. **94**, 80–88 (2016)
9. Ngai, E., Ohlman, B., Tsudik, G., Uzun, E., Wählisch, M., Wood, C.A.: Can we make a cake and eat it too? A discussion of ICN security and privacy. ACM SIGCOMM Comput. Commun. Rev. **47**, 49–54 (2017)
10. Nguyen, T., Cogranne, R., Doyen, G.: An optimal statistical test for robust detection against interest flooding attacks in CCN, Ottawa, ON, Canada, pp. 252–260, May 2015
11. Salah, H., Wulfheide, J., Strufe, T.: Lightweight coordinated defence against interest flooding attacks in NDN, Hong Kong, China, pp. 103–104, April 2015
12. Tourani, R., Misra, S., Mick, T., Panwar, G.: Security, privacy, and access control in information-centric networking: a survey. IEEE Commun. Surv. Tutor. **20**(1), 566–600 (2018). https://doi.org/10.1109/COMST.2017.2749508. ISSN 1553-877X
13. Wang, K., Zhou, H., Qin, Y., Chen, J., Zhang, H.: Decoupling malicious interests from pending interest table to mitigate interest flooding attacks. In: Proceedings of IEEE Globecom Workshops (GC Wkshps). Atlanta, GA, USA, pp. 963–968, December 2013

A Secure and Targeted Mobile Coupon Delivery Scheme Using Blockchain

Yingjie Gu[1,2], Xiaolin Gui[1,2(✉)], Pan Xu[1,2], Ruowei Gui[1],
Yingliang Zhao[1], and Wenjie Liu[1,2]

[1] School of Electronics and Information Engineering, Xi'an Jiaotong University, Xi'an, China
{gyj123wxc,panchance,r.w.gui,lwj19940706}@stu.xjtu.edu.cn,
xlgui@mail.xjtu.edu.cn, ylzhao.xjtu@xjtu.edu.cn
[2] Shaanxi Province Key Laboratory of Computer Network,
Xi'an Jiaotong University, Xi'an, China

Abstract. This paper presents a new secure and targeted mobile coupon delivery scheme based on blockchain. Our goal is to design a decentralized targeted mobile coupon delivery framework, which enables the secure delivery of targeted coupons to eligible mobile users whose behavioral profiles accurately satisfy the targeting profile defined by the vendor. It does not require trusted third-party meanwhile protects the mobile user and vendor's information security, including user privacy, data integrity and rights protection. We adopt Policy-Data Contract Pair (PDCP) to control the transfer of information between users and vendors and use encryption algorithm to ensure the data security. Once transactions containing signatures are recorded in the blockchain after consensus, they become non-repudiation. Theoretical analysis and simulation experimental results demonstrate that our model has higher security and lower computation than JG'16 scheme.

Keywords: Targeted coupon delivery · Blockchain · Policy-Data Contract Pair
Information security · Non-repudiation

1 Introduction

Mobile coupon targeted delivery is becoming increasingly prevalent. Vendors hope to increase sales by issuing coupons purposefully according to users' information. Users also want to cut down expenses in the goods of their interest, without wasting bandwidth for uninteresting information. Nowadays, mobile coupon targeted delivery has come to rely more heavily on behavioral targeting [1], since users' behavioral targeting is the only basis for the vendor to determine accurately whether a user meets delivery demands. Hence, before issuing coupons, vendors may collect users' behavior information such as location, network behavior, life style and so on.

However, it could arise users' privacy concerns [2, 3] and even the user's rights could be violated if some spiteful vendors issue fake coupons to users. Beyond that, vendors also do not want to disclose their coupon delivery strategy in advance, in case malicious users forge their behavioral targeting. That is to say both users and vendors want their

© Springer Nature Switzerland AG 2018
J. Vaidya and J. Li (Eds.): ICA3PP 2018, LNCS 11337, pp. 538–548, 2018.
https://doi.org/10.1007/978-3-030-05063-4_40

information to be honest and integrated, which cannot be tampered with or forged by malicious parties. Prior work aimed at achieving secure targeted coupon delivery either leaked vendor's coupon strategy to the user [4], or required vendors to offer coupons to the user who does not meet the demands [5]. To our best knowledge, secure and targeted coupon delivery is still challenging, and to design a secure, accurate and practical targeted coupon delivery system remains to be fully explored, especially for resource-limited mobile devices.

In this paper, we propose a scheme based on blockchain technology for mobile coupon targeted delivery in order to solve the potential security risks and the rights and interests risks caused by the traditional scheme based on privacy protection.

2   Background and Related Work

2.1   Blockchain Technology

Blockchain is the underlying technology for encrypted digital currency like Bitcoin system [6]. It is a distributed database that maintains a growing list of blocks which are linked one by one. More than that, from 2015 to now, blockchain has been widely applied in Internet of Things [7], Big Data [8], Resources Management [9], Edge Computing [10] and so on because of its unique data structure and internal algorithms (consensus mechanism, cryptographic algorithms, timestamps, smart contract, etc.). The features such as decentralized trust, timing data that cannot be tampered and forged, programmable contract and anonymity [11] provide a new solution to the security problem of the mobile coupon targeted delivery.

2.2   Motivation and Related Work

Secure coupon targeted delivery service is one type of secure advertising targeted delivery service. In recent years, there are many scholars studying on the secure coupons targeted delivery service scheme [1, 3–5, 12–14]. In this section, we compare our block-chain-based scheme with some of existing secure targeted mobile coupon deliveries in Table 1 and list their deficiencies.

Table 1. Comparison of four schemes.

Scheme	Technology	Security analysis
RU'14 [4]	Fuzzy commitment	Vendor's coupon delivery strategy may be disclosed
Picoda [5]	LSH, PAKE	Non eligible users may receive coupons
JG'16 [12]	Paillier homomorphic encryption, Garbled circuits, Random masking	Replay attack, Need trusted third party
Our scheme	Blockchain technology (P2P, Consensus mechanism, ECC, Hash and smart contract)	Secure, Data can be tracked, Data cannot be tampered or forged

Among them, RU'14 leverages fuzzy commitment technology to design secure coupon targeting delivery scheme, which may result in vendors' coupon delivery strategy to be disclosed. Picoda achieves privacy-preserving targeted coupon delivery based on local-sensitive hashing technology and password authenticated key exchange protocol but it may let non-eligible users receive coupons because of the false positives in LSH. The latest research scheme JG'16 adopts Paillier homomorphic encryption, garbled circuits and random masking to construct a secure and targeted mobile coupon delivery scheme. This scheme could protect the data privacy of users and vendors well, but it has the following hidden dangers. (1) JG'16 needs a credible third-party CSP but it cannot be guaranteed. (2) JG'16 is unable to resist replay attack from attackers. (3) As the number of users and vendors increases, the computational costs of the CSP may increase dramatically. Therefore, it is an urgent issue to develop a new scheme that can protect the information security of users and vendors as well as the rights and interests.

In this paper, we leverage a blockchain decentralized structure, consensus mechanisms, cryptography algorithm and smart contracts to achieve a privacy-preserving scheme for secure and targeted mobile coupon delivery whose data can be tracked and cannot be tampered or forged. Compared with existing schemes, our scheme could deliver coupons to eligible users securely while protecting data privacy of users and vendors, without the need of trusted third parties. Furthermore, our design could protect the rights and interests of users and vendors through data trace and tampering prevention.

3 Problem Statement

First, we show our key notations in Table 2. We consider the user's behavioral profile P_u as an n-dimensional vector, i.e., $P_u = (u_1, u_2, \ldots, u_n)$, where each element u_i is an integer that refers to the value of an attribute according to the protocol. For instance, u_1 is the value of attribute Diet which represents the combination of weight coefficient about preference of western food w_{11}, Japanese food w_{12} and Chinese food w_{13}, i.e., $u_1 = w_{11}||w_{12}|| \cdots ||w_{1k}$, here we consider each w_{ij} as a four bits binary number, and u_2 is the value of attribute Entertainment which represents the combination of weight coefficient about preference of movies w_{21}, singing w_{22}, games w_{23} and so on. Likewise, the targeting profile P_v is also represented as an n-dimensional vector, i.e., $P_v = (v_1, v_2, \ldots, v_n)$. Vendors set their own attributes and weighted values according to the protocol, and unrelated attributes should be set to zero. For example, a restaurant should set the value of attributes like Entertainment and Clothing to zero. Similar with P_u, each dimension is the combination of weight coefficient such as $v_1 = m_{11}||m_{12}|| \cdots ||m_{1k}$. The vendor should transform the targeting profile to P'_v according to the following rule when publishing their delivery strategy in order to hide specific information: if $v_i > 0$, then set $P'(v_i) = 1$, otherwise set $P'(v_i) = 0$.

Table 2. Key notations.

Notation	Definition
P_u	Behavioral profile of user u
P_v	Targeting profile of vendor v
P'_v	Published targeting profile of vendor v
P_{uv}	Behavioral profile of user u associated with vendor v
w_{ij}, m_{ij}	The value of each dimension attribute
sk_u, sk_v	Secret key of user u or vendor v
$<pk_u, A_u>$	Public key and node address of user u
$<pk_v, A_v>$	Public key and node address of vendor v
δ_u, δ_v	Signature of user u or vendor v
Tx_P, Tx_D	Eligibility test parameter
S	System parameters including timestamp and others in blockchain structure

The user generates a new behavioral profile P_{uv} on the basis of P_u and P'_v on his mobile device when he finds an interested vendor. Specifically, the user performs bitwise operations that if $P'(v_i) = 0$ then set $P_{uv}(i) = 0$, if $P'(v_i) = 1$ then $P_{uv}(i) = P(u_i)$, to get P_{uv}. The eligibility requirement for the user to obtain a particular coupon is that the distance (such as squared Euclidean) between the new behavioral profile P_{uv} and the targeting profile P_v is within a threshold ε, i.e., $Dist(P_{uv}, P_v) \leq \varepsilon$, and the vendor has the right to issue specific coupons to the user only in the case of the user having a subjective desire. Besides, we consider adopting a Policy-Data contract pair model to improve system security. We will describe in detail about Policy-Data Contract Pair (PDCP) in the next section.

4 Design of BC-Based Scheme for Secure and Targeted Mobile Coupon Delivery

4.1 Proposed Protocol

We now present the protocol for our scheme, and the detailed protocol proceeds as follows:

1. **System Setup.** Vendors will build a blockchain network platform in accordance of an original agreement which contains consensus mechanism, cryptographic algorithms, and data formats of transactions and attributes and so on. The genesis block that records the information of initial nodes will be backed-up permanently in users and vendors' device. The local client randomly generates the user's private key sk_u and saves it offline on the local device. Then, pk_u will be transformed into the user's public key through Elliptic Curve Cryptography and now the user gets his own key pair $<pk_u, sk_u>$. Similar to Bitcoin system, we have to convert pk_u to a network address A_u in order to increase readability. A_u is the address for sending and receiving

transaction. In the same way, the vendor obtains his own key pair $<pk_v, sk_v>$ and network address A_v when joining the system. The user must set his behavioral profile P_u at the local client when he joins in the blockchain network. Similarly, the vendor also sets his targeting profile P_v according to his scope of service.

2. **Policy-Data Contract Pair.** In the scheme proposed in this paper, the contract in the request transaction initiated by the user is called Policy Contract, and the contract in the response transaction initiated by the vendor is called Data Contract. Policy Contract and Data Contract are indispensable and restrict each other. The Policy Contract includes the operation of transmitting the user data to the specific vendor according to the output address when certain conditions are met. The purpose of the Policy Contract is to indicate to the vendor that a specific user has issued a coupon request and permit the vendor to obtain his personal data. Data Contract includes the operation of transmitting the coupon data to the specific user according to the output address when certain conditions are met. In particular, the transaction that contains Data Contract must have the hash value of previous transaction that contains Policy Contract. If a vendor broadcasts a transaction without the specific hash value, the Data Contract will be triggered and the transaction will be considered invalid.

3. **Secure and Targeted Coupon Delivery.** As illustrated in Fig. 1, our protocol supports secure and targeted mobile coupon delivery as follows:

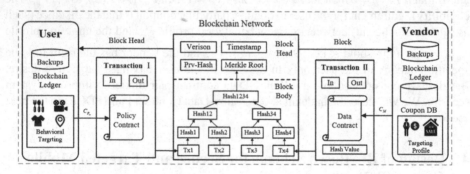

Fig. 1. BC-based secure and targeted mobile coupon delivery framework

(a) The user first preprocesses his behavioral profile P_u to produce P_{uv} related to the vendor when the user finds his interested vendor and hopes to acquire the coupons.

We use the vendor's public key pk_v to encrypt P_{uv} and then the ciphertext $C_{P_{uv}}$ is written into a Policy Contract (PC). The transaction that contains input address A_u, output address A_v, policy contract and other data is going to be broadcasted to the blockchain network. δ_u is the digital signature of the transaction by utilizing user's secret key sk_u. Here is our algorithm on the user side.

Algorithm 1. User Setting

$Input : P_u, P_v', sk_u, A_u, A_v$

$Output : Tx_p$

1: $C_{P_{uv}} \leftarrow Enc_{pk_v}(P_{uv}), P_{uv} \leftarrow P_u \otimes P_v'$

2: $Tx \leftarrow (PC, A_{ui}, A_v, S)$

3: $Tx_p \leftarrow (Tx \| \delta_u), \delta_u \leftarrow Sig_{sk_u}(Tx)$

(b) Upon receiving the transaction created by the user, vendor nodes first verify the validity of the transaction. If it is an illegal transaction caused by format error or signature error, nodes reject this transaction. If it is a legitimate transaction, this transaction and some other transactions which have already been verified but not been written into blockchain will be recorded permanently in current block after nodes consensus. In particular, vendor nodes backup full blockchain data while user nodes just backup the block head data in their blockchain ledger database.

(c) The Policy Contract in the transaction will be triggered after the backup is completed and then $C_{P_{uv}}$ is sent to the vendor by the output address A_v. The vendor decrypts $C_{P_{uv}}$ with his private key sk_v, and then calculates the distance between P_{uv} and P_v. If $Dist(P_{uv}, P_v) > \varepsilon$, the vendor sends a void message to the user. If $Dist(P_{uv}, P_v) \leq \varepsilon$, the vendor encrypts his coupon M with the user's public key pk_u and the coupon ciphertext C_M is written into a Data Contract (DC). Then the transaction that contains input address A_v, output address A_u, data contract and other data is going to be broadcasted to blockchain network. δ_v is the digital signature of the transaction by utilizing user's secret key sk_v. Here is our algorithm on the vendor side.

Algorithm 2. Vendor Setting

$Input: C_{P_{uv}}, P_v, sk_v, A_u, A_v, M$

$Output : Tx_D$

1: $P_{uv} \leftarrow Dec_{sk_v}(C_{P_{uv}})$

2: if $Dist(P_{uv}, P_v) \leq \varepsilon$ return $C_M \leftarrow Enc_{pk_u}(M)$

3: else return $False$

4: $Tx \leftarrow (DC, A_u, A_v, H(Tx_p), S)$

5: $Tx_D \leftarrow (Tx \| \delta_v), \delta_v \leftarrow Sig_{sk_v}(Tx)$

(d) Similar to (b), the vendor nodes (consensus nodes) first verify the validity of the transaction and then reach consensus, finally record effective transactions into a new block. In particular, the transaction that includes data contract must have the hash value of the transaction that includes policy contract and is signed by the same user.

(e) The Data Contract in the transaction will be triggered after the backup is completed. The coupon ciphertext C_M could be decrypted by the user's private key sk_u. In the end, the user gets the coupon.

4.2 Security Analysis

1. **Analyze the trust security between three entities.** (1) The proposed scheme in this paper does not require any third party, hence, there is no need to consider the safety assumption that each participating entity is honestly operating according to a predetermined protocol and does not collude with each other. (2) The consensus mechanism in blockchain directly solves the problem of trust and security between vendors and users. Even there are some dishonest nodes (less then 1/3), it will not affect the security of the system.

2. **Analyze the security of users and vendors' data and rights.** (1) It is extremely difficult to find the private key by traversing the entire private key space because the number of private keys could be 2^{256}. (2) P_{uv} is encrypted by ECC and it provides equivalent or higher levels of security by using smaller key space compared to RSA. (3) The integrity of coupon targeted delivery between users and vendors is guaranteed by the digital signatures, Merkle trees and policy-data contract pair. The system can present a complete transaction chain in the event of an infringement owing to the backup of blockchain, which could ensure the security of the rights and interests.

5 Performance Evaluation

5.1 Implement

We implement a preliminary system prototype for our proposed design in Java. Our user-side prototype is deployed on an Android VM, while our vendor-side prototype is deployed on a desktop PC which is equipped with a two-core 2.7 GHz processor and 8.0 GB RAM. For Blockchain, we adopt one-input-one-output transaction structure, ECDSA as signature algorithm and PBFT as consensus algorithm. Without loss of generality, we use the number n of dimensions ranging from 10 to 60 as example cases in our experiments, so as to thoroughly evaluate the performance. We remark that such a setting is reasonable to conform the real-world user targeting applications (e.g., Facebook uses 98 personal data points for user targeting [15]). We set the size of vendor's coupon as 128 Byte, which is reasonable because it only need to include text information such as the vendor name, discount, and time.

5.2 Performance Evaluation

We now investigate the performance overheads at the user and the vendor. Our performance evaluation will be conducted in two aspects: computation and bandwidth. All the results are averaged over 10 runs.

1. **Computation consumption.**
   (a) User Side. The computation overheads on the user consist of the generation of an asymmetric key pair, the encryption of his behavioral profile, the generation of the user's digital signature of the transaction and the decryption of coupon ciphertext.

   Firstly, we measure the key generation time on the user side, which turns out to be *221.07* ms. Note that this is a one-time cost during system setup. Secondly, we measure the decryption time of coupon cyphertext, which turns out to be *28.3* ms. Then we measure the signature generation time on the user side, which turns out to be *15.8* ms. Finally, we measure the encryption time of user's behavioral profile, when the number of profile dimensions n varies from 10 to 60, the encryption time ranges from *143.6* ms to *661.9* ms. Figure 2(a) shows the comparison with JG'16 scheme. The comparison results show that the computation consumption in encryption of our solution is smaller than that of JG'16 (average *48.22%*). Overall, our proposed design achieves practical computation performance on the user side.

   (b) Vendor Side. The computation overheads on the vendor consist of the generation of an asymmetric key pair, the decryption of user's behavioral profile, the generation of vendor's digital signature of the transaction and the encryption of coupon. In addition, as a consensus node, the vendor also has to pay the computational cost of consensus and digital signature verification in the Blockchain.

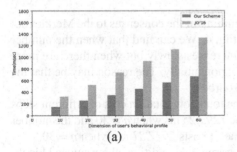 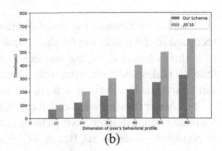

(a)　　　　　　　　　　　　　　(b)

Fig. 2. Time of encrypting and decrypting the behavioral profile on user/vendor side

Firstly, we measure the transaction verification time, which turns out to be *33.7* ms. Note that the key generation time and digital signature time on the vendor side are close to the user side, because the same encryption scheme has the same algorithm and key length. Secondly, we measure the encryption time of coupon, which turns out to be *59.6* ms. Then we measure the decryption time of user's behavioral profile, when the number of profile dimensions n varies from 10 to 60, the encryption time ranges from *66.9* ms to *323.2* ms, similar to user side, Fig. 2(b) shows the comparison with JG'16 scheme. Particularly, here is the homomorphic encryption time in JG'16 scheme. The comparison results show that the computation consumption in decryption of our solution is smaller than that in JG'16 (average *60.34%*).

2. **Bandwidth consumption.** The bandwidth overheads in our scheme is primarily targeted at the user side. This setting is reasonable because most of the vendors are covered with wireless networks and just need a bit cost. But bandwidth is still a kind of precious resources for mobile devices, especially when they operate in cellular networks. The bandwidth consumption mainly consists of transporting transaction to blockchain network, backing up block head from the blockchain and receiving the encrypted coupon. Firstly, the size of coupon ciphertext we got is 276 Byte and the size of a block head is 80 Byte. Then we measure the size of encrypted user's behavioral profile because it is the main part of transaction, when the number of profile dimensions n varies from 10 to 60, the size of encrypted profile ranges from *690* Byte to *4.14* KB. Figure 3 shows the comparison with JG'16 scheme. The comparison results show that the bandwidth consumption in our solution is smaller than that in JG'16 (average *27.60%*).

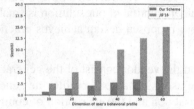
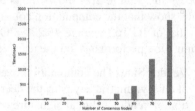

Fig. 3. Size of encrypted the behavioral profile on user side

Fig. 4. Time consumption from consensus to Merle root recorded

Finally, we measure the time from the beginning of the consensus to the Merkle root recorded in the block, the result is shown in Fig. 4. We can find that when the number of nodes is less than *70*, the consensus time increases slowly but when there are more than *70* nodes, the consensus time increases exponentially. The reason may be that the same physical host has limited computing resources.

For better illustration, we also calculate the total computation cost of different steps for once coupon delivery, which turns out to be *1293.25* ms when $n = 30$ and the number of consensus nodes is 50. But in JG'16 scheme, it costs *2027.31* ms when $n = 30$.

In summary, under the same data and experimental conditions the proposed blockchain-based secure and targeted mobile coupon delivery has less computational overhead than the JG'16 scheme and achieves practical computation performance on the users and vendors' sides.

6   Conclusion

In this paper we propose a blockchain-based secure and targeted mobile coupon delivery scheme combining with privacy protection technologies. Our scheme enables coupons only be delivered to eligible users whose behavioral profiles accurately match the targeting profile defined by the vendor, while protecting users and vendors' privacy. We implemented a preliminary system prototype for our proposed design, and conducted security analysis and experiments for performance evaluation compared with JG'16 scheme. The results indicate that our proposed design is superior to JG'16.

Acknowledgments. This work was partially supported by the National Natural Science Foundation of China (61472316, 61502380), the key Research and Development Program of Shaanxi Province (2017ZDXM-GY-011), the grant Basic Research Program of Shaanxi Province (2016ZDJC-05), and the Science and Technology Program of Shenzhen (JCYJ20170 816100939373).

References

1. Partridge, K., Bo, B.: Activity-Based Advertising. Human-Computer Interaction Series, pp. 83–101. Springer, Heidelberg (2011). https://doi.org/10.1007/978-0-85729-352-7_4
2. Nath, S.: MAdScope: characterizing mobile in-app targeted ads. In: Proceedings of the International Conference on Mobile Systems, Applications, and Services, pp. 59–73 (2015)
3. Hua, J., Tang, A., Zhong, S.: Advertiser and publisher-centric privacy aware online behavioral advertising. In: Proceedings of the International Conference on Distributed Computing Systems, pp. 298–307 (2015)
4. Rane, S., Uzun, E.: A fuzzy commitment approach to privacy preserving behavioral targeting. In: Proceedings of the ACM MobiCom Workshop on Security and Privacy in Mobile Environments, pp. 31–35 (2014)
5. Partridge, K., Pathak, M.A., Uzun, E., et al.: PiCoDa: privacy-preserving smart coupon delivery architecture. In: Proceedings of Hot Topics in Privacy Enhancing Technologies, pp. 1–15 (2012)
6. Nakamoto, S.: Bitcoin: a peer-to-peer electronic cash system. Consulted (2008)
7. Dorri, A., Kanhere, S.S., Jurdak, R.: Towards an optimized blockchain for IoT. In: Proceedings of the ACM 2nd International Conference on Internet-of-Things Design and Implementation, pp. 173–178 (2017)
8. Abdullah, N., Hakansson, A., Moradian, E.: Blockchain based approach to enhance big data authentication in distributed environment. In: Proceedings of the International Conference on Ubiquitous and Future Networks, pp. 887–892 (2017)
9. Imbault, F., Swiatek, M., Beaufort, R.D., et al.: The green blockchain: managing decentralized energy production and consumption. In: Proceedings of the IEEE International Conference on Environment and Electrical Engineering and 2017 IEEE Industrial and Commercial Power Systems Europe, pp. 1–5 (2017)
10. Stanciu, A.: Blockchain based distributed control system for edge computing. In: Proceedings of the International Conference on Control Systems and Computer Science, pp. 667–671 (2017)
11. Yuan, Y., Wang, Y.F.: Blockchain: the state of the art and future trends. Acta Automatica Sinica **42**(4), 481–494 (2016)
12. Jiang, J., Zheng, Y., Yuan, X., et al.: Towards secure and accurate targeted mobile coupon delivery. IEEE Access **99**(4), 8116–8126 (2017)
13. Banerjee, S., Yancey, S.: Enhancing mobile coupon redemption in fast food campaigns. J. Res. Interact. Market. **2**(4), 97–110 (2010)

14. Wray, J., Plante, D., Jalbert, T.: Mobile advertising engine for centralized mobile coupon delivery. Soc. Sci. Electron. Publ. **4**(1), 75–85 (2011)
15. 98 Personal Data Points That Facebook Uses to Target ADS to You. https://www.washingtonpost.com/news/theintersect/wp/2016/08/19/98-personal-data-points-that-facebook-uses-to-target-ads-to-you/. Accessed 1 Oct 2016

Access Delay Analysis in String Multi-hop Wireless Network Under Jamming Attack

Jianwei Liu[1(✉)] and Jianhua Fan[2]

[1] Army Engineering University of PLA, Nanjing 210007, China
619883059@qq.com
[2] National University of Defense Technology, Nanjing 210007, China

Abstract. Wireless networks can be easily attacked by jammers due to their shared nature and open access to the wireless medium. Jamming attack can degrade the network performance significantly by emitting useless signals to the wireless channel, i.e. the access delay of nodes' packets will increase under jamming scenarios. In order to analyze the impact of jamming attack, this paper investigates the access delay of nodes' packets in a string multi-hop wireless network. Specially, a ring-based model is put forward to calculate the existing probability of the jammer based on the stochastic geometry theory. Then, the collision probabilities of the nodes in different locations are derived while considering the impact of neighbor nodes and jammers. At last, the access delay of the packets under IEEE 802.11 protocols is obtained. A series of numerical tests are conducted to illustrate the impact of different jamming probabilities or jammer densities on the access delay.

Keywords: IEEE 802.11 · Access delay · String wireless network
Jamming attack

1 Introduction

In recent years, the String Multi-Hop Wireless Network (SMHWN) has been paid much attention by researchers due to its widely employment in several scenarios, such as Vehicular Network. In order to decrease the collision probability of nodes, IEEE 802.11 protocols have been employed in SMHWN. To be specific, 802.11 MAC protocol provides a distributed coordination function (DCF) mechanism based on the Carrier Sense Multiple Access with Collision Avoidance (CSMA/CA) scheme. According to the DCF mechanism, the node will sense the wireless channel firstly before sending packets. When the channel is idle for a period of DCF Inter-frame Space (DIFS), the packets can be sent out. Otherwise, the node will wait for a certain time before sending it again. Request to send (RTS)/clear to send (CTS) is a typical mechanism with four-way handshaking in DCF.

As another important factor in evaluating the network performance, delay analysis in the wireless network has been paid much attention by several researchers, especially for the network with delay sensitive applications. In order to obtain the delay of end-to-end transmission in the string-topology wireless network, Kosuke et al. employed the

© Springer Nature Switzerland AG 2018
J. Vaidya and J. Li (Eds.): ICA3PP 2018, LNCS 11337, pp. 549–559, 2018.
https://doi.org/10.1007/978-3-030-05063-4_41

'airtime' expressions to derive the correlation expressions of transmission probability and collision probability [14].

On the other hand, due to the open and sharing characteristics of wireless channels, jamming attack can be initiated from multiple layers with the aim to degrade the network performance maliciously. Xu et al. conducted a series of research on the jamming attack firstly and analyzed the impact of jamming attack on network performance through a series of simulations [15].

In conclusion, although [7] and [14] have analyzed the performance of 802.11 wireless network, the impact of jammer attack is not considered. In addition, [15] has analyzed the impact of jammer attacks on the wireless network based on the assumption of the nodes are homogeneous, which is not held for the nodes in SMHWN. To be specific, the collision probabilities of nodes are closely related to their locations in SMHWN.

Inspired by the above motivations, the impact of jamming attack on the access delay of nodes in SMHWN is investigated in this paper. Specially, a ring-based model is put forward to calculate the existing probability of the jammers based on stochastic geometry theory. Then, before calculating the collision probabilities, the nodes are divided into two categories according to their locations. Afterwards, the collision probabilities of these two kinds of nodes are discussed while taking the impact of neighbor nodes and jammers into consideration based on the ring-based model and jamming strategy. At last, the access delays of the nodes are derived after obtaining the transmission probabilities of each node. A series of numerical tests are conducted to illustrate the impact of jamming attack on the access delay under different jamming probabilities or jammer densities.

The rest of paper is organized as follow. Section 2 overviews related studies on the delay analysis of wireless network and the impact of jamming attack on the network performance. In Sect. 3, we present the network model, jamming model, and propagation model. The calculations of collision probability and access delay are discussed in Sect. 4. Section 5 presents a series of numerical test. Finally, the contributions of this paper are concluded in Sect. 6.

2   Related Work

Several studies have been presented to conduct the jamming analysis [10–13]. In [11], link-layer jamming algorithms that are based on minimal knowledge of the target protocols were purposed. In wireless senor network, authors put forward the corresponding effective measures to the link jamming attacks. Bayraktaroglu et al. studied the performance of the IEEE 802.11 MAC protocol under a range of jammers and derived the saturation throughput under different jamming ways [10].

Considering access delay is an important factor in evaluating the SMHWN performances. Many algorithms and models have been proposed to analyze the access delay in recent years [1–9]. In [3], big-O expressions for the end-to-end delay of static and mobile node networks were derived under full scheduling and routing conditions. Moreover, Carvalho et al. conducted a research on average service time of per node for an ad hoc network under saturation condition in [9]. There are many papers on the distribution of the access delay. Considering the hidden interfering terminal problem, Jiao et al. calculated the end-to-end delay distribution in multi-hop network under the general traffic arrival process and *Nakagami-m* channel model [1].

3 System Model

3.1 Network Model

A typical SMHWN considered in our analysis is shown in Fig. 1 and several basic assumptions of the network are illustrated as follows:

- IEEE 802.11 protocols are employed to conduct the wireless communication.
- The wireless nodes are all assumed to be equipped with omnidirectional antennas.
- The computing, transmission, and storage capabilities of nodes are assumed to be similar. The distance between neighbor nodes is equal to each other.
- Each node can sense the transmission of its neighboring nodes. Namely, node i can sense the transmissions from node $i - 1$ and node $i + 1$.
- The nodes are assumed to be under saturation condition. In other words, each node always has at least a packet to transmit.

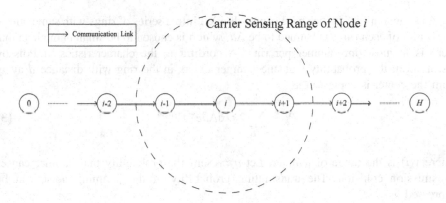

Fig. 1. Network model

3.2 Jamming Model

The memoryless jammer equipped with omnidirectional antenna is adopted in our analysis to model the jammers. To be specific, the jamming noise will be sent to the wireless channel at a certain probability for each jammer. Under jamming scenario, the normal transmission may be disturbed when the received jamming noise exceeds a certain threshold.

3.3   Propagation Model

Free space propagation model is adopted in our analysis and the calculation of the received power is shown in Formula (1)

$$P_{RX} = \frac{P_X}{d_x^2} \tag{1}$$

where P_{RX} is the receiving power of receiver, P_X is the transmitting power of transmitter, d_x is the distance between the transmitter and the receiver.

4   Analysis of Collision Probability and Access Delay

4.1   Jamming Analysis

The distribution of jammers is assumed to obey the Poisson distribution with parameter λ, which can be viewed as the jammer density. The probability of there being n jammer in an area S is

$$P_n = \frac{(\lambda S)^n}{n!} e^{-\lambda S} \tag{2}$$

As shown in Fig. 2, the space can be divided into a series of rings with same width. The width of each ring is assumed to be Δd, which is chosen to be small enough so that there is at most one jammer per ring. According to the characteristics of Poisson distribution, the probability that one jammer exists in the ring with distance d away from the center is expressed as

$$P_k = \sum_{v(i)} 2\pi\lambda \mathrm{d}\Delta d e^{-2\pi\lambda d\Delta d} \tag{3}$$

where $v(i)$ is the range of jammer. Let q present the probability that jammer causes transmission collision. The transmitting probability of the jamming noise can be expressed as

$$P_{ki} = qP_k \tag{4}$$

$$P_{ki} = qP_k$$

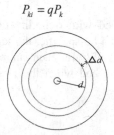

Fig. 2. Jamming model

From Formulas (1), (2), (3), and (4), $X_k(i)$ can be expressed as

$$X_k(i) = q \sum_{v(i)} \frac{2\pi\lambda\Delta dP_{JX}}{d} e^{-2\pi\lambda d\Delta d} \tag{5}$$

where $X_k(i)$ is the received jamming power, P_{JX} is the transmitting power of the jammer.

4.2   Collision Probability of Individual Node

If the SNR of the receiver is smaller than a certain threshold, the node cannot decode the received packets correctly. In other words, a transmission collision occurs. SNR is defined as ratio of received signal power to the sum of noise powers. Therefore, the collision probability is

$$P_c = P\{\frac{P_{RX}}{X} > \theta\} \tag{6}$$

where X is the sum noise of the receiving node and θ is the SNR threshold.

There are three types of noises in the network: jamming noise, interference noise and environment noise. Due to the independent character of these noises, the sum of noise powers of node i can be calculated by

$$X_i = X_k(i) + X_n(i) + X_e(i) \tag{7}$$

where $X_n(i)$ is the noise power of interference and $X_e(i)$ is the noise power of environment.

The collision probabilities of the nodes in SMHWN are related to their locations. Therefore, before analyzing the collision probabilities of nodes with different positions, the nodes in SMHWN can be divided into two categories.

Node is Located at the Penultimate Location

As shown in Fig. 3, node $H - 1$ is located at the penultimate hop of a multi-hop network, the carrier sensing range of node $H - 1$ is its neighboring node $H - 2$ and node H. When the packet is transmitted from the penultimate node to the last node, other nodes in the SMHWN have no effect on the transmission of node $H - 1$. Therefore, the collision probability of node i caused by interference is equal to zero.

Let P_{ci} represent the collision probability of node i. By plugging Formulas (5) and (7) into Formula (6), the relational expression of node i's transmission probability and its collision probability can be shown as follows:

$$P_{ci} = P\{(\frac{P_{TX}}{d_n^2 q \sum_{v(i)} \frac{2\pi\lambda\Delta dP_{TX}}{d} e^{-2\pi\lambda d\Delta d} + X_e(i)}) > \theta\} \tag{8}$$

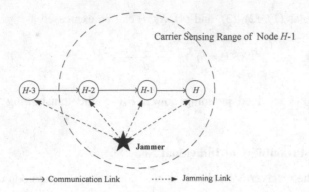

Fig. 3. Node is located at the penultimate hop of a multi-hop network

Node is Located in Other Location

As shown in Fig. 4, the node's previous node and the latter node are within its carrier sensing range. When node $i - 2$ is transmitting a packet, the interference can occur if a packets are sent out by node i since node i cannot sense the transmission of node $i - 2$.

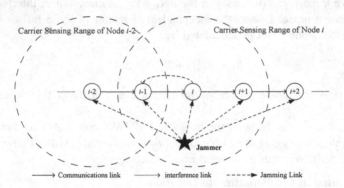

Fig. 4. Node is located at the source of a multi-hop network

Therefore, the collision probability caused by interference for node i is equal to the transmission probability of node $i + 2$, which can be expressed as follows:

$$P_{ni} = \tau_{i+2} \tag{9}$$

where τ_{i+2} is the transmission probability of node $i + 2$ in a randomly chosen slot time. From Formulas (1) and (9), $X_n(i)$ can be calculated by:

$$X_n(i) = \frac{\tau_{i+2}P_{TX}}{d_n^2} \tag{10}$$

where d_n is the distance between neighbor nodes. P_{TX} is the transmission power of the node. Due to the independence character of jammers and nodes, the collisions caused by jamming attack for all the nodes are equal. By plugging Formulas (7) and (10) into Formula (6), the collision probability of the transmitted packets P_{ci} can be expressed as follows:

$$P_{ci} = P\{(\frac{P_{TX}}{(q\sum_{v(i)} \frac{2\pi\lambda\Delta dP_{JX}}{d} e^{-2\pi\lambda d\Delta d} + \frac{\tau_{i+2}P_{TX}}{d_n^2})d_n^2 + X_e(i)}) > \theta\} \qquad (11)$$

Through the above analysis, it can be concluded that the collision probability is a function of the transmission probability τ, which is related to the network protocols. In order to derive the value of τ, the relationship between node's transmission probability and its collision probability can be obtained according to model proposed by Bianchi for the IEEE 802.11 network. The transmission probability τ is:

$$\tau_i = \frac{2(1-2p_{ci})}{(1-2p_{ci})(W_{min}+1) + p_{ci}W_{min}(1-(2p_{ci})^m)} \qquad (12)$$

where m is defined as "maximum backoff stage", meaning the maximum retransmission number, which can be expressed as

$$m = \log_2 \frac{W_{max}}{W_{min}} \qquad (13)$$

where W_{min} and W_{max} is the minimum and maximum value of the contention window. Based on the Formulas (11) and (12), the collision probability and transmission probability of the node can be derived.

4.3   Access Delay Analysis

The total access delay is the sum of the access delay of each node. Generally speaking, the access delay of each node includes the average backoff time and the average successful transmission time. Based on the delay analysis in reference [9], the average backoff time T_{ai} is:

$$T_{ai} = \frac{\alpha(W_{min}\beta - 1)}{2(1-P_c)} + \frac{P_c}{1-2P_c}T_c \qquad (14)$$

where

$$\beta = \frac{(1-P_c) - 2^m P_c^{m+1}}{1-2P_c} \qquad (15)$$

$$\alpha = \sigma(1-\tau) + \tau(1-P_c)T_s + \tau P_c T_c \qquad (16)$$

where α is defined as the average backoff step size, σ is the slot time, T_s is the duration that the channel is sensed to be occupied due to a successful transmission, T_c is the duration that the channel is sensed to be occupied by the collision. Assume the network adopts the RTS/CTS MAC scheme and the collision occurs only on RTS frame. From [7], we can obtain the T_s and T_c

$$T_s = RTS + SIFS + \delta + CTS + SIFS + \delta + H \\ + E[P] + SIFS + \delta + ACK + DIFS + \delta \tag{17}$$

$$T_c = RTS + DIFS + \delta \tag{18}$$

where δ is the propagation delay, H is the data frame header, and $E[P]$ is the data frame size. The access delay of each node can be expressed as

$$T_i = T_s + T_{ai} \tag{19}$$

In conclusion, the total access delay can be calculated by:

$$T_{delay} = \sum_{i=0}^{H} \left(\frac{\alpha(W_{\min}\beta - 1)}{2(1 - P_{ci})} + \frac{P_{ci}}{1 - 2P_{ci}} T_c + T_s \right) \tag{20}$$

5 Numerical Tests

In this section, we conduct a series of numerical tests to analyze the collision probability and access delay of the nodes by MATLAB simulator. According to the 802.11 standards, the parameters of MAC protocol and control frames are shown in the Table 1. In our experiments, we choose a SMHWN with 6-hop as the simulation scenario. The distance between neighbor nodes d_i is assumed to be 40 m. The jamming probability is assumed to be 0.10, 0.15, and 0.20 respectively.

Table 1. Related parameters

P_{TX}	10 dBm	ACK	112 bits + PHY header
P_{JX}	10 dBm	RTS	160 bits + PHY header
X_{ei}	−50 dBm	CTS	112 bits + PHY header
SNR threshold	25 dB	Channel bit rate	5 Mbps
Packet payload(P)	800 bits	Propagation delay	1 us
MAC header	192 bits	Slot time	30 us
PHY header	80 bits	SIFS	16 us
ACK	112 bits + PHY header	DIFS	34 us
RTS	160 bits + PHY header	W_{max}/W_{min}	1024/16

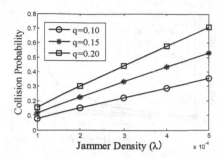

Fig. 5. Comparison of collision probability for different λ

In Fig. 5, the x-coordinate represents the jammer density and the y-coordinate represents the collision probability. From the figure, we can see that the relationship between λ and collision probability is linear. As the jammer density increases, the collision probability increases. Besides, it can also be concluded from the figure that the greater the jamming probability is, the larger the collision probability is.

Figure 6 shows the impact of λ, which is defined as the jammer density, on received jamming power. The x-coordinates are the jammer densities, and the y-coordinates are the received jamming powers. As λ increases, the received jamming power increases with it linearly.

In Fig. 7, the x-coordinates are the jammer densities, and the y-coordinates are the access delays. We compare the impact of different λ on the access delay, and it can be concluded that the access delay increases exponentially with the increase in jammer density. Comparing the results of flow1, flow2 and flow3, we also can find that the access delay increases non-linear with jammer density.

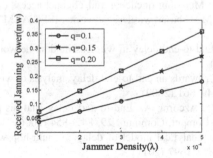

Fig. 6. Comparison of received jamming power for different λ

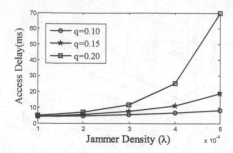

Fig. 7. Comparison of access delay for different λ

6 Conclusion

In this paper, we have proposed a ring-based jamming model to analyze the access delay in string multi-hop wireless network. At first, the existing probability of the jammers is derived based on stochastic geometry theory. According to different locations, the nodes are divided into two categories and the collision probability of each kind of node is derived. Then, the access delay of each node is discussed through the calculation of transmission probability of the transmitted packets. At last, a series of numerical tests are conducted to illustrate the impact of jamming attack on the access delay.

References

1. Jiao, W., et al.: End-to-end delay distribution analysis for stochastic admission control in multi-hop wireless networks. IEEE Trans. Wirel. Commun. **13**(3), 1308–1320 (2014)
2. Tickoo, O., Sikdar, B.: Modeling queueing and channel access delay in unsaturated IEEE 802.11 random access MAC based wireless networks. IEEE/ACM Trans. Netw. **16**(4), 878–891 (2008)
3. Yu, S.M., Kim, S.L.: End-to-end delay in wireless random networks. IEEE Commun. Lett. **14**(2), 109–111 (2010)
4. Xie, M., Haenggi, M.: Towards an end-to-end delay analysis of wireless multihop networks. Ad Hoc Netw. **7**(5), 849–861 (2009)
5. Banchs, A., Serrano, P., Azcorra, A.: End-to-end delay analysis and admission control in 802.11 DCF WLANs. Comput. Commun. **29**, 842–854 (2006)
6. Ghadimi, E., et al.: An analytical model of delay in multi-hop wireless ad hoc networks. Wirel. Netw. **17**(7), 1679–1697 (2011)
7. Bianchi, G.: Performance analysis of the IEEE 802.11 distributed coordination function. IEEE J. Sel. Areas Commun. **18**(3), 535–547 (2000)
8. Ziouva, E., Antonakopoulos, T.: CSMA/CA performance under high traffic conditions: throughput and delay analysis. Comput. Commun. **25**(3), 313–321 (2002)
9. Carvalho, M.M., Garcia-Luna-Aceves, J.J.: Delay analysis of IEEE 802.11 in single-hop networks. In: IEEE International Conference on Network Protocols, p. 146. IEEE Computer Society (2003)

10. Bayraktaroglu, E., et al.: Performance of IEEE 802.11 under jamming. Mob. Netw. Appl. **18** (5), 678–696 (2013)
11. Sagduyu, Y.E., Berryt, R.A., Ephremidesi, A.: Wireless jamming attacks under dynamic traffic uncertainty. In: Proceedings of the, International Symposium on Modeling and Optimization in Mobile, Ad Hoc and Wireless Networks, pp. 303–312. IEEE (2010)
12. Wei, X., et al.: Jammer localization in multi-hop wireless network: a comprehensive survey. IEEE Commun. Surv. Tutor. **PP**(99), 1 (2016)
13. Wei, X., et al.: Collaborative mobile jammer tracking in multi-hop wireless network. Future Gener. Comput. Syst. (2016)
14. Sanada, K., Komuro, N., Sekiya, H.: End-to-end delay analysis for IEEE 802.11 string-topology multi-hop networks. IEICE Trans. Commun. **E98**(07), 1284–1293 (2015)
15. Xu, W., et al.: Jamming sensor networks: attack and defense strategies. IEEE Netw. Mag. Glob. Internetw. **20**(3), 41–47 (2006)

Anomaly Detection and Diagnosis
for Container-Based Microservices
with Performance Monitoring

Qingfeng Du, Tiandi Xie[✉], and Yu He

School of Software Engineering, Tongji University, Shanghai, China
{du_cloud,xietiandi,rainlf}@tongji.edu.cn

Abstract. With emerging container technologies, such as Docker, microservices-based applications can be developed and deployed in cloud environment much agiler. The dependability of these microservices becomes a major concern of application providers. Anomalous behaviors which may lead to unexpected failures can be detected with anomaly detection techniques. In this paper, an anomaly detection system (ADS) is designed to detect and diagnose the anomalies in microservices by monitoring and analyzing real-time performance data of them. The proposed ADS consists of a monitoring module that collects the performance data of containers, a data processing module based on machine learning models and a fault injection module integrated for training these models. The fault injection module is also used to assess the anomaly detection and diagnosis performance of our ADS. Clearwater, an open source virtual IP Multimedia Subsystem, is used for the validation of our ADS and experimental results show that the proposed ADS works well.

Keywords: Anomaly detection · Microservices
Performance monitoring · Machine learning

1 Introduction

At present, more and more Web applications are developed in microservice design for better scalability, flexibility and reliability. An application in microservice approach consists of a collection of services which is isolated, scalable and resilient to failure. Each service can be seen as an application of its own and these services expose their endpoints for communicating with other services. With the adoption of a microservice architecture, a lot of benefits can be got. For example, software can be released faster, and teams can be smaller and focus on their own work.

To generate enough isolated resources for such a number of services, the following virtualization techniques are widely used. Virtual Machines (VMs) are traditional ways of achieving virtualization. Each created VM has its own operating system (OS). Container is another emerging technology for virtualization

© Springer Nature Switzerland AG 2018
J. Vaidya and J. Li (Eds.): ICA3PP 2018, LNCS 11337, pp. 560–572, 2018.
https://doi.org/10.1007/978-3-030-05063-4_42

which is gaining popularity over VMs due to its lightweight, high performance, and higher scalability [1]. And the created containers share host OS together.

The development of virtualization technologies, especially container technology, has contributed to the wide adoption of microservice architecture in recent years. And the service providers start to put greater demands on the dependability of these microservices. Service Level Agreements (SLAs) are usually made between service providers and users for specifying the quality of the provided services. They may include various aspects such as performance requirements and dependability properties [2]. And severe consequences may be caused by a violation of such SLAs.

Anomaly detection can help us identify unusual patterns which do not conform to expected patterns and anomaly diagnosis can help us locate the root cause of an anomaly. As anomaly detection and diagnosis require large amount of historic data, service providers have to install lots of monitoring tools on their infrastructure to collect real-time performance data of their services.

At present, there are two main challenges faced by these microservice providers. Firstly, for container-based microservices, what metrics should be monitored. Secondly, even if all the metrics are collected, how to evaluate whether the behaviors of the application are anomalous or not.

In this paper, an anomaly detection system (ADS) is proposed and it can address these two main challenges efficiently. The proposed ADS gives a prototype for service providers to detect and diagnose anomalies for container-based microservices with performance monitoring.

The paper is organized as follows: Sect. 2 reviews the technical background and some widely used anomaly detection techniques. Section 3 first presents our ADS and its three main components. Section 4 presents the implementation of the proposed ADS in detail. Section 5 provides validation results of the proposed ADS on the Clearwater case study. Section 6 concludes the contribution and discusses the future work.

2   Background and Related Works

2.1   Backgroud

Microservice architecture is a cloud application design pattern which shifts the complexity away from the traditional monolithic application into the infrastructure [3]. In comparison with a monolithic system, microservices-based arhitechture creates a system from a collection of small services, each of which is isolated, scalable and resilient to failure. Services communicate over a network using language-agnostic application programming interfaces (API).

Containers are lightweight OS-level virtualizations that allow us to run an application and its dependencies in a resource-isolated process. Each component runs in an isolated environment and does not share memory, CPU, or the disk of the host operating system (OS) [4]. With more and more applications and services deployed on cloud hosted environments, microservice architecture depends heavily on the use of container technology.

Anomaly detection is the identification of items, events or observations which do not conform to an expected pattern or other items in a dataset [5]. In a normal situation, the correlation between workloads and application performance should be stable and it fluctuates significantly when faults are triggered [6].

2.2   Related Work

With widely adoptions of microservice architecture and container technologies, performance monitoring and performance evaluation become a hot topic for the containers' researchers. In [7], the authors evaluated the performance of container-based microservices in two different models with the performance data of CPU and network. In [8,9], the authors provided a performance comparison among a native Linux environment, Docker containers and KVM (kernel-based virtual machine). They drew an conclusion that using docker could achieve performance improvement according to the performance metrics collected by their benchmarking tools.

In [2], the authors presented their anomaly detection approach for cloud services. They deployed a cloud application which consisted of several services on several VMs and each VM ran a specific service. The performance data of each VM was collected and then, processed for detecting possible anomalies based on machine learning techniques. In [6], the authors proposed an automatic fault diagnosis framework called FD4C. The framework was designed for cloud applications and in the state-of-the-art section, the authors presented four typical periods in their FD4C framework including system monitoring, status characterization, fault detection and fault localization. In [10–12], the authors paid attention to the system performance. To detect anomalies, they built models with historical performance metrics and compared them with online monitored ones. However, these methods require domain knowledge (e.g. the system internal structure). Although these papers only focus on VM-level monitoring and fault detection, they give us much food for thought and methods can be used in container-based microservices similarly.

This paper is aimed at creating an ADS which can detect and diagnose anomalies for container-based microservices with performance monitoring. The proposed ADS consists of three modules: a monitoring module that collects the performance data of containers, a data processing module which detects and diagnoses anomalies, and a fault injection module which simulates service faults and gathers datasets of performance data representing normal and abnormal conditions.

3   Anomaly Detection System

This section overviews our anomaly detection system. There are three modules in our ADS. Firstly, the monitoring module collects the performance monitoring data from the target system. Then, the data processing module will analyze the collected data and detect anomalies. The fault injection module simulates service faults and gathers datasets of performance monitoring data representing normal and abnormal conditions. The datasets are used to train machine learning models, as well as to validate the anomaly detection performance of the proposed ADS.

For the validation of our ADS, a target system composed of several container-based microservices is deployed on our container cluster. The performance monitoring data of the target system are collected and processed for detecting possible anomalies.

Usually, a user can only visit the exposed APIs from upper application and can not access the specific service deployed on the docker engine or VM directly. Thus, our ADS is not given any a priori knowledge about the relevant features which may cause anomalous behaviors. The proposed ADS has to learn from the performance monitoring data with machine learning models itself.

3.1 Monitoring Agent

A container-based application can be deployed not only on a single host but also on multiple container clusters [13]. Each container cluster consists of several nodes (hosts) and each node holds several containers. For applications deployed in such container-based environments, performance monitoring data should be collected from various layers of an application (e.g., node layer, container layer and application layer). Our work is mainly focused on the container monitoring and microservice monitoring.

Container Monitoring. Different services can be added into a single container, but in practice, it's better to have many small containers than a large one. If each container has a tight focus, it's much easier to maintain your microservices and diagnose issues. In this paper, container is defined as a group of one or more containers constituting one complete microservice, it's same as the definition of pod in Kubernetes. By processing the performance data of a container, we can tell whether the container works well.

Microservice Monitoring. In this paper, a container contains only one specific microservice and a microservice can be deployed in several containers at the same time. By collecting the performance data of all the related containers, we can obtain the total performance data of a specific microservice. And we can also know whether a microservice is anomalous by processing these service performance data.

3.2 Data Processing

Data Processing Tasks. Data processing helps us to detect and diagnose anomalies. Carla et al. defined an anomaly as the part of the system state that may lead to an SLAV [2]. We use the same definition of anomaly as stated in Carla's work. An anomaly can be a CPU hog, memory leak or package loss of a container which runs a microservice because it may lead to an SLAV. In our work, there are two main tasks: classify whether a microservice is experiencing some specific anomaly and locate the anomalous container when an anomaly occurs.

Data Processing Models. Anomaly detection techniques are based on machine learning algorithms. There are mainly three types of machine learning algorithms: supervised, unsupervised and semi-supervised. All of these algorithms can be applied to classify the behaviors of the target system with performance monitoring data.

To detect different types of the anomalies which may lead to SLAVs, supervised learning algorithms are used. In our ADS, supervised learning algorithm consists of two phases, shown in Figs. 1 and 2.

Figure 1 shows the training phase. It demonstrates how classification models are created. Firstly, samples of labelled performance data representing different service behaviors are collected and stored in a database. These samples are called training data. Then, data processing module trains the classification models with these training data. To simulate actual users requests, a workload generator is deployed. To collect more performance data in different types of errors, a fault injection module is deployed and it will inject different faults into containers. With more samples collected, the model will be more accurate.

The second phase is the detection phase. Once the model is trained, some real-time performance data can be collected and transferred to data processing module as inputs, and the data processing module can detect anomalies occurring in the system with the trained model. For the validation of the data processing module, some errors will be injected to the target system, and then the data processing module uses the real-time performance data to detect these errors.

The anomaly of a service is often caused by the anomalous behaviors of one or more containers belong to this service. To find out whether the anomaly is caused by some specific container, time series analysis is used. If several containers run a same microservice, they should provide equivalent services to the users. The workload and the performance of each container should be similar. For this reason, if an anomaly is detected in a microservice, the time series data of all the containers running this microservice will be analyzed. The similarity among the data will be measured and the anomalous container will be found.

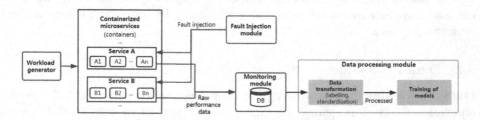

Fig. 1. Training phase, offline.

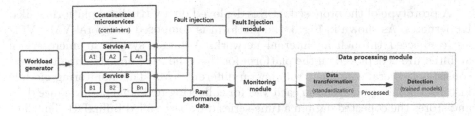

Fig. 2. Detection phase, online.

3.3 Fault Injection

Fault injection module is integrated for collecting the performance data in various system conditions and training the machine learning models. To simulate real anomalies of the system, we write scripts to inject different types of faults into the target system. Four types of faults are simulated based on the resources they impact: high CPU consumption, memory leak, network package loss and network latency increase.

This module is also used to assess the anomaly detection and diagnosis performance of our ADS. As shown in Fig. 2, after the classification models are trained, the fault injection module injects same faults to the target system, and real-time performance data are processed by the data processing module. The detection results are used for the validation.

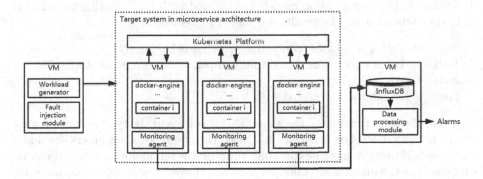

Fig. 3. Implementation of the ADS.

4   Implementation

This section presents the implementation of the three modules of the proposed anomaly detection system.

A prototype of the proposed ADS is deployed on a virtualized platform called Kubernetes. As shown in Fig. 3, the platform is composed of several VMs. VMs are connected through an internal network. A target system in microservice architecture is deployed on the platform for the validation and the target system consists of several containers running on different VMs. The monitoring module installs a monitoring agent on each VM for collecting real-time performance data and stores the collected data in a time-series database called InfluxDB. The data processing module gets the data from the database and executes processing tasks with the data. The fault injection module and the workload generator work by executing bash scripts on another VM.

4.1   Monitoring Module

As shown in Fig. 3, a monitoring agent is deployed on each of the VM. In a monitoring agent, several open-source monitoring tools are used for collecting and storing performance metrics of the target system such as cAdvisor and Heapster. CAdvisor collects resource usages and performance monitoring data of all the containers while Heapster groups these data and stores in a time series database called InfluxDB. The metrics in Table 1 are collected for each service and container including CPU metrics, memory metrics and network metrics.

4.2   Data Processing Module

The data processing module executes the two tasks for each service as discussed in Section 3. The classification models are trained with four algorithms included in library scikit-learn. The results are shown in Section 5.

- Support Vector Machines (configured with kernel = linear)
- Random Forests (configured witih max_depth = 5 and n_estimators = 50)
- Naive Bayes
- Nearest Neighbors (configured with k = 5)

After the detection phase, the anomalous service and the type of the anomaly can be got (e.g. CPU hog in Service A). Next, the anomalous containers should be diagnosed. If there is only one container running the anomalous service, it can be diagnosed as the anomalous container directly. However, if several containers are running the anomalous service, an algorithm is needed to diagnose the anomalous one. Clustering of time series data is a good solution and some algorithms can be used easily [14,15]. However, clustering needs a large amount of data, and people seldom deploy such a number of containers. In this case, we assume that there is only one anomalous container at the same time.

The distance between two temporal sequences $\mathbf{x} = [x_1, x_2, ..., x_n]$ and $\mathbf{y} = [y_1, y_2, ..., y_n]$ can be computed via Euclidean distance very easily. However, the length of the two given temporal sequences must be the same. DTW algorithm is a better choice to measure the similarity between two temporal sequences. It finds an optimal alignment between two given sequences, warps the sequences

Table 1. Monitoring metrics

Metric name	Description
cpu/usage	Cumulative CPU usage on all cores
cpu/request	CPU request (the guaranteed amount of resources) in millicores
cpu/usage-rate	CPU usage on all cores in millicores
cpu/limit	CPU hard limit in millicores
memory/usage	Total memory usage
memory/request	Memory request (the guaranteed amount of resources) in bytes
memory/limit	Memory hard limit in bytes
memory/working-set	Total working set usage Working set is the memory being used and not easily dropped by the kernel
memory/cache	Cache memory usage
memory/rss	RSS memory usage
memory/page-faults	Number of page faults
memory/page-faults-rate	Number of page faults per second
network/rx	Cumulative number of bytes received over the network
network/rx-rate	Number of bytes received over the network per second
network/rx-errors	Cumulative number of errors while receiving over the network
network/rx-errors-rate	Number of errors while receiving over the network per second
network/tx	Cumulative number of bytes sent over the network
network/tx-rate	Number of bytes sent over the network per second
network/tx-errors	Cumulative number of errors while sending over the network
network/tx-errors-rate	Number of errors while sending over the network

based on the alignment, and then, calculates the distance between them. DTW algorithm has been successfully used in lots of fields such as speech recognition and information retrieval.

In this paper, DTW algorithm is used to measure the similarity between the time series performance data of the given containers. Once an anomalous metric in a service is detected, the time series data of all the containers running that service will be analyzed by the algorithm. And the most anomalous container which has the maximal distance from the others will be found.

4.3   Fault Injection Module

An injection agent is installed on each container of a service. Agents are run and stopped through an SSH connection and they simulate CPU faults, memory faults and network faults by some software implementations.

CPU and memory faults are simulated using a software called Stress. Network latency and package loss are simulated using a software called Pumba.

Injection procedures are designed after the implementation of the injection agents. To create a dataset with various types of anomalies in different containers, an algorithm is designed and shown in 1. After the injection procedure is finished, the collected data are used to create anomaly datasets.

Algorithm 1. Fault injection procedure.

Input: $container\_list, fault\_type\_list, injection\_duration, pause\_time, workload$

1: $GenerateWorkload(workload)$
2: **for** $container$ in $container\_list$ **do**
3:   **for** $fault\_type$ in $fault\_type\_list$ **do**
4:     $injection =$
    $Injection(fault\_type, injection\_duration)$
5:     $inject\_in\_container(container, injection)$
6:     $sleep(pause\_time)$
7:   **end for**
8: **end for**

---

5 Case Study

5.1 Environment Description

Kubernetes is an open-source system for automating deployment, scaling, and management of containerized applications. The target system (Clearwater) runs on a kubernetes platform which consists of three VMs (which are rain-u2, rain-u3 and rain-u4). Each VM has 4 CPUs, a 8 GB memory and a 80 GB disk. VMs are connected through a 100 Mbps network. A monitoring agent is installed on each of the VM. The installed monitoring tools include cAdvisor, Heapster, InfluxDB and Grafana.

Clearwater is an open source implementation of IMS (the IP Multimedia Subsystem) designed from the ground up for massively scalable deployment in the Cloud to provide voice, video and messaging services to millions of users [16]. It contains six main components, namely Bono, Sprout, Vellum, Homer, Dime and Ellis. On our kubernetes platform, each container runs a specific service and can be easily scaled out. In this paper, our work is focused on Sprout, Cassandra and Homestead constituting the Call/Session Control Functions (CSCF) together, and we perform experimentations for these three services.

5.2 Clearwater Experimentations

First of all, Clearwater is deployed on our kubernetes platform. All the services are running in containers and the number of the replica of component homestead is set to three. It means there will be three containers running the same service homestead. The performance data of a service is the sum of all the containers running this service.

Then, two datasets (dataset A and dataset B) are collected with the help of the fault injection module. The injection procedures are shown in Table 2. By combining the two datasets together, a third dataset can be obtained as dataset C. After being standardized and labelled, a dataset has a structure as shown in Table 3.

Since these three services constitute the CSCF function together, there will be some relationships among their performance data. And the question whether we can detect the anomalies with the performance data of only one service comes. To answer this question, each dataset is divided to three smaller datasets according to the service, and the classification algorithms are also executed on these datasets for the validation. The structure of the divided dataset is shown in Table 4.

Table 2. Fault injection procedures

Experiment	Injection procedures
dataset A	container_list = {sprout,cassandra,homestead1}
	fault_type = {CPU, memory,latency,package_loss}
	injection_duration = 50 min
	pause_time = 10 min
	workload = workloadA (5000 calls per second)
dataset A	container_list = {sprout,cassandra,homestead1}
	fault_type = {CPU, memory,latency,package_loss}
	injection_duration = 30 min
	ause_time = 10 min
	workload = workloadB (8000 calls per second)

Table 3. Dataset structure

Time	Cassandra CPU	Cassandra Mem	Other metrics	Homestead metrics	Sprout metrics	Label
2018-05-08T09:21:00Z	512	70142771	...	...	...	nomal
2018-05-08T09:21:30Z	350	120153267	...	...	...	cass_mem_leak
2018-05-08T09:22:00Z	322	70162617	...	...	...	sprout_cpu_hog

As we inject four different types of faults to three different services, there will be 12 different labels. We also collect the data in a normal condition and in a heavy workload, thus, there are 14 different labels totally in these datasets.

5.3 Validation Results

Detection of Anomalous Service. Four widely used algorithms are compared in this paper for training the classification models of our datasets, which are

Table 4. Service dataset structure

Time	Cassandra CPU	Cassandra Mem	Other metrics	Label
2018-05-08T09:21:00Z	512	70142771	...	nomal
2018-05-08T09:21:30Z	350	120153267	...	cass_mem_leak
2018-05-08T09:22:00Z	322	70162617	...	sprout_cpu_hog

Table 5. Validation results of three datasets

Dataset	Measure	kNN	SVM	NB	RF
A	Precision	0.93	0.95	0.95	0.95
	Recall	0.93	0.92	0.93	0.92
	F1-score	0.93	0.93	0.93	0.92
B	Precision	0.98	0.75	0.98	0.99
	Recall	0.97	0.82	0.97	0.99
	F1-score	0.97	0.77	0.97	0.99
B	Precision	0.96	0.82	0.83	0.93
	Recall	0.96	0.80	0.79	0.91
	F1-score	0.96	0.78	0.78	0.91

Support Vector Machine (SVM), Nearest Neighbors (kNN), Naive Bayes (NB) and Random Forest (RF). The purpose of these classifiers is to find out the anomalous service with the monitored performance data.

There are 757 records in dataset A, 555 records in dataset B, and 1312 records in dataset C. For each of the dataset, 80% of the records are used as training set to train the classification model and the rest 20% are used as test set to validate the model. The validation results are shown in Tables 5 and 6.

Regarding the validation results in Table 5, the detection performance of the anomalous service is excellent for most of the classifiers with measure values above 0.9. For dataset A, all of the four classifier give excellent validation results. For dataset B, three of these classifiers give wonderful results except SVM. For dataset C, the performance of Random Forest and Nearest Neighbors still look excellent. These results shows that the dataset created by our ADS is meaningful, and both of the Random Forest and Nearest Neighbors classifiers have excellent detection performance.

To answer the question whether anomalies can be detected from the performance data of only one related service, we performed same experiments on the three divided datasets from dataset C. The classification results of the divided datasets (shown in Table 6) are not as good as the results using the entire dataset. However, Nearest Neighbors classifier still gives satisfying results on all of the three divided datasets. SVM seems to be the worst because it doesn't perform well on datasets with multiple classes. Consequently, Nearest Neighbors classifier is recommended if you have to use a dataset with only one service.

Table 6. Validation results of three services in dataset C

Service	Measure	kNN	SVM	NB	RF
Cassandra	Precision	0.91	0.48	0.61	0.89
	Recall	0.89	0.35	0.51	0.75
	F1-score	0.90	0.33	0.50	0.76
Homestead	Precision	0.92	0.27	0.56	0.71
	Recall	0.90	0.36	0.48	0.72
	F1-score	0.91	0.28	0.46	0.69
Sprout	Precision	0.88	0.31	0.47	0.85
	Recall	0.86	0.33	0.46	0.78
	F1-score	0.86	0.28	0.42	0.79

Diagnosis of Anomalous Container. The network latency anomaly of container homestead-1 is used for the validation. As discussed previously, there are three containers running the service homestead. As a microservice application, the workload and the performance data of these three containers should be similar. Thus, the container with the furthest distance from others will be considered as the anomalous container. A python program is implemented to help us diagnose the anomalous container, and it gets the latest 20 performance data from the InfluxDB, calculates the distance and shows the result as shown in Fig. 4.

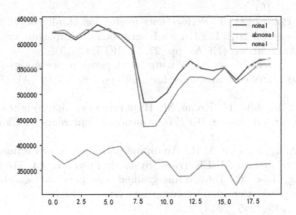

Fig. 4. Diagnosis of the anomalous container.

6 Conclusion and Future Work

In this paper, we analyzed the performance metrics for container-based microservices, introduced two phases for detecting anomalies with machine learning techniques, and then, proposed an anomaly detection system for container-based microserivces. Our ADS relies on the performance monitoring data of services and containers, machine learning algorithms for classifying anomalous and normal behaviors, and the fault injection module for collecting performance data in various system conditions.

In future, a more representative case study in microservice architecture will be studied. Currently, the fault injection module only focused on some specific hardware fault, and in future, some complicated injection scenarios can be added in this module.

References

1. Singh, V., et al.: Container-based microservice architecture for cloud applications. In: Computing, Communication and Automation (ICCCA) (2017)
2. Sauvanaud, C., et al.: Anomaly detection and diagnosis for cloud services: practical experiments and lessons learned. J. Syst. Softw. **139**, 84–106 (2018)
3. Rusek, M., Dwornicki, G., Orłowski, A.: A decentralized system for load balancing of containerized microservices in the cloud. In: Świątek, J., Tomczak, J.M. (eds.) ICSS 2016. AISC, vol. 539, pp. 142–152. Springer, Cham (2017). https://doi.org/10.1007/978-3-319-48944-5_14
4. Kratzke, N.: About microservices, containers and their underestimated impact on network performance. arXiv preprint arXiv:1710.04049(2017) (2017)
5. Chandola, V., Banerjee, A., Kumar, V.: Anomaly detection: a survey. ACM Computing Surveys (2009)
6. Wang, T., Zhang, W., Ye, C., et al.: FD4C: automatic fault diagnosis framework for web applications in cloud computing. IEEE Trans. Syst. Man Cybern.: Syst. **46**(1), 61–75 (2016)
7. Amaral, M., Polo, J., et al.: Performance evaluation of microservices architectures using containers. In: 2015 IEEE 14th International Symposium on Network Computing and Applications (NCA), pp. 27–34. IEEE (2015)
8. Ferreira, A., Felter, W., et al.: An updated performance comparison of virtual machines and Linux containers. Technical Report RC25482 (AUS1407-001). IBM (2014)
9. Kjallman, J., Morabito, R., Komu, M.: Hypervisors vs. lightweight virtualization: a performance comparison. In: IEEE International Conference on Cloud Engineering (2015)
10. Zheng, Z., Zhang, Y., Lyu, M.R.: An online performance prediction framework for service-oriented systems. IEEE Trans. Syst. Man Cybern. **44**, 1169–1181 (2014)
11. Mi, H., Wang, H., et al.: Toward fine-grained, unsupervised, scalable performance diagnosis for production cloud computing systems. IEEE Trans. Parallel Distrib. Syst. **24**(6), 1245–1255 (2013)
12. Zhang, S., Pattipati, K.R., et al.: Dynamic coupled fault diagnosis with propagation and observation delays. IEEE Trans. Syst. Man Cybern.: Syst. **43**(6), 1424–1439 (2013)
13. Pahl, C.: Containerization and the PaaS cloud. IEEE Cloud Comput. **2**, 24–31 (2015)
14. Liao, W.T.: Clustering of time series data–a survey. Pattern Recogn. **38**(11), 1857–1874 (2005)
15. Chen, Y., Keogh, E., et al.: The UCR time series classification archive, July 2015. www.cs.ucr.edu/~eamonn/time_series_data/
16. Clearwater: Project clearwater. http://www.projectclearwater.org/

Integrated Prediction Method for Mental Illness with Multimodal Sleep Function Indicators

Wen-tao Tan, Hong Wang[✉], Lu-tong Wang, and Xiao-mei Yu

School of Information Science and Engineering, Shandong Normal University,
Jinan 250358, China
wanghong106@163.com

Abstract. Sleep quality has great effect on physical and mental health. Severe insomnia will cause autonomic neurological dysfunction. For making good clinical decisions, it is crucial to extract features of sleep quality and accurately predict the mental illness. Prior studies have a number of deficiencies to be overcome. On the one hand, the selected features for sleep quality are not good enough, as they do not account for multisource and heterogeneous features. On the other hand, the mental illness prediction model does not work well and thus needs to be enhanced and improved. This paper presents a multi-dimensional feature extraction method and an ensemble prediction model for mental illness. First, we do correlation analysis for every indicators and sleep quality, and further select the optimal heterogeneous features. Next, we propose a combinational model, which is integrated by basic modules according to their weights. Finally, we perform abundant experiments to test our method. Experimental results demonstrate that our approach outperforms many state-of-the-art approaches.

Keywords: Mental illness · Sleep quality · Ensemble prediction
Multimodal sleep function indicator

1 Introduction

According to the World Health Organization survey for 25,916 primary care patients in 14 countries on 5 continents, 27% of people have sleep problems. More seriously, 50% of students have insufficient sleep. Although sleep disorders have a great negative impact on quality of life and even neurological functions, a considerable number of patients have not been properly diagnosed and treated. Therefore, sleep disorders have become prominent issues that threaten the public. To the best of our knowledge, there are still no effective means for extracting clinical features of sleep quality and predicting the associated mental illness. Therefore, both selecting appropriate features of sleep quality and predicting mental illness are crucial for us. So, in this study, we present a multi-dimensional feature extraction method and an ensemble prediction model for the mental illness. Our contributions are the follows.

© Springer Nature Switzerland AG 2018
J. Vaidya and J. Li (Eds.): ICA3PP 2018, LNCS 11337, pp. 573–580, 2018.
https://doi.org/10.1007/978-3-030-05063-4_43

(1) After detailed analyses, we find optimal heterogeneous features and obtain the relationship between sleep quality and these sleep indicators. And we verify that the Pittsburgh Sleep Quality Index (PSQI) is a good measure for sleep quality.

(2) We present an integrated model to predict the mental illness for patients by using multimodal features such as the PSQI and other indicators. It is more effective than other state-of-the-art approaches.

(3) We perform abundant experiments to test our method. The experimental results show that the indicators defined here can effectively describe different levels of sleep quality, and our method is effective and efficient in predicting mental diseases.

2   Related Work

In order to measure the sleep quality, Buysse proposed the Pittsburgh Sleep Quality Index (PSQI) in 1989 [1]. Based on the PSQI, Gutiérrez studied the relationship between anxiety and sleep quality through collecting questionnaires [5]. Mariman provided a model of the PQSI based on three factors to analysis the chronic fatigue syndrome [2]. Phillips analyzed the physiological status of the HIV patients by the PSQI [3]. Shin mined the relationship between sleep quality and Alzheimer's disease (AD) [4]. Sim analyzed the causes of insomnia in the elderly by clinically observing 65 elderly patients [6].

In summary, there are prior works for extracting suitable clinical features and predicting insomnia-related diseases. However, there are still many problems to be solved, such as how to extract multi-source heterogeneous clinical features of insomnia and how to predict various sorts of diseases more efficiently. Therefore, this paper proposes an effective combinational model to select optimal heterogeneous features for sleep quality, and further predict mental diseases.

3   Prediction Model for Mental Illness

We will construct our model in three steps. We first find a group of factors related to the sleep quality. Then, we analyze the relationship between these sleep-related indicators. Finally, we ensemble top-k approaches with advantages to predict mental diseases.

3.1   Feature Selection

We first perform univariate analysis to find the correlation between primary indicators. Among several correlation criteria in correlation analysis, the most common one is the Pearson correlation coefficient.

Then, we use the regression model to reduce the feature dimensions. Among models of regression analysis, the Polynomial regression is the most common one, in which the relationship between the independent variable x and the dependent variable y is modelled as a nth degree polynomial of x. That is, the Polynomial regression fits a nonlinear relationship between variables, denoted as follows.

$$y = \beta_0 + \beta_1 x + \beta_2 x^2 + \beta_3 x^3 + \varepsilon \qquad (1)$$

Where, ε is a random error.

3.2 Prediction Model Construction

We use the PSQI value as a measure of the sleep quality. It is described as Eq. 2.

$$\begin{aligned} PSQI = &\; Sleep\_quality + Sleep\_latency + Sleep\_time + Sleep\_efficiency \\ &+ Sleep\_disorder + hypnagogue + Daytime\_dysfunction \end{aligned} \qquad (2)$$

Based on the criterion of the PSQI, six kinds of multi-classification models are selected as basic ones. They are K-Nearest Neighbor (KNN), Classification and Regression Trees (CART), AdaBoost (ADAB), Gradient Boosting (GB), Support Vector Machine (SVM), and RandomForest (RF). In order to integrate appropriate models among them, we compare their relative errors on the verification dataset, and further, construct the combined forecasting model by taking the top-k models with minimum relative errors. The final forecasting results are the weighted average of predicting results of these basic models. The weights are represented by Eq. 3. Where, τ_i represents the Fit degree of a model and ω_i is the weight of a model.

$$\omega_i = \frac{\tau_i}{\sum\limits_{i=1}^{k} \tau_i} \qquad (3)$$

The Fit degree τ_i is depicted as Eq. 4. Where, σ_i indicates the standard deviation of a model when making prediction on the validation set, μ_i represents the mean value of a model, ξ_i is the relative error of a model, and σ and μ indicate the average standard deviation and mean value for all models. In order to obtain a more reliable and stable model, we adopt ten-fold cross validation to optimize the model.

$$\tau_i = \frac{1}{\xi_i} + (\sigma_i - \sigma)(\mu_i - \mu) \qquad (4)$$

4   Experimental Results

We preform three groups of experiments to test the effectiveness of our method.

4.1   Data Set

The data set used in this article is from a data mining competition in Asia, which contains a Type I and a Type II data set. The Type I data set is a sample set of sleep quality and related characteristics of 6349 persons. Among them, there are 2084 males and 4265 females, and all persons are between 16 and 87 years old. The related characteristics are Age, Sex, Source, Sleep quality, Reliability, Psychoticism, Nervousness and Character. The Type II data set includes 122 diagnose results for 6349 persons and seven sleep characteristics, such as sleep quality, sleep latency, sleep time, sleep efficiency, sleep disorder, hypnagogue and daytime dysfunction. There are totally 118 types of diseases to be identified.

4.2   Data Preprocessing

Obviously, data preprocessing is indispensable. We do this preprocess in three aspects, which are data specification, data segmentation, data cleaning.

(1) **Data Specification.** The sleep quality values in Type I data set are quantified as 0, 1, 2, 3, which represents good, normal, poor and very poor. According to the United Nations World Health Organization age segmentation criteria, we divide age values into four segments. Specially, the youth (16–44) is set to 0, the middle age (45–59) is set to 1, the young elderly (60–74) is set to 2, and the elderly (75–87) is set to 3. Therefore, we can use the uniform standard to measure the influence of age on the model.

(2) **Data Segmentation.** If a same person is diagnosed with two diseases, we divide the case into two cases and the sleep quality label remains unchanged. Observational data show that this phenomenon exists in 588 rows in the data set.

(3) **Data Cleaning.** Data with problems, such as blank data, missing data and non-disease label data are deleted, and then we get the new data set.

4.3   Correlation Between Sleep Quality and Features

Firstly, we divide the data into two groups which are the male group and the female group. In each group, we use the same method to analyze the correlation between sleep quality and other features. As an example, the relationship scatter plot for the sleep quality and the Age indicator is shown in Fig. 1.

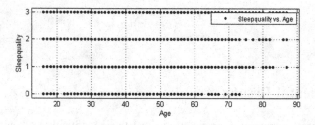

Fig. 1. Scatter plot of sleep quality and age

Similarly, we analyze the density distribution histogram for five indexes, as shown in the Fig. 2. Through the analysis, it is found that:

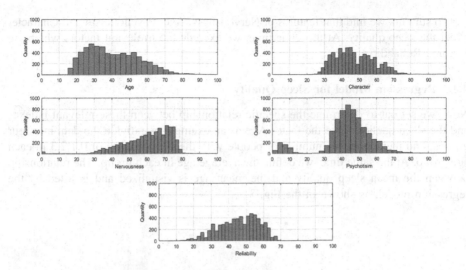

Fig. 2. The density distribution histograms

(1) For different genders, the data volumes of four-level sleep quality are roughly the same, so the feature Sex is not associated with the sleep quality.

(2) In different ages, the proportion of sleep quality in four grades is significantly different, which indicates that the distributions of the sleep quality of different age groups are different. Therefore, the feature Age is the key factor to affect the sleep quality.

In order to further verify the analysis above, we do the systematic correlation testing, whose results are as shown in Table 1.

Table 1. The Pearson correlation and significance value

		Reliability	Psychoticism	Nervousness	Character
Sleep quality	Pearson correlation	0.017	0.078**	0.083**	−0.031*
	Significance	0.179	0.000	0.000	0.012

Note: ** indicates confidence level of 0.01, and * is significant at 0.05

Seen from Table 1, on the one hand, the Pearson correlation coefficient between the Reliability and the sleep quality is 0.017 and the significant value 0.179 which is much higher than the threshold 0.05. So, the correlation between them is highly accidental and not relevant. On the other hand, the correlation coefficient between the sleep quality and the Psychoticism is 0.078 with a significance of 0.00 which is less than the significant threshold of 0.01. Similarly, the correlation coefficient between the sleep quality and the Nervousness is not significantly different from the above one. Therefore, Psychoticism criterion and Nervousness index have a greater impact on the sleep quality. In addition, the Pearson correlation between the sleep quality and the feature Character is -0.031 with a significance of 0.012. Although it is a negative correlation, it also shows that the Character is an effective factor affecting the sleep quality.

To sum up, we find that features of Nervousness, Age, Psychoticism and Character affect the sleep quality. At the same time, we exclude the irrelevant factors which are Sex and Reliability.

4.4   Regression Model for Sleep Quality

Now, we set out to determine the specific relationship between these relevant indexes and the sleep quality. Take the factor Age as an example, we divide the data into four groups, and then count the number of people with the sleep quality of 0,1,2,3 in each age group. At the same time, we define the average age in each group. The relationship between the mean sleep quality and the mean age is visualized and is fitted by the regression model, as shown in the Fig. 3.

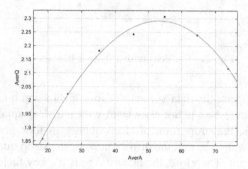

Fig. 3. The cubic polynomial regression curve of age and sleep quality

When getting the optimized polynomial regression curve, its parameters are determined, as shown in the Table 2.

Table 2. The Parameter result of fitting curve

Parameter	Parameter value	Confidence interval
β_3	$-1.065e^{-6}$	$(-6.482e^{-6}, 4.352e^{-6})$
β_2	$-2.207e^{-4}$	$(-9.747e^{-4}, 5.333e^{-4})$
β_1	$3.259e^{-2}$	$(3.585e^{-4}, 6.482e^{-2})$
β_0	1.343	$(9.306e^{-1}, 1.755)$
R^2: 0.9988 SSE: 0.001116		RMSE: 0.01928 Adjusted R^2: 0.9845

4.5   Mental Illness Classification

In this experiment, we analyze the relationship between the diagnosis and the sleep. It is considered as a multi-classification problem. The criterion for this task is the most common one, called accuracy.

Now, we use six machine learning models to train the model and test their validation set by cross validation. The mean, standardization, maximum and minimum of predicting accuracy of different models by ten-fold cross validation are as follows. Note that these models use their default parameters (Table 3).

Table 3. Predicting results with six models

Model	Mean	Standardization	Maximum	Minimum
KNN	0.5618	0.0082	0.5731	0.5488
CART	0.6143	0.0085	0.6341	0.6016
GB	0.4245	0.0099	0.4501	0.4108
RF	0.6201	0.0089	0.6375	0.6068
SVM	0.5247	0.0107	0.5447	0.5051
ADAB	0.3807	0.0094	0.3999	0.3639

In order to get optimized models, we need to adjust their super-parameters, respectively. In the KNN model, the parameter K, to a large extent, can affect the performance of the model, and its value always is less than 20. Therefore, we make the experiment to find the best K value. Seen from Fig. 4, the K value within the interval [2, 5] achieves the better accuracy. This accords with the fact that the sample number of each category in our data is smaller. So, the relatively smaller K can improve the effect of the KNN model.

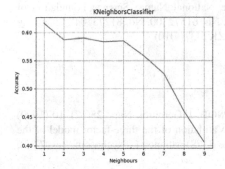

Fig. 4. Accuracy of the KNN

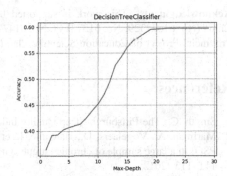

Fig. 5. Accuracy of the CART

While, the super parameter of the CART is the depth of the tree. If the decision tree is too deep, the model will overfitting. So, we make experiments to get the depth of CART. Seen from Fig. 5, when the max depth is greater than eighteen, the accuracy will not be improved. In similar way, we can get the number of weak classifiers and the learning rate of AdaBoost, the number of the decision trees and the max depth of every tree in Random Forest and Gradient Boosting algorithms and three parameters for SVM.

Table 4. Accuracy of the integrated model

Model	Accuracy
Random Forest	0.6321
Random Forest + Logistic	0.6438

According to the above experiments, we combine two models, the Random Forest and the Logistic Regression, to obtain the best model. In our best model, the number of estimators is 9 and the max depth of tree is 15 in the Random Forest model. The parameter C is 0.1 and multi-classification strategy is OVR in the logistic model. The C is reciprocal of the regularization coefficient to avoid overfitting. The results are shown in Table 4.

5 Conclusion

The article proposes a hybrid recognition method to find the relationship between sleep indicators and disease diagnosis results. First of all, we analyze the correlation between indicators and the sleep quality, and further do a regression fit to reduce feature dimensions. Then, we calculate the PSQI and initially obtained the relationship between diseases and the sleep quality. Finally, we mix the prediction models to predict the diagnosis results. Our model overcomes the shortcomings of the traditional models and innovatively proposes a reasonable sleep program. In further work, we will further improve the solution to reduce errors due to imbalanced data. In addition, the effectiveness of the proposed program needs a further evaluation as well.

Acknowledgments. This work is supported by the National Nature Science Foundation of China (No. 61672329, No. 61373149, No. 61472233, No. 61572300, No. 81273704), Shandong Provincial Project of Education Scientific Plan (No. ZK1437B010).

References

1. Smyth, C.: The Pittsburgh Sleep Quality Index (PSQI). J. Gerontol. Nurs. **25**(12), 10 (1999)
2. Mariman, A., Vogelaers, D., Hanoulle, I., et al.: Validation of the three-factor model of the PSQI in a large sample of chronic fatigue syndrome (CFS) patients. J. Psychosom. Res. **72**(2), 111–113 (2012)
3. Phillips, K.D., Sowell, R.L., Rojas, M., et al.: Physiological and psychological correlates of fatigue in HIV disease. Biol. Res. Nurs. **6**(1), 59–74 (2004)
4. Shin, H.Y., Han, H.J., Shin, D.J., et al.: Sleep problems associated with behavioral and psychological symptoms as well as cognitive functions in Alzheimer's disease. J. Clin. Neurol. **10**(3), 203–209 (2014)
5. Gutiérrez-Tobal, G.C., Álvarez, D., Crespo, A., et al.: Multi-class adaboost to detect Sleep Apnea-Hypopnea Syndrome severity from oximetry recordings obtained at home. In: Global Medical Engineering Physics Exchanges, pp. 1–5. IEEE (2016)
6. Sim, D.Y.Y., Teh, C.S., Ismail, A.I.: Improved boosted decision tree algorithms by adaptive apriori and post-pruning for predicting obstructive Sleep Apnea. Adv. Sci. Lett. **24**, 1680–1684 (2018)

Privacy-Aware Data Collection and Aggregation in IoT Enabled Fog Computing

Yinghui Zhang[1,2]($\boxtimes$), Jiangfan Zhao[1], Dong Zheng[1,2], Kaixin Deng[1], Fangyuan Ren[1], and Xiaokun Zheng[3]

[1] National Engineering Laboratory for Wireless Security, Xi'an University of Posts and Telecommunications, Xi'an 710121, People's Republic of China
{zjf291495791,dkx523121943,rfyren}@163.com
[2] Westone Cryptologic Research Center, Beijing 100070, China
yhzhaang@163.com, zhengdong@xupt.edu.cn
[3] School of Computer Science and Technology, Xi'an University of Posts and Telecommunications, Xi'an 710121, People's Republic of China
xiaokzheng@163.com

Abstract. With the rapid development of the Internet of Things (IoT), a large number of IoT device data has flooded into cloud computing service centers, which has greatly increased the data processing task of cloud computing. To alleviate this situation, IoT enabled fog computing comes into being and it is necessary to aggregate the collected data of multiple IoT devices at the fog node. In this paper, we consider a privacy-aware data collection and aggregation scheme for fog computing. Although the fog node and the cloud control center are honest-but-curious, the proposed scheme also ensures that the data privacy will not be leaked. Our security and performance analysis indicates that the proposed scheme is secure and efficient in terms of computation and communication cost.

Keywords: Fog computing · Data security · Internet of Things Privacy · Data aggregation

1 Introduction

In recent years, cloud computing has obtained rapid development [19,28] with its advantages of ultra-large-scale storage, powerful computing power, high scalability, and low cost [1,13]. However, with the advancement of IoT and wireless network technologies [22,23], all IoT data files are uploaded to the cloud for

Supported by National Key R&D Program of China (No. 2017YFB0802000), National Natural Science Foundation of China (No. 61772418, 61472472, 61402366), Natural Science Basic Research Plan in Shaanxi Province of China (No. 2015JQ6236). Yinghui Zhang is supported by New Star Team of Xi'an University of Posts and Telecommunications (No. 2016-02).

J. Vaidya and J. Li (Eds.): ICA3PP 2018, LNCS 11337, pp. 581–590, 2018.
https://doi.org/10.1007/978-3-030-05063-4_44

processing, which will bring performance bottleneck to the cloud service center [5,9,16]. Especially, it is difficult to meet the low latency requirements of real-time processing [10,20]. In 2012, Bonomi et al. proposed the concept of fog computing [2] to address the high latency, the lack of support for mobility and location awareness of cloud computing. In other words, fog computing is an extension of cloud computing and the perfect combination of cloud and fog makes the IoT network work more efficiently.

In IoT, vehicles, smart meters, smart homes, and even heart monitors of smart health system can send data to the control center through fog nodes [4,8,21]. These IoT devices often contain user's privacy [12,27], which has been considered in cloud computing [24–26]. Because the fog nodes are deployed at the edge of the network and low-traffic nodes [11], they are more vulnerable to hackers [18]. Once user's information is leaked, it will have a bad influence [6,7,14,17]. Therefore, we must encrypt the sensitive data before uploading. In addition, the data aggregation technology should be applied to fog devices to reduce the communication overhead.

Our Contribution. In this paper, we propose a privacy-aware data collection and aggregation scheme (PDCA) for fog computing. Firstly, the control center can only obtain the total data within the limited range instead of directly reading the data of a single IoT device. Secondly, the PDCA scheme realizes privacy protection. In fact, if the fog device and the control center are not honest and the data to be reported by a single IoT device or the aggregated data by the fog device is leaked, the attacker will not get any privacy about the user, nor can it forge or change the ciphertext to be sent to the fog device. Finally, the PDCA scheme adopts an efficient batch verification method based on bilinear pairings, which can verify the signatures of multiple users together instead of verifying them one by one. Performance evaluation shows that the PDCA scheme reduces the computation overhead of the fog device.

Organization. The remaining of this paper is organized as follows. Some preliminaries are reviewed in Sect. 2. In Sect. 3, we describe the proposed scheme in detail. In Sect. 4, we give the security and privacy analysis of the proposed scheme, followed by the performance evaluation in Sect. 5. Finally, we draw our conclusions in Sect. 6.

2   Preliminaries

2.1   Bilinear Pairings

Let G_1 and G_2 be a cyclic additive group and a cyclic multiplicative group of the same prime order q. Let $P_0 \in G_1$ be a generator. We call $\hat{e}$ a bilinear pairing if $\hat{e}: G_1 \times G_1 \to G_2$ is a map with the following properties: (1) Bilinear: For all $a, b \in Z_q^*$, $\hat{e}(aP_0, bP_0) = \hat{e}(P_0, P_0)^{ab}$; (2) Non-degenerate: $\hat{e}(P_0, P_0) \neq 1_{G_1}$; (3) Computable: For all $P_0, Q \in G_1$, it is efficient to compute $\hat{e}(P_0, Q)$.

2.2 Paillier Encryption

Paillier encryption consists of three algorithms: key generation, encryption, and decryption as below [15]:

(1) Key Generation: Given a security parameter κ, choose two large primes p and q, where $\mid p \mid = \mid q \mid = \kappa$, compute $N = pq$ and $\lambda = lcm(p-1, q-1)$, define the function $L(u) = \frac{u-1}{N}$, select the generator $g \in Z_{N^2}^*$ and get the public key $pk = (N, g)$ and the secret key λ.

(2) Encryption: Given a message $M \in Z_N$, a random number $r \in Z_N^*$ and calculate the ciphertext $C = g^M \cdot r^N \ mod \ N^2$.

(3) Decryption: Given ciphertext $C \in Z_{N^2}^*$, the corresponding plaintext is $M = \frac{L(C^\lambda mod N^2)}{L(g^\lambda mod N^2)} \ mod \ N$.

3 PDCA: Privacy-Aware Data Collection and Aggregation

In this section, a privacy-aware data collection and aggregation scheme for fog computing is proposed. The system model includes a control center (CC), some fog devices (FD) at the network edge, and some IoT devices $U = \{HID_1, HID_2, ..., HID_n\}$. During communication, CC generates system parameters and collects all IoT devices data $(m_1, m_2, ..., m_n)$ via FD periodically. We consider that the privacy data $(m_1, m_2, ..., m_n)$ should be encrypted based on the Paillier homomorphic encryption. In our paper, we assume all the entities are honest-but-curious. PDCA consists of the following parts: system initialization, data collection request, IoT devices report, privacy-aware aggregated data generation, privacy-aware aggregated data reading. The details are given as follows:

3.1 System Initialization

In the system parameters generation stage, firstly, the control center selects the security parameter κ and generates $(q, P_0, G_1, G_2, \hat{e})$ by running $gen(\kappa)$. Secondly, CC selects the security parameter κ_1 and two safe large prime numbers p, q, computing a homomorphic encryption public key pair $(N = p_1 q_1, g)$ and the corresponding private key $\lambda = lcm(p_1 - 1, q_1 - 1)$, where g is a generator of $Z_{N^2}^*$. Then CC defines a function $L(x) = \frac{x-1}{N}$ and chooses two secure cryptographic hash functions, $H_1 : G_2 \rightarrow Z_q^*$, $H_2 : \{0, 1\}^* \rightarrow G_1$, and a random element $sk_{cc} \in Z_q^*$ as its secret key and calculates $PK_{cc} = sk_{cc}P_0$ as its public key. Each fog device chooses a random element $sk_{fd} \in Z_q^*$ as its secret key and calculates $PK_{fd} = sk_{fd}P_0$ as its public key. Then, FD submits PK_{fd} to CC to issue a certificate to bind the public key to the fog device's identity. In like manner, each IoT device chooses a random element $sk_i \in Z_q^*, 1 \leq i \leq n$ as its secret key and calculates $PK_i = sk_iP_0$ as its public key. It also obtains a certificate for PK_i from CC. Finally, CC publishes the public parameters $\{q, P_0, G_1, G_2, \hat{e}, H_1, H_2, PK_{cc}\}$.

3.2   Data Collection Request

During every time slot T_s, the control center can collect data from related fog devices. Specifically, CC sends data collection request($Data\_Req$)packet that contains parameters $\{ID_{cc}, ID_{fd}, T_s, r_{cc}P_0, TS, \sigma_{cc}\}$ to FD. Where, ID_{cc} and ID_{fd} is the identity of the control center and fog device, $r_{cc} \in Z_q^*$ is a random number and $r_{cc}P_0$ is used by each IOT device covered by the fog device in establishing a one-time key shared with the control center. Finally, timestamp TS and $\sigma_{cc} = sk_{cc}H_2(ID_{cc}\|ID_{fd}\|T_s\|r_{cc}P_0\|TS)$ will be used for verifying by the fog devices.

After receiving the $Data\_Req$ packet, according to the difference between the current time and the timestamp TS, FD checks the freshness of $Data\_Req$ packet. Then, FD verifies the signature by computing if $\hat{e}\ (\sigma_{cc}, P_0) = \hat{e}\ (H_2(ID_{cc}\|ID_{fd}\|T_s\|r_{cc}P_0\|TS), PK_{cc})$ holds. If the above equation holds, the FD randomly chooses $r_{fd} \in Z_q^*$, calculates $r_{fd}P_0$, puts $r_{fd}P_0$ in the packet $Data\_Req$, and broadcasts the packet that contains parameters $\{ID_{fd}, ID_{cc}, T_s, r_{fd}P_0, r_{cc}P_0, TS, \sigma_{cc}\}$ in its area. Note that $r_{fd}P_0$ is used by IOT device HID_i covered by the fog device in establishing a one-time key shared with the fog device.

3.3   IoT Device Report Generation

After receiving the packet $Data\_Req$, IoT device HID_i will report its sensing data m_i to fog device at time slot T_s. HID_i chooses $r_i \in z_q^*$ and computers r_iP_0 which is used by ID_{fd} in establishing a shared one-time key between itself and the related fog device. Then, HID_i computes two shared keys as $k_i = H_1(\hat{e}(PK_{cc}, sk_ir_ir_{cc}P_0))$, $k_i' = H_1(\hat{e}(PK_{fd}, sk_ir_ir_{fd}P_0))$, which will be used for hiding HID_i's sensing data m_i. Next, it chooses a random number xi_i masks the sensing data m_i and computes ciphertext C_i and signature σ_i, where

$$C_i = g^{m_i+k_i+k_i'}\xi_i^N \bmod N^2, \tag{1}$$

$$\sigma_i = sk_iH_2(C_i\|ID_i\|ID_{fd}\|T_s\|r_iP_0\|TS). \tag{2}$$

Finally, HID_i sends data collection reply $Data\_Rep$ packet that contains parameters $\{C_i, ID_i, ID_{fd}, T_s, r_iP_0, TS, \sigma_i\}$ to fog devices.

3.4   Privacy-Aware Aggregated Data Generation

Upon receiving the $Data\_Rep$ packet, firstly, FD verifies n $Data\_Rep$ packets received to ensure that the packet are valid and have not been tampered or forged during communication. Verify that Eq. (3) holds, and if so, all IOT device $Data\_Reps$ are verified successfully, otherwise the verification fails.

$$\hat{e}(P_0, \sum_{i=1}^{n}\sigma_i) = \prod_{i=1}^{n}\hat{e}(PK_i, H_2(C_i\|ID_i\|ID_{fd}\|T_s\|r_iP_0\|TS). \tag{3}$$

Note that using the above verification method, the number of bilinear pairs is $n+1$ times. The traditional one-by-one verification method requires $2n$ bilinear pairing operations. Obviously, the above batch verification method is safer and more efficient. If the above verification is hold, the fog device calculates

$$k_i' = H_1(\hat{e}(PK_i, sk_{fd}r_{fd}r_iP_0)) = H_1(\hat{e}(PK_{fd}, sk_ir_ir_{fd}P_0)). \tag{4}$$

Then, It runs the following data aggregation operations and get the aggregate ciphertext C and the corresponding signature σ, the specific process are as follows:

$$C = \prod_{i=1}^{n}(C_i \cdot g^{-k_i'}) \; mod \; N^2$$

$$= \prod_{i=1}^{n}(g^{m_i+k_i+k_i'} \cdot g^{-k_i'}) \cdot (\xi_1\xi_2...\xi_n)^N \; mod \; N^2$$

$$= g^{\sum_{i=1}^{n}(m_i+k_i)} \cdot (\prod_{i=1}^{n}\xi_i)^N \; mod \; N^2, \tag{5}$$

$$\sigma = sk_{fd}H_2(C\|ID_{fd}\|ID_{cc}\|T_s\|r_{fd}P_0\|TS). \tag{6}$$

Next, the fog device sends the $Data\_Rep$ packet that contains parameters $\{C, ID_{cc}, ID_{fd}, T_s, \{r_iP_0\}_{1<i<n}, TS, \sigma\}$ to control center.

3.5   Privacy-Aware Aggregated Data Decryption

Upon receiving the fog device reply packet $Data\_Rep$, the control center first verifies the $Data\_Rep$ to ensure the packets' authenticity and integrity according to Eq. (7):

$$\hat{e}(P_0, \sigma) = \hat{e}(PK_{cc}, H_2(C\|ID_{fd}\|ID_{cc}\|T_s\|r_{fd}P_0\|TS)). \tag{7}$$

If it does hold, then further reading. CC calculates

$$k_i = H_1(\hat{e}(PK_i, sk_{cc}r_{cc}r_iP_0)) = H_1(\hat{e}(PK_{fd}, sk_ir_ir_{cc}P_0)). \tag{8}$$

Use the private key λ to decrypt the aggregated ciphertext C by calculating

$$M = \frac{L(C^\lambda \; mod \; N^2)}{L(g^\lambda \; mod \; N^2)} \; mod \; N - \sum_{i=1}^{n}k_i = \sum_{i=1}^{n}m_i \tag{9}$$

to recover M.

4   Security Analysis

4.1   Privacy Protection

In our scheme, according to the Paillier encryption algorithm, HID_i sends the sensitive data m_i that was encrypted by the public key to the associated gateway in the ciphertext and it is infeasible to decrypt without the private key, where, $C_i = g^{m_i + k_i + k_i'} \xi_i^N \bmod N^2$. In the IoT devices report generation stage, the secret key k_i and k_i' are added in the Paillier encryption algorithm to get the ciphertext C_i. Even if the adversary gets the data packet sent by tapping the wireless IoT device or the wireless communication channel, without knowing k_i or k_i', the adversary cannot know the sensitive data m_i. Despite the control center has the secret key k_i, it cannot get k_i', and thus cannot decrypt C_i to recover m_i.

In the data aggregation stage, the aggregation operation by the gateway is performed in a ciphertext manner. Even if the gateway is invaded by an adversary, any sensitive data about the IoT device cannot be obtained. For the control center, it only has the aggregated data $M = \frac{L(C^\lambda \bmod N^2)}{L(g^\lambda \bmod N^2)} \bmod N - \sum_{i=1}^n k_i = \sum_{i=1}^n m_i$ and just gets the data sum $\sum_{i=1}^n m_i$. Even if an adversary has intruded into the control center database, detailed data of a single device cannot be obtained. Like this, the individual sensing data privacy is still preserved.

4.2 Non-repudiation and Unforgeability

In the proposed PDCA system, each entity uses its own private key to sign the data to be sent before sending the message. Then, the data is received and is verified by using the sender's public key. The signature scheme we use is based on the issue of CDH security to ensure that adversaries cannot forge a new signature by eavesdropping on signed messages and thus cannot implement forgery attacks [3,22]. At the same time, the entities private keys are properly kept by themselves, their messages sent has non-repudiation. Our program has the ability to discover the dishonest behavior of entities.

5   Performance Evaluation

In this section, we evaluate the performance of the proposed PDCA scheme in terms of the computational complexity and communication overhead at the IoT devices, the fog device, and the control center.

5.1   Computational Complexity

For computation complexity, we assume that there are n IoT devices associated with a fog device and will focus on measuring the time required for performing the cryptographic operations in the proposed scheme. where, with T_{e_1}, T_{e_2}, T_{e_Z}, T_{m_Z}, T_p, T_{pai} denote the computational costs of an exponentiation operation in G_1, an exponentiation operation in G_2, an exponentiation operation in $Z_{N^2}^*$, a multiplication operation in $Z_{N^2}^*$, a bilinear pairing operation and a paillier decryption operation, respectively. We represent the computational complexity in Table 1.

In the security model [10], it consider a trusted authority is a trusted third party because the control center and fog device are honest-but-curious and may

Table 1. Computational complexity of PDCA

	Computation complexity
CC	$3T_p + 2T_{e_1} + T_{e_2} + T_{pai}$
FD	$(n+5)T_p + (n+1)T_{m_Z} + 2T_{e_1} + T_{e_Z} + T_{e_2}$
HID$_i$	$2(T_p + T_{e_2} + T_{e_Z} + T_{e_1})$

be affected by malicious cyber attacks that could result in the leakage of data from IoT devices. Although security is guaranteed, it also increases communication and time overhead. In [12], although there is no a trusted third party, We find that the proposed data aggregation scheme based on paillier homomorphic encryption does not completely protect sensitive information because the control center has the private key λ. The control center may be affected by undetected malware to steal a single user's data, it is possible to obtain directly sensitive information with the private key λ. It is worth mentioning that we don't consider the third-party trusted authority but there is no risk of privacy leakage as [12], and also the control center and fog device are honest-but-curious. Besides, the computational cost of generating an aggregated ciphertext C based on paillier homomorphic encryption is $(n+1)T_{m_Z}$, and the PDCA need $(n+1)T_{m_Z} + T_{e_Z}$.

5.2   Communication Overhead

In the proposed scheme, the privacy of IoT devices has been well protected. Denote the communication overhead of control center to fog device, fog device to IoT device, IoT device to fog device and fog device to control center by $l_{cf}, l_{fi}, l_{if},$ and l_{fc}, respectively. In order to show the communication cost of PDAF, we define the size of each identity as 2 bytes, 4 bytes for T_s or time stamp TS, the length of the Paillier ciphertext is 2048 bits. Let G_1 be a 160-bit elliptic curve, then the length of the signature is 160 bits. Under this setting, the length of $Data\_Req = \{ID_{cc}, ID_{fd}, T_s, r_{cc}P_0, TS, \sigma_{cc}\}$ is 52 bytes, that is $l_{cf} = 52$, the $Data\_Req$ packet is of the form $\{ID_{fd}, ID_{cc}, T_s, r_{fd}P_0, r_{cc}P_0, TS, \sigma_{cc}\}$ and $l_{fh} = 72$, the data collection request response $Data\_Rep$ of HID$_i (1 \leq i \leq n)$ contains $C_i, ID_i, ID_{fd}, T_s, r_iP_0, TS, \sigma_i$ and it length $l_{hf} = 308$ bytes, and the response message is of the form $\{C, ID_{cc}, ID_{fd}, T_s, \{r_iP_0\}_{1<i<n}, TS, \sigma\}$ and the size is $l_{fc} = 288 + 20n$ bytes where n is the number of hybrid IoT device. We represent the communication overhead in Table 2.

For the comparison with PDCA, in the following, we consider a traditional scheme, where all IoT devices blinded data C_i are not aggregated into a ciphertext C by the fog device. For n IoT device data, the length of l_{fc} for the traditional scheme will increase to $288 + 256n$ bytes. As shown in Fig. 1, we further show the change of the communication overhead with the hybrid IoT devices number n.

In general, the proposed PDCA scheme is privacy-aware and it is efficient in terms of computation and communication costs.

Table 2. Computation overhead of PDCA

	Communication cost (bytes)
l_{cf}	52
l_{fi}	72
l_{if}	308
l_{fc}	$288 + 20n$

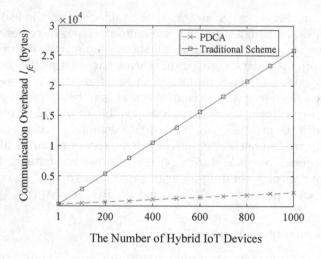

Fig. 1. The communication overhead comparison.

6   Conclusions

In this paper, we proposed a privacy-aware data aggregation scheme in fog computing. The proposed scheme realizes privacy protection, non-repudiation, and unforgeability. The data aggregation technology based on homomorphic encryption not only can effectively protect the privacy of IoT devices but also can reduce the communication overhead of the system. In order to improve the efficiency of data integrity checking, we consider an efficient batch verification mechanism. By analyzing the security and performance, we showed that the proposed scheme is secure and efficient.

References

1. Armbrust, M., et al.: A view of cloud computing. Commun. ACM **53**(4), 50–58 (2010)
2. Bonomi, F., Milito, R., Zhu, J., Addepalli, S.: Fog computing and its role in the internet of things. In: Proceedings of the First Edition of the MCC Workshop on Mobile Cloud Computing, pp. 13–16. ACM (2012)

3. Han, Q., Zhang, Y., Chen, X., Li, H., Quan, J.: Efficient and robust identity-based handoff authentication in wireless networks. In: Xu, L., Bertino, E., Mu, Y. (eds.) NSS 2012. LNCS, vol. 7645, pp. 180–191. Springer, Heidelberg (2012). https://doi.org/10.1007/978-3-642-34601-9_14

4. He, D., Kumar, N., Zeadally, S., Vinel, A., Yang, L.T.: Efficient and privacy-preserving data aggregation scheme for smart grid against internal adversaries. IEEE Trans. Smart Grid 8(5), 2411–2419 (2017)

5. Hosseinian-Far, A., Ramachandran, M., Slack, C.L.: Emerging trends in cloud computing, big data, fog computing, IoT and smart living. In: Dastbaz, M., Arabnia, H., Akhgar, B. (eds.) Technology for Smart Futures, pp. 29–40. Springer, Cham (2018). https://doi.org/10.1007/978-3-319-60137-3_2

6. Huang, J.Y., Hong, W.C., Tsai, P.S., Liao, I.E.: A model for aggregation and filtering on encrypted XML streams in fog computing. Int. J. Distrib. Sens. Netw. 13(5), 1–14 (2017)

7. Huang, Q., Yang, Y., Wang, L.: Secure data access control with ciphertext update and computation outsourcing in fog computing for internet of things. IEEE Access 5, 12941–12950 (2017)

8. Jia, W., Zhu, H., Cao, Z., Dong, X., Xiao, C.: Human-factor-aware privacy-preserving aggregation in smart grid. IEEE Syst. J. 8(2), 598–607 (2014)

9. Liu, Y., Zhang, Y., Ling, J., Liu, Z.: Secure and fine-grained access control on e-healthcare records in mobile cloud computing. Future Gener. Comput. Syst. 78, 1020–1026 (2018)

10. Lu, R., Heung, K., Lashkari, A.H., Ghorbani, A.A.: A lightweight privacy-preserving data aggregation scheme for fog computing-enhanced IoT. IEEE Access 5, 3302–3312 (2017)

11. Lu, R., Liang, X., Li, X., Lin, X., Shen, X.: EPPA: an efficient and privacy-preserving aggregation scheme for secure smart grid communications. IEEE Trans. Parallel Distrib. Syst. 23(9), 1621–1631 (2012)

12. Mahmoud, M., Saputro, N., Akula, P., Akkaya, K.: Privacy-preserving power injection over a hybrid AMI/LTE smart grid network. IEEE IoT J. 4(4), 870–880 (2016)

13. Mell, P.M., Grance, T.: SP 800-145. The NIST definition of cloud computing (2011)

14. Mukherjee, M., et al.: Security and privacy in fog computing: challenges. IEEE Access 5, 19293–19304 (2017)

15. Paillier, P.: Public-key cryptosystems based on composite degree residuosity classes. In: Stern, J. (ed.) EUROCRYPT 1999. LNCS, vol. 1592, pp. 223–238. Springer, Heidelberg (1999). https://doi.org/10.1007/3-540-48910-X_16

16. Stergiou, C., Psannis, K.E., Kim, B.G., Gupta, B.: Secure integration of IoT and cloud computing. Future Gener. Comput. Syst. 78, 964–975 (2018)

17. Stojmenovic, I.: Fog computing: a cloud to the ground support for smart things and machine-to-machine networks. In: 2014 Australasian Telecommunication Networks and Applications Conference (ATNAC), pp. 117–122 (2015)

18. Wang, H., Wang, Z., Domingo-Ferrer, J.: Anonymous and secure aggregation scheme in fog-based public cloud computing. Future Gener. Comput. Syst. 78, 712–719 (2018)

19. Xhafa, F., Feng, J., Zhang, Y., Chen, X., Li, J.: Privacy-aware attribute-based PHR sharing with user accountability in cloud computing. J. Supercomput. 71(5), 1607–1619 (2015)

20. Yannuzzi, M., Milito, R., Serral-Gracia, R., Montero, D., Nemirovsky, M.: Key ingredients in an IoT recipe: fog computing, cloud computing, and more fog computing. In: IEEE International Workshop on Computer Aided Modeling and Design of Communication Links and Networks, pp. 325–329 (2015)

21. Zhang, Y., Zheng, D., Deng, R.H.: Security and privacy in smart health: efficient policy-hiding attribute-based access control. IEEE IoT J. **5**(3), 2130–2145 (2018)
22. Zhang, Y.H., Chen, X.F., Li, H., Cao, J.: Identity-based construction for secure and efficient handoff authentication schemes in wireless networks. Secur. Commun. Netw. **5**(10), 1121–1130 (2012)
23. Zhang, Y., Chen, X., Li, J., Li, H.: Generic construction for secure and efficient handoff authentication schemes in EAP-based wireless networks. Comput. Netw. **75**, 192–211 (2014)
24. Zhang, Y., Chen, X., Li, J., Li, H., Li, F.: FDR-ABE: attribute-based encryption with flexible and direct revocation. In: 2013 5th International Conference on Intelligent Networking and Collaborative Systems (INCoS), pp. 38–45. IEEE (2013)
25. Zhang, Y., Chen, X., Li, J., Wong, D.S., Li, H.: Anonymous attribute-based encryption supporting efficient decryption test. In: Proceedings of the 8th ACM SIGSAC Symposium on Information, Computer and Communications Security ASIA CCS 2013, pp. 511–516. ACM, New York (2013)
26. Zhang, Y., Li, J., Chen, X., Li, H.: Anonymous attribute-based proxy re-encryption for access control in cloud computing. Secur. Commun. Netw. **9**(14), 2397–2411 (2016)
27. Zhang, Y., Zhao, J., Zheng, D.: Efficient and privacy-aware power injection over AMI and smart grid slice in future 5G networks. Mobile Inf. Syst. **2017**, 1–11 (2017)
28. Zhang, Y., Zheng, D., Chen, X., Li, J., Li, H.: Efficient attribute-based data sharing in mobile clouds. Pervasive Mobile Comput. **28**, 135–149 (2016)

A Reputation Model for Third-Party Service Providers in Fog as a Service

Nanxi Chen[1]([✉]) [iD], Xiaobo Xu[1,2], and Xuzhi Miao[1]

[1] Shanghai Institute of Microsystem and Information Technology,
Chinese Academy of Sciences, Shanghai, China
nanxi.chen@mail.sim.ac.cn,
{xiaobo.xu,xuzhi.miao}@wico.sh
[2] Shanghai Normal University, Shanghai, China

Abstract. Fog computing, as a mode of distributing computing resources, can process data directly at the network edge so becomes a promising solution towards the Internet of Things (IoT). To support various IoT services, many third-party fog resources providers participate in the service provisioning process, which accelerates the development of Fog as a Service (FaaS). Current solutions assume the existence of a reliable entity to maintain run-time information about such third-party fog resources providers, which is not feasible because of resource constraints at the network edge. To be aware of the dynamic availability of the fog resources, this paper proposes a graph-based decentralized reputation model for service provisioning in fog computing environment. This mechanism includes a verification model between fog nodes and a consensus mechanism for composite transactions in FaaS. This paper evaluates the proposed solution and proves its feasibility through the experimental result.

Keywords: IoT · Decentralized reputation model · Fog computing
Service composition

1 Introduction

With the continuous emergence of the Internet of Things (IoT) services, such as smart homes, smart grids, and intelligent transportation, countless sensors and devices have been employed by IoT [1]. IoT has penetrated into the people's daily life, industrial production, and so many other fields. According to the ITU-T study report, each person will generate 1.7 MB of data per second and the shipment of IoT wearable devices will reach 237 million by 2020 [2]. The types and number of services provided by IoT are also rapidly expanding. To deal with massive requests for services, how to provide high-quality services is an emerging problem. At present, IoT services and data processing mainly rely on cloud computing that alleviates the pressure of massive data storage, redundancy, and transmission of IoT [3]. However, as the data traffic continuously increases, the cloud center's calculation pressure can be extremely heavy, and it will consume a lot of network bandwidth. Such a centralized computing paradigm will eventually lead to excessive response delay [4].

© Springer Nature Switzerland AG 2018
J. Vaidya and J. Li (Eds.): ICA3PP 2018, LNCS 11337, pp. 591–599, 2018.
https://doi.org/10.1007/978-3-030-05063-4_45

In order to solve the problem of high latency for IoT, there have been many efforts on pushing some of the computing and data caching tasks to the edge of the network. Fog computing, as a distributed computing model at the network edge, has been highlighted by the IoT community [5]. Fog computing takes advantage of both cloud computing and edge computing, and it can utilize the terminal's computing capabilities and benefit from local processing. Fog computing creates a new market for many small infrastructure providers like little companies or even an individual person who is willing to share devices. This inspires the Fog as a Service (FaaS) business model. FaaS allows software vendors to rent a group of FaaS devices (a.k.a., fog nodes) to provide efficient end-to-end application services for IoT consumers. FaaS distributes application control logic, functions, information and resources to the participated devices. In the current FaaS model [10], multiple fog nodes can cooperate to meet users' requirements through service composition. However, it is necessary to ensure the availability of fog node resources. When the fog network cannot guarantee the participated fog nodes' availability, the QoS of IoT application is likely to be reduced, and ultimately IoT application fails to meet user requirements. Therefore, there is an urgent need for a verification mechanism, which can guarantee the availability of fog node resources under the distributed fog computing service model.

Nowadays, blockchain technology and the applications that use such technology are gradually changing the way of services being delivered. The blockchain is a decentralized distributed ledger technology that creates trust between users without having to go through trusted third parties. The recent market investigation indicates that such decentralized consensus technologies will become the future of the finance domain [15]. IOTA [12] is one of this kind that focuses on the machine-to-machine transaction. The core technology of IOTA is Tangle, a structure based on a directed acyclic graph, which provides efficient, secure, portable, real-time micro-transactions without transaction costs. In Tangle, consensus can be used to verify the node's trust value, and then the system determines the transaction.

Based on this, this paper proposes a decentralized reputation model for service providers in FaaS. It includes a trust verification mechanism determining the availability of fog node resources and the QoS of candidate services through mutual authentication between fog nodes in a distributed fog computing environment. Then we select a cost-effective service composition base on the resource and assign a reference quote to fog resource provider for the negotiation of service level agreement (SLA). The contribution of this paper is a reputation model to determine the availability of fog node resources and the SLA negotiation model.

The rest of the paper is structured as follows: Sect. 2 introduces the related work; Sect. 3 presents the system model of this solution, including the fog node verification mechanism based on Tangle and a new tips selection algorithm; Sect. 4 presents the simulation scheme of the proposed mechanism and evaluates the simulation results; and Sect. 5 presents the conclusions of this research and the future work.

2   Related Work

Existing papers have done a lot of research on the architecture of fog computing and service composition. A network service chaining model [6] integrates cloud and fog computing in the 5G environment that works in collaboration with the advanced technologies such as Software Defined Network (SDN) and Network Function Virtualization (NFV). This service model automates virtual resources by chaining in a series for fast computing in both computing technologies. In [7], the authors proposed an infrastructure with the collaboration of fog computing combined with machine-to-machine intelligent communication protocol followed by integration of the Service Oriented Architecture (SOA). This model aims to transfer data by analyzing reliably and systematically with low latency, less bandwidth, heterogeneity in less amount of time maintaining the QoS befittingly. In order to make better use of fog computing resources, some schemes consider layering fog computing structure. A multi-tier fog computing architecture that supports IoT service provision is devised [8]. This architecture optimizes the service decentralization on a fog landscape leveraging context-aware information such as location, time and QoS. Foggy [9] is a platform based on the open source technology, that coordinates application workloads, negotiates resources and supports IoT operations for multi-tier, distributed heterogeneous and decentralized cloud computing systems.

Context-aware service composition is a well-accept way to improve the reliability of composed services. In [16, 17], context awareness is introduced to adapt to the dynamic changes in the environment to realize the individualization of service composition. In order to obtain the most effective service, the service composition based on the maximum QoS was studied [18]. In [19], a framework for service selection and composition by the properties of QoS is proposed. According to the constraints of the service consumer and the service provider, the composition model performs service discovery and composition of microservices deployed on different nodes through semantic fragment information. Context-aware solutions require constant monitoring effort to aggregate run-time information about service providers, which can be resource-consuming in fog computing environments. Service composition models that use historical execution record as a reference when selecting services for a new composition [20]. But such a solution requires a centralized entity to maintain the record, which can cause a lot of communication overhead.

Current fog-based solutions either assume fog nodes are trustworthy or require the existence of a reliable entity to maintain run-time information about such third-party fog nodes, which is not feasible because of resource constraints at the network edge.

The trust model based on the social network technology [22–25] has been investigated to define the trustworthiness of the third-party participates in a service composition process. Multiple foreseen path-based heuristic algorithm [23] proposes a routing algorithm to find the optimal social trust path between a service provider and a service consumer. Although it targets a trustworthy issue in a routing problem, it has the potential to solve the composite service selection in the fog computing environment. LOCASS [25] introduces the social selfishness to a dynamic fog network using for mobile caching. It assumes a computing environment that consists of mixed cooperative and selfish service providers, which is close to the FaaS environment. However, LOCASS do not consider the trustworthy issue for service composition or SLA negotiation.

Decentralized consensus mechanisms have a great potential to address the trustworthy problem in fog computing. IOTA [12] is a type of transaction settlement and data transfer layer designed for IoT. The core technology in IOTA is called Tangle [13] that is based on a structure of DAG. This paper leverages the concept of Tangle's consensus mechanism and proposes a graph-based decentralized reputation model for service provisioning in fog computing environment. Compare with Tangle, the proposed solution provide an integrated model to represent a fog node's reputation and can support not only an individual transaction but also composite transactions.

3   System Model

The service composition model in the proposed solution is based on FogSEA [21]. FogSEA supports service composition by service discovery over a semantic service overlay network [14]. Such a network introduces Input/Output (I/O) dependency and maintains data dependency links between fog nodes, so the system can efficiently aggregate a composite service's information through the overlay network. This paper extends the overlay network with a reputation model to enhance service selection and SLA negotiation for composite services. In this paper, how the fog network discovers services and how the services being composed will not be described as it has been introduced in [14].

This paper proposes a Tangle-Fog network that is a DAG represented by $G(V, E)$. In this structure, we define a fog node that provides service in a transaction as a *site* and is represented by V, which means the fog node that has participated in a service composition process as a service provider. Edges E represents approvals provided by other fog nodes that consumes the service. A fog node that only provides but not consumes services in a transaction is defined as a *genesis*. In a Tangle-Fog, we define the leaf sites as *tips*. Tangle-Fog is maintained in the fog network and expands when a new transaction is issued. In a site, the arrow pointing to the site indicates that this site has been verified by another site, and the arrow pointing from site indicates that the site has verified an existing site.

In this paper, a verification indicates that a fog node has used the service provided by a site and confirmed that the actual quality of service (QoS) is close to the QoS claimed by the site. According to Tangle [13], new coming nodes have to verify two existing tips to join the system. Unlike that in Tangle, this paper defines if a fog node wants to issue a new transaction to a site, it must verify the service delivery process of the site and add a new edge directing to it. As shown in Fig. 1, ω is the weight of a site, which represents the number of calculations that the fog node pays for constructing Tangle-Fog. The more often a fog node consumes the service provided by a site, the greater the amount of calculations is contributed by the fog node. H(t) is the cumulative weight of a site or a genesis which is derived from the weight of its own site and the direct or indirect verification of the weight of the sites.

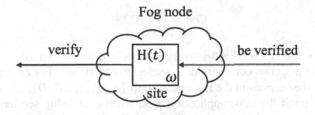

Fig. 1. The site.

Figure 2 illustrates an example of a Tangle-Fog network. The example shows two geneses and 9 sites. Site A and C have not been verified by any other site, so we call the two sites as tips. A is verified directly by B, C and D. C directly verifies A. For instance, since the cumulative weight of site B is its own weight plus the sum of the weights of D, E, and F. It can be calculated that at time t, the cumulative weight of B is $H_B(t) = 1 + 3 + 1 + 2 = 7$. A site's cumulative weight updates along with the added tips, and the site with a higher $H(t)$ value indicates that the site itself and its subsequent site were used and verified more times.

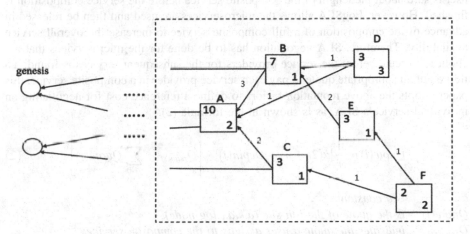

Fig. 2. The example of Tangle-Fog in a fog computing environment

In the Tangle-Fog network, a confirmation confidence (Con) is defined for each site, which represents the credibility of the resources provided by this fog node. When the confirmation confidence reaches a certain threshold, the fog node is trusted and can participate in the service composition. The confirmation confidence can be calculated by the formula (1), where m represents the total number of sites in Tangle-Fog, and n represents the number of sites that directly or indirectly verify a certain fog node, which is also the weight value for the edges in a Tangle-Fog network. As shown in Fig. 2, $n_{C \to A} = 2$. A higher Con indicates the site's service has been used and verified by more fog nodes.

$$Con = \frac{n}{m} * 100\% \tag{1}$$

Given this solution's service discovery and composition are based on FogSEA, any (micro-)services in a composite service are selected on demand. For example, assuming the two composite services in the fog node group $\{A, D\}$, $\{A, B, D\}$, $\{A, C, F\}$ and $\{A, B, E, F\}$ can support the same application task, when composing services for the task, FogSEA will select one fog node from B, D and C to hand over the administration of a service composition process only after A has provided its service (See Fig. 2). Therefore, we model the service selection on the fog node (site) i as a multi-attribute decision making (MADM) process with an attribute set $\{H(t), Con, Depth(G)\}$ and a discrete set of r $(r \geq 2)$ potential alternatives $\{i+1, i+2, \ldots i+r\}$. Depth(G) represents the depth of the sub-graph that include all alternative sites for the composite service, which is the length of the longest oriented path from the tips to the site. The value of Depth(G) can be calculated during the backward service discovery in FogSEA.

FogSEA's service discovery and composition model will compose a set of microservices from different service providers to satisfy one user task when there is not a single service provider can support the task independently, so we cannot assume a user is sure about the length of the composite service before the service composition is finished. However, FogSEA allows the microservices are used and then be released in advance of the composition of a full composite service to increase the overall service availability. Therefore, SLA negotiation has to be done for the microservices that are about to execute before the service providers for the subsequent services is found. To figure out an appropriate quote to pay each service provider in a composite service, this paper adopts the above reputation factors to define a reference cost for negotiating an individual service's SLA, as is shown in the formula (2).

$$Quote(i) = \frac{1}{r}[\alpha(2r + n) + Depth(i)] \cdot \left[Q_{request} - \sum_{j=0}^{i-1} Quote(j) \right] \tag{2}$$

α *is a constant.*

$Quote(i)$ *is the quote of the i-th site (a.k.a., fog node).*

$Q_{request}$ *indicates the quote a user assigns to the composite service.*

4   Evaluation

In order to prove the effectiveness of the proposed mechanism, we conducted a simulation on Matlab. We deployed 100 fog nodes and assumed each fog node only host one service for simplicity. 10% of these fog nodes were initialized as unreliable nodes. In this experiment, we deployed an IoT application that includes five tasks, each of which can be supported by a certain group of microservices. The group size is a random number from one to two. The workflow of the application is shown in Fig. 3. The price of each microservice follows a Gaussian distribution $\sim N(2, 0.5^2)$. Services were generated that can include a random number of tasks from one to five. Before sampling data, the simulation ran by using 500 service requests to build the Tangle-Fog network. We applied the self-adaptive combination approach in the literature [11] as a baseline to evaluate our proposed model, represented by CM-T. In this simulation, we used the linear weighted sum method to solve the MADM problem during service selection, but the other problem-solving methods can also be applied to the proposed model.

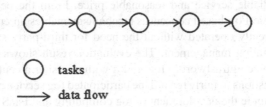

○ tasks

⟶ data flow

Fig. 3. The application workflow used in the evaluation.

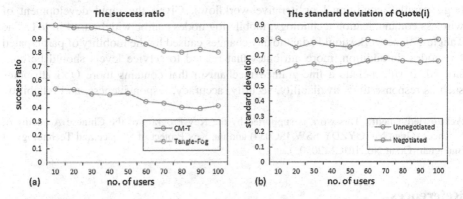

Fig. 4. The result of (a) the success ratio and (b) the standard diviation of with the increasing number of users.

Figure 4(a) presents the success ratio of the service composition with the increasing number of users. Both the two approaches' success ratio decreased when the number of users grows. This is because the average fog node availability for each user is reduced when a user has more competitors. The results show that the scheme proposed in this paper has a higher success ratio compared to the baseline as the increase in users' requests. Figure 4(b) illustrates the standard deviation of $Quote(i)$ for each participated fog node. A smaller value of the standard deviation indicates the participated fog nodes are more fairly paid in the service transaction. The result curves show that the negotiated service composition by using the proposed reference cost achieved more fair transactions.

5 Conclusion and Future Work

This paper proposes a reputation model for service providers in FaaS. It extends FogSEA and introduces a graph-based decentralized trust mechanism to ensure the availability of third-party fog nodes. It also presents a way to generate a reference cost to allow a part of the SLA negotiation can be conducted without the presence of all the service providers or the knowledge about the full composite service.

From the FaaS users' point of view, this solution helps them to obtain a good service experience with reliable service and reasonable price. From the perspective of FaaS providers, our Tangle-Fog-based consensus mechanism enables an end-to-end verification and can be directly operated without the need for third-party supervision, which saves costs on operation management. The evaluation result shows that the proposed solution can recognize untrustworthy fog nodes without using a centralized entity and gives the user suggestions to fairly reward the participated fog service providers. This has the potential to promote the development of fog computing and FaaS business model.

However, the proposed work only goes a small step towards the end of providing a fully functional trustworthy fog computing environment. First of all, the Tangle-Fog network will need to support the service composition with a more complex workflow (e.g., parallel, conditional or iterative workflow). Given the rapid development of wireless communication technology, mobile fog nodes can be widely used in IoT. The Tangle-Fog network should adapt to any changes caused by the mobility of participated fog nodes. In addition, more attributes that related to service levels should be considered. It will include a fine-grained mechanism that contains more QoS attributes such as response time, availability, security, accuracy, responsiveness, and reliability.

Acknowledgement. This work is supported by the Key Program of the Chinese Academy of Sciences (Grant No. QYZDY-SSW-JSC034) and the Key Project of Science and Technology of Shanghai (Grant No. 16JC1420503).

References

1. Pirbhulal, S., Zhang, H., Me, A.E.: A novel secure IoT-based smart home automation system using a wireless sensor network. Sensors **17**(1), 69 (2017)
2. Ming, L. (1999). http://www.dvbcn.com/2018/04/12-161148.html. Accessed 19 April 2018
3. Zheng, Z., Wang, P., Liu, J.: Real-time big data processing framework: challenges and solutions. Appl. Math. Inf. Sci. **9**(6), 3169–3190 (2015)
4. Bonomi, F., Milito, R., Natarajan, P., Zhu, J.: Fog computing: a platform for internet of things and analytics. In: Bessis, N., Dobre, C. (eds.) Big Data and Internet of Things: A Roadmap for Smart Environments. SCI, vol. 546, pp. 169–186. Springer, Cham (2014). https://doi.org/10.1007/978-3-319-05029-4_7
5. Skarlat, O., Nardelli, M., Schulte, S.: Resource provisioning for IoT services in the fog. Serv. Oriented Comput. Appl. **11**(4), 427–443 (2016)
6. Chaudhary, R., Kumar, N., Zeadally, S.: Network service chaining in fog and cloud computing for the 5G environment: data management and security challenges. IEEE Commun. Mag. **55**(11), 114–122 (2017)

7. Ashrafi, T.H., Hossain, M.A., Arefin, S.E., Das, K.D.J., Chakrabarty, A.: Service based FOG computing model for IoT. In: IEEE International Conference on Collaboration and Internet Computing, pp. 163–172. IEEE Computer Society (2017)
8. Minh, Q.T., Nguyen, D.T., An, V.L., Hai, D.N., Truong, A.: Toward service placement on Fog computing landscape. In: Nafosted Conference on Information and Computer Science, pp. 291–296 (2017)
9. Santoro, D., Zozin, D., Pizzolli, D., Pellegrini, F.D., Cretti, S.: Foggy: a platform for workload orchestration in a fog computing environment. IEEE International Conference on Cloud Computing Technology and Science, pp. 231–234. IEEE (2017)
10. Yang, Y.: FA2ST: Fog as a Service Technology. In: IEEE Computer Software and Applications Conference, p. 708. IEEE Computer Society (2017)
11. Chen, N., Clarke, S.: A dynamic service composition model for adaptive systems in mobile computing environments. In: Franch, X., Ghose, Aditya K., Lewis, Grace A., Bhiri, S. (eds.) ICSOC 2014. LNCS, vol. 8831, pp. 93–107. Springer, Heidelberg (2014). https://doi.org/10.1007/978-3-662-45391-9_7
12. Divya, M., Biradar, N.B.: IOTA-next generation block chain. Int. J. Eng. Comput. Sci. 7, 23823–23826 (2018)
13. Serguei, P.: Tangle. IOTA (2017)
14. Kalasapur, S., Kumar, M., Shirazi, B.A.: Dynamic service composition in pervasive computing. IEEE Trans. Parallel Distrib. Syst. 18, 907–918 (2007)
15. Tschorsch, F., Scheuermann, B.: Bitcoin and beyond: a technical survey on decentralized digital currencies. IEEE Commun. Surv. Tutor. 18(3), 2084–2123 (2016)
16. Cao, Z., Zhang, X., Zhang, W.: A context-aware adaptive web service composition framework. In: IEEE International Conference on Computational Intelligence & Communication Technology, pp. 62–66. IEEE (2015)
17. Madkour, M., Ghanami, D.E., Maach, A.: Context-aware service adaptation: an approach based on fuzzy sets and service composition. J. Inf. Sci. Eng. 29(1), 1–16 (2013)
18. Lin, C., Kavi, K.: A QoS-aware BPEL framework for service selection and composition using QoS properties. Int. J. Adv. Softw. 6(1 and 2), 56–68 (2014)
19. Rajeswari, M., Sambasivam, G., Balaji, N.: Original article: appraisal and analysis on various web service composition approaches based on QoS factors. J. King Saud Univ.-Comput. Inf. Sci. 26(1), 143–152 (2014)
20. Wang, Z., Xu, T., Qian, Z.: A parameter-based scheme for service composition in pervasive computing environment. In: Complex, Intelligent and Software Intensive Systems, CISIS 2009 (2009)
21. Chen, N., Yang, Y., Li, J., Zhang, T.: A fog-based service enablement architecture for cross-domain IoT applications. IEEE Fog World Congress (2017)
22. Jamali, M., Ester, M.: A matrix factorization technique with trust propagation for recommendation in social networks. In: ACM Conference on Recommender Systems, pp. 135–142 ACM (2010)
23. Liu, G., Wang, Y., Orgun, M.A., et al.: Finding the optimal social trust path for the selection of trustworthy service providers in complex social networks. IEEE Trans. Serv. Comput. 6(2), 152–167 (2013)
24. Ziegler, C.N., Lausen, G.: Spreading activation models for trust propagation. In: IEEE International Conference on e-Technology, e-Commerce and e-Service, pp. 83–97. IEEE (2004)
25. Yang, Y., Wu, Y., Chen, N., et al.: LOCASS: local optimal caching algorithm with social selfishness for mixed cooperative and selfish devices. IEEE Access PP(99), 1 (2018)

Attribute-Based VLR Group Signature Scheme from Lattices

Yanhua Zhang[1(⊠)], Yong Gan[2], Yifeng Yin[1], and Huiwen Jia[3]

[1] Zhengzhou University of Light Industry, Zhengzhou 450002, China
{yhzhang,yinyifeng}@zzuli.edu.cn
[2] Zhengzhou Institute of Technology, Zhengzhou 450044, China
yongg@zzuli.edu.cn
[3] Guangzhou University, Guangzhou 510006, China
hwjia@gzhu.edu.cn

Abstract. Attribute-based group signatures allow a group member who possesses certain attributes to anonymously sign messages on behalf the group, and an opening authority can reveal the real identity of the signer from a signature in case of any needed. Almost all of the existing schemes work only in the bilinear map setting and are insecure against quantum computers. The only exception is the lattice-based construction put forward by Kuchta et al. (ICISC 2017) that can handle the user enrollment, however, users cannot be revoked. As a flexible and practical revocation approach, verifier-local revocation (VLR) only needs the verifiers to own the up-to-date revocation information. In this work, we provide the first attribute-based VLR group signature from lattices, and thus, the first construction that supports for membership revocation and is quantum-resistant. The signature size of our scheme is linear in terms of the size of the threshold predicate and in the random oracle model, the security can be reduced to the worst-case lattice hardness problem, the approximating shortest independent vector problem (SIVP).

Keywords: Lattice-based cryptography
Attribute-based group signature · Verifier-local revocation
Quantum-resistant

1 Introduction

Group signatures, a cryptographic primitive introduced by Chaum and van Heyst [8], allow the group member who owns a private key certified by some authority to sign messages in the name of the group, while retaining its anonymity. Yet, given a valid signature, an opening authority can reveal the real identity of the signer. Attribute-based group signature [12] is a new variant of group signature, in which each member receives a private key depending on the assigned attributes, and

Supported by the National Natural Science Foundation of China under Grant No. 61572445.

J. Vaidya and J. Li (Eds.): ICA3PP 2018, LNCS 11337, pp. 600–610, 2018.
https://doi.org/10.1007/978-3-030-05063-4_46

a signed message will be accepted if the verifier convinces that the signature is produced by some member whose attributes set satisfies the signing predicate, that is to say, in attribute-based group signatures, the group members do not have the same signing privileges, instead, a member who only possesses sufficient attributes satisfying the predicate can sign a message on behalf of the group.

RELATED WORK. After its first put forward by Khader [12], there has been much progress as for the construction of attribute-based group signatures over the last few years. An attribute-based group signature scheme with member revocation [13] was constructed, while without achieving attribute anonymity. Subsequently, a dynamic attribute-based group signature scheme supporting a frequent change in attribute relationships [9], an attribute-based group signature with attribute anonymity and traceability [2], an attribute-based group signature with signature size independent of the number of attributes [3], an attribute-based group signature with verifier-local revocation and backward unlinkability [4] and a fully secure construction against adaptive adversary were proposed. Recently, Kuchta et al. first achieve an attribute-based instantiation of the generic group signature framework of [15], meanwhile, supporting the dynamic growth of memberships.

However, all of the attribute-based group signature schemes above-mentioned are based on the hardness of traditional number-theoretic problems, i.e. discrete logarithm problems, which are not secure against quantum computers and work only in bilinear map setting. To design secure and efficient attribute-based group signatures against quantum attacks is becoming an urgent task.

Lattice based cryptography, as one of the efficient candidates of post-quantum cryptography, has attracted a significant interest in recent years, and large numbers of lattice-based constructions are proposed, in particular, signature schemes, such as group signatures [16–22,25,28] and attribute-based signatures [6,26,27]. The only known attribute-based group signature from lattices that has a dynamic feature was put forward by Kuchta et al. [14]. Their scheme handles the user enrollment problem, however, users cannot be revoked.

The support for membership revocation is a desirable functionality for group signature scheme. As a flexible and practical revocation approach, verifier-local revocation (VLR) [7] only needs the verifiers to own some up-to-date revocation information. In a VLR group signature, the verifier is given a revocation list (RL) which contains a token for every revoked group member. The verifier accepts the signatures generated by the unrevoked members and obtains nothing else about the unrevoked member generating these signatures. If some member is revoked, the signatures from it are no longer accepted. Thus, apart from only supporting a dynamically growing population of users in attribute-based group signatures, an orthogonal problem of dynamic user revocation yields, and if we can construct an efficient attribute-based group signature scheme with membership revocation from lattices?

OUR RESULTS. In this work, we introduce the first attribute-based VLR group signature from lattices in the random oracle model (ROM) to reply to the above open problem positively, which is also the first construction that is secure against quantum computes. Although the proposed scheme only satisfies a weaker notion of *selfless-anonymity* [7]. Nevertheless, compared with the only known lattice-based construction, our construction enjoys several noticeable advantages:

1. Revocation: Our scheme is the first dynamic attribute-based group signature from lattices supporting for membership revocation, which is a desirable functionality for practical attribute-based group signature scheme.
2. Simplicity: Our scheme is constructed simply under the VLR approach and a new non-interactive zero-knowledge Stern-type protocol. Moreover, the revocation token can be used in tracing algorithm, thus, our scheme is free from any lattice-based encryption operations.
3. Security: Our scheme is provably secure and can be reduced to the worst-case hardness of approximating the shortest independent vector problem (SIVP) to within a factor $\gamma = \ell \cdot \widetilde{\mathcal{O}}(n^2)$ for general lattice with dimension n and $N = 2^\ell$ is the maximum number of the group members.
4. Efficiency: The group public key and the signer's private key enjoy bit-sizes $\ell \cdot \widetilde{\mathcal{O}}(n^2)$ and $(n'+p') \cdot \widetilde{\mathcal{O}}(n)$, respectively, where $n' = |\mathsf{Att}|$, and $p' \le n'$ is the number of attributes assigned to the signer. Compared with the lattice-based construction [14], there is a noticeable improvement.

Given the security parameter n, let $t \le p$ be the threshold value, while it is the number of attributes associated with the signature in other schemes. The terms IND-CPA and IND-CCA refer to indistinguishability under chosen plaintext attack and chosen ciphertext attack, respectively. User-Anon., Qua.-Res., Revo. are the abbreviations of user-anonymity, quantum-resistant and revocation, respectively. In Table 1, we compare our scheme with known attribute-based group signatures in details. The group key size, signer's key size and signature size of our scheme are larger than others except [14]. In fact, the main disadvantages of lattice-based cryptography are exactly large key sizes and large space complexity.

Table 1. Comparison with known attribute-based group signatures.

Scheme	Gpk size	Sig. size	Signer's key size	User-Anon.	Qua.-Res.	Revo.	Model
[13]	$\mathcal{O}(t)$	$\mathcal{O}(t)$	$p' \cdot \mathcal{O}(\log n)$	IND-CPA	no	yes	ROM
[9]	$\mathcal{O}(t)$	$\mathcal{O}(t)$	$p' \cdot \mathcal{O}(\log n)$	IND-CCA	no	no	ROM
[2]	$\mathcal{O}(t)$	$\mathcal{O}(1)$	$p' \cdot \mathcal{O}(\log n)$	IND-CCA	no	no	Standard
[3]	$\mathcal{O}(t)$	$\mathcal{O}(1)$	$p' \cdot \mathcal{O}(\log n)$	IND-CPA	no	no	Standard
[4]	$\mathcal{O}(t)$	$\mathcal{O}(1)$	$t \cdot \mathcal{O}(\log n)$	Selfless	no	yes	Standard
[14]	$2^\ell \cdot \widetilde{\mathcal{O}}(n^2)$	$p' \cdot \ell \cdot \widetilde{\mathcal{O}}(n)$	$p' \cdot \ell \cdot \widetilde{\mathcal{O}}(n)$	IND-CCA	yes	no	ROM
Ours	$\ell \cdot \widetilde{\mathcal{O}}(n^2)$	$p \cdot \ell \cdot \widetilde{\mathcal{O}}(n)$	$(n'+p') \cdot \widetilde{\mathcal{O}}(n)$	Selfless	yes	yes	ROM

To summarize, we solve the problem of dynamic user revocation for attribute-based group signature against quantum computers, and provide the first attribute-based VLR group signature from lattices in the random oracle model. Moreover, our construction is relatively simple and efficient.

2   Preliminaries

NOTATIONS. If S is a finite set, we use $|S|$ to denote its size. $S(k)$ denotes the set of permutations of k elements and $\leftarrow_R$ denotes that sampling elements from a distribution uniformly at random. The Euclidean and infinity norm of $\mathbf{e}$ are denoted by $\|\mathbf{e}\|$ and $\|\mathbf{e}\|_\infty$, respectively. Given $\mathbf{e} = (e_1, e_2, \cdots, e_n) \in \mathbb{R}^n$, $\mathsf{Parse}(\mathbf{e}, k_1, k_2)$ denotes a vector $(e_{k_1}, \cdots, e_{k_2}) \in \mathbb{R}^{k_2 - k_1 + 1}$ for $1 \le k_1 \le k_2 \le n$.

The standard notations $\mathcal{O}$ and ω are used to classify the growth of functions. All logarithms are of base 2.

2.1   Lattices

Definition 1. *For integers n, m, prime $q \ge 2$, $\mathbf{A} \in \mathbb{Z}_q^{n \times m}$, $\mathbf{u} \in \mathbb{Z}_q^n$, define,*

$$\Lambda_q^\perp(\mathbf{A}) = \{\mathbf{e} \in \mathbb{Z}^m \mid \mathbf{Ae} = \mathbf{0} \bmod q\}, \quad \Lambda_q^\mathbf{u}(\mathbf{A}) = \{\mathbf{e} \in \mathbb{Z}^m \mid \mathbf{Ae} = \mathbf{u} \bmod q\}.$$

For $s > 0$, define the Gaussian function on $\mathbb{R}^m$ with center $\mathbf{c}$,

$$\forall \mathbf{e} \in \mathbb{R}^m, \quad \rho_{s,\mathbf{c}}(\mathbf{e}) = \exp(-\pi \|\mathbf{e} - \mathbf{c}\|^2 / s^2).$$

For $\mathbf{c} \in \mathbb{R}^m, s > 0$, define the discrete Gaussian distribution over Λ,

$$\forall \mathbf{e} \in \mathbb{Z}^m, \quad \mathcal{D}_{\Lambda,s,\mathbf{c}} = \rho_{s,\mathbf{c}}(\mathbf{e}) / \rho_{s,\mathbf{c}}(\Lambda).$$

For convenience, we denote $\mathcal{D}_{\Lambda,s,\mathbf{c}}$ as $\mathcal{D}_{\Lambda,s}$ if $\mathbf{c} = \mathbf{0}$.

Lemma 1 [1,5,23]. *Let $n \ge 1$, $q \ge 2$ and $m = \lceil 2n \log q \rceil$, there exists a PPT algorithm $\mathsf{TrapGen}(q, n, m)$ that outputs a matrix $\mathbf{A}$ and a trapdoor $\mathbf{T_A}$ such that $\mathbf{A}$ is statistically close to uniform matrix over $\mathbb{Z}_q^{n \times m}$. Let $s = \omega(\sqrt{n} \cdot \log n)$, and for $\mathbf{u} \in \mathbb{Z}_q^n$, there is a PPT algorithm $\mathsf{SamplePre}(\mathbf{A}, \mathbf{T_A}, \mathbf{u}, s)$ that outputs $\mathbf{e} \in \mathbb{Z}^m$, which is drawn from a distribution statistically close to $\mathcal{D}_{\Lambda_q^\mathbf{u}(\mathbf{A}),s}$.*

2.2   Hardness Assumption

The (inhomogeneous) small integer solution (ISIS, SIS) problems are defined as follows.

Definition 2 [10]. *The $\mathsf{SIS}_{n,m,q,\beta}^\infty$ and $\mathsf{ISIS}_{n,m,q,\beta}^\infty$ problems in infinity norm are that given a prime q, uniformly matrix $\mathbf{A} \in \mathbb{Z}_q^{n \times m}$ and a vector $\mathbf{u} \in \mathbb{Z}_q^n$, to find a non-zero $\mathbf{e} \in \mathbb{Z}^m$ such that $\mathbf{Ae} = \mathbf{0} \bmod q$, $\|\mathbf{e}\|_\infty \le \beta$ and $\mathbf{A} \cdot \mathbf{e} = \mathbf{u} \bmod q$, $\|\mathbf{e}\|_\infty \le \beta$, respectively.*

Lemma 2 [10,24]. *For m, $\beta = \mathrm{poly}(n)$, $q \ge \beta \cdot \omega(\sqrt{n \log n})$, the average-case $\mathsf{SIS}_{n,m,q,\beta}^\infty$ or $\mathsf{ISIS}_{n,m,q,\beta}^\infty$ problem is as hard as SIVP_γ problem in worst-case to within $\gamma = \beta \cdot \widetilde{\mathcal{O}}(\sqrt{nm})$ factor. In particular, if $\beta = 1$, $q = \widetilde{\mathcal{O}}(n)$, $m = \lceil 2n \log q \rceil$, the $\mathsf{SIS}_{n,m,q,1}^\infty$ or $\mathsf{ISIS}_{n,m,q,1}^\infty$ problem is as hard as $\mathsf{SIVP}_{\widetilde{\mathcal{O}}(n)}$.*

3   The Interactive Zero-Knowledge Stern-Type Protocol

In this section, we present an efficient proof of knowledge protocol which allows a prover $\mathcal{P}$ to convince the verifier $\mathcal{V}$ that $\mathcal{P}$ is indeed a group member who can sign a message $\mathsf{m} \in \{0,1\}^*$, i.e., its attributes set satisfies the predicate $\mathcal{T}$ and its revocation token is not in RL.

Given $\mathsf{id} = (id_1, id_2, \cdots, id_\ell) \in \{0,1\}^\ell$, we define four sets:

1. B_{3m}: the set of vectors in $\{-1,0,1\}^{3m}$ having m coordinates -1, m coordinates 1 and m coordinates 0.
2. $B_{2\ell}$: the set of vectors in $\{0,1\}^{2\ell}$ having Hamming weight ℓ.
3. $\mathsf{Sec}_\beta(\mathsf{id})$: the set of vectors $\mathbf{e} = (\mathbf{e}_1, \mathbf{e}_2, id_1\mathbf{e}_2, id_2\mathbf{e}_2, \cdots, id_\ell\mathbf{e}_2) \in \mathbb{Z}_q^{(\ell+2)m}$ and $\|\mathbf{e}\|_\infty \leq \beta$.
4. $\mathsf{SecExt}(\mathsf{id}^*)$: the set of vectors $\mathbf{e} = (\mathbf{e}_1, \mathbf{e}_2, id_1\mathbf{e}_2, id_2\mathbf{e}_2, \cdots, id_\ell\mathbf{e}_2, \cdots, id_{2\ell}\mathbf{e}_2)$ $\in \{-1,0,1\}^{(2\ell+2)3m}$ for $\mathsf{id}^* = (id_1, id_2, \cdots, id_{2\ell}) \in B_{2\ell}$, where id^* is an extension of id and $\mathbf{e}_1, \mathbf{e}_2 \in B_{3m}$.

Given vectors $\big\{\mathbf{e}_i = (\mathbf{a}_i, \mathbf{b}_{i,0}, \mathbf{b}_{i,1}, \cdots, \mathbf{b}_{i,2\ell}) \in \mathbb{Z}_q^{(2\ell+2)3m}\big\}_{i \in \{1,2,\cdots,p\}}$, for permutations $\pi, \varphi \in S(3m), \tau \in S(2\ell)$ and $\phi \in S(p)$, we define a composition of these four permutations,

$$F_{\pi,\varphi,\tau,\phi}(\mathbf{e}_i) = (\pi(\mathbf{a}_{\phi(i)}), \varphi(\mathbf{b}_{\phi(i),0}), \varphi(\mathbf{b}_{\phi(i),\tau(1)}), \cdots, \varphi(\mathbf{b}_{\phi(i),\tau(2\ell)})).$$

In particular, given $\mathsf{id} \in \{0,1\}^\ell$, $\pi, \varphi \in S(3m)$, $\tau \in S(2\ell)$, $\phi \in S(p)$, and $\{\mathbf{e}_i\}_{i \in \{1,2,\cdots,p\}}$, it can be checked that,

$$\{\mathbf{e}_i\}_{i \in \{1,2,\cdots,p\}} \in \mathsf{SecExt}(\mathsf{id}^*) \Leftrightarrow \{F_{\pi,\varphi,\tau,\phi}(\mathbf{e}_i)\}_{i \in \{1,2,\cdots,p\}} \in \mathsf{SecExt}(\mathsf{id}^*).$$

As in [17,20], we now introduce the Decomposition-Extension technique.

Let $k = \lfloor \log \beta \rfloor + 1$, $\beta_1 = \lceil \frac{\beta}{2} \rceil$, $\beta_2 = \lceil \frac{\beta - \beta_1}{2} \rceil$, $\beta_3 = \lceil \frac{\beta - \beta_1 - \beta_2}{2} \rceil, \cdots, \beta_k = 1$.

Decomposition: Given $\mathbf{e} = (e_1, e_2, \cdots, e_m) \in \mathbb{Z}^m$ for $\|\mathbf{e}\|_\infty \leq \beta$, the goal is to represent $\mathbf{e}$ by k vectors in $\{-1,0,1\}^m$. The procedure Dec proceeds as follows:

1. For $i \in \{1, \cdots, m\}$, consider a representation of e_i as $e_i = \sum_{j=1}^k \beta_j e_{i,j}$ where $e_{i,j} \in \{-1,0,1\}$.
2. For $i \in \{1,2,\cdots,k\}$, let $\widehat{\mathbf{e}}_i = (e_{1,i}, e_{2,i}, \cdots, e_{m,i}) \in \{-1,0,1\}^m$. We observe that $\mathbf{e} = \sum_{i=1}^k \beta_i \widehat{\mathbf{e}}_i$.

Extension: Given a vector $\widehat{\mathbf{e}} = (e_1, e_2, \cdots, e_m) \in \{-1,0,1\}^m$, the goal is to extend it to $\mathbf{e} \in B_{3m}$. The procedure Ext proceeds as follows:

1. Denote the numbers of coordinates -1, 0 and 1 in vector $\widehat{\mathbf{e}}$ are λ_{-1}, λ_0 and λ_1, respectively.
2. Choose a random vector $\mathbf{e}' \in \{-1,0,1\}^{2m}$ which has $(m - \lambda_{-1})$ coordinates -1, $(m - \lambda_0)$ coordinates 0 and $(m - \lambda_1)$ coordinates 1. Let $\mathbf{e} = (\widehat{\mathbf{e}}, \mathbf{e}')$, for $\pi \in S(3m)$, we have $\mathbf{e} \in B_{3m} \Leftrightarrow \pi(\mathbf{e}) \in B_{3m}$.

Matrix Extension: Given a matrix $\mathbf{A}' = [\mathbf{A}|\mathbf{A}_0|\mathbf{A}_1|\cdots|\mathbf{A}_\ell] \in \mathbb{Z}_q^{n\times(\ell+2)m}$, the goal is to extend it to $\mathbf{A}^* \in \mathbb{Z}_q^{n\times(2\ell+2)3m}$. The procedure is as follows:

1. Append $2m$ zero-columns to each of component-matrices and ℓ blocks of $\mathbf{0}^{3m}$.
2. Output $\mathbf{A}^* = [\mathbf{A}|\mathbf{0}^{n\times2m}|\mathbf{A}_0|\mathbf{0}^{n\times2m}|\mathbf{A}_1|\mathbf{0}^{n\times2m}|\cdots|\mathbf{A}_\ell|\mathbf{0}^{n\times2m}|\mathbf{0}^{n\times3m\ell}]$.

The underlying Stern-type protocol can be summarized as follows:

1. The public parameters are $\mathbf{A}' = [\mathbf{A}|\mathbf{A}_0|\mathbf{A}_1|\cdots|\mathbf{A}_\ell] \in \mathbb{Z}_q^{n\times(\ell+2)m}$, a threshold predicate $\mathcal{T} = (t, \mathsf{S})$ where $\mathsf{S} = \{\mathbf{u}_{j_1}, \mathbf{u}_{j_2}, \cdots, \mathbf{u}_{j_p}\} \subseteq \{\mathbf{u}_1, \mathbf{u}_2, \cdots, \mathbf{u}_{n'}\} = \mathsf{Att}$, $t \leq |\mathsf{S}| = p$, and $\mathbf{u}_i \in \mathbb{Z}_q^n$ for $i \in \{j_1, j_2, \cdots, j_p\}$.
2. The witness for the prover $\mathsf{id} = (id_1, \cdots, id_\ell) \in \{0,1\}^\ell$ with index a and a set of attributes $\mathsf{S}_a \subseteq \mathsf{Att}$ are:
   a. t vectors $\mathbf{e}_i = (\mathbf{e}_{i,1}, \mathbf{e}_{i,2}, id_1\mathbf{e}_{i,2}, \cdots, id_\ell\mathbf{e}_{i,2}) \in \mathsf{Sec}_\beta(\mathsf{id})$ for $\mathbf{u}_i \in \mathsf{S}_0 \subseteq (\mathsf{S} \cap \mathsf{S}_a)$ where $|\mathsf{S}_0| = t$.
   b. $p - t$ vectors $\mathbf{e}_i = (\mathbf{e}_{i,1}, \mathbf{e}_{i,2}, id_1\mathbf{e}_{i,2}, \cdots, id_\ell\mathbf{e}_{i,2}) \notin \mathsf{Sec}_\beta(\mathsf{id})$ for $\mathbf{u}_i \in \mathsf{S}\backslash\mathsf{S}_0$.
   For convenience, we suppose that $\mathsf{S}_0 = \{\mathbf{u}_{j_1}, \mathbf{u}_{j_2}, \cdots, \mathbf{u}_{j_t}\}$. Moreover, $\mathsf{RL} = \{\mathbf{u}'_{a'} = (\mathbf{u}'_{a',1}, \cdots, \mathbf{u}'_{a',n'}) \in (\mathbb{Z}_q^n)^{n'}\}_{a'\leq N}$ is an additional input of the verifier.
3. The goal of the prover is to convince the verifier that:
   a. For $i \in \{j_1, j_2, \cdots, j_t\}$, $\mathbf{A}' \cdot \mathbf{e}_i = \mathbf{u}_i \bmod q$, where $\mathbf{e}_i \in \mathsf{Sec}_\beta(\mathsf{id})$, $\mathbf{u}_i \in \mathsf{S}_0$, while keeping id and S_0 secret.
   b. For $i \in \{j_{t+1}, \cdots, j_p\}$, $\mathbf{A}' \cdot \mathbf{e}_i = \mathbf{u}_i \bmod q$, where $\mathbf{e}_i \notin \mathsf{Sec}_\beta(\mathsf{id})$, $\mathbf{u}_i \in \mathsf{S}\backslash\mathsf{S}_0$.
   c. For $i \in \{j_1, j_2, \cdots, j_p\}$, $\mathbf{A} \cdot \mathbf{e}_{i,1} \bmod q \neq \mathbf{u}'_{a',i} \in \mathbf{u}'_{a'} \in \mathsf{RL}$.
   Let COM be a statistically hiding and computationally blinding commitment scheme as it was proposed in [11], and $\mathbf{A}^* \in \mathbb{Z}_q^{n\times(2\ell+2)3m}$ be an extension of $\mathbf{A}'$. For simplicity, we omit the randomness of COM.

The prover $\mathcal{P}$ does as follows:

1. For $i \in \{j_1, j_2, \cdots, j_t\}, j \in \{1, 2, \cdots, k\}$, $\mathcal{P}$ applies the Dec and Ext techniques on $\mathbf{e}_i$ to obtain $\mathbf{e}_{i,j} \in \mathsf{SecExt}(\mathsf{id}^*)$ such that $\mathbf{A}^* \cdot (\sum_{j=1}^k \beta_j\mathbf{e}_{i,j}) = \mathbf{u}_i \bmod q$.
2. For $i \in \{j_{t+1}, j_{t+2}, \cdots, j_p\}, j \in \{1, 2, \cdots, k\}$, $\mathcal{P}$ can decompose and extend $\mathbf{e}_i$ to obtain $\mathbf{e}_{i,j} \in \mathbb{Z}_q^{(2\ell+2)3m}$ such that $\mathbf{A}^* \cdot (\sum_{j=1}^k \beta_j\mathbf{e}_{i,j}) = \mathbf{u}_i \bmod q$.

Let $e_1 = \{j_1, j_2, \cdots, j_p\}$, $e_2 = \{1, 2, \cdots, k\}$, the details are as follows:

a. Commitments: $\mathcal{P}$ randomly samples $\{\mathbf{r}_{i,j}\}_{i\in e_1, j\in e_2} \in \mathbb{Z}_q^{(2\ell+2)3m}$, $\mathbf{r}_{\mathsf{id}} \in \mathbb{Z}_q^{2\ell}$, permutations $\{\pi_{i,j}, \varphi_{i,j}\}_{i\in e_1, j\in e_2} \in \mathsf{S}(3m), \tau \in \mathsf{S}(2\ell), \phi \in \mathsf{S}(p)$. Let $\mathbf{r}_{i,j,0} = \mathsf{Parse}(\mathbf{r}_{i,j}, 1, m)$, $\mathcal{P}$ sends the commitment $\mathsf{CMT} = (\mathbf{c}_0, \mathbf{c}_1, \mathbf{c}_2, \mathbf{c}_3)$ to $\mathcal{V}$,

$$
\begin{cases}
\mathbf{c}_0 = \mathsf{COM}(\tau; \phi; \{\pi_{i,j}; \varphi_{i,j}\}_{i\in e_1, j\in e_2}; \{\mathbf{A} \cdot (\sum_{j=1}^k \beta_j\mathbf{r}_{i,j,0}) \bmod q\}_{i\in e_1}), \\
\mathbf{c}_1 = \mathsf{COM}(\tau; \phi; \{\pi_{i,j}; \varphi_{i,j}\}_{i\in e_1, j\in e_2}; \{\mathbf{A}^* \cdot (\sum_{j=1}^k \beta_j\mathbf{r}_{i,j}) \bmod q\}_{i\in e_1}), \\
\mathbf{c}_2 = \mathsf{COM}(\tau(\mathbf{r}_{\mathsf{id}}); \{F_{\pi_{i,j}, \varphi_{i,j}, \tau, \phi}(\mathbf{r}_{i,j})\}_{i\in e_1, j\in e_2}), \\
\mathbf{c}_3 = \mathsf{COM}(\tau(\mathbf{r}_{\mathsf{id}} + \mathsf{id}^*); \{F_{\pi_{i,j}, \varphi_{i,j}, \tau, \phi}(\mathbf{r}_{i,j} + \mathbf{e}_{i,j})\}_{i\in e_1, j\in e_2}).
\end{cases}
$$

b. Challenge: $\mathcal{V}$ randomly chooses a challenge $\mathsf{CH} \leftarrow_R \{1, 2, 3\}$ and sends it to $\mathcal{P}$.

c. Response: Depending on the challenge CH, $\mathcal{P}$ replies as follows:
   - $\mathsf{CH} = 1$. For $i \in e_1$, $j \in e_2$, let $\mathbf{v}_{i,j} = F_{\pi_{i,j}, \varphi_{i,j}, \tau, \phi}(\mathbf{e}_{i,j})$, $\mathbf{v}_{\mathsf{id}} = \tau(\mathsf{id}^*)$, $\mathbf{w}_{i,j} = F_{\pi_{i,j}, \varphi_{i,j}, \tau, \phi}(\mathbf{r}_{i,j})$, and $\mathbf{w}_{\mathsf{id}} = \tau(\mathbf{r}_{\mathsf{id}})$. Then $\mathcal{P}$ sends,
     $$\mathsf{RSP} = (\{\mathbf{v}_{i,j}; \mathbf{w}_{i,j}\}_{i \in e_1, j \in e_2}; \mathbf{v}_{\mathsf{id}}; \mathbf{w}_{\mathsf{id}}).$$
   - $\mathsf{CH} = 2$. For $i \in e_1$, $j \in e_2$, let $\hat{\pi}_{i,j} = \pi_{i,j}$, $\hat{\varphi}_{i,j} = \varphi_{i,j}$, $\hat{\phi} = \phi$, $\hat{\tau} = \tau$, $\mathbf{y}_{i,j} = \mathbf{e}_{i,j} + \mathbf{r}_{i,j}$, and $\mathbf{y}_{\mathsf{id}} = \mathbf{r}_{\mathsf{id}} + \mathsf{id}^*$. Then $\mathcal{P}$ sends,
     $$\mathsf{RSP} = (\hat{\tau}; \hat{\phi}; \{\hat{\pi}_{i,j}; \hat{\varphi}_{i,j}; \mathbf{y}_{i,j}\}_{i \in e_1, j \in e_2}; \mathbf{y}_{\mathsf{id}}).$$
   - $\mathsf{CH} = 3$. For $i \in e_1$, $j \in e_2$, let $\tilde{\pi}_{i,j} = \pi_{i,j}$, $\tilde{\varphi}_{i,j} = \varphi_{i,j}$, $\tilde{\phi} = \phi$, $\tilde{\tau} = \tau$, $\mathbf{h}_{i,j} = \mathbf{r}_{i,j}$, and $\mathbf{h}_{\mathsf{id}} = \mathbf{r}_{\mathsf{id}}$. Then P sends,
     $$\mathsf{RSP} = (\tilde{\tau}; \tilde{\phi}; \{\tilde{\pi}_{i,j}; \tilde{\varphi}_{i,j}; \mathbf{h}_{i,j}\}_{i \in e_1, j \in e_2}; \mathbf{h}_{\mathsf{id}}).$$

d. Verification: Receiving the response RSP, $\mathcal{V}$ checks as follows:
   - $\mathsf{CH} = 1$. Check that $\mathbf{v}_{\mathsf{id}} \in \mathsf{B}_{2\ell}$ and for $i \in e_1$, $\mathbf{v}_{i,j} \in \mathsf{SecExt}(\mathbf{v}_{\mathsf{id}})$ is valid for t sets of vectors and all $j \in e_2$. Then, check that,

$$\begin{cases} \mathbf{c}_2 = \mathsf{COM}(\mathbf{w}_{\mathsf{id}}; \{\mathbf{w}_{i,j}\}_{i \in e_1, j \in e_2}), \\ \mathbf{c}_3 = \mathsf{COM}(\mathbf{v}_{\mathsf{id}} + \mathbf{w}_{\mathsf{id}}; \{\mathbf{v}_{i,j} + \mathbf{w}_{i,j}\}_{i \in e_1, j \in e_2}). \end{cases}$$

   - $\mathsf{CH} = 2$. For $i \in e_1$, $j \in e_2$, let $\mathbf{y}_{i,j,0} = \mathsf{Parse}(\mathbf{y}_{i,j}, 1, m)$, and check that,

$$\begin{cases} \forall\, \mathbf{u}'_{a'} = (\mathbf{u}'_{a',1}, \mathbf{u}'_{a',2}, \cdots, \mathbf{u}'_{a',n'}) \in \mathsf{RL}, \\ \mathbf{c}_0 \neq \mathsf{COM}(\hat{\tau}; \hat{\phi}; \{\hat{\pi}_{i,j}; \hat{\varphi}_{i,j}\}_{i \in e_1, j \in e_2}; \{\mathbf{A} \cdot (\sum_{j=1}^{k} \beta_j \mathbf{y}_{i,j,0}) - \mathbf{u}'_{a',i}\}_{i \in e_1}), \\ \mathbf{c}_1 = \mathsf{COM}(\hat{\tau}; \hat{\phi}; \{\hat{\pi}_{i,j}; \hat{\varphi}_{i,j}\}_{i \in e_1, j \in e_2}; \{\mathbf{A}^* \cdot (\sum_{j=1}^{k} \beta_j \mathbf{y}_{i,j}) - \mathbf{u}_i\}_{i \in e_1}), \\ \mathbf{c}_3 = \mathsf{COM}(\hat{\tau}(\mathbf{y}_{\mathsf{id}}); \{F_{\hat{\pi}_{i,j}, \hat{\varphi}_{i,j}, \hat{\tau}, \hat{\phi}}(\mathbf{y}_{i,j})\}_{i \in e_1, j \in e_2}). \end{cases}$$

   - $\mathsf{CH} = 3$. For $i \in e_1$, $j \in e_2$, let $\mathbf{h}_{i,j,0} = \mathsf{Parse}(\mathbf{h}_{i,j}, 1, m)$, and check that,

$$\begin{cases} \mathbf{c}_0 = \mathsf{COM}(\tilde{\tau}; \tilde{\phi}; \{\tilde{\pi}_{i,j}; \tilde{\varphi}_{i,j}\}_{i \in e_1, j \in e_2}; \{\mathbf{A} \cdot (\sum_{j=1}^{k} \beta_j \mathbf{h}_{i,j,0}) \bmod q\}_{i \in e_1}), \\ \mathbf{c}_1 = \mathsf{COM}(\tilde{\tau}; \tilde{\phi}; \{\tilde{\pi}_{i,j}; \tilde{\varphi}_{i,j}\}_{i \in e_1, j \in e_2}; \{\mathbf{A}^* \cdot (\sum_{j=1}^{k} \beta_j \mathbf{h}_{i,j}) \bmod q\}_{i \in e_1}), \\ \mathbf{c}_3 = \mathsf{COM}(\tilde{\tau}(\mathbf{r}_{\mathsf{id}}); \{F_{\tilde{\pi}_{i,j}, \tilde{\varphi}_{i,j}, \tilde{\tau}, \tilde{\phi}}(\mathbf{h}_{i,j})\}_{i \in e_1, j \in e_2}). \end{cases}$$

The verifier outputs 1 if and only if all the conditions hold, otherwise 0.

The associated relation $\mathcal{R}(n, k, \ell, m, \beta, p, t)$ in the above protocol can be defined as:

$$\mathcal{R} = \left\{ \begin{array}{l} \mathbf{A}' = [\mathbf{A}|\mathbf{A}_0|\mathbf{A}_1|\cdots|\mathbf{A}_\ell] \in \mathbb{Z}_q^{n \times (\ell+2)m}, \mathcal{T} = (t, \mathsf{S} = \{\mathbf{u}_{j_1}, \mathbf{u}_{j_2}, \cdots, \mathbf{u}_{j_p}\}), \\ \mathsf{id} \in \{0,1\}^\ell, \{\mathbf{e}_i\}_{i \in \{j_1, \cdots, j_p\}} \in \mathbb{Z}_q^{(\ell+2)m}, \mathsf{S}_0 = \{\mathbf{u}_{j_1}, \mathbf{u}_{j_2}, \cdots, \mathbf{u}_{j_t}\} \subseteq \mathsf{S}, \mathsf{RL}, \\ s.t.\ \mathbf{A}' \cdot \mathbf{e}_i = \mathbf{u}_i \bmod q, \mathbf{A} \cdot \mathbf{e}_{i,1} \bmod q \notin \mathsf{RL}, \{\mathbf{e}_i\}_{i \in \{j_1, \cdots, j_t\}} \in \mathsf{Sec}_\beta(\mathsf{id}), \\ \{\mathbf{e}_i\}_{i \in \{j_{t+1}, j_{t+2}, \cdots, j_p\}} \notin \mathsf{Sec}_\beta(\mathsf{id}). \end{array} \right\}$$

Theorem 1. *For a given commitment* CMT, *three valid responses* RSP_1, RSP_2 *and* RSP_3 *with respect to three different values of challenge* CH, *a statistically hiding and computationally binding commitment scheme* COM, *the protocol is a statistical zero-knowledge argument of knowledge for* $\mathcal{R}(n, k, \ell, m, \beta, p, t)$, *where each round has perfect completeness, soundness error 2/3, argument of knowledge property, communication cost* $\widetilde{\mathcal{O}}(p\ell n \log \beta)$. *The proof is given in the full version.*

4 An Attribute-Based VLR Group Signature Scheme from Lattices

4.1 Our Construction

ABGS.Setup(1^n): On input the security parameter n, and set the other parameters n', m, q, s, β as specified in Sect. 4.2 below. Then, do the following steps:

1. Define the universal set of attributes Att = $\{\mathbf{u}_1, \mathbf{u}_2, \cdots, \mathbf{u}_{n'}\}$, where vectors $\{\mathbf{u}_i\}_{i \in \{1,2,\cdots,n'\}} \in \mathbb{Z}_q^n$ is an uniform random vector. Here, attribute att_i is associated to $\mathbf{u}_i$ via a list L = $\{(att_i, \mathbf{u}_i)\}_{i \in \{1,2,\cdots,n'\}}$.
2. Let $\mathcal{H} : \{0,1\}^* \to \{1,2,3\}^\kappa$, $\kappa = \omega(\log n)$ be a hash function, modeled as a random oracle.
3. Output the public parameters PP = $\{Att, L, \mathcal{H}\}$.

ABGS.KeyGen(PP, N, id, a, S_a): On input the public parameters PP and the maximum number of the group members $N = 2^\ell$, then, do the following steps:

1. Generate the verification key $\mathbf{A}, \mathbf{A}_0, \mathbf{A}_1, \cdots, \mathbf{A}_\ell \in \mathbb{Z}_q^{n \times m}$ and a signing key $\mathbf{T_A}$ for the modified Boyen's signature scheme as in [23].
2. For member id = $(id_1, id_2, \cdots, id_\ell) \in \{0,1\}^\ell$ with an index $a \in \{1, \cdots, N\}$ and a set of attributes $S_a = \{\mathbf{u}_{j'_1}, \mathbf{u}_{j'_2}, \cdots, \mathbf{u}_{j'_{p'}}\} \subseteq$ Att, the manager defines a matrix $\mathbf{A}_{id} = [\mathbf{A}|\mathbf{A}_0 + \sum_{i=1}^\ell id_i \cdot \mathbf{A}_i]$ and runs SamplePre($\mathbf{A}_{id}, \mathbf{T_A}, \mathbf{u}_{i'}, s$) to generate a short vector $\mathbf{e}_{i'} = (\mathbf{e}_{i',1}, \mathbf{e}_{i',2}) \in \mathbb{Z}^m \times \mathbb{Z}^m$ such that $\mathbf{A}_{id} \cdot \mathbf{e}_{i'} = \mathbf{A} \cdot \mathbf{e}_{i',1} + (\mathbf{A}_0 + \sum_{i=1}^\ell id_i \cdot \mathbf{A}_i) \cdot \mathbf{e}_{i',2} = \mathbf{u}_{i'} \bmod q$ for $i' \in \{j'_1, j'_2, \cdots, j'_{p'}\}$.
3. For $\mathbf{u}_i \in$ Att$\backslash S_a$, the manager samples $\mathbf{e}_{i,1} \leftarrow_R \mathcal{D}_{\mathbb{Z}^m, s}$ and sets $\mathbf{e}_{i,2} = \perp$.
4. Let the private key of id with an index a be $gsk_a = \{(\mathbf{e}_{i,1}, \mathbf{e}_{i,2})\}_{i \in \{1,2,\cdots,n'\}}$, and revocation token be $grt_a = \{\mathbf{u}'_a = (\mathbf{u}'_{a,i} = \mathbf{A} \cdot \mathbf{e}_{i,1} \bmod q)_{i \in \{1,2,\cdots,n'\}}\}$.
5. Output the group public key Gpk = $(\mathbf{A}, \mathbf{A}_0, \cdots, \mathbf{A}_\ell)$, the members private key Gsk = $(gsk_1, gsk_2, \cdots, gsk_N)$, and the members revocation tokens Grt = $(grt_1, grt_2, \cdots, grt_N)$.

ABGS.Sign(PP, $\mathcal{T}$, Gpk, gsk_a, S_a, m): On input the group public key Gpk, private key gsk_a of a member id with an index a and a set of attributes $S_a \subseteq$ Att, a message m $\in \{0,1\}^*$ and a threshold predicate $\mathcal{T} = (t, S = \{\mathbf{u}_{j_1}, \mathbf{u}_{j_2}, \cdots, \mathbf{u}_{j_p}\} \subseteq$ Att) where $1 \leq t \leq |S| = p$, the member id does the following steps:

1. Select a random t-element subset $S_0 \subseteq (S \cap S_a) \subseteq \mathsf{Att}$, where $|S_0| = t$. For convenience, we suppose that $S_0 = \{\mathbf{u}_{j_1}, \mathbf{u}_{j_2}, \cdots, \mathbf{u}_{j_t}\}$.
2. For $i \in \{j_{t+1}, j_{t+2}, \cdots, j_p\}$, run basic linear algebra algorithm to generate a vector $\mathbf{e}_{i,2} \in \mathbb{Z}^m$ such that $(\mathbf{A}_0 + \sum_{i=1}^{\ell} id_i \cdot \mathbf{A}_i) \cdot \mathbf{e}_{i,2} = \mathbf{u}_i - \mathbf{A} \cdot \mathbf{e}_{i,1} \bmod q$, where $\beta < \|\mathbf{e}_{i,2}\|_\infty$ and reset $\mathbf{e}_i = (\mathbf{e}_{i,1}, \mathbf{e}_{i,2})$.
3. Generate a proof that the prover is indeed a valid group member owning at least t attributes among $S \subseteq \mathsf{Att}$ and having not been revoked. This can be achieved by repeating $\kappa = \omega(\log n)$ times the Stern-type protocol as in Sect. 4.3 with public inputs $(\mathbf{A}, \mathbf{A}_0, \cdots, \mathbf{A}_\ell, \mathbf{u}_{j_1}, \mathbf{u}_{j_2}, \cdots, \mathbf{u}_{j_p})$ and witness $(\mathsf{id}, \mathsf{gsk}_a)$, then making it non-interactive via the Fiat-Shamir heuristic as $(\{\mathsf{CMT}_i\}_{i \in \{1, \cdots, \kappa\}}, \mathsf{CH}, \{\mathsf{RSP}_i\}_{i \in \{1, \cdots, \kappa\}})$, where $\mathsf{CH} = \{\mathsf{CH}_i\}_{i \in \{1, \cdots, \kappa\}} = \mathcal{H}(\mathsf{m}, \{\mathsf{CMT}_i\}_{i \in \{1, \cdots, \kappa\}})$.
4. Output the signature $\sigma = (\mathsf{m}, \{\mathsf{CMT}_i\}_{i \in \{1, 2, \cdots, \kappa\}}, \mathsf{CH}, \{\mathsf{RSP}_i\}_{i \in \{1, 2, \cdots, \kappa\}})$.

$\mathsf{ABGS.Verify}(\mathsf{PP}, \mathcal{T}, \mathsf{Gpk}, \mathsf{RL}, \sigma, \mathsf{m})$: On input $(\mathbf{A}, \mathbf{A}_0, \cdots, \mathbf{A}_\ell, \mathbf{u}_1, \mathbf{u}_2, \cdots, \mathbf{u}_{n'})$, a threshold predicate $\mathcal{T} = (t, S = \{\mathbf{u}_{j_1}, \mathbf{u}_{j_2}, \cdots, \mathbf{u}_{j_p}\} \subseteq \mathsf{Att})$, a signature σ on $\mathsf{m} \in \{0, 1\}^*$, a set of tokens $\mathsf{RL} = \{\mathbf{u}'_{a'} = (\mathbf{u}'_{a',1}, \mathbf{u}'_{a',2}, \cdots, \mathbf{u}'_{a',n'})\}_{a' \le N} \subseteq \mathsf{Grt}$, the verifier does the following steps:

1. Parse the signature $\sigma = (\mathsf{m}, \{\mathsf{CMT}_i\}_{i \in \{1, 2, \cdots, \kappa\}}, \mathsf{CH}, \{\mathsf{RSP}_i\}_{i \in \{1, 2, \cdots, \kappa\}})$.
2. Check that if $\mathsf{CH} = \{\mathsf{CH}_1, \cdots, \mathsf{CH}_\kappa\} = \mathcal{H}(\mathsf{m}, \mathsf{CMT}_1, \cdots, \mathsf{CMT}_\kappa)$.
3. For $i \in \{1, 2, \cdots, \kappa\}$, run the verification step of the protocol from Sect. 4.3 to check the validity of RSP_i with respect to CMT_i and CH_i.
4. If the above are satisfied, then output 1 and accept σ, otherwise reject it.

4.2 Parameters

Given the security parameter n, to keep all algorithms can be implemented in polynomial time, correctly and the security properties hold, we set all the other parameters as follows: $N = 2^\ell = \mathrm{poly}(n)$,

$$q = \mathcal{O}(\ell n^2), \quad m = 2n\lceil \log q \rceil, \quad n' = \mathrm{poly}(n), \quad s = \omega(\log m), \quad \beta = \widetilde{\mathcal{O}}(\sqrt{\ell n}).$$

4.3 Security Analysis

Theorem 2. *The proposed scheme is correct with overwhelming probability. If* COM *is a statistically hiding commitment scheme, our construction are selfless-anonymous and attribute-anonymous in the random oracle model. Furthermore, if the* $\mathsf{SIVP}_{\ell \cdot \widetilde{\mathcal{O}}(n^2)}$ *problem is hard, then our construction is traceable and non-frameable in the random oracle model.*

Proof. Because the space is limited, the proof is present in the full version.

Acknowledgments. We thank the anonymous referees for their helpful comments.

References

1. Ajtai, M.: Generating hard instances of lattice problems (Extended Abstract). In: STOC, pp. 99–108. ACM (1996)
2. Ali, S.T., Amberker, B.B.: Dynamic attribute based group signature with attribute anonymity and tracing in the standard model. In: Gierlichs, B., Guilley, S., Mukhopadhyay, D. (eds.) SPACE 2013. LNCS, vol. 8204, pp. 147–171. Springer, Heidelberg (2013). https://doi.org/10.1007/978-3-642-41224-0_11
3. Ali, S.T., Amberker, B.B.: Short attribute-based group signature without random oracles with attribute anonymity. In: Thampi, S.M., Atrey, P.K., Fan, C.-I., Perez, G.M. (eds.) SSCC 2013. CCIS, vol. 377, pp. 223–235. Springer, Heidelberg (2013). https://doi.org/10.1007/978-3-642-40576-1_22
4. Ali, S.T., Amberker, B.B.: Dynamic attribute-based group signature with verifier-local revocation and backward unlinkability in the standard model. Int. J. Appl. Cryptogr. **3**(2), 148–165 (2014)
5. Alwen, J., Peikert, C.: Generating shorter bases for hard random lattices. Theory Comput. Syst. **48**(3), 535–553 (2011)
6. Bansarkhani, R.E., Kaafarani, A.E.: Post-quantum attribute-based signatures from lattice assumptions.https://eprint.iacr.org/2016/823
7. Boneh, D., Shacham, H.: Group signatures with verifier-local revocation. In: CCS, pp. 168–177. ACM (2004)
8. Chaum, D., van Heyst, E.: Group Signatures. In: Davies, D.W. (ed.) EUROCRYPT 1991. LNCS, vol. 547, pp. 257–265. Springer, Heidelberg (1991). https://doi.org/10.1007/3-540-46416-6_22
9. Emura, K., Miyaji, A., Omote, K.: A dynamic attribute-based group signature scheme and its application in an anonymous survey for the collection of attribute statistics. In: ARES, Fukuoka, pp. 1968–1983. IEEE (2009)
10. Gentry, C., Peikert, C., Vaikuntanathan, V.: Trapdoor for hard lattices and new cryptographic constructions. In: STOC, pp. 197–206. ACM (2008)
11. Kawachi, A., Tanaka, K., Xagawa, K.: Concurrently secure identification schemes based on the worst-case hardness of lattice problems. In: Pieprzyk, J. (ed.) ASIACRYPT 2008. LNCS, vol. 5350, pp. 372–389. Springer, Heidelberg (2008). https://doi.org/10.1007/978-3-540-89255-7_23
12. Khader, D.: Attribute based group signatures. http://eprint.iacr.org/2007/159
13. Khader, D.: Attribute based group signature with revocation. http://eprint.iacr.org/2007/241
14. Kuchta, V., Sahu, R.A., Sharma, G., Markowitch, O.: On new zero-knowledge arguments for attribute-based group signatures from lattices. In: Kim, H., Kim, D.-C. (eds.) ICISC 2017. LNCS, vol. 10779, pp. 284–309. Springer, Cham (2018). https://doi.org/10.1007/978-3-319-78556-1_16
15. Kuchta, V., Sharma, G., Sahu, R.A., Markowitch, O.: Generic framework for attribute-based group signature. In: Liu, J.K., Samarati, P. (eds.) ISPEC 2017. LNCS, vol. 10701, pp. 814–834. Springer, Cham (2017). https://doi.org/10.1007/978-3-319-72359-4_51
16. Libert, B., Ling, S., Mouhartem, F., Nguyen, K., Wang, H.: Signature schemes with efficient protocols and dynamic group signatures from lattice assumptions. In: Cheon, J.H., Takagi, T. (eds.) ASIACRYPT 2016, Part II. LNCS, vol. 10032, pp. 373–403. Springer, Heidelberg (2016). https://doi.org/10.1007/978-3-662-53890-6_13

17. Langlois, A., Ling, S., Nguyen, K., Wang, H.: Lattice-based group signature scheme with verifier-local revocation. In: Krawczyk, H. (ed.) PKC 2014. LNCS, vol. 8383, pp. 345–361. Springer, Heidelberg (2014). https://doi.org/10.1007/978-3-642-54631-0_20

18. Libert, B., Ling, S., Nguyen, K., Wang, H.: Zero-knowledge arguments for lattice-based accumulators: logarithmic-size ring signatures and group signatures without trapdoors. In: Fischlin, M., Coron, J.-S. (eds.) EUROCRYPT 2016, Part II. LNCS, vol. 9666, pp. 1–31. Springer, Heidelberg (2016). https://doi.org/10.1007/978-3-662-49896-5_1

19. Libert, B., Mouhartem, F., Nguyen, K.: A lattice-based group signature scheme with message-dependent opening. In: Manulis, M., Sadeghi, A.-R., Schneider, S. (eds.) ACNS 2016. LNCS, vol. 9696, pp. 137–155. Springer, Cham (2016). https://doi.org/10.1007/978-3-319-39555-5_8

20. Ling, S., Nguyen, K., Wang, H.: Group signatures from lattices: simpler, tighter, shorter, ring-based. In: Katz, J. (ed.) PKC 2015. LNCS, vol. 9020, pp. 427–449. Springer, Heidelberg (2015). https://doi.org/10.1007/978-3-662-46447-2_19

21. Ling, S., Nguyen, K., Wang, H., Xu, Y.: Lattice-based group signatures: achieving full dynamicity with ease. In: Gollmann, D., Miyaji, A., Kikuchi, H. (eds.) ACNS 2017. LNCS, vol. 10355, pp. 293–312. Springer, Cham (2017). https://doi.org/10.1007/978-3-319-61204-1_15

22. Ling, S., Nguyen, K., Wang, H., Xu, Y.: Constant-size group signatures from lattices. In: Abdalla, M., Dahab, R. (eds.) PKC 2018, Part II. LNCS, vol. 10770, pp. 58–88. Springer, Cham (2018). https://doi.org/10.1007/978-3-319-76581-5_3

23. Micciancio, D., Peikert, C.: Trapdoors for Lattices: simpler, tighter, faster, smaller. In: Pointcheval, D., Johansson, T. (eds.) EUROCRYPT 2012. LNCS, vol. 7237, pp. 700–718. Springer, Heidelberg (2012). https://doi.org/10.1007/978-3-642-29011-4_41

24. Micciancio, D., Peikert, C.: Hardness of SIS and LWE with small parameters. In: Canetti, R., Garay, J.A. (eds.) CRYPTO 2013, Part I. LNCS, vol. 8042, pp. 21–39. Springer, Heidelberg (2013). https://doi.org/10.1007/978-3-642-40041-4_2

25. Nguyen, P.Q., Zhang, J., Zhang, Z.: Simpler efficient group signatures from lattices. In: Katz, J. (ed.) PKC 2015. LNCS, vol. 9020, pp. 401–426. Springer, Heidelberg (2015). https://doi.org/10.1007/978-3-662-46447-2_18

26. Wang, Q.B., Chen, S.Z.: Attribute-based signature for threshold predicates from lattices. Secur. Commun. Netw. 8, 811–821 (2015)

27. Wang, Q., Chen, S., Ge, A.: A new lattice-based threshold attribute-based signature scheme. In: Lopez, J., Wu, Y. (eds.) ISPEC 2015. LNCS, vol. 9065, pp. 406–420. Springer, Cham (2015). https://doi.org/10.1007/978-3-319-17533-1_28

28. Zhang, Y.H., Hu, Y.P., Gao, W., et al.: Simpler efficient group signature scheme with verifier-local revocation from lattices. KSII Trans. Internet Inf. Syst. 10(1), 414–430 (2016)

Construction of VMI Mode Supply Chain Management System Based on Block Chain

Jinlong Wang[1], Jing Liu[1], and Lijuan Zheng[2(✉)]

[1] School of Information, Beijing Wuzi University, Beijing, China
wangjl2105@163.com, liujingbjwzxy@126.com
[2] School of Information Science and Technology, Shijiazhuang Tiedao University,
Shijiazhuang, China
zhenglijuan@stdu.edu.cn

Abstract. Block chain has become a hot research topic in recent years, such as the United Nations, the International Monetary Fund and other international organizations, as well as many governments. Industry has also increased investment efforts. At present, the application of block chain has been extended to the Internet of things, intelligent manufacturing, supply chain management, digital asset trading and other fields, which will bring new opportunities for the development of cloud computing, big data, mobile Internet and other new generation of information technology. On the basis of analyzing the disadvantages of the traditional VMI mode, this paper discusses the feasibility of applying the block chain technology in the VMI mode supply chain, and tries to construct the VMI mode supply chain management system based on the block chain technology. The purpose of this paper is to combine the blockchain technology and supply chain management in order to find a feasible way to implement the VMI supply chain mode.

Keywords: Block chain · VMI · Supply chain

1 Introduction

Block chain is a kind of distributed database, since the origin of bitcoin, it is a string of data blocks using cryptographic methods associated with the each data block contains a bitcoin network trading information is used to verify the validity of the information (Security) and generates the next block. With the development of industry 4.0 era and the arrival of big data era, the blockchain technology, as a new Internet technology, has been widely paid attention by the government and all walks of life, and has been extended to various professional fields to try to achieve technology application and cross-border development. Since October 2016, the Ministry of Industry and Information Technology issued the "China White Paper on Block chain Technology and Application Development, 2016" [1] and in December 2016, block chain has been used as a strategic frontier technology for the first time. Since the subversive technology was written into the State Council's Circular on issuing the Thirteenth Five-Year Plan on National Informatization [2], the block chain has received increasing attention and attention from the Chinese

© Springer Nature Switzerland AG 2018
J. Vaidya and J. Li (Eds.): ICA3PP 2018, LNCS 11337, pp. 611–616, 2018.
https://doi.org/10.1007/978-3-030-05063-4_47

government. Governments around the issue of block chain policy guidance and notification documents.

It can be predicted that block chain technology has a wide range of application scenarios. In view of this, based on the advantages of block chain technology, this paper analyzes the drawbacks of the traditional VMI mode. On the basis of analyzing the feasibility of the application of block chain technology in supply chain management in VMI mode, a supply chain management system of VMI mode based on block chain technology is constructed in order to provide a reference for the research of block chain technology and cross-border development of supply chain management.

2   Block Chain Technical Description

2.1   Definitions and Origins

The blockchain technique originated from a groundbreaking paper, "Bitcoin: a Point-to-Point Electronic Cash system", published in 2008 by a scholar named Satoshi Nakamoto. In recent years, experts and scholars at home and abroad have defined it from different perspectives. Yong [3] believes that block chain is a new decentralized infrastructure and distributed computing paradigm, which is gradually rising with the increasing popularity of digital cryptographic currency such as bitcoin; Wang et al. [4] in their paper, it is pointed out that block chain refers to the technical scheme of collective maintenance of a reliable database by means of decentralization and distrust; Baojun [5] will understand the block chain as a programmed, encrypted, networked, open data ledger, recording all transactions of users on the block chain; Mei et al. [6] it is written in their paper that block chain is a kind of distributed shared database based on cryptography. Its essence is to maintain a reliable database collectively by means of decentralization and distrust.

The white paper "China Block chain Technology and Application Development White Paper (2016)" issued by the Department of Information and Software Services of the Ministry of Industry and Information holds that block chain is a kind of chain data structure which combines data blocks in sequence according to time order and cannot be tampered with and unforgeable by cryptography. Each block contains all transaction information and block metadata for the current period of time. As shown in Fig. 1.

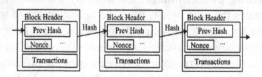

Fig. 1. Block chain schematic diagram

2.2   Block Chain Characteristics

Block chain involves key technologies, such as hash function, Meckel tree, asymmetric encryption, data block, chain structure, time stamp P2P network, propagation mechanism PoWO pos-DPoso, block chain finance, block supply chain and so on, combining with the connotation, technology and infrastructure of block chain. Its basic characteristics are summarized as follows.

Decentralization. Each distributed node in the block chain system is pedigree distributed, and trust each other through mathematical method rather than mandatory central management organization, so as to ensure that each node has equal rights and obligations.

Security and Transparency. Two asymmetric ciphers, Public Key and Private Key, are used in the encryption process. Combined with the hybrid encryption mechanism KEM and DEM (Data Encapsulation Mechanism), the security requirements and ownership verification requirements are satisfied [7].

Smart Contracts. The block chain has a transformable programming system that supports each node to build an efficient intelligent contract. Intelligent contract automatically judges the conditions and obligations of each node to execute the contract, and automatically executes the contract items that meet the conditions.

Verifiability. Block chain system uses timestamp technology to extend time dimension for data information to ensure that its data information storage and exchange can be verified [8].

3 Application of Block Chain Technology in VMI Supply Chain

3.1 Drawbacks of the Traditional VMI Model

"VMI (Vendor Managed inventory)" is a common agreement under which the vendor manages inventory and constantly monitors the implementation and revision of the agreement, aiming at the lowest cost to both the user and the supplier. Cooperative strategy for continuous improvement of inventory management. This inventory management strategy breaks the traditional inventory management mode and embodies the integrated management idea of supply chain. It is very important in the distribution chain at present, so people pay more and more attention to it. However, there are many factors leading to the VMI model has been difficult to implement.

Trust Issues. This kind of cooperation needs some trust. In the process of implementation, it is difficult to reach an absolute strategic partnership due to the consideration of its own business secrets and the security of personal information.

Technical Issues. Although the use of EDI technology has realized the transmission of point-of-sale information and distribution information to suppliers and retailers. Although the use of barcode and scanning techniques can basically ensure the accuracy of the data, it does not necessarily guarantee the disclosure of information in the course of transmission.

Traceability of Damage to Goods. Due to the increased workload of supplier management, the risk increases with the increase of VMI's ownership of goods from the previous relationship to the consignment relationship, and the safety and integrity of the goods themselves are inspected by the prior procurement process.

Payment of Funds. In the past, retailers used to pay the goods only one to three months after they received them, which required both parties to settle according to historical transaction data. Now they may have to pay the goods after the goods have been sold, and the payment period has been shortened. The question that follows is whether the information provided by several partners is accurate.

VMI is the integration and coordination across enterprise boundaries, which requires the supplier and supplier to establish a partnership of mutual trust. For these reasons, this model has encountered a lot of bottlenecks in its implementation, which can be said to be no exaggeration. It is impossible to achieve absolute information sharing and integration and coordination between enterprises before new and applicable technologies are introduced.

3.2   Application Analysis of Block Chain in Supply Chain Management of VMI Mode

First of all, from the perspective of the transaction mechanism, each distributed node in the block chain system forms a consensus mechanism through the chain structure, and each block forms a "chain" that can store data information permanently and continue continuously, which is tamper-proof and traceable. Safety, transparency, etc. In view of the existence of multiple and complex transactions among supply chain agents in VMI mode, a decentralization trust mechanism of block chain system is introduced to realize the true recording and verification of transactions and to reduce or eliminate the opportunity cost caused by the lack of trust among the agents. It can be seen that there is a coupling relationship between the two parties in the transaction mechanism.

Secondly, from the point of view of intelligent contract, the block chain supports transaction processing, preservation mechanism and a complete state machine, accepts and processes various intelligent contracts, and completes the connection between transaction preservation and state processing. After the transaction and event information are passed into the intelligent contract, the state machine judgment of the intelligent contract is triggered by updating the resource state in the contract information resource set in time. The supply chain guarantees the automatic execution of the transaction through a series of intelligent contracts. The intelligent contract based on the block chain can avoid malicious interference with the normal execution of the contract, and it also has the advantage of cost efficiency. It can be seen that there is a coupling relationship between them on the intelligent contract.

In summary, many attributes of block chain technology are suitable for supply chain management in VMI mode. The corresponding coupling analysis is shown in Fig. 2.

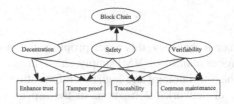

Fig. 2. Application analysis of block chain technology in VMI mode supply chain management

3.3 Supply Chain Management System Based on VMI Mode Based on Block Chain Technology

The application of the block chain can provide technical support for the supply chain management of "from point, chain to network". We construct a VMI mode supply chain management system based on block chain technology, as shown in Fig. 3.

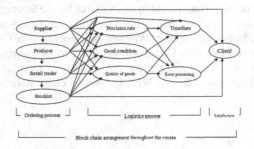

Fig. 3. Supply chain management system based on VMI mode based on block chain

"Point": for nodal enterprises, block chain technology is embedded in the internal Internet of things. IoT realizes information exchange by implanting intelligent perception. Behavior and rules can support the establishment and improvement of decentralization consensus mechanism in block chain systems.

"Chain": The introduction of block chain technology can transform the "series" relationship between nodal enterprises into "parallel" relationship, thus reducing the opportunity cost.

"Web": According to the time series, a unique and continuous "chain" is formed in the common "block", which can improve the efficiency of supply chain management and ensure the uniqueness, accuracy and traceability of transaction.

The block chain system has the technology of decentralization credit, automatic intelligent contract. Logistics and capital flow constitute the basis of supply chain structure, and information flow constitutes "neural network" of supply chain, which is the link between all parties.

4   Conclusion

Based on the block chain technology, this paper proposes the model of logistics information resource management of block VMI supply chain. In the aspect of logistics, the integration of block chain technology and logistics information technology effectively improves the security of network information. In the aspect of information flow, a smooth and transparent information flow is formed in the block supply chain, and the existing problems in the operation process are found and solved in time. The block chain data information with timestamp can solve the disputes among the participants. In terms of capital flow, the application of block chain technology can reduce the cost of reconciliation and dispute resolution between financial departments. At the same time, there is no central payment and clearing office in block chain technology. The introduction of block chain into supply chain management in VMI mode is beneficial to development of industrial clusters.

Acknowledgement. The study is supported by the National Nature Science Foundation of China "Research on the warehouse picking system blocking influence factors and combined control strategy" (No. 71501015), Beijing the Great Wall scholars program (No. CIT & TCD20170317), the Beijing Collaborative Innovation Center and the 2018 major project of China Society of Logistics: "Research on the connectivity of modern logistics network system" (2018CSLKT2-004), the project of Beijing Wuzi University Yunhe River scholar.

References

1. Ministry of Industry and Information Technology: China White Paper on Blockchain Technology and Application Development. http://www.cbdio.com/BigData/20-16-10/21/content_5351215.htm. Accessed 01 Mar 2018
2. State Council of the people's Republic of China: Circular of the State Council on the issuance of the "13th Five-Year" national informatization planning. http://www.gov.cn/zhengce/content/2016-12/27/content_5153411.htm. Accessed 01 Mar 2018
3. Yong, Y., Yue, W.: Current situation and prospect of blockchain technology. J. Autom. **3**, 481–494 (2016)
4. Wang, A., Fan, J., Guo, Y.: Application of block chain in energy internet. Power Inf. Commun. Technol. **9**, 1–6 (2016)
5. Baojun, Z.: Consideration on the application of block chain technology in banks. Chin. Financ. Comput. **9**, 47–48 (2016)
6. Mei, H., Liu, J.: Current situation, problems and policy recommendations of block chain. Telecommun. Sci. **11**, 134–138 (2016)
7. Changping, H., Shushu, H.: Protection of user's rights and interests in public cloud storage service. Inf. Theory Pract. **39**(11), 17–27 (2016)
8. Yong, Y., Yue, W.: Current situation and Prospect of Block chain Technology. J. Autom. **4**, 481–494 (2016)

H²-RAID: A Novel Hybrid RAID Architecture Towards High Reliability

Tianyu Wang[1], Zhiyong Zhang[1], Mengying Zhao[1], Ke Liu[1], Zhiping Jia[1(✉)],
Jianping Yang[2], and Yang Wu[3,4]

[1] School of Computer Science and Technology, Shandong University, QingDao, China
jzp@sdu.edu.cn
[2] State Grid Shanghai Municipal Electric Power Company, Shanghai, China
[3] NARI Group Corporation (State Grid Electric Power Research Institute),
Nanjing, China
[4] Beijing Kedong Electric Power Control System Co. Ltd., Beijing, China

Abstract. With the rapid development of storage technology, Solid State Drive (SSD) has received extensive attentions from industry and academia. As a promising alternative of the conventional Hard Disk Drive (HDD), SSD shows its advantages in terms of I/O performance, power consumption and shock resistance. But the natural constraint of write endurance limits the use of SSDs in large-scale storage systems, especially for scenarios with high reliability equirements. The Redundant Arrays of Independent Disks (RAID) technology provides a mechanism of device-level fault tolerance. To guarantee the performance, current RAID strategies usually evenly distributes the I/O requests to all disks. However, different from HDD, the bit error rate (BER) of SSD increases dramatically when it gets older. Therefore, simply introducing RAID technology into SSD array would result in the "correlated SSD failure" problem, that is, all the SSDs in array wear out at approximately the same time, seriously affecting the reliability of the array. In this paper, we propose a Hybrid High reliability RAID architecture named H²-RAID, which combines SSDs with HDDs to achieve the high-performance of SSDs and the high-reliability of HDDs. To minimize the performance degradation caused by the low-performance HDDs, we design an HDD-aware backup strategy to coalesce the small writes requests. We implement the proposed strategy on the simulator based on Disksim. The experimental results show that we reduce the probability of data loss from 11.31% to 0.02% with only 5% performance loss, in average.

Keywords: Solid state drive · Hard disk drive · RAID reliability
Hybrid architecture

1 Introduction

Recent development of NAND flash shows great potential to replace traditional hard drives (HDDs) with flash-based solid state drives (SSDs) in both personal

J. Vaidya and J. Li (Eds.): ICA3PP 2018, LNCS 11337, pp. 617–627, 2018.
https://doi.org/10.1007/978-3-030-05063-4_48

computers and enterprise servers [1]. Without the mechanical parts, SSDs deliver one order of magnitude greater throughput, and two orders of magnitude greater I/O operations per second (IOPS), than conventional HDDs. Moreover, SSDs exhibit the advantages of lower power consumption and higher shock resistance. All these features make SSDs play an important role in today's large scale storage systems and adopted by many commercial companies.

Although SSDs outperform HDDs in many aspects, they suffer from the limitation of write endurance. Moreover, to increase the capacity of SSDs, the technologies of NAND flash are from SLC (Single-Level Cell) to MLC (Multi-Level Cell) even the TLC (Triple-Level Cell), which further reduces the endurance of the SSDs. Therefore, the device-level fault tolerance becomes a necessary problem to be addressed.

Parity-based redundant array of inexpensive disks (RAID) [2] provides a good option to ensure device-level fault tolerance, and has been widely-used for decades. RAID is a data storage virtualization technology that combines multiple physical disks into one or more logical units for the purposes of data redundancy, performance improvement, or both. Depending on the required level of redundancy and performance, data is distributed across the disks in one of several ways, referred to as RAID levels. Once a disk has worn out, the RAID controller can recover the data by means of such as redundancy check technologies. Doing like this, the data error is fixed and the reliability of the storage system is enhanced.

However, the traditional RAID architecture is designed for HDD. For traditional HDD arrays, the Bit Error Rate (BER) of a disk is not correlated with its age. But for the SSD arrays, the bit error rate rapidly increases as the P/E cycles of NAND flash progress [3,4]. According to Kim and Lee [5], the Uncorrectable Page Error Rate (UPER) of commercial SSDs reaches 1E-15 when received 75T bytes written and exceeds 1E-11 when received 200T bytes written, while the UPER of HDDs maintains 1E-15 during their whole lifetime. Since the projected lifetime of many commercial SSDs is more than 200TBW (Total teraBytes Written), as the SSDs get older, they show worse reliability.

Due to the above feature of SSD, simply applying the RAID technology to the SSD array will encounter a serious problem, called "correlated failure". To take RAID-5 (the most widely used RAID architecture) as an example, it balances writes across devices by evenly distributing parity chunks into them. In this way, all the SSDs in the array will wear out at approximately the same time [6]. Since the RAID-5 can tolerate only one disk failure, the continuous failures of SSDs will result to large scale data loss, which seriously damages the reliability of the SSD array.

To address the problem of correlated failure in SSD array, this paper proposes a hybrid RAID architecture named H^2-RAID, which combines SSDs with HDDs to achieve the high-performance of SSDs and the high-reliability of HDDs. In this paper, for each SSD, we insert an extra HDD with the same capacity to protect data in SSD. Both HDDs and SSDs are connected to RAID controller.

Therefore, even if all the SSDs in the array are failed at the same time, we still have the HDDs to provide online services.

Although the use of HDDs significantly increases the reliability, the higher random-access latency of HDDs will reduce the performance of the storage array. To maintain the high reliability while minimizing the performance degradation, we use an I/O window to coalesce the small I/O requests into a larger one to reduce disk seek and rotation cost. Thus, the performance of the total array is guaranteed.

We develop a simulator based on DiskSim with SSD Extension [7], and integrate all the proposed techniques. Experiments have been conducted with various representative I/O-intensive benchmarks under RAID-5. The results show that our H²-RAID provides higher reliability than traditional SSD RAID with only 5% performance loss in average.

The main contributions of this paper can be summarized as follows:

- We propose a hybrid RAID architecture combining SSDs with HDDs to improve the reliability of SSD array.
- Based on the hybrid RAID architecture, we design an HDD-aware backup strategy to minimize the performance loss.

The rest of this paper is organized as follows. Section 2 describes the previous work and the motivation. Section 3 presents the hybrid RAID architecture and discusses its reliability. Section 4 details the HDD-aware backup strategy. Experimental results and analysis are presented in Sect. 5 and finally, this paper is concluded in Sect. 6.

2 Background and Related Work

In this section, we first describe the RAID architecture, then review studies focus on the SSD array and its reliability issue. We also review studies focused on the multi-level RAID architecture, as well as hybrid storage system using both HDDs and SSDs. Finally, we conclude these researches and bring our motivation up.

2.1 Traditional RAID for HDDs

RAID technology consists of multiple disks with the same capacity, which uses stripe technology to distribute the read and write requests across multiple disks [2]. It has been used successfully for decades with HDD. Due to its redundant mechanism, RAID significantly enhances the reliability of storage systems, and improves the performance by interleaving data across all disks in array.

In many levels of RAID, the RAID-5 is most popular today. However, RAID-5 can tolerate only one disk failure, which means that RAID-5 is fragile during its recovery period. When RAID-5 is reconstructing (in Degraded Mode), there is no redundancy for the whole disk array. Once the second disk fails during the recovery period, the RAID-5 array will come to nothing, which is unbearable for those applications with high reliability requirement. Unfortunately, there are many criminals that can lead to disk failure. The extreme high Uncorrectable Bit Error Rate (UBER) plays an important role. Because the recovery process will read all data blocks from remaining healthy disks and calculate the missing data block, the excessive UBER may likely cause a read failure in one of the remaining disks, hence that disk will fail continuously.

When applying RAID-5 in SSD array, due to the UBER increases when SSD ages [3,8], the above issue will become more serious. We will discuss this phenomenon in the following subsections.

2.2   RAID for SSD Array

Park et al. [9] introduce a new function for parity generation called EVE-NOOD, to enhance data reliability of SSD array. Wang et al. [10] present a scheme called i-RAID, which uses NVRAM to absorb the log writes. It also constructs the stripe on physical flash blocks instead of on the logical addresses, to obtain more freedom and control rights for the moment of parity calculating. Li et al. [11] introduce a workload-aware scheme with hot data identification for SSD Arrays. Which reduces the RAID-level GC cost so as to improve the performance and endurance of SSD Array. It separates data chunks with different hotness to reduce writes in them, thus it can significantly lengthen the lifetime of SSD array.

Multi-level RAID. To solve the correlated failure of SSD array caused by load-balanced writes, Balakrishnan et al. [6] propose a RAID scheme named Diff-RAID, which aims to enhance the reliability of SSD array by keeping the parity distribution imbalanced. Diff-RAID makes a trade-off between RAID-4 and RAID-5, lets one SSD of the array be used up in advance, to reserve enough time for RAID reconstruction. Wan et al. [12] propose a novel RAID architecture named S^2-RAID, which divides the disks of RAID-5 into three or more groups. It provides the ability of tolerating at most three SSD failures, meanwhile improves the speed of recovery via parallel processing. Wang et al. [13] present OI-RAID scheme using two-layer RAID-5, which can tolerant at least three SSD failures. They use Balanced Incomplete Block Design (BIBD) for the outer layer, which can provide higher degree of parallelism. Thus, it obviously reduces the recovery time, obtains better reliability.

Hybrid Scheme with SSDs and HDDs. On account of that the UBER of HDDs maintains constant and is lower than which of aged SSDs, adding HDD to SSD-based storage system can also relieve the pressure of reliability. Kwanghee et al. [9] propose an heterogeneous RAID-4 architecture whose parity disk is replaced with HDD. Because the frequency of parity-stored SSD in RAID-4 is much higher than the average frequency of data-retained SSDs, they use an HDD to store parity blocks instead of SSD, to prevent the parity-stored SSD from wearing out prematurely. Kim et al. [14] develop MixedStore to investigate performance and SSD lifetime for hybridizing SSDs and HDDs. It can improve the performance for about 71% as compared to an HDD-based system and extend by 33% the lifetime of SSD. Xiao et al. [15] develop a hybrid storage system called PASS which prominently improves the reliability of a SSD-based system. It backups data in multiple SSDs to one HDD with less performance loss, so it can recover data when any of the primary SSD suddenly fails.

2.3 Motivation

Reviewed all above researches, we found most of them focusing on how to prolong the lifetime of SSDs or SSD-based systems. However, they neglected one thing that the P/E cycle of SSDs will finally approach its upper limit, then SSDs become unsteady. And although SSDs have many merits compared with HDDs, their high UBER at later period is still a defect which HDDs have no need to worry. Therefore, we apply HDDs in SSD array, even if all SSDs fail due to their limited write endurance, there still has HDDs to protect data and provide online services. We also explore the new issue existing in our new architecture such as how to reduce the performance loss brought by HDDs.

3   Hybrid RAID Architecture and Reliability Analysis

In this section, we first introduce the new RAID architecture, then calculate its reliability. Furthermore, we discuss the new problem for the architecture, pave the way for the next section.

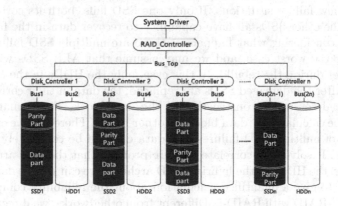

Fig. 1. H² RAID architecture

3.1   Hybrid RAID Architecture

As discussed above, the SSD array faces the problem of correlated failure even worse than HDD array. Since it is hard to improve its disk-failure tolerability with only SSDs, we introduce HDD into SSD array to build a hybrid RAID architecture shown as Fig. 1. Note that the space of each SSD has been divided into the data part and the parity part. It seems like that all the parity blocks are sequentially stored in a SSD, but in fact they are distributed all over. What Fig. 1 shows is only to express that each SSD has 1/N parity blocks and (N-1)/N data blocks.

Although the capacity of HDDs is identical to SSDs, the data stored in them has a little difference. HDDs only backup the data blocks of SSDs, which means that the parity blocks in SSDs will not be duplicated. Thus, the capacity of HDDs can be (N-1)/N of SSDs. But we still keep the same capacity between SSDs and HDDs, in order to have better extensibility.

What motivated us to give up copying parity blocks to HDDs is the characteristic of RAID-5: every write request will access its corresponding parity block, which means that one write request to the RAID system will be divided at least into two requests: one for data block while the other for parity block. HDDs have weak performance compared to SSDs, if all the write requests are duplicated to HDDs, it will be disaster for the performance of the whole array. Without parity blocks backup, the data in HDDs merely loses redundancy, while the original data is all preserved. However, we can reduce nearly half the write request of HDDs due to the characteristic mentioned above. This will make a prominent performance improvement.

3.2   Reliability Analysis

According to related works [5,8,9,15], HDDs have better reliability compared with aged SSDs. To analyse the reliability of the proposed H^2-RAID, let us first focus on a few failure situations. If only one SSD fails, both its corresponding HDD and the other SSDs all have capability to recover data in the failed SSD. It is worth considering what happens if there are multiple SSD failures. Then we consider the worst case, and we may assume that ALL SSDs will fail one after another during the rebuild. In this case, only the HDDs in the array work normally. After the damaged SSDs are replaced, the data in their corresponding HDDs is read to start reconstruction of the data block. The damaged parity blocks can be calculated by data blocks in other HDDs. Therefore, we ensure that in the case of multiple SSD failures, the data can still be completely recovered with no loss. It solves the correlated failure problem that the SSD array faces.

However, the HDDs in the hybrid RAID architecture can also be damaged. So we attempt to give a quantified calculation about the reliability comparing the proposed H^2-RAID with RAID-5. Different from other works, we directly use the Uncorrectable Page Error Rate (UPER) which is the most original probability causing the disk failure, rather than MTBF and MTTDL. Due to the low UPER of SSDs on the early stage, they show extremely reliable. Hence we only consider about the UPER of SSDs and HDDs in late period. We suppose the UPER of aged SSD (200TB written) is 5E-11 while HDD have the UPER of 1E-12 during its whole lifetime [5]. Because the probability of disk failure is correlated with its capacity, so we also fix the capacity of SSDs and HDDs to 400 GB. Therefore, the probability of disk failure Fail_{disk} can be calculated as follows:

$$Fail_{disk} = 1 - (UPER_{disk})^{\frac{Capacity_{disk}}{PageSize_{disk}}} \tag{1}$$

Then we plug the UPER and capacity of SSD and HDD into the formula, to calculate the failure probability of SSD: $Fail_{ssd} = 3.92\%$, and of the HDD: $Fail_{hdd} = 0.08\%$. Then we need to calculate the probability of data loss during the recovery period. For RAID-5, that is the probability of second SSD failure. But in our architecture, only the HDD next to its corresponding SSD fails, will data be damaged. And the probability of data loss is tightly correlated with the amount of disks N in the array, thus we fix it to 4. With definition above, the data loss probability in RAID-5 can be described as:

$$DataLoss_{raid-5} = 1 - (1 - Fail_{ssd})^{N-1} \tag{2}$$

And for the proposed H²-RAID, the probability of data loss is calculated as:

$$DataLoss_{H^2-raid} = 1 - Fail_{hdd} * (1 - Fail_{ssd})^{N-1}$$
$$- (1 - Fail_{hdd}) * (1 - Fail_{ssd} * Fail_{hdd})^{N-1} \tag{3}$$

For comparison, we also add two-layer RAID-15 architecture into the reliability calculation. Its data loss probability can be easily calculated by simply replacing the $Fail_{hdd}$ with $Fail_{ssd}$ in the above formulation:

$$DataLoss_{raid-15} = 1 - Fail_{ssd} * (1 - Fail_{ssd})^{N-1}$$
$$- (1 - Fail_{ssd}) * (1 - Fail_{ssd}^2)^{N-1} \tag{4}$$

Plugging the SSD and HDD failure probability calculated above into the formula, we can arrive at the probability of data loss in RAID-5: $DataLoss_{raid-5} = 11.31\%$, in RAID-15: $DataLoss_{raid-15} = 0.89\%$, and in H²-RAID: $DataLoss_{H^2-raid} = 0.02\%$. The result shows that the proposed H²-RAID significantly reduces the probability of data loss compard with RAID-5, and is even better than RAID-15.

3.3 Discussions

Because the proposed H²-RAID takes advantage of HDDs, it decreases the probability of data loss in SSD array by a large margin, improves the reliability of SSD array. However, there are still many problems which needs to be optimized. The first one is performance loss brought by HDDs. Although we throw the parity blocks out of HDDs, it still receives many write operations. So we develop an HDD-aware backup strategy using an I/O window to coalesce small and discrete writes. We will discuss the HDD-aware backup strategy in the following section.

4 HDD-Aware Backup Method

Although we have a considerable improvement of the SSD array reliability, there is still plenty of room to speed things up. In this section, we introduce the HDD-aware backup method.

All the operations can be simply divided into two types: reads and writes. Since the random access time of SSDs is much lower than HDDs, all the read operations may be directed to SSDs. HDDs are completely unnecessary during read operations. But write operations are quiet different. When a write operation is transferred to a certain SSD, the RAID controller detects whether the block involved is a parity block. If true, only the SSD will be written. Otherwise, the request will be handled to both the SSD and HDD, then disk controller responds to the RAID controller. Since the parity block will undergo more write operations than data blocks in RAID-5, canceling the backup operation of the parity block to the HDD will significantly reduce the number of write operations to the HDD. At the same time, for the characteristics that the HDD writes slowly if the request is not sequential, we use an I/O window to coalesce the backup request which can be aggregated [15], so as to reduce the performance loss. In order to assist its sequential operation, we maintain a flag for each stripe on the RAID controller, which records whether all data blocks in the stripe have been backed up to the HDD. This flag plays the role of data security monitor. The specific steps are as follows:

- (1) When a write request arrives, it is stored in the SSD first rather than backed up to the HDD immediately, and all the stripes which affected by the request will be marked as "unsafe" on the RAID controller;
- (2) Check whether current write request can be coalesced with the previous one. If it is possible, the current request is merged with the previous one. Otherwise, the previous write request will be backed up to the HDD, and the RAID controller will eliminate all the "unsafe" flags set by the previous write request.
- (3) Continue to service the next write request.

However, this kind of sequentialize operation may cause failure to completely recover all data when multiple disks fail at the exact same time. Thus we design a threshold T that can be set artificially, indicating that how many stripes can be in the "unsafe" state at most. Once the number of stripes involved in the sequentialize operation reaches or exceeds T, no matter whether the subsequent write requests can be sequentialized, they will be forcibly backed up into the HDD to ensure data security and prevent data loss when multiple disks fail.

How to set the threshold T depends on the working environment of the whole disk array. If the size of most write operation in the working set is small, especially smaller than the stripe size, that each write operation involves only one data disk and the parity disk. For this type of workloads, if the SSD which stores the data block is damaged at this time, although the backup operation is not performed timely, so long as the SSD with the parity block is still working, and the damaged data can be recovered. Therefore, the threshold T can be set larger to obtain higher overall performance of the disk array. If the size of predominant writes in the working set is large, even larger than several times of the stripe size, then each write operation will involve multiple data disks and the parity disk. If one of the SSD which contains the data block fails at this

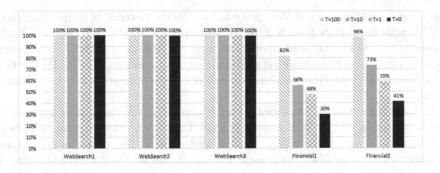

Fig. 2. Online processing performance of H^2-RAID (100% for RAID-5)

time, the data may not be able to recover once any other SSD which involved by the same write operation fails either. Therefore, the threshold T should be set smaller to ensure high reliability of the data.

5 Experimental Evaluation

5.1 Experimental Setup

We develop a simulator for the hybrid RAID architecture based on the widely-used Disksim with SSD Extension [7]. The simulator is running on a desktop computer which contains an Intel Core i7-6770HQ CPU running at 3.2 GHz and 32 GB memory. We implement our HDD-aware backup method in the simulator, and evaluate its performance compared with traditional RAID-5 architecture.

We use the real-world workload trace collected by University of Massachusetts, which includes the OLTP Application I/O traces and Search Engine I/O traces [16]. We fix the number of disks in the array to 4, which means we have a system consisting of four HDDs and four SSDs. Thus, the parity blocks occupy 1/4 of the whole SSD, which means the HDD only needs to backup 3/4 of the whole data. We set the capacity of SSDs and HDDs accurately. All the disks are connected to the disk controller in pairs, one SSD and its correlated HDD. And the disk controllers are all connected to the RAID controller, which contains the system driver and is abstracted to the system level.

5.2 Experimental Results

According to the experimental results, the proposed H^2-RAID and correlated HDD-aware strategy give a satisfactory answer. It reduces the probability of data loss from 11.31% (RAID-5) down to 0.02%, while only degrades 5% performance, in average.

Because the purpose of our method is to eliminate the performance impact caused by HDD, we replay these traces via our HDD-aware backup method. As Fig. 2 shows, the different values of T have different performance impacts. Let us firstly focus on the traces of Web Search. Due to the percent of write operations in Web Search 1, Web Search 2, Web Search 3 are 0.02%, 0.02%, and 0.03% respectively and all the read operations will not inflect the HDD, our hybrid RAID architecture has nearly no performance loss compared to RAID-5 which is the 100% standard. But the situation will not be so optimistic for the following traces.

In two OLTP traces, Financial 1 and Financial 2, the percent of write operations outdistances the Web Search traces. They have write operations about 79.56% and 15.20% respectively. According to Fig. 2, the performance impact declines as the threshold T increases. The condition of $T = 0$ means that we do not use any I/O window to coalesce the sequential write requests. It has the highest reliability because every write to SSDs is backed up to HDDs immediately without any delay, but will cause too much performance loss.

However, high performance may not lead to less reliability. Let us observe the condition of $T = 100$, which means there are at most 100 stripes being "unsafe". These stripes are not really "unsafe", because these "unsafe" stripes will be recovered at first. Calculated the size of 100 "unsafe" stripes, that is 128 KB (normally) * 100 = 12.5 MB, we find that too small compared to the recovery speed. Taking 100 MB/s for the recovery speed, which is much lower than the actual write speed of SSDs, it is even less than one second to recover 12.5 MB data. It is almost impossible that two disks fail continuously in one second, so that we can provide high reliability even $T = 100$. The benefits are obvious, in the trace of Financial 2, we achieve nearly full performance compared with RAID-5. For the writing intensive trace of Financial 1, we only lose 18% performance. Consider that we drop the data loss probability from 11.31% to 0.02%, this result can totally be accepted.

6 Conclusion

In the SSD array, correlated failure is a classical problem which drops the reliability. To address the problem, in this paper, we introduce a hybrid RAID architecture named H^2-RAID, which inserts backup HDDs to SSD array, so as to improve the reliability. After that, we design HDD-based strategy for backup, to gain high reliability while minimize the performance loss. We implement a simulator based on Disksim, and evaluate our architecture and strategy via real-world traces. The experimental results show our scheme effectively improves the reliability of SSD array with little performance loss, compared with the RAID-5.

Acknowledgements. This research is sponsored by the National Key R&D Program of China No. 2017YFB0902602 and State Key Program of National Natural Science Foundation of China No. 61533011.

References

1. Narayanan, D., Thereska, E., Donnelly, A., Elnikety, S., Rowstron, A.: Migrating server storage to SSDs: analysis of tradeoffs. In: Proceedings of the 4th ACM European conference on Computer systems, pp. 145–158. ACM (2009)
2. Patterson, D.A., Gibson, G., Katz, R.H.: A case for redundant arrays of inexpensive disks (RAID), vol. 17. ACM (1988)
3. Grupp, L.M., et al.: Characterizing flash memory: anomalies, observations, and applications. In: 42nd Annual IEEE/ACM International Symposium on Microarchitecture (MICRO), pp. 24–33. IEEE (2009)
4. Mielke, N., et al.: Bit error rate in NAND flash memories. In: IEEE International Reliability Physics Symposium (IRPS), pp. 9–19. IEEE (2008)
5. Kim, J., et al.: Improving SSD reliability with raid via elastic striping and anywhere parity. In: 43rd Annual IEEE/IFIP International Conference on Dependable Systems and Networks (DSN), pp. 1–12. IEEE (2013)
6. Balakrishnan, M., Kadav, A., Prabhakaran, V., Malkhi, D.: Differential raid: rethinking raid for SSD reliability. ACM Trans. Storage (TOS) 6, 4 (2010)
7. Agrawal, N., et al.: Design tradeoffs for SSD performance. In: USENIX Annual Technical Conference, vol. 57 (2008)
8. Lee, S., et al.: A lifespan-aware reliability scheme for raid-based flash storage. In: Proceedings of the 2011 ACM Symposium on Applied Computing, pp. 374–379. ACM (2011)
9. Park, K., et al.: Reliability and performance enhancement technique for SSD array storage system using raid mechanism. In: 9th International Symposium on Communications and Information Technology (ISCIT), pp. 140–145. IEEE (2009)
10. Wang, M., Hu, Y.: i-RAID: a novel redundant storage architecture for improving reliability, performance, and life-span of solid-state disk systems. In: Proceedings of the 31st Annual ACM Symposium on Applied Computing, pp. 1824–1831. ACM (2016)
11. Li, Y., Shen, B., Pan, Y., Yinlong, X., Li, Z., Lui, J.C.S.: Workload-aware elastic striping with hot data identification for SSD raid arrays. IEEE Trans. Comput.-Aided Des. Integr. Circ. Syst. 36(5), 815–828 (2017)
12. Wan, J., et al.: S2-RAID: parallel raid architecture for fast data recovery. IEEE Trans. Parallel Distrib. Syst. 25(6), 1638–1647 (2014)
13. Wang, N., Xu, Y., Li, Y., Wu, S.: OI-RAID: a two-layer raid architecture towards fast recovery and high reliability. In: 46th Annual IEEE/IFIP International Conference on Dependable Systems and Networks (DSN), pp. 61–72. IEEE (2016)
14. Kim, Y., et al.: HybridStore: a cost-efficient, high-performance storage system combining SSDs and HDDs. In: IEEE 19th International Symposium on Modeling, Analysis & Simulation of Computer and Telecommunication Systems, pp. 227–236. IEEE (2011)
15. Xiao, W., et al.: Pass: a hybrid storage system for performance-synchronization tradeoffs using SSDs. In: IEEE 10th International Symposium on Parallel and Distributed Processing with Applications (ISPA), pp. 403–410. IEEE (2012)
16. I/O. UMass trace repository (2007). http://traces.cs.umass.edu/

Sensitive Data Detection Using NN and KNN from Big Data

Binod Kumar Adhikari[1]([✉]) [iD], Wan Li Zuo[1], Ramesh Maharjan[2], and Lin Guo[3]

[1] College of Computer Science and Technology, Jilin University, Changchun 130012, China
`binodkumaradhikari14@mails.jlu.edu.cn, wanli@jlu.edu.cn`
[2] Amrit Campus, Tribhuvan University, Kathmandu, Nepal
`ramesh.anahcolus@gmail.com`
[3] School of Economic Management, Changchun University of Science and Technology, Changchun 130012, China
`guolin@cust.edu.cn`

Abstract. This paper focuses on the determination of sensitive data from huge mass of data collected from social network, cloud drives, local repository files etc. With the advancement of technology, numerous technologies have emerged and are actively being used in extracting useful and critical information about criminal activities from big data that get accumulated due to the use of communicating devices and applications. Numerous reduction techniques and data retrieval algorithm have been invented to extract sensitive information from accumulated data of criminals to prevent future criminal activities and to control unexpected events. In this paper, two different reduction techniques – Neural Network and K-Nearest Neighbor algorithms are used. Experiments for both algorithms were done in the similar environment by changing data size and node numbers in the processing cluster. From the experiment, it is found that Neural Network classification algorithm is more superior to retrieve sensitive data from big data than K- nearest neighbor algorithm.

Keywords: Terrorism · Hadoop Distributed File System (HDFS) · MapReduce Neurons · Cluster

1 Introduction

Big data, are collection of unstructured data sets, which are collected from diverse sources like social media, cloud drives, internet etc. which has been possible with wide spreading of information technologies to every aspect of society, expansion and use of internet, different types of services provided by the internet. Moreover, it is the exponential growth of data is due to the use of a number of application of the digital technology in health, bioinformatics, astrology, public administration, transportation.

Big data are assembly of a very large data sets obtained from different domains [1]. It is defined as a huge amount of data, composed of unstructured, semi-structured and structured data sets, making more complex form of the data which are difficult to process by the traditional data processing techniques. It is characterized by four Vs – volume,

J. Vaidya and J. Li (Eds.): ICA3PP 2018, LNCS 11337, pp. 628–642, 2018.
https://doi.org/10.1007/978-3-030-05063-4_49

velocity, variety and value [2]. The volume represents the size of the data, which are represented in exabytes or more; the velocity represents the rate of access of the data; the term variety is used for different forms of the data; the value defines the context and importance of the data [3]. The parallel and distributed systems of big data exceed the data size from exabytes and are increasing exponentially [4]. The volume of the big data is the most distinctive feature for big data analytics than general analytics [5].

Since 1970, there have been more than 12500 known terrorist events on the global scale [6]. A number of death, injuries, and property damage are resulted from the terroristic activities and huge amount of terroristic data have been collected by researchers, organizations and Alamieyeseigha and Strang [7]. It is found that anti-terroristic activities are more expensive for the administration [8]. With the rapid growth of technologies, people share their thoughts through social network, keep their data on the cloud, use latest technologies which share information through internet. As like normal people, criminals also share information through the internet. And all the data takes the shape of big data. It provides opportunities for big data analytics to determine sensitive data from big data. As the size of big data is voluminous, the probability of determination of sensitive data are high [9]. Researchers use social network architecture to understand structural characteristics of secret terroristic network [10]. Data reduction techniques play vital role in retrieving of useful information from big data.

To analyze and retrieve sensitive data from huge mass of data at once is the tedious work. But if the size of the large volume of documents which contains the sensitive information is reduced to the low volume and also terms are segregated from the documents, then it becomes easy to determine the sensitive data. Mascarenhas et al. [11] used data reduction techniques -principal component analysis and Monte Carlo methods to select sustainability indicators for demonstrating the views of different stakeholders. The supervised classification methods – Neural Networks and Support Vector Machines had been explored based on k-median clustering algorithm and showed that these techniques reduce the data size effectively [12]. The data reduction techniques were implemented in cyber scanning [13], intrusion detection [14], cluster analysis [15], mobile healthcare applications [16], etc. Distributed parallel processing plays another vital role in quicker analysis of big data.

Apache Hadoop, is written in java programming language [17] that processes large data sets in parallel and distributed computing environment. It uses Hadoop distributed file system [18] for storage and MapReduce architecture [19] for processing on a cluster made of few machines to several commodities computers. MapReduce architecture has two stage processing models i.e. Map and Reduce.

The artificial neural network focuses on different applications like data mining, weather forecasting, big data, image processing, traffic control etc. Thakur and Ramesh [20] determined the malaria abundances on the geographical location using environmental variable with Big Data and clinical datasets. The neural network captures both linear and non-linear data and after processing, provides results with high accuracy [21]. Zhang et al. [22] reviewed most typical deep learning models and their variants, implemented big data feature learning with deep learning models and discussed future trends and challenges of the big data learning.

K- nearest neighbor (KNN) is used as a classification method in machine learning or data mining. It estimates its class members. Maillo et al. [23] classified big datasets with large amount of unseen cases. The map phase determined k-nearest neighbor in different chunk of data and reduce stage computed absolute nearest neighbors from the list obtained from the map phase and showed the promising scalabilities capabilities of KNN. Dixon [24] presented an KNN imputation technique to deal with missing value in supervised classification in 1979. Inyaem et al. [25] used KNN with different classification algorithm to extract terrorism data and presented to intelligence officers to further analysis and prediction of terroristic events.

The purpose of this paper is to answer the following questions:

- Are sensitive data determined with the help of distributed computing and classification algorithms?
- Are data reduction techniques – Neural Network and K-nearest neighbor helpful for retrieval of sensitive data?
- From Neural Network and K- Nearest Neighbor, which algorithm will be more effective for detection of sensitive data from big data?

The rest of the paper is organized as follows: Sect. 2 defines terrorism, data sources of sensitive data, way of communication of criminals and use big data analytics as a tool for sensitive retrieval. Section 3 defines data reduction techniques, its aim and goal. Section 4 provides conceptual architecture of distributed computing with Hadoop, its storage and processing architecture. Section 5 gives outline of Neural Network and its implementation for retrieval of sensitive data. Section 6 provides method of implementation for KNN in distributed environment with map and reduce algorithm. Section 7 provides the outline of the proposed model. Section 8 gives the running environment of the experiment from software, hardware and cluster perspective. Section 9 shows the experimental results of Neural Network and K- nearest neighbor separately based on the number of the node used. Section 10 compares the experimental results obtained for both the algorithms. Section 11 draws the conclusion of this article and provides thought for the future enhancement for retrieval of sensitive data from big data.

2   Sensitive Data

Terrorism is a significant degrading factor for many countries because it influences the international politics and is harmful for the society. Here, sensitive data, represents the data related to the criminals, explosions, cyber criminals, druggists, thieves, domestic violence, burglaries, murder etc., which are present in the big data. These data are used to investigate the nature, place, pattern of crimes, people involved before and after the crime etc. For every crime, there are the interaction among criminals by social networks, phone calls, and text message, etc. which are in the form of big data. It creates opportunity for predictive analytics to find sensitive data from big data to take right action at right time. For this, security agency has to be one step ahead than terrorist to effectively prevent the terrorism [26].

By determining the sensitive data, the most fundamental investigative analysis can be done cooperatively by exploring terrorist activities effectively, discovering reasons of attacks by identifying geospatially between multiple terrorist groups and modes of attacks [27]. Criminal data are obtained from uniform crime reports (UCR), national incident base reporting system (NIBRS), national crime victimization survey (NCVS), Global Terrorism Database (GTD), Log files, Social network, cloud drives, etc.

Friends, colleagues, managers, staffs, employee communicate and share their thoughts in the social network. In the same way, the criminals also share their feeling, ideas, activities before and after the crimes. In this way, huge amount of data is collected, stored in local drive or cloud drive through the social network which may contain sensitive data. Big data analytical tools help to determine those sensitive data to control future criminal activities [28]. It helps to determine anomalies, pattern of incidents very fast. The analysis of huge amount of unstructured data should be done with high speed at right time to find criminal activities even if they change their policies and move quickly [29].

3 Data Reduction Techniques

Data reduction is the technique of minimizing the size of data that provides the meaning, required terms from the collection of huge amount of unstructured data sets. It increases the efficiency to determine the required terms and reduces the time to get the exact result and also increases the storage capacity to minimize costs. The reduced and relevant data are more useful than inconsistent, noisy, redundant, raw data. The big data have millions of variables datasets which requires unbounded computations to find actionable knowledge [30].

Classification is one the distinctive method of machine learning. The main goal of classification is to predict unknown objects, facts, concepts like sensitive data from huge amount of data. With the help of different classification model, required data, classes or concepts are obtained from unstructured datasets. The process of determining the classification model is known as learning process which helps to predict unknown terms or class labels.

4 Hadoop

Hadoop is an open source software based on Google MapReduce architecture. It was created by Doug Cutting, the creator of Apache Lucene. Hadoop is designed to process the huge amount of complex and unstructured data. It provides huge amount of storage for any kind of data, fast processing and ability to tackle unlimited concurrent jobs or tasks.

When there is massive amount of data, it is difficult to process all the data by a single computer. So, it becomes necessary to partition the massive data in a number of commodity computers. The parallel computing with efficient processing and suitable framework are the basic requirements for the processing of big data. Distributed File System [31] manages the data store across a number of computers in a cluster. Since all the computers are connected with each other through network, thus making distributed file system is more complex than regular file system. So, it is necessary to first rectify the problems related with the network, then manage computer in a cluster.

4.1 Hadoop Distributed File System

The file system used by Hadoop is called Hadoop Distributed File System (HDFS), which is designed for storing large files running on a cluster of commodity computers. It can store constantly increasing data volumes especially from social network and internet. It provides very high bandwidth across computers in a cluster. It gets reliability by replicating data across multiple nodes and there is no need of redundant array of independent disks (RAID) storage.

Hadoop uses a master/slave architecture both for distributed computation and distributed storage. In this architecture, master is represented by Namenode and Jobtracker while slave is characterized by Datanode and Tasktracker. Secondarynamenode is the assisting node for the Namenode. A Datanode may communicate with other Datanode to replicate data blocks to solve the redundancy problems. Each slave machine has Datanode to read and write HDFS blocks to actual files on the local file system. Input data is split in a number of blocks and each block is allotted a Datanode to be processed according to client needs.

4.2 MapReduce Architecture

MapReduce is the heart of Hadoop. It is the programming framework that provides scalability across a number of computers present in a cluster. It allows to write applications that process huge amount of data in a distributed environment in a large cluster of commodity computers in a reliable and fault-tolerance manner. It has two phases – map phase and reduce phase [32]. Each phase is defined by a function called mapper and reducer. Mapper takes input and results in key-value pairs as intermediate code and that intermediate code becomes input for the reducer and after processing intermediate code, reducer provides output. In easy term, mapper is used to filter and transform the input into intermediate code which is aggregated by the reducer.

5   Neural Network

Neural network, is the interconnection of a number of neurons, used to solve the complex problem easily by establishing communication among the neurons. In each and every neuron, a number of inputs are fed, after processing and based on the threshold, an effective output can be achieved. Each output is affected by the weight. It is the information processing technique to solve the problems irrespective of conventional problem techniques. Conventional computers use algorithmic approach to solve the problem by sequentially executing the instruction while neural network solves the problem by communication among a number of independent neurons, which has processing capabilities.

Figure 1 depicts the process of retrieving sensitive data from big data using neural network algorithm. In this method, all the documents which may contain sensitive criminal data are fed as an input with specific weight to the neural network. The document with the weighted sensitive data are processed in neurons of the different hidden layers. All the data are analyzed. And at last the criminal sensitive data are resulted as output.

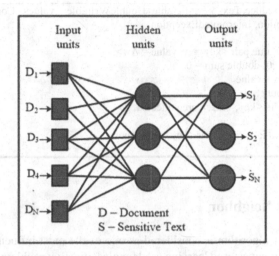

Fig. 1. Sensitive data detection using NN

The output of the perceptron is determined by the following equation

$$Output = \begin{cases} 0 & if \; \sum_i w_i x_i \leq threshold \\ 1 & if \; \sum_i w_i x_i > threshold \end{cases} \tag{1}$$

Where x_i is the input and w_i is the weight for perceptron.

Algorithm 1 is the mapper function for neural network where all the strings are broken down into words and generates key value pairs. For every value, weight w and its context weight Δw are calculated and passed to the reduce phase.

Algorithm 1. Mapper function for NN

Mappper map(key, value)

---

public void map (Object key, Text value, Context context) throws IOException, InterruptedException
{
    String line = value.toString()
    String [] parts = line.split(" ")
    Input key/value pair <key, value = parts>.
    For every value as the input of the network,
compute weight w   and get its weight Δw context
write pair <w, Δw>
    }

Algorithm 2, is the reducer function for NN, takes input from mapper, calculates the sum of value and total count of words and at last reduced form of output are generated.

Algorithm 2. Reducer function for NN

---

public void reduce(Text key, Iterable<DoubleWritable> values, Context context) throws IOException, InterruptedException
{
    Input key/value pair <key = w, value = Δw>.
    int count = 0; double sum = 0
    sum = sum + value
    count = count + 1
    If more pairs <key, value> are collected, go
    to step 1
    Else context key/value pair <key, sum/count>
}

---

6   K- Nearest Neighbor

K nearest neighbor algorithm is considered as one of the most influential data mining algorithms [33]. It is supervised learning used for classification problem solving method. It is also known as lazy algorithm [34] because it does not use training data sets for generalization of concept.

MapReduce framework can be implemented with K nearest neighbor. There are two phases for MapReduce architecture: Map phase and Reduce phase. For the efficient use of memory and to avoid out of memory issues, the training data is executed line by line. The distributed data is passed to the map phase for computing the distance. For each training data, distance of the data is provided as output in the form of key value pairs. In the reduce phase, each intermediate value is grouped by a key and a new HashMap (key, increment by 1 for each repetition) is created. The HashMap is repeated < k, where k is a number given by the user. The reducer produces the highest scoring key as output. Similarities of the terms are determined by using the distance formula. If query is executed with sensitive data, all the nearest sensitive data are grouped in one place.

Algorithm 3 is the mapper function for KNN, it takes input as training data sets which contains sensitive data. Training data are read and vectorized object produced and it also generate key value pairs as output.

Algorithm 3. Map function for KNN

Mappper map(key, value)

Input : key: misc/178445; value: misc; len: 10000; 0:0.014563; 1:0.05825; 2:0.009708737

Output : <RecordKey, RecordKey> pair

1 read the training data

2 for(String line = traingdata.readLine(); line != null; line = trainingdata.readLine())
{

    VectorizedObject vector = new VectorizedObject(line);

    ArrayList<VectorizedObject>.add(vector);

}

3 for(every dataline of the data)
{

    VectorizedObject data = new VectorizedObject(dataline);

    while(trainngDataVectorizedObject.hasNext())

        {

        VectorizedObject training = (VectorizedObject)trainngDataVectorizedObject.next();

        RecordKey key = new RecordKey(training.getKey(), Double.valucOf (training.getLocation().distance(training.getLocation())));

        RecordKey value = new RecordKey(data.getValue(),Double.valueOf training.getLocation().distance(training.getLocation())));

        context.write(key, value);

    }

}

Algorithm 4 takes input from mapper function as RecordKey pairs and generates text as output. It uses hashMap function to add value to each reputation key, gets key with highest value as an output.

Algorithm 4. Reduce function for KNN

Reducer reduce(key, Iterable(value))

Input : <RecordKey, RecordKey> pair
Output : <Text, Text> pair
1. Get the number of neighbors from input (nn)
2. while (RecordKey value of data.hasNext() and until the loop is less than n)
    {
    store in hashMap(key, add 1 to each repetition of key)
    }
3. Iterate over the hashMap from step 2 and get the key with highest value
4 context.write(training data key, highest scoring key from step 3)

7   Proposed Model

In the proposed model, there is the use of neural network and k-nearest neighbor to determine sensitive data from big data. There is the comparison of two different independent data reduction classification algorithm to retrieve criminal information effectively. Both the algorithms are executed in distributed environment by varying number of nodes and cluster size.

Jiang and Zhou [35] proposed neural network ensemble to manipulate the training data for KNN classifier and showed that the approach is more useful than the approaches derived from Depuration. Bagheri et al. [36] used two classification methods – artificial neural network with two hidden layer and k- nearest neighbor with k variable for the application of data mining and feature extraction.

The proposed model is demonstrated in Fig. 2. In this model, documents with sensitive data are taken as a source. The collected documents are tokenized to get tokens of words and then it is scrubbed. By using hash function, data are fed to the different algorithms for processing. In Fig. 2(a), there is the implementation of neural network to process voluminous data to retrieve sensitive data where all the documents are taken as input and sensitive terms are resulted as output. In Fig. 2(b), K nearest neighbor is used for processing of the documents containing sensitive data using mapper and reducer function.

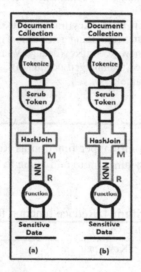

Fig. 2. Proposed model to retrieve sensitive data

8   Running Environment

8.1   Software Environment

- Operating System: Ubuntu 16.04 LTS
- Programming Language: Java jdk1.8.0 112
- Tool used: Hadoop, Yarn Resource Manager

8.2 Hardware Environment

- Processor: Intel Core i5-4430S CPU @ 2.70 GHz x 4
- Physical Memory: 8 GB
- Secondary Memory: 500 GB Sata

8.3 Cluster Size

- Single node cluster: 1 node
- Multi-node cluster: 3 nodes, 5 nodes, 7 nodes

9 Experimental Result

To retrieve sensitive data from big data based on MapReduce Programming model which was executed on Hadoop platform using HDFS, a number of experiments were done using NN and KNN algorithms.

The experiments were done by increasing the size of input data sets like 100 MB, 500 MB, 1 GB, and 5 GB in size. The MapReduce architecture is simple and provides powerful interface for the user. It is fault tolerance, highly scalable, and resilient to work failure.

9.1 Comparative Study

By using distributed concept of Hadoop Clusters, a number of experiments are performed for NN and KNN. In both case, experimental environment was same but size of Input data and number of nodes were kept different.

Figure 3 shows that total execution time taken for processing of 5 GB in 1 node, 3 nodes and 5 nodes clusters are 96, 88, 87 s and for the 100 MB, 500 MB, 1 GB, and 5 GB data for 5 nodes cluster are 73, 74, 81, 87 s. This result shows that as the number of nodes increase, time taken for processing is inversely proportion and as the data size increases for a particular cluster, execution time also increases.

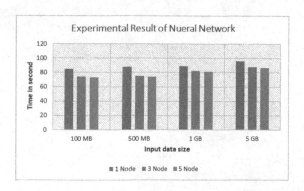

Fig. 3. Experimental result of neural network

Figure 4 shows that total execution time taken for 1 Node, 3 Node, and 5 Node for 1 GB data are 90, 64, 61 s and time taken for processing of 100 MB, 500 MB, 1 GB, 5 GB data in 5 node cluster are 35, 43, 61, 190 s respectively. This result also shows that as cluster size increases, time taken for execution decreases and as the data size increases, time taken for execution also increases. K – nearest neighbor based on the distance of the related terms were calculated. It is the technique to deal with the large-scale problems.

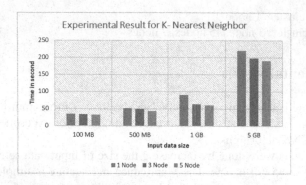

Fig. 4. Experimental result for K- Nearest Neighbor

10   Experimental Analysis

The graphical representation is important for the explanation of any process and explain the subject matter by the use of collected data. The comparative study of experimental result obtained for NN and KNN with different data size is demonstrated in this section.

Figure 5 shows that experimental result on 1 node cluster for NN and KNN with different input data size. The time taken for KNN are gradually increases as the data size increases but NN time taken for processing is slightly increases. The figure also shows that at 1 GB data, time taken for processing by KNN is drastically increases than NN. NN has smooth increment for the processing.

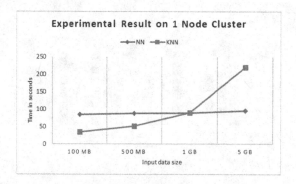

Fig. 5. Experimental result on 1 node cluster

Figure 6 shows the experimental result obtained for NN and KNN for 3 Node cluster. For both cases, as the data size increases, total time taken for execution also increases. It is found that at 1 GB data, total time taken for KNN has increases rapidly and total time taken for NN has gradually increases.

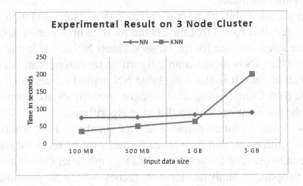

Fig. 6. Experimental result on 3 node cluster

Figure 7 shows the experimental result obtained for NN and KNN for 5 Node cluster. Time taken for NN and KNN at 500 MB, 1 GB and 5 GB data are 75, 43, 81, 61, 87, 190 s respectively. It also shows that time taken for NN is less than KNN for the processing of 5 GB data on 5 node cluster.

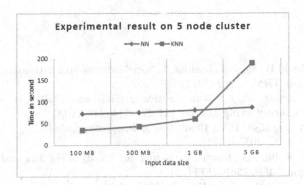

Fig. 7. Experimental result on 5 node cluster

Overall, the experiment shows that NN is suitable for sensitive data retrieval from big data than KNN.

11   Conclusion

This paper has made a significant contribution in the effort of eradicating terrorism, a harmful aspect of every society. Among many reduction techniques, this paper has implemented two reduction techniques - Neural Network and K-Nearest-Neighbor, for the determination of sensitive data from big data using Hadoop distributed system. The algorithms were designed to run in distributed system using Map-Reduce framework to extract useful and critical criminal information from big data. Experiments were carried out by altering the data size and cluster size to get processing speed in the distributed system of commodity hardware.

Both the classification algorithms were executed separately and their total execution time were calculated. It is found that time taken for determination of sensitive by KNN is low for smaller sized data but for the larger datasets NN algorithm is more effective. So, it is concluded that NN is more suitable algorithm for determination of sensitive data from huge amount of data. It is also found that NN is used for textual data while KNN is used for vector data. Compared against the existing methods, the proposed system has also compared the performance of two different algorithms.

We are interested to do future enhancement of our study. First, we plan to combine more than one algorithms so that time taken for retrieval of sensitive data will be less. Second, we intend to retrieve the sensitive data through other classification algorithms like principal component analysis, term-frequency - inverse document frequency, support vector machine etc. Third, we are doing research to implement the algorithm in real time so that right information can be obtained in real time.

Acknowledgment. Project supported by the National Nature Science Foundation of China (No. 60973040, No. 61602057), the Outstanding Young Talent Project of Jilin Providence (No. 2017052005954), the Key Scientific and Technology Projects of Jilin Province. (No. 20130206051GX).

References

1. Tan, W., Blake, M.B., Saleh, I., Dustdar, S.: Social-network-sourced big data analytics. IEEE Internet Comput. **17**(5), 62–69 (2013)
2. Chen, C.P., Zhang, C.-Y.: Data-intensive applications, challenges, techniques and technologies: a survey on big data. Inf. Sci. **275**, 314–347 (2014)
3. Labrinidis, A., Jagadish, H.V.: Challenges and opportunities with big data. Proc. VLDB Endow. **5**(12), 2032–2033 (2012)
4. Kambatla, K., Kollias, G., Kumar, V., Grama, A.: Trends in big data analytics. J. Parallel Distrib. Comput. **74**(7), 2561–2573 (2014)
5. Chen, H., Chiang, R.H., Storey, V.C.: Business intelligence and analytics: from big data to big impact. MIS Q. **36**, 1165–1188 (2012)
6. Rivinius, J.: Majority of 2013 terrorist attacks occurred in just a few countries, pp. 1–2. Press Release (2014)
7. Strang, K.D., Alamieyeseigha, S.: What and where are the risks of international terrorist attacks: a descriptive study of the evidence. Int. J. Risk Conting. Manag. (IJRCM) **4**(1), 1–20 (2015)
8. Jayo, M., Diniz, E.H., Zambaldi, F., Christopoulos, T.P.: Groups of services delivered by Brazilian branchless banking and respective network integration models. Electron. Commer. Res. Appl. **11**(5), 504–517 (2012)
9. Kwapien, A.: How big data helps to fight crime. https://www.datapine.com/blog/big-data-helps-to-fight-crime/
10. Herbert, M.: Understanding terror networks. Mil. Rev. **85**(4), 101 (2005)

11. Mascarenhas, A., Nunes, L.M., Ramos, T.B.: Selection of sustainability indicators for planning: combining stakeholders participation and data reduction techniques. J. Clean. Prod. **92**, 295–307 (2015)
12. Ougiaroglou, S., Diamantaras, K.I., Evangelidis, G.: Exploring the effect of data reduction on neural network and support vector machine classification. Neurocomputing **280**, 101–110 (2017)
13. Bou-Harb, E., Debbabi, M., Assi, C.: Cyber scanning: a comprehensive survey. IEEE Commun. Surv. Tutor. **16**(3), 1496–1519 (2014)
14. Herrera-Semenets, V., Pérez-García, O.A., Hernández-León, R., van den Berg, J., Doerr, C.: A data reduction strategy and its application on scan and backscatter detection using rule-based classifiers. Expert Syst. Appl. **95**, 272–279 (2018)
15. Wang, J., Yue, S., Yu, X., Wang, Y.: An efficient data reduction method and its application to cluster analysis. Neurocomputing **238**, 234–244 (2017)
16. Amor, L.B., Lahyani, I., Jmaiel, M.: Data accuracy aware mobile healthcare applications. Comput. Ind. **97**, 54–66 (2018)
17. Lam, C.: Hadoop in Action. Manning Publications Co., New York (2010)
18. Shvachko, K., Kuang, H., Radia, S., Chansler, R.: The hadoop distributed file system In: 2010 IEEE 26th Symposium on Mass Storage Systems and Technologies (MSST), pp. 1–10. IEEE (2010)
19. Laclavík, M., Šeleng, M., Hluchý, L.: Towards large scale semantic annotation built on MapReduce architecture. In: Bubak, M., van Albada, G.D., Dongarra, J., Sloot, Peter M.A. (eds.) ICCS 2008. LNCS, vol. 5103, pp. 331–338. Springer, Heidelberg (2008). https://doi.org/10.1007/978-3-540-69389-5_38
20. Thakur, S., Dharavath, R.: Artificial neural network based prediction of malaria abundances using big data: a knowledge capturing approach. Clin. Epidemiol. Glob. Health (2018)
21. Chen, A.-S., Leung, M.T., Daouk, H.: Application of neural networks to an emerging financial market: forecasting and trading the taiwan stock index. Comput. Oper. Res. **30**(6), 901–923 (2003)
22. Zhang, Q., Yang, L.T., Chen, Z., Li, P.: A survey on deep learning for big data. Inf. Fusion **42**, 146–157 (2018)
23. Maillo, J., Triguero, I., Herrera, F.: A MapReduce-based k-nearest neighbor approach for big data classification. In: Trustcom/BigDataSE/ISPA, 2015 IEEE, pp. 167–172. IEEE February 2015
24. Dixon, J.K.: Pattern recognition with partly missing data. IEEE Trans. Syst. Man Cybern. B Cybern. **9**(10), 617–621 (1979)
25. Inyaem, U., Meesad, P., Haruechaiyasak, C.: Named-entity techniques for terrorism event extraction and classification. In: 2009 Eighth International Symposium on Natural Language Processing SNLP 2009, pp. 175–179. IEEE (2009)
26. Sanderson, T.M.: Transnational terror and organized crime: blurring the lines. SAIS Rev. Int. Aff. **24**(1), 49–61 (2004)
27. Wang, X., Miller, E., Smarick, K., Ribarsky, W., Chang, R.: Investigative visual analysis of global terrorism. Comput. Graph. Forum **27**, 919–926 (2008)
28. How to Detect Criminal Gangs Using Mobile Phone Data (2014). https://www.technologyreview.com/s/526471/how-to-detect-criminal-gangs-using-mobile-phone-data/
29. Data Protection Act (1998). https://www.huntonprivacyblog.com/wp-content/uploads/sites/28/2016/11/big-data-and-data-protection.pdf
30. ur Rehman, M.H., Liew, C.S., Abbas, A., Jayaraman, P.P., Wah, T.Y., Khan, S.U.: Big data reduction methods: a survey. Data Science and Engineering **1**(4), 265–284 (2016)

31. Yalagandula, P., Nath, S., Yu, H., Gibbons, P.B., Seshan, S.: Beyond availability: towards a deeper understanding of machine failure characteristics in large distributed systems. In: WORLDS (2004)
32. Dean, J., Ghemawat, S.: MapReduce: simplified data processing on large clusters. Commun. ACM **51**(1), 107–113 (2008)
33. Wu, X., Kumar, V., Quinlan, J.R., Ghosh, J., Yang, Q., Motoda, H., et al.: Top 10 algorithms in data mining. Knowl. Inf. Syst. **14**(1), 1–37 (2008)
34. Zhang, M.-L., Zhou, Z.-H.: ML-KNN: A lazy learning approach to multi-label learning. Pattern Recogn. **40**(7), 2038–2048 (2007)
35. Jiang, Y., Zhou, Z.-H.: Editing Training Data for kNN Classifiers with Neural Network Ensemble. In: Yin, F.-L., Wang, J., Guo, C. (eds.) ISNN 2004. LNCS, vol. 3173, pp. 356–361. Springer, Heidelberg (2004). https://doi.org/10.1007/978-3-540-28647-9_60
36. Bagheri, B., Ahmadi, H., Labbafi, R.: Application of data mining and feature extraction on intelligent fault diagnosis by artificial neural network and k-nearest neighbor. In: 2010 XIX International Conference on Electrical Machines (ICEM). IEEE, pp. 1–7 (2010)

Secure Biometric Authentication Scheme Based on Chaotic Map

Jiahao Liang and Lin You(✉)

College of Communication Engineering, Hangzhou Dianzi University,
Hangzhou 310018, China
mryoulin@gmail.com

Abstract. Biometric authentication system has been widely used because of its convenience. But the development of science and technology has brought new challenges to biological information in the authentication system. In this paper, a revocable biometric template authentication scheme based on chaotic map is proposed. The scheme uses a piecewise Logistic chaotic mapping system to generate key sequences to encrypt biometric data and changes the way of traditional biometric authentication system which directly stored biometric templates in plaintext. Our scheme enables the storage and matching of biometrics in the encryption domain and it has improved the security of the biometric identity authentication in open network.

Keywords: Biometric authentication · Piecewise Logistic map
Biometric template · Security

1 Introduction

The acceleration of the digital information process has brought tremendous influence to most sectors of the society. In the era of big data, massive amounts of data have become the most valuable asset. Identity authentication security is a crucial part of data security protection. It is an important basis for network service providers to provide authorized services, and it is also the first line of defense for network security. However, most of the current biometric authentication systems are inadequate in security protection. User's biometric templates are usually stored in plaintext, and since the biometric information is unique, once it is compromised, the leakage is irreversible. The biometrics of human body that can be used for identity authentication are limited, thus the particularity of biometric data deserves a higher security protection.

In the absence of actual control for the data storage and operation, the security of the authentication system lies more in the security of the biometric

This research is partially supported by the National Science Foundation of China (No. 61772166, 61272045) and the Key Program of the Nature Science Foundation of Zhejiang province of China (No. LZ17F020002).

© Springer Nature Switzerland AG 2018
J. Vaidya and J. Li (Eds.): ICA3PP 2018, LNCS 11337, pp. 643–653, 2018.
https://doi.org/10.1007/978-3-030-05063-4_50

templates. In the face of various forms of attacks, protecting the user's biometric information from being stolen and leaked is a basic security requirement for the biometric authentication system.

Considering the characteristics and practicality of various technologies, we proposed a secure biometric authentication scheme based on chaotic map. The good pseudo-randomness, unpredictability of orbits, extreme sensitivity to initial values and the parameters of the chaotic systems are consistent with the requirements of cryptography [1]. Since biometric authentication has a natural association with the image processing technology, we can combine the technology of chaos theory with the image encryption for biometric template protection, and it will provide a novel way for the security protection of the biometric authentication system.

2   Related Work

The ideal biometric template protection scheme should satisfy the following four conditions [2]: diversity, revocability, irreversibility and high efficiency. Based on these requirements, a variety of biometric template protection technologies has been proposed. The mainstream biometrics protection technologies are divided into two types, biometric encryption technology [3,4] and biometric transformation technology [5]. Besides that, some researchers have applied homomorphic encryption technology to protect biometric templates [6], but the effect is not satisfactory. Due to the close relationship between chaos theory and cryptography, researchers have done a lot of work on chaotic cryptography, and chaos theory has been gradually developed from theoretical research to the practical application in the field of information security. Especially, chaos theory has been widely used for image encryption [7,8].

In recent years, some work which applied chaotic map to protect biometric authentication system has been put forward. In [9], the author has proposed a novel encryption strategy with 2D Bernoulli-Logistic map to protect the security of the biometric authentication system. They use retina, iris and fingerprint for scheme verification. Their encrypted images have good performance in volatility and correlation. However, they did not carry out authentication experiment with encrypted biometric features. In [10,11], researchers have proposed face template protection schemes based on Logistic map. Related experiments show that both scheme can ensure the security of the original template and the performance of their system is not significant degraded. In [12], a new cancelable biometric template transformation scheme based on Logistic map is proposed. They tested the effectiveness of the solution with the iris and achieved a good recognition performance.

3   Proposed Scheme

Here, we design a new privacy preserving biometric authentication scheme based on piecewise Logistic map. In our scheme, the user's biometric data to be stored are encrypted in advance. Even if an attacker invades the server and steals the template data, it is difficult to recover the original biometric data. And the system can immediately generate a new biometric template by replacing new parameters. The overall process of our scheme is shown in Fig. 1. Our scheme is specifically divided into two parts, that is, the enrollment process and the authentication process.

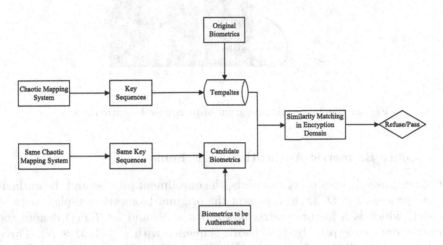

Fig. 1. The overall process of the secure biometric authentication scheme based on chaotic map.

3.1   Piecewise Logistic Map

For normal Logistic map, only when the branch parameter $\mu = 4$, the generated chaotic sequence will have ergodicity over the entire interval $[0, 1]$. In practical applications, the values of the sequences generated by Logistic map may be aggregated, overlapped and interlaced, and it cannot achieve the ideal chaos characteristics. In [13], the author has proposed a new piecewise Logistic mapping system. The new system allows a wider range of branch parameter μ to guarantee the ergodicity of the generated chaotic sequence over the interval $[0, 1]$. Its mathematical expression is as follows.

$$x_{n+1} = \begin{cases} 4\mu(0.25 - x_n)^2, & x_n \in (0, 0.5] \\ 1 - 4\mu(0.75 - x_n)^2, & x_n \in (0.5, 1) \end{cases} \tag{1}$$

Where $x_n \in (0, 1)$, μ represents the branch parameter of the piecewise Logistic map, n indicates the number of iteration, and x_0 is the initial value. The piecewise Logistic mapping bifurcation diagram is shown as Fig. 2.

According to the experimental results, the chaotic sequence generated by the system can exhibit ergodicity over the interval $[0, 1]$ when $\mu \in (2.01, 2.98) \cup (3.11, 4]$. It is much larger than that of the Logistic map.

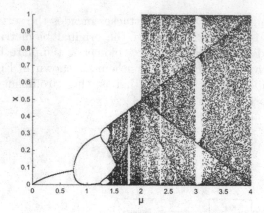

Fig. 2. The bifurcation diagram of piecewise Logistic map.

3.2   Secure Biometric Authentication Scheme

Our scheme mainly consists of two parts, the enrollment process and the authentication process. Let $OT(x, y)$ represent the original biometric template data of the user, which is a feature matrix of size $M \times N$, and let $ET(i)$ denote the biometric data encrypted by the chaotic sequence with $i \in [1, M \times N]$. Three chaotic sequences $KS = \{KS_1, KS_2, KS_3\}$ are generated by the piecewise Logistic chaotic system which are stored in a trusted third party. The elements in the sequence KS_1 are decimal numbers, while both KS_2 and KS_3 are binary sequences. The key sequence KS_1 is used to scramble the data in the original biometric template $OT(x, y)$, and then the scrambled biometric data $TT(i)$ will be obtained. Through the following operation by the encryption rules designed in this paper, we can achieve the purpose of the protection of the user's original biometric data.

Enrollment Process. The enrollment process mainly includes the generation of chaotic key sequences and the encryption of the original biometrics. The basic flowchart is shown in Fig. 3.

By setting the initial values and branch parameters, we can get the discrete real chaotic sequences from the piecewise Logistic chaotic mapping system. Since KS_2 and KS_3 are binary sequences and KS_1 is a decimal sequence, it is necessary to perform a naturalization operation on the generated chaotic sequence values to obtain a discretization sequence $\{s_i\}$ with $s_i \in \{0, 1\}$ as defined in Eq.(2).

$$s_i = \begin{cases} 1, x_i \geq 0.5 \\ 0, x_i < 0.5 \end{cases} \qquad i = 0, 1, 2, \ldots, n \qquad (2)$$

s_i denotes the element in the chaotic sequence after naturalized as 0 or 1. Where n represents the length of the chaotic sequence. The size of the original

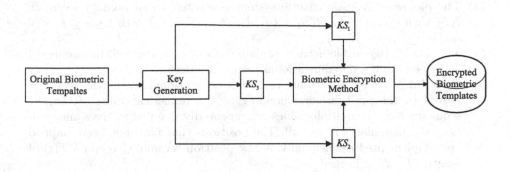

Fig. 3. Flow diagram of the enrollment process.

biometric template required for encryption is $M \times N$. For the sequences KS_2 and KS_3, they are binary sequences made up of s_i. For the sequence KS_1, set

$$
\begin{aligned}
b_1 &= s_1 s_2 ... s_k \\
b_2 &= s_{k+1} s_{k+2} ... s_{2k} \\
&\vdots \\
b_n &= s_{(n-1)k+1} s_{(n-1)k+2} ... s_{nk}
\end{aligned}
\tag{3}
$$

Where $b_1, b_2, \cdots, b_n$ are decimal integers made up of k binary values in each steam. Set $d_i = b_i \bmod n$ with $i \in [1, n]$, then $d_i \in [0, M \times N - 1]$, $KS_1 = \{d_1, d_2, \ldots, d_i, \ldots, d_n\}$. The flow diagram of key sequence generation is shown as in Fig. 4.

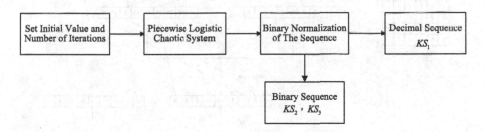

Fig. 4. Flow diagram of key sequence generation.

As described above, $OT(x, y)$ represents the user's original biometric template data in size $M \times N$ and $ET(i)$ denotes the biometric data encrypted by the chaotic sequences, where $i \in [1, M \times N]$. The biometric template data processed by the key sequence KS_1 is $TT(i)$. The detailed process of encryption are as follows.

(1) The piecewise Logistic chaotic system generates a real number sequence KS_1 with a length of n, $KS_1 = \{d_1, d_2, \ldots, d_i, \ldots, d_n\}$ with $1 \le i \le M \times N$ and $d_i \in [0, M \times N - 1]$.

(2) The user's original biometric template data of each row will be connected end to end into a one-dimensional vector of length $M \times N$.

(3) Each bit value of the transformed one-dimensional biometric vector is moved to the position corresponding to the numerical value of the key sequence KS_1. If multiple values are repeatedly mapped to the same position, the first map will prevail. The positions that have not been mapped are supplemented by 0. Finally, a new position scrambled vector $TT(i)$ of length $M \times N$ is formed.

(4) If $KS_1(i)$ is even and $KS_2(i) = 1$ or $KS_1(i)$ is odd and $KS_2(i) = 0$, perform the following operations.

$$ET(i) = TT(i) \odot KS_3(i) \tag{4}$$

In which the symbol $\odot$ is XNOR operation.

(5) If $KS_1(i)$ is odd and $KS_2(i) = 1$ or $KS_1(i)$ is even and $KS_2(i) = 0$, perform the following operations.

$$ET(i) = TT(i) \oplus KS_3(i) \tag{5}$$

In which the symbol $\oplus$ is XOR operation.

In Fig. 5, we use the feature data of size 6×6 as an example to illustrate the basic process of scrambling and encrypting the feature data through three key sequences KS_1, KS_2 and KS_3, respectively.

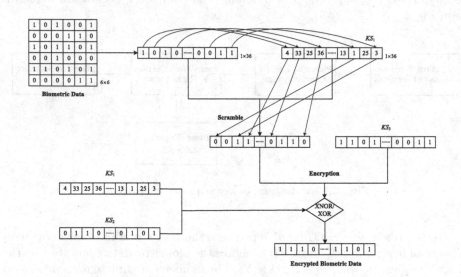

Fig. 5. Process of encryption.

Authentication Process. Our authentication process can be shown as in Fig. 6. In the enrollment phase, the user's biometric data is first encrypted by the chaotic sequences generated by the piecewise Logistic mapping system and then is stored as the template in the database. In the authentication phase, the user's extracted biometrics to be authenticated will be encrypted by the chaotic sequences generated using the same system initial values and parameter values. The Hamming distance between the biometric data to be authenticated with the prestored biometric template will be checked in the encryption domain. According to the threshold set based on the experiment, we can get the result of authentication.

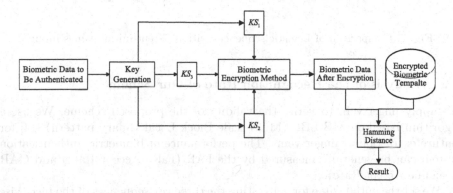

Fig. 6. Authentication process of the secure biometric authentication scheme.

4 Experimental Results and Analysis

In order to verify the effect of the chaotic sequences generated by the piecewise Logistic chaotic mapping system for biometric encryption, our scheme uses finger vein to verify the solution. The data used in the experiment comes from our laboratory's finger vein database with a total of 560 finger veins of 70 individuals. The image size of the finger vein is 140×300. The computer's hardware configuration is Intel Core i5 3470 main frequency 3.2 GHz, 8 GB memory, win10 operating system, and the compiler environment is Matlab2014b.

4.1 Piecewise Logistic Mapping System Analysis

First, in order to verify the initial value sensitivity of the piecewise Logistic mapping system, we set $\mu = 3.5000$ and two initial values as 0.3000 and 0.3001, respectively. We give a comparison of the last 100 elements of the sequence after 150 iterations as shown in Fig. 7.

It can be seen from Fig. 7 that in the case of only a 0.0001 difference between the two initial values, the distribution of the chaotic sequence generated by the piecewise Logistic mapping system almost has no coincidence points. It has high sensitivity to a very little change of the initial value.

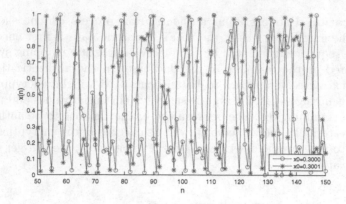

Fig. 7. Comparison of Logistic sequences with different initial values input.

4.2   Analysis of the Recognition Rate of Our Scheme

We apply finger vein to verify the validity of the proposed scheme. We use a algorithm based on MB-LBP (Multi-scale Block Local Binary pattern) [14] for feature extraction of finger veins. The performance of biometric authentication system can be generally measured by the FAR (False Accept Rate) and GAR (Genuine Accept Rate).

We set the initial value for generating the three key sequences of the piecewise Logistic mapping system to be 0.3456, 0.4567 and 0.5678, respectively, and then the branch parameters are selected as 2.8, 3.2 and 3.6, respectively. We have tested the performance of FAR and GAR for finger vein recognition system before and after the templates are encrypted. We have also compared the result with the scheme of using Logistic map to protect face features in [15]. The results are shown in Table 1.

Table 1. Performance of our scheme and its comparison.

GAR (%)	0.01% FAR	0.1% FAR	1% FAR	10% FAR
Unencrypted	76.04%	87.67%	97.19%	99.48%
Cheng et al. [15]	74.64%	81.43%	88.21%	96.79%
Our scheme	70.57%	82.91%	95.52%	99.14%

From Table 1, it can be found that the recognition rate of the finger vein authentication system using our encryption method is lower than the authentication system without encryption. However, the level of decline is within an acceptable range, and the impact on the authentication performance of our system is minimal. We sacrifice a small recognition rate for higher security.

In order to verify the sensitivity of the scheme to the initial value, we select five finger vein feature samples to analyze the small changes in the initial parameters for generating the three key sequences and the influence on the identity authentication results. The authentication results are shown in Table 2.

Table 2. Influence of initial value change on authentication result.

Finger vein	Initial value for generating key sequence (original/changed)			Result
	KS_1	KS_2	KS_3	
1	0.2568/0.2567	0.1489/0.1486	0.6789/0.6788	Refused
2	0.3846/0.3844	0.3698/0.3699	0.3468/0.3465	Refused
3	0.4178/0.4173	0.4236/0.4238	0.7468/0.7436	Refused
4	0.6459/0.6457	0.5896/0.5898	0.0147/0.0146	Refused
5	0.7965/0.7966	0.9636/0.9635	0.2264/0.2267	Refused

Figure 8 is the ROC curves for finger vein authentication when the image is encrypted using our method or not encrypted. From the ROC curves, we can see that the proposed scheme can still maintain a high recognition rate.

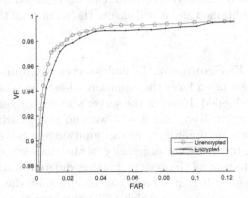

Fig. 8. ROC curves before and after encryption.

It can be seen from all the experimental data that when the finger vein features are encrypted using our method, it can not only ensure a certain recognition rate, but also make correct authentication judgments on the subtle changes in the initial values of the system. It is of practical significance to sacrifice a smaller recognition rate for a higher security guarantee.

5   Security Analysis

(1) Key Space. The size of key space is an important index to measure the security strength of an encryption algorithm. The current computer stores and calculates data in double precision, and its effective number is 16 bits. A chaos-based encryption algorithm can only provide $10^{16} \approx 2^{53}$ size of the key space [16], which is slightly smaller than the 2^{56} size of the key space of the DES encryption algorithm, and it is far smaller than the 2^{128} size of the key space provided by AES-128. Using the biometric encryption algorithm proposed in this paper, our algorithm has a total of six parameters (μ_1, μ_2, μ_3, x_1, x_2, x_3) for generating the three key sequences $KS = \{KS_1, KS_2, KS_3\}$, and it means that the size of the key space is $2^3 \times 10^{16} \times 10^{16} \times 10^{16} \approx 2^{162}$. It follows that our algorithm can provide 162-bit security strength, which is greater than the 128-bit security strength provided by AES-128. Compared with the traditional chaos-based scheme, the size of key space in our system is increased by three times, and so our security intensity is greatly improved.

(2) Revocability. In our authentication system, the biometric templates stored in the database are encrypted, hence, it can effectively resist conventional exhaustive attacks. Even if the stored biometric templates are leaked, it is difficult for the attacker to recover the original biometric information from the leaked templates. If the user's templates are stolen, the system only needs to replace the initial parameters to generate new key sequences to encrypt user's biometric data. Thus, the leaked biometric template can be replaced by a new encrypted biometric template obtained and it will ensure the security of the identity authentication system.

(3) Multi-server Environment. In multi-server environment, the biometric authentication system often faces the situation where the template data in multiple servers are overlapped. If one of the server's biometric templates are stolen, other servers will be involved, and it will weaken the security. In our scheme, the piecewise Logistic mapping system can guarantee a wide range for branch parameter selection to ensure the ergodicity of the chaotic sequences. It is flexible and convenient to control the system. Setting different initial parameters and branch parameters for different servers can ensure that the encrypt-generated biometric templates are different, which will guarantee the security of identity authentication systems in multi-server environments.

6   Conclusion

In this paper, a new revocable biometric template protection scheme based on chaotic map is proposed. Our scheme can store encrypted biometrics and implement the identity authentication process in the encryption domain. It is more secure than the traditional biometric authentication system in open network. Compared with other schemes based on Logistic map, our scheme has a larger key space. Experimental results show that our scheme can maintain a high recognition rate. Our scheme is not limited to the protection of finger vein, but also can be applied to other biometric authentication systems.

Data protection in biometric authentication process will be the focus of the future research work. Moreover, the biometric authentication technology itself is constantly developing, and the transition from contact identity authentication to contactless identity authentication requires higher requirements for biometric extraction technology and encryption technology. The extension of our scheme can be carried out from the selection and optimization of chaotic maps. Improving the applicability of different biometric matching algorithms to this encryption scheme is also one of the optimization options.

References

1. Deng, S.J., Li, C.D.: Chaos theory and its application in cryptography. J. Civil, Archit. Environ. Eng. **25**(5), 123–127 (2003)
2. Jain, A.K., Nandakumar, K., Nagar, A.: Biometric template security. EURASIP J. Adv. Sig. Process. **2008**(1), 1–17 (2008)
3. You, L., Yang, L., Yu, W., Wu, Z.: A cancelable fuzzy vault algorithm based on transformed fingerprint features. Chin. J. Electron. **26**(2), 236–243 (2017)
4. Kaur, M., Sofat, S.: Fuzzy vault template protection for multimodal biometric system. In: International Conference on Computing, Communication and Automation, pp. 237–243. IEEE, Greater Noida (2011)
5. Lim, M.H., Teoh, A.B.J., Kim, J.: Biometric feature-type transformation: making templates compatible for secret protection. IEEE Signal Process. Mag. **32**(5), 77–87 (2015)
6. Gomez-Barrero, M., Maiorana, E., Galbally, J., Campisi, P., Fierrez, J.: Multi-biometric template protection based on homomorphic encryption. Pattern Recognit. **67**(C), 149–163 (2017)
7. Teng, L., Wang, X., Meng, J.: A chaotic color image encryption using integrated bit-level permutation. Multimed. Tools Appl. **77**(10), 1–14 (2017)
8. Ahmad, M., Alam, M.Z., Umayya, Z., Khan, S., Ahmad, F.: An image encryption approach using particle swarm optimization and chaotic map. Int. J. Inf. Technol. **10**(3), 247–255 (2018)
9. Liew, C.Z., Shaw, R., Li, L., Yang, Y.: Survey on biometric data security and chaotic encryption strategy with Bernoulli mapping. In: 2014 International Conference on Medical Biometrics, pp. 174–180. IEEE, Shenzhen (2014)
10. Ghouzali, S., Abdul, W.: Private chaotic biometric template protection algorithm. In: Image Information Processing (ICIIP), pp. 655–659. IEEE, Shimla (2013)
11. James, D., Philip, M.: A novel face template protection scheme based on chaos and visual cryptography. Int. J. Appl. Inf. Syst. **2**(5), 31–35 (2012)
12. Supriya, V.G., Manjunatha, R.: Logistic map for cancellable biometrics. In: ICAMT (2016)
13. Bing, L.: A binary sequence scrambling encryption algorithm based on improved logistic mapping. J. China West Norm. Univ. (Nat. Sci.) **38**(3), 340–346 (2017)
14. You, L., Wang, J., Yan, B.: A secure finger vein recognition algorithm based on MB-GLBP and logistic mapping. J. Inf. Hiding Multimedia Sig. Process. **7**(6), 1231–1242 (2016)
15. Cheng, W., An, G.: Face template protection using chaotic encryption. In: 5th IET International Conference on Wireless, Mobile and Multimedia Networks, pp. 245–248. IET, Beijing (2013)
16. Fu, C., Zhu, Z.: A chaotic image encryption scheme based on circular bit shift method. In: International Conference for Young Computer Scientists, pp. 3057–3061. IEEE, Zhang Jiajie (2008)

Author Index

Printed in the United States
By Bookmasters